D0562647

COSTA RICA

'From forest floor to leafy canopy, it's just layer upon layer of plant life – mosses, lichens, ferns, trees, strangler vines, lianas, bromeliads, orchids and more; at times the forest seems to be almost at war with itself, a mass of battling greenery, hungrily competing for each rare shaft of sunlight.'

Joseph Fullman

About the Guide

The **full-colour introduction** gives the author's overview of the country, together with suggested **itineraries** and a regional 'where to go' map and **feature** to help you plan your trip.

Illuminating and entertaining **cultural chapters** on local history, wildlife, conservation and activities give you a rich flavour of the country.

Travel covers the basics of **getting there** and **getting around**, plus entry formalities. The **Practical A–Z** deals with all the **essential information** and **contact details** that you may need, including a section for disabled travellers.

The **regional chapters** are arranged in a loose touring order, with plenty of public transport and driving information. The author's top **'Don't Miss'** ✪ **sights** are highlighted at the start of each chapter and there are also **short-tour itineraries**.

A **language and pronunciation guide**, a **glossary** of cultural terms, ideas for **further reading** and a comprehensive **index** can be found at the end of the book.

Although everything we list in this guide is **personally visited and recommended**, our author inevitably has his own favourite places to eat and stay. Whenever you see this **Author's Choice** ⭐ icon beside a listing, you will know that it is a little bit out of the ordinary.

Hotel Price Guide

Luxury	$$$$$	US$120 and above
Expensive	$$$$	US$80–119
Moderate	$$$	US$40–79
Inexpensive	$$	US$26–39
Budget	$	US$25 and under

About the Author

Joseph Fullman admits that he is now something of a Costa Rica bore – if he can corner someone and enthuse about jungles and rainforests, he will. He hopes that this book will encourage everyone else to visit too – just not all at the same time. He has also written guides to Andalucía, Berlin, England, Las Vegas, London and Venice, and co-written the Cadogan guide to Belize.

1st Edition Published 2006

01

INTRODUCING
COSTA RICA

Costa Rica, the 'rich coast', is well named, even if it took nigh on five centuries for the people living there to realize that its real riches lay not in deposits of gold or precious stones – mistakenly expected by the first settlers from Europe – but in the very thing they'd spent all that time exploring, adapting and destroying in the hunt for treasure: the natural environment. What were once obstacles to be overcome – volcanoes, mountains, rivers, waterfalls, mangrove swamps, coral reefs, great stretches of rain-forest – are now tourist attractions to be showcased.

Today Costa Rica is one of the world's leading purveyors of that strangely oxymoronic form of modern travel – ecotourism. The tiny country's internationally lauded conservation programme has seen 25 per cent of its land protected in a network of national parks and private refuges, which provide a home for one of the greatest concentrations of wildlife on earth. Aside from its natural wonders, much of the credit for Costa Rica's growing popularity can be attributed to convenience. Few other countries offer such easy or comfortable access to the exotic. Costa Rica may have a biodiversity that compares with the Amazon basin or the Serengeti plains, but its dimensions are closer to those of Holland. Views and experiences of an intensity that will remain lodged in the memory forever are often just a short bus ride or plane hop away from your luxury air-conditioned hotel. Pay a visit to Arenal and you'll be rewarded with the comic-book sight of lava being flung straight out of the top of a volcano. In Monteverde, you can battle your way through a ludi-crously lush cloudforest, where near-total humidity creates a Hollywood-style jungle blanketed in thick, swirling mists. At the Parque Nacional Marino Ballena, you may see 50-tonne mother humpback whales frolicking with their young. Head inland to the depths of the rainforest and you may be greeted by the rumbling

Above: Sunrise, Volcán Arenal, p.271; Plant, La Paz Waterfall Gardens, p.138

Opposite page: Market fruits; La Guácima Butterfly Farm, p.131

*Above: Mangoes,
Mercado Central, Puerto
Limón, p.334*

*Opposite page:
Shoe shop*

roar of howler monkeys shouting out their ownership of the trees. Both Atlantic and Pacific coasts offer visitors the opportunity to see marine turtles clambering clumsily ashore to dig their nests and lay their eggs. And, who knows? You may end up being that one traveller in a million who catches sight of an elusive jaguar.

When you tire of watching, and feel a bit more like doing, Costa Rica offers all manner of activities – hiking up mountains, climbing down waterfalls, rafting along rivers, zip-lining between trees, horse-riding through forests, surfing over Pacific breakers and more. And, should you have some energy left by evening, you'll find there's still plenty of drinking, dining and dancing to be done, particularly in the main urban hotspots of Jacó, Tamarindo, Manuel Antonio and the capital, San José.

It seems strange to have got so far into an introduction to a country without mentioning the people who live there. Still, the Costa Ricans, or 'Ticos' as they call themselves, would understand. But then, they're a very understanding – not to mention tolerant, welcoming and, above all, non-argumentative – bunch. Costa Ricans hold just a handful of passionate beliefs – the chief one being not to get too passionate about things. Throughout their history they have been masters at avoiding confrontation, both internal and external. In fact, they became so good at it that in 1949 they felt able to abolish their armed forces, an act that put them in stark contrast to the rest of Central America. And with no wars to fight, the people have channelled their energies in other directions, such as education, healthcare and employment. Costa Ricans enjoy the highest standard of living on the entire isthmus, and one of the highest in the whole of Latin America.

Thus Costa Rica is not just a beautiful place, full of natural glories, it's also a safe, stable and relatively prosperous one. Tourism is now the largest generator of revenue and employment in the country – outstripping even coffee and banana production, the traditional economic giants. No wonder Ticos always look so pleased to see you.

Above: Monteverde Cloudforest Reserve, pp.241–3

Below: Iguana; Playa Junquillal, Tamarindo, at dusk, p.183; Church interior, Zarcero, p.135

Opposite page: Frog, Ranario, Monteverde, p.246

Where to Go

The capital, **San José**, which starts our guide, can come across as rather depressingly urban – a snarling mess of concrete and consumerism – despite the glorious fringing ring of mountains. Give it a chance, however, and you may find it growing on you. It certainly conforms to all the standard big city clichés – it's lively, bustling and energetic, and it possesses the only notable cultural scene in the entire country.

The serene frame surrounding the intense, noisy picture that is San José, the **Valle Central** offers a nice mixture of urban and rural attractions. It's the country's most populated area, home to the three biggest cities after San José – Alajuela, Cartago and Heredia – but it also boasts large swaths of forest (the Parque Nacional Braulio Carrillo), rolling coffee plantations and the huge volcanic peaks of Irazú and Poás.

The **Northwest** regions of Guanacaste and the Nicoya Peninsula are both the country's most deeply traditional area – a place where cowboys still trot horses down the main street – and its most rapidly changing, with new beachfront constructions going up by the year. Over the past few decades it's been the pioneer for Costa Rica's two main branches of tourism, providing the site for both the Reserva Natural Absoluta Cabo Blanco, the country's first ever protected area, and the Papagayo Project, the country's largest luxury tourist resort. If it's activities you're after – snorkelling, surfing, golf – this is definitely the region to come to.

The attractions of the **Central Pacific Coast and Monteverde** range from the first-world – Jacó and Manuel Antonio are two of the country's most built-up party towns – to the lost world – the Monteverde cloudforest is an ethereal environment unlike anywhere else in the region. Activities on offer range from bird-watching in Parque Nacional Carara, monkey-watching at Parque Nacional Manuel Antonio and sports fishing out of Quepos.

While the **North** may be one of the country's least visited, it does boast some of the country's most popular attractions, including Volcán Arenal, nearby Lake Arenal – a major windsurfing centre – and the white-water rafting centre of La Virgen.

Although parts of the **South and the Osa Peninsula** are becoming increasingly built-up, this region still boasts some of

most remote and untouched landscapes in the entire country, including the huge Parque Internacional La Amistad and the Parque Nacional Corcovado, one of most biologically intense places on the continent.

Finally, up in the northeast, the **Caribbean Coast** is one of Costa Rica's more distinct regions, its culture influenced as much by the offshore Caribbean islands as by the rest of the country. The coastal towns of Cahuita and Puerto Viejo de Talamanca have an easygoing charm, and provide access to some great natural wonders, including the country's largest barrier reef. The regional capital of Puerto Limón is a bit more rough and ready, but is the liveliest place in all Costa Rica during the week-long October carnival, while in the north is one of country's conservational pride and joys, the Parque Nacional Tortuguero, one of the world's most important nesting sites for green turtles.

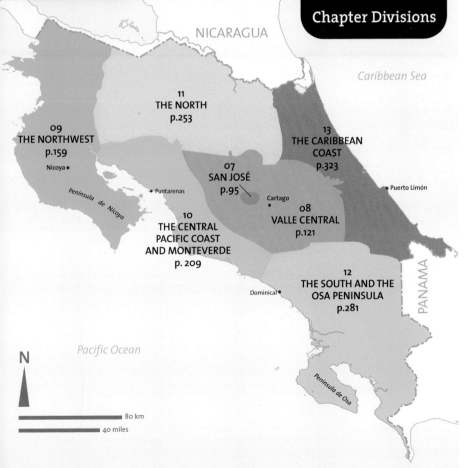

Chapter Divisions

NICARAGUA

Caribbean Sea

11
THE NORTH
p.253

09
THE NORTHWEST
p.159

Nicoya

Peninsula de Nicoya

13
THE CARIBBEAN COAST
p.323

07
SAN JOSÉ
p.95

Puntarenas

Cartago

Puerto Limón

10
THE CENTRAL PACIFIC COAST AND MONTEVERDE
p. 209

08
VALLE CENTRAL
p.121

12
THE SOUTH AND THE OSA PENINSULA
p.281

Dominical

PANAMA

N

Pacific Ocean

Peninsula de Osa

80 km
40 miles

Clockwise from top left: Festival, Barva, p.143; Cañas, p.274; Mercato Central, San José, p.106

Small Town Life

One of the oft-overlooked pleasures of touring Costa Rica, where the focus is usually on exploring natural wonders, is the chance you have to visit small towns and rural villages to see people going about their everyday lives – shopping at the Saturday market, having a bite to eat at the local soda or snack stall, attending a church service or having a kickabout on the local football pitch.

Each town holds its own fiesta – in addition to all the national holidays and celebrations – at some point during the year, which is when you'll see the community at its most exuberant and welcoming. This is often a rowdy, boisterous affair with lots of food, drinking and dancing, with perhaps a rodeo, a concert, a fancy-dress parade or a firework display laid on for good measure (*see* pp.79–80 for more details of festivals).

The Fertile Land

Costa Rica's gloriously fertile land produces an abundance of fresh produce – mangoes, pineapples, melons, coconuts and more. Every major town has a central covered market, usually called the Mercado Central, which is your best bet for picking up cheap fresh fruit and vegetables.

Until recently, the country's economic fortunes were largely dependent on what could be grown from the soil, with the production of coffee and bananas in particular leading the creation of vast international businesses. Today, these have been overtaken by tourism, with people now paying more attention to what the land can produce when it doesn't receive any artificial assistance.

Above: Coconut tree

Right: Teatro Nacional, San José, p.105

Opposite page: Iglesia de Santo Cristo de La Agonía, Alajuela, p.128

Architecture

Enjoy whatever architectural gems you can find. For all its undoubted natural beauty, Costa Rica doesn't boast that much in the way of man-made splendour; most of its cities and towns have been designed more with function than aesthetics in mind.

What elegance there is to be found on the skyline is usually provided by the town church – Alajuela and Zarcero boast fine examples – or theatre. San José's 19th-century Teatro Nacional, a

tropical re-creation of a European-style opera house, is one of the country's finest buildings. Liberia, the capital of the northwest province of Guanacaste, is perhaps the country's most stylish town, with its main street, Calle Real, lined with grand colonial-era constructions.

Saddle Up

Cattle-ranching is an important sector of the Costa Rican economy, particularly in the north-western province of Guanacaste where Costa Rican cowboys, known as *sabaneros*, have had a profound influence on the region's culture. Here these weatherbeaten horsemen enjoy an exalted status, held up as the epitome of rugged, taciturn self-sufficiency, celebrated for their horse-handling skills and bullfighting courage, which are regularly demonstrated at the region's various fiestas and rodeos. You'll see them both out on the open plains – much of the northwest has been cleared for pasture – and in the town centres, gently guiding their charges along the main street, thereby neatly illustrating the central role they play in Guanacastian society. Liberia, the regional capital, has a small museum, the Sala de Sabanero, celebrating the cowboy lifestyle (*see* p.165).

Above: Urban cowboy, Liberia, pp.163–8

Below: Central Pacific coast south of Quepos, pp.228–32

A Shore Thing – Beach and Sea Life

Costa Rica has a lot of coastline. Its Atlantic and Pacific margins boast a combined total of over 1,400km of shore, along which you'll find some of the most idyllic, brochure-perfect beaches imaginable – all golden sands, azure waters and gently swaying palm trees. Away from the major towns and resorts, the beaches are often completely empty, allowing you to walk for miles without seeing another soul, or even a single man-made construction. Costa Rica does also have its more crowded stretches of coast, particularly in the northwest, which is home to several of the country's most popular resorts, including Playa del Coco and Tamarindo, where you'll have plenty of company while you sunbathe, and where you can enjoy a wide range of water-based activities, such as snorkelling, diving, surfing, whale-watching, sea kayaking and sports fishing (*see* pp.55–62 for more details of activities).

Jungles, Forests and Beautiful Beasties

Costa Rica boasts an unparalleled abundance of natural wonders. Its national parks and refuges, which account for around a quarter of the country's total area, protect an extraordinary number of habitats – including desert-like tropical dry forest, sodden rainforest and mist-wreathed cloudforest – in which live an even greater number of creatures, from tiny iridescent tree frogs and primeval-looking lizards, to gloriously patterned butterflies, brightly coloured parrots and much, much more.

01 **Introduction** | Jungles, Forests and Beautiful Beasties

Above: Playa del Coco,
pp.176–8; Butterfly

Right: Poison arrow frog

Overleaf: Parrot

Itineraries

The Best of Costa Rica in Two Weeks

Day 1 Tour of San José, taking in the museums, the city centre bustle and one of the better restaurants.

Day 2 Catch a morning flight to Tortuguero, and in the afternoon take a boat tour of the Parque Nacional Tortuguero on the lookout for monkeys, caimans and crocodiles.

Day 3 Explore Tortuguero town, visit the turtle museum and in the evening (if visiting between July and October) go on a guided tour to watch marine turtles nesting on the beach.

Day 4 Fly back to San José. Pick up a rental car. Drive to La Fortuna. Spend the late afternoon and early evening relaxing in the Tabecón hot springs, taking in views of the volcano.

Day 5 Hike the lower slopes of Volcán Arenal, take a drive around Lake Arenal and pay a visit to the Hanging Bridges of Arenal.

Day 6 Drive to Monteverde. Spend the afternoon exploring the town of Santa Elena, and visiting some of area's smaller attractions, such as the Butterfly Garden, the Orchid Houses or Frog Pond.

Day 7 In the morning, hike through the Monteverde Cloudforest Reserve. In the afternoon, try a canopy tour at Selvatura.

Day 8 In the early morning, drive south to Manuel Antonio, followed by a short hike though the park to see squirrel monkeys and white-faced capuchins. Spend the rest of the afternoon lazing on the beach. Take your evening meal at El Avión, a restaurant set in a disused plane overlooking the Pacific ocean.

Day 9 Drive along the bumpy unpaved road to Dominical. If in season (Dec–March), take a boat trip out to see the humpback whales in the Parque Nacional Marino Ballena. Otherwise, try surfing (or a surfing lesson) off Dominical beach. In the evening, watch the sunset from the Tortilla Flats bar on the beachfront.

Day 10 Get up early for the long (3–4hr) drive south to Sierpe. You'll need to get there by 3.30pm. Park the car and take a *lancha* (boat) to Drake Bay, where you can stay in a beachfront lodge.

Day 11 A long hike into Parque Nacional Corcovado on the lookout for jaguars, pumas, tapir and scarlet macaws.

Day 12 A snorkelling trip out to Caño Island.

Day 13 Take a *lancha* back to Sierpe, pick up the car and drive to one of the lodges on the Cerro de la Muerte (*see* p.285).

Day 14 Take an early morning hike to look out for quetzals, then head back to San José.

A Week of Costa Rican Wildlife-spotting

Day 1 Begin your trip in relatively easy fashion with a short hike through the Parque Nacional Manuel Antonio to spot squirrel monkeys, sloths and white-faced capuchins.

Day 2 Drive north to the Parque Nacional Carara. Take a hike through its forested depths on the lookout for scarlet macaws. Afterwards, park at the Río Tárcoles Bridge to observe the basking crocodiles. Stay the night in the Tarcol Lodge.

Day 3 Take an early morning birdwatching tour of the Río Tárcoles tidal mudflats, followed by a drive northeast to one of the lodges on the lower slopes of Volcán Poás. In the afternoon, pay a visit to the Rainforest Aerial Tram for a canopy safari.

Day 4 In the early morning, climb up Volcán Poás, hoping to see hummingbirds, quetzals and Poás squirrels on the way. Around midday, take a drive southwest along HWY-32 through the Parque Nacional Braulio Carrillo down to Cahuita. Take a late afternoon stroll through the mainland section of the Parque Nacional Cahuita, listening out for howler monkeys.

Day 5 Go snorkelling out on Parque Nacional Cahuita's coral reef, which is Costa Rica's largest and home to 35 species of coral and over 120 species of fish.

Day 6 Drive west to Reserva Biológica Hitoy Cerere, and hike its humid depths on the lookout for various colourful frogs.

Day 7 Drive down to the Refugio Nacional Gandoca-Manzanillo. Begin with a snorkelling trip on the lookout for dolphins and manatees, followed by a hike through the coastal forest searching for pumas, sloths and monkeys.

Active Costa Rica

Day 1 Begin with a white-water rafting trip along the Río Sarapiquí, out of La Virgen, near Puerto Viejo de Sarapiquí.

Day 2 Take the bus west to La Fortuna. Follow this with a hike around the lower slopes of Volcán Arenal.

Day 3 If in season (December–April), try windsurfing on Lake Arenal, otherwise hike along the Hanging Bridges of Arenal.

Day 4 Get up early for a 6hr horse-ride along the El Castillo Trail southwest to Monteverde. If you still have some energy, try a couple of hours' zip-lining with the Original Canopy Tour.

Day 5 Take a short early morning hike through the Santa Elena Cloudforest Reserve, followed by a bus ride to Cañas, where you can connect with a bus up to Playa del Coco.

Day 6 Take a snorkelling or diving trip out to Islas Catalina or Islas Murciélago.

Day 7 Catch the bus south down to Tamarindo, where you can enjoy surfing the Pacific breakers.

Previous page, from top: Volcán Arenal, p.271; Playa Hermosa, Bahía Culebra, p.180

Above, from top: Leaf frog; Reserva Santa Elena, p.244; Playa del Coco, pp.176–8

CONTENTS

Maps and Plans

Reference

History
and Society

The 'rich coast' that took centuries to reveal its riches; the most Spanish of all the Central American colonies but one that was, for a long time, almost totally ignored by Spain; a peaceful, army-less nation in the heart of one of the most volatile regions on earth... Costa Rica's history is a little different.

O2

Pre-Columbian Times – Not Wholly Uncivilized

Costa Rica's pre-Columbian existence can be regarded as quite literally that, for it was Columbus himself who led the first European expedition to the region, landing near the site of present-day Puerto Limón on 18 September 1502, during his fourth and final journey to the Americas.

For a long time, it was assumed that Costa Rica had little in the way of civilization prior to this Spanish invasion and subsequent colonization. It's not that the area was uninhabited up to that point, rather that the people who lived here were until relatively recently regarded as lesser, more primitive cultures compared to the great Aztec and Mayan empires to the north. This view came about in part because the indigenous people left behind so little evidence of their existence. In contrast to the vast cities and monuments erected by the Aztecs and Mayans, the peoples here created almost no lasting architecture and, for the most part, had no written language. Furthermore, following the Spanish invasion, most of the region's inhabitants were either slaughtered, enslaved, died of diseases brought over by the Europeans (in particular smallpox and measles) or simply fled. Today, less than two per cent of Costa Rica's population is of indigenous descent, the lowest ratio in all of Central America.

It was the early Spanish chroniclers who first portrayed the indigenous people of Costa Rica as 'undeveloped' – largely, it seems, because they lacked the ostentatious wealth that was being hungrily plundered elsewhere in the Americas. However, painstaking work by archaeologists has revealed that before the arrival of the Spanish the region was home to several relatively advanced cultures who had populated the region since at least 1000 BC; in fact, archaeological evidence suggests that the very first settlers of the region may have arrived as far back as 10,000 BC. Just before the invasion there were over 20 separate identifiable communities, living in fortified villages of up to 20,000 individuals. These included the **Catapas** in the northeast, the **Diquis** in the southwest and, perhaps the most numerous and certainly the most advanced, the **Chorotegas**, who lived in present-day Guanacaste. Far from being 'undeveloped', these peoples utilized intensive farming methods, traded readily with their neighbours and were capable of great craftsmanship, producing exquisitely detailed jewellery, particularly gold and jade work, examples of which can be seen in San José's Museo de Oro Precolombino (Pre-Columbian Gold Museum, *see* p.104) and Museo de Jade (Jade Museum, *see* p.107). Much of this jewellery was in the form of totemic representations of animals, particularly jaguars, and it is believed it was used to ward off evil spirits, suggesting the existence of some form of religion. Also, according to contemporary accounts of the Spanish invasion, it is known that many of these communities spoke **Nahua**, the language of the Aztecs, from which we can deduce that native Costa Ricans had close cultural and trading links with the peoples to the north. Unfortunately, details on how these peoples lived – their social hierarchies, customs, and the precise nature of their relationships with the region's other cultures – remain frustratingly vague.

A fascinating glimpse into one of these 'lost' civilizations can be found 85km east of San José, at the **Monumento Nacional Guayabo**, Costa Rica's only significant example of pre-Columbian architecture. Though much less visually arresting and architecturally complex than the great Aztec and Mayan cities of Mexico and Guatemala (all that remains today is a collection of low walls), the site nonetheless shows that, prior to European interference, the native peoples were capable not just of building a sizeable permanent settlement, but of significant feats of civil engineering – many of the stones were brought here from great distances, and water for the settlement was provided via a technically advanced storage and irrigation system. Owing to a lack of funds, only a small part of the site has been excavated and so the purpose of many of the structures is still unclear (for more information, *see* pp.157–8).

Mysterious as Guayabo is, it's practically an open book when compared to the stone **spheres**, or '*bolos*', found all over the southern half of the country. The work of the Diquis, these exquisitely carved, perfectly spherical pieces of granite, ranging in size from a cricket ball to a truck, have turned up in some very strange places, including the Isla de Caño, 20km off Costa Rica's Pacific coast. How did they get here? What was their purpose? No one really knows, but their very existence suggests a high level of social organization. Though the lack of knowledge about these great rock spheres would seem to underline the lack of understanding about these cultures in general, it can nonetheless be said, with some degree of confidence, that by the 15th century Costa Rica was home to a number of highly developed communities who had managed to successfully forge for themselves a way of living in an environment often extremely hostile to human habitation. That, however, was all about to change, as the Old World came knocking on the door of the New (ready to kick it down).

The Spanish are Coming (Eventually): Colonization and Empire

It all seemed so promising to begin with. When, in 1502, Columbus and his crew disembarked on this remote stretch of the Atlantic coast following a heavy storm, they thought they had discovered a land of plenty and opportunity. The natives seemed friendly and largely unthreatening and, more to the point as far as the Spanish were concerned, wore large amounts of gold jewellery – bracelets, headbands, earrings, etc. – which the Spanish took as evidence that the area must be rich with precious metals. Indeed, so convinced were they of the bounty which lay in store that by the time they left (after just 17 days) they had christened the region 'Costa Rica', the 'rich coast'. Oh, how that name would come to taunt the Spanish over the succeeding decades.

Hearing tales of this wonderful, prosperous land ripe for the taking, the Spanish king, Ferdinand, lost no time in staking his claim to its riches. In 1506, he sent **Diego de Nicuesa** to colonize it for the Spanish crown. Unfortunately for Diego, by the time he had crossed the Atlantic the promised land was looking a little less promising. Not only did it soon become apparent that there was a good deal less wealth to be plundered here than had originally been believed, but this time the natives were not nearly so happy to see them. Almost as soon as the Spanish landed, the coastal Indians launched a sustained guerrilla campaign to drive them back out again. What had particularly provoked their fury was the Spanish attempt to impose 'encomienda', a system of tribute by which the natives would be forced to give up a quota of their food to the colonists. The natives' response was to burn their crops. This, combined with the ravages of tropical diseases (the area was rife with malaria and dengue fever), served to wipe out half the potential conquerors. The other half cut their losses after just a few years and returned home.

The Spanish monarchs were not to be denied, however, and so sent forth another expedition in 1522 led by **Gil González**. They were still convinced that, with a little perseverance, untold riches awaited. What the Spanish didn't know was that the gold Columbus had seen the natives wearing had all been acquired by trade, there being no gold deposits on the Atlantic side of the country. What small reserves there were existed in the as yet undiscovered southwest. This second colonizing mission was a much more determined, not to say much more brutal attempt at subjugation. The Spanish took the fight deep into the jungle, where many thousands of natives were slaughtered or forcibly baptized. But it was to no avail. Though the expedition did manage to plunder a good deal more wealth than the first, it, too, failed to establish a permanent colony, and in the end was forced to return to Spain.

If the natives thought they were winning, however, they were mistaken. Still the colonizing expeditions kept coming, and it soon became clear that the native Costa Ricans were fighting a gradually losing battle. Their numbers were being severely depleted, not just through warfare, but by a much more deadly enemy: European diseases. Measles, influenza and in particular smallpox killed thousands through-out the 16th century. Many other people simply chose to flee the area. The result was a complete crash of the indigenous population; according to official Spanish census figures, their numbers dropped from around 80,000 in 1563 to under 1,000 just a century and a half later. This was to have far-reaching consequences for the future of the Spanish colony.

Spain finally achieved a permanent foothold in Costa Rica following the despatch of yet another colonizing governor, **Juan Vásquez de Coronado**, in 1562. Coronado's first act was to found his colony not, as his predecessors had done, on the coast (the logical choice; after all, Spain was a seafaring nation and one of the primary reasons for establishing colonies was to ferry wealth back to Spain), but instead inland in the central highlands, where he built the country's first true town, **Cartago**. It many ways it proved an inspired decision. Cartago was located high on volcanic ground, away from the Atlantic swamps where malaria-ridden mosquitoes bred in such abundance, thereby immediately reducing the number of men lost to disease. However, its isolation caused its own set of problems. Communication links with Spain were necessarily strained owing to the vast distances involved. The lack of tangible assets being returned to the mother country, combined with the lack of need for reinforcements now that the native population had been 'removed', meant that it slipped out of Spain's public consciousness and for two centuries became something of a forgotten colony. As a consequence, it grew somewhat inward-looking, the Spanish rarely straying from their central stronghold – particularly as the coastal areas were a hotbed of pirate activity; the Pacific coast even welcomed a visit from the pirates' pirate himself, Sir Francis Drake, in 1579.

It was the reduction of the native population, however, that was to cause the greatest headache for potential Spanish colonists. By now, it had long been established that settlers came to the New World looking for prosperity, to become instant aristocrats over a subject population, demanding tribute and plundering wealth. But it was difficult to lead a tyrant life without anyone to tyrannize. Now that there were no natives to enslave, Spanish settlers were forced to toil their own fields (even the governor of the colony himself complained of having to do this in the early 18th century), with limited success. Agriculture remained determinedly small-scale until the 19th century – when coffee was introduced – with no export crops. The economy was so feeble that it didn't even justify its own currency; cacao beans were used for the majority of transactions right up till the 19th century. Costa Rica soon gained a reputation for being the least attractive colony in the entire Spanish empire. Anyone who came to Costa Rica in the hope of making his fortune was usually disappointed.

Historians now believe that it was during this period of adversity that the Costa Rican national character – based on egalitarianism and a lack of social hierarchy – developed. The only benefits to be had at this time came from hard work, not social status. And, with such a small native population, there developed a feeling among the settlers that they were 'all in it together'. Indeed, it is ironic that the most overwhelmingly Spanish of all Spain's colonies had come to be the least regarded by the mother country.

Hard as life was in Costa Rica, it went on and, little by little, the colony grew. By the 18th century, new towns were being established: **Heredia** in 1706, **San José** in 1737 and **Alajuela** in 1782. As the 19th century began, however, and revolutionary war raged in Europe, it was, in imperial terms at least, still little more than a provincial backwater.

Independence: Costa Rica Finally Reveals its Riches

Costa Rica's isolation at the beginning of the 19th century was neatly demonstrated when Central America declared independence from Spain on 15 September 1821. Not only was the Costa Rican government wholly unaware of this development at the time, but it didn't even find out what had happened until over a month later, when a pack mule arrived carrying the all-important message. In truth, far removed from the mainstream of Spanish political thinking, Costa Rica had been functioning as a de facto independent country for some time. Still, there were those who didn't feel quite ready to go it alone just yet. Two of Costa Rica's four main towns – Heredia and the capital, Cartago – wanted to join the Mexican Empire, while San José and Alajuela were four-square for independence, albeit within the looser agglomeration of a Central American Federation. A short **civil war** followed, in which the republicans proved victorious, after which the capital was moved to San José, where a new independent government was set up headed by **Juan Mora Fernández**, the country's first elected head of state. Costa Rica achieved **full independence** in 1848.

Fernández introduced a number of reforms, including the establishment of a fair judicial system and the expansion of the provision of education. The greatest influence on the Costa Rican way of life at this time, however, came about not as a result of a government programme, but from agriculture and, in particular, from the introduction from Cuba in 1808 of a brand new crop – **coffee**. Coffee plantations were soon thriving on the Valle Central's fertile volcanic slopes, and by the 1820s the export of the crop had begun in earnest. By the 1840s, Costa Rica was already one of the world's leading producers, providing the country with a hitherto unknown economic stability. Vast fortunes were being made by Costa Ricans finally reaping the wealth promised to settlers centuries before. Unfortunately, this wealth was not evenly distributed; Costa Rican society, previously noted for its lack of social hierarchy, began to develop a distinct class system, at the top of which sat the '*cafetaleros*', the wealthy coffee barons. Indeed, in 1849, one of the country's leading coffee-growers, **Juan Rafael Mora**, rose to the very top of society, becoming president, an office he would hold for a decade.

William Walker and Juan Santamaría

During his time in office, Juan Rafael Mora played a leading role in perhaps the most famous episode in Costa Rican history. In the 1850s, **William Walker**, a self-styled 'adventurer' from the USA, came up with a grand plan for Central America. He believed that the USA should invade the region and turn its countries into slave states serving US interests. When the US government declined to go along with his schemes, he decided to take matters into his own hands. He raised a small army and led an invasion into Mexico, but was quickly defeated and deported back to the States. This was merely a warm-up to the main event, however, and in 1855 Walker marched on Nicaragua, which quickly fell (Walker had himself declared president). Buoyed by his success, Walker and his army then turned their sights on Costa Rica, where the odds looked to be firmly in Walker's favour, as Costa Rica at that time had no army and seemed to be ripe for the taking.

Mora, however, issued a call to arms, getting together a force of 9,000 civilians armed with whatever they could lay their hands on (mostly machetes and a few rifles), and in March 1856 they headed north to confront Walker at Santa Rosa in the northwest of the country. In the event, Costa Rica's amateur troops won the day and Walker fled back to Nicaragua. The Costa Ricans followed in hot pursuit, eventually forcing Walker and his troops to make a stand at a wooden fort in Rivas. After a short stand-off, they were finally ousted when a lowly drummer boy from Alajuela, **Juan Santamaría**, daringly set fire to the fort. Realizing the jig was up, Walker and his army retreated. Tragically, Santamaría died in the fire, and is today remembered as one of the country's favourite national heroes.

Victory should have been Mora's crowning achievement, but it actually marked the beginning of his demise. A **cholera epidemic** followed soon after, killing an estimated 10 per cent of the population and leading to a severe economic slump. Mora, somewhat unfairly, was blamed for both, with many believing that his army had brought the disease back with them from Nicaragua. Mora was deposed in 1859 and, following a failed coup, executed in 1860. As for Walker, he was still up to his old tricks, convinced that his plans would one day pay off. Unfortunately (for him, if not the Central Americans), his luck did eventually run out: at his next target, Honduras, he was captured and executed.

Stability, Liberalism and Prejudice: Costa Rica in the Late 19th and Early 20th Centuries

The remainder of the 19th century saw the country enjoying greater liberalism (universal male suffrage was introduced in 1889) and increased prosperity, with coffee, and later banana, revenue used to build new bridges, roads and even a **railway**. It was the construction of the railway which showed that, for all the progress being made, the egalitarianism which had characterized the early Costa Rican character was woefully lacking when it came to race relations. When work began on a San José–Puerto Limón railway in 1871, a labour shortage led to the hiring of several thousand black Jamaican workers, many of whom stayed on after the project's completion to work on the newly established banana plantations around Limón. **Bananas** had actually been introduced to Costa Rica by the man charged with building the railway, the American **Minor Keith**, who had planted them alongside the line. They grew so well that he went on to found the United Fruit Company (later United Brands), known locally as 'Yunai', which would become one of the largest and most influential firms in all Central America. For a while, the black population enjoyed a relatively good standard of living, especially as, being English-speaking, they were often given high-ranking jobs liaising with US representatives. Unfortunately they also suffered from a good deal of prejudice from native Costa Ricans.

When, in the early 20th century, the plantations around Limón became infected with blight, United Fruit went looking for new plantation sites. The government allocated them land near Quepos on the central Pacific coast and Golfito in the south, on the understanding that the company must employ only native Costa Ricans. This, combined with a law that prevented Afro-Caribbeans from moving inland from Limón, drove the population into desperate poverty; Puerto Limón went into an abject decline from which it is only now just emerging.

Costa Rica spent much of the early 20th century deciding if it really wanted to be a democracy or not. Indeed, for a while it seemed that certain vested interests might succeed in taking over the state and halting progress, as they had (and would again do) in other Central American countries. Thankfully, they failed, although there were some close shaves, including a short-lived dictatorship following a coup led by the minister of war, **Federico Tinoco**, in 1917 (he was overthrown after a couple of years) and another wobble in the 1920s when talk among certain factions of trying to ape the Russian revolution threatened to get out of hand (but in the end came to nought).

In 1932, the **National Republican Party** was formed, which would come to dominate the political scene for the next couple of decades. Its leader, **Rafael Calderón Guardia**, was elected president and introduced many of the social reforms and state benefits for which the country is still known (and which put it in such stark contrast to many of its neighbours) – free schooling, workers' rights to organize, a minimum wage, social security, health insurance, etc.

1948: Revolution, Costa Rican Style

1948 was probably the most significant year in the country's history since 1856. The election that year was between **Teodorico Picado**, Calderón's successor, and **Otilio Ulate**, an ally of the wealthy coffee baron **José Figueres Ferrer**, known as 'Don Pepe', who had led a campaign to oust Calderón in the early forties and had subsequently been exiled to Mexico. Ulate was declared the winner, only for Picado to object, claim electoral fraud, and proclaim himself president. With both sides refusing to back down, the situation soon began to escalate. By this time, Figueres was back from Mexico and determined to force the issue. He raised a small army, supplied with modern weapons by the CIA, and launched an attack on the government in San José. As had happened a century earlier, Picado was forced to defend his position by raising an amateur army who had to supply their own weapons. But this time history was not to repeat itself. The several weeks of fighting that followed saw over 2,000 people killed and Picado's poorly equipped army defeated.

In the aftermath, Figueres was declared president of a short-lived dictatorship. However, far from overseeing a heavy-handed clampdown on liberties, he instigated a whole raft of liberal reforms, giving citizenship rights (including full freedom of movement) and the vote to Afro-Caribbeans, the vote to women, and abolishing the army (Costa Rica is still, uniquely for the region, army-less). Following the reintroduction of free elections in 1951, Figueres' party, the PLN or National Liberation Party, who despite their liberal reforms pursued vigorous free-market policies, became a firmly entrenched part of the political landscape, with Figueres himself being returned as president in 1953 and 1970 and his son, **José María Figueres**, in 1994. In fact, Costa Rican politics over the past 50 years has often given the impression of being something of a closed shop, with many of the presidential candidates emerging from the same families; Calderón's son, **Rafael Calderón Fournier**, was elected in 1990. Since the war, the presidency has tended to alternate between the PLN and the leading opposition party of the day (this is currently the PUSC or Social Christian Unity Party), partly, it has to be said, because of the law preventing presidential candidates from running for consecutive terms.

Debt, Default and Devising the Peace: Costa Rica in Recent Decades

In the 1960s and '70s, Costa Rica achieved a good level of economic and social stability. Its now famed welfare system was extended, large numbers of public schools were built and a bill was passed giving the country's tiny indigenous population rights for the first time to live on (although, crucially, not own) separate land reserves. But by the end of the 1970s trouble was brewing, although it was largely not of Costa Rica's making.

In the early 1980s, a dramatic slump in the international prices for the country's two principal exports – coffee and bananas – on which the entire economy was still over-reliant – resulted in 'prosperous' Costa Rica suddenly defaulting on its international loans, taken out in the '60s and '70s, prompting a wave of similar defaults across the region. This coincided with an escalation of the conflicts taking place within many of Costa Rica's regional neighbours, including Panama, El Salvador, Honduras, Guatemala and, above all, Nicaragua. Despite Costa Rica's overt declaration that it would remain neutral regarding these conflicts, economic pressures forced it to compromise its position slightly. As the Nicaraguan civil war grew in intensity, there was increased lobbying from the USA for Costa Rica to provide a supply route for the US-backed Contra rebels in Nicaragua. The government's eventual agreement coincided with a decision by the IMF to restructure Costa Rica's loans – something which left a sour taste in the mouths of many.

In 1986, the newly elected PLN president, **Oscar Arias Sánchez**, took it upon himself to try and sort out Costa Rica's problems by addressing the wider concerns facing the isthmus. He formulated a **Central American peace plan**, calling for a ceasefire, an amnesty for rebels who laid down their arms and the beginning of talks between opposing parties. The plan's initial success won Arias the Nobel Peace Prize in 1987 and brought Costa Rica to international attention, although the uneasy truces established in the plan's wake would soon begin to disintegrate.

Though Arias had managed to secure increased aid from the USA, he became increasingly unpopular at home, particularly following the imposition of strict economic conditions – a freeze on public sector wages and stiff price increases – to comply with IMF guidelines, and also because of his decision in 1989 to allow the USA to launch an attack on Panama's General Noriega from Costa Rican soil. In the 1990 elections, the opposition, as was by now traditional in Costa Rican politics, was returned to power.

Further problems awaited, however, including a devastating **earthquake** in 1991 which caused widespread damage to buildings and roads, just when the government was struggling to find money for public works and building projects. The number of refugees pouring into the country from conflicts in Nicaragua and elsewhere was also on the increase, causing tensions with the native population (not least because many of these countries, unlike Costa Rica, harboured yellow fever). These were offset by a few positive developments, including the signing of a **free trade agreement** with Mexico in 1995 to counter the damaging effects of NAFTA (the free trade agreement Mexico had joined earlier with the USA and Canada), and the decision by the computer giant Intel, around the same time, to build a new chip-making factory in the country.

Today, Costa Rica still faces severe economic problems. **Inflation** is high and its **international debts** are huge, accounting for some 30 per cent of government revenue. In the inevitable trade-off between providing public money for, on the one hand, welfare and education, and on the other the country's infrastructure, it's usually the infrastructure that loses out. In particular, many of the country's roads are in an extremely poor condition. This has led to the development of a 'neo-liberal' movement that has called for many of the country's state monopolies, including ICE (the national electricity company) and RECOPE (the national oil and petrol company) to be privatized. The economic situation has not been helped by the ever-expanding **population**, particularly in rural areas, where it is the fastest-growing in all Latin America, and there is still an over-reliance on the staple products of coffee, bananas and pineapples, particularly as profit margins are constantly being squeezed by competition from elsewhere, particularly Ecuador, with its low labour costs. Taxation revenue from **tourism**, which has increased vastly over the past decade (it's now the country's single biggest earner), has plugged some of the fiscal gaps, but causes problems of its own. The damage being done to the environment as a result of increased visitor numbers seems likely to, if not kill the golden goose outright, then at least wing her a little.

For all this, as it heads into the 21st century, Costa Rica remains, in comparison with the rest of Central America, a prosperous country, with its citizens enjoying the highest standards of living on the isthmus (the average life expectancy is 70) and one of the most generous welfare systems to be found anywhere.

Costa Rican Society Today

Costa Rica's population is of overwhelmingly Spanish descent. Of its estimated four million inhabitants, under two per cent are descended from the original indigenous inhabitants. Most of these live in a small network of reserves in and around Limón province, which is also home to the majority of the country's Afro-Caribbean population. These populations' extreme minority has, throughout the country's history, made it easy for the majority to neglect their concerns. Indeed, the black population suffered from official discrimination (they were unable to vote, hold Costa Rican citizenship or even travel to the Valle Central) until the latter half of the 20th century, while the indigenous peoples were only relatively recently allocated reserves of land.

A Coffee or a Banana Republic?

A rich brew versus yellow gold – which of the country's two main export crops has had the greater impact on Costa Rican life?

Of course, it all depends on how you define impact. To say that Costa Rica owes everything to coffee – its status, its wealth, its social cohesion, the strength of its economy, etc. – would be a bit of an overstatement, but not that much of one. For a good 70 or so years after the crop's introduction in the early 19th century, coffee remained the country's only major export. During that time, Costa Rica's economy was effectively a monoculture, its fortunes almost entirely dependent on the whims and fashions of European café society (to whom the majority of beans were supplied). A significant crash in the price of coffee at that time could easily have sent the country spiralling into a savage depression. Thankfully, no such crash occurred. Instead, coffee came to pervade all aspects of public life, paying for the construction of much of the country's urban infrastructure (particularly in San José) and becoming the major determinant of social stratification. In the late 1800s, people's place in the social scheme of things was almost entirely dependent on their position within the coffee-growing industry. The crop's influence continues to linger: even today, most of Costa Rica's political class is drawn from those same few wealthy coffee-growing families who emerged as the country's social élite in the mid-19th century.

And yet, though Costa Rica is perhaps more famed for its coffee, it could be argued that bananas have had an almost equally transforming effect on the country. Interestingly, the crop's initial success came off the back of a project designed to maximize coffee revenues. In the late 19th century, with the construction of the Jungle Train – the railway link designed to speed up the transportation of coffee beans from the Valle Central to the Atlantic coast – running into both logistical and financial difficulties, Minor Keith, the young US railroad magnate in charge of the project, decided to supplement his dwindling cash reserves by planting bananas alongside the tracks. In the event, these 'supplementary' bananas would prove much more profitable than the railway, which, owing to spiralling costs and a cash-strapped government unable to honour its debts, never made Keith much money at all. However, the company he founded in the early 20th century to administer his banana-exporting business, United Fruit, would go on to become one of the largest and most powerful in all the Americas, making Keith one of the continent's wealthiest men.

The mass growing of bananas effected profound changes on Costa Rica, for both good and ill. The towns of Puerto Limón, Quepos and Golfito all owe their initial expansion and success to the establishment of banana plantations by United Fruit, and all also owe their subsequent recessions to the company's abrupt decision to close down their operations. Throughout much of the 20th century, 'Yunai', as it came to be known colloquially, had the power to make or break areas almost at will, and became notorious for its draconian attitude towards workers' rights.

In the public arena, the influence of the banana-growing industry, though significant, has probably been less profound than that of coffee. With control of the industry concentrated in so few hands, bananas have never guided the affairs of the political classes or been used as a tool to determine social class to the extent that coffee has.

On the environment, however, the banana industry's effect has been truly significant. For such a major crop, bananas are surprisingly delicate, susceptible to a whole host of ailments and blights. In order to keep the plants healthy, banana-growing has become one of the most pesticide-intensive farming practices on earth. When driving past/through a banana plantation, you will see bunches of bananas encased in blue plastic bags designed to concentrate the levels of pesticides around the plants. Not only have these pesticides been blamed for causing sterility in plantation workers, but they often leak into local rivers where they are carried to surrounding 'wild' areas, causing widespread pollution. The ongoing demise of Cahuita's coral reef (*see* p.351) has been largely blamed on pollution from mainland banana plantations seeping into water courses and being taken out to sea.

So, which of these two mass-cultivated crops, for so long the bedrock of the Costa Rican economy, has the greater influence on Costa Rican life? Simple: neither. Today, both crops have been succeeded in revenue-generating terms by tourism, which in the past 15 years has had a greater influence on the use of land and the direction of the economy than both crops put together. It has spawned the creation of vast protected areas and inspired mass development of the tourist infrastructure throughout the country. And, more importantly, it has opened Costa Rica up to the outside world, attracting visitors to the country in hitherto undreamed-of numbers. Most of the major decisions to be taken about the direction of Costa Rica over the next 20 years will be tourism-, not agriculture-related.

Greater influence has been exerted by more recent arrivals, including Nicaraguan refugees from their country's civil war (who now make up six per cent of the population) and, in particular, by North Americans. Though there are only 10,000 US citizens residing officially in Costa Rica (plus, it is estimated, another 20,000 living 'unofficially'), their influence is disproportionately large. Many of the country's major hotels and resorts are American-owned and, of the million-plus people estimated to visit the country each year, half come from the USA.

Costa Rica, then, is no multiracial melting pot. The overwhelming homogeneity of its population gives it a great uniformity of character. Around 85 per cent of the population is Roman Catholic. Though church attendance is high and the majority of religious festivals strictly observed (Holy Week, in particular, involves the near shutdown of the entire country), Costa Rica's brand of religion could best be described as a sort of Catholicism-lite, partly because the church has never been able to play a dominant role in political life. Abortion may still be illegal but contraception and divorce are not, which may go some way to explaining why over

60 per cent of the nation's mothers are single parents. The majority of the population is urban, although, paradoxically, the rural population is the fastest-growing in all Central America.

'Ticos', as the Costa Ricans call themselves, like to define their society as peace-loving and egalitarian, both of which are largely true. Certainly, prior to independence there was no real class structure to speak of (it's difficult to distribute wealth unevenly when there's no wealth to distribute). But, since the advent of mass agriculture in the 19th century – particularly coffee-growing – some stratification has occurred, as demonstrated by the fact that the majority of presidents and politicians over the past century have been descended from just three families, all of whom have links to the coffee-growing industry.

For almost 60 years so far, Costa Rica has managed without an army (it was disbanded in 1949), which not only puts it in stark contrast to most of its neighbours, but also makes it unique in world terms. The country's admirable ability to avoid conflict has given it a reputation for procrastination. Some have commented, not unfondly, that the average Costa Rican would rather form a committee than a battalion. In fact, according to one story, the very derivation of the name 'Tico' comes from a corruption of the word '*momentico*' – 'in a moment'.

Costa Rica long ago decided to put health, welfare and education above defensive concerns, hence the 20 per cent of the national budget that now goes on education, which is compulsory until the age of 14. The result is a 95 per cent literacy rate, the highest in Latin America.

Just a few decades ago, the majority of Costa Ricans would have been involved in just a few professions – most involving some form of agricultural work. Recently, however, there has been a significant shift in the nature of Costa Rica's economy. More modern industries, such as electronics and pharmaceuticals, are now significant employers (which has in part fuelled the migration of the population from rural to urban areas), while tourist numbers have more than trebled since 1990, bringing in significant revenues.

Perhaps because of its abundance of natural wonders, perhaps because of its lack of an indigenous population, perhaps because life for its early settlers was so hard, or perhaps because the egalitarian nature of its society makes its people naturally suspicious of 'élite' pursuits, Costa Rica does not have a large cultural scene. The first artistic endeavours of any note did not take place until the late 19th century and were, in the main, affected attempts to ape European culture, as shown by the construction of the Teatro Nacional in San José (*see* p.105). What cultural and artistic events there are (including the International Arts Festival, the largest event) are generally put on in the capital.

So what can we conclude? Not much, other than, taken literally, the average Costa Rican would seem to be a Spanish, Catholic, city-dwelling, peace-loving, well-educated single mother with a job in the tourist industry and little interest in the arts. Generalizations will only get you so far, but here's another one. Costa Ricans are, in the main, warm and friendly, welcoming to visitors, proud of their country and eager to explain its peculiarities – all you could wish for, really. The only way to really get to know a people is to meet them. From here on in, it's up to you.

Wildlife and the Environment

To start with some statistics, Costa Rica consists of just over 50,000 sq km (less than 20,000 square miles) of land, which is roughly equivalent to the size of Wales. Though its climate can be generally characterized as 'tropical', the country is in fact home to dozens of separate microclimates and a huge variety of habitats – rainforest, cloudforest, deciduous forest, tropical dry forest, evergreen forest, mangroves, coral reefs – which support an amazing four per cent of all the world's known flora and fauna. It is a biodiversity unmatched anywhere outside the Amazon basin.

03

Indeed, in terms of species per square kilometre, Costa Rica is the most naturally diverse place on earth, with over 900 species of tree, 850 species of bird (more than in the whole of Europe), 260 species of mammal, 180 species of amphibian, 235 species of reptile and over 65,000 species of insect (although more are being discovered each year).

And it's all down to geography. Costa Rica's narrow mass of land – the Atlantic and Pacific oceans are less than a day's drive apart – has long acted as a gateway for species travelling between the temperate zones to the north and the tropics to the south. Thanks to the enormous differences in elevation found throughout the country (or, put simply, the number of hills, mountains and volcanoes), many of these species have been able to find habitats and ecosystems suitable to their needs, enabling them to stay, thrive and evolve. Costa Rica could be described as a sort of ecological bottleneck, with the natural variety that would normally be spread out over a continent squeezed into a country-sized space.

The Environment Today

Once upon a time, practically all of Costa Rica, save for its beaches and the very tips of its volcanic peaks, was swathed in tropical forest. Today, around three quarters of that forest has gone, most of it never to return, uprooted by successive generations of people. Indeed, the story of human habitation in Costa Rica could also be seen as the story of the taming, adaptation and removal of much of its natural environment.

Things started gently enough. The Pre-Columbian peoples who first settled in the region around 1000 BC were well adapted to living in harmony with the forest and, unlike their Aztec and Mayan contemporaries, created little in the way of forest-clearing architecture. The early Spanish colonialists began in a similarly low-key fashion. Though they had established towns by the 18th century, these were small-scale affairs and most of the population rarely strayed from the colony's Valle Central heartland. There was little in the way of mass agriculture until the 19th century, and until then it could be claimed that the forest was more or less winning.

Following the introduction of coffee, however, in the early 19th century, and bananas in the late, the amount of land given over to agriculture began slowly to increase, although until the middle of the 20th century much of the country remained heavily forested. The process of rainforest 'reclamation', as it is somewhat euphemistically called, only really began to accelerate alarmingly in the 1960s and '70s as cattle-ranching was introduced on a massive scale, leading to vast tracts of forest being cleared for pasture. By the 1980s, it was estimated that around 30 per cent of the country's land was given over to the production of beef. Pressure on the land was further increased by the fact that rainforest soil is thin, with few nutrients, and thus quickly exhausted, forcing farmers to indulge in a process of almost constant clearance. The international trade in tropical hardwoods also began to grow significantly in this period, leading to a huge expansion of the logging industry (both legal and illegal).

The arrival of mass ecotourism at the end of the 20th century called a temporary truce on the war between man and forest, although many minor battles do still take place. Costa Rica's network of national parks and private refuges now protect around 25 per cent of the country's territory from development (*see* pp.51–3 and 84–5). There are still pressures on this land from illegal farming and logging, and even greater ones on those areas of forest that lay in the 'buffer' zones on the parks' borders, beyond official control. But tourist revenues, which now exceed all other industries, have at least given the conservation movement a significant economic impetus, even if the rapid growth of tourist numbers has led to the creation of a whole host of new environmental problems, *see* pp.49–54.

Unfortunately, this 25 per cent pretty much represents nature's last stand. The vast majority of the forests already cleared cannot be regenerated. Biodiversity like this is thousands of years in the making and cannot be turned off and on like a tap.

That, then, is the bad news. The good news is that within Costa Rica's parks are some of the most thrilling natural vistas to be found anywhere. It may be somewhat reduced in size, but this is still nature's wonderland, comprising a bewildering array of environments and habitats (rainforest, wetforest, cloudforest, dry forest, etc.) filled with the greatest diversity of life on earth.

Habitats

Forests

Ecologists define Costa Rica's natural geography not so much in terms of separate environments – many of the country's habitats are highly interconnected – but rather, collectively, under the much broader definition of 'Life Zones', which may contain several different types of habitat. These include a number of often subtly different types of forest. Starting at the country's highest reaches, these include the following.

Tropical Montaine Rainforest
Of course, rainforest is what Costa Rica is known for, and is the main draw for the majority of visitors. This, however, is not typical forest – you'll find no sultry depths here, more a sort of moss carpet. Found near the summits of many of the country's central volcanoes, including Poás and Irazú, the vegetation is characterized by its diminutive stature, with mosses and ferns clinging close to the slopes to offset the effects of the strong, biting winds.

As with plants, few large animals can thrive here, and those that do tend to be airborne – vultures, raptors and so on.

Premontaine Wet Forest
Found at elevations slightly lower than tropical montaine rainforest, premontaine wet forest is still an overwhelmingly mossy environment, but interspersed with a greater number of trees, typically evergreens. Examples can be found in the Tapantí and Braulio Carrillo National Parks.

Cloudforest

Found on the lower slopes of some of the country's volcanoes and mountains, cloudforest, as the name suggests, is almost permanently submerged within thick mists, which create a near 100 per cent humidity. It is an extremely wet environment and, as a consequence, an extremely lush and fertile one. It's made up of layer upon layer of thick vegetation, beginning at ground level with dense mosses and ferns, from which strangler vines and lianas lead up to a crowded tree canopy where epiphytes, including orchids, nestle in the high branches. The forest is home to a vast wealth of wildlife, including seemingly billions of insects, as well as some of the region's superstar animals – quetzals, pumas and jaguars. The Monteverde region is home to the country's largest remaining area of cloudforest.

Tropical Wet Forest

This is what most people think of when they hear the term 'rainforest'. These lowland forests are where you'll find the country's greatest concentration of flora and fauna, where jaguars prowl the inner depths and monkeys patrol the canopy. Primary rainforest – i.e. forest that has been left *in situ* for hundreds of years – has certain characteristics, some of which may come as a surprise to the uninitiated. Least surprising is that it's very wet, with some areas receiving 5–6 metres of rainfall a year. It's also, at ground level, somewhat sparse, which does tend to come as news to travellers expecting to have to battle their way through thick, impenetrable jungle (most people's idea of rainforest is actually more akin to cloudforest, *see* above). But rainforest trees are, as a rule, very tall – typically over 70m – quick-growing and, as a consequence, somewhat short-lived (few make it past 100 years – come heavy rains, the forest will reverberate to the sound of toppling giants). The real arena for jungle life here is not the forest floor but the canopy, where flat-topped trees compete so effectively for the available sunlight that very little (less than 10 per cent where there's full coverage) gets through to the ground below. And it's here that the majority of species make their homes, hence the large number of treetop tours offered throughout the country.

Secondary rainforest – usually created as a result of human clearing of primary – is thicker and more jungly, as there's greater competition here between species. The largest areas of preserved primary rainforest left in Costa Rica can be found in Tortuguero and Corcovado National Parks (*see* pp.335–44 and pp.319–22).

Tropical Dry Forest

This seems like a pretty fancy name for something that is essentially a desert for large parts of the year. In fact, the term 'tropical dry forest' can be used to describe a whole variety of habitats, including grasslands and deciduous forests, the linking factor being that they enjoy two distinct seasons: a wet season and a dry season. The dry season can be very dry, often lasting up to six months, when many trees and plants shed their leaves, hence the desert-like appearance. Tropical dry forest was once common all along Central America's Pacific coast, but has come under severe threat over the past century because of its suitability (much more so than rainforest, with its weak, nutrient-poor soil) for agriculture. The largest remaining stretch of dry forest in Costa Rica is in the Parque Nacional Santa Rosa (*see* p.171).

Aquatic Habitats

Mangrove Forests

Mangroves, with their ability to thrive in coastal areas where the freshwater of rivers meets the saltwater of seas, provide a unique environment, their stilt-like root systems acting as ecosystems for a great variety of wildlife including crocodiles, caimans and vast numbers of birds (some of which, such as the mangrove cuckoo and mangrove hummingbird, live nowhere else).

As with many of Costa Rica's natural environments, mangroves are becoming increasingly rare. The most significant remaining examples are to be found on the Pacific coast in the Parque Nacional Marino Las Baulas and the Parque Nacional Marino Ballena, both of which are home to all five of the native species of Costa Rican mangrove.

Rivers

Costa Rica's rivers, when not full of white-water rafters (*see* p.61) are home to a great abundance of wildlife, including crocodiles, herons, egrets, lizards and freshwater turtles.

For the best wildlife-spotting opportunities on rivers, head to the large Parque Nacional Tortuguero on the northern Atlantic coast or book a jungle cruise up the Río Sarapiquí.

Coral Reefs

Coral reefs are one of the most sensitive of all marine habitats, and their health or otherwise is a good indicator of the general state of the environment. The extraordinary community of creatures that live here – including fish, octopus, crabs, sponges and anemones – combine to form an extremely delicate ecosystem, highly susceptible to changes in the natural order.

Unfortunately, Costa Rica's reefs, of which there are just a handful (the most accessible lying just off the coast at Cahuita), are coming under increasing threat. Pollution, particularly from pesticides entering the water system, and deforestation (soil washing into the sea can block the filter-feeding mechanism of the coral) are reducing the coral's extent year by year. The coral's achingly slow growth rate means that these losses cannot easily be regenerated. *See* p.351.

Beaches and Seas

Costa Rica's beaches provide some of the world's most important nesting sites for marine turtles, including green, hawksbill, leatherback and olive ridley turtles. The main sites are located in the Parque Nacional Tortuguero on the Atlantic coast (green and hawksbill), and the Parque Nacional Marino Las Baulas (leatherback) and the Parque Nacional Santa Rosa (olive ridley) on the Pacific coast.

Offshore, dolphins and porpoises are common in Costa Rican waters, while humpback whales come to breed each year in the Parque Nacional Marino Ballena on the Pacific coast.

Wildlife Guide

Jaguars are the main draw, of course. They are the creatures that every visitor comes to Costa Rica in the hope of seeing. Unfortunately, almost everyone is disappointed; sightings of these shy, nocturnal and extremely scarce creatures are extraordinarily rare. However, your disappointment shouldn't last for long: even if few people get to tick the box at the top of their list, Costa Rica is still a wildlife-spotter's paradise, its national parks and refuges thick with all manner of beautiful birds, chattering monkeys, slithery reptiles and more. You will need rolls and rolls of film, or a very large memory card for your digital camera.

Whatever you want to spot, be it spider monkeys leaping through the canopy, scarlet macaws nesting in coastal trees, caimans gliding silently along a river or dolphins zigzagging their way through the open ocean, you're best off doing it in the company of an experienced guide. This particularly applies to wildlife-spotting in the rainforest, where much of the activity takes place 60 metres above your head and requires an expert eye to pick out. If you are staying near a national park, your hotel should be able to put you in touch with a good local guide or tour operator. Otherwise, see pp.68–70, and **Active Costa Rica**, pp.55–62.

Mammals

Cats

Jaguars

It's not just visitors to the region who find jaguars endlessly fascinating; these elusive jungle killers have long held a near mystical status in Central America. The Maya, in particular, considered them to be sacred animals. In part, it's the very nature of the beast – the silent, invisible assassin that reveals itself only at the moment of attack – that lends itself so well to mythologizing.

Jaguars are the largest carnivores in the Americas, a fully grown male weighing up to 150kg and measuring over two metres, nose to tail. Despite their relative bulk, they are extremely graceful creatures, their distinctive patterning – yellowy-orange fur marked with clusters of black rosettes – allowing them to blend in seamlessly with their jungle surroundings and to creep up unawares on their prey, which consists mainly of smaller mammals such as peccaries and coatis, as well as fish and birds.

In theory, jaguars have a range that stretches from the tip of Argentina to the bottom of Mexico, but in truth the population is restricted to a few isolated pockets. Hunting for jaguar pelts, which was legal in Costa Rica right up until the 1980s, combined with the destruction of their habitat (they're highly territorial animals, each requiring a large stretch of forest in which to hunt), has severely depleted their numbers.

There is talk of trying to establish a wildlife corridor linking the jungles of seven Central American countries – Belize, Guatemala, Honduras, El Salvador, Nicaragua, Costa Rica and Panama – into a Paseo Pantera (Path of the Panther), allowing jaguars, and other wildlife, to extend their ranges, but this is still in the early stages.

• **Chances of spotting:** Virtually nil.

• **Best locations for spotting:** Your best chance of seeing a jaguar ('best' in this instance means almost no chance, as opposed to absolutely no chance) is in the national parks of La Amistad and Corcovado, although the closest you are likely to get is to some of the animals' droppings. The camouflage, wariness and predatory skill of these animals means that, even if you were close by, chances are you'd never know. If you're particularly determined on tracking one down, you could listen out for their call – which apparently sounds a bit like a large dog gently clearing its throat.

Pumas

The puma (or mountain lion) may sport a slightly duller coat than the jaguar – being essentially a uniform sandy brown with a paler throat and belly – but it is also a good deal bolder in character. Though almost no one in Costa Rica has a jaguar encounter story to tell, you'll hear plenty of puma anecdotes. Unlike the jaguar, which usually restricts itself to the forest depths, pumas, which are almost as large as jaguars, have often been encountered on well-worn paths, and there are even tales of them wandering right into forest-side hotel complexes. These sightings would seem to give a good indication, not just of the animals' lack of fear, but of the relative strength of their numbers. Though still on the endangered list, the puma population would appear to be a good deal higher than the jaguars'.

• **Chances of spotting:** Low, but there's a chance.

• **Best locations for spotting:** Parque Nacional Corcovado; Parque Internacional La Amistad; Reserva Biológica Bosque Nuboso Monteverde.

Other Cats

Costa Rica is home to three other wild cats, all considerably smaller than the jaguar and puma. The most distinctive are **ocelots** and **margays**, both of which look a bit like miniature jaguars (ocelots are slightly bigger) with yellow fur and black markings. The **jaguarundi**, despite its name (which, unlike 'ocelot' or 'margay', does suggest a miniature jaguar), is actually a small reddish-brown cat. It's extremely shy, living deep in the forest depths, and, as a consequence, little studied or understood.

• **Chances of spotting:** Low. The margay is the most confident and numerous of the three, but sightings are still rare.

• **Best location for spotting:** Parque Nacional Corcovado.

Monkeys

If cats are the wildlife guide's curse, rarely putting in an appearance, then monkeys are their saviour, being relatively common and easy to spot. Every guide worth his or her salt will know the favourite nesting sites of several troops.

There are four species of monkey native to Costa Rica.

Howler Monkeys

You'll probably hear them before you see them, especially if you're staying near an area of lowland forest. True to their name, male howler monkeys greet and bid farewell to each day with a prolonged chorus of loud, low, reverberating whoops, which they produce by forcing air past a hollow bone in their throats. The sound, which can be a little unnerving for the uninitiated, can travel for several miles in the forest and, it is believed, is used to literally 'sound out' a group's territory.

Living in small groups of about a dozen individuals, howler monkeys can often be spotted in the day lazing at the tops of their favourite trees (all that howling must take it out of them) and, even when active, tend not to stray too far. They operate across a small range of territory (which has made them less susceptible to forest clearance than other species of monkey), slowly moving from tree to tree on the hunt for leaves, fruit and flowers.

• **Chances of spotting:** Good. Howler monkeys are relatively common, have small territories and are pretty slow-moving – the perfect spotting combination.

• **Best location for spotting:** Many parks, reserves and refuges have sizeable resident howler populations, including: Parque Nacional Cahuita; Parque Nacional Corcovado; Parque Nacional Rincón de la Vieja; Parque Nacional Tortuguero; and Reserva Natural Absoluta Cabo Blanco.

Spider Monkeys

In contrast to howler monkeys, which when they're not howling tend to be sleeping, spider monkeys seem to be always on the move. Smaller than howlers, with distinctive reddish fur, they are at times quite spectacularly gymnastic. Indeed, it's a privilege to watch them make their acrobatic way across the jungle, flinging themselves from branch to branch using all four of their long, spidery limbs (hence the name) and strong prehensile tail, which often seems to act as a safety harness – and they do need one: with such daring comes great risk. Spider monkeys often seem to miss the branch they're aiming for, but miraculously also always seem to manage to grab the one below just in time and recover.

Feeding primarily on fruit, spider monkeys require a lot of territory. Forest clearance in recent decades has severely reduced their numbers.

• **Chances of spotting:** Good, if in the company of a guide who knows his or her stuff. Spider monkeys tend to follow well-worn paths through the forest, known (believe it or not) as 'monkey highways'.

• **Best locations for spotting:** Parque Nacional Tortuguero. Its waterways provide good viewing opportunities of the monkeys making their way through the waterside canopies. There are also healthy populations in the Parque Nacional Cahuita, Parque Nacional Rincón de la Vieja and Parque Nacional Santa Rosa.

White-Faced Capuchins

This is not the most common monkey in Costa Rica, but it is perhaps the one you are most likely to encounter, partly because of its highly inquisitive nature. White-faced capuchins give the impression of being as keen on wildlife-spotting as we are, and will often descend to the low branches of trees in order to get a close-up look at the strange pink-faced creatures staring up at them. Occasionally, they can take offence at this intrusion and, though unlikely to attack, will chatter and bare their teeth aggressively. If they do, it's best to move away quickly, for, if you don't, their next mode of defence is to urinate (highly accurately) on their 'attackers'. Their inquisitive nature is born of a high intelligence, which in turn is due to their varied diet, which includes insects and shellfish as well as fruit and leaves. Capuchins are constantly exploring their environment, poking their fingers into holes and peeling away bark in the hunt for food. Unfortunately this 'cute' behaviour, combined with their cute appearance (they're about 70–100cm long, half of which is tail, with thick black fur offset by a bright white face) has often led to them being captured and kept in private zoos or as pets.

- **Chances of spotting:** Good, especially if they spot you first.
- **Best locations for spotting:** A variety of different parks and reserves, including: Parque Nacional Barra Honda; Parque Nacional Cahuita; Parque Nacional Corcovado; Parque Nacional Manuel Antonio; Parque Nacional Rincón de la Vieja; Parque Nacional Tortuguero; Reserva Biológica Bosque Nuboso Monteverde; and Reserva Natural Absoluta Cabo Blanco.

Squirrel Monkeys

The smallest (just 65cm long) and scarcest of Costa Rica's monkeys, squirrel monkeys are now found in only a few isolated patches of forest along the Pacific coast, the largest of which is in the Parque Nacional Manuel Antonio. Light brown with a 'cute' white face, they have, like the capuchins, often been taken from the wild for display in private zoos, where they rarely thrive. In the wild, they live and travel in small groups and feed mainly on fruit.

- **Chances of spotting:** Relatively good. Though rare, there is a large population in the Parque Nacional Manuel Antonio. In fact, you may find them coming to you. The number of visitors to the park has, so it has been claimed, had a detrimental effect on the animal's behaviour, with reports of monkeys approaching humans and begging for food, rather than keeping a safe 'wild' distance.
- **Best locations for spotting:** Parque Nacional Manuel Antonio; Parque Nacional Corcovado.

Sloths

Considering their quite extraordinary lack of activity – they can sleep for up to 23 hours a day – sloths are surprisingly difficult to spot. They spend so long rooted in one place, usually in the crook at the top of a tree, that over time their fur gets a covering of moss and algae which enables them to blend in perfectly with their surroundings (and helps protect them against attack from their most common predator – eagles).

Their lack of movement is due to their having an extremely low metabolic rate, which means they need to eat very little (they feed exclusively on leaves, which they can take up to two days to digest) and move even less. They also have an extremely low core temperature, with the result that, even though they live in the sweltering tropics, they occasionally die of hypothermia, being extremely susceptible to even small drops in temperature.

There are two types of sloth in Costa Rica: the **brown-throated three-toed sloth**, which is diurnal, and **Hoffman's two-toed sloth**, which is nocturnal (although for creatures that are barely awake, such characterizations are somewhat redundant, certainly from a spotter's perspective). They are both around 50–75cm in length and 'officially' brown, although more usually the colour of the adjacent tree. Their 'toes' are in fact long, very strong claws, which they use to grip branches and, *in extremis*, fend off attackers. That's if they can pick them out: in addition to all their other foibles, they also have extremely poor eyesight.

• **Chances of spotting:** Fair to middling if on your own. Relatively good in the company of a guide. Sloths have 'favourite' trees (i.e. ones they can't be bothered to move from), which an experienced guide will know.

• **Best locations for spotting:** Parque Nacional Tortuguero, where they can often be seen sleeping (what else?) in waterside trees; or slightly more accessibly in Puerto Limón, whose Parque Vargas is home to a small population.

Tapirs

Though near the top on most people's must-see list, tapirs are not often spotted in the wild (although I did see one during one of my first-ever trips into the rainforest). Despite their bulk – an adult male can weigh up to 300kg, making them Costa Rica's largest land animal – they are very shy, rarely straying from the forest depths. They're strange, primeval-looking beasts with short, dark grey (verging on black) fur, and small ears and eyes set behind a long prehensile snout, which makes them look a bit like a missing link diagram showing the evolution of the elephant (although, they are in fact a distant relative of the rhino).

Slow and lumbering (when out of water, where they spend much of their time feeding) with poor eyesight (which I can vouch for: the tapir I encountered plodded contentedly around a group of people without giving the slightest indication of realizing we were there), tapirs are peaceful vegetarians and unlikely to be aggressive, unless with young. Their distinctive appearance, though odd, has clearly been very successful. According to the fossil records, tapirs have existed in this area for at least 20 million years.

• **Chances of spotting:** Slim, but you might get lucky.

• **Best locations for spotting:** Parque Nacional Braulio Carrillo; Parque Nacional Corcovado; Parque Internacional La Amistad, particularly near rivers and streams where they spend a lot of time feeding.

Bats

Statistically speaking, you are more likely to see a bat than anything else. Half of all Costa Rica's mammal species are bats. These include **fishing bats**, **fruit bats**, three species of **vampire bat** (don't panic: they prey mainly on cattle) as well as many types of **insect-eating bat**, which are the most common.

Come dusk in any low-lying rural area, and quite a few urban ones, and you'll see them darting around the skies on the hunt for insects; they are distinguishable from birds in low light by their unique flying style, which makes them look as if they are doing a sort of front crawl through the air. In the day, if you know where to look, you can often spot groups of bats nesting on the undersides of branches. With their wings wrapped tightly around their bodies, they look like rows of leathery chocolates.

• **Chances of spotting:** Good. Though nocturnal, they become active at twilight and in the daytime you may be able to spot them roosting.

• **Best locations for spotting:** Throughout the country, but particularly in the Estación Biológica La Selva; the Murciélago Sector of the Parque Nacional Santa Rosa; the Hacienda Barú lodge and private reserve (*see* p.293); and the Parque Nacional Tortuguero, whose waterways, overlooked by countless branches, provide good opportunities for spotting roosting bats.

Peccaries

Tales of fearful confrontations in the jungle usually involve not, as you might suspect, jaguars or pumas or even tapirs with young, but these small, dark-haired wild pigs. There are two types – the **collared peccary** and the **white-lipped peccary** – neither of which is particularly large (70–80cm and up to 20kg when full grown), but they do move around in large packs of up to 50 individuals and can be highly territorial. They have been known to surround unwary travellers and clack their teeth aggressively, although they are unlikely to attack. The standard advice, if you come across a group that looks threatening, is to climb a tree, after which they should quickly lose interest and move on.

• **Chances of spotting:** Reasonable, although, considering their reputation for aggression you may not actually want to.

• **Best locations for spotting:** Parque Nacional Corcovado; Parque Nacional Rincón de la Vieja; Parque Nacional Santa Rosa; Reserva Biológica Bosque Nuboso Monteverde; Reserva Natural Absoluta Cabo Blanco.

Coatis

Coatis are members of the racoon family. They're about twice the size of North American racoons, with brown fur, white markings around their snout and a ringed tail, which they hold upright when they walk. Despite their somewhat lumbering gait, they are agile climbers, scampering up trees in the search for insects and fruit.

• **Chances of spotting:** Good: they are diurnal and relatively common.

• **Best locations for spotting:** Pretty much all over the country. Coatis can live in a variety of habitats and altitudes, and are common in both montane and rainforest. The Parque Nacional Barra Honda, Parque Nacional Cahuita, Parque Nacional Carara, Parque Nacional Corcovado, Parque Nacional Santa Rosa and Reserva Biológica Bosque Nuboso Monteverde all have healthy populations.

Other Land Mammals

Opussums are the Americas' only marsupial, the mothers carrying their young in a pouch in the manner of their Australian cousins. There are nine species in Costa Rica, the most common of which is the appropriately named **common opossum**, which lives in lowland forest areas, although, being nocturnal, is infrequently seen.

Costa Rica is home to three species of **anteater**: the very rare **giant anteater**, the **silky anteater** and, the one most likely to put in an appearance, the **lesser anteater**, also known as the **tamandua**. They live in rainforest and lower montane forest and, though primarily nocturnal, do occasionally come out to feed during the day. They're about 1.5m long with sandy brown and black fur and have an astonishing 40cm-long tongue which they use to lap up vast quantities of ants and termites. Be careful if you do come across one, as they can be dangerous. They have very large foreclaws for tearing open termite nests, which they will use against a potential attacker if they feel threatened.

The **armadillo**, the anteater's more heavily armoured cousin, is also nocturnal (which seems a strange choice for an animal that is practically blind), but is occasionally spotted, or more likely heard, bumping its myopic way around the foliage at twilight.

Otherwise, the mammals you're most likely to encounter in Costa Rica include **racoons**, **deer**, three types of **skunk**, **red-tailed squirrels**, **pacas** (a large water-dwelling rodent) and **coyotes**, common to the open plains of Guanacaste.

Marine Mammals

Humpback whales from the Arctic and Antarctic return each year (roughly December to March) to breed and calve in the coastal waters of the Parque Nacional Marino Ballena, which is also home, year-round, to **common** and **bottle-nosed dolphins**. 'Watching' tours are popular and offer a reasonable chance of success, particularly of dolphins.

Manatees, also known as sea cows, can still be found in the waters around Tortuguero. They're certainly difficult to miss if you come across one, being around 4m long and weighing up to 600kg (they look a bit like enormous, inflated seals), but their population is in decline because of pollution and, owing to their habit of drifting near the surface, injuries caused by boat collisions.

Birds

For its size, Costa Rica is home to an astonishing variety of birdlife. In total, including migratory birds, 850 species have been recorded here. That's roughly 10 per cent of all the world's species in a country that accounts for less than 0.03 per cent of the world's landmass.

Every day, whether actively spotting or not, you are bound to see several different species. Birdwatching tours are big business here, and many jungle lodges offer spotting packages (see also **Active Costa Rica**, p.58, and Travel, pp.69–70).

The best places for watching are on the edge of an area of forest, on open plains and, for wildfowl, in wetland areas such as Parque Nacional Palo Verde, Parque Nacional Tortuguero and Refugio Nacional de Vida Silvestre Caño Negro.

Quetzals

The quetzal, with its dazzling green and red plumage, is to birdwatchers what the jaguar is to mammal-watchers. It's the big one, the must-see species. And, like the jaguar, it has long played a major role in the region's culture. Its feathers were used as currency in pre-Columbian times (the Guatemalan currency is still called the quetzal) and adorned the headdress of one of the most important Aztec gods, Quetzalcoatl, while in the colonial era the bird became a symbol of liberty owing to its hatred of captivity.

Though spotting one can take some effort – what seems so brilliant and distinctive in a photograph actually blends in very effectively with the cloudforest foliage where the birds make their homes – they are a good deal easier to track

The Mythical Mystery Tour

Early European settlers in Central America were intrigued by tales of the quetzal, but soon became convinced that these were nothing other than powerful local legends. This was mainly due to the fact that the Europeans, lacking specialist knowledge of the region's geography, were unable to find the birds, while the natives for their part were probably unwilling to show them. The killing of a quetzal was punishable by death under Mayan law.

No European set eyes on a quetzal until 1861, when an English naturalist, Osbert Salvin, led a dedicated expedition into the jungle to determine once and for all whether the bird truly existed. He was amazed at what he found. The quetzal, he declared, was indeed a reality, with plumage 'unequalled for splendour among the birds of the New World'. That sort of beauty couldn't be left to escape, so he shot it, had it stuffed and took it back to England, where hats adorned with quetzal plumes were soon all the rage.

down than jaguars. As is traditional, the male has more resplendent plumage than the female, with red headfeathers and two long green and white tailfeathers that can grow to over 60cm (the bird itself is about the size of a large pigeon).

• **Chances of spotting:** Reasonable. There's a whole tourist infrastructure in place dedicated to quetzal-watching. A good guide will know the location of some aguacatillo trees, the birds' favourite source of food. Sightings are also more common during the March–June breeding season.

• **Best locations for spotting:** The upper elevations of Parque Nacional Braulio Carrillo, Parque Nacional Volcán Poás; Parque Nacional Chirripó; and, in particular, the cloudforests of the Reserva Biológica Bosque Nuboso Monteverde and the Reserva Santa Elena.

Scarlet Macaws

After quetzals, these large, brightly coloured members of the parrot family are perhaps the most sought-after by birdwatchers. Though they were relatively common until just a few decades ago, deforestation has reduced their numbers so severely that there are now just two sizeable colonies left – in the national parks of Carara and Corcovado, both of which are on the Pacific coast.

However, once they have been located, there's certainly no mistaking them with their stunning primary-coloured plumage – a red head and tail blending into yellow and blue wings for both males and females – which acts as a sort of anti-camouflage, making them easy to pick out against the green forest background. They're highly gregarious, living in large groups, and can often be spotted perching or flying in pairs (they mate for life), squawking raucously to each other as they glide in perfect multicoloured formation.

The bulk of their diet is made up of seeds and nuts, which they break open using their hooked beaks (in fact, their beaks are so powerful that they can even crack those kings of nutty security, brazils).

Costa Rica is also home to **great green macaws** (predominantly green with touches of blue on the wings and red on the head), which live on the Caribbean side, and several species of parakeet, common throughout the country.

• **Chances of spotting:** Reasonable, if you go to the right place.

• **Best locations for spotting:** There are only two spotting locations: the Parque Nacional Carara, which is home to about 200 individuals; and the Parque Nacional

Corcovado, which is home to around 1,600. Large numbers have often been seen roosting in the coastal trees near the La Leona ranger station in Corcovado.

Hummingbirds

These tiny, hyperactive, brightly coloured whirligigs are among the most wondrous of all birds and, thankfully, also some of the easiest to spot in the wild. Costa Rica's 50 species come in a mad variety of shimmering shades (oranges, blues, violets, blacks and iridescent greens – their feathers acting as tiny prisms refracting the light) and an even stranger array of names: the **green-crowned brilliant**, the **white-necked jacobin**, the **long-tailed hermit**, the **green violet-ear**.

What they all have in common is their size – they're absolutely minute: the largest, the **violet sabrewing**, is a mighty 15cm long; most are under 10cm. And there is their unique ability to hover. Specially jointed bones and super-fast-twitch muscles allow hummingbirds to beat their wings at up to 100 times per second (impossible for the naked eye and even most high-speed cameras to pick out), enabling them to hover motionless in front of the flowers on which they feast. This frenzied beating produces the faint whirring sound from which they get their name. They use their long tongues to feed on nectar, which they must consume in vast quantities in order to keep their feverish metabolism ticking over – their pulse beats at an astonishing 1,200 times per minute. Some species can eat up to eight times their own body weight in a single day. To compensate for their hectic lifestyle, many hummingbirds go into a sort of mini-hibernation each night, lowering their heartbeat and body temperature and slowing their metabolism until morning.

Their speed and tiny size can make it quite difficult to tell species apart, although any hummingbird is a wonder to behold, whether correctly identified or not.

• **Chances of spotting:** Good. They are relatively common and largely unafraid of people. In fact, during the breeding season, male hummingbirds will often fly right up to people to inspect them (presumably to check whether they are a potential rival). Some refuges and lodges have set up artificial hummingbird feeders with adjacent observation platforms allowing you to see them at close quarters.

• **Best locations for spotting:** The Reserva Biológica Bosque Nuboso Monteverde is home to the country's highest concentration of hummingbirds.

Waterbirds

Costa Rica's coastal areas are home to several migratory species including **gulls**, **sandpipers**, **plovers** and, one of the most distinctive, **frigate birds**, the males of which have bright red inflatable neck pouches (they are common along the Guanacaste coast and around the Gulf of Nicoya).

Inland, the prime wetland areas for birdwatching are the Parque Nacional Tortuguero, Parque Nacional Palo Verde and Refugio Nacional de Vida Silvestre Caño Negro. Birds here range from the common – **herons**, **cormorants**, **ibis**, **kingfishers** (there are six types) and **anhingas** (a larger relative of the cormorant) – to rarer birds, including the **jabirú stork** and the beautiful **roseate spoonbill**, which has bright pink wings and a distinctive long, flat bill which it swills around underwater, sifting for food.

Birds of Prey

There are over 50 species, including **hawks**, **eagles**, **kites** and **falcons**, although, as with many other animals that require a large territory in which to hunt, deforestation has severely reduced their numbers. Indeed, the **harpy eagle** is reckoned to be now almost extinct.

Those that remain can be difficult to spot owing to the great height and speed at which they fly, and, once spotted, they can be even trickier to identify accurately because of the similarity of plumage and wing-shape of many species. Some of the most common types include: **ospreys**, which still patrol the Caribbean coast in relatively healthy numbers; the **common black hawk**, another coastal inhabitant; the **black-shouldered hawk**, which is often seen in agricultural areas; the **laughing falcon**, which you should be able to pick out by following the sound of its distinctive 'wa-co' call (from which is derived its Spanish name 'guaco') and, perhaps the most common, the **roadside hawk**, which, true to its name, often perches on low posts by the roadside in rural areas.

There are also 17 species of **owl**, which, being nocturnal, are rarely seen, although you may hear the slightly eerie call of the screech owl.

Vultures

Vultures, of which there are several species, are common in Costa Rica. If you spend any length of time driving around the countryside, you're almost guaranteed to come across the rather ominous sight of a group of these naked-headed carrion-eaters perched on a fence at the side of the road, waiting for something to go wrong (at which point, you can't help but check the petrol gauge).

Reptiles and Amphibians

Turtles

Costa Rica's beaches make up one of the world's most important nesting sites for four types of marine turtle – **green turtles**, **hawksbill turtles**, **leatherback turtles** and **olive ridley turtles**. The sight of these great aquatic giants clambering clumsily up the shore to dig their nests and lay their eggs is one of the most magical, and heavily observed, in the natural world. What was once an excuse for a mass feast of turtle meat is now one of the main events on the tourist calendar, with hundreds flocking to the shores of Tortuguero and elsewhere to watch the '*desove*' (egg-laying) each year. It's a vulnerable time for the turtles, who, being wholly adapted for life at sea, face grave dangers during the small proportion of that life they spend on land. Their strategy for coping with the inevitable attention of predators (who, even in these heavily protected times, still include human poachers) is to arrive *en masse* at night, with each mother turtle laying thousands of eggs, which they then bury carefully in the sand.

Though predators claim many young turtle lives, with coatis and racoons digging up nests, and seabirds, vultures and crabs preying on the newly hatched offspring as they make their hazardous journey to the sea, the sheer volume of baby turtle numbers ensures that at least some survive.

• **Chances of spotting:** Good, if you're prepared to wait. Access to all the main nesting sites is strictly controlled, but viewing opportunities can be very good if you pick the right night.

• **Best locations for spotting:** Tortuguero's Atlantic beaches are the main nesting site for green and hawksbill turtles. Leatherback turtles, who at up to 500kg and 5m long are the world's largest reptile, nest predominantly at the Parque Nacional Marino Las Baulas, while olive ridley turtles, the country's most numerous species, also nest on the Pacific side, principally in the Parque Nacional Santa Rosa and the Refugio Nacional de Fauna Silvestre Ostional.

Frogs and Toads

At times, the country can seem as if it's literally heaving with frogs and toads. It's a rare jungle lodge indeed that can keep its swimming pool amphibian-free for a whole evening.

Marine toads, which, despite their name, are common to most of the country, seem to be the keenest midnight paddlers. Other notable species include that perennial postcard favourite, the bright green **leaf frog**, as well as several varieties of **poison arrow frog**. One of the most common – particularly in Tortuguero – is about 2cm long with a crimson red body and blue legs (it's known locally as the 'blue jeans frog'). These should on no account be touched, as their highly toxic poison can be transmitted through the skin.

Crocodiles and Caimans

Despite the ever-present attention of hunters servicing the demands of the handbag industry, Costa Rica still has relatively healthy populations of caimans and crocodiles. The waterways of Tortuguero and Caño Negro offer the best spotting opportunities, where you'll often see **caimans**, a smaller relative of the crocodile (they're about 1.5m long), bobbing near the surface like partially submerged logs – which is the intention; they use their camouflage to drift towards their prey unnoticed. **Crocodiles** are larger and tend to be found nearer the sea, often as not basking on mud and sandbanks.

Snakes

First the good news – of Costa Rica's 162 species of snake, just 22 are venomous. Not only do these species tend to advertise their potential danger with gaudy coloration, but they're mostly nocturnal, rarely seen and, if encountered, are more likely to slither away than attack. Still, you should always take special care when walking through dense undergrowth or grassland, particularly at dawn and dusk when snakes are most likely to be active.

The species you should be most wary of include the **fer-de-lance**, which lives predominantly near streams and rivers, the **coral snake** with its distinctive red, yellow and black stripes (you should also watch out for the false coral snake, which is not poisonous, but looks identical; only an expert can tell them apart), and the **bushmaster**, which has a reputation for aggression. However, there is no need to be overly alarmed. Most visitors to Costa Rica do not encounter a single snake during their time in the country.

Lizards

There are plenty of lizards in Costa Rica. The most common is probably the **green iguana**, a strange primeval beast with a knobbly head and side-set legs which make it look a bit like a mini-dinosaur (which, essentially, is what it is). They can often be spotted basking on branches at the side of rivers, which is also a good location for spotting **basilisk lizards**. If surprised, these bright green reptiles will escape by 'running' across the water on large webbed feet in a strange cartwheeling motion (hence their nickname, **'Jesus Christ lizards'**).

Fish

Starting inland, the determined fish-spotter can encounter **trout** and **rainbow bass** in freshwater rivers; **parrotfish**, **angelfish**, **starfish** and **manta rays** at the coral reefs off the coast of Cahuita and the Isla del Caño; **tarpon**, **snook**, **marlin** and other fighting fish in the deep waters of the north Caribbean; and **marlin** and **sailfish** in the south Pacific. Barra del Colorado, Quepos and Golfito are the country's prime sports-fishing destinations.

Insects and Spiders

This is where statistics give way to guesstimates. So far, over 65,000 species of insect have been recorded in Costa Rica, including ants, moths, butterflies, beetles, praying mantises, bees and wasps. Though no one knows how many more may be out there, all the experts agree that this inventory is far from complete and there are probably thousands of species as yet undiscovered (so get looking; you may find something entirely new to science).

Unlike the rest of the country's wildlife, when it comes to insects there are probably as many species you want to avoid – including **mosquitoes**, **purrujas** (a type of midge) and **chiggers** – as to seek out. For these, make sure you have plenty of DEET-based repellent (not to mention the appropriate anti-malarials) and good luck. **'Killer' bees** have also colonized certain parts of the country, including the Parque Nacional Palo Verde. Though not quite as murderous as they're often portrayed, they can be aggressive and you should certainly not approach a nest. They are unlikely to attack unless directly threatened.

On the opposite side of the scale are **butterflies**, which are extremely plentiful. There are thousands of species (again, no one is sure exactly how many), many of which are large, brightly coloured and active during the day – in other words, a spotter's delight. The top spot is probably the **Blue Morpho**, with its vibrantly coloured 15cm wings, which is common along riverbanks.

Moving your gaze from the skies to your feet, you'll find the forest floor alive with all manner of **ants** (it is estimated that for every hectare of forest, there are nine million ants), including **leaf-cutters**. They move in regimented lines, each individual carrying a tiny piece of vegetation back to the nest where it is collected for food (the ants don't actually eat the plant matter itself, but rather a fungus which they cultivate on its surface).

Slightly less charming are **army ants**, which launch voracious campaigns through the forest, devouring any small creatures in their path. If you encounter them, simply move to the side and let the column continue on its way.

The creepy-crawly you're perhaps most likely to encounter is not an insect at all, but an arachnid. The **golden orb spider**, which has a bright green body with yellow spots and yellow and black legs, can grow up to 16cm across and looks like the quintessential tropical nightmare spider. In fact, it's perfectly harmless. It's also extremely common, found in most Pacific forest areas, so you'd best get used to it.

Conservation and Ecotourism

Famously, 25 per cent of Costa Rica's territory is protected in a network of national parks and private refuges. The country is often held up as some sort of gold standard of conservation, an ecological fortress standing firm against the attacks and ravages of modern development. But there's trouble in paradise, and it has been brewing for some time.

Costa Rica's commitment to conservation is a relatively recent phenomenon. So much of the environment has already been adapted for human use that this 25 per cent, though a significant proportion (certainly compared to other western hemisphere nations), pretty much marks the outer limits of protection, representing almost all of the large tracts of forest left in the country, and even this land is by no means totally secure.

04

Throughout much of its history, Costa Rica, like so many other nations, seemed to regard its natural environment merely as something to be exploited and adapted for human gain. Indeed, until relatively recently the clearing of forest was officially known as 'improvement'. With forests blanketing much of the country, there was perhaps an assumption that resources were somehow inexhaustible (or, at least, would only become a problem for generations far in the future), leading to massive forest clearances for agriculture, timber and pastureland, particularly in the latter half of the 20th century. Pressure to conserve the environment has been growing since the 1950s as the dangers of constantly ransacking the environment have become increasingly apparent, but a truly national conservation strategy was only put in place in the late 1980s, when the growth of ecotourism began to give environmentalism an economic as well as a scientific or moral rationale.

However, the tourist dollar has proved to be no universal panacea. While it provides an important impetus for protection, the development that tourism necessitates, and the number of visitors involved, create their own set of environmental problems.

Awakening to the Dangers

Not so long ago, over 75 per cent of Costa Rica was covered in **forest**. As the country's economy grew, however, in the 1960s and '70s – fuelled not just by the expansion of traditional exports such as coffee, bananas and pineapples, but by the growing international trade in tropical hardwoods and the introduction of large-scale cattle-ranching – so demand for land became ever greater. Forests began to be cleared at a frenzied rate. In the 1970s and '80s it was estimated that over two per cent of the country's primary forests was being cleared each year, mostly with the full support of the government. This destruction didn't go entirely unnoticed or unprotested. Costa Rica's richly diverse environment had long attracted the attention of naturalists and scientists, and it was they who were the first to raise the alarm regarding the potential long-term dangers of such wholesale destruction of the environment.

Forest clearances damage the environment on a number of different levels. Though tropical forests account for just a small part of the earth's surface (they exist in a thin band of territory extending just ten degrees either side of the equator), they play a hugely important role in regulating **global climates**, and their destruction, particularly if accompanied by the creation of pastureland, can be a significant cause of global warming. On a more local scale, high-altitude forests also act as important **watersheds**, absorbing much of the rainfall that would otherwise deluge and wash away the topsoil at lower elevations – which is exactly what has happened in areas where mass clearances have taken place.

Aside from the mass extinction of species, the clearance of forests also removes the potential for making discoveries that could be of benefit to mankind as a whole. According to some estimates, only around 20 per cent of tropical forest flora has been properly classified and studied. And yet in that 20 per cent many plants with important **medicinal qualities** have already been found. Owing to their sheer overwhelming diversity, most tropical forests cannot be regenerated. Species that live here often live nowhere else. Once gone, they are gone for ever, taking with them their secrets. To combat this, since 1989 the **Instituto Nacional de Biodiversidad** has been conducting an inventory with the aim of identifying and classifying every species of plant and animal in the country. Much of their funding is provided by pharmaceutical companies, including the US giant Merck, in return for primary access to this research.

By the 1960s, thanks to the concerted efforts of a small, dedicated band of campaigners, the first few conservation initiatives were put in place, resulting in the creation of the country's first **national park**, Santa Rosa, in 1971. But noble talk of dwindling diversity, species extinction and watersheds could only advance the arguments so far. What really brought the preservation of the environment to the centre of Costa Rican affairs was precisely what had made all those forest clearances so attractive in the first place – money. The discovery of Costa Rica's wondrous diversity by the outside world and the subsequent **tourism** boom in the 1980s and '90s focused attention on the environment as never before, at a stroke turning the conservation movement into the conservation industry.

Ecotourism: The Perfect Solution?

In 1982, there were an estimated 35,000 visitors to Costa Rica. Within a decade this had trebled, and today over a million people visit the country each year, the vast majority with the intention of visiting the national parks and experiencing at first hand their famed natural diversity. By the late 1990s, tourism had overtaken coffee and banana production as the country's principal industry. Suddenly, everyone wanted to be involved in preserving and showcasing Costa Rica's natural environment. It seemed like the perfect conservational solution: the people coming to observe the natural environment would pay for its upkeep.

Unfortunately, it wouldn't prove quite that easy. Pristine natural environments, hordes of visitors and the demands of maintaining a major industry don't always add up to responsible conservation. Costa Rica's newfound popularity soon began to cause problems. Fragile ecosystems do not respond well to being constantly trampled over, and many supposedly 'unspoilt' areas are beginning to show increasing signs of distress owing to the amount of human (albeit benignly intended) interference. But with more and more people in Costa Rica dependent on the tourist dollar, it can be difficult to agree limits on visitor numbers (and even harder to enforce them). Nobody wants to kill the golden goose, but similarly no Costa Rican involved in the tourist industry wants to jeopardize his or her livelihood. The trick, of course, is to keep visitor numbers high but to make sure these visitors interact with the environment in a way that does not adversely affect it. It's a difficult one to pull off.

It is not just tourists' interaction with the environment that can cause problems. Tourists need somewhere to stay, transport on which to travel, restaurants in which to eat, etc. In the 1980s and '90s, developers were quick to spot the new industry's potential, buying up chunks of land, particularly on the Pacific coast of Guanacaste, in order to turn them into hotel complexes and 'eco' lodges. Unfortunately, their attempts to touristify the environment often resulted in its damage, as they cut down areas of forest and drained mangrove swamps to build lodges, extended roads and power lines, and installed shoddy waste disposal systems that often caused pollution. Of course, not all tourist developments are like this. Many are scrupulously environmentally friendly – using solar and hydro power and wood from sustainable forests and making genuine efforts to maintain natural habitats – but for a significant minority terms like 'environmentally friendly', 'ecotourism' and 'green' are not so much noble intentions as very effective marketing slogans. For tourists concerned about what is genuinely eco-friendly and what is not, the tourist board has recently introduced a **'green leaf' programme**, rating hotels according to a set of environmental criteria – whether they recycle, conserve electricity, use sustainable building materials, etc.

The problems of excessive development are particularly apparent in the so-called **'buffer' zones** bordering national parks. These stretches of forest are supposed to act as an outer layer of protection for the parks, but are often open to abuse owing to the lack of official regulation. Evidence of this can be seen on the stretch of Pacific coast running south from the town of Dominical, bordering the Parque Nacional Marino Ballena (a protected cove and stretch of shoreline where humpback whales come each year to breed). Though the park only stretches for around 50 metres inland, it was until recently fringed by grand swaths of forest. However, since the paving of the coastal road a few years ago (and even more so following the recent laying down of electricity and phone lines), tourist developments have begun to spring up on either side of the park. Property speculators have moved in *en masse*, buying up chunks of coastline and forest to be turned into beach resorts and holiday homes. Of course, this process isn't meant to go unchecked: before it can sanction the purchase of a plot of land for development, the local council is meant to commission an environmental impact study. Unfortunately, this doesn't always happen. There is a lot of money to be made from tourism; council officials are poorly paid, and can on occasion be swayed by non-environmental inducements. Recently, a large American hotel chain managed to 'convince' the local council to pass its plans for building a new resort on a pristine stretch of coast south of Dominical without going through the usual regulatory procedures. It was only because somebody on the council got an attack of conscience and decided to turn whistleblower that the plan was stopped following an exposé in the national press.

Trouble at the Top

The lack of control over the development of the tourist industry is in part due to the sheer speed at which it has grown. But the government has also been guilty, at times, of failing to provide strong leadership and unequivocal support for conservation. Tourism may raise vast revenues, but that does not mean this money will necessarily go towards the upkeep of the environment. Despite controlling the country's major tourist draws, the **National Parks Service** is still severely under-financed, lacking the funds even to adequately patrol its territories, with the result that illegal logging and farming do still take place within the parks' borders. Furthermore, the name 'national park' is something of a misnomer, seeming to indicate state ownership. In fact, the government directly owns around half of the land in its national parks; the rest is in private ownership. Though development is technically restricted on this private land, some landowners have managed to exploit loopholes to circumvent the law.

Matters are complicated even further by disagreements between official bodies as to how to manage the growth of tourism. The two bodies entrusted with overseeing the development of tourism in Costa Rica are **MINAE**, the Ministry of Energy and the Environment (Ministerio del Ambiente y Energia, *www.minae.go.cr*), which directly controls the National Parks Service, and the **tourist office** (or **ICT**, the Instituto Costarricense de Turismo), and it is generally accepted that they don't always see eye-to-eye on how best to manage their resources. Whereas MINAE is, despite severe underfunding, widely seen as having done a reasonably good job in ensuring that tourism doesn't overwhelm the parks' fragile ecosystems (imposing limits on visitor numbers and, in the case of some parks, such as Tortuguero, ensuring that nobody is allowed to enter unless accompanied by a certified guide), the ICT is often portrayed as putting commercial interests above environmental ones. In contrast to the somewhat impoverished state of MINAE, the ICT makes a lot of money out of tourism, much of it derived from the three per cent tax collected on every occupied hotel room. This has led some to accuse the ICT of being more concerned with generating new accommodation (and thus money) than with the possible impact the increase in visitors could have on the environment and local communities. A few years ago, the head of MINAE even went so far as to initiate a public row with the ICT, who, he claimed, were using the lure of the national parks to increase the amount of tourist revenue but were failing to donate enough of this revenue towards the parks' upkeep. When the ICT denied these claims and refused to give the parks any more money, the head of MINAE responded by threatening to close the national parks to all visitors. The ICT, realizing what this would do to visitor numbers, backed down and coughed up.

Conservation – Who Benefits?

It is striking how many of Costa Rica's larger tourist complexes (beach resorts, rainforest lodges, etc.) are owned, funded and run by **foreigners** (principally Americans). There is also a noticeable disparity between the standard of living enjoyed by many Costa Ricans living in rural areas and the luxurious nature of the Western-owned accommodation in these parts. Though the principal business for the majority of the people living in the areas surrounding the national parks is tourism, there is often a glaring contrast between the type of tourist accommodation offered by locals – basic, cheap – and that offered by Americans – luxurious and sumptuously appointed. It seems very difficult for locals to raise the capital needed to fund the larger, more upmarket tourist projects.

That is not to say that what the Americans are doing is necessarily wrong. Many are performing a vital role in preserving the environment, as well as providing jobs for local people as guides, cleaners, cooks, etc. But some Costa Ricans take a more hostile view, seeing what the Americans are doing as a form of eco-imperialism, protecting the environment for the 'greater good', while ignoring the more day-to-day needs of the country's native inhabitants. Easy as it is to criticize people involved in illegal logging or forest clearance, it's also easy to understand why locals, denied access to the material benefits of conservation, might be forced to engage in more harmful pursuits. The fact that forests continue to be cleared for agriculture does not, in itself, mean that rural Costa Ricans are not interested in protecting the environment, rather that they simply do not have the economic wherewithal to do it. If the environment is to be maintained for the benefit of everybody, then everybody needs to benefit from it. If the profits from conservation are largely being enjoyed by foreigners, it is perhaps no surprise if occasionally the locals decide it's not worth the effort.

The ideal solution would see Costa Rica's natural wonders preserved, tourism managed in a way that doesn't impact on the environment (or at least only minimally), and the profits of tourism used both to directly help maintain the environment and to get local communities involved with, and benefiting from, its preservation. It's a difficult circle to square. For conservation to work, there must be in place a **single, cohesive strategy** and a distinct **unity of purpose**. The founding of the **Costa Rican Reserve Network** in 1996 was a major step towards this goal, bringing together, for the first time, over a hundred of the reserves that lay outside official park borders under a single administrative control. There are also plans to try to link all the protected areas in the country into just eleven **conservation areas**, the idea being both to establish larger protected blocks (important for animals such as jaguars, who require sizeable hunting territories) and to involve local communities in conservation, getting them to train as guides, rangers, etc.

Of course, environmental problems are by no means unique to Costa Rica, which is why there are also plans to try and establish a **unified conservation strategy** across MesoAmerica, linking up protected areas in different countries into a series of giant conservation zones. Unfortunately, given that this would require seven different countries to agree upon, adopt and implement a single plan, this ideal is still a long way from being realized.

Active Costa Rica

For the majority of visitors, Costa Rica's appeal can be broken down into just two main categories: nature (exploring the country's diverse environments – its rainforests, volcanoes and palm-fringed beaches, and spotting its abundant wildlife); and adventure (engaging in adrenaline-fuelled activities – rafting down rivers, zip-lining between trees, fishing for marlin, etc.).

NICARAGUA

Caribbean Sea

COSTA RICA

Pacific Ocean

05

Sometimes, however, the two categories of nature and adventure overlap, with some activities undertaken primarily in order to get closer to nature and provide better viewing opportunities of the wildlife (such as, for example, hiking, horse-riding, diving). Others seem almost wilfully designed to scare away any animals that might possibly be in the vicinity; ATV (quad-bike) tours and canopy tours fall firmly into this category.

You will find details of tour operators offering many of the activities outlined in the following pages on pp.68–70, as well as throughout the book. Some also offer a few slightly more esoteric pursuits – microlight flights, bungee jumps, paintball afternoons, and so on. Unsurprisingly, you'll find the greatest range of activities offered at the major tourist hubs of Playa del Coco, Tamarindo, Jacó and Quepos/Manuel Antonio.

ATV Tours

Bumping and banging your way along a dirt track on an 'all-terrain vehicle', also known as a quad bike, is certainly a very enjoyable (if not a particularly eco-friendly) way of exploring the country.

It has become an increasingly popular pursuit in recent years, particularly on the Pacific coast, around Quepos and Manuel Antonio, where tours are led along the unpaved roads traversing the nearby palm oil plantations. See p.225 for details and a list of operators.

Canopy Tours and Aerial Walkways

'Canopy tour' is a rather gentle-sounding name for what is, in truth, not a particularly gentle pursuit. If you didn't know what it entailed, you might initially be a little confused, perhaps imagining it to be a leisurely ascent into the treetops on the lookout for wildlife.

In fact, done properly and well, there's almost no activity more liable to scare away animals than a canopy tour. Its other name, 'zip-lining', gives perhaps a clearer indication of what is taking place – attached to a harness, zipping your way along high-strength steel cables between the canopies of tall forest trees. It can be a hugely exhilarating experience; just don't expect to see much nature, especially as you will probably have your eyes closed most of the time. Its popularity is growing all the time, with dozens of tours now operating throughout the country, including several in Monteverde, where the practice originated. See p.246 for more details.

Less extreme ways of exploring the forest canopy are available, although, just to confuse matters, these tours are normally prefixed with the word 'aerial' rather than 'canopy'. Some of the best include: the 'aerial walkways' (i.e. a series of treetop platforms) of the Sky Trek in Monteverde (see p.248) and the Hanging Bridges of Arenal (see p.273); and the Rainforest Aerial Tram in Braulio Carrillo, which offer nature-watching rides through the canopy in purpose-built suspended gondolas (see p.146).

Hiking and Wildlife-watching

Costa Rica's various protected areas, which amount to some 25 per cent of the country's total landmass, offer plenty of great hiking and wildlife-watching opportunities: trekking through the humid depths of the rainforest; climbing to the tops of extinct volcanoes; admiring the lower slopes of active volcanoes; strolling along palm-lined beaches, etc. You can undertake as much or as little as you like. In fact, if you're not an experienced hiker, it is perhaps best to start with something gentle, such as the Parque Nacional Manuel Antonio, whose short, well-maintained beach-fringing trails can provide a relatively undemanding start to your investigation of the country's natural vistas. Once you've built up a head of steam, you can then turn your attention to the Parque Nacional Corcovado's multi-day La Leona–San Pedrillo hike (*see* p.322) or the Parque Internacional La Amistad's 20km Sendero Valle del Silencio trail (*see* p.307), both of which offer hiking that's as challenging as you could possibly wish for. If it's really hardcore trekking you're after, you should come in the dry season; despite the inevitable heat, you'll have access to a good deal more territory, as sections of several parks, including Corcovado, become impassable in the rainy months.

If the purpose of your hike is to spot wildlife, you should also consider hiring a guide. Not only will they know the best places to go where the chances of encountering animals will be highest, but from a safety perspective they can also help prevent you getting lost, eaten or drowned or succumbing to any other potential disaster. Conversely, they can also steer you away from indulging in any activities that might cause damage to the environment. Finally, a good guide will prove invaluable in spotting things you might miss. This particularly applies to wildlife-watching in the heart of the rainforest where much of the activity takes

Tips for Spotting Wildlife in the Jungle

Don't believe the hype. Your guidebook may have a close-up image of a jaguar on its front cover, but your chances of seeing one in the wild are virtually zero (in fact, the cover picture may well have been taken in a zoo – why do you think it's a close-up?). You may see plenty of wildlife during your time in the forest – although this is more likely to be birds and monkeys than big cats – or you may not see anything much at all. Adjust your expectations accordingly and be patient. This is a natural environment, not a theme park.

There are, however, a few tips you can follow in order to give yourself the best chance possible of seeing as much as possible.

• Set out as early as you can. Most diurnal animals are at their most active shortly after dawn.

• Keep looking. In the forest, most of the activity takes place in the canopy. Keep scouring the tops of the trees for telltale signs of movement.

• Bring a good pair of binoculars.

• Move slowly so as not to alarm the animals.

• Listen. You'll often hear things – such as monkeys crashing their way along branches – way before you see them.

• Be quiet. You're not going to hear anything if you make too much noise. And nothing is more likely to drive the animals away than constant chatter.

• And, once again, be patient.

Safety Tips

Note: tips tailored for each major park and reserve are included throughout the guide.

• It may seem obvious, but if you are planning to do several hours' worth of hiking through thick, humid jungle, you'll need to make sure that you are physically up to the task. There have been too many examples of couch potatoes using some of Costa Rica's jungle trails to undertake their first serious piece of exercise in years, only to succumb to exhaustion after just a few kilometres. If you know you're coming here, get in training early.

• Try to travel as light as possible...however...

• ...be sure to bring plenty of water with you.

• Bring a hat and regularly reapply sunscreen.

• Try to rest in the shade during the hottest part of the day.

• Bring light, easily portable waterproof clothing.

• Wear proper fitted hiking shoes.

• Bring a strong DEET-based insect repellent and reapply regularly. Bugs love humid conditions.

• Bring a torch and matches.

• Bring a supply of energy-rich food.

• If visiting one of the country's volcanoes or mountains, be sure to bring a couple of extra layers of warm clothing; it can get very chilly near the summits.

• If exploring without a guide, never leave the marked trail.

place 30 metres above your head and requires an expert eye to pick out. A guide will help you to spot animals camouflaged in the undergrowth, will identify tracks and calls, and will recognize that log-shaped silhouette for what it truly is. And, if the animals aren't putting in the required appearances, guides can also draw your attention to the many and varied plants of the forest, which to the uninitiated can look like an indistinguishable mass of greenery. You should be able to find a guide for any of the country's national parks simply by contacting the relevant office of MINAE (the official government body that oversees the parks). If you are staying near a private protected area, your hotel should be able to put you in touch with a recommended local guide. Otherwise, *see* pp.68–70.

Birdwatching

With over 850 species of resident and migratory bird – to put that into context, that's more than in the whole of Europe, or the whole of the USA and Canada combined – Costa Rica is unsurprisingly one of the world's major birdwatching destinations, and many tour operators offer dedicated birding tours (*see* **Travel**, pp.69–70). Some of the best areas for birding include Corcovado (home to the country's largest population of scarlet macaws); Monteverde (for hummingbirds and quetzals); the Cerro de la Muerte (for quetzals); Caño Negro (for wildfowl) and Palo Verde (also for wildfowl).

Diving and Marine Wildlife-watching

Despite the supreme abundance of wildlife inhabiting Costa Rica's coastal waters, the country is not a particularly renowned snorkelling or diving destination, certainly not when compared with Belize further north up the isthmus, with its barrier reef and crystal-clear waters. Costa Rica's waters, by contrast, offer rather poor visibility – rarely exceeding a few metres – especially in the wet season when heavy rains wash large amounts of silt into the sea. There are only a few stretches of coral along the entire coast, the most notable examples being the small reefs at Cahuita (*see* p.351) and the Isla del Caño (*see* p.317), but these are nothing like the quality you'll find in Belize.

The news is slightly better when it comes to some of the ocean's larger inhabitants. Costa Rica has a couple of decent dive sites off the northern Nicoya Peninsula, at Murciélago and Catalina islands near Playa del Coco (*see* p.177), where dolphins, sharks, octopuses, rays and groupers are often spotted.

You can also take dolphin- and whale-watching trips at the Parque Nacional Marino Ballena from December to April (*see* pp.295–7); and at certain times of the year it is possible to watch marine turtles laying their eggs on the beaches. You can see olive ridley turtles at Parque Nacional Santa Rosa (*see* pp.171–2), leatherback turtles at the Parque Nacional Marino Las Baulas (*see* pp.188–90) and green and hawksbill turtles at Parque Nacional Tortuguero (*see* pp.335–44).

Horse-riding

Trotting along on horseback is a great way to see the Costa Rican countryside, whether it is made up of forest, beach, mountain, savannah or anything else. Horse-riding tours are available in pretty much every major tourist destination in the country, San José and the Caribbean northeast excepted. In certain areas, where road coverage is minimal, riding actually represents the easiest and most convenient way of getting around. There's a particularly well-worn horse trail between Monteverde and La Fortuna, which has been established in lieu of a formal road network (for more details, *see* p.248).

Unfortunately, the pastime's growing popularity has led to problems, with some stables overworking their animals or using horses that are past their prime. You should book your ride only through an approved, scrupulous operator, and be sure to check on the condition of the horses before saddling up.

As much fun as horse-riding is, it can be rather hard on the behind. If you're not used to riding, don't attempt anything too ambitious; a couple of hours in the saddle will be more than enough for a beginner.

Responsibilities when Wildlife-spotting

Exploring the jungle is not just about getting your fill of wildlife-spotting. Remember, you also have responsibilities.

• Never try to attract animals by offering them food. This can upset their natural feeding patterns.

• Never leave any litter in the forest. Bring an extra bag with you for its disposal (forests tend to be a bit light on litter bins).

• Never remove any vegetation.

• Obey all the signs at all times.

Prices can begin as low as US$15 per hour (more typically $20 and above). Some of the most popular riding spots include Monteverde, Tamarindo and La Fortuna.

Sports Fishing

Sports fishing has become such a popular activity in the past few years that several towns have become specialist sports-fishing centres, catering almost exclusively to the needs of enthusiasts hoping to bag something big and scaly out on the open ocean. This is hardly surprising given that sports fishermen are often willing to pay top dollars to indulge their passion – upwards of $750 a day in some instances (which is a lot more than most birdwatchers are prepared to pay). The pursuit has helped to revive the fortunes of a number of previously rather run-down coastal towns, including Quepos and Golfito.

Most fishing trips involve the catch-and-release method, so as to preserve stocks, although a number of specimens are retained as trophies each year. There's no official season, but December to April is generally considered the best time to fish on both coasts.

The main centres on the Caribbean side, where the prime catches are snook and tarpon, are Barra del Colorado and Parismina; and on the Pacific side, whose waters provide a home to sailfish and marlin, Quepos and Golfito.

Surfing

Costa Rica's renowned waves and breaks have been drawing international surfers since the 1960s. Today, it boasts a number of dedicated 'surf towns', filled with surf schools offering lessons, shops offering board rental, *cabinas* offering simple (and cheap) accommodation and plenty of bars and restaurants offering the all-important 'party atmosphere' with which the sport is traditionally associated.

Most of the main surf sites are on the Pacific side and include Playa del Coco, Witches Rock (in the Parque Nacional Santa Rosa), Tamarindo, Playa Avellana (nicknamed 'Little Hawaii'), Playa Negra, Playa Junquillal, Playa Grande, Jacó, Playa Hermosa and Dominical. However some of the country's most fearsome waves batter the Caribbean side, where Puerto Viejo de Talamanca is the main surf town. Lessons start at around $20 per hour.

Swimming

As inviting and enticing as Costa Rica's seas look, swimming is an activity best undertaken with a good deal of caution, as many beaches are pounded by fearsome waves, more suitable for surfing than frolicking. In truth, choppy seas are not the main danger you have to watch out for. Every year, several dozen people die in the country's coastal waters after being caught in a riptide, a fast-moving underwater current that can quickly drag a swimmer out to sea. Most fatalities occur when the victim panics and tries to swim against the tide, soon becoming exhausted. In fact most riptides are very short-lived phenomena, whose energy is soon dissipated. If caught in one, the standard advice is to relax and let yourself be carried out until the tide's pull wanes (which shouldn't be too far out), then swim back to the shore at a 45° angle so as to avoid getting caught in another one.

White-water Rafting and Kayaking

White-water rafting rivals zip-lining (also known as 'canopy tours', see pp.56 and 246) for the title of the most popular outdoor activity in Costa Rica, with dozens of firms offering trips along the rapids of the three principal rafting rivers: the Reventazón, the Sarapiquí and the Pacuare. Indeed, Costa Rica has become one of the most renowned rafting destinations in all Central America, with several international Olympic teams using it as a training base.

Prices start at around $75 per day, which should include transport, lunch and all the necessary safety equipment, including lifejackets and helmets. You should only need to bring with you a change of clothing, sunscreen, insect repellent, a good level of fitness and strong nerves. The minimum age for rafting is typically 10, sometimes 12 on the more challenging sections.

Though the vast majority of people who undertake rafting trips come to no harm, do bear in mind that it can potentially be a rather dangerous pursuit. Only use established firms with good safety records, the appropriate medical rescue certifications and, if you don't speak Spanish, bilingual guides.

It's an activity that can be enjoyed year-round, although the rainy season, particularly June to October, provides the most challenging conditions, when heavy rains cause the rivers to swell significantly and turn the rapids ever more rapid. Thankfully, for the more faint of heart, many firms also offer the gentler alternative of kayaking along calmer stretches of river, which is perhaps the preferred option if you just want to look at some wildlife – focusing on monkeys in nearby trees can be a bit tricky when you're hanging on to a raft for dear life. It's also possible to go sea kayaking out on the open ocean, although this should only be undertaken in the company of a guide.

Though ostensibly more about achieving a high-adrenaline thrill than interacting with the environment, white-water rafting's popularity has had an important conservational side effect. The contribution made to the local economy by rafting companies – combined with a concerted campaign by environmentalists – recently led to the cancellation of a plan to build a hydroelectric dam on the Río Pacuare.

Some of the country's more well-established rafting operators for short trips once you are already in the country are listed in **Travel**, p.69. Also see **Travel**, pp.68–9 for countrywide tour operators offering longer multi-activity packages, p.156 for Turrialba-based tour operators, and p.262 for Puerto Viejo de Sarapiquí/ La Virgen-based tour operators.

Windsurfing

It's not exactly a countrywide sport, but in the shape of the Laguna de Arenal 'Lake Arenal', Costa Rica possesses one of the top windsurfing spots in the whole of the Americas, where powerful and (more importantly) consistent winds are pretty much guaranteed throughout the December–April high season.

Several companies in the lakeside towns of Nuevo Arenal and Tilarán (*see* p.274) offer windsurfing lessons and equipment hire. Prices start at around $40 for a half-day, $70 for a full day.

Travel

06

Getting There

By Air

The overwhelming majority of visitors to Costa Rica arrive on flights from the United States. This includes visitors from the UK, Europe and Australasia, who will usually have to connect via one of the US cities of New York, Chicago, Atlanta, Houston, Dallas, Los Angeles or, most commonly, Miami.

There are two international airports in Costa Rica: **Juan Santamaría**, near the small city of Alajuela on the outskirts of San José, which processes most of the country's air traffic; and the smaller **Daniel Oduber Airport**, near Liberia, the provincial capital of Guanacaste, in the country's northwest. The latter, an increasingly popular choice since the expansion of its terminal a couple of years ago, welcomes mainly package holidaymakers *en route* to the all-inclusive resorts of the northern Pacific.

The number of flights to both is increasing all the time, as Costa Rica's tourist industry continues to boom. Increased competition on routes means there are also plenty of deals to be found, if you have the time to shop around. It's certainly worth putting in the research time if you are coming from the UK or Australasia, as the flight itself will probably represent the single biggest investment of your holiday. The cheapest prices become available during the low (or 'green') season of May to November. Fares inevitably rise during the high season, December to April, reaching a peak during the six-week period either side of Christmas.

From the UK

At the time of writing, it is still not possible to fly direct to Costa Rica from the UK. Total travelling time ranges between 12 and 24 hours, depending on which part of the country you're coming from and how many connections you need to make.

Flights from London are offered by British Airways via Dallas and Miami, Continental via Houston, and United Airlines via Chicago and New York. Fares range from £450–750 depending on the season. Strange as it may seem, the very cheapest deals involve heading (initially) in the wrong direction, to Madrid with Iberia, Spain's national carrier, and then

Exit Tax

Although there's no entry tax to Costa Rica, do bear in mind when calculating your budget that you need to keep back $26 to pay the exit tax, which applies to all tourists departing the country by air. This must be paid before checking in, either in cash (US dollars only) or by credit card – Visa is accepted but, at the time of writing, not MasterCard.

flying either direct to San José (there are 4 services a week) or connecting via Miami. Door-to-door, even if you live in London and stay in San José, this can still take nigh on 24hrs, especially via the USA, but may end up costing under £400.

From Ireland

There are no direct flights from Ireland to Costa Rica. You'll have to make your way to the USA and connect from there. Aer Lingus offer flights from Dublin and Shannon to New York, Boston and Chicago, and from Dublin only to Los Angeles. Fares range from below €700 to over €1,000.

From the USA

Most direct flights from the USA to Costa Rica depart from Dallas, Houston, Atlanta and Miami, all of which offer several daily services. There are also four direct flights each week from New York operated by American Airlines; six direct flights a week out of Washington, DC operated by United Airlines; one direct daily flight out of Chicago operated by United; two direct daily flights out of Newark operated by Continental; one direct daily flight out of Philadelphia operated by US Airways; and one daily flight out of Los Angeles via Guatemala City, operated by United. The majority of services out of New York, Los Angeles and Chicago, however, involve a change of planes, often in San Salvador in El Salvador.

Miami–San José is the shortest, most convenient and most frequently flown route, taking just under 3hrs. Prices start at under $400 for direct flights from Miami and Dallas, rising to over $700 for New York/Los Angeles flights, which can take in excess of 8hrs, including changes.

If you are staying in northwest Costa Rica, it is worth checking out direct flights to the country's second international airport, Daniel

Oduber in Liberia, which depart from Atlanta (daily with Delta), Houston (daily with Continental) and Miami (daily with American Airlines), as this will save considerably on your total journey time.

From Canada

You cannot fly direct from Canada to San José, although, unlike from the USA, it is possible to fly there via Havana in Cuba.

Grupo Taca operates flights from Toronto via the Cuban capital, while Mexicana operates flights from Toronto via Mexico City. You can also fly from Vancouver via Miami. Fares range from under $700 to over $900.

In total, Taca operates services from the following cities: Chicago, Dallas, Houston, Los Angeles, Mexico City, Miami, New York, San Francisco, Washington, DC and all the Central American capitals.

Airline Carriers

UK and Ireland

Aer Lingus, UK t 0870 876 5000, Ireland t 0818 365 000, www.aerlingus.com.

American Airlines, UK t 0845 778 9789, Ireland t (01) 602 0550, www.aa.com.

British Airways, UK t 0870 850 9850, Ireland t 1-800 626 747, www.ba.com.

Continental, UK t 0845 607 6760, Ireland t 1-890 925 252, www.continental.com.

Delta, Ireland t (01) 407 316, www.delta.com.

Iberia, UK t 0845 601 2854, Ireland t (01) 407 3017, www.iberia.com.

United Airlines, UK t 0845 844 4777, www.unitedairlines.co.uk.

USA and Canada

Air Canada, USA/Canada t 1-888 712 7786, www.aircanada.com.

American Airlines, USA t 800 433 7300, www.aa.com.

British Airways, USA t 1-800 AIRWAYS, www.ba.com.

Continental Airlines, USA/Canada t 800 044 0005, www.continental.com.

Delta Airlines, USA/Canada t 800 056 2002, www.delta.com.

Iberia, USA/Canada t 1-800 772 4642, www.iberia.com.

Mexicana de Aviación, Canada t 1-800 531 7921, www.mexicana.com.

Taca, t 1-800 400 8222, www.taca.com.

United Airlines, USA t 800 052 1243, www.united.com.

US Airways, t 800 622 1015, www.usairways.com.

Australia and New Zealand

Air New Zealand, Australia t 1-800 809 298, New Zealand t 0800 737 000, www.airnz.co.nz.

British Airways, Australia t (1 300) 767 177, New Zealand t 0800 274 847, www.ba.com.

Qantas, Australia t (13) 1313. New Zealand t 0800 808 767, www.qantas.com.au.

Discounts, Special Deals and Online Travel Sites

The online marketplace represents your best bet for finding a cheap flight to Costa Rica, though you'll need to be as flexible as possible with dates, while willing to accept the most rigid, non-refundable tickets going.

www.airbrokers.com
www.arrowtravel.com
www.cheapflights.co.uk / www.cheapflights.com / www.cheapflights.com.au
www.cheap-flight-finder.com
www.cheaptickets.com
www.ebookers.com
www.expedia.ca / www.expedia.co.uk / www.expedia.com
www.flightfareshop.co.uk
www.flights.com / www.flights.co.uk
www.flyaow.com
www.hotwire.com
www.kayak.com
www.lastminute.com / www.lastminute.com.au / www.lastminute.co.nz
www.moments-notice.com
www.opodo.co.uk
www.site59.com
www.skyauction.com
www.travelocity.ca / www.travelocity.co.uk / www.travelocity.com

Student and Youth Deals

Students are entitled to significant discounts. Note that the term 'student' in this instance is taken to mean anyone under 26, or anyone under 32 in full-time education.

STA Travel, UK t 0870 163 0026, www.statravel.co.uk; USA t 800 781 4040, www.statravel.com; Canada t 888 427 5639, www.statravel.ca; Australia t 1300 733 035, www.statravel.com.au; New Zealand t 0508 782 872, www.statravel.co.nz.

Student Flights (UK), t 0870 499 4004, www.studentflight.co.uk.

Travel Cuts (USA and Canada), t 1-866 246 9762, www.travelcuts.com.

Usit (Ireland), t (01) 602 1904, www.usit.ie.

From Australia and New Zealand

Qantas and Air New Zealand both offer services from Australia to San José via Los Angeles and Houston, for around Aus$2,500–3,000 from the country's eastern cities and Aus$2,800–3,200 from Perth. Air New Zealand also flies via Mexico City.

From New Zealand, Qantas, Air New Zealand and American Airlines fly via Los Angeles and Houston for NZ$2,500–3,500.

By Sea

There are no dedicated international ferry routes to Costa Rica, although several US cruise ships do stop by during their tours of the tropics, usually at the Caribbean port of Puerto Limón, or the Pacific ports of Puntarenas and Caldera.

By Land

Entering Costa Rica by **rail** is impossible – there's no longer a railway – and by **car** practically so, owing to the number of legal hurdles to be overcome, not to mention the cost of the petrol, which can make it more expensive than flying. Still, if you're determined, try and track down of copy of *You Can Drive to Costa Rica in 8 Days* by Dawn Rae Wessler, which will tell you how to do it.

This makes the **bus** the only practical land option. Costa Rica has good bus links to all other Central American countries. Some routes are time-consuming – over three days in some instances – and the buses themselves rather uncomfortable, even if most these days have air-conditioning, TVs and toilets, but the savings that bus travel offers, when compared to air travel, make it popular.

The longest and most hardcore route into the country is the **Tica Bus** service from Tapachula in Mexico to San José. The journey takes three days, with overnight stops in San Salvador in El Salvador and Managua in Nicaragua (you'll have to arrange and pay for your own accommodation), and costs $122. Almost equally demanding is the Tica Bus

from Guatemala City, which also stops *en route* at San Salvador and Managua (again, where and if you sleep is up to you), but takes half a day less and costs $92. Tica Bus also runs: a 48hr service from San Pedro Sula in Honduras, with an overnight stop in Managua, for $60; a 2-day service from San Salvador (overnight in Managua) for $40; a 10hr service from Managua for $20; and an 18hr service from Panama City for $50.

Services from Guatemala City, San Salvador and Managua are also operated by **Transnica** and **King Quality**.

Entry Formalities

There's not much paperwork involved when travelling from North America, the UK, Western Europe or Australasia. Citizens of the USA, Canada and most Western European nations, including the UK, need only a valid passport to enter Costa Rica for a period of up to 90 days, while citizens of Australia, New Zealand and Ireland can stay for up to 30 days. You will be issued with a passport stamp upon arrival informing you of the official duration of your stay. In theory, all visitors are meant to be assessed upon arrival to ensure that they have a return ticket out of the country and adequate funds for the proposed length of their stay (i.e. are not looking for work), but these enquiries are usually reserved for residents of other Central American countries, not tourists.

If you want to stay longer than 90 days, you can either make a formal application for a visa extension from the **Departmento de Migración** (t 220 0355) in San José, a lengthy and complicated procedure or, less formally, you can simply exit the country across one of its various land borders for a period of no less than 72 hours, after which you will be issued with a new passport stamp upon your return, enabling you to stay for a further 90 days. Many people actually manage to unofficially 'live' in Costa Rica using this method.

Note, you are obliged by law to carry ID with you wherever you go in Costa Rica. A photocopy of your passport is accepted as ID, so avoid carrying the real thing. Most hotels have safes – use them.

For further information on entry requirements, visit *www.migracion.go.cr*.

Bus Companies

Tica Bus, **t** 221 8954, *www.ticabus.com*.
Transnica, **t** 221 3318, *www.transnica.com*.
King Quality, **t** 223 4123.

Travel Agents and Tour Operators

As Costa Rica's popularity as a tourist destination continues to grow, so the number of foreign-based operators specializing in holidays to the country continues to expand, offering all manner of activities – rainforest hikes, volcano walks, birdwatching, whitewater rafting – and itineraries taking in pretty much every corner of the country.

While it is perfectly possible to plan every aspect of your holiday before you leave, the majority of visitors to Costa Rica arrive with the intention of improvising their holiday as they go along. What tours and activities they do decide to indulge in will be booked on Costa Rican soil, which is where the country's bulging brood of domestic tour operators comes in. Most are based in San José and are fairly evenly split between those offering general tours taking in a number of country highlights – Volcán Arenal, Tortuguero, Monteverde, Manuel Antonio, etc. – and those offering high-adrenaline activities – white-water rafting, canopy tours, sports fishing, etc. Several, of course, offer both. *See* chapter 04, **Active Costa Rica**.

UK-based Tour Operators

The Adventure Company, t 0870 794 1009, *www.adventurecompany.co.uk.* Adventure travel specialist. Tours include a 15-day 'Costa Rica Adventure', taking in San José, Volcán Irazú, Tortuguero, Volcán Arenal, Monteverde Cloudforest, Manuel Antonio and white-water rafting on the Pacuare river, from £1,649.

Condor Journeys and Adventures, t (01700) 841 318, *www.condorjourneys-adventures.com.* Tours include an 8-day 'Costa Rica Highlights' package, taking in San José, Volcán Irazú, Braulio Carrillo National Park, Tortuguero, Volcán Arenal and the Tabacón Hot Springs, from £631. Birdwatching, white-water rafting and combined Guatemala-Costa Rica tours.

Exodus, t 0870 240 5550, *www.exodus.co.uk.* Tours include: a 15-day package to Costa Rica, taking in San José, Tortuguero, Volcán Arenal, Monteverde Cloudforest Reserve, Manuel Antonio and Golfito, from £1,085 (excluding flights); a 15-day 'Trails of Central America' taking in Costa Rica and Panama; and a 20-day 'Pan-American Tour', taking in Costa Rica, Nicaragua, Honduras and Guatemala.

Explore!, t 0870 333 4001, *www.explore.co.uk.* Adventure travel specialist. Tours include a 16-day 'Active Costa Rica' tour, hiking, horse-riding, snorkelling and white-water rafting, and taking in Corcovado, Caño Island, Rincón de la Vieja National Park and Volcán Arenal. Also offers a combined 'Beneath the Volcanoes' tour to Costa Rica and Nicaragua.

Journey Latin America, t (020) 8747 3108, *www.journeylatinamerica.co.uk.* Offers flights, tours (honeymoons, family holidays, nature breaks and wine tours) and travel throughout Latin America. Tours include a 'Highlights of Costa Rica' option (San José, Tortuguero, Monteverde, Volcán Arenal, Manuel Antonio,

Corcovado and white-water rafting on the Pacuare river), from £1,198 (excluding flights).

Kumuka Worldwide, t 0800 389 2328, *www.kumuka.co.uk.* Tours include: a 6-day 'Caribbean Costa Rica' option, seeing San José, Tortuguero and Cahuita National Park, from £299; and a 9-day 'Pacific Costa Rica', visiting San José, Volcán Arenal, Monteverde and Manuel Antonio, from £350. Prices exclude air fares. Multi-country tours (Costa Rica, Nicaragua, Guatemala and Honduras) are also available.

Last Frontiers, t (01296) 653 000, *www.last frontiers.com.* Tours include a 16-day 'Costa Rica Self-drive' option, taking in San José, Volcán Poás, Turrialba, Puerto Viejo, Malpaís and the Nicoya Peninsula beaches, from £1,990.

North South Travel, t (01245) 608 291, *www. northsouthtravel.co.uk.* Small travel agent whose profits go to charitable projects in Africa, Asia and Latin America.

Reef and Rainforest Tours, t (01803) 866 965, *www.reefandrainforest.co.uk.* Wildlife-watching specialist. Offers a number of different options, including a 'Budget Tour', a 'Self-drive Tour', a 'Wildlife Adventure Tour', a 'Remarkable Diversity Tour', a 'Naturally Family Friendly Costa Rica Tour', a 'Romantic Style Tour' and a 'Nature de Luxe Tour'.

Responsible Travel, *www.responsibletravel.com.* Travel agent that encourages 'responsible' tourism, working only with Costa Rican guides and locally owned accommodation. Tours include a 16-day option including San José, Turrialba, Volcán Irazú, Guayabo National Monument, Puerto Viejo, Gandoca-Manzanillo National Park, Tortuguero, Volcán Poás, Volcán Arenal, Monteverde and Manuel Antonio, from £1,459 (excluding flights).

South American Experience, t (020) 7976 5511, *www.southamericanexperience.co.uk.* Tours include a 14-day 'Forests and Volcanoes' option, taking in San José, Tortuguero, Volcán Arenal, Tabacón Hot Springs, Monteverde and Tamarindo, from £995 (excluding flights).

Trips Worldwide, t (0117) 311 4000, *www.trips worldwide.co.uk*. Despite its name, this firm actually specializes in just one part of the world – Latin America – offering a wide range of Central American options. Tours include 'Highlights of Costa Rica', from £1,695.

Wildlife Worldwide, t 0845 130 6982, *www. wildlifeworldwide.com*. Wildlife-watching specialist. Tours include: a 14-day 'Costa Rica Odyssey', visiting San José, Braulio Carrillo National Park, Tortuguero National Park, Volcán Arenal, Monteverde Cloudforest Reserve and the Nicoya Peninsula, from £1,595.

USA-based Tour Operators

The Adventure Center, t 1-800 228 8747, *www. adventurecenter.com*. Adventure travel specialist offering a number of Costa Rican options: 9-day 'Costa Rica Quest' (from $635); 10-day 'Costa Rica Highlights' (from $685); 12-day 'Costa Rica Family Adventure' (from $1,095); 15-day 'Active Costa Rica' (from $2,410) and a 15-day 'Costa Rica Hike, Bike and Raft' ($1,295).

Back Roads, t 1-800 462 2848, *www.backroads. com*. Adventure travel specialist. Tours include: a 6-day 'Costa Rica Biking Tour', from $2,398; a 6-day 'Costa Rica Walking Tour', from $2,298; and a 6-day 'Costa Rica Family Multisport Tour', from $3,298.

Concord World Travel, t (877) 287 5505, *www. costaricadreamin.com*. A number of 8-day tours including: 'Nature Escapade', from $850; 'Adventure Escapade', from $870; 'Jungle Beach and Volcano Tour', from $675; and 'Pure Nature Tour', from $1,380.

Ecotour Expeditions, t (401) 423 3377, *www. naturetours.com*. Tours include a 10-day 'Costa Rica Explorer' option (San José, Volcán Poás, Monteverde, Arenal, Tabacón Hot Springs and Tortuguero), from $1,998 (excluding air fares).

Geographic Expeditions, t 1-800 777 8183, *www.geoex.com*. Specialist in 'out-of-the-way' destinations. Tours include a 10-day 'Costa Rica Connoisseur' option: San José, Monteverde, Volcán Arenal and Tortuguero, from $2,008.

International Expeditions, t 800 6333 4734, *www.internationalexpeditions.com*. Nature travel specialist. Offers a 9-day Costa Rica tour, taking in San José, Tortuguero, Monteverde, Ballena Marine National Park and Corcovado National Park, from $2798 (excluding air fare).

Journeys International, t 800 255 8735, *www.journeys-intl.com*. Adventure travel specialist. Tours include: a 9-day 'Costa Rica

Adventure Call', from $2,560; a 9-day 'Costa Rican Natural Wonders for Families' tour, from $2,290; and a 9-day 'Costa Rica Tropical Treasures' tour, from $2,695.

Tico Travel, t 1-800 493 8426, *www.ticotravel. com*. Offers a wide range of options, from canopy safaris and weekend getaways to diving tours (at Caño Island), sports fishing packages, white-water rafting and 'retirement tours'.

Wilderness Travel, t 1-800 368 2794, *www. wildernesstravel.com*. Tours include an 11-day 'Costa Rica Wildlife Tour', taking in San José, Monteverde, Volcán Arenal, Tortuguero and Corcovado, from $2,695 (excluding air fare).

Costa Rica-based Tour Operators

Multi-destination Tours

Camino Travel, C 1, Av 0/1, San José, t 234 2530, *www.caminotravel.com*. Tour include: a 7-night 'Costa Rica Verde' tour of Volcán Poás, Volcán Arenal, Tabacón Hot Springs, Caño Negro Wildlife Refuge, Monteverde Cloudforest Reserve, Carara National Park and Jacó, from $809 per person; and an 8-night 'Jungle Escapade' tour taking in Corcovado, Caño Island and white-water rafting on the Pacuare river, from $1,474 per person in the low season.

Costa Rica Expeditions, C 0, Av 3, San José, t 257 0766, *www.costaricaexpeditions.com*. One of the oldest (founded in 1978) and best-known tour operators in the country, Costa Rica Expeditions operates three properties: Tortuga Lodge in Tortuguero, the Corcovado Tent Camp on the edge of Parque Nacional Corcovado, and Monteverde Lodge. It also offers a variety of itineraries and customized tours throughout the country. Standard tours include: a 9-night 'Costa Rica Explorer' tour, taking in Monteverde Cloudforest Reserve, Volcán Arenal and Tortuguero National Park, from $1,908; and an 8-night 'Costa Rica River and Rainforest' tour, taking in Corcovado National Park, a hike on the Cerro de la Muerte and white-water rafting on the Pacuare river, from $1,538.

Costa Rica Nature Adventures, Av 5, C 33/35, San José, t 225 3939, *www.costaricanatureadven tures.com*. Tours include: a 7-day self-guided (i.e. you drive yourself in a rented car following a pre-set itinerary) 'Family Adventure', taking in San José, white-water rafting on the Río Sarapiquí, Volcán Arenal, Tabacón Hot Springs, Monteverde Cloudforest Reserve and beaches of Guanacaste from $3,235 (2 adults, 2 children); 'Explorer's Adventure Tour', taking in San José, Parque Nacional Marino Ballena, an ultralight flight, horseback riding and the Parque Nacional Corcovado, from $2,050 (for two); 2-night tours to Tortuguero ($251); Volcán Arenal ($454) and Monteverde Cloudforest Reserve ($415); and 3-night tours to the Parque Nacional Corcovado ($1,115). White-water rafting on the Sarapiquí and Pacuare rivers is also offered.

Ecole Travel, Gran Hotel Costa Rica, Plaza de la Cultura, San José, **t** 256 0295, *www.ecoletravel. com*. One-day combined highlights tours to: Volcán Irazú, Lankester Gardens and the Orosi valley ($58); Volcán Poás, La Paz Waterfall Gardens, Café Britt and Braulio Carrillo ($79); Volcán Poás, Grecia and Sarchí ($56); Volcán Arenal and Tabacón Hot Springs ($79). Canopy tours ($77) and white-water rafting on the Reventazón and Pacuare ($75) also offered.

Ecoscape Nature Tours, Av 5, C 7/9, San José, **t** 297 0664, *www.ecoscapetours.com*. Tours include the 'Sunset Jungle Tour', comprising a boat journey along the Río Sarapiquí, lunch at the Selva Verde Jungle Lodge and a torchlit night walk through rainforest ($65); and a one-day Highlights Tour taking in Volcán Poás, La Paz Waterfall Gardens, lunch at the Selva Verde Lodge and a boat ride up the Río Sarapiquí ($79). The overnight version also involves white-water rafting and a canopy tour ($250).

Expediciones Tropicales, Av 11/13, C 3 bis, **t** 257 4171, *www.costaricainfo.com*. Offers a wide range of one-day tours, including a '4 in 1' tour, taking in Volcán Poás, La Paz Waterfall Gardens, Parque Nacional Braulio Carrillo and a white-water rafting trip on the Río Sarapiquí ($82); Volcán Arenal and Tabacón Hot Springs ($79); Volcán Poás, Grecia and Sarchí ($29); Volcán Irazú ($36); Monteverde Cloudforest Reserve ($125); Parque Nacional Tortuguero ($75); Parque Nacional Carara and Jacó ($80); and San José City ($26). Horse-riding ($77), white-water rafting on the Reventazón and Sarapiquí rivers ($75–95) and canopy tours are also offered.

Horizontes Nature Tours, C 28, Av 1/3, San José, **t** 222 2022, *www.horizontes.com*. Long-established (founded 1982), well-respected operator. Tours include: an 11-day/10-night 'Costa Rica Rainforest Tour', taking in Tortuguero National Park, La Paz Waterfall Gardens, Volcán Arenal, Monteverde Cloudforest Reserve and Manual Antonio National Park, from $1,582 per person low season; a 9-day/8-night 'Multisport Activity Tour': horse-riding in Rincón de la Vieja National Park, mountain biking around Lake Arenal, hiking around Volcán Arenal, canyoning, a canopy tour and white-water rafting on the Pacuare river, from $1,441 per person. Customized, family and honeymoon packages.

Rainforest World, Turrialba, **t** 556 0014, *www.rforestw.com*. Tours of this Turrialba-based operator include: a 10-day/9-night 'Costa Rica

Adventurer' tour visiting Tortuguero National Park, Volcán Arenal, Tabacón Hot Springs, Monteverde Cloudforest Reserve and Manuel Antonio National Park, as well as a canopy tour, horseback riding and white-water rafting on the Pacuare river, from $2,231 per person. Customized tours also available.

Multi-activity Tours

Aventuras Naturales, **t** 225 3939, *www. adventurecostarica.com*. Run by Costa Rica Nature Adventures, Aventuras Naturales offers horse-riding, kayaking, sailing, jet-skiing, ATV hire, white-water rafting on the Pacuare, zip-lining at Pacuare Canopy Adventure and accommodation at Pacuare Lodge.

Desafío Adventure Company, **t** 645 5874, *www. monteverdetours.com*. Offers horse-riding, rafting and canopy tours in the Monteverde area; *see* p.247 for more details.

Hacienda Pozo Azul, La Virgen de Sarapiquí, **t** 761 1360, *www.haciendapozoazul.com*. One-day activity tours at its adventure centre located 90 minutes north of San José near Puerto Viejo de Sarapiquí. Tour includes transport, meals and a choice of two activities from canopy tours, horseback riding and white-water rafting.

Serendipity Adventures, Turrialba, **t** 507 1358, *www.serendipityadventures.com*. Turrialba-based company offering white-water rafting, horse-riding, mountain biking, sea kayaking, tree-climbing, canopy tours, canyoning, hiking, hot-air ballooning and more.

White-water Rafting

See also the multi-activity operators.

Costa Sol Rafting, **t** 431 1183, *www.costasol rafting.com*. Offers one- and two-day rafting tours (including transport from San José, meals and overnight camping) on the Reventazón and Pacuare rivers, from $75.

Exploradores Outdoors, **t** 222 6262, *www. exploradoresoutdoors.com*. Offers one- and two-day trips along the Reventazón, Sarapiquí and Pacuare rivers from $75. Canopy tours and snorkelling also available.

Ríos Tropicales, **t** 233 6455, *www.riostropicales. com*. 20-year-old company offering trips along the Pacuare, Reventazón, Pacuare and Naranjo rivers (price includes lunch and San José pick-up). Kayaking in Tortuguero and on Lake Arenal.

Birdwatching

With Costa Rica home to 850 species of bird (which is more than either the USA or Europe), it's little wonder that the country has come to be regarded as something of a mecca by bird-watchers, with a growing number of companies offering tours to the prime ornithological hotspots of Caño Negro, Carara, Corcovado, Palo Verde and Tortuguero.

Caligo Tours, 426 Petronia Street, Key West, Florida, USA, t 800 426 7781, *www.caligo.com/ costarica*. Offers several 9-night birdwatching tours including: 'Classic Highlights', taking in Volcán Poás, Río Sarapiquí, Monteverde and Carara National Park; 'Southern Region', visiting Corcovado and the Cerro de la Muerte; and the 'Caribbean Region', visiting Tortuguero and the Río Sarapiquí, from $2,050 pp, low season.

Sunny Travel, San Isidro El General, t 771 9686, *www.sunnycostarica.com*. Offers a choice of four birdwatching tours: Caribbean lowlands and Talamancan highlands; Monteverde and the Central Pacific, the Central Valley and the Caribbean Lowlands; the Southern Pacific Highlands, Lowlands, Rainforest and Seashore.

Volunteer Projects

If you feel like contributing a little bit more to the country than just a few footprints and a bunch of extra tourist dollars, there are plenty of volunteer projects available, enabling you to help out with Costa Rica's ongoing conservation work – helping to preserve rainforests, studying endangered species, monitoring animal migrations, planting trees... You'll be expected to commit to at least a few weeks of work, pay your own air fare and contribute towards the (usually pretty basic) food and lodging.

Amigos de los Aves, *info@parrotfund.org*, *http:// amigosdelosaves.org*. Parrot-conservation project dedicated to breeding and reintroducing endangered species back into the wild.

Asociación ANAI, Costa Rica t 224 3570, *www. anaicr.org*. Conservation project in Costa Rica's Talamancan region, offering a number of volunteer options, including working on an

environmentally friendly farming project (minimum commitment 6 weeks) for around $300 and sea turtle conservation (minimum commitment seven days) for $79.

Asociación de Voluntarios para el Servicio de las Areas Protegidas (ASVO), Costa Rica t 233 4989, *www.asvocr.org*. Volunteer projects throughout Costa Rica's national parks; trail maintenance, etc. Minimum commitment 2 weeks (4 weeks if working on a turtle project). $14 a day.

Caribbean Conservation Corporation and Sea Turtle Survival League, Costa Rica t 373 6441, *www.cccturtle.org*. The country's oldest and most famous turtle conservation group, the organization primarily responsible for setting up Tortuguero National Park offers a number of projects, including tagging turtles for monitoring purposes. A 15-day commitment is required.

Earthwatch, UK t 01685 318 838, USA t 1-800 776 0188, Aus t 03 9682 6828, *www.earthwatch. org*. Venerable conservation organization, overseeing worldwide projects for over 35 years. In Costa Rica this can involve saving sea turtles, conducting research into sustainable coffee-growing, studying the habits of howler monkeys, tree-planting and more.

Estación Biológica la Selva, Costa Rica t 766 6565, *laselva@sloth.ots.ac.cr*. Respected tropical research station run by the Organization for Tropical Studies: various volunteer programmes.

Genesis II Cloud Forest Reserve, Costa Rica t 381 0739, *http://genesis-two.com*. Four-week placements working in a cloudforest reserve, helping with reforestation, for $150 per week.

Global Volunteers, USA t 800 398 8787, *www. globalvolunteers.org*. Organizes a variety of volunteer projects in the country, including several around Santa Elena in conjunction with CASÉM (Cooperativa de Artesanas de Santa Elena y Monteverde), an artisans' co-operative.

Getting Around

By Air

Domestic air connections are good, and getting better all the time, with most of the country's major towns – including Golfito, Liberia, Nosara, Drake Bay, Puerto Jiménez, Quepos, Sámara, Tamarindo and Tambor – served by daily flights from San José. And, because Costa Rica is such a small country (something that's not always apparent when driving on its interminably winding, potholed roads), no destination lies much more than an hour's flight away from the capital.

If you have the money, flying certainly represents the most convenient way of getting to some of the country's more isolated destinations, including Corcovado on the Osa Peninsula, where the roads are often impassable, and Tortuguero and Barra del Colorado in the northeast, otherwise only reached via a boat journey of several hours.

There are two domestic carriers, which offer flights on small 14–19-seat, propeller-powered airplanes (typical baggage allowance 12kg): **Sansa**, which is affiliated to the country's national carrier, Grupo Taca, and flies out of Juan Santamaría International

Airport (**t** 221 9414, *www.flysansa.com*); and **NatureAir**, which flies out of Tobías Bolaños Airport, 7km west of San José (**t** 220 3054, *www.natureair.com*). Fares start at around $75 return. For details of flight times and frequencies, *see* **San José**, p.104.

Do note that, because of the small size of the planes and Costa Rica's ever-changing weather, delays and cancellations are common, particularly in the wet season. It's also worth bearing in mind that the flights can be a bit hairy, with the planes landing on tiny airstrips just a few hundred yards long.

Still, if you're a good flyer, are hoping to see a lot of the country and have the funds, it might be worth investing in Sansa's **Costa Rica Air Pass**, which allows unlimited travel around the country for one week ($199) or two weeks ($249).

There are also several charter companies operating out of Tobías Bolaños Aiport, who can offer much the same range of flight options as the scheduled airlines, albeit for around twice the cost: **Aerobell** (**t** 290 0000, *www.aerobell.com*) and **Paradise Air** (**t** 231 0938, *www.flywithparadise.com*).

By Boat

In certain parts of the country, where the road system is either minimal or non-existent, boats represent the main form of transport. This particularly applies to Puerto Viejo de Sarapiquí), Tortuguero and Barra del Colorado in the northeast, and Bahía Drake on the Osa Peninsula in the southwest. Most journeys here are undertaken in flat-bottomed river craft known as *lanchas*.

There are also regular **ferry** services between Golfito and Puerto Jiménez across the Golfo Dulce and between Puntarenas and Paquera across the Golfo Nicoya.

By Bus

Regional Buses

Costa Rica's bus network is extensive, taking in almost all of the country's major tourist destinations. Its services are regular and cheap – no journey, of whatever length, should cost more than $8. In fact, the only downside to taking the bus is the time it will take to get to your destination. Because of the number of stops buses have to make –

even the supposedly 'direct' services tend to stop for whoever hails them – and the poor state and winding nature of many of the country's roads (*see* 'By Car'), journeys to more far-flung destinations can be inter-minable. If you're hoping to cover a lot of the country during your trip, and aren't going to invest in either flights or a hire car, you're going to find yourself spending a significant amount of time sitting on buses. It's up to you whether you consider the savings worth the wasted hours and discomfort – and things can get very uncomfortable. Much of the country's bus fleet is made up of old, noisy converted US school buses that offer little room for people – they were designed with children, not adults in mind – let alone luggage. Few have air-conditioning or toilets.

As with air travel, **San José** is the main hub for bus routes. Slightly frustratingly, getting from one regional centre to another will usually involve backtracking to the capital. The sheer number of services available out of San José can be rather confusing, as the capital has no single **bus station**, but rather a sort of diffuse bus station area covering much of downtown. It can take a while tracking down the stop you want, especially as these tend to change from year to year. And, just to confuse things further, the bus schedules are also notoriously fluid, which is not such a big problem on commonly travelled routes – there'll be another service along shortly – but can cause major headaches on less travelled ones. Your best bet is to phone the relevant bus company in advance and check, although you will need to have pretty good Spanish for this. *See* pp.102–3 for details of the current bus stops and bus company phone numbers.

You can pick up a **bus schedule** (*itinerario de buses*) for all routes from San José's tourist office, although you should treat even this with a degree of scepticism. In fact, you'll probably be told as it's being handed over that 'there have been some changes lately'. On good days a helpful member of staff may write these alterations onto the schedule by hand. On other occasions, the best you'll get will probably be an encouraging smile.

Many of the longer regional bus routes are covered by two services: a fast **direct service** (the *directo*) and a slower **stopping service**.

Make sure you get on the right one, although do also be aware that the direct service often isn't that much faster than the stopping one.

It's not normally necessary to **book** in advance for frequently run services, although it is advisable for less regular ones, particularly those serving destinations in the far south. Buses tend to be much more crowded around the big public holidays of Christmas and, in particular, in the run-up to Easter, partly because the entire service shuts down from Thursday to Easter Sunday.

Bus fares are payable in *colones* only, and you should ideally have the right change ready. To get off, you can get the bus to **stop** by pressing the bell or by politely calling out *'la parada, por favor'* ('this stop, please'). You may also hear locals requesting their stop by whistling at the driver, but as this seems to irritate them greatly, you should probably avoid following suit.

Finally, it should be said that, while the majority of Ticos are honest and helpful, happily bunching up to allow you onto a crowded bus, there are, as everywhere, a few bad apples. Theft is a worryingly common phenomenon on the region's buses, particularly from the overhead storage racks. If possible, keep your bags with you during your journey and always keep an eagle eye on your belongings, particularly at stops, as it has been known for thieves to pass bags out of windows to accomplices waiting outside.

See pp.102–3 for details of regional services from San José.

Shuttle Buses

This is the faster, more convenient, more comfortable and much more expensive alternative. There are currently three companies offering speedy, air-conditioned, cushion-seated shuttle bus services to the main tourist centres. But be warned, these are as costly as they are convenient – $27 from San José to Arenal or the Nicoya beaches, $38 to Monteverde.

Grayline Fantasy Bus, t 232 3681, *www.fantasy.co.cr.*

Interbus, t 283 5573, *www.interbusonline.com.*

Montezuma Expeditions Tur Bus Shuttle Service, t 440 8078, *www.montezumaexpeditions.com.*

Local Buses and *Colectivos*

Some of the country's major urban centres, including Puerto Limón, Puntarenas and, of course, San José, also operate **local bus** routes around the city. No urban bus journey should cost more than c250 ($0.50). In more rural areas, where the roads are too poor to support a regular bus service (most notably on the Nicoya and Osa peninsulas), communities rely instead on *colectivos* – open-back truck taxis that trundle along 'collecting' passengers as they go (hence the name).

By Car

The guidelines for drivers about to tackle the Costa Rican road network always seem to resemble the advice given out to potential Mogwai owners at the start of the film *Gremlins* – avoid the wet, keep your wits about you and, whatever you do, don't risk anything after dark. The poor state of Costa Rica's roads is almost legendary. Aside from a few half-decent well-maintained stretches – most notably the Pacific coastal highway south of Dominical, and some (though by no means all) sections of the Pan-American Highway (Interamericana, HWY-1/HWY-2) – Costa Rica's roads run the gamut from pretty awful to downright terrible. The country's admirable commitment to education and health, not to mention its sizeable foreign debts, means that very little money is set aside for road maintenance.

However, it's not just the state of the road surface you have to worry about. Additional hazards include ever-changing climatic conditions, which at high altitudes, such as on the stretch of highway passing over the Cerro de la Muerte (*see* p.285), can mean the sudden arrival of dense fogs or, at lower elevations, such as on the Osa Peninsula road between Puerto Jiménez and Carate, swollen rivers (which must be driven through). You'll also have to keep a keen lookout for dead animals lying on the road, live animals running across the road, groups of school-children meandering alongside the road and, last but not least, other drivers all over the road. This last factor, perhaps the most significant of all the variables, can take a myriad different forms: slow-moving tractors and lorries trundling uphill, fast-moving lorries hurtling downhill, badly misjudged over-taking manoeuvres, aggressive tail-gating, trucks churning up clouds of dust and, in San José at least, choking congestion. That said, outside the capital – where driving tends to take the form of inching your way forward amid a honking maelstrom – Costa Rica's highways actually support remarkably little traffic. A typical cross-country drive will usually see you either whizzing along empty roads making good time, or – as most high-ways are single-lane affairs – dawdling along in a convoy behind a slow-moving truck.

Putting all dire warnings aside for the moment, it's worth saying that, whatever travails you may face, driving still represents the most convenient way of getting around the country.

Tips for Driving in Costa Rica

• **Big and bulky is best.** Unless you're planning to do all your travelling in and around San José, get a 4WD. This particularly applies to wet sea-son months when, if you're intent on visiting some of the country's more challenging areas, your rental firm will probably insist on it. A Daihatsu Terios, the standard budget 4WD car, is fine for most conditions and routes, although you might want something a little sturdier, with a touch more ground clearance, for when the rains start coming down and rivers really start to swell.

• **Drive defensively.** i.e. not the way the locals do. Despite the many and various hazards of their roads, and the country's fearsomely high road accident rate, many Ticos continue to drive in a way that could most charitably be described as a tad aggressive. Avoid following suit. If somebody wants to pass, let them. Drive extremely cautiously at all times in the expecta-tion that anything could be around the next corner – a traffic jam, a herd of cows, a huge axle-breaking pothole, a missing section of the road that's been washed away by the rains...

• **Start early.** Before you begin any drive, look at a map. Estimate how long you think it will take you to reach your destination, and then double it. This is not just so as to avoid potential delays on the roads, but because Costa Rica's roads, particularly those traversing the central moun-tains, are extremely winding. A route that looks straight on a map is often anything but, instead wending its way around several peaks. Give yourself ample time to complete your journey.

• **Finish early.** Don't drive at night. It's hard enough in the day, but things are even worse once darkness falls. Most highways are entirely unlit and many have sharp drops on either side. It's the tropics, so daylight comes to an abrupt end around 6–6.30pm throughout the year. Plan to be off the road well before then.

• **Watch your speed.** Speed limits, which range from 60–90km on major highways, should be painted on the road, although they're often not. Police with radar guns do make regular patrols of the highways and will issue fines of up to $150 for speeding, which must be paid at a bank (and *not* direct to the police officer). If you see an oncoming driver flashing their headlights at you, this means there is probably a police speed trap up ahead. But it makes sense to comply: not only are Costa Rica's roads not designed for fast travel, but most highways pass through the centre of a number of towns, where you'll often see groups of children wandering along the road. The word '*escuela*' painted on the road indicates that you are passing a school and are legally obliged to drop your speed to 25kmph.

• **Pay attention.** You'll need your wits about you, not just to avoid any hazards, but simply to work out where you're going. Signposting in much of the country is extremely poor, and in certain parts entirely non-existent. Ideally you should travel with a companion who possesses both good map-reading ability and fluent Spanish.

• **Don't get ripped off.** And finally, if you've managed to successfully navigate a path around everything the Costa Rican road net-work can throw at you, the last thing you want is for someone to break into your car – after all, you can get that at home. Car crime is, as every-where, common, and you will no doubt hear tales of the various cunning ploys thieves have devised to get you to pull over and be robbed: telling you there's something wrong with your car; telling you there's something wrong with their car and asking for help; deliberately engi-neering an accident; and, most elaborate of all, putting a slow puncture in your tyre while you are parked and then following you till it goes flat. Almost all problems can be avoided if you follow the same common sense rules you would anywhere: keep doors locked and win-dows rolled up when driving through town; never stop for anyone other than a policeman or another official; don't pick up hitch-hikers; don't leave valuables on display in the car; don't leave your vehicle parked on the street overnight; and if you think you're being followed, drive to the nearest busy, well-lit area and call the police.

Car Hire

Renting a car in Costa Rica is a relatively straightforward process. Tourists need only show their passport, a valid photo driving licence from their home country and an internationally accepted credit card (Visa or MasterCard) in order to hire a car for the duration of their visitor's permit. The credit card will need to have enough credit to cover both the full cost of the hire period and the excess (or 'deductible'), typically $1,500, due should the vehicle be damaged beyond repair. With hire rates at around $30–40 per day and insurance (a necessity) around $15–18 per day, you're looking at a total hire cost of around $350–400 a week, which is pretty expensive by US or (some) European standards. This price is, however, slightly offset by relatively low petrol prices (certainly by UK standards) of around c65 per litre, around $30 per tank for a small 4WD.

Unsurprisingly, as it's the entry point for the vast majority of visitors, San José is home to most of the country's car hire firms, with numerous offices located both at the airport and downtown (there are several along the Paseo Colón). There are also offices in Liberia, site of the country's other international airport, as well some of the country's other major tourist destinations, including Quepos and Jacó and Tamarindo. It's also possible to hire a car through many of San José's tour operators, as well as some of its major hotels.

As with hiring anywhere, you should make sure that an official note has been made of any damage – which on a rental pool 4WD that's spent the last few years bumping and banging its way around Costa Rica's roads is liable to include a whole host of minor bumps and scratches – before you sign the contract. Your rental firm will probably hand over the car with a full tank of petrol and expect it to be returned in the same state. Most rental cars have manual gear shifts.

On Foot

Costa Rica is a country in which you'll end up doing a lot of walking – tramping through the rainforest, strolling along the beach, tiptoeing around the edge of a swimming pool to the hot tub, etc. Its urban centres – including even its great sprawling capital, San José – are all best explored on foot, although you'll need to make sure you have a good, up-to-date map (*see* p.89).

Most Costa Rican towns and cities are laid out according to a grid system of interconnecting *avenidas* (running east–west) and *calles* (running north–south), which are numbered, rather than named; they have a small park, most often named the Parque Central, at their centre; and they have almost no street signs. Even those towns that aren't laid out in a grid pattern still tend to observe the no street sign rule.

While official addresses are usually given using a combination of *avenidas* and *calles* – e.g. C 1, Av 1/3, which means that the desired location is on Calle 1, between Avenidas 1 and 3 – **directions** almost never are. Instead Ticos guide each other using a combination of prominent local landmarks and distances, e.g. 100m south of the Mas X Menos supermarket, 200m north of the gas station. The 100m in this instance does not mean an exact distance, but is rather used to denote the average length of a city block. If taking a taxi, always give the driver the name of the place you want rather than its official address, unless you want to be met with a blank, uncomprehending stare.

Car Hire Firms

Adobe, t 258 4242, *www.adobecar.com*. Offices in San José, Juan Santamaría Airport, Liberia, Tamarindo and Quepos.

Avis, t 293 2222, *www.avis.co.cr*. Offices in San José, Juan Santamaría Airport and Liberia.

Budget, t 255 4750, *www.budget.co.cr*. In San José, Jacó, Liberia, Sámara and Tamarindo.

Europcar, t 257 1158, *www.europcar.co.cr*. Offices in San José, Juan Santamaría Airport, Liberia and Tamarindo.

Mapache, t 586 6300, *www.mapache.com*. In San José, Liberia and Tamarindo.

National, t 242 7878, *www.natcar.com*. In San José, Juan Santamaría Airport, Jacó, Quepos, Sámar, Tamarindo and at the Four Seasons Hotel, Papagayo.

Payless, t 233 8605, *www.paylesscr.com*. Offices in Juan Santamaría Airport, Jacó, Liberia, Quepos and Tamarindo.

Thrifty, t 257 3434, *www.thrifty.com*. At Juan Santamaría Airport, Liberia, Quepos and Tamarindo.

Practical A–Z

07

Climate and When to Go

Costa Rica lies in the heart of the tropics, between 8° and 11° north of the equator. As such, you'd expect it to be hot, and much of it is. Temperatures of 20–30°C are standard in the Valle Central where the majority of the population lives, rising to over 35°C in the northwest, the country's hottest region.

In tourism terms, Costa Rica's year is split into two seasons, although these don't tell the whole story. The **high season**, which runs from roughly late November to the end of April, sees the highest amount of sunshine and the least amount of rain, while the May to mid-November **low season** (or 'Green Season', as it has been rechristened by the tourist board) represents the year's wetter months. These are by no means catch-all definitions, however. Only the **Valle Central** and **Pacific coast** enjoy a distinct dry season. The **Caribbean coast** tends to remain lush, green and very wet all year round.

And within this general picture lie a myriad different details, with the climate of many areas affected as much by local topography as by more general weather systems. Costa Rica's rolling countryside, its central spine occupied by a string of volcanoes and mountains (see 'Geography', pp.83–5), has led to the formation of hundreds of separate microclimates; just a short 3hr drive from San José to the Central Pacific coast will see you passing through many different weather patterns – from the moderate temperatures and sparse clouds of the lowlands up into the cool mist-covered peaks of the Cerro de la Muerte, down through lush jungle-fringed roads and out to the dry heat of the coast.

As for the best time to go, different advice applies to different regions (and different activities). Most people visit in the high season when skies are at their bluest, temperatures at their hottest, prices (flights, hotel rooms, etc.) at their highest and room occupancy at its greatest, with everything coming to a peak around the public holidays of Christmas and Easter. For economy's sake, you may want to consider visiting in the low season; and some activities – e.g. watching turtles nesting on the beaches of Tortuguero – are only possible during certain off-season months (July–October). Guanacaste, the country's hottest, driest province, which can look a bit desert-like during the high season, is also a much more pleasant place to be once temperatures have come down a little, there's a bit of moisture in the ground and the vegetation has had a chance to spruce up a bit. Unfortunately, it's not always feasible to visit some of the more out-of-the-way places – particularly those which lack paved roads, such as the southern Nicoya Peninsula, Monteverde and Corcovado – during the wet season; in these areas, the roads here can quickly become impassable once the rains begin to come down.

Because Costa Rica lies close to the equator it enjoys a more or less uniform-length day throughout the year, with the sun rising around 5am and setting around 6pm.

Crime and Safety

Emergencies t 911. Operators will reroute calls to the appropriate emergency service.

Travelling around the country, you'll hear lots of stories about the various cunning scams employed by the nation's fiendish gangs of criminals to separate you from your valuables: feigning illness on the street, obliging you to go to their aid, thus leaving your bag to be stolen by an unseen accomplice; 'accidentally' tipping food on you, and then helping to clean you up (and out); offering you a drugged drink on a bus and then stealing your luggage; 'accidentally' driving into the back of your car and then holding you up when you get out to investigate. To be honest, you'll probably hear more stories about potential elaborate criminal set-ups than you will reports of actual crimes. That's not to say these scams haven't happened. They have, but the frequency with which the stories are repeated does give some of them an urban myth-like quality, and conveys the impression that the country is much more crime-ridden than is the case. The crimes you're most likely to fall victim to are not muggings or convoluted stings, but pickpocketing, petty thievery and minor scams – a petrol pump attendant carrying on pumping after the tank is full; being handed a foreign coin in your change or being sold a non-existent tour by a street-corner hustler.

See also p.73 for tips on car safety, p.72 for buses, and p.58 for safety when hiking.

Safety Precautions

• Although you are obliged to carry ID with you wherever you go in Costa Rica, a recent change in regulations means that the authorities now accept photocopies of passports as proof of ID. Wherever possible, avoid travelling with the real thing; store that in a hotel safe.

• Make photocopies of other important documents – airline tickets, travellers' cheques, etc. When travelling with the real things, keep the photocopies in a separate part of your luggage to where you store the originals.

• Make sure you bring phone numbers with you in case you need to cancel credit cards, have airline tickets reissued, etc. If you lose your passport (or it gets stolen), contact the relevant embassy or consulate, see p.79.

• Don't keep all your money in one place. Divide it into separate stashes – some in your pocket, some in your money belt etc.

• Keep your documents and money in a waterproof money belt tucked beneath your waistband. It can be a bit uncomfortable, but it's not as bad as having all your documents stolen.

• In major towns, try to rely on credit cards (which can be cancelled) as much as possible.

• Don't carry your bag or rucksack over one shoulder. Always use both straps or loop the strap over your head.

• Don't display ostentatious wealth. Keep your camera hidden away unless actually using it.

• Don't walk around unfamiliar areas of town on your own after dark. Try to find out which are the 'dodgy' areas of town and steer clear. If you don't know where the dodgy areas are, stick to the busy main streets.

• Try to look as little like a tourist as possible. Act confidently and stride purposefully, as if you know exactly where you're going and what you're doing (even if you're completely lost). If you need to check your bearings on a map in an unfamiliar town, try and do so inside a shop or café rather than on a street corner.

• And finally, if you are mugged, make no attempt to keep hold of your valuables. Give the thieves what they want with the minimum of fuss. The vast majority of hold-ups are non-violent. Don't do anything to unnecessarily provoke your assailant.

The Authorities

If you are victim of a crime, you will have to report it to the local police. The chances of anything being recovered are, of course, slim, but you will need to make an official report for insurance purposes. In San José, go to the **Organismo de Investigación Judicial (OIJ)**, Av 4/6, C 15/17, **t** 295 3643. Most major towns have a police station. Take along a phrasebook, as you won't be able to count on the policemen speaking English.

Women Travellers

Women may be singled out for special attention, especially if wearing skimpy clothing, although this is rarely anything worse than one of the country's would-be casanovas trying to attract your attention with a complimentary whistle or hiss. As everywhere, these demonstrations of admiration are usually done less for your benefit than for the benefit of the whistler's associates. Studious, haughty indifference is the best response. Treat all unwanted attention the same way you would anywhere. Be polite but firm, and keep walking.

Tight jeans and crop tops are all the rage in the capital, and bikinis are acceptable on the beach (although topless sunbathing is not), but fashion tastes are a good deal more conservative in rural areas. Try to avoid offending local sensibilities. Rapes and sexual assaults do happen in Costa Rica, but no more frequently than anywhere else. Simply take the same precautions you would in any country. Don't walk alone through unfamiliar areas, particularly late at night. Don't use unlicensed taxis. Don't hitch-hike.

Prostitution

'Free choice' prostitution is legal in Costa Rica, so long as both parties are over 18, although the promotion or advertisement of prostitution is not. You won't find any tour operators offering 'special packages', or guidebooks telling you the best places to go, but it's an all too obvious fact that a lot of men come to Costa Rica in order to drink cheap beer and have sex with the country's large number of prostitutes. It's been going on a long time. Paul Theroux reported on the phenomenon in The Old Patagonian Express 25 years ago, and things have only increased.

The sex tourism industry is centred on the country's main tourist towns, in particular San José and Jacó, and ports, including

Puntarenas, Golfito and Puerto Limón. Prostitute pick-up bars in the latter usually have large boards positioned outside the entrance to stop casual passers-by from seeing in, and thus are quite easy to recognize and avoid. Things are slightly less clearly demarcated in San José, where prostitution is more mainstream, with scores of women operating out of the glitzy Gringo bars and casinos of the downtown area. Though the prostitute bars here do not have any exterior markings (which would be illegal, in any case), they're still quite easy to spot should you accidentally stumble into one – the clientele will be made up exclusively of scantily clad ladies and paunchy middle-aged men. As a man entering one, you will immediately be earmarked as a potential customer and approached (repeatedly); as a woman you may find yourself at the centre of some even less welcome attention. If you do find yourself sitting in a prostitute bar having bought a drink, never leave that drink unattended or unwatched for even a short while, as it has been known for them to be spiked. Never accept sweets from prostitutes for similar reasons. STDs, including AIDS, are common.

Also be aware that Costa Rica has an increasing problem with illegal child prostitution. If you believe the exploitation of minors is taking place, you should report it.

Disabled Travellers

The situation for disabled travellers can perhaps best be described as problematic but improving (slowly). Of course, it is understood that many of the country's more remote attractions – rainforests, volcanoes, etc. – do, by their very nature, pose serious problems for anyone with mobility difficulties, although efforts are being made to provide disabled provision to the country's national parks, with the Parque Nacional Volcán Poás and Parque Nacional Carara now both offering limited wheelchair access. What is slightly less understandable is the number of urban hotels and restaurants that still do not accommodate disabled guests. Laws are now in place obliging all new businesses to make their premises wheelchair-compatible; unfortunately, these cannot be retrospectively enforced.

Disability Organizations

In Costa Rica

International Institute for Creative Development/Foundation for Universal Access to Nature, t 771 7482, *www.empowerment access.com*.

Serendipity Adventures, t 558 1000 (USA t 1-877 507 1358), *www.serendipityadventures.com*.

Vaya con Silla de Ruedas (Go with a Wheelchair), t 454 2810, *www.gowithwheelchairs.com*.

In the USA

Accessible Journeys, 35 West Sellers Avenue, Ridley Park, PA 19078, t 800 846 4537, *www.disabilitytravel.com*.

In the UK

Disability Now, 6 Markets Road, London N7, t (020) 7619 7323, *www.disabilitynow.org.uk*.

Most public transport is not wheelchair-friendly either, although the country's bus companies have made a collective commitment to try and adapt 8 per cent of the total bus fleet for wheelchair use in the near future – a tiny proportion, but a start.

If you have mobility difficulties, your best bet would be to get in touch with one of dedicated official bodies or tour operators listed above, for expert detailed advice.

Electricity

Costa Rica's electric current is supplied at 110v AC at 60Hz. The country's outlets take US-style flat-pronged two-pin plugs. Note, if you are travelling from Europe, adapters can be very difficult to track down in Costa Rica. Bring your own. Be sure to unplug your electrical equipment if there's a storm.

Rather admirably, Costa Rica does not use fossil fuels to provide its electricity (vehicles excepted). Instead, it relies solely on renewable energy sources. Unfortunately, this is not quite as eco-friendly as it sounds, as the government has categorized hydroelectric dams as renewable (which technically they are), despite the significant and long-term environmental impact their construction can have – flooding areas of forest, diminishing local water supplies, etc. Nonetheless, the country's dams have proved very successful, today supplying over 80 per cent of the country's electricity. In fact, despite the fact that Costa Rica is currently a net exporter of electricity, there are plans to build more. The Dos Montañas Ravine on the Río Pacuare had long been earmarked as a potential site for a dam. Thankfully, a combined protest by environmentalists, residents and the white-water rafting industry – which would effectively be ended by the dam's construction – led to the project's being put on hold, at least for now.

Embassies and Consulates

Australia and New Zealand do not operate embassies in Costa Rica. Citizens from these countries should contact the UK embassy. See www.rree. go.cr for information (in Spanish).

Foreign Embassies in Costa Rica

Canada: Third Floor, Ejecutivo La Sabana, Edificio 5, Sabana Sur, San José, **t** 242 4400, *sjcra@internacional.gc.ca*.

UK: 11th Floor, Edificio Centro Colón, Paseo Colón, San José, **t** 258 2025, *britemb@ sol.racsa.co.cr*.

USA: Pavas, in front of the Centro Comercial Oeste, San José, **t** 519 2000, *info@ usembassy.or.cr*.

Costa Rican Embassies Abroad

Australia: PO Box 205, Spit Junction, Sidney, NSW 2088, **t** (09) 969 4050, *congenrica@ ozemail.com*.

Canada: 325 Dalhousie Street, Suite 407, Ottawa, ON, K1N 7G2, **t** (613) 562 2855, *embcrica@travel-net.com*.

UK: Flat 1, 14 Lancaster Gate London W2 3LH, **t** (020) 7706 8844, *costaricanembassy@ btconnect.com*.

USA: 2114 S Street, NW Washington D.C. 20008, **t** (202) 234 2945, *embassy@ costarica-embassy.org*.

Festivals and National Holidays

Costa Rica's year sees a whole host of events taking place – national holidays, music festivals, carnivals, local village fairs. Many celebrations are religious in origin, or are at least based on the Christian calendar, even if some have subsequently acquired a more secular, hedonistic veneer. Christmas and Easter are strictly observed. The latter sees the entire country more or less shut down from Thursday to Easter Sunday when, incidentally, no alcohol is served throughout the country (in theory, anyway).

Calendar of Events

January

Jan 1 New Year's Day (national holiday).

Jan 16 *Fiesta de Santa Cruz*. Santa Cruz, the 'National Folklore City', celebrates Guanacaste province's traditional way of life with folk dances, parades, rodeos and bullfights.

February–March

Some time in month Monteverde Music Festival. The Monteverde Institute (*www. mvinstitute.org*) lays on a month's worth of classical, jazz and Latin music performances at venues throughout the region.

Some time in months *Fiesta de San Isidro El General*. Agricultural-themed fiesta with rodeos, cattle shows, parades and parties.

Some time in month *Fiestas Cívicas de Liberia*. Lively fiesta-cum-agricultural fair in the capital of Guanacaste: rodeos, parties and parades.

March 19 *Día de San José*. The capital honours its patron saint, St Joseph, with parades and special church services.

April

April 11 *Día de Juan Santamaría* (national holiday). Celebration of the country's victory over the US invader William Walker at the 1856 Battle of Rivas. Festivities are centred on Alajuela, the home town of Juan Santamaría, whose arsonist activities turned the conflict in Costa Rica's favour (*see* **History**, p.24, for more information on the story).

Easter Easter in Costa Rica is both a time of strict religious observance – many towns stage re-creations of Christ's crucifixion and hold special masses – and relaxation, as families take the opportunity to head off to the beach. With no business taking place between Thursday and Sunday, don't count on getting anywhere (there are no buses), buying anything (most shops are closed) or getting any money out (all banks are closed) during this time.

Last week San José University Week. Exhibitions, displays and concerts put on by the University of Costa Rica during the last week of the month.

May

May 1 Labor Day (national holiday). The president gives his 'State of the Nation' address.

May 29 Corpus Christi (national holiday).

June

June 29 *Día de San Pedro y San Pablo* (St Peter's and St Paul's Day). Processions in villages of those names.

July

During month *Festival de los Mangos*, Alajuela. Nine-day arts and crafts fair.

July 25 *Día de Guanacaste* (national holiday). The day on which Guanacaste voted to become part of Costa Rica, rather than neighbouring Nicaragua, is celebrated nationwide. Liberia, the capital of the province, hosts the biggest party, with parades, horse shows, rodeos, music, folk-dancing and bullfights.

August

During month Costa Rica International Music Festival (**t** 282 7724, *www.costaricamusic.com*). The country's most prestigious classical musical festival: performances throughout the month at the Teatro Nacional in San José, as well as at selected 'superior' venues around the country, including the Hotel Si Como No in Manuel Antonio, the Amphiteatre Villa Caletas on the Pacific coast, the Hotel Arenal Lodge and the Hotel Cala Luna on Tamarindo Beach.

Aug 2 *Día de la Virgen de Los Angeles*, Cartago. Important religious festival held in Cartago's Basílica de Nuestra Señora de Los Angeles, honouring a miracle believed to have taken place in the town in 1635. It attracts thousands of pilgrims from all over the country (*see p.148*).

Aug 15 *Día de la Madre* (national holiday). Mother's Day.

September

Sept 15 *Día del Independencia* (national holiday). Costa Rica's 'Day of Independence' celebrates the country's release from the Spanish Empire in the early 19th century. It's marked with parades, a nationwide singing of the national anthem at 6pm, and an inter-country relay race in which a 'freedom torch' is carried from Guatemala to Cartago – symbolizing the fact that all of Central America achieved independence at the same time, and that Cartago was capital of Costa Rica at that time.

October

Oct 12 *Día de las Culturas* (national holiday). Also known as Columbus Day, the 'Day of the Cultures' commemorates the moment when Columbus became the first European to set foot on Costa Rican soil when he landed on Uvita Island, just off the coast of modern day Puerto Limón, in 1504. It also marks the end of the Limón Carnival, one of the country's biggest and liveliest events, comprising a whole week of music, dancing, parades, food, fireworks, drinking and general overindulgence (*see p.333*).

November

Nov 2 *Día de los Muertos* (national holiday). The 'Day of the Dead' or 'All Souls' Day' is observed throughout much of Latin America. Families honour their ancestors by visiting cemeteries and holding special church services.

December

2nd week *Fiesta de la Luz*, San José. San José's 'Festival of Lights' is held during the second week of the month and consists of parties, fireworks and parades of floats adorned with illuminations.

Dec 24–6 Christmas (national holiday 25th). For tourists, Christmas is the busiest and most expensive time of year. It can also be hugely atmospheric in the weeks before, with funfairs, fireworks, carol singers, nativity scenes and hordes of shoppers on the streets. You won't find any respite from the masses on the coast, as many Tico families take trips to the beach at this time. Midnight mass on 24 December is strictly observed by a large proportion of the population, while 26 December sees a horse parade, or '*Tope*' in downtown San José.

Dec 31–Jan 2 *Fiesta de los Diablitos*, Boruca. The 'Festival of the Little Devils' is held in the small indigenous town of Boruca over three days at New Year, with a symbolic re-enactment of the battle between the Spanish conquistadors and the native peoples (*see pp.290–91*).

Food and Drink

Local Cuisine

Costa Rica's native cuisine, known as *comida típica* ('typical cuisine'), is nothing if not consistent, with rice and beans (*arroz y frijoles*) making up the principal ingredients of around two-thirds of all meals. Just to get things rolling, the traditional Costa Rican breakfast is *gallo pinto* (literally 'red rooster'), a hearty combination of rice, beans (both red and black), onions, sweet red peppers and coriander, often served up with a portion of scrambled eggs. This is labourer's food, carbohydrate-rich fare for people going out to do a day of hard manual slog. Despite its lowly origins, it has over the years achieved the status of a sort of unofficial national dish, available pretty much everywhere – Costa Rican branches of McDonald's even do a version. If you don't feel you can face something so hearty so early on, many hotels do also offer continental breakfasts, or a selection of tropical fruits, typically pineapple, banana, mango and melon.

The lunchtime staple in traditional Costa Rican restaurants (known as sodas) is the *casado*, a 'marriage' (the word's literal meaning) between rice and beans, a selection of vegetables – usually sautéed with garlic and onions and known as *picadillos* – and a piece of chicken, meat or fish. Sodas also usually serve a range of *empanadas* – deep-fried turnovers with either savoury or sweet fillings – Mexican-style tacos and, at Christmas, *tamales*, a mixture of ground cornmeal, vegetables, meat and raisins wrapped in a banana leaf.

The food does vary as you travel, albeit often quite subtly. Essentially you should expect to find rice and beans everywhere, accompanied by a shifting assortment of regional specialities. In **Guanacaste**, much of the food is corn (maize)-based. Look out in particular for *rosquillos* (a sort of corn doughnut), *chorreados* (cornflour pancakes) and *pozol* (pork and corn soup). The country's most distinctive cooking is served up on the **Caribbean coast**, where the strong Afro-Caribbean influence has led to the introduction of spicy Creole flavours, as typified by the slow-cooked coconut stew *rondón* (see p.334). In general, however, Costa Rican cooking is not particularly spicy, which sometimes comes as a surprise to visitors expecting the region's cuisine to take its culinary cue from Mexico. Some have even described Tico cooking as bland, which is a bit harsh, although it is rather predictable.

Most of the country's major towns, particularly those that welcome significant numbers of tourists, do also boast a selection of international restaurants, most typically Chinese (the country has a large Chinese population), Italian and Mexican. San José offers, as you'd expect, the widest range of cuisines, with everything from Middle Eastern and Japanese to Peruvian and Spanish available, along with a good deal of American fast food – McDonald's, Burger King, Taco Bell, etc.

Drinks

Coffee

Finding a good cup of coffee in Costa Rica is not quite as straightforward as you might think. Considering the country's status as one of the world's major coffee-exporters, widely renowned for the quality and smoothness of its product, the general awfulness of much of the coffee served here can come as a bit of a shock. Unfortunately, most of the good stuff, the *grano de oro* ('golden bean') is reserved for export, although you will find it sold in the country's better hotels and restaurants. The majority of cafés and restaurant sell lower-quality blends, some of which are even pre-sweetened in accordance with local sweet-toothed tastes and are pretty ghastly.

Café Britt is the country's main and most visible supplier of quality coffee. You'll see their bags for sale in pretty much every supermarket in the country. They also operate a very good café serving speciality coffees in the Teatro Nacional in San José (*see* p.118), and you can take a tour of their Valle Central plantation to see the coffee-harvesting process in action (*see* pp.142–3).

Soft Drinks

All the main American super-brands – Coca-Cola, Pepsi, Sprite, etc. – are widely available, although you might like to try the healthier local alternative, the *refresco* (sometimes also known simply as a *fresco*). This is a whizzed-up combination of water (or milk), ice and a mixture of fruits. The fruit can be anything from the expected – banana, pineapple, mango, melon, etc. – to the more esoteric – passion fruit (*maracuya*), star fruit (*carambola*) or blackberry (*mora*).

Alcoholic Drinks

The country's sole brewery, the Cervercería Costa Rica, produces a number of different **beer** brands. The most common, sold in every bar in the country, is Imperial, whose bottles bear a distinctive logo of a black stylized eagle on a yellow background. Other varieties include Pilsen, a light beer served on beer mats featuring pictures of bikini-clad ladies known as La Chicas Pilsen ('The Pilsen Girls', also available in calendar form), the American-style Rock Ice and the European-style Bavaria Dark. The brewery also has a licence to bottle and distribute Heineken.

Wine is not produced domestically, although it is available in most tourist-orientated restaurants, with Chilean imports being the most common. Imported **spirits** – including vodkas and whiskies – are also available, but can be pretty pricey, although you may consider the extra expense worth it once you've considered the alternatives. Domestic liquor production is the preserve of a state-owned monopoly, the Fabrica Nacional de Licores (FANAL), whose principal product is *guaro*, which is made from fermented sugar cane and tastes like a slightly less smooth version of methylated spirits. Rather smoother on the palate, albeit not much more appealing, is Café Rica, a creamy coffee-flavoured liqueur like of a cross between Baileys and Nescafé.

No alcohol is served anywhere from Easter Thursday–Sunday, or on national election days.

Eating Out

Restaurants and Sodas

Outside the big urban centres, the main Costa Rican dining experience is represented by a meal at the local **soda**. Usually family-run, a soda is a small, street-corner restaurant-café, often with a counter and stalls on the street or a takeaway window, aimed primarily at locals, not tourists. The emphasis is on serving basic hearty fare at low prices: most dishes cost less than $5. These are definitely the places to take advantage of if you're on a budget, as the prices in tourist-orientated 'international' eateries are inflated by a 13 per cent food tax and a 10 per cent service tax, usually added as standard. Thankfully, this practice makes tipping redundant, unless you feel the service particularly merits it; it's not expected.

In tourist restaurants, expect main courses to start at $6–8, over $10 in the top-end places; a full meal for two with wine will cost $30–35.

Costa Ricans tend to eat early. Breakfast can usually be had any time after 7am (sometimes earlier), and many restaurants, particularly outside the main tourist centres, close by 10pm. Things are, of course, different in the capital, where cafés catering to the gambling crowd stay open late into the night. There are even a couple of 24hr sodas in downtown San José.

While no-smoking sections are becoming more common in restaurants, you should expect smoking to be taking place in most Costa Rican eateries.

Bars

As with restaurants, where there's one type of eatery for locals (simple and cheap), and another for tourists (fancy and expensive), so it is with bars. Those aimed at locals tend to be rather basic affairs, both in terms of their décor and the range of drinks sold, which rarely stretches much beyond bottles of the ubiquitous Imperial and shots of *guaro*. At a local level, bar drinking in Costa Rica is an overwhelmingly male-dominated, macho pursuit and something best avoided by lone female travellers. Do also watch out for (and avoid) bars which double as pick-up joints for prostitutes. Those frequented by locals often have large boards positioned outside to prevent you from seeing what's going on inside. Tourist-orientated bars, however, are another world entirely – welcoming, well-equipped and stocking a wide range of drinks. Many of those in the main visitor hot spots – San José, Tamarindo, Jacó, Cahuita – transform into clubs at the weekend and stay open till the early hours. Bars aimed at locals usually close a littler earlier, often by around 10pm. You must be 18 to drink in a bar in Costa Rica. You may be asked for ID to prove your age if you look young.

Gay Costa Rica

The situation for gay and lesbian travellers in Costa Rica is a lot better than you might expect, and also a lot better than in most other Central American countries. That's not to say it exactly exhibits an open San Francisco-like tolerance, but gay lifestyles have a higher profile here than anywhere else on the isthmus. And unlike a number of other countries in the region, such as Belize, homosexual acts between consenting adults (over 18) are not illegal. In practice, the gay scene is restricted to just a handful of areas, principally San José and Manuel Antonio, where there are a few openly gay hotels, clubs and tour operators. Here at least, gay travellers can expect little hassle. Rural communities tend to be slightly more conservative and intolerant, influenced in part by the Catholic Church, which takes a predictably strong line against such things. However, the Church's relative political weakness – historically it has never played a dominant role in Costa Rican affairs – has prevented it from being able to dictate policy.

Most of the population have adopted a *de facto* 'don't ask, don't tell' position on the matter. In fact the country's famous tolerance and 'live and let live' attitude means that even those people who might be prejudiced probably wouldn't dream of bringing the subject up. The tourist board doesn't actively encourage gay tourism, but neither does it actively discourage it. The gap in information is provided by a couple of dedicated gay-friendly tour operators (*see* box).

Gay-Friendly Organizations

Hotels

San José: Bohemian Paradise, t 258 9683, *www.seecentralamerica.com/costa_rica/home.html*; **Colours Oasis Resort**, t 877 932 6652, *www.colours.net*; **Keköldi** (*see* p.115); **Sleep Inn**, Av 3, C 9/11, t 222 0101, *www.sleepinnsanjose.com*. **Manuel Antonio: Hotel Villa Roca**, t 777 1349, *www.villaroca.com*; **Keköldi**, t 248 0804, *www.kekoldi.com*.

Clubs

San José: La Avispa, C 1, Av 8/10, t 223 5343, *www.laavispa.co.cr*; **Déjà Vu** (*see* p.120); **La Metro**, C 19, Av 2/4, t 222 7167, *www.lametro.co.cr*; **Puchos Nightclub**, C 11, Av 8, t 256 1147, *www.puchosnightclub.com*.

Tour Operators

Gaytours Costa Rica, t 297 3556, *www.gaytourscostarica.com*. Gay travel agent with special expertise in San José and Manuel Antonio, between which they operate a daily 'Gaybus'. **Tiquicia Travel**, t 256 6429, *www.tiquiciatravel.com*. Long-established gay-owned and -operated travel agent.

Further Resources

The gay-orientated monthly newsletters *Gayness* and *Gente 10*, are available from select San José bars and bookstores, as is *Manuel Antonio Circuit* in Manuel Antonio.

Café Uno@Diez, C 3, Av 7, San José, t 258 4561, *www.1en10.com*. The 'place where you can be yourself' is a net café-cum-gay and lesbian traveller information centre. It also operates a website listing gay-friendly establishments and providing travel tips.

www.purpleroofs.com Worldwide accommodation listing service for gay and lesbian B&Bs, inns, guesthouses, hotels and tour operators.

www.planetout.com General gay travel site.

www.gaycostarica.com Spanish-language site which has a forum, a message board, a dating service and listings of gay-friendly hotels and tour operators.

Geography

Costa Rica lies at the centre of the Central American isthmus, sandwiched between Nicaragua to the north and Panama to the south, at a latitude of 8–11° north, and a longitude of 82–85° west. It's not a very large country, measuring less than 500km north to south and encompassing a total area of just over 50,000 sq km (or just under 20,000 square miles), making it just over twice the size of Wales or around half the size of the US state of Kentucky. Still, it has managed to squeeze an awful lot of geography into its rather limited confines – volcanoes, mountains, swaths of thick jungle, rolling open plains and sandy beaches.

At the country's narrowest point, the Atlantic and Pacific oceans lie just 275km apart. In fact, if Costa Rica were flat and its roads straight, it would only take a few hours to drive from one to the other. But Costa Rica is not flat and its roads are not straight. The oceans are separated by vertical as well as horizontal obstacles, chief among them the great ranges of volcanoes and mountains forming the country's central spine. Starting in the far northwest are the **Cordillera de Guanacaste**, which boasts a number of active volcanoes – notably Volcán Rincón de la Vieja (1,895m), Volcán Miravalles (2,028m) and

Volcán Tenorio (1,916m) – although these are active only in a low-key sort of a way; think steam vents, bubbling mud pools and hot springs rather than explosions of lava and ash. Slightly more impressive views are provided by the range south of here, the **Cordillera de Tilarán**, whose principal peak, Volcán Arenal (1,633m), puts on regular displays of spectacular pyrotechnics, flinging lava and superheated gases up into the air.

The next range you come to as you head south is the **Cordillera Central**, which boasts several of the country's most visited peaks, including Volcán Poás (2,704m), Volcán Irazú (3,432m) and Volcán Barva (2,906m). It also marks the northern extent of the Valle Central, an 'inter-mountain plateau' that represents a brief respite from the otherwise overwhelmingly mountainous terrain, with elevations hovering at around 1,000–1,500m. This is the most populated area in the country, home to the capital, San José, and the country's next three biggest cities, into which are crammed over half of the total number of Costa Rican citizens.

The mountains begin again just south of San José in the shape of the **Cordillera de Talamanca**, whose peaks are not volcanic. Rather, they are the topmost parts of an enormous granite batholith, a geological feature formed when magma (molten rock) deep underground tries to force its way to the surface, but can't. Instead, it sort of spreads sideways, cooling to form a giant rock intrusion that is gradually revealed by tectonic uplift and erosion. The range has over a dozen peaks, stretching all the way down to the border with Panama and beyond, the tallest of which, Cerro Chirripó, is, at 3,819m, the country's tallest mountain. In fact, it is so high that it occasionally even sports a light covering of snow. Much of the range's southern end is taken up by the **Parque Internacional La Amistad**, the country's largest protected area, which also extends into Panama

Either side of the great mountain ranges, the land gradually becomes less elevated as it slopes down to the lowland coastal areas. The shorter **Caribbean coast** – it's just over 200km long – is in general a good deal wetter than its Pacific counterpart, its low-lying areas thick with swamps, water-

ways and forests. The **Pacific coast** displays more climatic variation, but then there's a good deal more of it. Including its two **peninsulas** – the Nicoya and the Osa – which jut out from the mainland, the entire coast stretches for over 1,200km, from the dry desert-like expanses of Guanacaste in the north to the lush primary rainforest of Corcovado in the south.

Seismic Dangers

Costa Rica owes its existence to the continuous seismic activity rumbling away beneath its surface. Around three million years ago the movement of the Cocos tectonic plate into its Caribbean neighbour, forcing it upwards, created much of the country's land. Since then, Costa Rica's area has been greatly added to by the matter regularly expelled from the country's numerous volcanoes. Unfortunately this creative force can – from a human perspective – also be incredibly destructive, with the country extremely prone to both serious volcanic eruptions and earthquakes. A particularly devastating earthquake in 1991, which measured over 7.5 on the Richter scale, killed over 50 people, destroyed numerous buildings and caused so much damage to the country's railway that it had to be abandoned. Another, measuring 6.2 in November 2004 caused less damage, but no little unease, a feeling which was further exacerbated by the Indian Ocean tsunami two months later. The latter has served to focus attention on the state's readiness to deal with a truly major quake or tidal wave, and has led to calls for the installation of an early warning system on both coasts.

The country endures numerous quakes throughout the year, most of which are too small to be felt. If you are caught in a sizeable one, however, the standard advice is to move away from anything that might possibly fall on you. If in a building, head for the nearest load-bearing doorframe. If outside, steer clear of any walls, trees, lamp-posts or anything else liable to topple over.

National Parks and Private Refuges

Call t 192 for information (in English) on the national parks.

The Costa Rican national parks system is the country's pride and joy, and the main draw for the majority of tourists. As anyone who has read any sort of pamphlet or brochure produced by the Costa Rican tourist board will know, 25 per cent of the country's total area is protected against future development. This amounts to over a hundred protected areas, which are split into a number of categories: 27 national parks, 8 biological reserves and 63 wildlife refuges.

The distinctions between the different types of protected area can be subtle. A **national park** tends to be a large tract of land encompassing a significant swath of the environment, usually with areas that have been specifically designed for use by tourists. **Biological reserves** are usually less developed, maintained more for the benefit of scientists and naturalists than casual visitors, while **wildlife refuges** are set up to help protect specific (and often endangered) species.

The country's national parks contain all manner of different environments, including tropical dry forest (Parque Nacional Santa Rosa), lush primary rainforest (Parque Nacional Corcovado) whale-breeding grounds (Parque Nacional Marino Ballena), coral reefs (Parque Nacional Cahuita), turtle-nesting sites (Parque Nacional Tortuguero), volcanoes (Parque Nacional Volcán Arenal) and mountains (Parque Nacional Chirripó).

All of these protected areas come under the overall control of **MINAE** (Ministerio del Ambiente y Energía, *www.minae.go.cr*), the Ministry of Energy and the Environment, whose job it is to patrol the parks' borders, prevent poaching, maintain trails and train guides using the proceeds from the park entrance fees, which vary between $6–8. Despite this revenue, the parks system is still severely underfunded (*see* pp.49–54 for an in-depth look at financial problems facing the country's conservation movement). Help is provided by the private sector: in addition to the state-controlled parks there are around 30 **private refuges**, the largest being the Monteverde Cloudforest Reserve.

Health and Insurance

Costa Rica may be in the tropics – conjuring up images of terrible exotic diseases, deadly insects burrowing their way beneath your skin where they remain undetected for years (by which time they've grown several metres long) and fearsome jungle-dwelling creatures – but it's really a pretty safe place. Very few travellers encounter any health problems at all during their trip.

Obviously precautions still need to be taken, both before you leave – making sure you take out the necessary travel insurance and get the recommended inoculations – and once you're there – avoiding contaminated food and drink, staying out of the sun and evading the attentions of mosquitoes, particularly on the wetter, more humid Caribbean side of the country.

Insurance

It is vital that you take out travel insurance before your trip. This should cover, at a bare minimum, cancellation due to illness, travel delays, accidents, lost luggage, lost passports, lost or stolen belongings, personal liability, legal expenses, emergency flights and medical cover. The latter is, of course, the most important part of any policy. You need to establish whether your policy will pay out as and when you require treatment or (the more common option) only when you return home, in which case you'll have to pay your medical bills up front and claim the money back later – so be sure to keep hold of all the relevant paperwork.

In the USA and Canada, you may find that your existing insurance policies give sufficient medical cover, and you should always check them thoroughly before taking out a new one. Canadians, in particular, are often covered by their provincial health plans. However, things may not be so straightforward if you're planning to undertake any of the extreme sports for which the country is renowned – white-water rafting, canopy tours, scuba diving, etc. – as this may require the negotiation of a bespoke policy and, unfortunately, higher premiums.

Medical provision in Costa Rica is generally good. After all, the government spends a lot of money on the health service. However, if you are particularly concerned, it should be possible to arrange a policy whereby you can be flown out of the country to receive medical treatment elsewhere (i.e. in the USA), although this will be very costly.

Inoculations and Vaccines

There are no inoculation requirements to enter Costa Rica, unless you're coming from a country harbouring yellow fever, such as Colombia, in which case you'll need to present a current, valid certificate of inoculation. It is recommended that you have inoculations (or boosters) against hepatitis A and B, typhoid, polio and tetanus, although you should note that none of these is a major concern. You'll need to get your jabs done a few weeks in advance for them to be effective. It's also worth taking a course of antimalarials, particularly if you're going to be travelling on the Caribbean coast.

Food and Drink Dangers

As is the case with most trips, the ailment you're most likely to succumb to in Costa Rica is an upset stomach. Costa Rica's drinking water is pretty safe, at least in the major towns, although you might want to exercise a degree more caution in rural areas and port towns, notably Puerto Limón and Puntarenas. Bottled water is available throughout the country. If camping, sterilize any water drawn from outdoor sources by boiling it (for at least five minutes) or treating it with chemical purifiers, even if you have taken your supply from a clear running stream.

Most infections are caused, not by infected drinking water, but by unhygienically prepared food, although, again, standards of hygiene are pretty good throughout the country. Always wash and peel fresh fruit and vegetables. When eating out, stick to hot meals. Don't drink milk or eat any dairy product you suspect may not have been pasteurized. If you do get diarrhoea, the most important thing is to keep drinking. Most of the pain you feel is the result of lost fluid, so you need to replenish constantly, ideally with a rehydration solution, which will also replace some of the lost minerals. In Costa Rica you can pick up packets of reydration solution, '*suero oral*', at most pharmacies, although you should ideally bring your own supply; the last thing you want to do when you've got diarrhoea is go searching for a pharmacy. When you're feeling a bit stronger, you can begin to eat light, easily digestible food, but make sure you're fully recovered before eating out again.

Occasionally the ingestion of contaminated food or water can lead to the development of something more serious, such as hepatitis A. Seek medical help if your diarrhoea continues for more than three days, if your stools are bloody, if you develop a prolonged fever, or if you have constant severe stomach pains.

Sun Dangers

Costa Rica gets a lot of sunshine. Even its wetter areas get a lot of sunshine, in between all the downpours, as do the summits of its volcanoes and mountains, which can feel misleadingly cool. The dry northwest endures blazing temperatures all year round, frequently exceeding 35°C. For the rest of the country, temperatures of between 20–30°C are common.

Stay out of direct sunlight as much as possible, especially around midday when the ultraviolet rays will be at their fiercest. Use a strong sunscreen – at least factor 15 – wear a wide-brimmed hat and drink plenty of water. Try to avoid getting sunburnt. Not only will it be extremely unpleasant, but it could lead to something worse, such as heatstroke or, if you're fair-skinned, perhaps even skin cancer, cases of which are increasing by the year.

Insect Bites and Insect-borne Diseases

Unfortunately the nagging discomfort of insect bites is pretty much guaranteed, unless you are very lucky or extraordinarily careful, and somehow manage to keep your entire body either swaddled in insect repellent or within a hole-less mosquito net for the entire duration of your trip.

Mosquitoes are present in all lowland areas. You'll find the greatest concentrations – and thus should take the greatest precautions – on the Caribbean coast, whose swampy ground provides the perfect breeding conditions for the blood-sucking beasts. Ankle-biting sand flies (also known as chiggers or 'no-see-ums' because of their diminutive size) are common to most beaches. You should also watch out for ticks in the jungle. Protect yourself by covering up as much of yourself as is comfortably possible. If trekking through forest, this means long trousers and sleeves. Wear proper hiking boots, not sandals.

Use a strong DEET-based insect repellent on all areas of exposed skin and keep reapplying according to the maker's instructions – typically every 5–6 hours for a solution containing 35 per cent DEET. However, be careful not apply repellent to cuts or areas of sensitive skin. Take special care at dusk when insects are at their most active. If possible, bring your own mosquito net. Many hotels will supply them as a matter of course, and will have screened windows, but they may have holes. The mosquitoes will still get you, of course, they always do, but hopefully not in such great numbers.

Dengue Fever

It happens very rarely, but sometimes an insect bite can lead to something a good deal more serious than an itchy leg. The biggest concern is dengue fever, a viral affliction transmitted by the Aedes mosquito. If contracted, the virus usually produces nothing worse than flu-like symptoms – a fever, aches, a rash, vomiting – at least on the first infection. Unfortunately, a second infection can be much more severe and in some instances can even result in death, although this is usually only true of young children or the very old. Still, it's a worry, not so much for the likelihood of your catching it – it's pretty rare, with fewer than a thousand cases reported each year, though these do tend to be given the full 'epidemic sweeping the nation' treatment by the press – but because there's no vaccine and no cure, so there's not a great deal you can do once you've got it, other than take plenty of fluids and ride it out. The majority of cases are recorded on the Caribbean coast, the central Pacific coast and in Guanacaste.

Malaria

Malaria is still present in all Central American countries. However, Costa Rica sees very few cases each year, certainly a good deal fewer than for dengue fever, and only a tiny number of these prove fatal. Symptoms include headaches, muscle pains, severe fevers, alternating periods of feeling very hot and extremely cold, shaking, and, occasionally in severe cases, hallucinations and coma.

The country's wetter regions – Limón province and Alajuela province – are the most prone to outbreaks, principally because they have the largest numbers of mosquitoes, with pockets of still water providing ideal breeding conditions. There is no cure for malaria, but there are preventative measures you can take. Costa Rica's malarial strain can be effectively combated by taking a simple course of chloroquine, which involves taking a couple of tablets once a week on the same day. You need to start the course a couple of weeks before arriving in the country for it to be effective. Remember, no prophylactic is entirely foolproof, and you should still use plenty of insect repellent to give yourself added protection.

HIV/AIDS

It's not a huge problem (yet), but, as everywhere, it is a concern and, because of the country's prominent sex industry, a growing one. The same worldwide rules apply. If you're going to have sex with a stranger, use a condom. For preference bring a supply from home, as Costa Rica's versions are not of a very high quality.

Rabies

Contracting rabies is a possibility – the disease is present in the country – but an extremely remote one. Only a handful of cases have been reported in the past couple of decades. There is a vaccine you can take, but, as it involves an intensely unpleasant procedure involving three injections, and must be begun a month in advance of your trip, it is only recommended for people who are going to be directly handling animals, such as volunteers on conservation projects.

Animal Nasties

The number of people who are scared of big scary spiders is always a lot greater than the number of people who actually encounter big scary spiders. Several species of **tarantula** – those stalwarts of travellers' nightmares – live in Costa Rica, but you'd probably have to put in several hours of dedicated searching to find one, as they are primarily nocturnal and live in camouflaged subterranean burrows. And, as the bite of most tarantulas is no worse than a bee sting, there's no need to be unduly concerned.

Snakes are a bit more of a worry, albeit only relatively so. Judging the potential danger of snakes is always a matter of subdivisions, of finding the Russian doll within the Russian doll. So, of Costa Rica's 160-plus species of snake, only around 20 are venomous. Of these, only a handful have venom strong enough to kill a human. And none has managed to do so in recent years. There are just three species you really need to watch out for. The first is the **coral snake**, the most venomous of all Central American snakes, which is around 60cm–1m long and has a black body adorned with thick red bands and thin yellow ones. However, it's not aggressive and will only attack if directly threatened (or trodden on). The second, the **bushmaster**, does have a reputation for aggression, but is extremely rare and infrequently seen. It can grow up to 2m long and is a sort of light brown colour with darker, diamond-shaped patterns along its back. The final snake, the **fer-de-lance**, is the smallest Russian doll of all (despite its 1.5–2.5m length), responsible for most of the region's fatal snake bites. Though its venom is not as deadly as that of the coral snake, it is supposedly extremely bad-tempered and liable to attack at the slightest provocation. Thankfully, it's nocturnal and rarely seen, although its brown, black and white camouflage can make it difficult to pick out. There is no need to be overly alarmed. Most visitors to Costa Rica do not encounter a single snake during their time in the country. Just be sure to take special care when walking through dense undergrowth or grassland, particularly at dawn or dusk, when snakes are most likely to be active. And always wear closed hiking boots or shoes, never sandals, if walking in an area where there could possibly be snakes.

If bitten, get yourself to hospital as soon as possible. Ideally, you should provide the medical staff with a description (or even a positive identification) of the snake so that the correct antivenin can be administered, although this may not be possible for obvious reasons.

For all the talk of snakes and spiders, the animal attack you're most likely to succumb to is a **bee** or **wasp** sting. If you are allergic to insect stings, be sure to bring injectable adrenaline (epinephrine) or an EpiPen. And keep away from the Palo Verde area, which supports populations of African 'killer' bees.

Hospitals

Costa Rica spends a large proportion of its national budget on healthcare provision. Medical services are generally very good, compared with the rest of Central America.

Costa Rican citizens' entitlement to health-care depends on their keeping up monthly subscriptions to the national social security system, known as the Caja. Official foreign residents can also register with the Caja. However, foreign visitors whose insurance polices don't allow for immediate medical payouts must pay their medical costs up front. At a public hospital, expect to pay around $50 for a basic emergency procedure (stiches, dressing a wound, etc.), rising to over $300 for an overnight stay, and upwards. Prices are even higher at private hospitals.

As pricey as medical work can be, it's still a lot cheaper than in the USA, which is why the past decade has seen Costa Rica welcoming increasing numbers of **medical tourists**, many of whom come to take advantage of cheap plastic surgery and cosmetic dentistry procedures. For more information, contact the **Asociación Costarricense de Cirugía Plástica Reconstructiva y Estética** (Costa Rican Association of Plastic, Reconstructive and Aesthetic Surgery), *www.accpre.org*, or the **Costa Rican Surgeons' and Dentists' Association**, **t** 256 3100, *dentista@racsa.co.cr*.

Pharmacies

Most Costa Rican towns have at least one well-stocked *farmacia* (sometimes also known as a *botica*), selling a wide range of drugs and medications. Most drugs, including birth control pills, are available without

Public Hospitals in Costa Rica

San José: Hospital San Juan de Dios, **t** 257 6282.
Alajuela: Hospital San Rafael, **t** 440 1333.
Heredia: Hospital San Vicente de Paúl, **t** 261 0001.
Cartago: Hospital Max Peralta, **t** 550 1999.
Liberia: Hospital Emilio Baltodano, **t** 666 0011.
Puntarenas: Hospital Monseñor Sanabria, **t** 630 8000.
Puerto Limón: Hospital Tony Facio, **t** 758 2222.

prescription, the main exceptions being antibiotics, psychotropic drugs and 'sexual performance' drugs (i.e. Viagra). It's worth learning the correct scientific name of any drug you may require, as this is more likely to be stocked than a specific brand name drug.

The Internet

These days, most towns have at least one Internet café; larger tourist towns often have several. Several post offices also offer Internet access and an increasing number of hotels can provide wireless connections. Coverage is more limited in remoter areas, although the telephone network has been extended in recent years by RACSA, the state-owned telephone company and the country's main Internet provider – which, incidentally, is why the majority of the country's businesses have email addresses with the suffix racsa.co.cr.

Expect to be charged around $1–2 per hour for access in an Internet café.

Maps

Owing to the peculiarities of the Costa Rican address system (see p.74), not to mention the country's seeming abhorrence of clear, regularly spaced signposts, you're best off bringing a supply of maps with you, rather than relying on picking up mapping material once you get here. The tourist board in San José can provide a decent city map of the capital, plus plans of a few other major tourist centres, but its countrywide map is very basic. And, considering the tourist board's subterranean location, you may have trouble locating it in the first place without a map. Outside of the capital city, there are precious few map sources.

Recommended published maps include: *Berndtson & Berndtson 1:650,000*; *Globetrotter 1:470,000*; *ITMB International Travel Map 1:330,000*. These will be available from specialist travel bookshops including the following:

UK

Stanfords, 12–14 Long Acre, London, WC2 9LP, **t** (020) 7836 1321, *www.stanfords.co.uk*.

Travel Bookshop, 13 Blenheim Crescent, London W11 2EE, **t** (020) 7229 5260, *www.thetravelbookshop.co.uk*.

USA

Distant Lands, 56 South Raymond Ave, Pasadena, CA 91105, **t** 800 310 3220, *www.distantlands.com*.

Longitude Books, Suite 1206, 115 West 30th Street, New York, NY 1001, **t** 800 342 2164, *www.longitudebooks.com*.

Money and Banks

Costa Rica's national currency is the *colón* (plural *colones*), named in honour of Christopher Columbus (Cristóbal Colón in Spanish), the first European to set foot here. Though the *colón*'s fortunes are obviously largely dependent on the region's strongest currency, it is not officially tied to the dollar, with the result that it tends to depreciate against the world's major currencies by around 8–10 per cent a year.

Approximate **exchange rates** (2006): US$1=c475; €1=c600; £1=c875.

The currency is issued in both coins and notes. Coins come in two colours: older silver coins in denominations of 5, 10 and 20 colones and new gold-coloured ones in denominations of 5, 10, 25, 100 and 500. And, just to make things confusing, the two sets of coins are different sizes. It can take a few days to get used to handling your change. The colourful notes come in denominations of 1,000, 2,000, 5,000 and 10,000 *colones*, the last of which is decorated with pictures of the country's four most famous volcanoes: Arenal, Irazú, Poás and Rincón de la Vieja.

US dollars are used throughout the country as a sort of secondary currency, effective in around 75 per cent of all transactions. They're accepted in almost all hotels and tourist-orientated restaurants. Indeed, prices for hotel rooms and tours are usually quoted in dollars. This is very handy as it can be quite difficult to get hold of *colones* outside Costa Rica. If staying in San José or one of the other major urban centres, it's perfectly possible to get through your entire holiday using only small-denomination dollar bills (nothing bigger than $20), although you will be given your change in *colones*, so you will have to handle them at some point. Many grocery stores now have computerized tills on which the shopkeeper can work out the current exchange rate before giving you your change.

On buses you can only pay in *colones*, and in most street-corner sodas you'd be expected to. The majority of taxi drivers accept dollars. All San José taxi drivers do.

Most **prices** in this guide are given in dollars, except for services which can only be paid in *colones*. Prices in Costa Rica are generally a good deal higher than in surrounding countries, particularly if you're using services aimed at tourists – upmarket hotels, restaurants car hire. However, locally orientated services – budget hotels, sodas, bus travel – are usually pretty cheap.

You can **exchange money** in all state banks (Banco Nacional , Banco de Costa Rica, Banco de Crédito Agrícola) and, albeit slightly more expensively, at most private ones (Banco Popular, Banco de San José, Scotiabank, Banco de Comercio). Many upmarket hotels also change money, although their rates are not always so favourable. There are a few dedicated *bureaux de change* (*casa del cambio*) at the international airports of San José and Liberia, but none anywhere else.

Most banks have **ATMs** that will issue money on **debit/credit cards** affiliated to the Visa/Plus or MasterCard/Cirrus networks. The majority of the top-end establishments will accept internationally recognized credit cards (i.e. Mastercard, Visa and American Express), and the number of smaller places that accept them is growing all the time, although you may still have a hard time 'living on plastic' in more rural areas; there you should make sure you bring enough money to cover expenses.

In extremis, it is possible to get money wired to you via **Western Union,** t 1-800 777 7777, *www.westernunion.co.cr*, which has branches operating out of many Mas X Menos supermarkets around the country. You'll need to show your passport.

Opening Times

In general, everything stays open longer and for more days in the capital and the main tourist towns than in the rest of the country. In less visited, more rural areas, most businesses are shut on Sundays. **Shops** usually open Mon–Fri 9–6, though some supermarkets may stay open a bit longer. Some also open on Saturday mornings. **Post offices**

(*correos*) open Mon–Fri 7.30–5.30, Sat 7.30–12, and **banks** from Mon–Fri 8.30–3.30. Again, some urban branches may open for a few hours on Saturday mornings.

Post and Faxes

Almost every town in the country boasts a **post office**, or *correo*. The Costa Rican postal service is relatively efficient, particularly from the main towns, although letters can take a while to be despatched from more rural branches. To **send a postcard or letter** (up to 20g) costs c135 to the US, c165 to Europe and c175 to Australia.

You can **receive post and parcels** in Costa Rica via the general delivery (or *poste restante*) method, whereby the post office will hold the mail for you until you come to collect it, although this is probably only a good idea at major branches, such as the main one in San José. You'll have to show your passport to claim your mail. Make sure that the sender addresses the envelope with your name exactly as it appears on your passport or it may not be handed over. You'll probably be charged a minimal fee of around c100 per item. Try to avoid having anything sent to you that will require the payment of duty, as this will add considerably to the time it will take to retrieve your post.

For more details, *see www.correos.go.cr*.

Shopping and Crafts

The most notable development to have taken place in the Costa Rican shopping scene in recent years has been the advent of the mall. It was only a matter of time. Costa Rica has long been the most Americanized of all the Central American countries, and the arrival of US-style air-conditioned shopping centres – filled with chain stores, fast food courts, neon-lit bars and, after school and, at weekends, hordes of disaffected teenagers – had a certain inevitability to it. San José now has over a dozen such malls, and you'll also find examples in some of the country's other major towns, including Liberia and Tamarindo.

As Westernized as the Costa Rican shopping experience has become in places, most towns still boast outlets catering primarily to local needs, and maintain a central food market, usually known as the Mercado Central, which usually offers the cheapest source of fresh produce for self-caterers.

In terms of keepsakes, Costa Rica is not a renowned shopping destination. With just a small indigenous population, it doesn't have much of an arts and crafts tradition. Most souvenirs take the form of kitschy represen-tations of the country's natural icons: toy monkeys, parrot mobiles, plastic toucans, jaguar T-shirts, as well as some generic 'Central American'-looking crafts. You'll find the widest choice of souvenirs, as you'd expect, in San José, particularly in the suburb of Moravia in the northwest of the city where there are a number of dedicated shops.

Some of the better souvenirs on offer include replicas of small gold charms of the type once worn by the Diquis indigenous tribe and now on display in San José's Museo de Oro Precolombino (see pp.104–5); and bags of high-quality premium coffee. The last is certainly the easiest souvenir to track down. The products of the Café Britt Finca (see pp.142–3), the country's main coffee exporter, can be found in pretty much every super-market in the country. They also operate a couple of outlets at the airport.

However, the country's most popular souvenirs are probably Sarchí ox-carts, minia-ture versions of brightly coloured agricultural vehicles that were once used to haul coffee beans down from Valle Central plantations and are now employed as ornaments, drinks cabinets and plant-holders in hotels and restaurants throughout the country (and beyond). A huge industry has grown up in Sarchí turning out the carts, as well as wood and leather rocking chairs (see pp.133–4).

Do avoid buying any souvenirs that utilize animal products, particularly anything made from turtle shells, coral, feathers or fur, or anything made from rare hardwoods, such as mahogany or purple heart.

Telephones

Making an international phone call from your hotel can be fiendishly expensive, although local calls are often free. Check first.

The cheapest way to make an international call is to purchase a **phone card** for use in a public pay phone. Most Costa Rican towns have banks of public phones. There are two types of phone card. The first, known as a **Chip Card**, comes in denominations of ₡1,000 and ₡2,000, and can only be used in the less common modern digital phone booths. Making a call is a pretty straightforward procedure: simply insert the card into the slot and then follow the instructions (in Spanish and English) that appear on the screen. More widely available is the old-fashioned **Viajero 199** card, which comes in denominations of ₡3,000, ₡5,000 and ₡10,000, and can be used on all touch-dial public phones and mobile (cell) phones. Dial t 199, then 2 for instruc-tions in English, which will prompt you to type in the code printed on the card, after which you can begin to make your call. A card of ₡3,000 will get you around 10–12 minutes to the USA, or 8–10 minutes to Europe.

Many US **mobile (cell) phones** can be used in Costa Rica. Contact your network provider for more information. For visitors from the UK, Europe or Australasia, whose phones may not work here, an increasingly common option is to hire a mobile phone. This is certainly more convenient than constantly hunting down phone booths, particularly if you're doing a lot of travelling about, but it's not cheap. Rates start at around $6–8 per day, $35–40 per week, $125 per month, plus a $300–400 credit card deposit, with local calls from $0.50 per minute and international calls from $1.25 per minute.

To **call Costa Rica from abroad**, dial 00 and then the country code, 506, followed by the 7-digit local phone number. Costa Rica has no area codes.

To **call abroad from Costa Rica**, dial 00 and then the country code (UK 44; Ireland 353; USA and Canada 1; Australia 61; New Zealand 64), then dial the number, omitting the first zero of the area code.

Time

Costa Rica occupies the same time zone as the central United States (US Central Time), six hours behind Greenwich Mean Time.

Tipping

It's welcome but in most instances not expected. Tipping is certainly not a mainstay of the Costa Rican service economy, as it is in certain other countries, most notably the USA. Tipping hotel porters and maids around $1 a day is standard. Tipping taxi drivers and waiting staff is not, particularly as most restaurants levy an automatic 10 per cent service charge. You should only venture an extra gratuity if you feel the service has genuinely merited it.

Toilets

Costa Rica doesn't have public conveniences. In the capital and several other major towns, people do treat the rest rooms of fast food restaurants as if they were public conveniences, even though they're officially for patrons only, and often have signs up warning you not to use them if you haven't purchased any food. Otherwise, it's usually a question of buying a drink in a bar in order to earn the right to use their facilities, which is not really an ideal solution when you're in a hurry and it may just lead to your needing to repeat the experience an hour later. The situation is a good deal simpler out in the wilds of the national parks, where it's just you, nature and (if you've been clever and remembered to bring it) a roll of toilet paper.

Tourist Offices

Costa Rica doesn't have many tourist offices. The only one of any size – and the main resource for tourists – is the **Instituto Costarricense de Turismo (ICT)** in the Plaza de la Cultura in San José (**t** 223 1733, *www. visitcostarica.com; open Mon–Fri 9–5*), which can provide information on attractions and destinations throughout the country, and hands out free city maps of San José (plus a number of other tourist towns), bus timetables and accommodation lists, many of which can also be downloaded from its website.

There are also a few ICT booths at the main entry points to the country, at San José's Juan Santamaría Aiport, at Pasa Canoas on the Panamanian border and Peñas Blancas on the Nicaraguan border, although these are less well equipped.

Some towns do also have their own regional offices, but these are usually locally operated initiatives, not officially affiliated with the national tourist board. In fact, wherever you're going in the country, you

should assume that it doesn't have a tourist office. If in San José for a portion of your trip – and considering its status as the main transport hub for the entire country, you probably will be – try and pick up as much information as you can about other destinations before you leave.

The situation isn't much better outside the country. There's no official tourist office in the USA, Canada, the UK or Australia, although each country's respective embassy (*see* p.90) should be able to provide some tourist information. North Americans can also call a toll-free number, **t** 1-800 343 6332, to speak to tourist board staff in Costa Rica. Otherwise, your best bet is to do as much research as possible before you arrive; *see* p.366 for some useful websites.

Where to Stay

There's no shortage of accommodation options in Costa Rica. The tourism boom of the past 15 years has spurred the creation of thousands of new hotel beds throughout the country. Though pre-booking is advisable at top-end and moderate places, if backpacking your way around you should be able to just turn up and find somewhere quite easily on an ad hoc basis. The country's major tourist destinations offer a good deal of choice in all price categories, and even less visited towns usually have one or two options.

Although there's little about the hotel scene here that will seem wholly unfamiliar – a dood geal of it is aimed squarely at Western tastes – there are a couple of terms in the Costa Rican accommodation lexicon that may require a little explaining. The first is '*cabinas*', which is used as a sort of loose, all-purpose description for much tourist town accommodation. There is no one single definition of *cabinas*. It can be used to refer either to rooms in a motel-like block, or separate units, but it is primarily used to describe rooms aimed at the budget and lower mid-range sector of the market. You'll find large concentrations of *cabinas* in all the country's major backpacking destinations, including Cahuita, Dominical, Montezuma and Puerto Viejo de Talamanca,

The other term is '**eco-lodge**', which is usually used to describe places that are both

San José

Around a million Costa Ricans live in the greater San José area, making it extremely populous, if not exactly popular. Perhaps it's resentment at the city's all-encompassing influence, but for many Costa Ricans living outside its confines (and, it has to be said, for a good deal living within), San José would seem to represent everything that is wrong with modern living – too frenetic, too polluted, too congested. Telling gleeful tales of the latest urban horror – particularly the latest crime scam – is almost a national pastime.

With this in mind, it is perhaps best to get all the things that are wrong with San José out of the way first, before moving on to what's

---

rural (hence 'lodge') and environmentally friendly (hence 'eco'). Unfortunately, the latter is not always the case. The prefix 'eco' is often used as much as a marketing slogan as a statement of conservational intent. If you're concerned about the potential environmental impact of your visit, be sure to check your proposed lodge's 'ecological' credentials a little more closely. To help you in your task the government has recently introduced a 'Green Leaf Scheme', rating hotels according to a set of environmental criteria – whether they recycle, conserve electricity, use sustainable building materials and utilize local resources responsibly. This last criterion particularly applies to water supplies, as there have been examples of some of the mega-resorts of the dry Pacific northwest siphoning off the water supplies of entire communities and ecosystems.

Prices, Facilities and Booking

Room rates are at their most expensive during the high season of mid-November–April, reaching a peak around the main public holidays of Christmas and Easter. In fact, prices are in general a bit higher in Costa Rica than in the rest of the isthmus, but then standards are a bit higher too. And there are still plenty of bargains to be had if you're prepared to lower your standards a little, or travel in the low (or 'green') season.

Bear in mind when room-hunting that the price often provides only a general guide to the level and standard of facilities you can expect. An inexpensive place may turn out to be much better equipped, and a good deal nicer, than a more expensive one, but may not be able to charge as high prices because it lies off the main tourist trail. Remember that posted room rates often don't include the 16.39 per cent **tax**, comprising a 13 per cent sales tax and a 3 per cent room tax.

In the past few years, it has become much easier to reserve in advance via the Internet or e-mail, although correspondence can be slow coming back from more far-flung places that may lack their own Internet connection, where the owners have to travel to the nearest large town to pick up e-mails. Some places require that you place a deposit using a credit card. Some even ask that you pay the full amount of your intended stay in advance.

Accommodation Price Codes

Prices quoted throughout the guide represent the cheapest rate you can expect to pay for a double room in high season. Prices often drop considerably, particularly at the top-end places, in the low season. Self-catering options can be available in all categories.

luxury	$$$$$	$120 and above
expensive	$$$$	$80–119
moderate	$$$	$40–79
inexpensive	$$	$26–39
budget	$	$25 and under

Be sure to check what's being requested carefully before committing yourself. It goes without saying that you shouldn't provide your credit card details unless the website is using a secure server with a valid safety certificate. If possible, bring a printout of your confirmation e-mail with you as proof of your reservation.

Levels of Accommodation

Camping

Camping is as popular an option with Ticos as it is with tourists, and many of the country's major destinations – including a good number of its beach resorts and national parks – have campsites. In the main, these are not overly well equipped – the best you can usually hope for are toilets and cold showers – and during the Tico holidays they can be very crowded, but they are cheap, typically under $7 per night. Some hostels and budget hotels also allow camping in their grounds, and may rent out tents if you haven't brought your own. Be sure to bring plenty of insect repellent with you, particularly if you're planning on pitching your tent on the more humid, bug-infested Caribbean coast.

Budget and Inexpensive Options

After campsites, the country's cheapest, most basic accommodation is provided by its network of **hostels**, which includes a number of places affiliated with Hostelling International. In truth, the 'basic' tag can only really be applied to the sleeping and abluting arrangements – expect communal dorms, and shared showers with a limited supply of hot water – rather than the general facilities.

The Local Alternative

Rather than stay in official hotel or hostel accommodation, another option is to opt for a home stay – actually living with a Tico family in a domestic house. It's an option often taken up by language students, and arranged through their universities. If your language skills are up to it, it can be a great way to learn more about the country from the people who know it best, giving you something more than the usual tourist experiences. A minimum commitment of at least a week is expected, although you may be able to stay for considerably longer. The price often includes your evening meals and a laundry service.

Bells' Home Hospitality, t 225 4752, *http://homestay.thebells.org*. Experienced home stay specialist, specializing in finding lodgings for people in the San José metropolitan area.

Cooprena R.L., t 248 2538, *http://turismoruralcr.com*. Puts travellers in touch with seven co-operatives around the country – in Rincón de la Vieja, Tenorio, Monteverde, Arenal, the Central Pacific coast, Limón and the Osa Peninsula – that can arrange stays with rural communities.

Some hostels are very well equipped – indeed better than a number of low-end hotels – offering kitchens, tour desks, laundry service, luggage storage, Internet access, hammocks and book exchanges. Some even have gardens and swimming pools.

You don't get a lot of privacy, but hostels can be great places to meet fellow travellers and find out information – many have noticeboards providing travel tips and telling you hottest new places to go. The very cheapest charge around $8 a night, more typically $10–12, and slightly more again for Hostelling International places if you're not a member.

UK: HI International Youth Hostel Federation, **t** (01707) 324170, *www.hihostels.com*. Also contact YHA, **t** 0870 770 8868, *www.yha.org.uk*.

USA: Hostelling International USA, **t** (301) 495 1240, *www.hiayh.org*.

Canada: Hostelling International Canada, **t** (613) 235 2595, *www.hihostels.ca*.

Australia: AYHA, **t** (02) 9218 9000, *www.yha.com.au*.

Moving up the price scale come the budget and inexpensive places, which are often motel-style rooms in simple purpose-built blocks. The standard and level of facilities varies enormously. Depending on where you are and the time of year, your $25 might not get you much at all – perhaps a small boxy room with thin walls, basic furniture, a shared bathroom and cold water – or it might get you something rather nice with a private bathroom, hot water, decent décor, a fan and free breakfast. Essentially, the further from the main tourist trail you are, the further you can expect your money to go.

At lower-end places (and some mid-range ones) watch out for the (not entirely ironically named) 'suicide showers'. These are strange boxy plastic contraptions that sit over the shower head housing an electric element that heats the water up as it comes out. As alarming as they look – all random wires sticking out all over the place – they shouldn't be dangerous unless touched when you or it are wet – avoid this even if it means having a cold shower. As a simple rule of thumb, the lower the water pressure, the hotter the temperature.

Moderate, Expensive and Luxury Options

From $40–80, you can expect a higher level of quality – nicer furnishings, private bathrooms, guaranteed hot water, fans (often air-conditioning). You might also get cable TV, a restaurant, a garden and a swimming pool. And for $80 and above, you can expect even better. As the price rises, so should the level of facilities until you reach the country's ultra-luxurious places, the sort that come with their own swimming pools, stretches of jungle, Jacuzzis and spas. In truth, the term 'luxury' in Costa Rica can mean anything from a generic, but well-equipped, business hotel in a city centre to somewhere gloriously remote that provides a gateway to the country's natural wonders. As always, price is rarely a definitive guide. However, you should expect the facilities in this category to be generally excellent. And if they're not, you're paying too much.

San José

There's no need to ask the way. All roads eventually lead to Costa Rica's capital and one true metropolis. Its Valle Central siblings of Heredia, Cartago and Alajuela may technically be classified as cities, but these are, in truth, little more than glorified towns. San José is properly city-sized and fully city-like – big, noisy, vibrant, confusing, bustling and, above all, packed full of people.

It is hard to exaggerate San José's dominance over Costa Rican affairs. It's the seat of government, the administrative capital, the main transport hub, location of the headquarters of all the country's major businesses (both national and international), as well as the site of its main cultural scene.

COSTA RICA

Pacific Ocean

08

Don't mi

⭐ Intense
bustling
Mercado Ce

⭐ Fine ja
all shad
Museo de

⭐ Old, i
crafted
Museo
Precolo

⭐ Gra
Parqu

⭐ A
on
op
Tea

See

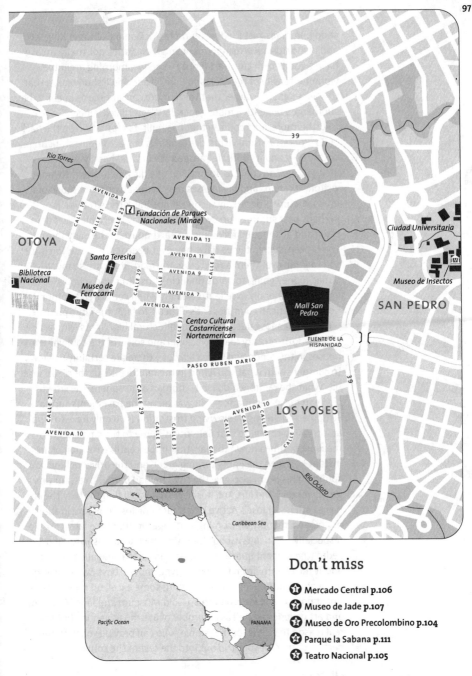

Río Torres

AVENIDA 15

CALLE 19
CALLE 21
CALLE 23

Fundación de Parques
Nacionales (Minae)

OTOYA

AVENIDA 13

AVENIDA 11

Santa Teresita

AVENIDA 9

CALLE 29
CALLE 31
CALLE 35

Biblioteca
Nacional

AVENIDA 7

Museo de
Ferrocarril

AVENIDA 5

CALLE 33

Centro Cultural
Costarricense
Norteamerican

Mall San
Pedro

SAN PEDRO

Ciudad Universitaria

Museo de Insectos

FUENTE DE LA
HISPANIDAD

PASEO RUBEN DARIO

39

CALLE 21

CALLE 29

LOS YOSES

AVENIDA 10

CALLE 31
CALLE 33

AVENIDA 10

CALLE 37
CALLE 39
CALLE 41
CALLE 43

CALLE

NICARAGUA

Caribbean Sea

Pacific Ocean

PANAMA

Don't miss

① Mercado Central **p.106**

② Museo de Jade **p.107**

③ Museo de Oro Precolombino **p.104**

④ Parque la Sabana **p.111**

⑤ Teatro Nacional **p.105**

good – and there's much that is good, although this can take some
seeking out. It's certainly the most Americanized of all the Central
American capitals, with streets lined with department stores,

shopping malls, fast food restaurants (McDonald's, Burger King, KFC) and billboards advertising American products. It's not that San José hasn't got its own cultural identity – spend a morning amid the vibrant intensity of the Mercado Central and you'll soon realize that this ain't Kansas – rather that this culture can, at times, appear to be submerged beneath a more generally Westernized veneer.

Furthermore, for a country that has built its reputation on the back of its glorious natural vistas, the capital is in places quite stupendously ugly, and its pothole-ravaged streets and hastily built architecture can come as something of a disappointment to many visitors. Its shops and businesses may be first world, but much of its infrastructure is decidedly second, if not third. The situation is perhaps best summed up by the city's railway line, which was devastated and abandoned following an earthquake in the early 1990s. The broken, decrepit lines have, however, been left in place, forcing you to jump over them as you cross the road. Still, with so much public money going towards financing hospitals and schools – which are generally excellent, certainly when compared to other Central American countries – it's difficult to fault the city's priorities.

Though San José does have its architectural highlights – in particular the 19th-century Teatro Nacional and some of the colonial-era houses in the Amón and Otoya *barrios* – there are certainly no views to compare with what you'll find in the rainforest. But then, San José has what the rainforest doesn't – human atmosphere. The crowds that can make negotiating your way along the pavements such a struggle and driving so slow and frustrating (you only have to stop at a crossing to realize that San José is home to the smallest measure of time known to man, that imperceptible fraction of an instant between the lights turning green and the driver behind you sounding his horn) also give the city's myriad bars and restaurants a great vibrancy and life. And it is here that you'll find the best the city has to offer. San José's native inhabitants, or 'Josefinos', are in the main open, friendly, welcoming and eager to share the latest gossip (especially the insults) about their city. The bars of Los Yoses and San Pedro (the student quarter) are great places to come and find out about the country from the people who know it best. San José also has a good cultural infrastructure with some excellent museums (most notably the Pre-Columbian Gold Museum and Jade Museum) and art galleries as well as a number of live music venues, but the real reason to visit is for the people, who can provide you with the perfect primer for your trip out into the rest of the country.

History

Costa Rica had already been a Spanish colony for nearly 200 years when the small religious community of San José was founded in 1737, although it was originally known by the significantly less catchy rural (hence 'lodge') and environmentally friendly (hence 'eco'). Unfortunately, the latter is not always the case. The prefix 'eco' is often used as much as a marketing slogan as a statement of conservational intent. If you're concerned about the potential environmental impact of your visit, be sure to check your proposed lodge's 'ecological' credentials a little more closely. To help you in your task the government has recently introduced a **'Green Leaf Scheme'**, rating hotels according to a set of environmental criteria – whether they recycle, conserve electricity, use sustainable building materials and utilize local resources responsibly. This last criterion particularly applies to water supplies, as there have been examples of some of the mega-resorts of the dry Pacific northwest siphoning off the water supplies of entire communities and ecosystems.

Prices, Facilities and Booking

Room rates are at their most expensive during the high season of mid-November–April, reaching a peak around the main public holidays of Christmas and Easter. In fact, prices are in general a bit higher in Costa Rica than in the rest of the isthmus, but then standards are a bit higher too. And there are still plenty of bargains to be had if you're prepared to lower your standards a little, or travel in the low (or 'green') season.

Bear in mind when room-hunting that the price often provides only a general guide to the level and standard of facilities you can expect. An inexpensive place may turn out to be much better equipped, and a good deal nicer, than a more expensive one, but may not be able to charge as high prices because it lies off the main tourist trail. Remember that posted room rates often don't include the 16.39 per cent **tax**, comprising a 13 per cent sales tax and a 3 per cent room tax.

In the past few years, it has become much easier to reserve in advance via the Internet or e-mail, although correspondence can be slow coming back from more far-flung places that may lack their own Internet connection, where the owners have to travel to the nearest large town to pick up e-mails. Some places require that you place a deposit using a credit card. Some even ask that you pay the full amount of your intended stay in advance.

Accommodation Price Codes

Prices quoted throughout the guide represent the cheapest rate you can expect to pay for a double room in high season. Prices often drop considerably, particularly at the top-end places, in the low season. Self-catering options can be available in all categories.

luxury	$$$$$	$120 and above
expensive	$$$$	$80–119
moderate	$$$	$40–79
inexpensive	$$	$26–39
budget	$	$25 and under

Be sure to check what's being requested carefully before committing yourself. It goes without saying that you shouldn't provide your credit card details unless the website is using a secure server with a valid safety certificate. If possible, bring a printout of your confirmation e-mail with you as proof of your reservation.

Levels of Accommodation

Camping

Camping is as popular an option with Ticos as it is with tourists, and many of the country's major destinations – including a good number of its beach resorts and national parks – have campsites. In the main, these are not overly well equipped – the best you can usually hope for are toilets and cold showers – and during the Tico holidays they can be very crowded, but they are cheap, typically under $7 per night. Some hostels and budget hotels also allow camping in their grounds, and may rent out tents if you haven't brought your own. Be sure to bring plenty of insect repellent with you, particularly if you're planning on pitching your tent on the more humid, bug-infested Caribbean coast.

Budget and Inexpensive Options

After campsites, the country's cheapest, most basic accommodation is provided by its network of **hostels**, which includes a number of places affiliated with Hostelling International. In truth, the 'basic' tag can only really be applied to the sleeping and abluting arrangements – expect communal dorms, and shared showers with a limited supply of hot water – rather than the general facilities.

The Local Alternative

Rather than stay in official hotel or hostel accommodation, another option is to opt for a home stay – actually living with a Tico family in a domestic house. It's an option often taken up by language students, and arranged through their universities. If your language skills are up to it, it can be a great way to learn more about the country from the people who know it best, giving you something more than the usual tourist experiences. A minimum commitment of at least a week is expected, although you may be able to stay for considerably longer. The price often includes your evening meals and a laundry service.

Bells' Home Hospitality, t 225 4752, *http://homestay.thebells.org*. Experienced home stay specialist, specializing in finding lodgings for people in the San José metropolitan area.

Cooprena R.L., t 248 2538, *http://turismoruralcr.com*. Puts travellers in touch with seven co-operatives around the country – in Rincón de la Vieja, Tenorio, Monteverde, Arenal, the Central Pacific coast, Limón and the Osa Peninsula – that can arrange stays with rural communities.

Some hostels are very well equipped – indeed better than a number of low-end hotels – offering kitchens, tour desks, laundry service, luggage storage, Internet access, hammocks and book exchanges. Some even have gardens and swimming pools.

You don't get a lot of privacy, but hostels can be great places to meet fellow travellers and find out information – many have noticeboards providing travel tips and telling you hottest new places to go. The very cheapest charge around $8 a night, more typically $10–12, and slightly more again for Hostelling International places if you're not a member.

UK: HI International Youth Hostel Federation, **t** (01707) 324170, *www.hihostels.com*. Also contact YHA, **t** 0870 770 8868, *www.yha.org.uk*.

USA: Hostelling International USA, **t** (301) 495 1240, *www.hiayh.org*.

Canada: Hostelling International Canada, **t** (613) 235 2595, *www.hihostels.ca*.

Australia: AYHA, **t** (02) 9218 9000, *www.yha.com.au*.

Moving up the price scale come the budget and inexpensive places, which are often motel-style rooms in simple purpose-built blocks. The standard and level of facilities varies enormously. Depending on where you are and the time of year, your $25 might not get you much at all – perhaps a small boxy room with thin walls, basic furniture, a shared bathroom and cold water – or it might get you something rather nice with a private bathroom, hot water, decent décor, a fan and free breakfast. Essentially, the further from the main tourist trail you are, the further you can expect your money to go.

At lower-end places (and some mid-range ones) watch out for the (not entirely ironically named) 'suicide showers'. These are strange boxy plastic contraptions that sit over the shower head housing an electric element that heats the water up as it comes out. As alarming as they look – all random wires sticking out all over the place – they shouldn't be dangerous unless touched when you or it are wet – avoid this even if it means having a cold shower. As a simple rule of thumb, the lower the water pressure, the hotter the temperature.

Moderate, Expensive and Luxury Options

From $40–80, you can expect a higher level of quality – nicer furnishings, private bathrooms, guaranteed hot water, fans (often air-conditioning). You might also get cable TV, a restaurant, a garden and a swimming pool. And for $80 and above, you can expect even better. As the price rises, so should the level of facilities until you reach the country's ultra-luxurious places, the sort that come with their own swimming pools, stretches of jungle, Jacuzzis and spas. In truth, the term 'luxury' in Costa Rica can mean anything from a generic, but well-equipped, business hotel in a city centre to somewhere gloriously remote that provides a gateway to the country's natural wonders. As always, price is rarely a definitive guide. However, you should expect the facilities in this category to be generally excellent. And if they're not, you're paying too much.

San José

There's no need to ask the way. All roads eventually lead to Costa Rica's capital and one true metropolis. Its Valle Central siblings of Heredia, Cartago and Alajuela may technically be classified as cities, but these are, in truth, little more than glorified towns. San José is properly city-sized and fully city-like – big, noisy, vibrant, confusing, bustling and, above all, packed full of people.

It is hard to exaggerate San José's dominance over Costa Rican affairs. It's the seat of government, the administrative capital, the main transport hub, location of the headquarters of all the country's major businesses (both national and international), as well as the site of its main cultural scene.

08

Don't miss

⭐ Intense, bustling city life
Mercado Central p.106

⭐ Fine jade in all shades
Museo de Jade p.107

⭐ Old, intricately crafted goldwork
Museo de Oro Precolombino p.104

⭐ Grassy spaces
Parque la Sabana p.111

⭐ A tropical take on a Parisian opera house
Teatro Nacional p.105

See map overleaf

Around a million Costa Ricans live in the greater San José area, making it extremely populous, if not exactly popular. Perhaps it's resentment at the city's all-encompassing influence, but for many Costa Ricans living outside its confines (and, it has to be said, for a good deal living within), San José would seem to represent everything that is wrong with modern living – too frenetic, too polluted, too congested. Telling gleeful tales of the latest urban horror – particularly the latest crime scam – is almost a national pastime.

With this in mind, it is perhaps best to get all the things that are wrong with San José out of the way first, before moving on to what's name of Villa Nueva de la Boca del Monte del Valle de Abra. For the next 80-odd years it would remain little more than a ramshackle backwater, far removed from the centre of Costa Rican affairs in the then capital, Cartago. According to an account in 1751, the country's future capital was at that time home to just 150 people who lived in 26 houses '...which form no plaza or street...(lacking) water which was then carried by open channels; the church is the most narrow, humble and indecent from all those...in the province...'.

The most (indeed only) notable incident in the town's early history was its rechristening after the patron saint of that 'humble and indecent' church, St Joseph. San José's ascension to dominance only came about after Central America declared its independence from the Spanish crown in 1821 (a development which not even the governor in Cartago, let alone the inhabitants of San José, was aware of for several weeks). Trouble soon arose when Mexico, having just removed itself from an empire, decided it wanted one of its own and began making plans for the annexation of Costa Rica. The citizens of the capital and nearby Heredia declared themselves in favour of Mexican rule, while those of San José and Alajuela were firmly opposed. The brief civil war that followed saw the oppositionists victorious and San José declared as the country's new capital.

It would remain a pretty unimpressive first city for some decades to come. While under Spanish rule, Costa Rica had come to be regarded as the runt of the imperial litter, with little in the way of natural resources or viable agriculture, and by the early 19th century San José's population was still only around 5,000. The country's and the capital's relative impoverishment would change, however, from the 1830s onwards, following the development of successful coffee- and tobacco-growing industries on the fertile Valle Central slopes surrounding San José. By the middle of the 19th century, the capital had achieved a significant level of prosperity, which saw the paving of its mud track roads, the creation of a university and the emergence of a new class of wealthy coffee barons – *finqueros* – who began building mansions for themselves in the San José neighbourhoods of Amón and Otoya, and taking a leading role in municipal and government affairs. With no great native cultural tradition to draw on, this coffee bourgeoisie began to use their newly disposable income to ape, somewhat self-consciously, European and particularly French customs and culture, adorning their homes with French-style filigree ironwork, adopting French modes of dress and sending their daughters for language lessons. The apotheosis of this Euro-affectation was the creation of the Teatro Nacional in the 1890s, a literal attempt to import high European culture to the tropics (every stone was shipped across the Atlantic). By this time San José had become one of the leading cities in Central America, and one of the first in the world to introduce electric lights and public telephones.

Getting to San José

By Air

Juan Santamaría International Airport's recently built terminal, located 17km northwest of San José, just south of Alajuela, welcomes the vast majority of international flights. For **flight information**, call t 443 2622. Though there isn't an entrance tax, there is a departure tax, which currently stands at $26 and must be paid before check-in, either in cash or by credit card (Visa, but not MasterCard, is accepted).

A **taxi** is the most convenient way of getting into town. Don't worry about finding one. As you leave Customs, you'll see cabs lined up outside the arrivals hall with the drivers standing immediately outside the exit soliciting for fares. Do be sure to take one of the official taxis, which are orange with a yellow triangle on the door. The journey should take around 20–30mins, depending on the traffic and the time of day, and cost around c5,000 ($12–14). Drivers will accept low-denomination dollar bills (nothing higher than a twenty). It's unlikely to happen, but don't let the driver take you to a hotel other than the one you've booked, or try to claim that your hotel is 'full' before you get there. This is a scam designed to get you to go to an associate's establishment, for which the driver will receive a commission.

Buses are cheaper than taxis and pretty plentiful, but are also rather uncomfortable, with little luggage space. And, unless you're travelling early in the morning or late at night, they're also likely to be crowded. This is a commuter service, not a dedicated airport bus. Buses depart about every 5mins from 5am–10.45pm, and then every half-hour through the night, depositing you at Av 2, C 12/14. The fare is c220, payable in *colones* only.

By Bus

Arriving by bus can be a great way of getting to see the glorious scenery, not just of Costa Rica but of its neighbouring countries, but there are problems and safety issues to take into account, both when travelling and after you arrive. For more information, *see* p.72. If travelling on from Costa Rica, remember that the land exit tax has recently been abolished, although the entry taxes to both Nicaragua and Panama still apply.

Tica Bus (t 221 8954) operates the majority of international bus routes, offering daily services to San José from Panama (Panama City), Nicaragua (Managua), Guatemala (Guatemala City), El Salvador (San Salvador), Honduras (Tegucigalpa) and, if you really want to make a journey of it, Mexico (Tapachula), arriving at Av 4, C 9/11. **Tracopa** (t 255 2981) also runs services from Panama, while **TransNica** (t 223 4242) and **NicaBus** (t 223 0293) offer daily services from Nicaragua. Fares range from around c5,000 ($12) for the one-day trip from Nicaragua to c28,000 ($60) for the three-day trip from Mexico.

Most domestic services, including those from Nicoya, Monteverde, Liberia and Puntarenas, pull into the area around the **La Coca-Cola bus station** (named after a long since demolished bottling plant) at Av 1/3, C 16/18. This is without question one of the grimmest and most unpleasant parts of town and a favourite stamping ground for pickpockets and thieves. It's certainly not the sort of place you want to be caught hanging around with a lot of luggage. Depart quickly after arrival, preferably in a taxi. Be sure to keep an eye on your luggage while travelling, especially if you have placed it in the overhead lockers. It's probably best to retrieve your bags during any stops *en route* – it's been known for thieves to pass bags out of windows to accomplices outside.

Getting around San José

On Foot

The city can get very crowded, particularly in the centre, and its uneven, potholed roads and pavements can take some getting used to (particularly the deep storm drains lining the edges of the roads which, in places, have to be jumped over), but San José is still a city best explored on foot. It's pretty flat, fairly compact – you can walk from the Parque la Sabana in the west to San Pedro in the east in under an hour – and a good stretch of the Avenida Central in the centre of the city, where you'll find many of the main sites and shops, is now pedestrianized. As always, the dangers of walking around alone increase after dark, especially for women, when you should probably switch to buses (which run till around 11pm) and taxis (which run throughout the night). This particularly applies to streets around the La Coca-Cola bus terminal and the Parque Central.

By Bus

Buses are regular, plentiful and pretty cheap (but can also be crowded during peak times) and run from roughly 5am to 11pm daily. Owing to ongoing pedestrianization, bus stops are gradually being moved further and further out from the centre, which has at least slightly improved the quality of the air (the buses here are mostly belching diesel behemoths). As it stands, buses heading west for the Parque la Sabana (marked Sabana Cementerio) can be caught at Av 2, C 5/7, those for Escazú at Av 0/1, C 16, while those heading east to Los Yoses and San Pedro leave from Av 0, C 9/15. Check the front windscreen for the destination and fare, typically c100 in the centre, rising to c150 for trips out to the suburbs.

You have to ring the bell to get the driver to stop, although many Josefinos prefer to shout or whistle to get their attention, which seems to irritate the driver greatly. It's probably best to stick to official procedure.

By Taxi

Taxis are a good way of getting around the city, particularly at night when there's less traffic. You'll see hordes of them lined up outside all the main nightspots in the centre, and at San Pedro and El Pueblo. They're also common in the day, although most seem to vanish – or at least fail to stop – when it's raining.

Official **city taxis** are red (except for airport taxis which are orange) and have a yellow triangle on the door marked with SJP (San José Publico) or TSJ (Taxi San José). Watch out for '*piratas*', illegal cab drivers who often use similar-looking cars, but without the telltale yellow triangle. **Fares** are reasonable, especially since the higher post-10pm tariff has been abolished (and don't let any cab driver try to persuade you otherwise). A journey within the city shouldn't cost more than c1,400 ($3.50). Either agree on the fare before you depart or make sure the driver turns on his meter: '*ponga la maría, por favor*'. Drivers will probably be unable to change large-denomination bills, so try to have the correct change handy. **Tipping**, though welcome, is not expected.

By Car

While hiring a car to explore the rest of the country does make sense, driving in San José itself is not recommended, for a number of reasons. The city's relatively small size and the excellence of its public transport system make the cost prohibitive – hire prices are steep by North American standards. Congestion is fierce during the day and the local driving style can perhaps best be described as a tad impatient. There's also the city's impenetrable one-way system to negotiate. Most roads are single direction only, usually (but crucially not always) the opposite direction to the adjacent street. And, once you've stopped driving, the question arises of what you do with the car. Some hotels have private garages, but by no means all (the class of hotel is no indicator – several hostels have garages, while a number of four-star hotels do not) and a car left unguarded on a city centre street is liable to be broken into. Some areas do employ guards to watch over cars parked on the street – they're not in uniform, but they do carry a truncheon, which is how you recognize them; you should tip them c300–500. And if all that hasn't put you off and you're still intent on driving, you'll find plenty of rental firms throughout the city (*see* 'Getting Away', p.103, for details).

In the 20th century, San José's dominance over its metropolitan rivals (and the entire country) continued to grow as more and more power came to be concentrated here. Today nearly every major domestic business and multinational company has its headquarters here, as do many Central American non-governmental agencies. And yet, until the 1940s, San José was still a relatively compact city of just 70,000 people, or around a tenth of the country's population. It was not until after the Second World War that the city really began to mushroom, as people began moving from rural to urban areas and more and more suburbs were created to accommodate them. Today, around a quarter of the population call San José home.

The City

Central San José

Plaza de la Cultura

The closest thing San José has to an official city centre, this large concrete plaza provides a neat overview of the city's history and influences. Below lie the subterranean riches of the **Museo de Oro**

Getting away from San José

Even if you decide not to sample the city's delights, you'll inevitably end up spending a portion of your trip here as you await connections to or make arrangements for excursions. To call San José the nation's main transport hub is something of an understatement: San José welcomes nearly all international flights, and is also the start and end point for the vast majority of domestic ones. All of the country's major domestic bus routes connect here, as do most of the major highways and, just for good measure, San José is also home to the majority of the country's car rental firms (although you will find branches in many of the other towns).

By Bus

Listed below are the bus stops for all the major domestic routes, as well as contact details for the relevant bus. For more information on travelling by bus, see p.100.

Destination	Bus Stop	Frequency	Duration	Bus Company
Valle Central				
Alajuela	Av 2, C 12/14	every 5–10mins, 5am–12 midnight	35mins	Tuasa
	Av 2, C 10/12			Station Wagon
Cartago	C 5, Av 18/20	every 5mins, 5am–9pm	30–45mins	Sacsa
Heredia	C1, Av 7/9	every 10–15 mins, 6am–10pm	30mins	Microbuses Rápidos Heredianos
	Av 2, C 10/12			Busetas Heredianos
	C 4, Av 3/5			Transportes Unidos
Parque Nacional Volcán Irazú	Av 2, C 1/3	2 a week, 8.15am Sat and Sun	1¼hrs	Buses Metrópoli
Parque Nacional Volcán Poás	Av 2, C 12/14	1 a day, 8am	1½hrs	Tuasa
Sarchí	Av 3, C 16/18	3 a day, 12.15pm, 5.30pm, 6.05pm	1½hrs	Tuan
Turrialba	C 13, Av 6/8	hourly 5.30am–10pm	1hr 40mins	Transtusa
The Northwest				
Liberia	C 24, Av 5/7	hourly, 6am–8pm	4½hrs	Pulmitan
Nicoya	C 14, Av 3/5	6 a day, 6am, 8am, 10.30am, 12.30pm, 2pm, 6.15pm	4–6hrs	Tracopa-Alfaro
Nosara	C 14, Av 3/5	1 a day, 6am	6½hrs	Tracopa-Alfaro
Peñas Blancas (and La Cruz)	C 20, Av 1	6 a day, 5am, 7am, 7.45am, 10.30am, 1.20pm, 4.10pm	5hrs	Transportes Deldú
Playa del Coco	C 24, Av 1/3	3 a day, 8am, 2pm, 4pm	5hrs	Pulmitan
Sámara	C 14, Av 3/5	2 a day, 12.30pm, 6.15pm	5hrs	Tracopa-Alfaro
Tamarindo	Av 5, C 14	2 a day, 11am, 3.30pm	5hrs	Tracopa-Alfaro
Central Pacific				
Jacó	C 16, Av 1/3	5 a day, 7.30am, 10.30am, 1pm, 3.30pm, 6.30pm	3hrs	Transportes Jacó
Monteverde/S. Elena	C 12, Av 9/11	2 a day, 6.30am, 2.30pm	5hrs	Transportes Tilarán
Puntarenas	C 16, Av 10/12	hourly, 6am–7pm	2hrs 20mins	Empresarios Unidos
Quepos/ Manuel Antonio	C 16, Av 3/5	4 a day, 6am, 12noon, 6pm, 7pm	3½hrs	Transportes Delio Morales
The North				
Ciudad Quesada (San Carlos)	C 12, Av 7/9	hourly, 5am–7.30pm	3hrs	Transportes San José–San Carlos
La Fortuna	C 12, Av 7/9	3 a day, 6.15am, 8.40am, 11.30am	4½hrs	Transportes San José–San Carlos
Los Chiles	C 12, Av 7/9	2 a day, 5.30am, 3.30pm	5hrs	Transportes San José–San Carlos
Puerto Viejo de Sarapiquí	C 0, Av 11	hourly 7am–6pm	2–4hrs	Empresarios Guapileños
Upala (Caño Negro)	C 12, Av 7/9	2 a day, 3pm, 3.45pm	4–5½hrs	Transportes Upala
The South				
Golfito	C 14, Av 5	2 a day, 7am, 3pm	8hrs	Tracopa-Alfaro
Palmar	C 14, Av 5	7 a day, 5am, 7am, 8.30am, 10am, 1pm, 2.30pm, 6pm	6hrs	Tracopa-Alfaro

Paso Canoas	C 14, Av 5	5 a day, 5am, 7.30am, 11am, 4.30pm, 6pm	9hrs	Tracopa-Alfaro
Puerto Jiménez	C 12, Av 7/9	1 a day, 12 noon	8hrs	Transportes Blanco-Lobo
San Isidro El General	C 0, Av 22/24	hourly, 5.30am–6.30pm	3½hrs	Musoc
San Vito	C 14, Av 5	4 a day, 5.45am, 8.15am, 11.30am, 2.45pm	7hrs	Tracopa-Alfaro

The Caribbean Coast

Cahuita	C 0, Av 11	4 a day, 6am, 10am, 1.30pm, 3.30pm	4hrs	Transportes Mepe
Guápiles/Siquerres	C 0, Av 11	every 30mins, 5am–7pm	1½–2hrs	Empresarios Guapileños
Puerto Limón	C 0, Av 11	every 30mins, 5am–7pm	3hrs	Transportes Caribeños
Puerto Viejo de Talamanca	Co, Av 11	4 a day, 6am, 10am, 1.30pm, 3.30pm	4½hrs	Transportes Mepe
Sixaola	Co, Av 11	4 a day, 6am, 10am, 1.30pm, 3.30pm	6hrs	Transportes Mepe

Bus Company Contact Details
Buses Metrópoli, t 530 1064.
Busetas Heredianos, t 261 7171.
Empresarios Guapileños, t 222 0610.
Empresarios Unidos, t 222 0064.
Microbuses Rápidos Heredianos, t 233 8392.
Musoc, t 222 2422.
Pulmitan, t 222 1650.
Sacsa, t 551 0232.
Station Wagon, t 222 7532.
Tracopa-Alfaro, t 222 2666.
Transportes Blanco-Lobo, t 771 4744.
Transportes Caribeños, t 221 2596.
Transportes Deldú, t 256 9072.
Transportes Delio Morales, t 223 5567.
Transportes Jacó, t 223 1109.
Transportes Mepe, t 257 8129.
Transportes San José–San Carlos, t 255 4318.
Transportes Tilarán, t 222 3854.
Transportes Unidos La 400, t 222 8986.
Transportes Upala, t 221 3318.
Transtusa, t 556 4233.
Tuan, t 258 2004.
Tuasa, t 442 6900.

By Car

There are plenty of car rental offices at Juan Santamaría International Aiport and most of the city's major hotels operate car hire desks (whereby the rental firm will bring the car to you). Otherwise try these:

Car Hire Companies
Adobe, C 7, Av 8/10, **t** 258 4242, *www.adobecar.com.*
Avis, C 42, Avenida las Americas, **t** 293 2222, *www.avis.co.cr.*
Budget, Av 0, C 30, **t** 223 3284, *www.budget.com.*
Dollar, Av 0, C 34/36, **t** 257 0671, *www.dollarcostarica.com.*
Europcar, Av 0, C 36/38, **t** 257 1158, *www.europcar.co.cr.*
Hertz, Av 0, C 38, **t** 221 1818, *www.hertz.com.*
Thrifty, C 3, Av 13, **t** 257 3434, *www.thrifty.com.*

By Air

Where driving on Costa Rica's maddeningly winding, under-maintained, traffic-clogged roads can make the country seem infinitely larger than it is, flying reminds you of its true reduced dimensions. No flight takes much longer than an hour; most last around 30–45mins. Flights need to be booked a good two weeks in

08

San José | Getting away from San José

advance during the high season (either directly or through one of the major tour operators) and should cost in the region of $70–80 return. There are currently two companies offering daily domestic flights within Costa Rica: **Sansa**, C 24, Av 0/1, **t** 221 9414, *www.flysansa.com*, who fly out of Juan Santamaría International Airport; and **NatureAir**, **t** 220 3054, *www.natureair.com*, who fly out of Tobías Bolaños airport in Pavas, 7km west of the city. Both serve all the following destinations:

Destination	Frequency		Duration		Return Cost ($)	
	Sansa	NatureAir	Sansa	NatureAir	Sansa	NatureAir
Barra del Colorado	1 daily	1 daily	1hr	1hr 20mins	126	140
Drake Bay	3 daily	2 daily	1hr 20mins	40mins	160	184
Golfito	5 daily	N/A	1hr	N/A	156	N/A
Liberia	4 daily	3 daily	1hr 15mins	1hr 15mins	156	176
Nosara	2 daily	1 daily	1hr 5mins	50mins	156	172
Palmar	3 daily	1 daily	1hr 20mins	1hr	144	160
Puerto Jiménez	2 daily	4 daily	1hr 10mins	50mins	156	184
Puerto Limón	N/A	1 daily	N/A	35mins	N/A	140
Quepos	8 daily	3 daily	25mins	25mins	96	108
Sámara	2 daily	N/A	50mins	N/A	156	N/A
Tamarindo	12 daily	4 daily	50mins	50mins	156	176
Tambor	3 daily	1 daily	30mins	30mins	126	138
Tortuguero	1 daily	1 daily	1hr	1hr	126	140

Precolombino, the country's finest collection of pre-Columbian gold. To the south is the neoclassical **Teatro Nacional**, built using the coffee money that provided such an impetus for the city's (and indeed the country's) growth in the 19th century. To the west is the 1930s-built **Gran Hotel Costa Rica**, the country's first ever hotel, the acorn from which the mighty sprawling oak of mass tourism has subsequently grown (now represented by the country's main **tourist office** located by the entrance to the Gold Museum on the plaza's eastern side, *see* p.112); while flanking the square's northern and eastern sides are an assortment of American stores and fast food restaurants (including McDonald's and Taco Bell) highlighting the city's current increasingly western-orientated direction. The square's pedestrianized confines, though hardly beautiful, are a popular meeting point, which in turn attracts a regular succession of buskers. The pavement café of the Gran Hotel Costa Rica provides a good spot for taking it all in.

The **Avenida Central**, the city's main artery, traverses the plaza's northern edge. The pedestrianized section stretching west from here to Calle 4 and east to Calle 11 is one of the city's main shopping areas, filled with all manner of clothes, shoes and department stores – including Universal, which has a small collection of English-language titles in its book section.

Museo de Oro Precolombino

Costa Rica's pre-Columbian cultures are still little understood. Unlike their contemporaries in Mexico or Guatemala, they left behind scant evidence of their existence, which makes this museum's collection of pre-Columbian goldwork – there are over 2,000 separate pieces – all the more fascinating, providing one of

Museo de Oro Precolombino
*t 243 4202,
www.museosdel
bancocentral.org; open
Tues–Sat 10–4; adm*

the few tangible insights into the country's ancient civilizations. The museum's somewhat gloomy subterranean confines – it's located beneath the Plaza de la Cultura, reached via a ramp on the square's eastern side – actually provides a very effective showcase for the gold, with spotlights picking out the pieces' dazzling forms against a dark background. Almost all the pieces were created by the Diquis, a tribe native to southwest Costa Rica who panned for gold in the Osa river. The work they created is highly detailed, showing a high level of craftsmanship and, by implication, civilization. Most are resp-resentations of animals – jaguars, alligators, snakes, sharks, lobsters, etc. – used, it is thought, as charms to protect the wearer against evil spirits, which the Diquis believed resided in animals and were the main cause of illness (the greatest number of diseases seem to have been caused by birds of prey, of which there are more representa-tions than any other creature).

The museum has recently been revamped, resulting in the addition (at long last) of English-language information panels as well as a number of new displays designed to place the craft in its historical and geographical context. You will find maps showing the main centres of gold production, models of gold-making settlements, and an exhibit showing how the pieces were created (basically via the clever use of wax models and clay moulds). There's also a film theatre where you can watch a somewhat portentous account of the rise and fall of Costa Rican gold-making.

Your ticket to the gold museum also entitles you to entry to the adjacent **Museo de Numismática**, a small, mildly diverting museum of Costa Rican currency.

Museo de Numismática
same opening hours as gold museum

Teatro Nacional

🟊 Teatro Nacional
t 252 0863, www. intent.co.cr; open for tours Tues–Sun 8.30– 4.30 (call ahead for performance times)

San José's one true architectural highlight, the neoclassical Teatro Nacional (*see* box, overleaf), stands on the southern side of the Plaza de la Cultura. Though somewhat grey and boxy from the outside, with a restrained columned façade, the inside is a lavish hotchpotch of marble, gilt, velvet and hardwoods overlooked by exuberant ceiling frescoes, much of which had to be extensively repaired following damage inflicted by the 1991 earthquake.

Today, the theatre stages a full repertoire of opera, ballet and classical performances (it is home to the National Symphony Orchestra), although outside of performance times you can tour its grand confines for $3, or have an elegant coffee and a slice of cake in its café (*see* p.118).

Parque Central and Mercado Central

The name is something of a misnomer. This is no leafy park, rather a fairly grim-looking paved plaza just off a heavily busy stretch of the Avenida Dos (2). It does have some greenery in the shape of a

The Teatro Nacional: Bringing the Mountain to Mohammad

The Teatro Nacional's overtly European appearance – it was supposedly modelled on the Paris Opera – is quite deliberate. Indeed, its construction in the late 19th century can be seen as the ultimate physical manifestation of the city's coffee bourgeoisie's desire for élite European-style culture. European, and in particular French, modes of dress, architecture and artistic tastes had long been *de rigueur* among the upper echelons of San José society when, in 1890, the famous opera singer Adelina Patti announced that she was to undertake a concert tour of the Americas. Her decision not to perform in San José, because it did not have a suitable venue, stung the city's coffee barons deeply. In response, they levied an export tax on coffee, from which they derived the funds necessary to construct a new opera house. This was to be no New World theatre, however – no attempt to forge a Costa Rican style of architecture. The coffee barons had no desire to explore Costa Rican culture; they simply wanted to be part of the greater 'high culture' as exemplified by Europe, and if that meant hiring European craftsmen and importing every single piece of stone for the building from Europe in order to construct an opera house that wouldn't look out of place on the Grands Boulevards of Paris, then so be it.

Despite the logistical problems of the exercise, the coffee barons' determination to see the project through saw the theatre constructed and opened for its inaugural performance by 1897. It's a suitably opulent affair. The main auditorium is a riot of gilt and red plush with hardwood parquet floors, and is flanked by elegant boxes. The coffee barons, eager to celebrate their own (and their businesses') contribution to the project, adorned the upstairs salons with sombre portraits of themselves, alongside a grand painting representing the harvest and export of coffee, which went on to become one of the country's most famous images (it used to decorate the five-*colón* note).

few trees where green parrots roost and chatter each night, and a pretty(ish) central bandstand, but this is not an area that should detain you long. It's bordered to the east by the city's modern and rather soulless **Catedral Metropolitaneo**, and to the north (across a fiendishly busy street) by the **Teatro Mélico Salazar**, the city's second most prestigious theatre (*see* p.119).

★ Mercado Central

Of much more interest is the **Mercado Central** to the northwest. Charmingly chaotic, this covered market would seem to pretty much exemplify the dictionary definition of 'bustling', particularly at lunchtime when the whole city seems to descend here *en masse* looking for a bite to eat. Its stalls sell some of the cheapest meals to be found anywhere in town. It's also a great source of fruit, vegetables, meat (including live poultry), fish and coffee, as well as leather goods and assorted crafts. It can be a fascinating place to wander, if you manage to avoid the crowds, taking in the oh, so typically Latin American sights and sounds, although do be on your guard: the market and its surrounding area are one of the favourite stamping (or should that be stealing?) grounds for the city's pickpockets, so be sure to keep your valuables safe (ideally back in your hotel room).

Museo Postal, Telegráfico y Filatélico
open Mon–Fri 8–4

The city's main post office, which has a small museum of postal history and philately, the **Museo Postal, Telegráfico y Filatélico**, is just a couple of blocks east.

Plaza de la Democracía and Museo Nacional

To the east you can easily spend a cheery 20 minutes browsing the arts and crafts of the **open-air market** on the plaza's western edge, but it's probably best to draw a veil over the concrete, car park-like expanse of the plaza, which could justly claim the title of 'ugliest square in San José' (which, considering the competition, is quite a claim). It certainly makes a poor (or perhaps fittingly imperfect) monument to democracy – it was built in 1989 to commemorate the winning by Costa Rica's then president, Oscar Arias, of the Nobel Prize for his formulation of a Central American peace plan.

Museo Nacional

Museo Nacional
t 257 1433, www. museocostarica.com; open Tues–Sat 8.30–4.30, Sun 9–4.30; adm

The museum's somewhat militaristic-looking exterior provides a clue as to its origins. It's housed in a converted fortress and some of its thick walls still bear bullet holes from the 1948 Civil War (*see p.26*). Entrance is via a pretty garden, adorned (appropriately enough) with cannons, after which you'll find displays taking you through a more or less chronological history of the country from pre-Columbian times (represented via exhibits of jade and goldwork, the most significant remaining items from this period), through colonial times (there are contemporary accounts of the often bloody conflict) and on to independence (lots of fine-looking furniture, period costumes and religious iconography).

Parque España and Around

One of the city's more pleasant open spaces, the Parque España is lined with towering trees where flocks of chattering, colourful tropical birds roost each night. Bordering its western side is the **Edificio Métalica** or 'Metal Building', which, true to its name, is a building made entirely out of metal plates. And, just to make the construction process that much harder, every single one of these plates was shipped over from Belgium at the end of the 19th century. The best views of this strange, shiny building (now a school) are afforded from the INS (Instituto Nacional de Seguros) building on the plaza's north side, a grimly functional skyscraper whose 11th floor is home to one of the city's foremost museums, the **Museo de Jade** (Jade Museum). The square's eastern flank is occupied by the monolithic **Centro Nacional de Arte y Cultura**, while just to the east is the small, paved **Parque Morazán**, whose only claim to fame, other than being supremely ugly, is its central domed bandstand, known rather floridly as the Templo de Música.

Museo de Jade

 Museo de Jade
t 287 6034; open Mon–Fri 8.30–3; adm

There are two reasons for visiting this museum. The first, of course, is to see the world's foremost collection of Central American jade, and it is a fine collection. The second is to enjoy the views out of the museum's windows over the city. What at street level seems so functional and ordinary-looking takes on a whole new aesthetic when viewed from 11 floors up, with buildings fading gently into a mountain-fringed horizon. It's a pity the museum shuts at 3pm; the night views must be quite something.

The museum displays are arranged according to regions, with lots of ceramics (animal-shaped pots, etc.) and stonework, although it's the jade that's the main draw. The pieces, which have been discovered all over Meso-America, including Costa Rica (despite there being no natural sources of jade here), come in both a huge range of shapes, representing their variety of functions – axe heads, pendants and necklaces (used both as jewellery and funerary offerings), fertility symbols – and, perhaps more surprisingly, shades. The colour of jade runs the gamut from deep green (which was seen as a symbol of agricultural fertility) to browns, greys and even soft whites. Much of the jade is displayed using backlighting to pick out the gemstone's delicate translucent patterns. The labelling, which is in both English and Spanish, is a tad incomplete, but you should be able to get the general idea.

Centro Nacional de Arte y Cultura

Museo de Arte y Diseño Contemporáneo
t 257 7202, www. madc.ac.cr; open Tues–Sun 10–5; adm

This vast building is usually referred to either by its acronym, CENAC, or (particularly by older Josefinos) as the 'Liquoría', a reference to the building's former role as the city's liquor factory. Though much of the space here is taken up by the government ministry in charge of art and culture, the complex does have two theatres, a dance studio and, its main visitor attraction, the **Museo de Arte y Diseño Contemporáneo** (Museum of Contemporary Art and Design), an ever-changing, terribly modern look at all that's best and brightest on the contemporary art scene.

Parque Nacional and Around

Galería de Arte Contemporáneo
t 257 5524; open Mon–Sat 10–1 and 2–5; adm

Museo Ferrocarríl
open Mon–Fri 9–4; adm

A few years ago this was something of a no-go area, particularly after dark, when it was rife with pickpockets, muggers and prostitutes. Thankfully, the simple measure of installing additional lighting seems to have sent the undesirables packing, and the park is now shady in the right way, its collection of fine old trees providing pleasant cover against the midday sun. Elegantly laid out, the park can provide a relaxing half-hour detour after all the hurly-burly of the city centre. It is bordered to the north by the **Biblioteca Nacional**, the country's most prestigious (and largest) library, and to the south by the **Galería de Arte Contemporáneo**, a small gallery dedicated to up-and-coming artists. The **Palacio Nacional**, Costa Rica's legislative assembly, is just south of the park.

A short walk east of here is a small museum dedicated to the city's now defunct railway, the **Museo Ferrocarríl**. The railway ran from San José to Puerto Limón from the late 19th century until 1991, when a great earthquake damaged it beyond repair (or, at least, beyond a cost of repair which the government was prepared to bear). Much of the now disused line still sits in place on the city streets (you'll be forced to cross it at several points as you make your way around the

Orientation

This is where things get tricky. Lying in the middle of the Valle Central at an elevation of around 1,150m and ringed by volcanic mountains, San José enjoys a beautiful, simple setting which its city planners have singularly failed to replicate. The city centre is divided into a basic grid pattern which gets less and less uniform the further from the centre you go. All streets are numbered rather than named, with *avenidas* running east to west and *calles* north to south, making the official centre of the city the intersection between Avenida 0 (also known as the **Avenida Central**) and Calle 0 (**Calle Central**), just west of the Plaza de la Cultura. From here, odd-numbered *calles* stetch off to the east, even-numbered to the west, while odd-numbered *avenidas* are to the north, evens to the south. Thus, Calles 19 and 20 are actually some considerable distance apart. '*Bis*' means a small street next to the main one, i.e. Av 3 bis is behind Av 3.

With no street names or building numbers, most addresses are written as a combination of *avenidas* and *calles* – e.g. Av 0, C 2/4, which means the location is on Avenida 0 on the block between Calles 2 and 4. Av 3, C 2 means on the corner of Avenida 3 and Calle 2. However, as a great many streets do not have signs, it can be very difficult finding your way around using this method (unless you're good at keeping count), which is why the majority of Josefinos give directions using landmarks – such as, 100m north of the Omni cinema, or 200m west of the Mas X Menos supermarket. The 100m is not a specific distance, but rather is used to denote the average size of a city block. And, just to complicate matters further, Josefinos have a great fondness for referring to landmarks that don't even exist any more – such as the La Coca-Cola bottling plant, which was pulled down decades ago (but at least lives on as the name of the bus station) or, even more arcanely, the '*antiguo higuerón*' or 'old fig tree', which, in this instance, refers to a tree that fell down in 1975. Be prepared to ask for directions, repeatedly. Josefinos understand the idio-syncratic nature of the addresses and are used to helping disorientated tourists.

Leaving directions to one side (it's not as complicated as it seems and it's actually quite easy to famili-arize yourself with the city's layout in a day or two), you'll find most of the city's main sights located in the centre. Around this are grouped several neighbourhoods, or *barrios*, the most interesting of which are the **Barrio Amón** to the north, which has several lovely 19th-century houses, and the lively student district of **San Pedro** to the east. Heading west along the Avenida Central (which out of the centre turns into the **Paseo Colón**), you eventually reach the city's largest open space, the **Parque la Sabana**, laid out on the site of the city's former airport. Further west still (around 7km from the centre) is the suburb of **Escazú**, home to most American expats.

southern and eastern stretches of the city), and is itself a sort of slowly rusting outdoor museum exhibit of a departed age.

Northern San José

Barrios Amón and Otoya

The city's most elegant neighbourhoods can be found directly north of the city centre, up a slightly gradiented hill. In the late 19th and early 20th centuries, these districts (particularly Amón) were the favoured addresses of the city's great coffee barons, who built dozens of French-inspired mansions here, adorned with great surrounding verandas and filigree ironwork. The area went rather out of fashion for a while in the 20th century, which at least saved it from redevelopment, but it has recently been rediscovered and many of its grand houses have now been converted into hotels. Just north of the Barrio Otoya is the depressingly small and cramped **Parque Zoológico Simón Bolívar**, which, considering the country's glorious national parks, seems almost insultingly redundant.

Parque Zoológico
Simón Bolivar
*open Tues–Fri 8–4, Sat
and Sun 9–5; adm*

El Pueblo

This purpose-built entertainment complex is officially called the Centro Comercial El Pueblo, but is nearly always referred to by the abbreviated form. Relatively new it may be, but the complex has been deliberately designed to look old, with its scores of bars, restaurants and clubs inhabiting traditional-style adobe houses. However, what could have been a ghastly exercise in retro tweeness actually works rather well, and it has proved highly popular with the locals, who flock here at weekends. The complex lies to the north of the Barrio Amón across the Río Torres. The walk is largely unlit and uphill – best to take a taxi. For details of the complex's bars, restaurants and clubs, *see* pp.117–20. There's a small butterfly garden next door, the **Spirogyra Jardín de Mariposas**.

Spirogyra Jardín de Mariposas
open daily 8–4; adm

Centro Costarricense de la Ciencia y la Cultura

The highlight of this small science and cultural centre, housed in a former prison a couple of blocks west of El Pueblo, is the **Museo de los Niños**, which is full of science-related interactive games and experiments for children. The centre is also home to a small penal history museum, the **Museo Histórico Penitencio**, where you can see one of the prison's original cells.

Centro Costarricense de la Ciencia y la Cultura
open Tues–Fri 8–4, Sat and Sun 10–4; adm

Eastern San José: Los Yoses and San Pedro

Just east of downtown San José, the *barrio* of **Los Yoses**, slightly unremarkable in itself, marks a sort of buffer zone between the city centre and the student district of San Pedro. Here, the city pauses for breath slightly, before gearing up again as it heads east. Primarily residential, the neighbourhood has some nice hotels, a few of which occupy former mansions, as well as a good collection of bars and restaurants. Its main sight, such as it is, is the **Mall San Pedro**, a vast American-style leisure complex of shops, restaurants, bars and clubs, which is hugely popular with almost everyone in the city under 20. More sedate pleasures can be found at the **Centro Cultural Costarricense-Norteamerican**, the library of which stocks English-language (mainly American, obviously) books and newspapers. The complex also boasts an art gallery and theatre.

To reach the student district of **San Pedro** via the Avenida Central, you have to cross the fearfully busy **Fuente de la Hispanidad** roundabout, just east of the Mall San Pedro. It can be quite tricky (not to say rather hairy) doing this on foot, as there is no official pedestrian crossing. You'd be better off taking the bus.

As you'd expect of a district whose population is largely made up of people in their late teens and 20s, San Pedro is a lively place,

Centro Cultural Costarricense-Norteamerican
Av 0, C 37; t 255 9433 for library, www.cccncr. com; open Mon–Fri 7–7, Sat 9–12 noon

packed full of bars, restaurants and discos (*see* pp.117–20), most of which are located a few blocks north of the Avenida Central (which in this part of the city is noisy and congested, its businesses of the type that cater mainly to commuter traffic – car dealerships, petrol stations, shopping malls), around the campus of the **University of Costa Rica**, one of the country's most prestigious educational institutions, which enjoys a pleasant, leafy setting. There are a number of entertainment options on campus which can be enjoyed by members of the public, including the open-air **Teatro de Bellas Artes** where classical concerts are held, the **Cine Universitario**, which specializes in arthouse offerings and, housed somewhat incongruously in the basement of the faculty of musical arts, the **Museo de Insectos**, one of the largest collections of creepy crawlies in Central America with over a million species from all over the world: beetles, butterflies, dragonflies, etc.

Teatro de Bellas Artes
t 207 4327

Cine Universitario
t 207 4717

Museo de Insectos
t 207 5318; open Mon–Fri 1–5pm; adm

Western San José

Heading west past the Mercado Central, the no longer pedestrianized Avenida Central widens as it reaches the San Juan de Dios Hospital, the city's principal hospital, and changes its name to become the **Paseo Colón**. Here, on either side of the traffic-choked boulevard, you'll find large shopping malls, fast-food eateries and, towards its western end, upmarket hotels and restaurants. Right at its western end, across the multi-lane Calle 42 (which becomes the Autopista General Cañas just north of here) is the **Parque la Sabana**, the city's largest and nicest open space, laid out on what was, until the 1950s, the city's main airport. The former airport terminal building is now home to the **Museo de Arte Costarricense** (Museum of Costa Rican Art), which is well worth an hour or so with its collection of paintings and sculptures by Costa Rican artists from the 19th century onwards, many showing idealized representations of the country's history – Columbus' heroic arrival, the indigenous peoples welcoming the conquering Spanish with open arms, workers happily toiling on coffee plantations, etc. – as well as colourful interpretations of its landscape. Just south of the park, housed in a former school building is the **Museo de Ciencias Naturales** (Museum of Natural Sciences) filled with all manner of dead nature – stuffed animals, mounted butterflies, giant turtle shells, fossils.

Behind these museums, the park itself is pleasant and leafy, with an almost English-style layout: large expanses of grass punctuated by shady trees and colourful modern art installations. There's also a large central lake, a jogging track and a sports complex with an Olympic-sized swimming pool and tennis courts. The affluent suburb of **Escazú**, filled with upmarket hotels and restaurants, is about a 15-minute drive from here.

 Parque la Sabana

Museo de Arte Costarricense
open Tues–Sun 10–4; adm

Museo de Ciencias Naturales
open Mon–Fri 8–3; adm

Tourist Information in San José

(i) San José >
Plaza de la Cultura,
t 223 1733 or t 223 1090,
www.visitcostarica.com;
open Mon–Fri 9–5

San José's **main tourist office** can take some finding. It's located on, or rather beneath, the eastern edge of the Plaza de la Cultura. A ramp leads you down to the entrance it shares with the Museo de Oro Precolombino. There are no signposts and it can be quite easy to overlook unless you are specifically searching for it. Though it doesn't offer an accommodation- or trip-booking service, it does hold leaflets and pamphlets on hotels, restaurants and excursions throughout the country. It can also provide free city and country maps as well as an up-to-date copy of the national bus schedule (with the latest additions often drawn in by hand). The **airport information booth**, as is usually the case, is smaller and provides a rather a more limited source of information.

(i) Juan Santamaría Airport >
t 443 1535 or t 443 2883; open Mon–Fri 9–5

(i) MINAE >
Fundación de Parques Nacionales, Av 15, C 23/25, Barrio Escalante, t 257 2239, azucena@ns.minae.go.cr, or call t 192 for free up-to-date information (in English and Spanish)

The main office for **MINAE** (the energy and environment ministry), the body that directly controls the country's network of national parks, is also worth a visit. In addition to providing information about the parks, the office also operates a ticket- and accommodation-booking service. It's always worthwhile checking in here first to see whether your desired destination has space available, rather than just turning up.

Services in San José

Banks: Banco de Costa Rica, Av 2, C 4/6; Banco Nacional, Av 0/1, C 2/4; Banco Popular, C 1, Av 2/4; Banco de San José, C 0, Av 3/5.

Books: Lehmann, Av 0, C 1/3, t 223 1212; 7th Street Books, C 7, Av 0/1, t 256 8251. Books, maps and guides in English.

Hospital: San Juan de Díos, Paseo Colón, C 14/16, t 257 6282.

Internet access: Internet Café Costa Rica, Av 0, C 0/2, t 255 1154; Café Digital, Av 0, C 5/7.

Laundry: Lavandería Sixaola, Av 2, C 7/9, t 221 2111.

Library: Biblioteca Nacional, C 15, Av 3, t 221 2436; Centro Cultural Costarricense-Norteamericano, Barrio Dent, www.cccncr.com (for English-language publications).

Pharmacy: Clinica Biblica, Av 14, C 0/1, t 257 5252. *Open 24hrs.*

Post office: Correo Central, C 2, Av 1/3. *Open Mon–Fri 7–5, Sat 7–12 noon.*

Supermarket: Mas X Menos, Av 0, C 9/11.

Shopping and Markets in San José

As with many big cities, the majority of San José's souvenir shops seem to specialize in overpriced tourist tat – Aztec T-shirts, maracas, *ocarinas*, bottles of Café Rica liqueur and the ubiquitous Sarchí ox-carts. However, there are also a number of craft co-operatives, which not only stock good-quality handicrafts produced by local artisans and indigenous tribal groups, but also try to ensure that profits are directed back to the artisans.

Atmósfera, C 5, Av 3, t 222 4322. Sells replicas of pre-Columbian gold jewellery of the type displayed in the Museo de Oro Precolombino (p.104).

Biesanz Woodworks, Bello Horizonte, Escazú, t 289 4337. Environmentally conscious wood carvings made from trees felled from sustainable plantations. Their designs have proved so successful that the workshop now has an ongoing commission to provide state gifts for the Costa Rican government.

Boutique Annemarie, Hotel Don Carlos, Av 9, C 9, t 221 6707, *www.doncarlos hotel.com*. Perhaps the city's best souvenir shop, selling a wide range of handcrafted goods – crystal, jewellery, ceramics, wooden sculptures, etc.

La Casona, Av 0, C 0, t 222 7999. Two-storey artisan workshop featuring items from across Central America.

Mercado Central, Av 0/1, C 6/8. The archetypal bustling, hectic, noisy tropical market, this is the one San José shopping experience you don't want to miss. It's a great source of fresh fruit and veg as well as cheap export-standard coffee (also *see* p.106).

Mercado Plaza de la Democracia, Av 0/2, C 15. Small, tented open-air market on the square next to the Museo Nacional. There's some good stuff to be found here – jewellery, hammocks, wood crafts, etc. – among all the usual tourist staples.

Where to Stay in San José

It hasn't always been the case, but San José now has decent accommodation options in all price categories. The vast rise in tourism in the 1990s saw a concomitant increase in the number of hotel rooms, which, in turn, was accompanied by an inevitable steep rise in prices. Thankfully, the inflationary bubble did eventually burst and there are now plenty of bargains to be had, even at high-end establishments, particularly outside December–May.

Several international chains – including Radisson, Best Western and Occidental – have opened grand if somewhat generic branches in town, and there are also some privately owned luxury hotels, many housed in restored mansions, offering a more authentic Costa Rican experience at very reasonable rates. The best hotels tend to be located in quieter *barrios* away from the centre.

The biggest improvement, however, has come at the bottom end of the spectrum. A decade ago, a budget hotel in San José was where you stayed only if you were truly desperate. Usually located in the worst parts of town, with few if any facilities (if you managed to get access to a shower at all, it would inevitably be cold), these were strictly the last resort. Today, there are several excellent cheaper choices offering en suite rooms, TVs, ceiling fans and tour-booking facilities for under $40 for a double room. The city's hostels, which are of a good standard, are even better value – $10 for a bed in a dormitory or $20 for a double room (though these tend to be booked up quickly) – and usually offer a range of extra facilities, including Internet access, a laundry service and parking.

Luxury ($$$$$)

Amon Plaza, Av 11, C 3 bis, t 257 0191, *www.hotelamonplaza.com* ($120). The strength of any large hotel chain is the uniformity and familiarity of its product, the guarantee that a hotel in New York or Paris will provide the same level and type of accommodation as one in San José. Of course, this is also their weakness. The Amon Plaza, a 'Choice Hotel', has all the facilities you'd expect from a top-end chain – clean, comfortable rooms (all with TVs, private baths and safes), 24hr room service, 24hr taxi service, a gym, a sauna – with the lack of character this often entails. It does have a good bar/restaurant with pavement seating, **El Cafetal de la Luz** (named in honour of San José's becoming only the third city in the world, after New York and Paris, to install electric streetlights in 1884), where live music is staged every Friday.

Intercontinental Real San José, Prospero Fernandez Hwy, t 208 2100, *www.ichotelsgroup.com* ($180). This huge resort in Escazú, a 15-minute drive southwest of downtown San José, has every facility and luxury you could want – two restaurants, two bars, a tour desk, a car rental desk, 24hr room service, Internet access – and its 261 rooms, which are spread out over three five-storey wings, all come with TV, coffee-maker, writing desk and private bathroom. It's fairly pricey, $180 upwards for a double and $269 for a junior suite on the 'Club Intercontinental' floor, although this does entitle you to 'butler service'.

Expensive ($$$$)

Best Western Irazú, Km3 Autopista General Cañas, t 232 4811, USA t 800 528 1234, f 232 4549, *www.bestwestern. com* ($89). Outside the city proper, 5km west of downtown San José, the 214-room Irazú is more of a resort than a hotel. Indeed, many of its guests never leave its confines during their stay, but instead spend their time happily shuttling between pool, gym, sauna, casino, restaurant and bar before jetting back home. The Irazú was designed to offer familiarity and comfort – which it does, in spades. If you do fancy popping out, a free shuttle bus can take you into San José or out to the chain's sister property at Jacó Beach (*see* p.220).

Fleur de Lys, C 13, Av 2/6, t 223 1206, f 257 3637, *www.hotelfleurdelys.com* ($89). The address might not sound promising – it's near the abandoned railway line, around the corner from the Tica Bus stop – but this is actually a quiet, tranquil place, the alarming pink of its façade notwithstanding. The public rooms of this 1920s mansion are bright and cheerful, filled with tropical plants, while the 31 colourful bedrooms are adorned with examples of Costa Rican art. All have cable TV, telephones and private baths (and all are non-smoking). There's also a tour desk and a very good restaurant, **Obelisco**, specializing, inevitably, in 'New Costa Rican' cuisine. There are good bargains to be had out of season, when you can splash out on a suite (and, indeed, splash around *in* a suite – three have Jacuzzis) for $135.

(★) Grano de Oro >

Grano de Oro, C 30, Av 2/4, **t** 255 3322, **f** 221 2782, *www.hotelgranodeoro.com* ($95). These days, San José is overflowing with late 19th- and early 20th-century mansion conversions, but few have been done as lovingly as this. It may not have all the facilities of some of its big chain rivals, but in terms of atmosphere this is the best luxury choice in town. Just 13 years old, the hotel has been revamped in antique style with brass fittings, hardwood furniture, wrought-iron beds and sepia-tinted pictures. The standard rooms are large, with TVs, ceiling fans and private bathrooms, while the four deluxe rooms are absolutely huge, each coming with its own private tropical garden. On the ground floor, there's an excellent restaurant with an outdoor courtyard (*see* p.117), while on the roof, they have recently installed a sun deck with twin hot tubs. It tends to attract an older, mainly American clientele. Non-smoking throughout.

Occidental Torremolinos, C 40, Av 5 bis, **t** 222 5266, **f** 255 3167, *www.occidental hotels.com* ($85). Built in 1994, this is a reasonably priced three-star business hotel on a quiet street near Parque la Sabana, to the west of the city centre. Some of its 84 rooms are a touch small, but they're all well equipped and there's a large pool, a tropical garden, a restaurant, bar, gym and sauna.

Moderate ($$$)
Ara Macao Inn, C 25 bis, Av 0/2, **t** 233 2742, **f** 257 6228, *www.hotels.co.cr/ aramacao.html* ($50). Small, 11-room B&B just east of the centre in Barrio La California. All rooms have private baths and TVs and three have kitchenettes – perfect for longer stays. There's also a nice outdoor courtyard.

Hotel Le Bergerac, C 35, Av 0, **t** 234 7850, **f** 225 9103, *www.bergerac.co.cr* ($70). Designed 'in the style of a French

inn', which seems to translate as large patio windows, wooden floors and lots of wrought iron, the Bergerac is situated on a quiet street, but within easy walking distance of the bars and restaurants of Los Yoses and San Pedro (although its own French restaurant, **L'Ile de France**, is one of the city's best, *see* p.117). Its 24 rooms, several of which have private gardens (all have TVs, telephones, ceiling fans and baths), are very competitively priced, and even its deluxe honeymoon suite, which has views of the mountains beyond the city, is still a very reasonable $115.

Hotel Don Carlos, C 9, Av 7/9, **t** 221 6707, **f** 255 0828, *www.doncarloshotel. com* ($70). 'Don' Carlos Balser was a leading European archaeologist and expert in pre-Columbian art who, in the 1930s, founded the city's second ever hotel (the first was the Gran Hotel Costa Rica), a simple guesthouse catering to the needs of visiting scientists and archaeologists. The hotel that bears his name today is a much grander affair – it's housed in a former president's mansion – with 33 large, well-equipped rooms, and it is decorated throughout with reproductions of pre-Columbian artefacts. There's also a lovely tropical garden with a hot tub and sun deck. The hotel's gift shop, **Boutique Annemarie**, is one of the city's main sources of Costa Rican art.

Hotel Don Fadrique, C 37, Av 8, **t** 225 8186, **f** 224 9746, *www.hoteldon fadrique.com* ($60–70). The former home of the early 20th-century architect, Fadrique Gutierrez, this is just across the street from Le Bergerac (*see* above) and offers similarly refined fare. Decorated with contemporary Costa Rican art, there are 20 rooms – all with hardwood floors, TVs, ceiling fans, telephones and private baths – a good restaurant and bar and a patio courtyard festooned with tropical foliage, including a large lopsided mango tree.

Hotel 1492 Jade y Oro, Av 1, C 31/33, **t** 256 5913, **f** 280 6206, *www.hotel1492. com* ($70). This strangely titled hotel is about equidistant between downtown San José and San Pedro. It's laid out around a nice, cool, high-ceilinged atrium (filled with antiques and examples of contemporary Costa Rican art) with a lovely small tropical garden at the back, where breakfast is served (and where hummingbirds are occasionally spotted). One of the city's most eco-friendly hotels, it has achieved a level three award for sustainable tourism. However, don't expect to endure any conservational hardships – its 10 rooms all come equipped with private showers, TVs, telephones and ceiling fans.

Gran Hotel Costa Rica, Av 0/2, C 3 t/f 256 8585, *www.granhotelcr.com* ($60–75). It was the city's first hotel, opened way back in the 1930s, and there are still few better situated. Its restaurant-bar, **Café Parisienne**, has long been one of the city's favourites, with its pavement tables on the Plaza de la Cultura. A good location is not everything, however, and you do get the feeling that the hotel has been resting on its laurels slightly; its 110 rooms are adequate but hardly inspiring. Facilities include a tour desk, 24hr room service and a 24hr casino.

Hotel Keköldi, Av 9, C 5/7, t 248 0804, *www.kekoldi.com* ($65). One of the city's few openly gay-friendly hotels, the Keköldi occupies a lovely Art Deco building. It has a hip young vibe with a nice, secluded garden and 10 good-sized rooms, all with queen-size beds, telephones, cable TV and safes. The hotel has a sister establishment in Manuel Antonio.

Hotel Rincón de San José, Av 9, C 13/15, t 221 9702, f 222 1241, *www.hotelrincondesanjose.com* ($52.50). Just across the street from the Café Mundo, one of the city's best restaurants (*see* p.117), this pretty, bright white hotel has recently been revamped – previously known as the Hotel Edelweiss, it's now under Dutch ownership. All of its 27 rooms have ceiling fans, wooden floors and private showers. The free buffet breakfast is served in a plant-filled room.

Hotel Rosa del Paseo, Paseo Colón, C 28/30, t 257 3213, f 223 2776, *www.rosadelpaseo.com* ($70). First the bad news – it's right on the busy Paseo Colón. The good news is that, with its efficient soundproofing, you should hardly notice the constant rumbling traffic. A sensitively restored 19th-century coffee exporter's mansion, the Rosa del Paseo has 18 large, comfortable rooms laid out around a central courtyard, all with TVs, private baths,

hardwood floors and Victorian-style fittings (some have air-conditioning). The master suite has its own Jacuzzi.

Hotel Santo Tomás, Av 7, C 3/5 , t 255 0448, f 222 3950, *www.hotelsantotomas.com* ($70). Located on a quiet street, with an unobtrusive façade hidden behind wrought-iron gates, this can take some finding. The bijou exterior, however, of this early 20th-century French-style plantation owner's house belies an extensive interior with 20 good-sized high-ceilinged rooms (TVs, telephones and en suite bathrooms in all), leading on to a lovely tropical garden with a mini-waterfall and a small heated pool, above which sits a hot tub. Extra facilities include a tour desk, Internet access, a very reasonable restaurant (three courses for under $15) and a real estate service for people looking to invest in land.

Inexpensive ($$)

Hotel Aranjuez, C 19, Av 11/13, t 256 1825, f 223 3528, *www.hotelaranjuez.com* ($38 with private bath, $25 with shared). A great budget choice on a quiet street, the Aranjuez has 23 rooms spread out over five interlinked houses, behind which sits a lush tropical garden where breakfast is served. Free local calls, wireless Internet and private parking are all part of the package. The tour desk can arrange trips to the Laguna Lodge in Tortuguero (*see* p.342). English and French spoken.

Hotel Cacts, C 28/30, Av 3 bis, t 221 2928, f 221 8616, *www.tourism.co.cr/hotels/cacts/cacts.htm* ($35). Cacts, which sits on a quiet west San José back street (where the grid system begins to fall apart a little), has a charmingly higgledy-piggledy layout. Recently renovated and expanded, its 25 rooms do vary greatly in size – at times, you do get the impression that the building has been designed completely at random – but all have TVs and ceiling fans, and most have private baths. Its main draws, however, are its roof terrace, tropical garden, swimming pool and hot tub.

Kap's Place, C 19, Av 11/13, t 221 1169, f 256 4850, *www.kapsplace.com* ($38). Perhaps the city's best hotel in any category, Kap's Place is presided over by the delightful Karla Arias, who goes out of her way to make guests feel

 Hotel Santo Tomás >>

 Kap's Place >>

welcome and fill them in on the intricacies of San José living. Behind a slightly unprepossessing exterior (basically, a green garage door) lies an object lesson in budget accommodation – 18 very comfortable, simple rooms (14 en suite, 4 with shared bathrooms), a communal kitchen, a rest area with hammocks and, for longer stays, a large two-floor apartment with its own kitchen, washing machine and fridge. Luggage storage and laundry service also offered. If there's a criticism – and it's a small one – it has the longest reservation form in the world.

Pension de la Cuesta, Av 1, C 11/15, t/f 255 2896, *www.suntoursandfun. com/lacuesta* ($27–35). A B&B with the feel of a hostel, this charming 80-year-old wood-framed house is a real travellers' haunt. With shared baths, a communal kitchen and a nice tranquil garden-cum-meeting spot, the bedrooms, which are clean and simple, are strictly for sleeping only. Laundry service and luggage storage also offered.

Budget ($)

Casa Ridgway, C 15, Av 6 bis between Av 6/8, t/f 233 6168 (dorms $10; double rooms $24). The hostel for the less raucous backpacker, Casa Ridgway is run by Quakers and was formerly known as the Peace Center. In addition to all the usual facilities – dormitories, a communal kitchen, laundry – there's also a library full of contemplative pamphlets. 'Quiet time' is from 10pm to 7am. A nice, peaceful budget choice.

★ Costa Rica
Backpackers >

Costa Rica Backpackers, Av 6, C 21/23, t 221 6191, f 223 2406, *www.costarica backpackers.com* (dorms $10 per person; double bedrooms $20). This independent hostel is a very popular meeting spot for backpackers (perhaps because it has mixed as well as single sex dormitories) who throng here during the season. It has got a great laid-back atmosphere, with a large garden and swimming pool where impromptu parties are held, and a communal kitchen with two large fridges which, despite their size, always seem to be full. Luggage storage, laundry service, TV room, free Internet and parking.

Galileo Hostel, Av 2, C 38/40, t 248 2094, *www.galileohostel.com* (dorm $7 per person; double room $16). The city's cheapest hostel is just a block east of

Parque la Sabana. It's well equipped, offering free Internet access, laundry service, free coffee and tea, luggage storage and a reading room, although, as with many hostels, the showers tend to be hot in name only.

Hostel Toruma, Av 0, C 29/31, t/f 224 4085, *www.toruma.com* (dorms $8 Hostelling International members, $10 non-members; double rooms $16 HI members, $20 non-members). Part of Costa Rica's official hostel network, the Toruma is clean, well-maintained and, as with all hostels, one of the best places to meet fellow travellers. Its single-sex dormitories sleep 4–6 and there are three double rooms, which seem to be permanently booked up, but you might get lucky. Luggage storage, a laundry service, free Internet access and free parking.

Eating Out in San José

It's hardly New York or Paris or London, but as far as Costa Rica is concerned San José is gourmet central, a welcome gastronomic oasis amid the beans-and-rice desert that makes up so much of the rest of the culinary landscape. Unlike most of the country's other urban centres, San José can offer a wide variety of international cuisines – Chinese, French, Italian, Mexican, Thai – as well as traditional Costa Rican fare. In fact, it's the latter which is becoming increasingly scarce. At the top end, this has been transformed into the slightly fanciful 'New Costa Rican' cuisine, while at the bottom end the street corner soda, for so long the staple of the Costa Rican culinary experience, and still prevalent in much of the country, is coming under increasing threat from the rapid growth in the fast food industry that's taken place over the past decade. However, you won't find many Josefinos bemoaning the threat this poses to their gastronomic culture. The younger generation, in particular, are enthusiastic consumers of fast food, hence the large numbers of McDonald's, Taco Bells, Burger Kings and KFCs you'll find around the city. These, and the remaining sodas – where you can pick up a simple *casado* or sandwich for under $5 – represent the cheapest eating options. Just above them on the price

Café Mundo >>

scale are the bakeries and cafés catering to the Ticos' sweet tooth and serving export-standard coffee.

At the top end the cuisine is more varied and more imaginative but also more expensive, with prices inflated by a 13 per cent food tax and a 10 per cent service tax, added automatically.

Restaurants

Unless otherwise stated, you can expect to pay around $6–8 for main courses; $30–35 for a full meal for two with wine.

Los Antojitos, Centro Comercial Cocorí, Av 0, **t** 225 9525. A fun kitschy Mexican opposite the Mall San Pedro, this is popular with the city's youth. As is often the case with Mexican restaurants, the cuisine has been adapted to suite local tastes, so what you get is a sort of Mexa-Tico hybrid of (cheap and filling) *burritos*, *enchiladas* and *casados*. It makes a good (if noisy) weekend pit-stop when mariachi bands perform.

Ave Fenix, San Pedro, 150 east of Mall San Pedro, **t** 225 3362. Long-established Szechuan Chinese restaurant just east of the Fuente de la Hispanidad roundabout. It's popular with the local Chinese community – a good sign.

Aya Sofya, Av 0, C 21, **t** 221 7785. San José's only taste of the Middle East – spiced meats and kebabs served with cooling yoghurts and finished off with ultra-thick Turkish coffee.

 **Balcón de Europa >**
Grano de Oro >>

Balcón de Europa, C 9, Av 0/1, **t** 221 4841. A great place to come and see what San José used to look like. The walls are adorned with sepia-tinted pictures of the old city – all dirt tracks, horse carts and trams – alongside framed aphorisms of the 'truth is the child of time' ilk. It's been going since the first decade of the 20th century (the head waiter has been here since 1952) and is still extremely popular, so they must be doing something right. The food is reasonable Italian fare, but you come for the atmosphere.

La Bastille, Av 0, C 22, **t** 255 4994. In an elegant dining space adorned with brightly coloured contemporary art, this is one of the city's top gourmet choices, offering a hybrid French-Italian menu of sherry-infused consommés, caviar, *filet mignon* and sea bass in wine sauce. It's not cheap.

Café Mundo, Av 9, C 15, **t** 222 6190. In a Barrio Amón converted mansion, this has a nice ambience and attracts a young, hip crowd who can sit chatting on its shady outdoor terrace until late into the evening. The food is pretty good too, a 'nouveau' mixture of Italian and Costa Rican staples – the grilled chicken is particularly recommended.

Le Chandelier, Los Yoses, 100m west and 100m south of the ICE building, **t** 225 3980. The directions may be as Costa Rican as they come, but the food is strictly French, and superbly prepared – try the trout with almonds or sea bass in Pernod sauce. Dinner here can be pricey (expect to pay $40–50).

Cocina de Leña, Centro Comercial El Pueblo, **t** 255 1360. The restaurant's ostentatiously 'authentic' rustic décor gives it a bit of a kitschy feel, but this has long been regarded as the best purveyor of Tico food in town, although prices have risen since its move to El Pueblo just north of the city centre over the Río Torres. The menus, which are printed on paper bags, feature such traditional dishes as *pozol* (corn and pork soup), stuffed peppers and plenty of steaks and fish, much of it cooked in the eponymous 'wood oven'.

La Galeria, Los Yoses, behind the Apart-hotel Los Yoses, **t** 234 0850. Specializes in central European (including German and Swiss) cuisine, including a fine line in fondues, in the Los Yoses district next to San Pedro, east of the centre.

Grano de Oro, Hotel Grano de Oro, C 3, Av 2/4, **t** 253 3322. Perhaps the city's best hotel restaurant (not to mention one of the most expensive), this occupies an elegant *hacienda*-style dining space with an open courtyard. The menu is made up of Costa Rican takes on traditional dishes – *filet mignon* stuffed with tropical fruits; lettuce, orange and macadamia nut salad; *piña colada* cheesecake, etc. They also do wonderful margaritas. Non-smoking.

L'Ile de France, Hotel Le Bergerac, C 35, Av 0, **t** 234 7850. Top-notch French restaurant serving up Gallic delicacies – onion soup, rabbit liver pâté, salmon in basil sauce, duckling 'Landais-style'. There's an elegant indoor dining space as well as an outdoor courtyard. Costs above average. *Closed lunch and Sun.*

 L'Ile de France >>

Machu Picchu, C 32, Av 1, **t** 222 7384. Authentic Peruvian cuisine (you can tell it's authentic because of the pictures of llamas on the walls), including a very good seafood *ceviche*. Wash it down with their trademark cocktail, the 'pisco sour' a potent combination of pisco, lemon juice, egg whites, sugar and aromatic bitters.

Marbella, San Pedro, Centro Comercial Calle Real, **t** 224 9452. The city's best Spanish restaurant is renowned for its paellas, although its salads and steaks aren't bad either.

Parrillada El Churrasco, Barrio Escalante, 500m east and 100m north of Santa Teresita church, **t** 228 1598. A meat-lover's paradise serving huge juicy steaks and burgers cooked up on an outdoor grill.

La Piazzetta, Av 0, C 38, **t** 222 7896. Near Parque la Sabana on the Paseo Colón, this has a reputation as one of the finest Italians in town. It certainly serves an excellent range of pizzas, *antipasti*, soups, seafood and risottos and has an extensive wine list.

Il Pomodoro, San Pedro, 100m north of San Pedro Church, **t** 224 0966. Lively raucous pizzeria always filled with students and revellers from local bars tucking into giant pizzas and great tankards of beer. It's pretty cheap, especially if you share (the pizzas are big).

Tin-Jo, C 11, Av 6/8, **t** 221 7605. This is always recommended by local hotels. Perhaps because it serves Chinese, Malaysian, Japanese, Thai, Indian and Vietnamese cuisine, they figure it's probably got something for everyone. It's certainly very elegantly laid out, and they do a very good green curry.

Zermatt, Av 11, C 23, **t** 222 0604. Costa Rica's finest Swiss restaurant (although, to be fair, there's not that much competition) serves up all manner of fondues – *fondue bourguignonne* (with chunks of veal), *fondue du pêcheur* (fish fondue) – as well as some very good seafood dishes.

Sodas and Cheap Eats

Manolo's Churrería, Av 0, C 0/2. As with Chelles (below), this 24hr café is popular with the late-night crowd. There's a cheap downstairs café (famed for its *churros* and black bean soup) with tables on the pavement under an awning, and a slightly more formal restaurant upstairs adorned with tiles, which serves good grilled meats.

Soda Castro, Av 10, C 2/4. Great local neighbourhood family soda with a kids' play areas, offering *casados* and sandwiches for around $2–3. Kids they approve of, but don't get any ideas about making your own, certainly not any time soon; public displays of affection are banned here.

Soda Chelles, Av 0, C 9, **t** 221 1369. Open 24 hours, this downtown stalwart is the place to eat yourself sober after a hard night's drinking (try their excellent Cuban sandwich), while in the day it makes a good spot to sit and watch the world go by along this pedestrianized stretch of the Avenida Central. The décor and food are simple and basic.

Soda Isabel, C 19, Av 9. Archetypal street-corner soda that's as much a meeting point for the local community as a place to eat. Cheap, simple Tico fare – sandwiches, pastries and *casados* – and raucous conversation. There's also a kiosk selling food on the go.

Soda Tapia, C 42. Next to the busy ring road across from Parque la Sabana (which you can just make out through the constant procession of cars and trucks), this is a popular late-night hangout. The menu is more fast food than traditional soda fare, offering good burgers and sandwiches.

La Vasconia, Av 1, C 3/5. The food is cheap (*casados* start around $2), basic and filling, but varied with a huge range of dishes on their ever-changing chalkboard menu. Crowded at lunch.

Cafés

Café Britt, Teatro Nacional, Av 2, C 3/5. The Teatro Nacional's in-house café is a very grand affair, and its rarefied European-style elegance provides a neat contrast to the bustling human maelstrom of the Plaza de la Cultura just outside its windows. Serves wonderfully decadent cakes and export-standard coffee from the famous Café Britt Finca (*see* pp.142–3).

Café Parisienne, Gran Hotel Costa Rica, Av 2, C 3/5. San José's prime people-watching spot since the 1930s, Café Parisienne sits on the Plaza de la Cultura, just across from the Teatro Nacional. Its outdoor tables are a

⭐ **Café Britt** >>

great place to while away an afternoon while dickie-bowed waiters ply you with coffee and cake.

News Café, Av 0, C 7/9. Another good place to sit and watch the world go by, the News Café is on the ground floor of the Hotel Presidente overlooking a pedestrianized stretch of the Avenida Central. It serves simple meals as well as coffee in the traditional style.

Spoon, Av 0, C 5/7 and several other locations. Long the favoured pit-stop of harassed workers popping in for a quick coffee and a slice of cake before heading back to the office. Offers a wide selection of sticky treats, which you order by filling out a printed form.

Vishnu, Branches at Av 1, C 1/3; Av 3 C1; Av 8, C 9/11. One of the city's few vegetarian options, this self-service cafeteria sells all manner of soups, salads and *casados* as well as tasty fruit *refrescos*. The vegetarian club sandwich is a very reasonable c1,475.

Entertainment in San José

Theatre

San José has a vibrant theatre scene, although this is coming under increasing threat owing to cuts in subsidy. Most performances are in Spanish, and many of the larger institutions, particularly the Teatro Nacional and Teatro Mélico Salazar, also stage a full repertoire of classical music and dance. For listings, see the *Tico Times*.

Teatro Nacional, Plaza de la Cultura, Av 2, C 3, t 252 0863, *www.intent.co.cr*. The proud creation of the city's 19th-century coffee élite (*see* p.106), the elegant auditorium is still the city's (and the country's) pre-eminent venue for classical music, opera and ballet.

Teatro Mélico Salazar, C 0, Av 2, t 221 4952. The most prestigious venue, after the Nacional, this 1920s theatre stages a wide range of dramatic events, including native dance performances.

Teatro Arlequin, C 13, Av 0/2, t 221 5485. New dramatic and comedic works.

Teatro de Bellas Artes, School of Fine Arts, University of Costa Rica, San Pedro, t 207 4327. High-standard student productions in this open-air venue. Also stages classical concerts.

Teatro de la Aduana, Av 3, C 25, t 257 8305, *www.cntnet.co.cr*. Home of the National Theatre Company.

Teatro El Angel, Av 0, C 13/15, t 222 8258. Chilean drama company specializing in musicals and comedies.

Teatro Eugene O'Neill, C 37, Av 0/1, t 207 7554, *www.cccncr.com*. Hosts performances staged under the auspices of the North American-Costa Rican Cultural Center.

Teatro Laurence Olivier, Av 2, C 28, t 222 1034. Jack-of-all-trades arts venue that stages concerts and art exhibitions as well as theatrical performances.

Cinemas

Most of San José's cinemas show US blockbusters, usually with Spanish subtitles, although occasionally dubbed. There are also a couple of good arthouse cinemas. Check the *Tico Times* for listings and language options.

Cinemark Escazú, Multiplaza Mall, t 288 1111, *www.cinemark.com*.

El Semáforo, San Pedro, 80m west of Liceo Vargas Calvo, t 253 9126. Spanish and Latin American productions only.

Magaly, C 23, Av 0/1, t 223 0085.

Multicines San Pedro, Mall San Pedro, t 280 9585.

Omni, C 3, Av 0/1, t 221 7903.

Outlet Mall, San Pedro, Av 0, opposite San Pedro church, t 234 8868.

Sala Garbo, Av 2, C 28, t 223 1960. Arthouse and independent films.

Nightlife in San José

San José is absolutely packed full of bars, although, as with any big city, for the best places it's always wise to go where the locals go. The bars in downtown San José cater mainly to tourists, and, indeed, many cater to tourists looking to buy a little bit more than a drink. A man standing at the bar in any downtown drinking hole, particularly those on Avenida 1 between Calles 9 and 3, will soon find himself attracting a steady stream of female admirers. The scantily clad young ladies vying for attention are not being 'flirtatious', they're looking to do a little 'business'. Prostitution is legal in Costa Rica and, in its capital, extremely prevalent.

Native Josefinos tend to head out to Los Yoses, El Pueblo or the student quarter of San Pedro to do their drinking. Here, the bars are relaxed and friendly, with many becoming impromptu discos come midnight at weekends, although there are also several dedicated clubs for which you'll have to pay a small cover charge (usually around $4). The music tends to be a lively combination of Latin beats, American hits and reggae. The dress code is relaxed, with little sense of élitism. Bars tend to close early during the week (11pm), but are usually open till the early hours at weekends. You need to be at least 18 to drink. San José also has one of the most visible gay nightlife scenes in Central America.

Casinos

24hr casinos, where you can play roulette, poker, craps and 21 (a Tico rules version of blackjack) are operated by several of the larger hotels including the Gran Hotel Costa Rica, Aurola Holiday Inn and the Hotel Del Rey. However, as is the case with the bars, many downtown establishments have a dual-edged purpose, acting as semi-official pick-up joints for the city's sizeable prostitute population. It's probably best to stick to those establishments operated by the larger international chains away from the centre.

Bars, Discos and Live Music

Bar Rio, Boulevard Los Yoses, **t** 225 8371. Popular, noisy sports bar. The outside terrace is for talking and watching the Avenida Central, while the inside is for watching whichever football match is showing on its assortment of TVs (apart from at weekends, when the crowds move to the dance floor at the rear). Live music is staged on Tuesdays and some weekends.

Chelles, Av 0, C 9, **t** 221 1369. Not the most relaxing of venues with its harsh strip lighting – but this is still a popular late-night spot, especially once all the other clubs have wound down.

Cielo, Av 1, C 21, **t** 222 7419. In the past couple of years, this has taken over from El Cuartel opposite (see below) as downtown's hippest bar. It has a more laid-back vibe than its rival, with a funky upstairs lounge bar, and is one of the best places to meet Ticos.

Cocoloco, Centro Comercial El Pueblo, **t** 222 8782. Latin and reggae beats pre-dominate at this perennial El Pueblo favourite. It can get very sweaty and intense at weekends.

El Cuartel de la Boca del Monte, Av 1, C 21, **t** 221 0327. This big, brash neon-clad restaurant-cum-bar has long been a firm favourite with the city's youth, who flock here on Mondays and at weekends – when live bands and Djs play – to sweat it out till the small hours on the venue's small (and generally packed) dance floor. It's one of the few places in town that still serves *bocas* – mini-snacks, Costa Rican tapas.

Déjà Vu, C 2, Av 14/16, **t** 223 3758. The city's most famous gay venue has two large dance floors and a happy, fun atmosphere. The only downside is that it's in a slightly insalubrious area – best to take a taxi.

Gravity, Centro Comercial El Pueblo, **t** 233 5516. Pumpingly popular disco in among a glut of similar El Pueblo places. There are several dance floors (the one on the top floor is open-air), all of which are packed to bursting at weekends, with DJs serving up a mixture of salsa, reggae and US hits.

Jazz Café, San Pedro, next to the Banco Popular, **t** 253 8933. Dedicated to all things jazz, with live bands performing most nights from 10pm onwards. There's a cover charge of around $8.

Meridiano al Este, Av 0, C 21, **t** 256 2705. Upmarket, earnestly intellectual restaurant, bar and arts venue that puts on a variety of concerts and shows by local acts – jazz, Latin music, a capella groups, spoken word, etc.

Salsa 54, C 3, Av 1/3, **t** 233 3814. The city's best dancers come here to cut a rug to hip-shaking Latin beats. It can be fun watching, although joining in can be a bit intimidating (they are very good).

Terra U, San Pedro, 100m east of San Pedro church, **t** 225 4261. The current pick of San Pedro's discos, Terra U is spread over three open-air floors, each with its own dance floor and all blaring out a different style of music – salsa, reggae, hip hop, etc.

La Villa, San Pedro, 150m north of the old Banco Anglo, **t** 280 9541. Always full of students and intellectuals putting the world to rights. The music is laid-back, alternative and background to let the conversation flow.

Valle Central

What Costa Rica is to the natural biodiversity of the Americas, the Valle Central is to the country's cultural institutions, political establishment and human population – it's the bottleneck, where everything and seemingly everybody ends up. Just as the country of Costa Rica, though accounting for less than 0.1 per cent of the world's land mass, supports some four per cent of the world's known species of flora and fauna, so the Valle Central is home to two-thirds of the country's population and nearly all of its human infra-structure, despite amounting to less than six per cent of its area.

09

Don't miss

⭐ **An introduction to coffee beans**
Café Britt Finca **p.142**

⭐ **Seeking jaguars and quetzals**
Parque Nacional Braulio Carrillo **p.143**

⭐ **Bubbling crater**
Parque Nacional Volcán Poás **p.136**

⭐ **Moonlike dream landscapes**
Volcán Irazú **p.150**

⭐ **A guided tour of the jungle canopy**
Rainforest Aerial Tram **p.146**

See map overleaf

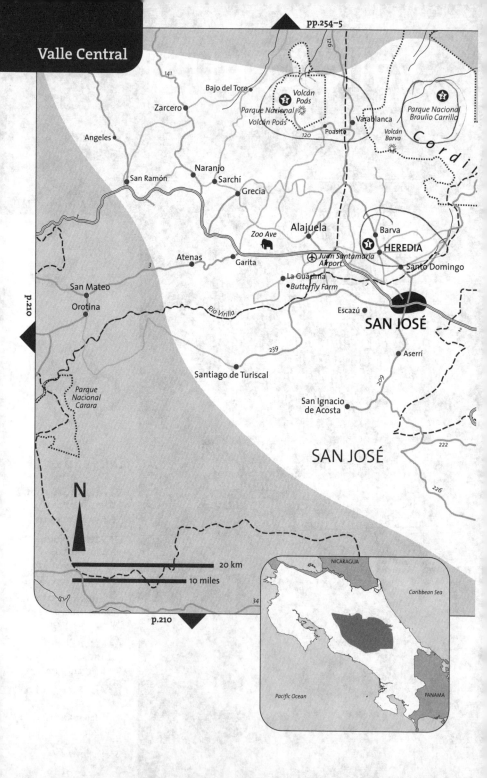

p.210

p.210

141

126

Bajo del Toro

Volcán
Poás

Parque Nacional
Volcán Poás

Parque Nacional
Braulio Carrillo

Zarcero

120

Vārablanca

Poasito

Angeles

Volcán
Barva

Cordi

Naranjo

San Ramón

Sarchí

Grecia

Barva

Zoo Ave

Alajuela

HEREDIA

Atenas

Garita

Juan Santamaría
Airport

Santo Domingo

La Guácima
Butterfly Farm

3

San Mateo

Río Virilla

Escazú

Orotina

SAN JOSÉ

239

Aserrí

209

Santiago de Turiscal

San Ignacio
de Acosta

Parque
Nacional
Carara

222

SAN JOSÉ

226

N

20 km

10 miles

34

NICARAGUA

Caribbean Sea

Pacific Ocean

PANAMA

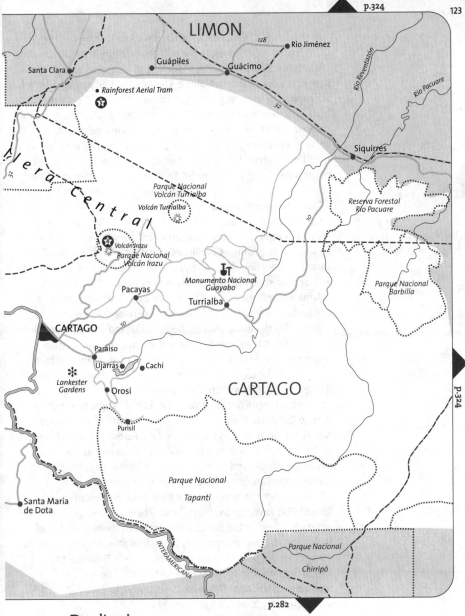

Don't miss

⭐1 Café Britt Finca **p.142**

⭐2 Parque Nacional Braulio Carrillo **p.143**

⭐3 Parque Nacional Volcán Poás **p.136**

⭐4 Volcán Irazú **p.150**

⭐5 Rainforest Aerial Tram **p.146**

At the centre of Costa Rican affairs since the founding of the original Spanish colony here in the mid-16th century, the Valle Central today is home to the country's four largest cities: San José (covered in the previous chapter), **Alajuela**, **Heredia** and **Cartago**, all of which are capitals of their respective provinces. Inevitably, it's the most built-up and urban of Costa Rica's regions, although perhaps less so than you might expect, given the statistics. San José's metropolitan sprawl aside, none of the cities is of an overwhelming size, and they might more accurately be described as towns. Furthermore, owing to the area's geographical peculiarities, the cities all lie very close together, with the most outlying, Cartago, just 22km from San José.

Despite its name, the Central Valley is technically classified as an 'inter-mountain plateau', and is often referred to locally as the **Meseta Central** or 'Central Tableland'. To the north lies the volcanic mountain range of the **Cordillera Central**, which boasts two of the country's most famous (and most visited) peaks, Poás and Irazú, while to the south are the northern slopes of the **Cordillera de Talamanca**. This means that the region's cities actually occupy a comparatively small area of flat land in between the two ranges (a sort of bottleneck within the bottleneck). As a consequence, the region is a good deal more rural than the size of its population might suggest. Aside from the coffee plantations lining the mountains' lower slopes, from which the region (and indeed the country) derives much of its wealth, the region is home to four large national parks – the **Parque Nacional Volcán Poás** and **Parque Nacional Braulio Carrillo** to the north of the urban heartland, the **Parque Nacional Volcán Irazú** to the east and the **Parque Nacional Tapantí** to the southeast – and several smaller ones, as well as a whole host of private refuges and reserves including the La Paz Waterfall Gardens, the Rainforest Aerial Tram and Lankester Gardens.

To the east of the region's urban heartland, the beautiful, heavily forested **Río Reventazón** churns its way between the two mountain ranges heading for the Caribbean coast. With several sections of rapids, the river has become very popular with white-water rafters, many of whom base themselves in the town of **Turrialba**, the region's main water sports centre. Just north of here is the **Monumento Nacional Guayabo**, the country's largest and most significant pre-Columbian settlement.

San José aside, the region's cities and towns are not in themselves great tourist attractions, being rather functional (not to say ugly) and boasting few tourist facilities, although they can make convenient bases for exploring nearby attractions. Alajuela, which lies less than 3km from the country's main international airport, has the best selection of hotels. The region's most pleasant (not to mention most scenic) accommodation, however, is provided by the rural lodges that dot the region, particularly near Poás, Irazú and Turrialba.

Getting around the Valle Central

As with much of the country, travelling around the Central Valley can be a tricky proposition. Though **driving** affords the greatest degree of freedom, it can be quite a challenge finding your way along narrow, winding, congested, poorly signposted, unlit roads.

Public transport offers greater peace of mind – and is also significantly cheaper – but there are still a couple of attractions, most notably Irazú (during the week) and the Parque Nacional Tapantí, which do not as yet have a bus service. For this reason, multi-destination **organized tours**, of which there is a multitude offered out of San José (*see* pp.68–9), often represent the best way of getting to see the region's attractions.

History

This is where it all began, at least in terms of modern Costa Rica. The Valle Central's fertile slopes – its soils regularly replenished by the ash popping out of the top of the region's still (semi-)active volcanoes – were the site of the Spanish Empire's first sustainable colony in the 'Rich Coast'. Juan Vásquez de Coronado established the country's founding colony and capital (Cartago) here in the name of the Spanish crown in the 1560s, although, as related in the **History** chapter, the next three centuries would not prove to be the most auspicious for the Spanish settlers.

By the time the colony was up and running, the native population, which the Spanish had hoped to enslave and put to work on its farms, had either fled or (ironically) died of diseases brought over by the Europeans, forcing the Spanish to toil their own fields, with limited success. With no enslaved population to help them and little idea about what crops to grow in the Central Valley's tropical climes, the Spanish were able to achieve little more than subsistence agriculture. There was no export economy to speak of.

Spain itself, after its initial push to colonize, soon lost interest when the riches it had counted on flowing from the new colony failed to materialize, with the result that there was little further investment from the mother country. Costa Rica's infrastructure remained at the most basic of levels until well into the 19th century. Perhaps nothing sums up the situation so well as the currency. From the early 1700s till the 1850s, most transactions that weren't purely barter were conducted using cacao beans. The majority of Spanish settlers were overwhelmingly poor, living a hand-to-mouth existence far removed from the promises of untrammelled wealth that had prompted their arrival in the first place and had been the inspiration for the creation (and naming) of the new country.

Life in the colony was hard and its growth slow. Nonetheless, some growth did take place with new towns being founded – Heredia in 1706, San José in 1737 and Alajuela in 1782 – although these remained little more than collections of dusty back streets until well into the 19th century. Settlement of the country's more outlying regions was almost non-existent. Though the country's borders stretched from the Atlantic to the Pacific ocean and from Panama in the south to

Nicaragua in the north, the vast majority of settlers then, as now, were concentrated in the country's Central Valley heartland.

Historians often point to this period as the time when Costa Rica's famously egalitarian society was formed, claiming that the lack of racial tensions (which came about largely because the native population was no longer there) and the absence of a class system in the first few centuries of the country's existence (it's difficult to assume social airs when you're using beans to buy things) served to limit the development of a rigid social hierarchy. In truth, if Costa Rican society was a level playing field when there was no wealth to be had, that field soon began to turn into a hill, and social stratifications soon emerged once wealth did finally become available, three centuries after the first settlers' arrival.

That wealth came about as a direct result of the introduction of coffee from Jamaica in the early 19th century. The coffee plants, unlike most other crops the settlers had tried, thrived in the Central Valley's highlands. The crop's success, and the potential for viable agriculture it promised, served to send the government slightly giddy with excitement. Vast inducements were now offered to the region's farmers – in the form of free land, tax breaks and supplies of seedlings – in order to get them to turn their land over to coffee production. Happily, the government's keenness paid off. By the 1830s, the Central Valley's coffee harvest was already large enough for export, and by the 1840s – when the lucrative London market opened up – it looked as if Costa Rica had finally hit the big time. Wealth, growth, urban construction – all the things the settlers had been waiting for for 300 years – seemed to be finally within their grasp.

Once the coffee money started pouring in, so the region's towns began to grow, although one town, San José (which had taken over from Cartago as the nation's capital in the 1820s), grew at a significantly faster rate than the others, prompted in no small part by the activities of the newly wealthy coffee-growing barons. The country's first social élite poured so much money into San José's regeneration that, by the end of the 19th century, the region's other three cities, Alajuela, Heredia and Cartago, had been reduced almost to the status of satellite towns.

Though this urban growth has continued unabated in the 20th century, the Central Valley remains an overwhelmingly rural area. Its four cities occupy a compact urban heartland at its centre, surrounded by the coffee terraces that still make up the region's principal agricultural industry (albeit now augmented by fruit plantations and cattle ranches) as well as large tracts of unspoilt forest contained within the national parks of Poás, Braulio Carrillo, Irazú and Tapantí.

Alajuela and Around

Alajuela, 18km north of San José, is often described as a sort of San José in miniature, although a more accurate description might be a San José stuck in a time warp, or a San José shorn of the majority of its modern influences. Take away all the billboards, malls, fast food eateries, car dealerships and most of the vehicles and people from downtown San José, and what you'd be left with would be a pretty fair approximation of San José in the 1970s. Or Alajuela now.

Alajuela may be the second largest city in Costa Rica, but it's still just a fraction of the size of San José, with just over 200,000 inhabitants (compared with over a million). It's a quiet, sleepy place and seemingly always has been. Though founded in the late 18th century, Alajuela has, with just one notable exception, created little in the way of history. No buildings from the city's earliest times survive, and for the most part it has been happy to muddle along in the background. A small agricultural town, its fortunes have, in the main, been tied into the health of the local fruit and coffee plantations, rather than the machinations of government. It has taken a leading role in national affairs just twice: first during the Civil War of the 1820s, when it sided with San José against Cartago and Heredia, and later, and most famously, during the 1856 war against the invading mercenary William Walker (*see* p.24); Alajuela was the birthplace of the national hero, Juan Santamaría, the drummer boy whose arsonist capabilities secured the country's future against the American invaders.

In recent decades, the exponential growth of San José's suburbs has threatened to swallow Alajuela up entirely, although for the time being it remains a separate entity – the capital city's quieter, less ostentatious sibling. Alajuela may have few attractions of its own – the most notable are the Juan Santamaría Museum, which details the story of the 1856 war, and a large farmers' market, known as the *mayoreo*, held every Saturday – little nightlife and, as yet, no tourist office, but its proximity to the international airport just 3km south means that it has a decent selection of hotels. It's also a good deal less smoggy and traffic-filled than San José and, because it occupies an elevation some 200m lower, slightly warmer, making it

Orientation

The Parque Central marks the nexus of the city's street grid system, which, as with San José, is made up of numbered streets, with *calles* running north–south and *avenidas* running east–west. Avenida 1 traverses the Parque's northern edge, Avenida Central (0) its southern, Calle Central (0) its eastern and Calle 2 its western. Again, as with San José, road numbers ascend in twos, with even-numbered *calles* heading west and odd-numbered *calles* heading east. And, again as with San José, locals pay almost no notice to this system whatsoever when giving directions, preferring to use prominent landmarks, such as the Parque Central, the Mercado Central and the Museo Juan Santamaría.

Getting to Alajuela

Buses from San José (where you're most likely to be arriving from) are quick (35mins, although this can rise to over an hour at peak times), cheap (c220) and plentiful (every 5–10mins, 5am–midnight). Two bus companies currently provide a service: **Tuasa**, whose buses depart from Av 2, C 12/14 in San José, arriving at Alajuela's main bus terminal at Av 0, C 8/10, four blocks west of the centre; and **Station Wagon**, which departs from Av 2, C 10/12 in San José, arriving at Av 4, C 2/4 in Alajuela, two blocks south of the centre.

A **taxi** from San José to Alajuela should cost $12–20 depending on the traffic and the time of day. Be sure to stress to the driver that you want to visit the 'town' of Alajuela, otherwise they may take you to the airport. Unless you state a specific destination (such as a hotel), you'll be dropped off by the taxi rank on the south side of the Parque Central.

Getting to Alajuela by **car** is pretty straightforward. From San José, head north up the General Cañas Highway for 17km, then turn right for Alajuela. Whatever you do, avoid turning left for the underpass or you'll end up at the airport.

Getting around and away from Alajuela

Tourist Alajuela is tiny, with all the main sites (such as they are) and hotels grouped together within just a few blocks, making **walking** by far the easiest way of getting around. For seeing attractions beyond the city centre, **driving** is the simplest and most practical solution (although it's not without its difficulties), particularly for outlying sites, such as Volcán Poás. Though there are no car hire offices in town – the nearest being at Juan Santamaría Airport and San José – several of the town's hotels can arrange hire and drop-off for you.

Buses depart from Alajuela's main terminal at Av 1, C 8/10 for all the major local sites including La Guácima Butterfly Farm, Café Britt Finca, Sarchí and Volcán Poás (although not for the La Paz Waterfall Gardens). However, the easiest way to take in the greatest number of attractions in the shortest period of time is to go on an **organized tour**. Several of Alajuela's hotels offer multi-destination tours, or you can consult one of the plethora of tour operators in San José (*see* pp.69–9).

Taxis are available from the south side of the Parque Central, but only make economic sense for trips to attractions in the local vicinity – such as the Butterfly Farm ($12) or San José itself ($15) – or for more outlying attractions if you're travelling in a large group.

a nice place to base yourself while exploring some of the nearby attractions, which include the La Guácima Butterfly Farm and Zoo Ave, just a few kilometres away, the arts and crafts centre of Sarchí to the northwest, and the Parque Nacional Volcán Poás, which lies due north along Highway 130.

Sightseeing in Alajuela

There's not a great deal to Alajuela. Anything you might possibly want to see is either on, or within a few blocks' walk of, the **Parque Central**, the official centre of the city. As is usually the case, the Parque is not a park at all, but a square, albeit quite a pleasant one. Heart of the city it may be, but this is still a fairly sleepy, quiet place with a pedestrianized centre bedecked with mango trees and dotted with benches where you can relax in the afternoon sun. There's also a bandstand where brass bands play on Sunday mornings.

The Parque is flanked by some sturdy, distinguished-looking colonial-era buildings. To the east is the city's 19th-century **cathedral**, which, though by no means ugly, has a sort of make-do aesthetic to it, as exemplified by its corrugated iron cupola. The neo-Baroque

1930s **Iglesia de Santo Cristo de La Agonía**, five blocks east of the park, has an interior adorned with naïve Latin American art and is a good deal prettier. The **Mercado Central**, a sort of smaller, slightly less bustling version of the one in San José, lies a block west of the Parque Central and is a good source of cheap food.

On the square's north side stands the city's former prison, which has been turned into the town's main tourist attraction, the **Museo Histórico Cultural Juan Santamaría**, named after the city's most famous son, who played the defining role in perhaps the most famous event in the country's history. In 1856, when the country looked as if it was about to be conquered by the American adventurer, William Walker, it was Juan Santamaría, a lowly drummer boy from Alajuela, who turned the conflict in Costa Rica's favour by setting fire to Walker's Nicaraguan stronghold, forcing him to flee. Santamaría died performing this action, instantly turning himself into a national hero (*see* **History**, p.24).

The museum that bears his name tells the story of the conflict from Walker's initial incursions into Central America (which he hoped to turn into a slave state serving US interests) to his eventual defeat. Exhibits include period paintings (including several 19th-century representations of Santamaría, as often as not holding aloft a flaming torch), uniforms, maps, compasses and weapons.

The museum also houses a small theatre where lectures are given and, outside, an orchid garden.

Museo Histórico Cultural Juan Santamaría
Av 1, C 0/2; t 441 4775, www.mhcjs.go.cr; open Tues–Sun 10–6

09 Valle Central | Alajuela

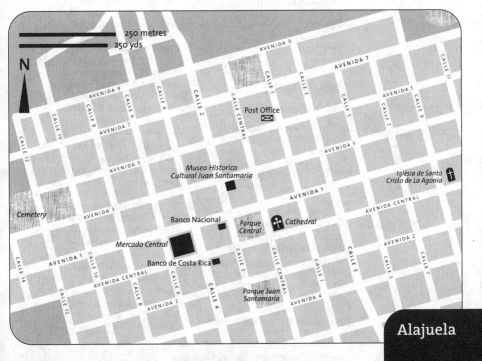

Alajuela

Tourist Information in Alajuela

As it stands, there isn't any, at least not in Alajuela itself. Many of the city's hotels do offer tours of local attractions and can provide tourist information, although they obviously tend to be biased in favour of their own services. Otherwise, your best bet is to find out what you can from the tourist office in San José before arriving.

Services in Alajuela

Banks: Banco de Costa Rica, Av 0, C4; Banco Nacional C 2, Av 0/1.
Supermarket: Mas X Menos, Av 0, C 0/2.
Post office: Av 5, C 1.

Festivals and Events in Alajuela

There's an annual arts and crafts fair held here every July, known as the *Fiesta de los Mangos*, but the city's biggest blowout takes place on and around 11 April, the national holiday celebrating the country's victory at the 1856 **Battle of Rivas** (and, in particular, honouring the role played by Juan Santamaría) which, unsurprisingly, is celebrated with an especially intense fervour in Alajuela – parades, parties, fireworks, etc.

Where to Stay in Alajuela

Alajuela may be small, but its proximity to the airport means that its hotels attract a good deal more trade than a town of this size might normally expect. It's therefore a good idea to book in advance, especially if your visit is going to coincide with the national holiday on 11 April.

(★) Xandari >

Xandari, 6km north of Alajuela, signposted off the main road to Poás, **t** 684 7879, *www.xandari.com* ($$$$$; $175). The Xandari is not just the best hotel in the Alajuela area, it's also one of the very best hotels in the whole of Costa Rica. Enjoying an unsurpassed setting in the hills north of the city, the Xandari occupies vast grounds that contain both a coffee plantation and a stretch of forest (complete with five waterfalls), with marked trails through both. At the estate's centre are 17 'designer' villas, the décor and design of which – a combination of Central American rainforest motifs and Western-style abstract expressionism – are the work of Californian architect Sherrill Broudy. The standard villas are supremely luxurious, the ultra villas even more so – vast bathrooms, huge beds and balconies providing stunning views out over Alajuela. Guests have the use of two pools, a Jacuzzi, a spa and a top-notch restaurant. Tours of local attractions, including Poás. Low-season rates start from $145.

Orquideas Inn, 5km west of Alajuela, signposted off the road to Grecia, **t** 443 9346, **f** 443 9740, *www.orquideasinn. com* ($$$$; $99). This delightful rural lodge has been specifically designed to resemble an authentic Spanish inn (the main exception being the Marilyn Monroe-themed restaurant), offering large, air-conditioned, wooden-floored rooms (several with volcano views), lush gardens, a pool, a gift shop and tour desk.

Hampton Inn Aeropuerto, t 443 0043, *www.hamptonhotel.co.cr* ($$$; $75). Just a kilometre east of the airport (free transfer offered), this large US-style hotel is now the main dormitory for people with early-morning flights to catch. The rooms are bland and generic, but perfectly suited to their function as airport stopovers with soundproofing, air-conditioning and cable TV. There's also a small pool and a cocktail lounge.

Hotel 1915, C 2, Av 5/7, **t** 440 7163, **f** 441 0495 ($$$; $55). A pretty hotel set in what used to be the owner's family house, with good, spacious rooms (all with private bathrooms) lining a plant-filled courtyard where breakfast is served. There's also a separate self-catering apartment sleeping up to six ($105). Parking available.

Los Volcanes, Av 3, C 0/2, **t** 441 0525, **f** 440 8006, *www.montezuma expeditions.com/hotel.htm* ($$$; $45). This friendly establishment, just north of the Museo Juan Santamaría, is the headquarters of Montezuma Expeditions, who organize tours to all the major sites in the region. The ooms are a touch on the small side, but clean and well maintained, and those without bathrooms are just $35.

Charly's Hotel, Av 5, C 2/0, **t/f** 441 0115, www.charlysplacehotel.com ($$; $35). Attracting a mainly American clientele, Charly's has 13 smallish rooms (some with private showers), as well as a couple of larger rooms that sleep up to six. There's also a small restaurant, a kitchen and tour desk.

Hostel Cortéz Azul, Av 5, C 2/4, **t** 443 6145, hostelcorteazul@yahoo.com ($; $15). Backpackers' favourite with basic (but clean) rooms – shared bathrooms only – a communal kitchen, laundry and Internet access.

Eating Out in Alajuela

Though you won't find the same level of choice here as you will in San José, there are still a reasonable number of eating options. In addition to the town's legion of street-corner sodas, Alajuela also has a growing number of international restaurants, including an Italian, a couple of Mexicans, a Chinese and even a McDonald's on the south side of the Parque Central.

Unless otherwise stated, expect to pay around $6–8 for main courses, $30–35 for a full meal for two with wine.

Ambrosia Café, Av 5, C 2. Italian-style café offering a decent range of pastries, sandwiches and coffees. There's a pleasant outdoor patio.

Heladería Soda, Av 0, C 6. This no-nonsense soda on the corner of the Mercado Central is a great source of ceviche, casados and local gossip.

Primer Sabor, A3, C2/4. Alajuela's most exotic offering is this reasonably priced Chinese in the hotel district just west of the museum. A few Tico and international dishes have been added to the otherwise authentic menu to cater to local tastes.

Restaurante Mixto Vegetariano, Av 0, C 2/4. Just west of the Parque Central on the second floor, the 'Mixto' is a clean and bright self-service café specializing in vegetarian versions of Tico staples.

Taco Miendo, C4, A 8/10. The pick of the town's Mexican restaurants, Taco offers the usual spicy fare – burritos, enchiladas, fajitas, etc. – as well as killer margaritas.

Entertainment and Nightlife in Alajuela

Alajuela's small cultural scene is centred on the **Museo Juan Santamaría**, which stages occasional concerts (mainly jazz and classical), and the small **Carpe Diem Theater**, **t** 442 7773, which puts on Spanish language plays.

As for nightlife, Alajuela is no party town, with few late-opening bars, although some of the restaurants do keep extended hours. Things are slightly more lively away from the centre. **La Jarra Garibaldi**, **t** 441 6708, ten blocks west of the Parque Central on the corner of Av 0 and Calle de la Feria, is a popular drinking spot, serving Mexican snacks and offering live music and dancing on Wednesdays, Fridays and Saturdays. There are also a couple of clubs on the road to the airport including **El Spectro**, located above **Pub 99**, **t** 440 1828, and the nearby **Bongo**, both of which offer several dance floors, live music and bocas. Both charge a cover of around $3.

South of Alajuela

La Guácima Butterfly Farm

La Guácima Butterfly Farm t 438 0400, www.butterflyfarm.co.cr; open daily 8.30–5; tours 9am, 11am, 1pm and 3pm; adm exp

About 8km southwest of Alajuela, this may be one of the region's main tourist attractions, but the vast butterfly ranch is first and foremost a commercial operation. While the idea of tying the fluttering elusive beauty of the butterfly to the demands of big business might not seem immediately obvious, whoever thought of it was clearly onto something. The Butterfly Farm, which when it

Getting to La Guácima

To get to the farm by **car** from Alajuela, take the airport road south and then follow signs for La Guácima. Otherwise, **buses** leave from San José, Av 1, C 20/22, at 11am and 2pm, and from Alajuela, C 8, Av 2, at 9am, 11am and 1pm (the bus sign should say 'La Guácima Abajo'). The Butterfly Farm also organizes its own tours with hotel pick-up, which can be combined with a visit to the Café Britt Finca (*see* pp.142–3).

opened in the early 1980s was the first of its type in Latin America, today breeds its multicoloured charges on an industrial scale for export to zoos and botanical gardens around the world. Everything about this place seems to work with mechanized precision – a consequence of the extreme brevity of the butterfly's lifespan. Breeding cycles have been carefully synchronized so that the pupae of dozens of different species can be ready for packing and export every Monday (it's the pupae rather than the butterflies themselves that are sold). Two-hour guided tours are offered throughout the day, in a multitude of languages including Spanish, English, French and German. These begin with an audiovisual presentation before you head off to the farm itself, a genuinely fascinating place comprising a series of tropical gardens where thousands of brightly coloured fluttering butterflies are carefully nurtured. Bright, sunny days are the best time to see the creatures in all their resplendent glory (they tend not to fly if it's raining), when, often as not, they'll be joined by a procession of tropical birds.

West and Northwest of Alajuela

Zoo Ave

Zoo Ave
t 433 8989,
www.zooave.org;
open 9–5 daily; adm

If you're planning on going bird-spotting during your time in Costa Rica, but aren't quite up to speed yet on all the different species, it might be worth your while paying a preliminary visit to this aviary 10km west of Alajuela, the largest in Central America, where you can get acquainted with the appearance of some 80 different types of native bird. Impressive as this sounds, it is by no means an exhaustive itinerary; Costa Rica is home to an estimated 850 species. Here you'll meet macaws, parrots, owls, falcons, toucans and more, either living in large cages or flying free in the park's tropical gardens. The zoo, which plays an important role in the captive-breeding of rare species – particularly scarlet macaws – also has a small collection of mammals (including several monkeys) and reptiles.

El Mundo de las Serpientes (The World of Snakes)

El Mundo de los
Serpientes
t 494 3700; open 8–4
daily; adm exp

Just as the Zoo Ave provides the perfect introduction to the country's bird life, so this small snake collection 16km west of Alajuela, 2km south of Grecia acts as a good primer for the country's scalier residents. Of course, familiarizing yourself with the country's

Getting to Zoo Ave and El Mundo de las Serpientes

To get to **Zoo Ave** by **car**, head west along the Interamericana to the Atenas exit, then follow the signs. **Buses** leave for the zoo from Alajuela's main bus terminal throughout the day and take just 15mins. Look for buses bearing the sign '**La Garita**', the name of the small town 5km west of the zoo, which is notable for two things: its famously clement weather and for the **Fiesta del Maiz** restaurant, **t** 487 7957, which serves dishes made only from corn. Strange as it may seem, it's the latter that really draws the crowds.

The **World of Snakes** lies a couple of kilometres south of the small, sleepy agricultural town of **Grecia**, famed for its metal church, on the main Alajuela–Grecia road. Regular **buses** depart for Grecia from San José, Av 4, C 16/18, and from Alajuela's main bus terminal, all of which stop at the menagerie's entrance.

---

various species of snakes does serve a sound practical purpose. Should you be unlucky enough to be bitten during your travels (and you would have to be very unlucky; for more information on snake safety, *see* p.88), it's vital that you correctly identify your attacker so that the correct antivenin can be administered. There are some 45 species on display here, most native to Costa Rica (though there are a couple of foreign interlopers as well) in addition to a few other reptiles. The snakes live in fairly large glass cages, which have been designed to replicate the animals' natural environments as closely as possible. The entrance fee includes a highly informative guided tour (in English) by one of the keepers. This is highly recommended as, it has to be said, a snake that's not eating tends to be a snake that's not moving, unless it's being directly handled by its keeper, who sometimes also lets visitors handle the snakes.

Sarchí

If you've ever wondered where those painted miniature ox-carts you see loitering garishly in hotel lobbies throughout the country come from, then this is your answer. Sarchí, an otherwise unremarkable town in the midst of a coffee-growing valley 30km northwest of Alajuela, has long been the country's main centre of arts and crafts (particularly woodworking). Its streets are lined with factories turning out multicoloured *carretas* (ox-carts) and items of furniture by the thousand for the dozens of tour groups who arrive here daily.

The carts themselves, which in recent times seem to have evolved into the iconic souvenir of the country, were once functional objects, used in the late 19th and early 20th centuries to transport coffee. It's believed that this particular design of cart was originally introduced to the country by settlers from Andalucía in Spain, who painted colourful Moorish-influenced designs on them as a way of denoting ownership. Today, long after the advent of mechanized transport, the carts serve a purely decorative purpose, acting as garden ornaments, lobby statues and bars – the only time you're likely to see a cart in action is during a fiesta. They can be bought in all sizes – from full-size (over $1,000) to miniature ($150–300) – and sport every shade of colour known to man, the simple designs of the original workers having long since been replaced by great Technicolor extravaganzas.

Getting to Sarchí

Three direct **buses** link San José with Sarchí each day, from Av 3, C 16/18, although, as the last two leave after 5pm, only the 12.15pm is a viable option, unless you plan on staying the night. It takes 90mins and costs c370. Otherwise, your best bet is to take one of the more frequent services to Grecia, a few km southeast of Sarchí, which depart from the same stop in San José every half-hour from 5am, and connect there with the Alajuela–Sarchí service, which runs every 25mins from Alajuela's main bus terminal.

Despite the commercialism of the town, Sarchí is still an interesting place to visit. The ox-carts may be produced on an industrial scale – think hi-tech factory rather than back-street workshop – but that's not to say that the process has been entirely mechanized. One of the great joys of visiting here is the chance you get of watching skilled craftsmen at work, assembling furniture (particularly leather rocking chairs, the town's second most popular item, $80–100) and painting patterns on ox-carts. The carts themselves can be disassembled for transportation and most factories offer shipping.

The majority of the factories and showrooms are located in modern Sarchí, known as **Sarchí Sur**. The Río Trojas separates this from the older, residential part of town, **Sarchí Norte**, which will be of less interest to tourists, although it does boast a striking pink and blue church. Showrooms include the **Fábrica de Carretas Joaquín**

Fábrica de Carretas Joaquín Chaverri
t 454 4960

Chaverri near the entrance to Sarchí Sur, the oldest (1903), largest and most famous of the town's ox-cart factories; it is a vast complex where you can watch every size of cart imaginable being assembled and painted. Credit cards are accepted and shipping arranged. There

Plaza de la Artesanía
t 454 4271

is also the **Plaza de la Artesanía** in Sarchí Sur, a large, bustling craft mall laid out around a courtyard with shops selling leatherwork, jewellery, furniture, ceramics and, of course, ox-carts. There are also several restaurants in the mall.

Where to Stay in Sarchí

Touristy as it is, Sarchí has just a handful of hotels; the majority of its visitors tend to arrive on day trips or as part of an organized tour.
Vista del Valle Plantation Inn, 8km south of Sarchí, t 450 0800, *www.vistadelvalle.com* ($$$$$; $135). On the border of the Zona Protectora Río Grande, a small nature reserve with a section of cloudforest, this inn boasts extensive grounds containing coffee and orange plantations, areas of forest, a botanical garden and even a waterfall. The rooms, in the beautiful hardwood house, are well equipped, several having balconies with volcano views. There are also a couple of self-catering cottages as well as a pool, Jacuzzi and

restaurant. Tours of the area and horse-riding ($20) are also offered.
Hotel Zamora, at the northern end of Sarchí, t 454 4596 ($$; $30). Generally regarded as the pick of the small bunch of hotels in town, with large, clean rooms, all with fans and also cable television.

Eating Out in Sarchí

Several of Sarchí's factories have restaurants attached, the best being the **Las Carretas**, next to the Fábrica Joaquin Chaverri, which specializes in Costa Rican cuisine.

There's also a good Mexican, **Helechos**, on the Plaza de la Artesanía, which also doubles as a coffee shop and has seating on the plaza.

Getting to Zarcero

Around a dozen **buses** (roughly hourly) leave San José's La Coca-Cola bus terminal for Zarcero every day. From Alajuela, take one of the services to Naranjo, which leave from Av 1, C 8/10 every half-hour between 6am and 10pm, where you can connect with the San José–Zarcero bus.

Getting to the Los Angeles Cloudforest Reserve

By **car**, the reserve can be reached from the town of **San Ramón**, which lies around 20km south. Follow the signs to the small town of Los Angeles Norte, where you should pick up signs for the Hotel Villa Blanca. If you don't have your own transport, **buses** run from Alajuela to San Ramón every hour, from where you'll have to take a taxi the rest of the way.

Zarcero

Set high on a peak, some 1,740m up, at the western end of the Cordillera Central, the lovely mountain town of Zarcero lies some 52km northwest of Alajuela. With few specific tourist attractions, the rewards of a visit here come from the joyous views the town affords of the soaring mountainous countryside and fertile agricultural slopes, long famed for the quality of the vegetables. Aside from its setting, the town is principally known for the collection of topiary sculptures created outside its church: local landscape gardener Evangelisto Blanco has spent years shaping bushes into all manner of strange shapes – elephants, birds, lightbulbs, etc.

Los Angeles Cloudforest Reserve

Los Angeles Cloudforest Reserve t 228 4603, www.villablanca-costarica.com; open daily 8–5; adm $12 for self-guided tour, $24 with guide

40km northwest of Alajuela, 20km north of San Ramón, this small 20 sq km area of cloudforest occupies a private reserve on land owned by the former Costa Rican president, Rodrigo Carazo. As with its more famous counterpart in Monteverde, the Los Angeles Reserve is mostly made up of dense, Hollywood-style jungle – all sodden, impenetrable foliage and snagging creepers. Its sultry depths are thick with wildlife, although the denseness of the vegetation can make it difficult to pick out individual animals. Access to the refuge

(i) Camara de Turismo Zarcero (CATUZAR) › on the main street, t 463 2120, catuzar@ costarricense.com

Where to Stay in Zarcero

Hotel Don Beto, north side of main square, t/f 463 3137 ($25 shared bathroom, $35 private). The best hotel.

Eating Out in Zarcero

There are a handful of places to eat in town, most clustered around the main square, although these are nothing special. Better fare is provided by **La Cocina de Turno de Doña Chila**, to the south of the town, which conjures up excellent traditional Costa Rican dishes from its wood-fired oven.

Where to Stay and Eat at the Los Angeles Cloudforest Reserve

Hotel Villa Blanca, t 228 4603, *www. villablanca-costarica.com* ($$$$; $75). The refuge's own swish jungle retreat, which consists of a main lodge as well as hotel-style rooms as well as over 40 adobe-style *casitas* nestling in amongst the foliage at the outer limits of the forest – all with baths and fridges. There's also a restaurant serving buffet-style meals for an extra $15 per night.

is via the **Hotel Villa Blanca** (*see* p.135), which is also owned by the former president, from where a couple of short **trails**, marked with wooden walkways, head off into the forest. These can be explored freely, although there's a longer, third trail which extends for 8km and which can only be attempted in the company of a guide. The hotel also offers birdwatching, night and horseback tours for $24 per person. On a different tack entirely, the hotel grounds contain a large church, **La Mariana**, built by the ex-president in honour of the Virgin Mary.

North of Alajuela

Parque Nacional Volcán Poás

⭐ Parque Nacional
Volcán Poás
*t 482 2424; open
daily 8–3.45; adm*

55km northwest of San José, 37km north of Alajuela, this is one of the best known and most popular of all Costa Rica's national parks, principally because it offers visitors the relatively rare opportunity of staring down into the mouth of a still (semi-)active volcano. The mighty Volcán Poás, which lies at the park's heart, is a 2,704m tall basalt cone, the top of which blew off centuries ago, leaving behind a large classically volcanic-looking crater measuring 1.5km across and 300m deep, which is filled with a bluish, sulphurous liquid.

Though largely quiet these days, the volcano is still prone to the occasional outburst. The last, in 1989, sent clouds of superheated ash and smoke flying a kilometre into the air, while an even more devastating eruption in 1910 covered the surrounding area with over 640,000 tonnes of ash. For the time being, however, the volcano is bubbling away in enough of a low-key fashion for it to be considered safe to visit. Nonetheless, you should bear in mind that, while there may be no immediate prospect of a major eruption, the volcano does still pose a few minor dangers. The sulphurous fumes that bubble up and rise off the surface of the volcanic lake are so toxic that visitors are forbidden to descend into the crater. These fumes can, in the rainy season, combine with clouds to form acid rain, which, if severe enough, can lead to the park's being closed to visitors (though this rarely happens). The strength of these chemical gurglings is ably demonstrated by the state of the vegetation near the volcano's summit, which is in the main sparse and stubby, made

Tips for Visiting Volcán Poás

• Get there early before the clouds roll in, which tends to happen late morning most days, regardless of the season. As the official bus service to the park doesn't arrive till 10am, you should, upon arrival, head straight to the summit to see what you can before the views become obscured, and explore the visitor centre near the entrance upon your return.

• It can get cold quickly near the summit, so be sure to bring warm clothing.

• You'll also need supplies of water and wet-weather clothing as, away from the summit, it can get very humid in the forest depths.

Getting to Volcán Poás

The most convenient way of visiting the park is as part of an **official tour**, which would usually involve pick-up from your hotel (either in San José or Alajuela), lunch and the service of a guide for around $45. *See* pp.68–70 for a list of San José-based tour operators. If you really feel like packing the sites in, you can combine a trip to the volcano with a variety of other attractions. **Expediciones Tropicales, t** 257 4171, *www.costaricainfo.com*, offer a '4 for 1' tour taking in Poás, La Paz Waterfall Gardens, Parque Nacional Braulio Carrillo and a boat trip on the Río Saripiquí for $82.

If travelling independently, you'd be best off coming by **car** or taxi, which will enable you to arrive early in the morning before the summit becomes shrouded in clouds and mist. A **taxi** from Alajuela should cost in the region of $30, from San José $50.

Otherwise, **buses** leave for Volcán Poás from San José at 8am from Av 2, C 12/14, stopping *en route* at Alajuela's main bus terminal at 9.15am, before arriving at the park at around 10am, which unfortunately is the time it usually starts getting misty. The trip costs around $2 each way. The return bus leaves at 2pm.

Getting to La Paz Waterfall Gardens

The gardens are 15km east of Poás, just north of the town of **Varablanca**, off HWY-126. There is no bus service to the gardens. Several tour operators, including Expediciones Tropicales, offers tours for around $45.

---

up of patchy expanses of lichens, mosses and stunted trees that struggle to cope with the atmosphere's overwhelming acidity. At lower elevations, the vegetation gradually thickens out to become full montaine forest. Indeed, Volcán Poás is surrounded by some 65 sq km of forest, home to a wide variety of wildlife, including some 79 species of bird (including hummingbirds and quetzals) coyotes, weasels, skunks, small cats (such as margays) and, perhaps most notably, the small green and yellow Poás squirrel, which is found nowhere else in the world.

Just by the entrance to the park is a small **visitor centre** (and even smaller snack shop) where a video about the volcano is shown on the hour from 9am to 3pm. From here, it's a relatively easy 1km walk up to the edge of the crater, which is traversed by a paved pathway known as the **Crater Overlook Trail** that provides spectacular views of the volcanic lake. There's also a trail leading from here to a nearby extinct crater which is filled with a freshwater lake known as **Laguna Batos** (the water of which is supplied by the adjacent Río Angel) and another trail, known as the **Escalonia Trail** (it's named after a tree common to the area), which takes you on a 30-minute forest trek.

Where to Stay around Volcán Poás and La Paz

(★) Peace Lodge >

(★) Poás Volcano Lodge >>

Peace Lodge, t 482 2720, *www.waterfallgardens.com* ($$$$$; $215). The area's most upmarket accommodation is provided by the super-swish hotel at the La Paz Waterfall Gardens. This is a peaceful, relaxing place with four large, luxuriously appointed rooms, all of them with canopy beds, Jacuzzis and balconies offering views out over the gardens – which you can explore at your leisure away from the crowds, outside official opening times.

Poás Volcano Lodge, 16km southeast of the park entrance, between Poasito and Varablanca, **t** 482 2194, *www.poasvolcanolodge.com* ($$$; $75). Despite its name, this is a 20min drive from Volcán Poás, on a former dairy farm near the

Parque Nacional Braulio Carrillo. It's run by an English family who've been residents here for over 30 years and are committed environmentalists, currently lobbying to establish a nature corridor linking Poás and Braulio Carrillo. Their hotel comprises a main lodge with nine rooms (some with private bathrooms) and one large separate apartment, all done out in a comfortable style. Great dinners are served each evening in the main lodge for around $10 per head and there's also a cosy sunken fireplace and a games room (with snooker and ping-pong tables). Nature trails have been marked out through the hotel's extensive grounds, which are home to a wealth of wildlife, though if the weather is bad you can always content yourself with the views from the lodge windows. Horse treks of Poás and Braulio Carrillo are available with specialist guide Romero – one of no fewer than 17 siblings, he knows this area like the back of his hand.

La Que Tu Quieres Lodge, 5km south of park entrance, **t** 482 2092 ($; $20). The 'whatever you want' lodge is the cheapest option in this area (especially if you camp, which is allowed in the grounds) with just three small, simple *cabinas*, all with showers and fireplaces. There's also a good restaurant, butterfly garden and horses for hire.

La Providencia Reserva Ecológica, 1km south of park entrance, **t** 232 2448 ($$$; $45). The closest accommodation to the park, this 'rustic' lodge is set on a 230ha private reserve on Poás' lower southern slopes, right on the park's borders. The reserve contains a working dairy farm as well as swaths of secondary forest, in amongst which are three good-sized *cabinas* (all have showers), an excellent restaurant (which is open to and extremely popular with the public) and trails through the grounds. Horse-riding trips up the volcano and into the forest depths are also offered for $25.

La Paz Waterfall Gardens

La Paz Waterfall Gardens
t 482 2720, www. waterfallgardens.com; open daily 8.30–5.30; adm $21 ($27 with lunch)

This attraction, one of the region's most visited, has been designed to showcase a series of spectacular waterfalls on Poás' eastern slopes. A 3.5km network of trails has been laid out around a stretch of the Río La Paz, linking up observation platforms for no fewer than six cascades, with lots of prime photo opportunities. The largest fall, **Magia Blanca**, is over 40m high, and pretty fearsome, so be sure to bring some waterproof clothing. The complex also boasts a visitor centre (where you can see a video on the history of the gardens), a large butterfly garden (about the size of a football pitch), an aviary (home to 16 species of hummingbird), a rather good restaurant serving Costa Rican cuisine and offering good views of the area, and even a hotel (*see* p.137). Though the gardens are clearly laid out, with easy-to-follow gravel paths, you can also hire a guide to take you round for $25. Note – if you haven't got time to explore the gardens in full, you can get a taster by driving along HWY-126 north of the town of **Varablanca**, from where the La Paz waterfall is clearly visible.

Heredia and Around

Though the sleepy coffee town of Heredia lies just 12km north of San José, and a similar distance east of Alajuela, the province of which it is the capital extends all the way to Nicaragua. Thankfully, most of the sites that make a journey here worthwhile are within

Getting to Heredia

Three **bus** companies currently operate services from San José to Heredia between 6am and 10pm daily, leaving every 10–15mins from C 1, Av 7/9 (Microbuses Rápidos Heredianos), Av 2, C 10/12 (Busetas Heredianos) and C 4, Av 3/5 (Transportes Unidos La 400), arriving around half an hour later at Co, Av 4, just south of the Parque Central.

A **taxi** from San José or Alajuela or the airport should cost $10–15 (more during the rush hour).

Getting around and away from Heredia

Heredia's diminutive size and straightforward layout makes **walking** the only sensible means of travel. Even its most outlying landmark, the Universidad Nacional, is just five blocks east of the Parque Central.

However, getting out of Heredia to the various surrounding attractions is a slightly trickier proposition, as the town has no central **bus** terminal, just a collection of bus stops. Thankfully, most (but crucially not all) services depart from the roads between the Parque Central and the town's twin markets: buses for San José leave every 10–15mins from the same stop at which they arrive, C 0, Av 2/4; those for the town of Barva leave every half-hour from C 0, A 1/3; while those for Volcán Barva and the Parque Nacional Braulio Carrillo leave from from C 4, Av 6/8 at 6.30am, 11am and 4pm. Services to Alajuela leave from near the university campus at Av 0, C9 every 20mins or so.

easy reach of the town. These include **Café Britt Finca**, just a couple of kilometres northwest, the country's largest and most famous coffee exporter (and one of the region's most important employers); and the dormant **Volcán Barva** – a popular excursion for the views it affords from its summit – which lies due north, at the western end of the vast 325 sq km (32,500ha) **Parque Nacional Braulio Carrillo**. Despite its size and the wealth of wildlife it contains, the park itself doesn't attract that many visitors, as its lack of facilities tends to put off all but the hardiest adventurers. A more convenient introduction to the area's natural wonders is provided, however, by the **Rainforest Aerial Tram** (which, as the name suggests, is a tramway through the forest canopy) located just outside the park's northeastern confines.

Heredia

Heredia by no means a beautiful or particularly interesting town, although its architecture does perhaps hold a degree more aesthetic appeal than Alajuela's, with several colonial-era buildings surviving. But the presence of the **Universidad Nacional** gives it a young, lively, bustling feel, even if the proximity of San José means there's little nightlife away from the student campus.

Orientation

By the time you reach Heredia, you'll probably have realized that the layout of most large Costa Rican towns conforms to a basic, simple template. So, as with Alajuela and Cartago, Heredia's centre is its Parque Central, which in this instance is a rather pleasant, leafy, mango tree-lined open space laid out around a central bandstand (where concerts are held on Sunday mornings) and a late 19th-century wrought-iron fountain (imported from England). From here, the city's grid of streets extends outwards, with *avenidas* running west to east and *calles* north to south. The town's two produce and household goods markets, the old and the new (Viejo and Nuevo), are located a couple of blocks south of here.

A tour of the town's main sites could easily be accomplished in half a day, beginning on the **Parque Central**'s eastern side with the **Basílica de la Immaculada Concepción**, the town's main church, which was completed in 1804. Unfortunately, the price for this longevity – when so many other churches and buildings from this era have succumbed to the region's numerous earthquakes – seems to have been beauty. The church's low-set, boxy aesthetic could only appeal to the most hardcore of cathedral devotees, although it does boast some interesting stained glass, imported from Europe.

To the north of the square sits the magnificently useless **El Fortín**, a late 19th-century brick fort whose gun windows were constructed the wrong way round, with the wide opening on the outside narrowing to a thin slit on the inside. The advantage this conferred on the enemy (with the gun windows essentially acting as targets rather than defences) meant that the tower was never employed in battle, but was turned instead into a prison. Unfortunately, the interior is currently closed to the public.

Casa de la Cultura
t 262 2505; open Mon–Sat 9–6

Just east of the tower sits the **Casa de la Cultura**, an attractive colonial-era building that was once the home of President Alfredo González and today has displays of local art and historical exhibits.

⭐ **Finca Rosa Blanca** >>

Tourist Information and Services in Heredia

There is no tourist office in Heredia. Pick up information in San José.

Banks (with ATMs): Banco Nacional, C 2, Av 2/4; Scotiabank, Av 4, C 0/2.

Books: The Literate Cat, 2nd Floor, Plaza Heredia, t 262 5206. Second-hand bookshop, stocking a good assortment of English language titles.

Hospital: Hospital San Vincente de Paul, C 14, Av 8/10, t 261 0001.

Markets: Mercado Viejo, C 2, Av 6/8; Mercado Nuevo, C 2, Av 8/10. Both serve wide range of fresh produce (including coffee) and household goods.

Police: C 0, Av 5/7, t 237 0011.

Post office: Av 0, C 2 (in the northwest corner of the Parque Central).

Internet access: PlanetWeb, Av 1, C 6/8.

Supermarket: Mas X Menos, Av 6, C 4/6.

Where to Stay in Heredia

With San José so close, few foreign travellers choose to spend the night in Heredia. Nonetheless, the town does have a number of hotels, mainly catering to families of students. There are a number of more upmarket lodges located in the countryside.

Finca Rosa Blanca, on the San Pedro de Barva–Santa Bárbara de Heredia road, t 269 9392, *www.finca-rblanca.co.cr* ($$$$$; $195). One of the region's top choices, northwest of Heredia near the small town of Santa Bárbara. Set in extensive grounds with expanses of forest and a trail leading to a waterfall, this has just nine rooms, all sumptuously decorated with handmade furniture and large patios. There's also a swimming pool, a games room, and an excellent restaurant where lavish meals made with fresh ingredients from the hotel's own gardens are served. Nature trails and horse-riding.

Hotel Bougainvillea, south of Heredia, near Santa Domingo de Heredia, t 244 1414, *www.bougainvillea.co.cr* ($$$$; $87). Lovely country retreat set in amongst rolling coffee fields and fruit orchards with 83 rooms, all with balconies (some with views out towards San José), a pool, tennis courts, a gift shop and restaurant. A free shuttle service to San José is offered.

Hotel America, C0, Av 2/4, t 260 9292 ($$$; $40). Handy if you've got a bus to catch in the morning, this bland if serviceable lower mid-range hotel is located opposite the San José bus stop just south of the Parque Central and offers basic, simply furnished rooms – all with bathrooms – and a decent restaurant (*serving 6am–9pm*).

Hotel Valladolid, C 7, Av 7, **t** 260 2905, *valladol@racsa.co.cr* ($$$; $77). The only town centre choice with genuine character – the rooms of this five-storey establishment are nicely decorated and have all mod cons – minibars and cable TV. There's also a roof terrace with a Jacuzzi, as well as a bar and restaurant.

Hotel Ceus, Av 1, C 2/4, **t** 262 2628, **f** 262 2639 ($$; $25). Basic, budget choice in an old house north of the Parque Central. It's a bit frayed around the edges but reasonable for the price. Its public rooms are decorated with old photos of the town and there's a decent restaurant.

Eating Out in Heredia

As always, the cheapest fare tends to be served up by the sodas in and around the markets (Av 6/10, C 2/6). Less adventurous bargain-hunters will have to make do with the selection of American fast food eateries near the entrance to the university campus. There are also a couple of good cafés bordering the Parque Central, most notably Café Heladería Azzuria, on the west side, which serves good-quality coffee and Italian ice creams.

Fresas, Av 1, C 7, **t** 262 5555. A sort of upmarket soda selling a variety of *bocas* (at the bar only) and *casados* as well as its speciality fruit concoctions – fruit cups, fruit shakes and fruit salads, all featuring the eponymous strawberries. Mains from around $5.

Le Petit Paris, C 5, Av 0/2, **t** 262 2564. Small, good-quality French restaurant, which lays on live music (usually jazz) on Wednesdays and Saturdays and good cooking the rest of the week. Crêpes are the house speciality. Try to get a table in the nice garden at the rear and expect to pay around $15–20.

Vishnu Mango Verde, Av 0, C 7, **t** 237 2526. Part of a popular vegetarian chain, this is perhaps the town's healthiest choice, offering a range of salads, fruit smoothies and vegetable platters for $2–5.

Nightlife in Heredia

While anyone looking to have it really large on the weekend will doubtless head to San José, there is a residual scene of sorts in Heredia offering a more low-key sort of hedonism for those students disinclined (or too poor) to make it to the capital. Though most of the more popular places are inevitably located near the university campus (**Champs Disco** at Av 4, C 9, **t** 260 2511, is a perennial favourite), there are also a few lively downtown places including **Miraflores Disco y Taverna** (Av 2, C 2/4, **t** 237 1880) which puts on live music and has regular karaoke evenings, and **Océanos** (C 4, Av 2/4, **t** 260 7809), a marine-themed disco decorated with an assortment of nautical paraphernalia, which is very popular with students, particularly at weekends (when they get reduced price drinks). In addition to all the drinking and dancing, it also serves very good *bocas*.

South of Heredia

INBioparque

INBioparque
t 244 4730, www.inbio.ac.cr; open daily 8–4; you can explore the site freely, although 2hr guided tours are available Tues–Sun; adm exp

The small 19th-century town of Santo Domingo, a few km south of Heredia, is the location for INBioparque, the research facility, educational centre and all-round public face of the Instituto Nacional de Biodiversidad. This not-for-profit organization, founded in the late 1980s, is engaged in the production of one of the world's largest nature inventories. As has already been noted elsewhere, in terms of species per square kilometre, Costa Rica is believed to be the most biologically diverse country on earth. This contention is all the more

Getting to INBioparque

Buses run from both San José and Heredia to the park, or you can take a **taxi** from either for around $10.

remarkable when you consider that it has been based on just those species so far discovered. And, according to some estimates, over 80 per cent of Costa Rica's flora and fauna may as yet be unknown to science. This is where the institute comes in. It has made it its mission to produce an exhaustive and definitive catalogue of the country's all-encompassing natural biodiversity, sending out field-workers (or taxonomists as naturalists who define species are technically known) to discover, categorize and label what they find, ready for it to be collated into a huge central database. This is not just some giant exercise in ecological stamp-collecting, however. Not only does the information gathered provide important pointers for the future conservation of the country's natural wonders, it can also be a vital human resource, identifying plants that may have as-yet-untapped medicinal benefits. For this reason, much of the funding for the project is provided by pharmaceutical companies, notably the American giant Merck who receive primary access to this research in return for their investment. As the foundation says in its mission statement, 'The institute works under the premise that the best way to conserve biodiversity is to utilize the opportunities it offers to improve the quality of life of human beings.'

INBioparque itself is a sort of glossy visitor centre aimed at explaining all this, as well as providing an introduction to the country's biodiversity to the lay visitor. There's an exhibition hall with audiovisuals and displays on the country's extremely varied but crucially interconnected habitats; exhibits of flora (including orchids and heliconias); an aquarium with glass windows looking beneath the surface of an outdoor lagoon; and four small gardens designed to replicate four of the country's main ecosystems – wetland forest, tropical dry forest, humid forest and Valle Central forest – filled with over 500 species of native plant, and dotted with a number of 'wildlife stations' where you can meet snakes, frogs, ants, butterflies, caimans and alligators and other examples of native fauna. There's also a decent restaurant and a small gift shop selling the foundation's publications (as well as souvenirs).

North of Heredia

Café Britt Finca

Café Britt Finca
t 260 2748, www. coffeetour.com; tours daily 9am, 11am (plus 3pm in summer); adm

If coffee is the lifeblood of Costa Rica (*see* **History**, pp.28–9), then this coffee farm, the country's largest and principal exporter, is its heart, pumping the caffeine-rich brew around the world. It's also one of the industry's major promoters, offering 'coffee tours' of its

Getting to Café Britt Finca

For $15, the *finca* can arrange for you to be picked up from your San José hotel. You can also combine a visit here with a visit to either the Rainforest Aerial Tram (*see* p.146) or the La Guácima Butterfly Farm (*see* p.131). The price includes admission, transportation and lunch at the Café Britt Finca.

grounds (in English), which, considering the modern coffee-growing industry's highly commercialized nature, are suitably slick. They begin with a multimedia presentation in which costumed actors don period dress in order to a enact a short 'comical' piece of theatre designed to show the central role coffee has played in the development of the country's democracy and national character (not as outlandish as it sounds, despite the inevitable cheesiness).

From here, it's on to the more interesting part of the tour – into the great rolling plantation itself, where you learn about the planting, nurturing and harvesting of the beans before visiting to the roasting factory and drying patios. The tour ends with a tasting lesson in the company of one of the farm's 'expert' tasters, designed to get you to learn how to distinguish between different coffee types (not as easy as it sounds). And, if you fancy making a day of it, there's also a reasonable Costa Rican restaurant, **Don Prospero**, on site.

Café Britt Finca lies a couple of kilometres north of Heredia near the town of **Barva**, which, founded in 1561, is one of the country's oldest colonial settlements. Its **church**, constructed in the late 1700s, is one of the region's prettiest.

Parque Nacional Braulio Carrillo and Volcán Barva

2 Parque Nacional
Braulio Carrillo
open daily 8–4; adm

If you were asked to come up with a list of activities likely to cause the most amount of environmental damage, road-building would probably be somewhere near the top. In this instance, however, it could be argued that the construction of a major highway was actually the primary impetus behind the preservation of an important swath of territory.

In the 1970s, when plans were first drawn up to build a highway linking San José with the Caribbean coast, it was assumed that this would cause significant environmental destruction. Not only would the highway's proposed path go straight through a section of virgin rainforest but, if the examples of previous schemes were any indication, the construction of the road would lead to the construction of new roadside settlements, an accompanying expansion of the logging industry, and increased deforestation.

However, a concerted campaign by environmentalists persuaded the government to preserve a large section of forest either side of the new highway against future development. That section is the

Getting to Braulio Carrillo

There are four official **entrances** to the parks, all marked by **ranger stations** (*puestos*). The one at Volcán Barva is the only permanently staffed station. It also has the most facilities for tourists, and hence is the most visited. Of the other stations, two are on the main Guápiles Highway, at Zurquí on the southern border of the park, and at Carrillo on the eastern border near the Rainforest Aerial Tram.

San José–Guápiles **buses** leave around every 30mins (or when full) from C 0, Av 11 between 5am–7pm Mon–Sat (till 9pm Sun) passing both ranger stations (you may have to request the driver to stop) and the Rainforest Aerial Tram. There are short trails leading into the forest from both stations, although the park authorities have issued warnings regarding the Carrillo station, where a high spate of car break-ins have been reported. As is usually the case, the earlier you travel, the better, to avoid hiking the humid depths in the midday heat.

The park's fourth station, located right at the park's northern reaches at Magsasay, is extremely difficult to reach. You'll need a 4WD, even in dry weather. In wet weather the dirt track leading to the station from HWY-126 may well be impassable. Furthermore, this stretch of the park has only underdeveloped, unmarked trails and should only be attempted in the company of a guide with expert local knowledge.

huge Braulio Carrillo National Park (named after the country's third president), which was officially designated as such in 1978 and has remained largely unmolested ever since. Its preservation is all the more remarkable when you consider that the park's borders start just 20km north of San José.

The park encompasses a huge area made up of a variety of different altitudes (ranging from nearly 3,000m at the summit of Volcán Barva, the park's highest peak, down to just 50m above sea level), landscapes (cloudforest, rainforest, mountains, volcanoes, rolling hills, waterfalls) and comprising at least seven separate life zones – the interconnected habitats by which tropical forests are categorized). Over 300 species of bird and more than 6,000 species of plant have been recorded here, though there may be many more, as much of the area remains largely unexplored (again remarkable considering its location). What is known is that it is an unremittingly wet environment, receiving over 4.5m of rain each year. While it may enjoy a nominal dry season from December to April, the vegetation cover is such – with an abundance of palms, ferns and large-leafed gunnera plants (known locally, and tellingly, as 'poor-man's umbrellas') – that parts remain thoroughly sodden all year round. Wet-weather clothing is an essential.

The lack of development and tourist infrastructure means that this is one of the country's least-visited parks. Most people only get to glimpse its lush vegetation on a journey to the coast as it rises up on either side of the highway, or on a day trip to the park's most developed section, around the dormant Volcán Barva. The denseness of the vegetation is such that exploring away from the main marked trails is inadvisable unless in the company of an experienced guide. Therefore you shouldn't go expecting an encounter with any of the superstar animals that make the park their home – which include jaguars, pumas, tapirs and bushmaster snakes. That said, the slopes of Volcán Barva are one of the country's best quetzal-spotting locations.

The President's Park

Unless you were aware of the history, it might seem a pretty uncontroversial decision to name one of Costa Rica's largest parks after the country's third president. But Braulio Carrillo Colina was nothing if not a controversial head of state. He was returned to office in 1838 following a brief period as president from 1835–8, but he so resented the restrictions to his rule imposed on him by elected office that, two years later, he led a military coup, installing himself as 'President for Life' (in effect dictator). Unfortunately for Carrillo, the country disagreed with his decision. His lifetime presidency lasted just a few months before he was overthrown and sent to live in exile in El Salvador, where he was later assassinated. Not, you might think, the sort of résumé that tends to inspire a grateful nation to start erecting monuments in your honour. What prompted Carrillo's ecological immortalization was one of the few success stories of his time in office – his decision to order the construction of a road linking San José to the Pacific coast (see pp.328–35), so as to improve the country's economy (which it did). The building of the motorway linking San José to the Pacific coast in the 1970s was seen as the completion of Carrillo's vision, and so his name lives on as the name both of the motorway itself and the national park preserved on either side.

Volcán Barva

Volcán Barva
t 283 5906; open Tues–Sun 7–4; adm; you can camp near the ranger station, which has water and toilets, for around $2 per person, although you should arrange this in advance, as there is only space for around 10 tents

This is the most visited and most visitor-friendly section of the Parque Nacional Braulio Carrillo, but that's not to say it's exactly a walk in the park. If coming by bus, you'll need to take one of the three daily services from Heredia to the small village of **Sacramento** (at 6.30am, 12noon and 4pm), from where it's a 3km (1–1½ hr) uphill walk along a very bumpy dirt track to the ranger station. Alternatively, you can take a taxi from the town, providing you can find one and providing the driver is willing to tackle the road (which will depend on the amount of recent rainfall). Things are slightly easier by car, although you'll need a 4WD (and strong nerves) to negotiate the ascent to the **ranger station**.

From here, the main 3km **trail** leads up to the summit of the dormant volcano which, at an altitude of just under 3,000m, is the highest point. The hike, if tackled without detours, should take around another 1–1½ hours, during which time you'll encounter numerous spectacular views. You ascend through the coffee fields that dot the peak's lower slopes, through the cedar and oak forests of the middle reaches, before emerging into cloudforest near the summit, where the volcano's three large crater lakes come into view: **Laguna Barva**, **Laguna Copey** and, at 500m across, **Laguna Danta**, all of which are filled with a strange, blue-green liquid. True to the forest's name, cloud cover near the summit can be high, especially later in the day. To avoid the worst of the mists, aim to arrive as early as possible, particularly as, if walking from Sacramento, it will take you 2–3 hours to reach the summit. Early morning also represents your best chance of seeing the quetzals that inhabit these parts.

If you've really got your walking boots on, there are paths leading off from the main trail which can be followed, although these will add considerably to your climbing time. The most rewarding is perhaps to the **Mirador La Vara Blanca**, the turning for which comes around halfway up and leads around 1km away from the main trail to where, on a clear day, a lookout point allows you to see over the plains to the Caribbean.

As the climb will take you nearly 3km above sea level into some very humid climes, be sure to bring with you adequate protection against wet and cold. Do not stray from the marked trails.

Rainforest Aerial Tram

⭐ **Rainforest Aerial Tram**
t 257 5961, www. rainforesttram.com; open Mon 9–4, Tues 6.30–4; adm exp ($49.50); the tram also operates 10 rustically furnished cabinas and has a restaurant

Fun as it is exploring the forest floor, it doesn't take long to realize that, by remaining so resolutely earthbound, you are missing out on a lot of the action. Birds, monkeys and many types of insect spend all or most of their lives high above our heads cavorting in the canopy. And it's a rare wildlife-spotter indeed who finds the object of his or her attention descending for closer inspection. Still, if the mountain won't come to Mohammed...

This 4 sq km reserve, which opened in 1994, 5km east of the Parque Nacional Braulio Carrillo, 2km east of the Guápiles Highway, offers an ingenious solution to this problem in the shape of 1.7km of aerial track beneath which hanging gondolas, each containing five passengers and a multilingual guide, take a 1½ hour round trip through the forest's upper reaches. While this elevated viewing experience does provide a great chance to see the birds, orchids, monkeys and insects of the canopy, there is, of course, no guarantee that the animals you want to see will put in an appearance during your ride. The best spotting opportunities are probably afforded during the early-morning birdwatching trips or the torchlit night rides (until 9pm), as many canopy inhabitants only become active and visible in the dark. The park also has a network of ground trails that can be explored on foot.

Of course, done without due sensitivity, you could easily see how a scheme such as this could have an extremely deleterious effect on the environment. Thankfully, the man behind the project, the American biologist Dr Donald Perry, whose labour of love this has been since the 1970s, is a committed conservationist who took every precaution to make sure that the environmental impact of the scheme remained as low-key as possible. He insisted that all the construction materials for the tramway were carried on site manually, apart from the large metal towers that support the track, which were dropped into position by Sandinista-supplied helicopters from Nicaragua (when the search for suitable Costa Rican airborne transport proved fruitless), while the gondolas have been designed to glide almost silently so as not to disturb the wildlife.

The scheme has proved so successful that there are now two more aerial trams, one near Jacó on the Pacific coast, the other on the Caribbean island of Dominica.

Getting to the Rainforest Aerial Tram

Buses leave from San José's Caribbean bus terminal at C 0, Av 11 every 45mins or so between 5am and 10pm Mon–Sat (till 9pm Sun), stopping at the entrance to the park *en route*, from where a free shuttle will take you to the tram. Alternatively, you can arrange with the Aerial Tram to be picked up from (and dropped back to) your San José hotel for $79.50.

Several San José-based **tour operators** offer tours to the tram, which can be combined with trips to the Café Britt Finca (*see* p.142) or INBioparque (*see* p.141).

Cartago and Around

The charms of the town of Cartago, the capital of the surrounding Cartago province, are perhaps best summed up by the fact that most tour operators offering trips to its nearby attractions, most notably the mighty Volcán Irazú, start their itineraries in San José. Of course, had things turned out differently, Cartago might now be the largest, prettiest and most influential city in the country, the hub around which the tourist industry revolved. Founded in the mid-16th century, it was Costa Rica's first capital and remained the seat of government for over 200 years. But, just as its namesake, Carthage, eventually succumbed to Rome, so Cartago, following the country's brief civil war in the early 1820s, found itself superseded by San José (you can't help feeling that naming it Carthage was tempting fate slightly).

Cartago

Now entering its 6th century, Cartago has witnessed a lot of history. Unfortunately, it has also seen a lot of earthquakes, so little evidence of this illustrious past survives. Most of its architecture is modern, functional and soulless. Indeed, Cartago can probably justly claim the title of the Central Valley's ugliest provincial capital. And it's not as if it makes up for its architectural paucity with a signifi-cant cultural infrastructure, having no museums, theatres or nightlife. For most visitors, Cartago's attractions are religious rather than aesthetic or cultural; its lavish cathedral – the city's one true architectural highlight – is home to the country's most venerated icon. Other than the time spent visiting the church, and the ruins of another cathedral, the length of your stay in Cartago will depend upon your interest in sleepy provincial towns, and the availability of accommodation in the town's only decent hotel.

Cartago's layout follows the usual Valle Central template with a grid of streets converging on a central square, the **Parque Central**, the western end of which marks the nexus of the Avenida Uno and Calle Uno (unusually, Cartago does not have either a Calle Central or an Avenida Central). The square itself is uninspiring; a gloomy expanse of concrete surrounded on three sides by shops and cafés

Getting to Cartago

From San José, **buses** depart for Cartago every 5mins from 5am–9pm from C 5, Av 18/20, taking around 30–45mins (depending on the traffic) and depositing you at the Parque Central in the centre of town.

Getting around and away from Cartago

Cartago is a two-sight town and, as such, there isn't a great deal of getting around to do. Upon disembarking from the bus at the Parque Central, most people's itinerary consists of looking at Las Ruinas at the eastern end of the park, walking the six blocks east along Av 2 to the Basilica, and then walking back again to the bus stop – a round-trip, not including time spent looking at the attractions, of around 20mins. If you fancy speeding the process up, there's a **taxi** rank outside Las Ruinas.

Getting away from Cartago, however, is a slightly less straightforward proposition. The town has no central bus terminal, rather a scattering of bus stops. Buses for San José leave from Av 4, C 2/4; for Paraíso and the Lankester Botanical Gardens from Av 5, C 2/4; and for Orosi from C 6 Av 1/3. For details of how to get to Volcán Irazú, *see* p.151.

and on the fourth, the eastern side, by the ruins of the town's first church, known appropriately enough as **Las Ruinas**. The church, which was dedicated to St Bartholomew, was constructed in 1575 and managed to withstand almost three centuries of seismic tremors before a particularly severe earthquake in 1841 almost completely destroyed it. The locals interpreted the destruction as a test of their faith and so took it upon themselves to restore the church to its former glory. Another major earthquake in 1910, however, proved a test too far and the church was left to fall into its current picturesque state of disrepair. Today, it's surrounded by charming, rambling **gardens** that provide a nice spot for a picnic.

The town's major draw lies a 5–10-minute walk east of here, along Avenida 2 or 4 to Calle 16/18. The **Basílica de Nuestra Señora de los Angeles** is not just Cartago's main church, it's the most important (and visited) house of worship in the whole of Costa Rica and home to the country's most venerated religious object, the **La Negrita** icon, a small doll-sized representation of the Virgin of Los Angeles. Every 2 August, thousands upon thousands of pilgrims visit the church to commemorate a miracle they believe took place on this day (and for

A Cartagan Miracle

The story behind La Negrita, Costa Rica's most venerated icon, is known by heart by every Tico, and goes something like this. A young Cartago girl was collecting firewood in the forest when she came upon a small, dark stone statue of the Virgin Mary lying on a rock, which she picked up and took home. When she awoke the next day, she found that the statue had been returned to the rock. Determined to keep her prize, the girl took the statue home again and locked it in a box, only to find that the next day the statue was back on the rock. Confused, the girl told her priest what had happened; initially he didn't believe her. But when he himself took the statue home and found the same thing happening – each day the statue would reappear on the rock – he became convinced that a miracle was taking place.

The local townspeople built a shrine on the spot where the statue was discovered, and in 1824 La Negrita was declared Costa Rica's patron saint. Today the site inspires an intense religious fervour on the saint's day, *El Día de la Virgen*, with pilgrims walking all the way from San José to the basilica and then shuffling down the aisle on their knees to pay homage.

Tourist Information and Services in Cartago

There is no tourist office; pPick up what information you can in San José.

Banks: Banco Nacional, C 1, Av 2; Banco Popular, Av 1, C 2/4.

Hospital: Hospital Dr Max Peralta, C 3, Av 5/7, **t** 550 1999.

Internet access: Café Internet, Av 4, C 12/14.

Police: Av 6, C 2/4, **t** 551 0455.

Post office: Av 2, C 15/17.

Where to Stay in Cartago

Cartago's hotels are, in the main, so poor, and San José so close by that, business travellers aside, few people choose to spend the night here.

Los Angeles Lodge, Av 4, C 14, **t** 591 4169 ($$; $35), next to the Basílica. The only semi-decent town centre choice, though rather boxy and soulless, is at least clean and well maintained. All rooms have private baths and TVs and there's a reasonable restaurant specializing in seafood on the ground floor.

Eating Out in Cartago

The eating out situation is slightly better than the accommodation situation, but only slightly. Bordering the Parque Central, there are a few decent, cheap sodas, and a couple of excellent cafés – try **Roxy's Gourmet Coffee**.

several successive days) in 1635. The Byzantine-style basilica, which was constructed in the mid-20th century (its predecessor having been destroyed, like Las Ruinas before it, by an earthquake), provides a suitably grand repository for its precious relic, with glorious stained-glass windows and a large gold altar. The populace's devotion to La Negrita and their belief in her healing powers is demonstrated by a side chapel filled with ex votos – tiny statues offered up for blessing by the virgin. These usually represent something in the worshipper's life which they believe requires divine intervention – body parts they wish cured, hearts they wish unbroken, houses they need to find the money to pay for, etc. Steps lead from here down to a **crypt**, where you can see the very boulder on which the statue was first discovered.

Around Cartago

Lankester Gardens

Lankester Gardens
*t 552 3247; open daily
8.30–4.30; adm*

Six kilometres east of Cartago is one of the world's most important collections of orchids. Begun in the 1950s by the British naturalist Charles H. Lankester, but now administered by the University of Costa Rica, the collection boasts over 800 species occupying a carefully tended site. As orchids are nearly all epiphytes (i.e. they live on other plants, particularly the upper branches of trees, utilizing the tree's height to gain access to sunlight and rainfall but in an entirely benign way to the host plant), the site is also filled with an assortment of the various tropical plants on which the orchids make their homes – bromeliads, heliconias, palms, etc. It's a fascinating place, like a sort of formally planted forest, and attracts a wealth of wildlife, particularly birds.

Getting to Lankester Gardens

Buses for the nearby town of **Paraíso** leave Cartago from C 6, Av 3/5 every 10–15mins from 5am to 10pm. Ask the driver to be let off at the 'Jardín Botánico'. It's a 15-minute ride, followed by a 15-minute walk to the garden. The route is signposted. Alternatively, a **taxi** from the rank outside Las Ruinas in Cartago should cost $3–4.

There are marked **trails** through the gardens and guidebooks (in English) are available from the ticket office. The best time to visit is January to April, when most of the species of orchid are in bloom.

Parque Nacional Volcán Irazú

⭐ Parque Nacional
Volcán Irazú
open daily
8.30–3.30; adm

From the summit of Volcán Irazú, Costa Rica's highest active volcano, it is claimed that, if it's clear enough, it is possible to see both the Atlantic and Pacific oceans. Needless to say, the weather is rarely clear enough, especially outside the December–April dry season. Still, trans-oceanic views aside, this is still a popular day-trip destination, particularly as a paved road leads right up to the summit, thus allowing you to forgo the thigh-burning hike that characterizes the trip to nearby Volcán Barva.

The volcano's eruptions, which have occurred at least 15 times since records began in the early 18th century, have played an important role in the local economy, the fertile ash spewing out of its craters replenishing the pastureland and coffee fields on the region's slopes. Of course, they've also caused their fair share of destruction. The last major eruption in 1963 is still well remembered locally, not least because it coincided with a state visit by US President John F. Kennedy. It also flattened a good deal of the surrounding countryside, destroyed over 300 houses, precipitated a huge mudslide and covered Cartago in a blanket of ash. Nevertheless, the volcano is currently regarded as being safe enough to visit, despite the ominous-looking sulphurous clouds, known as fumaroles, that roll off the surface of its main crater.

Whether travelling by car or bus, you'll eventually arrive at the summit car park, ticket office and **visitor centre**, from where a paved **trail** leads to a lookout area over the summit's edge. Here you can see the volcano's four craters, three of which are no longer active. The two largest are the **Crater Diego de la Haya** (named after a former mayor of Cartago who, in 1723, became the first person to

---

Tips for Visiting Volcán Irazu

• Remember, there's no public bus service to the volcano during the week.

• The summit enjoys an average daytime temperature of 7°C, so be sure to wrap up warm. The visitor centre sells hot drinks.

• The summit also enjoys a lot of rainfall, so bring wet-weather clothing. *In extremis*, waterproof capes are available from the visitor centre.

• Do be careful when walking near the crater edge. Try to stick to the concrete path, as the volcanic ash that makes up much of the ground does tend to crumble underfoot.

Getting to Volcán Irazu

During the week, there's no public transport to the volcano. You can go either as part of an **organized tour** from San José for around $30 (or $60 if you want to combine it with a trip to one of the nearby attractions, such as Lankester Gardens); take a **taxi** from Cartago (which, with waiting time, could well set you back $40–50); or **drive** yourself. The road you're looking for is HWY-8, which passes through the villages, coffee fields and pastureland of the volcano's lower slopes all the way to the summit.

On Saturdays and Sundays, a single public **bus** leaves for the volcano from in front of the Gran Hotel Costa Rica in San José (Av 2, C 1/3) at 8.15am, though you should get there a good deal earlier to be sure of getting a seat. It stops off at Las Ruinas in Cartago to pick up more passengers (providing there's room) at 8.45 before arriving at the summit at around 9.30. It makes the return journey at 12.30pm and costs c1,550.

record an eruption), which measures 690m across and contains a strange lizard-green lake; and the **Crater Principal** (the only active crater), whose 1km-wide, 300m-deep expanse is a constantly bubbling mass of gurgling chemicals and sulphurous mists. Both are well worth the couple of rolls of film or memory card you'll expend on them, especially as there's not that much else to photograph, Irazú offering little in the way of wildlife-spotting opportunities. At lower elevations, much of the land has been turned into pasture and, though there is a small band of tropical montaine forest at about the 2,000m mark, above 3,000m much of the vegetation has either been destroyed or tamed by volcanic eruptions. That which does survive tends to be stunted and slow-growing – shrubs mainly, a consequence of the extreme and constant cold at this elevation. The lack of vegetation gives the landscape a strange, almost alien appearance, giving you some idea of what a holiday on the moon might be like.

The Orosi Valley

The famously picturesque valley of the Río Grande de Orosi begins 2km south of the otherwise unremarkable town of **Paraíso** (its name, 'Paradise', seems more wishful thinking than an accurate description), just 8km southwest of Cartago. The area lends itself well to a driving tour (though it is also served by public transport) following HWY-224, which splits at Paraíso to form a loop engulfing the 1960s-built Cachí Dam and reservoir, passing through several historic villages, most notably Ujarrás and Orosi, and past rolling hills, coffee terraces, stretches of forest and tumbling waterfalls. The Parque Nacional Tapantí, one of the country's least visited national parks, lies to the southeast.

Orosi

Small, quiet and charming (if only all Valle Central towns were like this), Orosi, 7km south of Paraíso, lies off the main tourist trail, which only adds to its appeal. Surrounded by heavily wooded hills, it makes

Getting to the Orosi Valley

Buses depart from Cartago to Orosi every half-hour from 7am–10pm from C 6, Av 1/3, depositing you by the football field. The journey takes around 40mins. Buses making the return journey leave from the main road by the football field. There's also an hourly service from Cartago to Cachí, stopping at Paraíso and Ujarrás.

A **taxi** from Cartago will cost around $12–15.

By **car**, head southeast to Paraíso where the road then divides at the Parque Central. Take the left fork for Ujarrás and Cachí, or go straight on for Orosi. The road, HWY-224, forms a loop around the Cachí resevoir, so whichever direction you take, you'll eventually end up back in the same spot.

a pretty and relaxed base from which to explore the Parque Nacional Tapantí to the south, itself one of the more underexplored national parks (something that might be explained by its status as the country's wettest region). In truth, there's not much to Orosi; everything you may need is either on or just off the main road, which runs north–south through the town. Its attractions are low-key, but still worthy of your time. Chief among them is the **Iglesia de San José de Orosi**, one of the country's oldest continually used churches, which was constructed in 1735 in a simple, elegant design with a red terracotta tile roof. Next door is the **Museo Franciscano**, containing an interesting collection of religious art, icons and relics.

Museo Franciscano
*open Tues–Sat 1–5,
Sun 9–5; adm*

The town is also home to two thermal pools – a great way to while away an afternoon – fed by a hot spring emerging from the base of a nearby volcano. These are the **Balneario de Aguas Termales Los Patios**, where the water is a positively balmy 41°C, and the **Balneario Termal Orosi**, which, located slightly further from the spring's source, can only manage a temperature of 35°C.

Ujarrás and Cachí

Seven km southeast of Paraíso, the small town of **Ujarrás** makes more regular appearances on the itinerary of local tour groups than its neighbours, mainly because it is home to one of the region's most celebrated churches. The **Iglesia de Nuestra Señora de la Limpia Concepción** was, according to whom you believe, either the first or the second church ever built in Costa Rica, way back in the 1560s. In fact, it hasn't been a functioning house of worship since 1833, when it was abandoned following a devastating flood, although you can still visit its picturesque ruins, which sit looking charmingly decrepit in amongst landscaped gardens. Dedicated to the Virgin Mary, who supposedly appeared to a local fisherman on this spot, the church was credited with miraculously saving the town from the attention of British pirates in the 1600s, an event that is celebrated every spring with a march from Paraíso to the church grounds, where a mass is said.

Heading east from here, the road rises to provide great views of the **Cachí Reservoir**, formed in the 1960s following the creation of the Cachí hydroelectric dam. Though the town of **Cachí** itself is

Tourist Information in Orosi

ⓘ Orosi Tourist Information and Adventure Centre >

t 533 1113

Though Orosi doesn't have an official tourist office, the **Orosi Tourist Information and Adventure Centre** just south of the football pitch can provide useful information about the local area. The Montaña Linda lodge (see below) will also be happy to provide information on (and, of course, sell you their) tours of the region, even if you're not staying with them.

Where to Stay and Eat in the Orosi Valley

Orosi

Orosi Lodge, next to the Balneario Termales Orosi, **t** 533 3578, *www. orosilodge.com* ($$$; $45). This German-owned hotel occupies a pretty white-washed *hacienda*-style building. The rooms are attractively furnished, with furniture made by local craftsmen, and all have private baths, ceiling fans and coffee-makers. Some of the second-floor rooms have balconies with volcano views. There's also a lively on-site café selling good-quality coffee and home-made cakes while a vintage jukebox plays in the background. And you can always combine your trip with a dip in the thermal baths next door.

★ La Casona del Cafetal >>

★ Montaña Linda >

Montaña Linda, south of the football field, signposted from main road, **t** 533 3640, *www.montanalinda.com* ($; dorm bed $6.50, double $17, camping $3, tent hire $3). This low-budget backpackers' favourite has a great communal feel, with two single sex dormitories, a couple of double rooms, camping space and a shared kitchen. A wealth of local tours are offered (to Irazú and Monumento Nacional Guayabo, among other destinations), bikes can be hired, and you can even brush up your Spanish at the on-site language school.

Restaurant Coto, next to the football field, **t** 533 3032. This is the town's stand-out eatery (from an admittedly small pool of rivals) offering hearty traditional fare in the restaurant as well as lighter *bocas* at the bar. There's outdoor seating facing the church.

Paraíso

Sanchiri, just south of Paraíso; look for the large white sign set, Hollywood-style, on the hillside, **t** 574 8586, *www. sanchiri.com* ($$$; $47). The Sanchiri restaurant is simply furnished and offers a range of basic Tico staples (of the *arroz con pollo* variety), but with the spectacular views it offers out over the Orosi Valley, these small deficiencies hardly matter. There's also a butterfly garden and, if you're taken with the vistas, you can rent out one of the *cabinas* in the adjacent lodge for around $47 a night. Tours offered.

Albergue Linda Vista, 1km south of Paraíso on the road to Orosi, **t** 574 5534 ($$; $38). Well-kept B&B with stunning views and reasonably priced, reasonably decorated rooms with balconies. There's also a communal kitchen for guests.

Cachí

La Casona del Cafetal, 1km south of Cachí Dam on main road, **t** 577 1414. Generally regarded as one of the region's top restaurants, this attracts tour groups throughout the day (which can make getting a table difficult), who come to admire its views of the nearby dam and the surrounding coffee plantations, and sample its traditional Tico cooking. There's also a souvenir shop selling similar carvings to those offered at the Casa del Soñador (see below).

somewhat nondescript, it welcomes its fair share of tourists coming to look at the dam (Costa Rica's largest) and, as often as not, pay a visit to the **Casa del Soñador** ('House of the Dreamer'), 2km south, the workshop of a celebrated dynasty of local sculptors who turn out intricately carved figurines (principally religious) fashioned from coffee-root wood.

Parque Nacional Tapantí

**Parque Nacional
Tapantí**
open daily 7–5; adm

Little visited it may be, but people from all over the country have cause to be thankful for the existence of this 60,000ha park on the northern flanks of the Cordillera de Talamanca. Occupying one of the wettest regions in the whole of Costa Rica, the park's dense vegetation acts as a giant watershed, absorbing much of the estimated 7m of yearly rainfall here and channelling it down to the Cachí Dam, whose giant turbines provide electricity. This overwhelming wetness, combined with the relative difficulty of access – there's no public transport and only one poorly maintained road in and out – does seem to put off a lot of visitors, and as a consequence the park's infrastructure is still somewhat underdeveloped, with just three relatively short marked trails. The upside to this, of course, is that it increases your chances of seeing some of the park's abundant wildlife. Indeed, you'll probably find yourself exploring Tapantí's misty depths either on your own or in the company of just a few other hardy souls, rather than behind the procession of tour groups that can characterize visits to other natural parks and refuges.

Tapantí's rain-sodden climate produces an extremely verdant, fertile landscape of thick montaine jungle and, at higher elevations, cloudforest; the whole area is traversed by a multitude of rivers, streams, ponds and waterfalls. There are estimated to be over 150 waterways in the park. It's an environment that has proved extremely attractive for wildlife. Some 45 species of mammal have been recorded here, including jaguars, jaguarundi, ocelots and tapirs, as well the more common monkeys, racoons and pacas. There are also 280 species of bird, including hummingbirds, toucans and quetzals (who apparently nest quite near the ranger station), as well as an assortment of reptiles, snakes, frogs and various other amphibians that thrive in the humid conditions.

It perhaps goes without saying that, for comfort's sake, the park is best visited during the short dry season from January to March. It will still be wet at this time – the dense canopy cover sees to that – but with a little luck you should avoid the seething, all-consuming downpours that soak the area for the rest of the year. Regardless of

Where to Stay in Tapantí

Other than the hotels at Orosi, basic accommodation is available at the park's **ranger station** for a few dollars, although, with just 15 bunks available, this needs to be booked in advance. **Camping** is also permitted (depending on the state of the ground), but again you'll need to confirm this in advance.

Kiri Mountain Lodge, 1km from park entrance, **t** 533 2272, *www.kirilodge. com* ($$; $35). The area's best lodging; its 20 hectares adjoin the park and there are trails providing an introduction to the area's flora and fauna. Its six rooms are simply furnished but comfortable, with private bathrooms, and all have great views. There's also a good restaurant that will cook up anything you catch in the trout pond.

Getting to the Parque Nacional Tapantí

There is no **bus** service going all the way to the park. You can take a bus from Cartago to Orosi (C 6, Av 1/3; every half-hour 7am–10pm), from where it's a 10min **taxi** ride ($10–12; there's a rank by the football field) or a 12km **walk** along a gently rising and, as you approach the park, increasingly bumpy road to the entrance. There's also a bus service to the village of Purisil, from where it's a 5km walk to the entrance. Several **tour companies** in San José offer tours of the park for around $100, including transport, lunch and admission charges.

the weather forecast, however, you should bring raingear, as well as a supply of easily donned or removed warm clothing, as temperatures can vary enormously as you move from the forest depths to sunny clearings, and from low to high elevations.

From the **ranger station**, just to the right of the park entrance, three **trails** lead off into the forest: the longest, the slightly worryingly named **Sendero Árboles Caídos** ('Fallen Tree Trail'), meanders its way through 2.5km of thick jungle; the 1.2km **Oropéndola Trail** (named after a type of small tropical bird with black wings, an orange belly and yellow tail feathers) leads to a picnic area and a swimming hole filled with inviting-looking (but usually freezing cold) water; while the **La Pava** ('Turkey') **Trail**, though just 500m long, climbs a fairly stiff 75m up to a waterfall and a viewing spot out over the Orosi Valley (it's marked by a sign with an eye on it).

Turrialba

For a while Turrialba was the Bates Motel of the Central Valley. Located 58km east of San José, it was once an important staging post on the main route from the capital to the coast, but fell into something of a decline when the construction of the Guápiles Highway in the 1970s (and the subsequent discontinuation of the old 'Jungle Train') diverted the flow of traffic – and thus the flow of visitors and business – north. Of course, those hardy souls who did venture to the town during those lean years could expect, at worst,

River Rafting and Kayaking near Turrialba

Upon learning that the rapids of the rivers Reventazón and Pacuare are considered so challenging that several Olympic kayaking teams use Turrialba as a training base, you could be forgiven for thinking that this was a pursuit best left to the experts, or at least not attempted without several years of experience under your paddle. In fact, while stretches of both rivers are graded as having Class IV white-water (i.e. very foamy), there are also more placid stretches well suited for beginners. In fact, if you can manage to raise your eyes from your paddle for a few moments as you try desperately to steer a course through the water, you'll find that both rivers (but particularly the Río Pacuare) also provide plenty of opportunities for wildlife-spotting, their heavily forested banks home to kingfishers, herons, otters and more.

There are companies in Turrialba (*see* p.156) and San José (*see* p.69) offering white-water rafting and kayaking tours. All offer lessons for beginners as well as adventure tours for more experienced paddlers. They will usually require that you wear shorts or trousers (not jeans), laced trainers or sandals with ankle straps (not flip-flops) and bring with you a light waterproof jacket and sunscreen. Everything else will be provided. Prices for kayaking start at around $75–100 a day, for white-water rafting $100–150 a day.

Getting to Turrialba

San José–Turrialba **buses** leave hourly from C 13, Av 6/8 between 5.30am and 10pm. The journey takes 1hr 40mins direct (over 2hrs on a stopping service) and costs c650. A **taxi** from San José will cost around $60.

Getting around and away from Turrialba

Turrialba, like all its Valle Central siblings, is laid out in an easy-to-follow grid pattern with (what else?) a Parque Central at its centre. The main Turrialba **bus station** is at C2, Av 4, where services depart for San José, Cartago and Siquerres. However, buses for the Monumento Nacional Guayabo leave from C 2, Av 2.

a bit of a dull night, rather than a visit from 'mother', but things were still looking rather grim there for a few years. Thankfully (for the purposes of this metaphor), Turrialba's proximity to the Reventazón and Pacuare – and, specifically, to the rivers' sections of white-water rapids – has given the town the chance to reinvent itself in the past decade as a major centre of watersports, in particular kayaking and white-water rafting. During the rainy season, everyone from enthusiastic amateurs to professional canoeists descend on the town ready to test themselves against the local currents.

Even if the thought of hurtling down a river at breakneck speed in an inflatable dinghy doesn't appeal, you may still consider Turrialba worthy of a visit. Though by no means pretty and boasting no attractions as such, the town does have good tourist facilities – including several decent hotels – and is surrounded by some breathtaking countryside (most notably in the valley separating the volcanoes Irazú and Turrialba). Most of the town's lodges and tour operators, in addition to their various rafting packages, offer hiking, horse-riding and mountain-biking tours of the area.

Tourist Information and Services in Turrialba

While Turrialba doesn't have an official tourist office, most of the town's lodges and tour operators can provide information on the area's attractions, though they obviously tend to be biased in favour of their own services.

Banks: Banco Popular, Av 2, C 1/3; Banco Nacional, Av 0, C 1.

Internet access: Turrialba.net, C 2, Av 2/4.

Post office: C 0, Av 8.

Turrialba Tour Companies

Costa Rica Ríos, t 556 9617, *www. costaricarios.com*.

Jungla Expeditions, t 556 2639.

Tico's River Adventures, t 556 1231, *www.ticoriver.com*.

Where to Stay in and around Turrialba

Turrialba

Hotel Wagelia, Av 4, C 2/4, **t** 556 1566, *www.wagelia.com* ($$$; $69). One of the town centre's more upmarket offerings, the Wagelia has nicely decorated rooms, all with TV, phones and private baths (some have air-conditioning), set in landscaped gardens. There's also a decent, affordable restaurant. A range of tours and trips is offered.

Hotel Interamericano, three blocks south of the Parque Central, just south of the old railway line between Av 0 and Av 1, **t** 556 0142, *www.hotelinter americano.com* ($$; $35 with private bathroom, $22 shared). This cheerful orange and red budget hotel is a firm favourite with the rafting community,

(★) Volcán Turrialba Lodge >>

perhaps because it offers a laundry service – something of a necessity after a day spent getting covered by a significant portion of the Río Reventazón. Indeed, for comfort's sake, if you're here on a rafting trip it's perhaps worth spending extra for a room with a private bath. The bar area is always full of people discussing their adventures, and the owners, can provide advice about local tours.

Hotel Turrialba, Av 2, C 2/4, t 556 6396 ($$; $38). Just around the corner from the bus stop for Guayabo, this makes a simple, clean, if hardly outstanding base for exploring the area. All the rooms have TVs, ceiling fans and private baths.

Around Turrialba

Turrialtico, 7km from Turrialba, past the Río Reventazón on the road to Limón, t 538 1111, www.turrialtico.com ($$$; $62). The Turrialtico lodge's wood-panelled structure can seem flimsy when the winds start to blow. The 14 rooms all have private bathrooms, but are a touch threadbare and badly soundproofed. But, when the clouds clear and the views of the surrounding countryside come into view, little of this will seem to matter. The open-sided ground-floor restaurant overlooks the valley and serves an excellent array of Costa Rican specialities. Tours of the area are offered.

Volcán Turrialba Lodge, 15km north of Turrialba, near the village of Pacayas, t 273 4335, www.volcanturrialbalodge. com ($$$; $45). Clearly going for a 'rustic retreat' sort of a vibe, this lodge can take a bit of getting to. Its access road is impassable (and deliberately kept so) to all but the sturdiest 4WDs, but that just adds to its air of isolation. The hotel occupies an impressive setting on the flanks of Volcán Turrialba and all of its 14 rooms have private baths and (a nice touch) wood-burning stoves. A wood-burning oven is also used to cook the *típico* meals in the lodge's locally renowned restaurant. Prices include three meals a day, making it pretty good value. Hiking, horse-riding and birdwatching tours.

Eating Out in Turrialba

As noted above, the Hotel Wagelia, Turrialtico and, if you can make your way there, the Volcán Turrialba Lodge all have good restaurants.

La Feria, next to the Hotel Wagelia. Generally regarded as operating the best kitchen in town. Open throughout the day (to cater for rafters looking to fortify themselves both before and after their trips) it serves a menu made up of Costa Rican staples – *casados* with beef, chicken and fish, etc. – augmented by a few international choices – pasta, pizza, etc.

Around Turrialba

Monumento Nacional Guayabo

Monumento Nacional Guayabo
t 556 9507; open daily 8–3.30; adm

The significance of the Monumento Nacional Guayabo, the only sizeable pre-Columbian settlement ever found in Costa Rica, is a good deal greater than its current appearance might suggest – today, little more than the foundations of most structures survive. Until the site's discovery in the late 19th century, many historians had assumed that the pre-Columbian peoples of Costa Rica were much less culturally developed than their northern Central American counterparts, lacking the sophistication to create the great cities and monuments that characterize Aztec and Mayan civilizations. However, the unearthing of Guayabo forced them to revise their opinions. While Guayabo may not have the 'wow' factor of somewhere like Machu Picchu, it nonetheless shows that Costa Rica's indigenous population was capable of building a considerable

Getting to Guayabo

Two **buses** a day make the trip from Turrialba Mon–Sat, although, as the second doesn't leave till 5.15pm (2hrs after the site closes), the 11am is the only viable option. It should take around 45mins. Return services leave at 12.30pm and 5.30pm. The Sunday service leaves at 9am but doesn't return until 4pm, by which time you may have had your fill of pre-Columbian Costa Rican culture. **Driving** is more convenient, although the road leading into the site is somewhat uneven. From Turrialba, it should take around half an hour. A **taxi** from Turrialba will cost in the region of $15. Many of the area's hotels and lodges offer **organized tours**.

settlement furnished with a relatively advanced system of water provision – many of the site's structures are either irrigation channels or water storage containers.

Though its very existence presupposes a certain level of sophistication, there is still much about Guayabo that remains unexplained. This is partly due to the fact that the site has never been fully excavated. Indeed, a lack of funding (and interest) meant that the first major archaeological dig here didn't take place until the 1960s, and even that was incomplete. Much of Guayabo still remains hidden beneath the earth, waiting for a donor to fund its uncovering.

What *is* known is that the settlement was inhabited from around 500 BC to AD 1400, after which it was abandoned, perhaps because of an epidemic of disease or a war, no one is sure, although it is believed that this took place well before the Spanish invasion. The stone foundations that comprise much of the site would once have supported wooden structures, although, again, their precise nature and function remains largely a matter of guesswork. Many, of course, would have been houses, and the differentiation in size of these structures perhaps suggests the presence of a social hierarchy. It has been assumed that the settlement would have been presided over by a single chief, as was customary at the time. One thing on which archaeologists are agreed is that the stones themselves were not locally sourced, but were probably quarried on the banks of the Río Reventazón and then transported along the 8km paved road that leads into the site. Other than this, there are few concrete facts. The petroglyphs – stylized representations of animals – that have been carved onto the surface of many of the stones would probably tell us a great deal, if only anyone understood them.

You can pick up a leaflet explaining what is known and presumed at the entrance, where you may also be able to engage a guide (though most rangers only speak Spanish). In truth, so little of the original settlement remains and so little is known that you will have to use your imagination to get the best out of a visit here. For this reason, it's perhaps a good idea to visit as part of an organized tour out of Turrialba. Until the site is fully excavated and more questions are answered, the site's appeal will arise principally from its context, and the fact that no other comparable settlements exist (or, at least, have been found) in Costa Rica. You can't help thinking that, if Guayabo were situated in Mexico, it wouldn't get any visitors at all.

The Northwest

Most of northwestern Costa Rica lies within the province of Guanacaste, which stretches from Nicaragua right down almost to the tip of the Nicoya Peninsula. The tip itself, owing to an administrative quirk, is actually part of Puntarenas province (most of which lies on the central Pacific coast), but for the purposes of this chapter will be treated as honorary Guanacastean.

This is a very large area, offering much for the visitor to enjoy, from the national parks of Rincón de la Vieja and Santa Rosa to the north (with active volcanoes, tropical dry forest and marine turtle-nesting sites), to the stately city of Liberia at its centre, with its refined colonial-era buildings, and a lush line of beaches (both developed and otherwise) stretching south along the Nicoya Peninsula, renowned as one of the country's prime surfing and snorkelling destinations.

10

Don't miss

⭐ **Laid-back beach relaxation**
Montezuma p.203

⭐ **Turtles by night**
Parque Nacional Santa Rosa p.171

⭐ **Costa Rica's first protected region**
Reserva Natural Absoluta Cabo Blanco p.208

⭐ **Surfing paradise and party town**
Tamarindo p.182

⭐ **Mud pools and suphurous vents**
Volcán Rincón de la Vieja p.168

See map overleaf

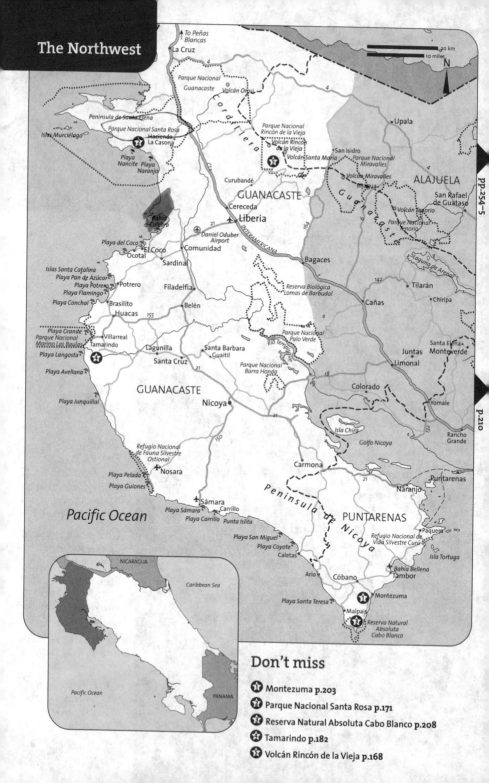

The Northwest

To Peñas Blancas
La Cruz

20 km
10 miles

N

Parque Nacional Guanacaste
Volcán Orosí

Península de Santa Elena
Parque Nacional Santa Rosa
Hacienda La Casona
Islas Murciélago

Parque Nacional Rincón de la Vieja
Volcán Rincón de la Vieja
Volcán Santa María

Upala

San Isidro
Parque Nacional Miravalles
Volcán Miravalles

ALAJUELA

San Rafael de Guataso

Playa Nancite
Playa Naranjo

Curubandé

GUANACASTE
Cereceda
Liberia
Daniel Oduber Airport
Comunidad

Bahía Culebra

Guayabo

Volcán Tenorio
Parque Nacional Tenorio

Playa del Coco
Ocotal
El Coco

Sardinal

Bagaces

Reserva Biológica Lomas de Barbudal

Laguna de Arenal

Tilarán
Chiripa

Islas Santa Catalina
Playa Pan de Azúcar
Playa Potrero
Playa Flamingo
Playa Conchal
Potrero
Brasilito
Huacas

Filadelfia
Belén

Cañas

Playa Grande
Parque Nacional Marino Las Baulas
Playa Langosta

Villarreal
Tamarindo
Lagunilla

Santa Barbara
Guaitil

Parque Nacional Palo Verde
Río Tempisque

Juntas
Limonal

Santa Elena
Monteverde

Colorado

Yomale

Rancho Grande

Playa Avellana

Santa Cruz

Parque Nacional Barra Honda

Playa Junquillal

GUANACASTE

Nicoya

Isla Chira

Golfo Nicoya

Refugio Nacional de Fauna Silvestre Ostional

Nosara

Carmona

Puntarenas

Playa Pelada
Playa Guiones

Naranjo

Pacific Ocean

Sámara
Playa Sámara
Playa Carrillo
Carrillo
Punta Islita

Península de Nicoya

PUNTARENAS

Paquera

Playa San Miguel
Playa Coyote
Caletas

Refugio Nacional de Vida Silvestre Curú

Isla Tortuga

Ario
Cóbano

Bahía Bellena
Tambor

Playa Santa Teresa

Montezuma

Malpais

Reserva Natural Absoluta Cabo Blanco

NICARAGUA

Caribbean Sea

Pacific Ocean

PANAMA

PP.254–5

p.210

Don't miss

Montezuma p.203

Parque Nacional Santa Rosa p.171

Reserva Natural Absoluta Cabo Blanco p.208

Tamarindo p.182

Volcán Rincón de la Vieja p.168

Getting to and around Guanacaste and the Nicoya Peninsula

The northern national parks and certain coastal stretches of the Nicoya Peninsula aside, getting around Guanacaste is as straightforward a process as you'll encounter anywhere in the country – i.e. the road network is extensive and regularly repaired, but still essentially Costa Rican in nature, which means, if you are **driving**, maintaining concentration as you negotiate the winding turns, savage potholes and poor signposting. **Bus** coverage is also good, although unfortunately not total.

There are three main routes for driving into the region. You can use the Interamericana (HWY-1) to get to mainland Guanacaste, the Nicaraguan border and the northern Nicoya Peninsula (via Liberia). Or you can access the southern end of the Nicoya Peninsula via the ferry from Puntarenas (*see* p.213) or its central areas across the Puente La Amistad ('Friendship Bridge'), which opened in 2003, at the mouth of the Gulf of Nicoya.

From Liberia, HWY-21 is the main artery running down through the centre of the Nicoya Peninsula. As yet, there is no major road linking the coastal beaches, just a collection of sometimes very minor ones, many of which quickly become impassable once the rains begin. You'll need a 4WD. Slightly inconveniently, getting from one beach to another will often involve backtracking to the main highway.

In one respect, this section of the Pacific coast bears comparison with its Atlantic counterpart, as both seem to be regarded by the rest of the country as being somehow 'other' from mainstream Tico society. Both certainly have their own distinct cultural identities. For the Atlantic coast, this is the result of a strong Afro-Caribbean influence, while for the northwest this has come about largely because of the historic importance of the region's cowboys. These *sabaneros*, as Costa Rican cowboys are known, were the lynchpins of the cattle-ranching industry that dominated the region's economy from the 19th century until just a couple of decades ago (when tourism took over), and today they enjoy a mythic status within Costa Rican society similar to that of their US counterparts – held up as ideals of lone, taciturn, rugged manhood. Even today, there are towns in the region's interior where horses still outnumber cars.

This shared cultural 'separateness' aside, there probably couldn't be two more dissimilar regions than the northern Pacific and Atlantic coasts. Where the Caribbean coast is wet and verdant almost all year round, the northwest is often dry and parched. Some parts of the northwest receive less than half a metre of rain a year compared with over five metres on the other side of the country. The weather can be so blindingly hot here that it is actually best to visit during the traditional 'low' season of May to November. This unforgiving climate has helped to give inland Guanacaste a landscape unlike anywhere else in the country – unremittingly flat, open and sun-baked. Indeed, the region's most famous environments – its swaths of tropical dry forest – can take on an almost desert-like appearance at times, although they can also achieve a temporary lushness when the rains come. Unfortunately, most of these forests have over the past hundred years been cleared for pasture, leaving in their wake vast, prairie-like expanses, offering 'big sky' vistas not unlike those of the US midwest.

As with Costa Rica as a whole, tourism to the northwest is increasing all the time, prompted by a huge spate of development over the past decade. The Nicoya Peninsula now boasts some of the most developed resorts in the entire country, acting as winter playgrounds to hordes of US package tourists. Thankfully, there are for the time being still some quieter stretches remaining, particularly further south along the peninsula, where the basic level of the transport infrastructure has acted as a curb on touristification.

History

It's probably fair to say that more is known about the **Chorotegas**, Guanacaste's pre-Columbian peoples, than all the other indigenous peoples of Costa Rica put together. As impressive as this sounds, this body of knowledge still doesn't amount to a great deal, it's just comparatively larger than all the others. There is still much about the lives, customs and culture of the Chorotegas that remains a mystery. Part of the reason why the Chorotegas are better understood than most of their contemporaries is that they, unlike any of the country's other tribal groups (as far as is known), had a written language, utilizing a form of hieroglyphs similar to those employed by the Maya. And part of the reason why there are still so many unanswered questions is that Chorotegan society – along with most other indigenous society in Costa Rica – collapsed shortly after the arrival of the Spanish thanks to a deadly combination of military defeat, disease and enslavement.

The Chorotegas are believed to be the descendants of Aztecs from near the site of present-day Mexico, who migrated south in the 7th century AD, possibly following conflicts with a neighbouring tribe. Once in Guanacaste, it is thought, their organizational sophistication and superior weaponry allowed them to rapidly defeat the less sophisticated peoples already living in Nicoya and take over the area. Unsurprisingly, the culture of the Chorotegans seems to have had much in common with its Aztec antecedents. They certainly seem to have placed a similarly strong emphasis on performing spectacular human sacrifices – throwing virgins into the mouths of volcanoes, etc. – and their priests played an important role in secular as well as religious affairs, acting as leaders of the community. While not quite reaching the giddy heights of Aztec civilization, the Chorotegans were capable of relatively advanced forms of social organization. Indeed, their society seems to have adopted a form of proto-Communism, with the community owning its land and benefiting from its development. Each year's harvest of crops – which included tobacco, cotton, maize and cacao beans – was apparently distributed evenly among the community members. Though no large Aztec-style architecture has been discovered, the Museo Nacional in San José does hold numerous examples of the Chorotegas' distinctive, sophisticated style of pottery, with typically stylized representations of the region's 'mythic' animals – jaguars, snakes, alligators, etc.

As with all Costa Rica's indigenous tribes, the Chorotegas were removed from history in double-quick time following the European conquest. Against the odds, a few individuals did manage to survive the twin onslaughts of smallpox and Spanish soldiers to co-exist with their conquerors, and today Guanacaste has the country's largest population of people claiming mixed heritage, although this is still a minimal amount by Latin American standards.

Once they had the province in their hands, it seems that the Spanish didn't really know what to do with it, passing it backwards and forwards between Nicaragua and Costa Rica over the next few centuries. By the time Central America declared independence from the Spanish crown in the 1820s, Guanacaste found itself in the schizophrenic position of being claimed by both countries. A referendum settled the matter, with the province declaring itself (just) in favour of Costa Rican ownership.

Since the 19th century, the province has developed a reputation as a centre of cattle-ranging, its character defined in the popular consciousness by the image of the lone cowboy battling against the elements. Although, as tourism has come to the fore in recent decades as the region's leading industry, its character might be better exemplified these days by the image of a surfer dude or a rich American tourist on a sports fishing trip.

Northern Guanacaste

Liberia

Few cities or towns in Costa Rica have as much character or are as steeped in tradition as Liberia, the Guanacastean capital, which lies 235km northwest of San José on the Interamericana. Presiding over a great network of surrounding cattle ranches, for whom it is the major market town, it has a proud provincial air, wearing its city status casually with little of the urban bustle that characterizes San José. Life here is cowboy- not business-paced – slow, thoughtful, plodding. It may be the province's major metropolis, but it is still an overwhelmingly rural place; somewhere where you can still see horses being gently trotted up the main street.

Liberia is also one of Costa Rica's few genuinely attractive towns, with wide, mango-tree-lined streets filled with pretty whitewashed colonial buildings, particularly on Calle Real, the city's main north–south thoroughfare. Since the opening of the country's second international airport here in the early 1990s (the other is in San José), Liberia has also developed into a minor tourist town, servicing visitors *en route* to the beaches of the Nicoya Peninsula (the northern ones are less than an hour's drive away) or travelling up to

Getting to Liberia

Daniel Oduber airport, 12km east of town, welcomes an increasing number of international **flights**, all of which originate in the USA, principally from the cities of Atlanta, Miami and Houston. If you are holidaying at one of the Nicoya Peninsula's coastal resorts, it is certainly worth investigating flying direct to Liberia, as this will prove a significantly quicker option than the usual route of connecting via San José. Both major domestic carriers, Sansa and NatureAir, operate daily flights from San José to Liberia (for more information, *see* p.104). There's no **bus** service from the airport, obliging you to take a **taxi**, which should cost around $7–10.

Buses leave San José for Liberia hourly 6am–8pm, from C 24, Av 5/7, taking around 4½ hours and costing c1,565, arriving at the town's main bus terminal at Av 7, C 12/14.

The **drive** from San José is as easy as any you'll encounter in Costa Rica. Just head north straight up the Interamericana, the country's main and best-maintained highway, until you reach the right-hand turn-off into town (marked by no fewer than three petrol stations).

Getting away from Liberia

Liberia is Guanacaste's main transport hub. As one of the country's main entry points, it has a number of **car hire** firms, although there is a strange absence of rental desks at the airport, obliging you either to head into town (perhaps the town's car rental firms and restaurateurs have come to a cunning arrangement to maximize revenue) or to book in advance, in which case your vehicle will be brought to the airport to meet you. If travelling anywhere other than the major resorts at the northern end of the Nicoya Peninsula (Playa del Coco, Tamarindo, etc.) you'll need a 4WD, and it's probably a good idea to get one anyway.

There are regular **bus** connections from Liberia's main terminal, Av 7, C 12/14, to all the major regional destinations, including Bagaces, Cañas, La Cruz, Peñas Blancas (the Nicaraguan border), Playa del Coco, Playa Flamingo, Playa Hermosa, Playa Panama, Playa Tamarindo, Puntarenas and Santa Rosa. Buses for San José leave at 3am, 5am, 6am, 7am, 8am, 10am, 12noon, 2pm, 4pm, 6pm and 8pm. There are also five international bus services a day to Managua in Nicaragua, which leave from in front of the Hotel Guanacaste, Av 1, C 12. You can buy tickets inside the hotel.

There is a **taxi** rank on the north side of the Parque Central.

Car Hire

Avis, t 666 7585, *www.avis.co.cr*.
Budget, t 668 1024, *www.budget.com*.
Elegante, t 668 1054, *www.eleganterentacar.com*.
Europcar, t 668 1022, *www.europcar.co.cr*.

---

the national parks of Rincón de la Vieja and Santa Rosa. However, if the mooted expansion of this airport does go ahead in the next few years, then Liberia may well be in line to become a major tourist town. Right now, the city welcomes just a spattering of international flights, compared to the deluge arriving in San José every week. But it has been argued that a significant increase in arrivals could result in Liberia's tourist infrastructure being expanded to almost San José-like proportions. After all, the vast majority of visitors to Costa Rica are not coming to see San José, but, as they're obliged to travel through it, often they will end up spending a good deal of time there – and, more importantly, spending a good deal of money in its hotels, restaurants, bars and shops – while they await their connections to elsewhere. Should this expansion come to pass, then it can only be hoped that it is managed sensibly and sensitively. Nobody would want to deny Guanacaste's sleepy capital a much-needed economic fillip, but it would be a shame if the town's search for tourist revenue served to dilute its charms.

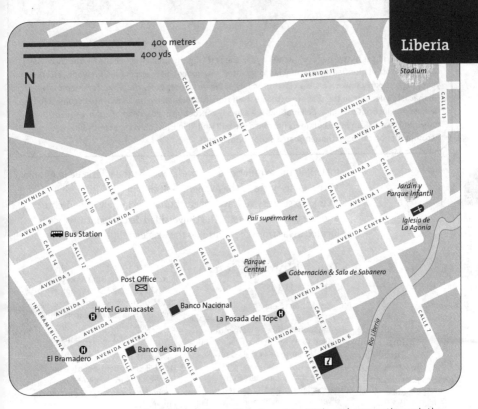

The Interamericana (Pan-American Highway) passes through the western edge of Liberia on its way up to Nicaragua, connecting with the **Avenida Central** (also known as the **Avenida 25 de Julio**), which heads from here into the town centre. This is marked by the **Parque Mario Cañas Ruiz** (also known, inevitably, as the **Parque Central**), which is named after a 20th-century Costa Rican singer famed for his wistful, elegiac songs about the region's cowboys. The park is a very large, very pretty, neatly laid-out open space overlooked by tall, shady trees and dotted with benches where you can sit and daydream the afternoon away. On the eastern side of the park, across the **Calle Central** (also known as **Calle Real**), is Liberia's slightly odd, almost modernist-looking church, while in the square's southeast corner is the town's only formal tourist attraction, the **Sala de Sabanero**, a museum dedicated to cowboy culture which occupies part of the **Gobernación**, the local government headquarters. Displays consist mainly of lots of cowboy paraphernalia – chaps, boots, spurs, whips, branding irons, etc. – as well as faded photographs of ranch life.

Sala de Sabanero
operates irregular and ever-changing opening hours; contact the tourist office to find out the latest times

Around this fulcrum Liberia is laid out according to a standard grid pattern, with *avenidas* running east–west and *calles* north–south, although, with the town boasting few road signs (as is customary in Costa Rica), most directions are given using major landmarks,

Festivals

Liberia plays host to two major blowouts a year. The first (slightly smaller) affair, the **Fiestas Cívicas de Liberia**, is a sort of glorified agricultural fair, celebrated with rodeos, parties, parades, fireworks, etc. The year's biggest party, however, takes place on 25 July, **El Día de la Independencia**, which commemorates Guanacaste's decision in the 1820s to extricate itself from Nicaraguan control in order to become a fully fledged province of Costa Rica. Celebrations are a heady concoction of parades, horseshow, rodeos, live music and Costa Rican-style bullfights (in which the bull isn't killed, just chivvied about a bit). Accommodation can be extremely scarce during both events.

including those mentioned above, as well as the **Iglesia de la Agonía** at the eastern end of the Avenida Central, a pretty, although – thanks to successive waves of earthquakes – largely ruined, church, and the town's university, the **Universidad de Costa Rica**, which is located away from the centre on the western edge of town.

Tourist Information and Tours in Liberia

ⓘ **Centro de Información Turística >**

C 1, Av 6, three blocks south of Parque Central, t 665 0135; open Mon– Sat 8–12 and 1.30–5

In addition to providing information on the town and surrounding area, the small **tourist office** also organizes guided tours to the nearby national parks of Rincón de la Vieja, Santa Rosa and Palo Verde.

Tours and/or transport to the national parks are also offered by several of the town's hotels, including the Hotel Guanacaste, the Hotel La Posada del Tope and the Hotel Liberia (*see right*).

Services in Liberia

Banks: Banco Nacional, Av 0, C 6/8; Banco de San José Av 0, C 10/12.

Hospital: Hospital Dr Enrique Baltodano Briceño, t 666 0011, in the northern suburbs.

Internet access: Cyberm@nía, Parque Central, Av 1, C 0/2; Planet Internet, Av 2, C 0.

Post office (*correo*): C 8, Av 3/5.

Supermarket: Supermercado Palí, Av 3, C 0.

Where to Stay in Liberia

The choice and standard of accommodation in Liberia is getting better all the time, with new places opening every year, although there's still not much in the way of out-and-out luxury to be found, with the top end of the market catered to by just a few rather bland business hotels. Prices have been rising recently as the town has become increasingly popular, but there are still bargains to be had, particularly in the off season. You'll need to book in advance during peak-month weekends and national hols.

Moderate ($$$)

Hotel El Bramadero, opposite Burger King Food Court, Av 1, t 666 0203, *bramadero@racsa.co.cr* ($45). Convenient and clean accommodation near the Interamericana. Room come with private bathroom, air-conditioning and TV (those at the front can be a touch noisy), and there's a swimming pool and a good open-air Tico restaurant, which does a fine line in seafood and steaks.

Hostal Ciudad Blanca, Av 4, C 1/3, t 666 3962 ($45). Very pretty choice with lots of character set in a former mansion. The rooms are a touch on the small side, but well equipped with private bathrooms, air-conditioning, cable TV and telephones, and there's a small, atmospheric restaurant/bar. Breakfast is included in the price.

Best Western Hotel Las Espuelas, 2km south of town, t 666 0144, *www. bestwestern.co.cr* ($65). Set next to a large Guanacaste tree, the Las Espuelas offers a decent standard of business comfort – large, generic, comfortable rooms (all with private bathrooms, air-conditioning, telephones, TVs and terraces), a swimming pool, a Jacuzzi, a steak restaurant and a business centre. Car hire and tours offered.

Best Western Hotel El Sitio, t 666 1211, *www.bestwestern.co.cr* ($65). Liberia's other Best Western, situated west of the centre heading out towards the airport, offers the highest (but also the blandest) level of comfort in town. It's very well equipped with two swimming pools, a gym, a casino and a restaurant/bar. All rooms come with air-conditioning and private bathrooms (with hot water). Car rental and tours are offered.

Budget ($)

La Casona, C 0, Av 4/6, **t** 666 2971 ($15). Good-value budget choice offering simple but quite spacious rooms with shared bathrooms for $10, and slightly more elegant ones with air-con and (small) private bathrooms for $15. Its single rooms are just $7, which is cheaper than many hostel dorms.

Hotel Guanacaste, Av 3, C 12, **t** 666 0085, *htlguana@racsa.com.* This backpackers' favourite is affiliated with Hostelling International and offers cheap dorms with fans and shared cold-water bathrooms ($7 per bunk), as well as some double rooms with private bathrooms, which are a touch more expensive ($30), although you do get a 15 per cent discount if you're an HI member. There's also a cheap café and a tour desk selling tickets for the daily bus to Managua (the bus stop is just outside), as well as for the hotel's own daily service to the Parque Nacional Rincón de la Vieja.

Hotel Liberia, C 0, Av 0/2, **t** 666 0161, *hotelliberia@hotmail.com* ($20–10). One of the most basic choices, just south of the Parque Central, the Liberia is aimed squarely at the itinerant backpacker market passing through town en route to the national parks/ beaches/Nicaraguan border. Although the accommodation itself is pretty spartan – $10 gets you four walls, a bed, access to a cold-water shared bathroom and not much else, while $20 will get you a slightly larger room with a private bathroom – it's a convivial and friendly place, with a central courtyard adorned with hammocks. Daily trips to Rincón de la Vieja and transport to Santa Rosa are organized.

La Posada del Tope, C 0, Av 2, **t** 666 3876 ($12). Another of the town's good budget choices, a block south of the Parque Central. Though the hotel enjoys a nice setting in an attractive 19th-century house, the rooms themselves are extremely basic and in need of a refit. Shared bathrooms (with cold water) only. There are some newer, smarter rooms in an annexe, the **Hotel Casa Real,** across the street, which come with private bathrooms and TVs and are around $10 more expensive. But, as is often the case with places of this type, the lack of amenities is more than made up for by the abundance of ambience. The central courtyard of the hotel is usually filled with chatting groups of backpackers and the friendly owner organizes trips to Palo Verde and Rincón de la Vieja.

Eating Out in Liberia

All tastes and budgets are catered for: there are a couple of supermarkets and an outdoor produce market, Av 7, C 10/12, for self-caterers; plenty of sodas (serving the Guanacastean take on *comida típica,* which tends to feature a lot of maize) and fast-food places (including a Burger King Food Court) for the budget-conscious; and several restaurants serving the ubiquitous 'international cuisine' for diners looking to splurge a little.

Restaurant El Café, Av 0, C 8/10. Serving snacks with a French accent (rather a singular experience for Liberia) – pastries, cakes, baguettes and a range of pâtés and cheeses – as well as good coffee, roasted fresh on the premises, which you can drink while browsing the excellent on-site book exchange. Baguettes from $3. *Open Mon–Fri* 10–7.

Restaurant La Cocina de José, Av 2, C 4/6, **t** 666 1202. A sort of sophisticated soda. Although the dining space looks rather dowdy and functional, the kitchen here is one of the finest purveyors of Costa Rican cuisine in town, turning out particularly fine spicy steaks, as well as excellent hearty soups and fish dishes. Mains $6–8.

Restaurant Paso Real, Av 0, C 0/2, **t** 666 3455. Tuck into *ceviche* and other traditional seafood delicacies from a balcony overlooking the Parque Central at one of Liberia's most upmarket restaurants. Mains $8–12.

Restaurant Pizza Pronto, t 666 2098. In a pretty 19th-century whitewashed house, this offers over 20 different pizza recipes ($4–10), all cooked up in a traditional wood-fired brick oven. In fine weather, you can eat alfresco in an attractive courtyard.

Soda Rancho Dulce, C 0, Av 0/2. Just south of the Parque Central, the Rancho Dulce offers good, cheap soda fare – *casados*, sandwiches, *gallo pinto*, etc., with nothing costing more than $4 – all served up at ancient wooden tables.

Entertainment and Nightlife in Liberia

Liberia is still a quiet town, although there are a few decent bars. Try **Las Tinajas** on the west side of the Parque Central, or **Tsunami**, just west of the Interamericana, which is pretty lively, particularly on Thursday nights (Ladies' Nights). The town's most happening place is the long-established **Kurú**, near the Best Western El Sitio, west of the Interamericana, a heaving disco that gets particularly packed at weekends.

Parque Nacional Rincón de la Vieja

Parque Nacional Rincón de la Vieja
t 661 8139; open daily 8–4; adm

Located roughly 25km northeast of Liberia, this national park encompasses many of the landscapes and environments for which Guanacaste is famous, including a sizeable swath of tropical dry forest and one of region's more active volcanoes, the eponymous Volcán Rincón de la Vieja. Unlike Volcán Arenal to the southwest, with its spectacular spewing lava, Rincón's activity takes the slightly less incendiary form of hot springs, bubbling mud pools and wafting sulphurous fumes. Experts seem to be divided as to whether this low-key activity makes Rincón more or less likely to explode in a major way in the near future. Some believe the vents covering the volcano's sides act as valves allowing it to regularly (and literally) blow off steam, thereby reducing the internal pressure and the likelihood of a significant explosion. Others contend that increased activity, particularly in the late 1990s, when the park was temporarily closed and local residents evacuated, may be indicative of a sizeable event on the horizon.

As it stands, the park has been judged safe to visit, although you should be aware that, even if you're not going to encounter red-hot lava flying through the air, this can still be a very dangerous environment, in fact perhaps more so than a volcano putting on a more obvious show of fireworks, as its hazards are not so readily apparent. For instance, several visitors have been severely injured falling through the brittle crusts of earth surrounding the volcano's inviting-looking, chocolatey (but boiling hot) mud pools.

 Volcán Rincón de la Vieja

The park covers an area of over 12,000ha, containing several minor peaks and two major ones: **Volcán Rincón de la Vieja** (1,895m) in the northwest corner of the park, and **Volcán Santa María** (1,916m), which is more or less in the centre. As has been the case with several of the country's national parks, Rincón was created in the early 1970s not so much to protect the area's flora and fauna, or even to protect local communities from the volcano, but in order to maintain the integrity of the watershed feeding the dozens of rivers and streams

Getting to the Parque Nacional Rincón de la Vieja

There is no official **bus** service to the park, but several of the hotels in Liberia offer transportation and guided tours (*see* p.166), as do the hotels listed below.

If **driving**, the turn-off for the Las Pailas ranger station via Curubandé is on the Interamericana around 5km north of Liberia. It's unpaved, but in pretty good condition, making it accessible to ordinary cars in the dry season, although, as always, it's preferable to take a 4WD, and you'll certainly need one if you're attempting to reach the Santa María entrance, the access road to which is in a much worse state.

A 4WD **taxi** from Liberia will cost around $25 – less if you can get people to share the ride.

that emerge in the high peaks of the park. The happy by-product of this water conservation has been the creation of an important refuge for a great deal of the region's wildlife, with the park being home to over 300 species of bird (curassows, eagles, hummingbirds, owls, parrots, quetzals, toucans, trogons, woodpeckers and more); lots of mammals (spider, white-faced and howler monkeys, jaguars, pumas, ocelots and margays, as well as tapirs, peccaries and sloths) and a huge abundance of insects, from the beautiful (the giant Blue Morpho butterfly, which can often be spotted near the park's water courses) to the irritating (chiggers, which can often be found biting lumps out of your ankles).

There are two main entrances to the park. Most people use the **Las Pailas ranger station**, which provides the easiest access to the summit of the volcano, rather than the **Santa María ranger station**, 8km away, which offers rather more testing hiking. Several well-marked **trails** lead into the park from Las Pailas: one takes you on a short tour through a section of tropical dry forest, where you may be able to spot some of the park's abundant wildlife; another heads west to a set of waterfalls, with an adjacent swimming pool; while a third takes you on a tour past several of the park's more note-worthy geothermal attractions, including a miniature volcano, some bubbling, burping mudpools and a number of steam vents (known as *hornillas*), which regularly exhale little train-engine puffs of gas. These are all very pretty but, as noted, a bit more dangerous than they look; exercise due caution and be sure not to get too close to anything active.

The **main trail** takes you on a hike all the way from Las Pailas to the summit of Rincón de la Vieja. This can be rather gruelling, involving a

Tips for Visiting Rincón de la Vieja

• Check the local weather conditions before setting out for the park (unless you're travelling as part of an official tour group, in which case they should do this for you) as Rincón's summit is often closed during very cloudy weather.

• Be sure to bring both wet-weather gear and plenty of warm clothing, as temperatures can quickly plummet near the summit, particularly when the winds start up.

• Bring something to cover your nose. The smell of sulphur near the summit is very strong, not to say rather unpleasant.

• Bring a strong DEET-based insect repellent and (if staying nearby) a mosquito net.

round trip of over 15km and a vertical ascent of over a kilometre. You'll need to start early in the day in order to be sure of completing your journey by the time the park closes. As you hike, you'll pass through several landscapes, including dry forest on the lower slopes and more lush forests at higher elevations until, near the summit, the vegetation dies away to practically nothing. As is common near the top of most active volcanoes, Rincón's summit is a barren, lifeless place where plants struggle to cope with the biting cold and the cocktail of toxic chemicals being spewed into the atmosphere.

If the weather is clear at the top, you'll be rewarded with some wonderful views, both close up – of the ominously smoking crater and nearby freshwater lake, the **Lago Los Jilgueros** – and futher afield to Lake Nicaragua to the north, the Pacific ocean to the west, and the Cordillera Central mountains to the south. Unfortunately, unrestricted views are by no means guaranteed. The weather here is unpredictable in the extreme, with banks of clouds rolling in and departing seemingly in an instant. Indeed, if the clouds become so thick as to severely reduce visibility, the park authorities may take the decision to close the summit. This is not an environment in which you wish to become disorientated, as the crater's edge is both brittle and unprotected. If dense mists descend while you're already at the summit, you should move away from the crater's edge and begin your return to the ranger station as soon as possible.

The walk from the Santa María ranger station to the summit of Rincón de la Vieja is even longer and more arduous, although equally rewarding, passing through areas of forest and past hot springs which are often cool enough to swim in – i.e. they are at sauna heat rather than coffee heat, although you should be sure to check the temperature first.

Where to Stay in and around the Parque Nacional Rincón de la Vieja

Camping is available at both ranger stations for $2. Toilets and showers are provided, but you'll need to bring your own toilet paper, food, camping stove and tent. You're also allowed to camp in certain areas within the park, although you'll need to check first with the ranger station to see if there's anywhere currently off limits.

The local area also has some reasonably priced and well-equipped lodges, all of which offer tours to the park.

Hotel Hacienda Guachipelín, t 666 8075, www.guachipelin.com ($$$; $65).

Just off the turning from the highway, with large cabins (with private bathrooms and terraces) and a decent restaurant set on over 800 hectares of a former cattle ranch that's gradually returning to a state of secondary forest.

Rincón de la Vieja Lodge, t 661 8198 ($$$; $70). Close to Las Pailas entrance, with good-sized, rustic-looking rooms, a few self-catering cottages, and a whole heap of facilities, including a swimming pool, a butterfly garden, mountain bikes, a restaurant, Internet access and a 21-platform canopy tour. Electric light and the somewhat intermittent hot water are provided by hydroelectric power.

Parque Nacional Santa Rosa

22 **Parque Nacional**
Santa Rosa
t 661 8150; open
daily 8–4; adm

This was Costa Rica's first national park, established way back in 1971, and it is still one of the largest and most popular. Encompassing over 36,000 terrestrial hectares, including the whole of the Peninsula de Santa Elena in the far northwestern corner of the country, plus a good deal of mainland territory, it offers a vast range of attractions, from the environmental (it's home to Central America's largest remaining swath of tropical dry forest, and its beaches are the world's largest nesting site for olive ridley turtles) to the historical (it is the site of and is named after the most famous battle in Costa Rican history) and the activity-based (its coast has long been famed for the quality of its surfing).

Tropical dry forest, a landscape that was once common throughout the isthmus, has over the past century been reduced to just a few isolated pockets, of which this is the most significant. It is perhaps best described as sort of opposite to cloudforest. Where cloudforest is lush, luxuriant and astoundingly thick, dry forest is (outside of the wet season, at least) sparse, stubby and almost desert-like, its trees shedding their leaves to conserve water. Despite the harshness of the conditions, Santa Rosa's forests are nonetheless home to a great concentration of wildlife, including over 250 species of bird (parrots, parakeets and trogons among them), dozens of species of reptiles and amphibians, thousands of species of butterfly and over a hundred species of mammal, including three species of monkey (howler, spider and white-faced capuchin), deer, coatis, peccaries, armadillos, coyotes, racoons, ocelots and many species of bat – best seen at an adjoining section of the park called, appropriately enough, the **Murciélago ('Bat')**
Sector, accessed via a different entrance. Intriguingly, dry forest's apparent lack of life actually makes it rather better for wildlife-spotting than its lusher counterpart. While it's difficult to see anything in cloudforest apart from the mass of foliage in front of your face, dry forest offers greater visibility, particularly in the dry season when animals tend to gravitate towards and congregate around the few remaining water holes.

The entrance to the park lies off the Interamericana, over 30km north of Liberia, from where a paved road leads to the park's **administration centre** 7km further on. **Trails** lead from here both into the dry forest and to the **La Casona Historical Museum**, which marks the spot where, in 1856, Costa Rica's ragtag army succeeded in defeating the invading forces of the US adventurer, William Walker (for the full story, *see* **History**, p.24). The original Hacienda La Casona was burned to the ground in 2001 by a couple of local farmers as a protest against being banned from hunting in the park (they were arrested and imprisoned), but has subsequently been rebuilt.

Getting to the Parque Nacional Santa Rosa

Buses running from Liberia to the Nicaraguan border pass by the entrance to the park, from where it's a 7km hike along a paved road to the administration centre. Ask the driver to let you off. The Hotel Liberia runs daily transport to the park for $15 (*see* p.167), although the easiest and most convenient way is to **drive** yourself in a 4WD. In the dry season, you can follow trails through the park all the way down to the coast.

Another trail heads west from here for 13km all the way to the white-sand **Playa Naranjo** on the coast (where there's another smaller, less well-equipped campsite), which is open to 4WD traffic in the dry season, December to April, and to hikers and horse-riders throughout the year. Playa Naranjo has been a popular surfing destination since the 1960s, with its offshore features – particularly the famous Witch's Rock – creating giant, almost cylindrical waves. Surfing tours to here are offered by many of the tour operators in Playa del Coco and Tamarindo, although you should be aware that the beaches are sometimes closed during the turtle laying season.

Further north of here, and also reachable by 4WD in the dry season, is **Playa Nancite**, the site of the world's largest *arribada* (annual mass laying, from July to November, with a peak from September to October) by olive ridley turtles, the smallest (typically less than 1m long) but also the most numerous of Costa Rica's marine turtles. And mass in this instance really does mean mass. Over 200,000 turtles are estimated to lay their eggs here every year (or several thousand per night). At peak times the beach can become an absolute sea of reptile flesh, with turtles clambering over the sand (and each other) to reach the high tide line, beyond which they lay their eggs. This great procession of procreative turtles used to be watched by almost equally sizeable levels of tourists, but access to the beach has become much more restricted in recent years. Permits to watch the laying are now issued on a case-by-case basis, with usually no more than 20 tourists a day allowed onto the beach. Enquire at the administration centre as to what the current limit is. Note that torches, flash photography and indeed any form of illumination are banned on the beach, as the turtles are extremely susceptible to light, using the stars and the moon to navigate themselves ashore.

Where to Stay in the Parque Nacional Santa Rosa

There are two main **campsites**: one at the park headquarters, which is well equipped with cold-water showers, toilets, picnic benches and drinking water; and a slightly less well-equipped one at Playa Naranjo (no drinking water), plus a few other basic ones dotted around the park. Space also sometimes becomes available in the **accommodation block** of the park's **research station**, although this is usually reserved for visiting scientists and students. If you do get lucky, $20 will get you a bunk in a dorm, cold showers and, best of all, access to the park in early morning, when wildlife-watching is at its best.

Parque Nacional Guanacaste

Guanacaste National Park is still something of a work in progress. Though its 30,000ha adjoin Santa Rosa National Park (or, at least, they would do if the Interamericana wasn't in the way), it is a very different beast. Whereas Santa Rosa is the country's oldest national park, set up to protect an existing environment, and is well geared up for tourism, Guanacaste is one of the country's more recently established parks, set up to give an adapted environment a chance to revert back to its wild state, and has very few facilities. Much of the national park is taken up by former pasture that it is hoped will one day transform back into tropical dry forest, thus providing the animals of Santa Rosa with a good deal more territory. Those small pockets of dry forest that do remain here are home to much the same wildlife as Santa Rosa, just in much smaller concentrations.

The park has been established more with science and research in mind than tourism, with precious few facilities for casual visitors. If you are interested in visiting, you'll need to contact Santa Rosa's administration centre, which can enquire as to whether there's any space available at one of the research stations. To be honest, for the next 10–20 years or so, you're probably better off sticking to Santa Rosa, whose environment is more pristine in any case.

La Cruz, Peñas Blancas and the Nicaraguan Border

Though it's a good 20km from Nicaragua, **La Cruz** has a real border town feel to it, principally because it is the last major town on the Interamericana before Nicaragua, and is usually camped out with people waiting to make the morning crossing. It's not a particularly awful place by border town standards, although, if it were not where it was, it wouldn't attract half the visitors or have a fraction of the facilities it does. There are a couple of banks (useful for getting money for the all-important entry fee to Nicaragua), a few decent sodas and some sleeping options if you're obliged to spend the night

Crossing the Border

It can be an expensive process getting into Nicaragua, particularly as the entry fee increases over the course of the day – $7 before noon, $9 after (and at weekends). This can be paid in dollars only. *In extremis*, if the bank is closed, you can change *colones* for dollars with one of the hordes of money-changers you'll see hanging around, although expect to pay well over the odds. It can also be quite a long-drawn-out process, another reason to get here early, with teams of border officials on both sides carefully scrutinizing your documents. The process is slightly speeded up if you're coming on the Tica Bus (*see* p.66), as passengers' passports and documents will be checked *en masse*. The crossing is open 6am–8pm daily. It's a 1km walk between the Costa Rican and Nicaraguan border posts, after which you can catch a bus, or take a taxi, to Rivas, the first sizeable city on the Nicaraguan side around 30km past the border.

Getting to Peñas Blancas

Buses leave San José, C 20, Av 1, daily for Peñas Blancas at 5am, 7am, 7.45am, 10.30am, 1.20pm and 4.10pm. It costs c1,035. There are also frequent services from Liberia.

(*see* bottom of this page). The crossing point is at **Peñas Blancas**, a town in name only, consisting of little more than a bank and a couple of sodas.

Parque Nacional Palo Verde and Reserva Biológica Lomas de Barbudal

Parque Nacional Palo Verde and Reserva Biológica Lomas de Barbudal
t 671 1062; open daily 8–4; adm; book tickets at the MINAE office in Bagaces, t 200 0125

People may be thin on the ground in the 18,000ha **Palo Verde**, one of the country's least visited national parks located around 50km southwest of Liberia, but birds are never in short supply. Bordering the Río Tempisque, the park's rolling limestone landscape supports a soggy network of mangrove swamps, marshes, swamps and lakes that provide perfect conditions for wildfowl, who exist here in greater numbers than anywhere else in Central America. Over 300 resident and migratory species have been recorded, including herons, storks, roseatte spoonbills, egrets, grebes, ibis and ducks.

Much of the park is inaccessible during the wet season, when heavy rains turn its surface into a patchwork of temporary lakes, swamps and rivers. However, most of these dry out and recede in the dry months, making it much easier both to get around the park and to spot its wildlife, who are obliged to congregate in ever denser clusters as the park's bodies of water shrink. The best time to visit is from September to March, when good spotting opportunities are offered from a raised viewing platform near the ranger station.

The 3,000ha **Reserva Biológica Lomas de Barbudal** adjoins the northern edge of Palo Verde, and together they form a single conservation unit administered by the same MINAE office in **Bagaces**, where you can book tickets for both. The park's swaths of tropical dry forest (some of the largest remaining in the region) seem to provide as compelling an environment for insects as Palo Verde's lakes do for wildfowl. Incredibly, over a quarter of all the world's known species of bee live here, feasting on the abundant wet-season flowers. They are less common at the height of the dry season, when the baking sun sucks all the moisture from the earth

Where to Stay in La Cruz

Amalia's Inn, 100m south of Parque Central, **t** 669 9618 ($; $25). The best choice, with large rooms, private bathrooms and a friendly atmosphere. It only has seven rooms, however.

Cabinas Santa Rita, across the street, **t** 679 9062 ($; $15). More spartan accommodation – small rooms with shared cold-water bathrooms, as well as a few fancier ones with private bathrooms and TVs.

Getting to Palo Verde and Lomas de Barbudal

Both parks can be reached via the Interamericana. The **Palo Verde** entrance lies 30km southwest of the town of **Bagaces**. There's no bus service, so if travelling without your own transport, you'll either have to take a **taxi** ($15), or book a tour with one of the operators in San José (*see* pp.68–70) or Liberia (*see* p.166). You'll need a 4WD to reach the park independently.

Tours (both on foot or horseback) can be booked at the ranger station for $15/30. The ranger station can also offer dormitory accommodation ($13), with shared bathrooms, and camping space for $7 (meals are $7 extra).

The entrance to the **Lomas de Barbudal Reserve** is reached via a turn-off from the Interamericana around 10km north of **Bagaces**. Again, there's no bus service, although you could catch a service travelling north along the highway and get dropped off at the turning, from where it's a 7km walk to the entrance. It's much more convenient to drive; the road is unpaved but in reasonable condition, but as always, for comfort, use a 4WD.

and the forest trees shed their leaves, giving the area a parched, desert-like appearance.

The Nicoya Peninsula: Northern Beaches

The Nicoya Peninsula boasts Costa Rica's most developed coastline. Indeed, the section of coast bordering Bahía Culebra at the northern end of the peninsula may be one of the most developed in the whole of Central America. It is the site of the infamous Papagayo Project, an attempt to create a vast Cancun-like, city-scale tropical resort (*see* p.179). While other ventures in the area have been slightly less extreme, much of the coast's transformation has been conducted in a way that might most charitably be described as less than sensitive. Though regulations have been tightened in recent years, there are parts of the northern Nicoyan coast that have had to endure some of the most first-world-orientated, environmentally damaging forms of development possible – the sort that destroys forests, drains mangroves and creates great water-sapping, climate-changing golf courses, those ultimate symbols of managed, tamed, neutered nature. And yet, for all this, there are still parts of the coast,

Getting to and around Playa del Coco

The **drive** to El Coco is pretty straightforward. The roads are paved and in reasonably good condition all the way from San José, a good 4hrs' drive away – and there are not too many other routes of a similar distance in the whole of the country you can say that about. Simply head up the Interamericana to Liberia, where you connect with HWY-21. Follow this south into the peninsula for around 20km, before exiting for the El Coco turning on your right just past the town of **Comunidad**. El Coco lies around 7km west of **Sardinal**, where you may want to check your fuel levels; there are no petrol stations on this stretch of coast, so if you're running low, you'll need to fill up here.

Three **buses** a day leave San José from C 24, Av 1/3 for Playa del Coco at 8am, 2pm and 4pm. The journey takes around 5hrs and costs c1855. There are also six services a day from Liberia, just under 40km away, which take just under an hour.

A **taxi** from Liberia to El Coco will cost between $15–20.

There's a **taxi** rank by the Parque Central.

particularly further south, that are pristine and untouched. Development on the peninsula has mostly been concentrated in a number of hot spots, with each new project latching onto and hoping to ride the coat-tails of the last. The lack of a single unifying coastal road has helped to reduce coastal sprawl, with most resorts, for the time being, lying separated from each other, rather than blending, Costa del Sol-like, into a single unbroken line.

The most aggressively touristic stretch of coast is the section between Bahía Culebra and Tamarindo. Here it's all about partying, beach life and comfort, offered in convenient all-inclusive, packaged slices. Having said that, even here there are still a few isolated bays and beaches that have as yet managed to escape the developers' predatory gaze. The further south you go, the weaker mass tourism's grip on the environment becomes. Despite the huge amount of building that has taken place, and the sheer volume of visitors arriving each year, particularly since the opening of the international airport at Liberia around a decade ago, this is still a region where, if you're willing to expend the effort, it's just about possible to get away from it all – head far enough away from the main tourist areas and you'll find yourself walking on some of the most idyllic stretches of coast in the entire country.

Playa del Coco

It's probably its facilities and the excellence of the transport links, from both San José and Liberia (just under 40km northeast), that have made Playa del Coco ① one of the most visited and popular of the Nicoyan beaches, rather than the stretch of sand itself, which is actually one of the region's least attractive. Still, it does lie within easy reach of several places with a good deal more aesthetic appeal. For the majority of visitors, El Coco's charms are twofold: in the daytime it offers great scuba-diving and snorkelling, with various firms offering trips out to observe the teeming wildlife of the coastal waters, while at night it becomes something of a party town. Its lively (occasionally bordering on seedy) collection of bars and discos are frequented by both tourists and Ticos, who pour down from the capital at the weekend to drink and dance their cares away.

El Coco boasts a layout common to many of the beach towns in this region, with just two main roads, the one leading into town, and the one running along the seafront, the junction of which is marked by a tiny **Parque Central**. There's also a slightly raggedy **pier** extending from the front. However, unlike many other nearby towns, El Coco does boast a few side streets as well, making it practically labyrinthine by the area's standards, although it's still a pretty simple place to find your way around.

Services in El Coco

Most of the services you require are located on the main road leading into town, including three Internet cafés – Leslie Internet, Café Internet and E-Juice Bar Internet – a branch of the Banco Nacional (from the front, it's about a 7–10-minute walk inland, on the left) which can change traveller's cheques and has an ATM, and a supermarket (near the bank).

Activities in El Coco

A number of companies in town arrange snorkelling and diving trips. The nearby **Islas Santa Catalina** and **Murciélago ('Bat Island')** are the prime dive sites, although the waters here are by no means crystal-clear. There are very few spots where visibility exceeds 20m, but the superabundance of wildlife in these waters means that this is rarely a major problem, as there's usually something fascinating swimming around in close proximity. Dolphins, sharks, octopuses, turtles and a chocolate-box assortment of tropical fish are all regularly spotted. The main dive season runs from April to September, just after the traditional high season.

The following dive companies are long-established and have good reputations.

Deep Blue Diving Adventures, Hotel Coco Verde, **t** 670 1004, *www.scuba-diving-in-costa-rica.com*.

Rich Coast Diving, **t** 670 0176, *www.richcoastdiving.com*.

Where to Stay in El Coco

There are plenty of options, from the upscale to the very, very low-scale, including a good number of extremely basic, no-frills *cabinas* aimed at absorbing the weekly migration of Josefinos on Friday and Saturday nights. Many are very spartan, offering four walls, a bed, access to shared cold-water showers and not much besides. In the high season, you'll need to book ahead for the more the more upmarket places, many of which are located on the town's outskirts.

Hotel La Flor de Itabo, **t** 670 0108, *www.flordeitabo.com* ($$$$; $80). Popular with Americans – it has a casino and offers sports fishing trips – this well-equipped, if slightly generic, hotel on the road into town has rooms with air-conditioning, telephones and cable TV, as well as some cheaper bungalows without air-conditioning. The restaurant serves up some pretty good Italian cuisine and there's a bar, a swimming pool and a Jacuzzi.

Hotel La Puerta del Sol, **t** 670 195 ($$$$; $80). An upmarket choice, The rooms of the Puerta del Sol boast some of the town's most elegant décor – all blues and oranges, designed to give it a Mediterranean feel. Each comes with a private bathroom, air-conditioning, cable TV, a telephone and safe, and overlooks the hotel's neatly laid-out gardens and swimming pool. There are also some luxury suites available for $110, as well as a Jacuzzi and gym. The Italian restaurant is one of the town's best (*see* below).

Hotel Villa Flores, t 670 0269, *www. hotel-villa-flores.com* ($$$; $55). Now under American ownership, the recently renovated property just north of the town centre on a road running parallel to the beach road has nine pleasantly appointed rooms, all with colourful décor, air-conditioning and gleaming white bathrooms. Some also have balconies and TVs. Additional features include a swimming pool, a Jacuzzi, lush gardens and, in high season, a restaurant.

Hotel Villa del Sol, t 670 0085, *www. villadelsol.com* ($$$; $45). North of the centre on the beach road, this has nice, bright, airy rooms. The cheapest have shared bathrooms and fans, the most expensive ($30 more) air-conditioning and ocean views from their balconies. There are also some self-catering units with kitchens, cable TV and telephones, as well as an attractive tropical garden with a swimming pool. It's just a short walk to the beach. The room rates include breakfast.

Cabinas Coco Azul, t 670 0431 ($; $10 per person). Near the football field, just back from the front, this is clean and tidy and pretty well equipped considering the price. All of the brightly coloured rooms have private tiled bathrooms, as well as balconies with hammocks.

Hotel Luna Tica, t 670 0127 ($; $20). The best thing to say about the Luna Tica, in the centre of town near the beach, is that it's cheap, but this is pretty basic stuff – small, slightly poky rooms and crumbling bathrooms. Get yourself an oceanside room and console yourself with the views. There's also a small annexe and a not too bad seafood restaurant, **Restaurante Luna Tica**, just across the street.

⭐ El Sol y Luna >>

Eating Out in El Coco

The restaurant scene is probably pretty much as you'd expect it to be – aimed primarily at American tastes and sensibilities, with lots of places offering 'genuine' Tex-Mex and Louisiana cooking. European sensibilities are catered to with a number of Italian eateries, a couple of which are actually pretty decent, and

there are even a few Costa Rican restaurants aimed at the local population which, as always, represent the best value, particularly if you go for the locally caught fish and seafood.

Chile Dulce, t 670 0465. The town's healthiest offering, the Chile Dulce offers a variety of salads and vegetarian dishes, as well as plenty of seafood. Its walls are adorned with artwork, much of it for sale.

El Sol y Luna, Hotel Puerta del Sol, **t** 670 0195. There are several Italian restaurants in town, but this is definitely the pick of the bunch, offering superior cuisine whipped up by a genuine Roman chef. Recipes are as Mediterranean as they come: a wide range of pasta, pizza and risotto choices, but there are also a few dishes that at least tacitly acknowledge the restaurant's location, such as the famous volcano-shaped Arenal cake. The dining space is suitably elegant, with candlelit tables and there's a good selection of wines (mostly Italian, of course).

Papagayo, on the seafront. This serves good quality, reasonably priced seafood – mixed seafood platters, catch of the day, *ceviche*, etc. all for around $7.

Tequila Bar and Grill, t 670 0741. Slighty rowdy Mexican restaurant that has proved a very popular watering hole with the town's sizeable Gringo population over the years. The food is actually pretty good, spicy fajitas, tacos and *tortas*, washed down with potent margaritas.

Nightlife in El Coco

El Coco turns into a full-on party town in the high season with plenty of lively places to choose from. Some of the most popular include: the **Banana Surf Bar/Disco,** above the El Tucán souvenir shop, which has tables surrounding a small dance floor and stays open till 2am most nights; the **Lizard Lounge,** where the crowds go if the Banana Surf isn't proving suitably lively (and vice versa) with an open-air dance floor under a thatched roof; and, for when these begin to wind down, the **Disco Coco Mar** on the beach where the party carries on all night.

North of Playa del Coco: Bahía Culebra

Coco provides a good base from which to explore the area, with several decent bays and beaches within easy (and, depending on the condition of the coastal road, not so easy) reach.

Around 7km north of Coco is **Bahía Culebra**, a beautiful, sheltered south-facing bay that protects a body of clear, calm water perfect for snorkelling and swimming. Unfortunately, these visitor-friendly qualities have not gone unnoticed by the country's developers. In the 1970s, **Playa Panamá** ② at the northern end of the bay became the site the country's biggest and most ambitious tourism development, the **Papagayo Project**. This was to be no gentle, subtle showcasing of the bay's charms, however, but rather a grandiose attempt to completely re-sculpt the environment according to the needs of mass tourism – flattening forests, re-routing water courses – in preparation for the creation of over 15,000 hotel rooms. This would have effected a threefold increase in the total number of hotel rooms in the country, at a stroke turning Costa Rica into one of Central America's prime tourist destinations (or so it was hoped). Of course, this scheme was conceived at a time before Costa Rica had fully woken up to the potential of its natural environment – its forests, mountains and beaches in their wild, unchanged state – as a tourist attraction. Back then, it was assumed that if you wanted to attract first-world visitors, you had to alter your landscape in order to make it look as first world as possible. However, as the conservation and eco-tourism movements grew over the next decade, and the protests of environmentalists became ever more vocal, so people's outlooks began to change. While protestors were never going to be able to stop a project of this size and momentum once it was under way, they did at least get it to pause for breath. A series of

Golfing in Northwest Costa Rica

For non-golf fans, the game's overwhelming popularity and seemingly ceaseless global expansion continues to astonish. It's difficult to understand how something so bland and mundane can take over the world. The growing interest in and demand for golf in Costa Rica is particularly perplexing. What is the thinking behind the decision to go for a round? Let's go to the most biologically diverse country on earth, a landscape littered with natural wonders, and play a game we could play anywhere in a landscape altered to look as if it could be anywhere. That said, objections to Costa Rican golf arise less from some sort of trivial dislike of the sport's identikit ubiquity as from serious environmental concerns. They may be green, but golf courses are not very ecologically friendly. A full 18-hole course takes up a lot of space and requires a lot of water to maintain – and this, remember, in one of the country's driest provinces.

Still if golf is your bag (and you may have worked out by now that it's not mine, at least not here), there are a number of courses in northwest Costa Rica where you can get a round. The following all have 'championship-standard' 18-hole courses:

Four Seasons, Playa Panamá, t 696 0009, www.fourseasons.com (see p.180).
Paradisus Playa Conchal Beach and Golf Resort, t 654 4123, www.solmelia.com (see p.182).
Hacienda Pinilla, t 680 3000, www.haciendapinilla.com.
Royal Pacific Golf and Country Club, t 383 3759.

environmental impact studies were commissioned which led to the original plans being significantly altered. Areas of tropical dry forest earmarked for destruction were saved, and the number of hotel rooms revised downwards. Nonetheless, a good deal of environmentally damaging construction did go ahead (and, indeed, continues to go ahead; the project is far from complete), resulting in a landscape that has been significantly altered. In the place of gently forested hills at the northern end of the bay now stand some of the country's most expensive resorts, offering all the luxury amenities its first-world package guests could possibly want – casinos, swimming pools, tennis courts, golf courses, etc.

Playa Hermosa ②at the southern edge of the bay (not to be confused with the beach of same name in the Central Pacific), has for now managed to escape the very worst ravages of this development. It's quiet and idyllic, if not totally pristine. Some construction has taken place here, but mostly in the form of villas, home to communities of expat Americans and Canadians who give the place a nice, villagey (if not exactly Costa Rican) feel. The swimming, snorkelling and sunset views are all particularly fine from here.

Where to Stay around Bahía Culebra

Four Seasons, Playa Panamá, **t** 696 0009, www.fourseasons.com ($$$$$; $465). The Four Seasons is one of the country's largest, most lavish, most well-equipped and most expensive resorts, and a perfect example of what the Papagayo Project is all about – hermetically sealed, all-inclusive tropical opulence. It offers restaurants, bars, casinos, swimming pools, tennis courts, saunas and spas by the bucketful, with every indoor space air-conditioned to the optimum temperature. The whole thing is undeniably sumptuous, but you do get the feeling that you're almost in a different country. Then again, that's probably the point. When accommodation reaches this sort of scale, it's the hotel, not the country, that's the destination; Costa Rica is just there to provide a tropical backdrop.

Cabinas Playa Hermosa, Playa Hermosa, **t** 672 0046 ($$$; $40). At the southern end of the beach, this has a nice laid-back vibe, with friendly owners and pretty gardens where hammocks are strung up between the trees. Its 20 rooms are well equipped, with fans, private bathrooms (hot water) and cable TV, albeit rather simply decorated. But then, with clear blue, snorkel-friendly waters right on your doorstep, you're probably not going to be in much. The hotel also operates a small restaurant, **Seabreeze**, where breakfast is served.

Playa Hermosa Inn, Playa Hermosa, **t** 672 0063, www.costaricabeach-hotel. com ($$$; $50). The Inn is, for the area, a fairly plain and simple choice, with just nine rooms (either with fans or, for $30 more, air-conditioning) and a small swimming pool. The apartment, which can sleep up to seven, represents good value for groups. The room rates include breakfast.

Hotel El Velero, Playa Hermosa, **t** 672 1017 ($$$; $72). On the beach road, this elegant-looking whitewashed hotel has large, stylish rooms – all with air-conditioning, private bathrooms (with hot water) and two double beds. There is also a swimming pool and a restaurant/bar serving tasty barbecue suppers. The hotel offers sailing and snorkelling cruises in its own boat.

South of El Coco

South of Playa del Coco is a line of slightly less accessible beaches, some fairly developed, some less so (and some just very pretty), but all with something to offer.

The dark-sand **Playa Ocotal** ③, 3km southwest, is considerably quieter and less built-up than Coco. Its waters are calm and good for swimming, and there's snorkelling, diving and fishing available. Heading south from here, you come to a very rough road known as the 'Monkey Trail' (because it's bordered by a swath of jungle where monkeys are often spotted), which is only passable in the dry season, and then only in a 4WD. Following this for around 13km takes you to the charming and secluded **Playa Potrero** ④, which can be used as a base to explore some even more charming and secluded beaches nearby, including the delightfully named **Playa Pan de Azúcar** ④ (Sugar Bread Beach). Buses only go as far as Potrero.

Three kilometres south of Potrero, and clearly visible (though thankfully separated by a rocky headland) is another of the coast's more built-up resorty stretches, **Playa Flamingo** ④. It is named (or rather re-named, it was originally called Playa Blanca) not after the local wildlife (there are no flamingos here), but in honour of one of the region's first hotels, the Flamingo Beach Resort, which still stands, looking pink and expensive at the end of the bay. The beach, which is actually rather pleasant, with tour operators offering sports fishing and diving trips, is overlooked almost along its entire length by great concrete monstrosities – mega-resorts, condos, beach hotels, etc. It's been nicknamed 'Flagringo' by some locals because of the high volume of US tourists.

Eight kilometres south of here, at **Playa Conchal** ⑤, the scene changes again. 'Shell Beach' (named not after a major local business but after the shells littering its sands) is as quiet and secluded as Flamingo is brash, noisy and touristy, although the Paradisus Playa Conchal resort, one of region's largest, looms menacingly nearby.

Where to Stay
South of El Coco

Flamingo Marina Resort, Playa Flamingo, t 654 4141, *www.flamingo marina.com* ($$$$$; $120). This isn't *the* Flamingo, i.e. the Flamingo Beach Resort, the opening of which put the area on the map and inspired the renaming of the beach in its honour. That's further down the hill (and, to be honest, is looking slightly worn around edges these days). This is a new, albeit no less pink, holiday complex comprising a great assortment of buildings spread up a hill, commanding good views of the area. The standard rooms are swish with air-conditioning, cable TV, telephones and nice detailing – wooden furniture, terracotta lamps, etc. – while the 'Sportsman Suites' ($170) are absolutely huge with leather sofas and kitchenettes. If you fancy a dip, there are no fewer than five swimming pools to choose from, as well as tennis courts and a dive shop. Diving and sports fishing tours are offered. The resort attracts, as you have probably already guessed, a primarily American clientele.

El Ocotal Beach Resort, Playa Ocotal, t 670 0321, *www.ocotalresort.com*

($$$$$; $150). Very well-equipped holiday complex perched imperiously on a cliff overlooking the ocean with three pools, three restaurants, a Jacuzzi, a spa, tennis courts, a gym, a souvenir shop, a dive centre and a sports fishing boat. It's not cheap: $150 will get you one of the least expensive rooms (air-conditioning, telephone, coffee-maker and terrace); $230 one of its bungalows (the same, but with a plunge pool; one pool per every two bungalows), while $280 will get you a suite (all of the above, plus Jacuzzi). All have great panoramic views.

Paradisus Playa Conchal Beach and Golf Resort, Playa Conchal, just south of Playa Brasilito, t 654 4123, *www. solmelia.com* ($$$$$; $209 per person). Only the super-rich need apply, for the Paradisus is one of the area's most renowned mega-resorts; its suites are palatial, its public areas awash with marble and its pool almost unswimmable (it's the largest in Central America, apparently). The hotel offers all those little touches that go towards the perfect holiday – such as an 18-hole golf course, tennis courts, shops, a beauty salon, a gym, Internet access, five restaurants, four bars, a casino and, of course, a private beach.

Hotel Sugar Beach, Playa Pan de Azúcar, t 654 4242, *www.sugar-beach. com* ($$$$$; $158–28). Set on a tree-lined hill just back from the beach, the Sugar Beach is one of the area's oldest hotels, but has managed to stay competitive with more recent arrivals via a process of near constant renovation. Its bedrooms still look fresh and modern (the bright colour schemes help), and come with private bathrooms, air-conditioning, cable TV and hand-carved doors featuring representations of local wildlife. The superior rooms have ocean views ($158) and there are also a couple of large apartments with two bedrooms, as well as two beach houses that can sleep up to 10. Surfing trips north up to Witch's Rock in the Parque Nacional Santa Rosa, and turtle-watching trips down south to the Parque Nacional Marino Las Baulas, are offered. There's a good open-air fish/seafood restaurant. The hotel is only accessible by car.

B&B Villa Casa Blanca, Playa Ocotal, t 670 0518 ($$$$; $87). Set just back from the beach on the top of a hill amid abundant tropical foliage, the Casa Blanca has a peaceful, secluded feel to it. The large rooms are decorated in a Victorian style, which seems to translate as ornate mirrors, and twiddly wooden detailing, and come with private bathrooms and a choice of ceiling fan or air-conditioning. Suites with ocean views, plus a couple of self-catering units with kitchenettes, are also available. Pool and Jacuzzi.

Hotel Guanacaste Lodge, Playa Flamingo, t 654 4494, *portolsa@ racsa.co.cr* ($$$; $60). One of the area's less overwhelming choices, this small Costa Rican-run lodge on the road heading south out of town towards Playa Brasilito offers large, bright, airy rooms, all with attractive wooden furniture, air-conditioning, cable TV, two double beds and private bathrooms, as well as a swimming pool and a very good open-air hybrid Tico/ Spanish/Mexican restaurant. It's something of a bargain for the area.

Cabinas Isolina Beach, Playa Potrero, t 654 4333, *www.isolinabeach.com* ($$$; $50). North of Potrero towards Playa Brasilito, this is, despite its name, actually set just back from the beach in attractive gardens. Recently renovated, it now offers a decent standard of mid-range comfort. Rooms have air-conditioning, cable TV and private bathrooms, and there are a couple of self-catering villas with kitchens, as well as a swimming pool. The rate includes breakfast.

Tamarindo

 Tamarindo

Once a quiet fishing village (weren't they all?), right now Tamarindo may well be the most popular resort in the whole of Costa Rica – and the most built-up. As with Coco to the north, a happy combination of ease of access (there's an airfield), great

Getting to Tamarindo

Both NatureAir and Sansa operate daily **flights** to Tamarindo's small airfield, 3km north of town, from where you can take a **taxi** to the centre of town for around $3.

If **driving**, the conditions aren't too bad, although if you are coming via Santa Cruz, the final 20km or so will be on an unpaved and pretty bumpy road. A smoother journey is provided by the slightly less obvious route of turning off HWY-21 before you reach Santa Cruz, just after Belén, following the road west to Huacas, then south to Villrreal, and then west again for the final couple of kilometres to Playa Tamarindo.

Two **buses** a day link San José with Tamarindo. They leave from Av 5, C 14 at 11am and 3.30pm and take 5hrs (c1,940). There are also six services a day from Liberia, at 5.30am, 9am, 11.30am, 1pm, 2pm and 4.30pm (c400).

---

surfing, a clement climate and loads of prime beachfront real estate has led to massive growth in the past couple of decades. Foreigners, Americans in particular, have arrived here *en masse* looking for their slice of the tropical pie, setting up homes and businesses by the hundred – hotels, shops, restaurants, bars, tour operators, estate agents, etc. – with more opening all the time.

Part of the attraction of the place – and what keeps new arrivals pouring in – is that there is so much to do. Surfing has long been the main daytime activity (*see* below), with a well-established surfing community (in fact it's so well established that some of the older members have begun graduating to the town's almost equally

Surfing around Tamarindo

Surfing was the activity that first put Tamarindo on the tourist map, and it continues to draw the crowds, with an absolute plethora of surf schools and shops on hand to service their needs, offering lessons for around $35 for 2hrs. The waters here particularly lend themselves to board-riding because of the number of physical features dotting the offshore landscape – sandbars, rock reefs, river mouths, sloping beaches, etc. – which shape and channel the incoming waves into those all-important 'breaks' on which surfers do their thing.

Unfortunately, the downside of all this wave channelling is that the swimming isn't great (too many riptides), while the overwhelming popularity of the sport means that the waters here get very crowded. Anyone with a bit of experience hoping to jump straight up onto their board will often find themselves waiting on the efforts of the hordes of learners making their first tentative attempts to catch a wave.

Happily, there are some much quieter, less crowded stretches of coast which offer equally good (if not better) surfing to the south of here, although these can be quite difficult to get to. The stretch of coast beginning around 13km south of Tamarindo – which includes the white-sand **Playa Avellana** ⑥, the somewhat dark and rocky **Playa Negra**, and the 2km-long remote and unspoilt **Playa Junquillal** ⑦ – is one of the country's most revered, and has been since its appearance in the 1960s film *The Endless Summer* first brought Costa Rica's surf scene to international attention. Indeed, Playa Avellana's breaks are of such a high quality that it's been given the nickname Pequeño Hawaii (Little Hawaii).

To get to these beaches independently, you'll need a 4WD and strong nerves, as the coastal road here is little more than a rough track that passes through several rivers. None is particularly deep outside the rainy season (but the best surfing is in the rainy season). Nonetheless, it can still be a little unnerving driving through them, especially as you sometimes can't make out the bottom clearly. You can't access the coast road directly from Tamarindo, but must retrace your tracks inland for a few kilometres first.

For a slightly less worrisome journey, leave it to the professionals. Most of Tamarindo's surf schools (*see* pp.184–5) offer trips out to here.

The surfing is also quite good just south of town at **Playa Langosta** ⑥, and just north at **Playa Grande**, which lies within the Parque Nacional Marino Las Baulas (*see* pp.188–90).

Orientation

The town's lack of formal planning shows in its layout, which is somewhat sprawling and unfocused. There are two main roads (plus a variety of side lanes and tributaries). The first, the beachfront road, runs south from the Parque Nacional Las Baulas for around 2.5km to a loop of shops and restaurants which marks the town's (unofficial) centre. Just north of here, the other main road heads southwest inland to a further concentration of businesses – tour operators, hotels, etc.

Just south of town and separated at high tide by a rocky headland is **Playa Langosta**, a sort of slightly less populated, slightly more genteel adjunct of Tamarindo.

populous golfing community) and numerous surf schools and shops in town. But there are also plenty of other distractions for when the appeal of the constantly breaking waves begins to pall – horse-riding, bike-riding, scootering, ATV tours, canopy tours, sailing, sports fishing, diving, turtle-watching (*see* pp.188–90) or simply watching the region's fabulous sunsets. And once darkness has fallen, a whole new array of entertainments becomes available. Tamarindo has one of the liveliest nightlife scenes in the country. Its status as a party town has been further enhanced in the past few years, following its adoption as a party venue by US college kids on 'spring break', with all the reckless hedonism those words imply.

For many, Tamarindo represents the unacceptable face of coastal development, and an all too likely template for the future direction of the area. And it's true, there's much about the place to criticise – the way foreigners massively outnumber locals, the way English seems to be the first language, the way there doesn't seem to be any overt Tico culture here whatsoever, the lack of planning and environmental forethought that's accompanied much of the development, how crowded the beaches get, the rising drug problem – but to do so in too strong a fashion would be missing the point slightly. The sheer volume of humanity here, and the sheer amount of business taking place here daily, gives the place a great vibrancy. And, unlike some other nearby resorts, Tamarindo at least functions as a genuine town rather than as some sort of sealed-off private community. There are plenty of other places around here doing a much worse job of co-existing with the local community and looking after the environment. That may only make it relatively better, but at least it's better. And it's fun. There really are few better places to come for a quick blast of unfettered hedonism before heading back off in search of the country's natural wonders.

Services in Tamarindo

You'll find all the services on or near the front – **banks** (there's a branch of the Banco Nacional, with an ATM, just north of the loop), **supermarkets**, **Internet cafés**, **shops** and a **petrol station** (at the northern end of town).

Sports and Activities in Tamarindo

Surf Schools

Chica Surf School, t 827 7884, *chicasurfschoolcr@hotmail.com*. A women-only surf school.

Iguana Surf, **t** 653 0148, *www.iguanasurf.net*. Surf school, surf shop and surfer-friendly café.

Tamarindo Adventures and High Tide Surf Shop, **t** 653 0108, *www.tamarindoadventures.net*.

General Activity Operators

Should you tire of surfing, there are dozens of other activities to engage in. The tour operators below can arrange most of them, and most of the area's hotels can also arrange tours.

Horse-riding on the beach is particularly popular, although you should be sure to pick a horse that looks healthy and is in good condition (and which hasn't just spent the morning giving rides to all and sundry), as there have been reports of some operators overworking their animals. You should also refrain from galloping on any occupied stretch of beach (even if you see other people doing this, which you probably will). This is extremely dangerous, not to say rather annoying for anyone attempting to sunbathe. You can also hire scooters, mountain bikes and ATVs for zipping about town and the local area.

Papagayo Excursions, **t** 653 0254, *www.papagayoexcursions.com*.

Tamarindo Tourist Information Center, **t** 653 0031, *www.crparadise.com*.

Where to Stay in and around Tamarindo

There's an absolute superabundance of choice, with new places opening up all the time. Even in high season, you'll probably be able to just turn up and find somewhere relatively quickly, although it is always advisable to book in advance if possible. Unfortunately, while there may be plenty of variety, there are no great bargains to be had – in high season, at least. With the town welcoming so many new visitors daily, hoteliers have little need to offer price incentives; they know there will always be someone willing to pay the full amount just around the corner. The area's nicest places are located away from the town centre towards Playa Langosta, a couple of km to the south. There are also a few hotels lining the surfing beaches of Playa Avellana, Playa Negra and Playa Junquillal, around 13–17km south of town.

Luxury ($$$$$)

Casa Cook, Tamarindo, **t** 653 0125, *www.tamarindo.com/cook* ($200). Owned by a friendly US couple, the Casa Cook is small but extremely well packaged. Its beachfront cabins come with kitchens, hot water, cable TV, sitting rooms (with sofa beds) and a choice of fans or (for $10 more) air-conditioning, and there's a swimming pool and a pleasant garden. A path leads down from the hotel to the beach.

B&B Sueño del Mar, Playa Langosta, **t** 653 0101, *www.sueno-del-mar.com* ($185). Right on the beach, this up-market 'adult' retreat (no children under 12 allowed) has 'rustic chic'- style rooms – all with four poster beds, an assortment of antiques, a choice of fan or air-conditioning and private bathrooms. Some have ocean views. There are also a a couple of large *casitas* ($160) set in the leafy grounds, which have outdoor 'Bali-style' showers. The price includes breakfast and use of the B&B's mountain bikes, boogie-boards and snorkelling equipment.

Hotel Tamarindo Diria Beach and Golf Resort, Tamarindo, **t** 653 0031, *www.tamarindodiria.com* ($137). The Diria is one of Tamarindo's oldest, largest, best-known and most conveniently located choices – right in the centre of town, next to the beach. Venerable it may be, but it hasn't let the town's recent expansion pass it by, regularly renovating its rooms, of which there are over a hundred, all with air-conditioning, cable TV, telephones and private bathrooms. You have a choice of views – the cheaper ones take in the hotel's nice garden, which is adorned with native artwork, and large serpentine pool, while the more expensive ones look out over the sea. The hotel has also rebranded itself lately as a 'golf resort', although it doesn't actually have its own course, merely offering its guests preferential rates at two of the region's major courses, the Hacienda Pinillia and Paradisus Playa Conchal (*see* p.182 for details). A range of tours and activities – surfing, snorkelling, horse-riding, ATV tours, etc. – is offered.

Expensive ($$$$)

Hotel El Jardin del Edén, **t** 653 0137, *www.jardindeleden.com* ($110). A very classy choice set in a hillside garden, the French-owned Jardin's rooms are terribly tasteful – lots of polished wood and subtle uplighting – and very well equipped, with air-conditioning, cable TV, telephones, private bathrooms (hot water) and either terraces overlooking a tropical garden (ground floor) or balconies overlooking the ocean (top floor). There are also a couple of self-catering apartments, a swimming pool, a Jacuzzi and a very well-respected Mediterranean restaurant. Tours, activities (tennis, golf, surfing, diving, etc.) and car rental are offered.

Hotel El Milagro, Tamarindo, **t** 653 0042, *www.elmilagro.com* ($99). This is a compact little place centred on a smallish pool and lounging area, around which 32 tightly packed bungalows have been carefully arranged, all with private bathrooms and (small) terraces. The hotel's good alfresco seafood restaurant is open to the public. Rates include breakfast. Lots of tours – coastal cruises, turtle-watching, canopy tours, scuba-diving – offered.

Tamarindo Vista Villas, Tamarindo, **t** 653 0114, *www.tamarindovistavillas. com* ($89). The Best Western Vista Villas is more than just another hotel, it's also a major local landmark. Occupying a prominent position perched on a hill near the entrance to town, it's more often than not cited as a reference point when giving directions, so you'll get used to its presence even if you don't end up staying here. It enjoys a relaxed, almost bohemian sort of vibe, influenced no doubt by the surfers who make up a large proportion of its clientele. The rooms are well equipped with air-conditioning, telephone, cable TV, coffee-makers and private bathrooms, although, as several have tempting views right out over the breaks, they're probably unoccupied most of the time. There are also a few self-catering suites with kitchens, VCRs and terraces sleeping 4–8 ($150–190), a pool with ocean views (and a swim-up bar) and a very popular late-night bar, the Monkey Bar. Diving trips are offered.

(★) **Hotel Iguanazul >>**

Moderate ($$$)

Cabinas Arco Iris, Tamarindo, **t** 653 0330, *www.hotelarcoiris.com* ($40). These pleasant but somewhat over-decorated (and rather randomly themed) *cabinas* are very comfortable – all with private bathrooms (hot water), fans, porches and hammocks – and there's a communal kitchen. Yoga classes are offered.

Hotel Iguanazul, Playa Junquillal, 17km south of Tamarindo, **t** 658 8123, *www. iguanazul.com* ($70). This cheery hotel, located at the north end of the beach, is one of the region's best, with 24 rooms, all offering a decent level of comfort with two double beds (private bathrooms) and either garden or beach views. The open-air restaurant-bar serves Tico cuisine (and is seemingly always filled with surfers talking through the day's thrills and spills) and there's a swimming pool. A variety of tours is offered, including surfing, snorkelling, fishing, kayaking and horse-riding. The lodge also operates a number of long-stay condos.

Cabinas Marielos, Tamarindo, **t** 653 0141 ($45). Overlooking the beach, a reasonable mid-range choice set in appealing gardens. The rooms have fans or (for $5 more) air-conditioning and private bathrooms (cold water only). Guests have access to a communal kitchen.

B&B Mono Congo Lodge, Playa Negra, on the road towards Playa Avellana, 15km south of Tamarindo, **t** 658 8261, *www.monocongolodge.com* ($65). In this surf-crazy part of the world, it's nice to find a hotel that's as interested in what's going on inland as well as out on the waves. The lodge occupies a large building in the centre of a swath of jungle that provides a home to a sizeable population of mono congos (or 'howler monkeys' as they're more commonly known) as well as plenty of other wildlife. It's very 'eco', but still extremely comfortable. The rooms have been fitted out to a very high standard with polished wood floors, Indian cotton sheets and tiled bathrooms, and there's a well-respected international restaurant. Surfboards can be rented. Tours offered.

Cabinas Las Olas, Playa Avellanas, 13km south of Tamarindo, **t** 658 8315, *www.cabinaslasolas.co.cr* ($65). Just a minute from the beach, Las Olas is set between a swath of monkey-friendly jungle and a protected area of mangroves – a raised boardwalk leads from the hotel to the sands. It offers ten large 'glass and stone' bungalows – all with fans, hot-water showers, gleaming furniture and private terraces – as well as a restaurant/bar and a variety of activities including kayaking, biking and snorkelling in addition to the obligatory surfing.

Hotel Pasatiempo, Tamarindo, **t** 653 0578, *www.hotelpasatiempo.com* ($79). This friendly mid-range hotel offers a choice of well-equipped standard rooms – all with air-conditioning, private bathrooms (ot water) and small terraces with hammocks – and some superior suites ($110), with living rooms and sofa beds. Additional facilities include a pool and a lively bar/restaurant, which draws quite a crowd on Tues when live music is played.

Inexpensive ($$)

★ Villas Macondo >

Villas Macondo, Tamarindo, **t** 653 0812, *www.villasmacondo.com* ($35). Owned and run by a young (and very friendly) German couple, this is one of the very best (upper) budget choices. Its bright yellow, cabin-like rooms are large and cheerfully decorated with ceiling fans, hot water showers (solar-heated), and porches with hammocks. There are also a couple of two-storey self-catering apartments with kitchens, cable TV and air-conditioning, as well as a swimming pool. It's a 200m walk to beach. Tours offered.

Hotel Mono Loco, Tamarindo, **t** 653 0238 ($35). Surrounding a pretty central garden with a small pool, this offers a rather expensive dormitory ($15 per person) as well as some tastefully decorated private rooms with bathrooms (with hot water) in a thatch-roofed building. It's perfectly adequate although, for what you get, a good $10 more expensive than you'd pay for something similar in one of the less popular parts of the country.

Budget ($)

Cabinas Coral Reef, Tamarindo, **t** 653 0291 ($20). There's not much true budget accommodation in Tamarindo, and what there is tends to be very

popular, so if you're coming here expect to find it pretty much permanently packed out with cost-conscious surfers. It's not as grotty as you might imagine, considering the price, but it is pretty basic. The rooms are small, but clean. Shared bathrooms only.

Eating Out in Tamarindo

You'll find plenty of average places, offering unimaginative facsimiles of US menus, but you'll also find plenty of very decent ones. Tamarindo has one of the most cosmopolitan dining scenes anywhere outside the capital. After all, there are a lot of people here with a lot of money to spend, and the town's restaurants have had to up their game. Expect a good deal of 'fusion' food.

Frutas Tropicales, on the main road at the northern end of town. This is a great place to pick up a snack if you're heading up towards Playa Grande, selling all manner of tropical fruit, both in its natural state and pulped into tasty *refrescos*, as well as an assortment of filling (but cheap) sandwiches, hamburgers and *casados* (nothing here will cost much above $4).

★ Lazy Wave Food Company >>

Lazy Wave Food Company, just inland from the loop, **t** 653 0737. More than meets the eye – the Lazy Wave offers a very high standard of cooking in what looks at first glance like a rather simple, typical alfresco restaurant. The menu changes daily, but always features a large selection of seafood (tuna steaks, shrimp salad, red snapper, etc.) plus a few hearty meat concoctions (beef Wellington, jambalaya) whipped up by the French-trained chef and served in very generous portions on stone plates. The outdoor dining area is set around a large tree, from which hangs a shady awning. The only downside to the experience is the restaurant's ever-growing popularity, which means you might have to wait a while for a table. Mains $7–10.

Nogui's, on the loop. Simple, unpretentious café where you can order from a menu of basic seafood dishes (fish-filled tacos, seafood salads, etc.), pastries and sandwiches, at plastic tables overlooking the beach.

Panadería de Paris, Hotel Laguna del Cocodrilo. The Panadería offers as clear a symbol of the town's cosmopolitanism as you could want. After all, there are very few other towns in Costa Rica where you can get genuine, fresh-baked Parisian-style croissants and baguettes. And, once you've finished your breakfast, take a wander out to the lagoon at the back where the hotel's eponymous crocodiles can often be spotted. *Open 6am–6pm.*

Shark Bite Deli, t 653 0453. On the road towards Playa Langosta, this well-named sandwich shop sells great bulging filled baguettes that would test the resolve of the hungriest great white, packed full of meat, cheese, salad, roasted vegetables and anything else you might desire. It also does a good line in desserts, and offers unlimited refills on coffee, a particularly useful feature if you are taking advantage of the in-store Internet access or browsing the book exchange. The only slight criticism is that it is a touch expensive ($5 plus for most sandwiches, but they are very large).

Stella's Fine Dining, a 5min walk inland, t 653 0127, www.stella-cr.com. It may be making a rod for its own back with the name, but this does (more or less) live up to its advertising. It certainly enjoys a very elegant dining space in a circular, ranch-style building – all starched white tablecloths and candlelight. Foodwise, the best choices tend to be the simplest – large pizzas cooked in a traditional wood-fired oven, catch of the day served with a tangy sauce, seafood platter. Although the kitchen does turn out its own interpretation of some more complicated international dishes (pasta primavera, Wiener schnitzel, chicken stroganoff), these can be of varying quality. Live music is put on some nights. Pizza delivery service.

Nightlife in Tamarindo

This is where the town really comes into its own, with streets packed with an ever-changing line-up of bars and discos. Though nobody could accuse Tamarindo of providing the most 'authentic' of Costa Rican experiences – most of the music you'll hear blaring out from bars will be the latest (or more precisely six-month-old) US hits, and indeed most of the people you'll be dancing with will probably be American – but it can be thoroughly enjoyable, partying the high season nights away on the beach till the sun comes up. If that sounds just too horrendous for words, try to visit in the off season when things are a lot quieter and mellower.

The biggest parties are held on Saturday at the **Big Bazar**, near Iguana Surf, with barbecues laid on in the early evening to get everyone fortified for a night of carousing on the sand. Other regular events include: the hugely popular ladies' nights on Wednesdays at the **Cantina Las Olas**, where women drink for free and men try their luck from 9.30pm–11.30pm; Thursday night live music at the **Monkey Bar** at the Best Western Vista Villas (although entertainment is provided every night by the congregation of surfers camped out around the circular bar retelling tales of that day's best manoeuvres); and the Tuesday night open-mike session at the **Hotel Pasatiempo** (all efforts accompanied by the house band). The **Mambobar** on the loop is the place most revellers head when all the other places have begun quietening down.

Parque Nacional Marino Las Baulas

Parque Nacional Marino Las Baulas
t 653 0470; open 9–6; adm $7 if visiting at night for a turtle tour, otherwise free

Set up in 1991, this national park located just a few kilometres north of Tamarindo represents a working compromise between the needs of surfers, who have been coming to **Playa Grande** in their thousands since the 1960s, and the needs of the leatherback turtles (*baulas* in Spanish), who have been coming here for slightly longer (at least several million years) to lay their eggs, albeit in increasingly

Getting to the Parque Nacional Marino Las Baulas

Most of the local hotels offer **tours** for around $35, including transport and park fees, although it is also possible to book directly through the **ranger station**. Travelling independently, you'll need your own transport as there's no bus service to the park. Entrance is via the ranger station at the southern end of the beach.

smaller numbers of late. Surfing is still permitted here throughout the year, except from dawn till dusk during the laying season, which runs from mid-October to mid-February, when the beach is closed to everyone apart from groups on official turtle-watching tours.

The park comprises over 20,000 hectares of sea, as well as over 300 hectares of land, which include areas of forest (home to monkeys, racoons and coatis) and mangroves (home to crocodiles), although the beach is undoubtedly the main draw. It's one of the last remaining nesting sites for what is both the world's largest reptile – leatherback turtles can grow up to 2.5 metres long and weigh over 500kg – and, until very recently, one of its most successful. Fossil records show that leatherback turtles have been around in more or less their current form, and in significant numbers, from around 120 million years ago until around 20 years ago, when, thanks to a combination of factors – pollution, over-hunting, the development of nesting beaches – their population suddenly began to dwindle drastically. Today, a little over 200 turtles nest here annually, compared to many thousands in previous decades. On some nights, none nests at all, and if that's the time you've picked to go on a turtle tour to try and see one in action, you're going to be disappointed. Instead, you'll have to make do with a visit to the park's small turtle museum, **El Mundo de la Tortuga**, at the northern end of the beach, which has an audioguide on the history of turtle protection, a good collection of turtle photos (no substitute for the real thing, but still, it's something) as well as a café and souvenir shop.

El Mundo de la Tortuga
t 653 0471; open 4pm–dawn

Tours are offered throughout the laying season, but numbers are limited, so you should book well in advance. To help preserve the leatherbacks, strict rules apply to these tours. All visitors must be part of an official group (of no more than 15 people), and can only set foot on the beach in the company of a certified guide. These guides are the only people licensed to carry any form of illumination – in this instance, a small, weak torch. Flash photography and smoking are banned. As a further precaution, visitors are obliged to wait away from the beach until a turtle has actually hauled itself ashore and begun laying. If disturbed before egg-depositing has begun, it's been known for a turtle to turn and flee (albeit in a rather slow and inelegant way) back to the sea without laying. However, once laying has started, the turtle will almost invariably see the process through, even if slightly disturbed. Guides work in teams: one on the beach spotting turtles, the other waiting with the tourists for a radio message to confirm that it is safe to come into range. There are no guidelines as to how long this might take. You may be waiting for some considerable time before you get the call (which, of course, may never come) or you may be summoned more or less immediately. Bring something interesting to help pass the time – a book, cards, Travel Scrabble, your diary, someone else's diary...

Should you be lucky enough to encounter one of these great primeval beasts in the flesh, be sure to show it due respect – they undertake vast annual migrations to get here, and the last thing they need when they're trying to concentrate on their reproductive business is to be bothered by some noisy tourist. Most conservationists agree that, in an ideal world, the beach would be closed off entirely to the public and the turtles left to get on with things in peace. However, it's not an ideal world, and the tours do contribute valuable revenue towards the turtles' conservation and, if managed sympathetically, don't seem to cause the animals any great harm. Indeed, of more pressing concern is the amount of continuing development going on near the nesting beach, as it is believed that bright electric lights (the number of which increases year on year) can interfere with the turtles' navigational systems. The outskirts of the park are much more built-up than you might expect of an area that borders an officially protected area, but this is simply indicative of the intense pressure on land in this part of Costa Rica.

Once the laying process is over, the turtles are given one last piece of help by the park rangers: they stand guard over the baby turtles as they hatch several months later in order to stop them from being eaten before they've made it into the waves. Of course, once in the sea, they're on their own; there's nothing to stop a fish from snaffling one up 10cm from the shore.

Outside the laying season, Playa Grande reverts to being a simple tourist beach, frequented more by surfers than wildlife. At these times entrance is free and unrestricted to all.

Where to Stay around Las Baulas

Hotel Las Tortugas, t 653 0423, *www.cool.co.cr* ($$$$; $85). North of Tamarindo, near the entrance, this is the closest hotel to the park. Its rooms are slightly overpriced (as you might expect considering the location), but well equipped with tile floors, air-conditioning and private bathrooms with hot water. There are also a couple of larger suites for $125. The restaurant/bar is pretty decent, the pool inevitably turtle-shaped, and a variety of tours are offered, including horse-riding, sports fishing and turtle-watching.

Hotel Villa Baula, t 653 0493, *www.hotelvillabaula.com* ($$$; $70). In the woods behind the beach, close to the park's southern entrance, the Baula has 20 nicely furnished rooms as well as five stilt-set bungalows with kitchens ($120). Private bathrooms (with hot water) are available in both. There are two swimming pools, a restaurant serving Indonesian cuisine and you can hire bikes and surfboards. Tours, including horse-riding and turtle-watching, are offered.

The Central Nicoya Peninsula: Inland

Nicoya

The centre of the peninsula has a very different flavour from the coastal regions. Its towns are as traditional, staid and provincial as the coastal resorts are modern, transitory and cosmopolitan. This is cowboy country, where life moves slowly in tune with the agricultural, not the tourist seasons. Nicoya, the peninsula's unofficial 'capital', acts as the administrative centre for the region and is the main point of contact with the outside world for the various surrounding cattle ranches. It's also a major transport hub. The continuing lack of a coastal road means that many tourists continue to pass through here *en route* to Sámara and Nosara, although only a fraction decide to stay for any length of time. While through traffic has increased since the opening of the 'Friendship Bridge' in 2003, tourism has yet to have any great transforming effect on the town. It remains a sleepy, quiet and ostentatiously rural place, where you can still see horses on the street, cows grazing the outlying pastures and window-boxes full of tumbling flowers. It's probably for the best, as the town doesn't seem to have had much luck with tourists down the years. The very first, the Spanish conquistador Gil González Dávilas, was welcomed with open arms by the local chief, Nicoya, who believed that the Spaniard's intentions were peaceful. He soon found out how wrong he was.

Though you won't find the vast all-encompassing tourist infrastructure you will in places like El Coco and Tamarindo, nor the number of attractions, you may find the town's laid-back, uncommercial, provincial charm a welcome change from all the resort bustle of the coast. Unlike most of the region's coastal towns, Nicoya is laid out according to the recognizable grid pattern, with *calles* running north–south and *avenidas* east–west. At its centre is the shady **Parque Central**, in the northeast corner of which sits the town's church, the **Iglesia de San Blas**, parts of which date back to the 17th century. Although, as it has had to spend the past five centuries being buffeted by a succession of earthquakes, there are

The Friendship Bridge

The opening of the 780m Puente La Amistad in 2003 across the Río Tempisque, just north of where the river feeds into the Golfo Nicoya, has significantly speeded up land journeys to the Nicoya Peninsula, which previously had to be undertaken either north via Liberia, or on a ferry via Puntarenas. Furthermore, as one of the largest and most impressive engineering projects undertaken in recent times – its 80m-high suspension towers are the country's tallest buildings – the bridge's construction has been a huge source of national pride, despite being largely funded with Taiwanese money. Taiwan stumped up the cash as a reward for Costa Rica's showing true 'friendship' (hence the bridge's name) by being one of the few countries in the world to recognize Taiwan as a separate sovereign government, and not part of mainland China (which must have Beijing quaking in its boots). A c90 toll is in force.

Getting to and away from Nicoya

Nicoya lies on HWY-21, the Nicoya Peninsula's main artery, making the drive down from Liberia pretty straightforward. The journey from San José (by either car or bus) has also been considerably eased by the opening of the **Puente La Amistad** bridge across the Río Tempisque in 2003 (c90 toll), which has chopped a good couple of hours off the journey time (*see* box, p.191). It will still take around 4–5 hours by car and 5–6 hours by bus, depending on the traffic, however.

Six **bus** services a day leave San José for Nicoya from C 14, Av 3/5 at 6am, 8am, 10.30am, 12.30pm, 2pm and 6.15pm. Buses arrive at the main bus terminal two blocks east and two blocks south of the Parque Central. Buses also leave from here for all major local destinations, including Liberia (10 a day), Playa Sámara (five a day), Nosara (four a day) and Santa Cruz (every 45mins).

also parts from almost every era since. Like the town itself, it's not a particularly beautiful place, but it is rather peaceful. Indeed, round about the only time that Nicoya isn't peaceful is on July 25, *Día de Guanacaste*, when the town has a big blowout to celebrate the province's decision in the 1820s to become part of Costa Rica rather than Nicaragua (the vote was actually rather marginal, although nobody seems to mention that now). Across from the church is the town's main cultural offering, the **Casa de la Cultura**, which has displays of local history and art.

Around Nicoya

Nicoya provides a convenient base from which to explore some of the peninsula's interior attractions, including the Parque Nacional Barra Honda with its network of limestone caverns to the north (*see*

Services in Nicoya

Banks: You'll find branches of the Banco de Costa Rica on the western side of the Parque Central and the Banco Nacional on C 3, just north of the park.

Internet access: There's an Internet café on C 1, just south of the Parque Central.

Post office: At the Parque Central's southwest corner.

Where to Stay in Nicoya

While it's certainly no major tourist town, Nicoya does boast a few decent sleeping options, if you're hoping to use it as a base to explore the nearby Barra Honda National Park.

Hotel Chorotega, C 0, Av 4/6, t 685 5245 ($; $12), south of Río Chipanzo. Basic, comfortable rooms with private baths (cold water only).

Best Western Hotel Curim, around half a kilometre south of town on the road towards Sámara, t 685 5238 ($$$; $55). Offers a slightly grander level of comfort – large bedrooms, hot water in the bathrooms, a swimming pool, an open-air restaurant, etc.

Hotel Las Tinajas, Av 1, C 3/5, t 685 5081 ($; $15), in the centre of town. Clean (though slightly worn) rooms with private bathrooms (cold water).

Eating Out in Nicoya

Nicoya has a sizeable Chinese population, the descendants of labourers brought over to work on the region's railways in the 19th century, and as a consequence a surprisingly large number of Chinese restaurants. Try **Restaurante Teyet** at C 1, Av 2/4. There's also a decent Italian, **Un Dulce Momento**, on the east side of park, or for something more typically Costa Rican, try the nearby **Soda Colonial**.

Getting to the Parque Nacional Barra Honda

If you're travelling by **car**, the route is clearly signposted from both Nicoya and the Puente La Amistad. If you're relying on public transport, the easiest method is to get a **taxi** from Nicoya for around $10, although you'll also have to remember to arrange a pick-up time. Otherwise, you can catch a **bus** from Nicoya to the village of **Santa Ana** at 8am, 12.30pm and 3.30pm and then walk the final 1km to the park entrance.

below); the town of **Santa Cruz**, 25km north along HWY-21, also known as 'National Folklore City', which is a major centre of traditional Guanacastrean music and dance; and **Guaitíl**, 12km east of Santa Cruz, one of the country's most important centres of pottery, where an artisans' co-operative has been set up turning out replicas of traditional Chorotegan designs – you'll see pots for sale throughout the town, and there's also a shop selling the town's wares on the highway about 10km north of Nicoya.

Parque Nacional Barra Honda

**Parque Nacional
Barra Honda**
*t 659 1551; open
daily 8–4; adm*

This 1,800-plus hectare national park is located 22km northeast of Nicoya, and around the same distance inland from the Río Tempisque. Most of its area is taken up by a vast limestone ridge, beneath which sits the park's main attraction, a tangly, twisting network of slimy caverns that have been eroded into existence by millions of years' worth of steadily dripping water. There are over 40 in total, although only around half have been fully explored (of these, some have been discovered to be over 200m deep), and only one, **Terciopelo**, is open to the general public. A 'mere' 25m deep, Terciopelo can nonetheless only be explored in the company of an official guide, who can be hired through the ranger station. The descent into the cave can be a touch hairy and you must wear a rope harness for safety.

Once down in the depths, you can see great, gnarly collections of stalactites and stalagmites, as well as some other less recognizable organic formations, which have been given emotive names such as 'fried eggs', 'popcorn' and 'shark's teeth', although, it has to be said, some bear an almost constellation-like lack of resemblance to their titles. At least **El Organo** ('the organ') lives up to its billing – an enormous limestone tube that sounds a distinct note when struck, just like an organ pipe. The cavern's seeping depths provide a home to a rather specialized collection of wildlife, including bats and sightless salamanders, although you're unlikely to see any (and, being blind, they definitely won't see you). You can book a guided tour at the **ranger station** from 8am to 1pm, although these can be quite expensive – $30 for the tour and equipment rental, not including the admission fee to the park.

Not all of the park's attractions are subterranean or expensive, which will no doubt come as a relief to cash-strapped visitors. The hills above the caverns are enveloped in deciduous **forest** where

Where to Stay in Barra Honda

You can **camp** at a special area near the entrance to the park for $2, and there are also a few dorm beds available for $12. Both have access to shared cold-water bathrooms only. You'll need to contact the ranger station well in advance to book your space (**t** 659 1551).

white-faced capuchins, coatis, armadillos, howler monkeys and various other animals live. **Trails** lead to the top of **Cerro Barra Honda**, the park's tallest peak, from where there are great views.

The Central Nicoya Peninsula: The Coast

Nosara

Nosara is the name both of a beach, located 35km southeast of Nicoya and 25km northeast of Sámara, and the town a few kilometres inland. In fact the distinction is rather vague, and most people use the name to refer to the whole area, from the Refugio Nacional de Fauna Silvestre Ostional in the north (a major nesting site for olive ridley turtles) to the lovely tranquil beaches of Playa Pelada and Playa Guiones to the south. All the region's white-sand beaches offer good swimming and are backed by abundant swaths of tropical forest that provide a home to good deal of wildlife – including monkeys, toucans and parrots.

The town itself is small and rather anonymous-looking, consisting of little more than a **football field** and a few roads, although it does have most of the area's main **services** – a post office, a supermarket, Internet access, laundry (although no bank). But, with the local beaches so inviting, you are unlikely to spend much time here.

As with many places along this stretch of coast, Nosara has a sizeable American expat community, although they exist in a much quieter, less ostentatious way than at Tamarindo further up the coast. You're more likely to encounter senior citizens than spring-breakers here. Development in the area has for the most part been rather restrained, with the local community banding together to keep the more avaricious of the region's developers at arm's length. There seems little chance of Nosara going the way of some of the other coastal resorts and becoming bloated and overdeveloped in the near future (although they probably said that about Tamarindo a few years ago). The town is at its most rowdy in January and February, when raucous Costa Rican-style rodeos are held, although, as this is Tico rather than tourist rowdiness, it's well worth joining in. All manner of bull-besting competitions are held, and the locals party themselves silly.

Getting to Nosara

Both of the main domestic carriers, Sansa and NatureAir, operate daily **flights** from San José to Nosara (*see* p.104 for more details). The **drive** is relatively easy from either Nicoya or Sámara, in dry weather at least. The 'coastal' road (it actually runs a few kilometres inland for much of its length) is unpaved, but not too taxing, unless it's been churned up by a prolonged downpour. A 4WD is still recommended, however, whatever the time of year.

One **bus** service a day connects San José with Nosara at 6am. It takes around 6½ hours and costs c2,290. It is also possible to catch one of the more regular services from Nicoya (at 5am, 10am and 2.30pm). All buses drop off and pick up passengers at the *pulpería* by the football field.

Getting to the Refugio Nacional de Fauna Silvestre Ostional

The refuge enjoys a relatively isolated position, about a 15min **drive** north of Nosara, or a $10 taxi ride. There is no **bus** service.

Sports and Activities around Nosara

There are plenty of activities to enjoy in the area, including **turtle-watching tours** (*see* p.196), **wildlife-watching** in the Reserva Biológica Nosara (*see* 'Where to Stay', Lagarta Lodge), as well as **kayaking**, **snorkelling** and **horse-riding**, most of which can be organized through the local hotels.

Surfing is also popular here, though the breaks are minimal compared to what you'll find further north up the coast at Tamarindo (*see* p.183). The **Nosara Surf Shop**, t 682 0186, *www.nosarasurfshop.com*, and **Coconut Harry's Surf Shop**, t 682 0574, *www.coconutharrys.com*, rent out boards (for around $20 a day), while **Crock Caroll's Surf School**, t 682 0385, can teach you how to do it for around $25 for 2hrs.

And for a little land-based hi-octane fun, **Gunter's Quads**, t 682 0574, offer **ATV/quad bike tours** of the coast.

All the above are located in or near Playa Guiones.

Where to Stay and Eat in Nosara

Bargain-hunters should head into town where the accommodation is at its cheapest (and consequently most basic). Be aware that it's quite a walk – around an hour or so – to the beach from here. Hotels get progressively more expensive – with more facilities – the closer to the coast you get. Several of those on the seafront are, in truth,

a touch overpriced, although they do offer lovely views. Many of the area's hotels also operate restaurants, which are open to the public.

Hotel Café de Paris, Playa Guiones, t 682 0087, *www.cafedeparis.net* ($$$; $60). Perched high on a hill, just inland from the beach, the Café de Paris is a very well-equipped, almost self-consciously stylish place. The rooms are sleek and modern with lots of shiny services and highly polished woodwork, and come with private bathrooms and air-conditioning. There are also some larger bungalows ($115) and a couple of two-storey villas with three bedrooms, two and a half bathrooms and terraces with ocean views ($150) which sleep up to six (a bargain if everyone pays). There's also a French bakery-café serving breakfast, which turns into a bistro serving dinner as the day wears on.

Cabinas and Pizzería Giardino Tropicale, near Playa Guiones, t 682 0258, *www.giardinotropicale.com* ($$$; $50). Just back from the front, this recently expanded complex now has 11 cool and welcoming cabins that have been simply (but nicely) furnished with fans and hot-water showers. The real draw here, however, is the thatched-roof restaurant, one of the area's most renowned, which turns out crispy pizzas from a traditional wood-fired stove, served alfresco in the eponymous tropical gardens.

Harbor Reef Lodge, near Playa Guiones, t 682 0059, *www.harborreef.com* ($$$; $70). A sort of upscale surfers' lodge offering nicely decorated rooms – with tile floors, native artwork, air-conditioning, private bathrooms (with hot water) – plus a couple of superior suites with fridges, coffee-makers and kitchens. There are also some long-stay houses ($800–1,200 per week), as well as a swimming pool, a souvenir shop, a mini-supermarket and a good 'international' fish restaurant. The waves of Playa Guiones are just a 5min walk away. Surfboards can be hired.

⭐ Lagarta Lodge >

Lagarta Lodge, 2km west of Nosara, towards Playa Pelada, t 682 0035, *www.lagarta.com* ($$$; $75). The area's most famous lodge, the Lagarta is set above its own private wildlife reserve, the **Reserva Biológica Nosara**, which offers great bird- and monkey-spotting opportunities. There are just seven rooms, all with fans, showers and views of the reserve from their balconies. There's also a small pool and an excellent restaurant (the Sunday barbecues are particularly popular) with good views of the surrounding jungle and, as the day draws to a close, the setting sun. Paths lead from the hotel into the forest. Non-guests can visit the reserve for $5.

Cabinas Chorotega, Nosara, t 827 4142 ($$–$; $30–15). In the centre of the village near the supermarket, this is a good, basic choice – no-frills rooms with fans, shared bathrooms and not much else. It's a bit dingy but perfectly serviceable. And $15 extra will get you one of the larger rooms with air-conditioning and a private bathroom.

Refugio Nacional de Fauna Silvestre Ostional

On the beaches of this small, locally administered refuge just north of Nosara, you may see the local people engaged in an activity liable to get them arrested if undertaken at any other reserve – collecting turtle eggs. Don't bother calling the police, however, as what they're doing is perfectly legal, so long as it's being done at the right time. Numbers of olive ridley turtles, for whom this is an important nesting site, are so healthy, with thousands arriving here between July and November, that the local community has been given official permission to harvest the eggs during (and only during) the first three days of the season. These are then sold for consumption in local bars and restaurants – they're supposed to be a powerful aphrodisiac, and certainly there are a lot of olive ridley turtles! Because so many turtles nest here, with peak concentrations not occurring until September, it has been assumed that the nests of the first arrivals would probably be disturbed by successive procreative waves anyway, so no great harm is being done by collecting some of the early batches.

There is no official entrance to the reserve, although the beach is intermittently patrolled by guards drawn from the local community who enforce egg-harvesting regulations, and offer tours for around $3. If you're very lucky, you might get to visit during an *arribada* (mass laying), which usually takes place during the first few days of a new moon (and usually in the early evening, rather than late at night as is common with other species), when the beach becomes almost submerged beneath a mass of feverishly laying turtles.

If no turtles are present, you'll have to content yourself with exploring the beach's fringing forest, which is home to monkeys and coatis as well as numerous species of tropical bird.

Getting to and away from Sámara

Sansa operates daily **flights** from San José to Sámara airfield (*see* p.104 for more details), which lies 5km east of town, from where you can catch a taxi into town for around $5.

If travelling by **car**, Sámara lies 26km southeast of Nosara via a rough, unpaved road, or 36km southwest of Nicoya via a paved road. Though it will take a good 4–5hrs, the drive from San José is relatively uncomplicated. Just head up the Interamericana, take the turning for the Puente La Amistad (c90 toll) and follow the signs.

Two **buses** a day make the journey from San José, following more or less the same route, from C 14, Av 3/5, at 12.30pm and 6.15pm. The cost is c2,120. Passengers are disgorged right by the beach in the centre of town.

From here, **buses** leave for Playa Carrillo, 6km east, four times a day at 11am, 1pm, 4.30pm and 6.30pm, and for Nicoya roughly every hour and a half between 5.30am–4.30pm. There's also one direct service a day to Nosara, which leaves from the northern end of town at about 11am, but this is a very slow and bumpy journey and liable to cancellation in poor weather.

Sámara

The calmer alternative to Tamarindo, Sámara has waters that are as tranquil, placid and swim-friendly as Tamarindo's are rough, wavy and surfer-friendly. Credit for the serenity of the seas must go to a reef lying around a kilometre offshore, which deflects the more aggressive waves away from Sámara towards other shores. With sandy, well-looked-after beaches and a town centre that's managed to avoid becoming too touristy, Sámara offers a peaceful, relaxing holiday experience – although things may be about to change. While the town may not as yet be as developed as some of the more northerly resorts, the potential is certainly there, and the number of businesses here is increasing by the year. Transport links are good – there's an airport, the roads are paved – and the opening of the Puente La Amistad (*see* p.191) has made this section of coast more accessible than ever before. Give it a few years, and Sámara could well be the next party town. Thankfully, for now, it's still a good deal more relaxed than that, somewhere to lie back on the beach and forget about it all. And it's not just Americans who appreciate the town's charms, though there is a sizeable contingent here; many Ticos have holiday homes in Sámara.

Services in Sámara

You'll find all the services in the centre of town – the Banco Nacional, Internet cafés, laundry, a pharmacy, supermarkets, tour operators, etc.

Activities in Sámara

Though Sámara can offer many of the same pursuits you can experience at the resorts to the north – **kayaking** (from $35), **surfing** (from $25 for a 2hr lesson), **snorkelling** (from $35), **boat rides**, **dophin-watching** (from $50), **horse-riding** – they seem to be done in a much calmer, more easygoing manner, in keeping with the town's relaxed, laid-back vibe. Indeed, the surfing can't help but be more sedate.

Tio Tigre, t 656 0127, *www.samara beach.com/tiotigre*. Kayaking, snorkelling, dolphin-watching and more.

Sámara Sub Sport Diving, t 656 0700, *samarasub@hotmail.com*. Offers lessons and dive trips.

Jesse's Gym and Surf School, t 676 0055. Rents out boards, offers lessons and has a fully equipped gym ($3 to use the equipment).

Wingnuts, t 656 0153, *www.samara beach.com/wingnuts*. Runs daily canopy tours (12 platforms) for $50, including transport and meals.

Where to Stay in Sámara

There's plenty of choice in all categories, and prices are pretty reasonable – perhaps because this is a popular destination with Ticos.

Hotel Villas Playa Sámara, 2km south of town on road towards Playa Carrillo, **t** 656 0372, *www.villasplayasamara.com* ($$$$$; $150). Well-equipped beachfront resort patronized as much by Ticos as foreign tourists. It offers large units – all with separate bedrooms and living areas, kitchens, terraces with hammocks and air-conditioning – and a range of activities, including fishing trips, mountain biking, ATV tours, badminton and volleyball. They also hold regular discos. In truth, despite all the abundant facilities – which also include a restaurant, a swimming pool and a Jacuzzi – there's something a bit retirement village-like about the place.

Hotel Casa del Mar, t 656 0264, *www. casadelmarsamara.com* ($$$; $40). Just back from the front, set in a small, neat garden (where there's an even smaller swimming pool), this is a good, dependable choice with large, simple rooms, all with fans (or air-conditioning for an extra $10, though the rooms all have cool tile floors) and a choice of shared or private bathrooms. Upper floors have sea views.

Hotel Giada, t 656 0132, *www.hotel giada.net* ($$$; $45). Just north of the beach, occupying a bougainvillea- and bamboo-adorned garden, this offers brightly coloured, fresh rooms, clean tiled bathrooms (hot water) and breezy views from its upstairs rooms. There's also an Italian restaurant serving an unadventurous but perfectly agreeable selection of pizza and pasta dishes, as well as a small swimming pool. The price includes breakfast.

Cabinas Casa Valeria, t 656 0511 ($$; $26). Right on the front, this quiet, easygoing hotel offers a hotchpotch selection of rooms of different sizes and styles (some decorated with shells, others strangely bare), as well as a couple of bungalows sleeping up to four ($40), all with fans and private bathrooms (with hot water). There's also a sleepy garden with hammocks and a communal kitchen where you can cook up your evening meals. Breakfast, however, is included in the price and served alfresco on a terrace.

Eating Out in Sámara

Sámara's beachfront is the best place for snacks and fast food. The town also boasts several reasonably priced sodas, catering to the Costa Rican visitors, as well as an array of 'international' restaurants aimed at more cosmopolitan tastes.

Anana's Heladería, at the northern end of town near the entrance. A great place to cool down after a hard morning's sunbathing, this offers a wide selection of home-made ice creams, as well as snacks, shakes, juice drinks and some pretty decent coffee. *Open from breakfast until 6pm.*

Pizzería Al Manglar, just off the main road. This agreeable Italian serves up some rather unusual (but very tasty) pasta and seafood combinations – shrimp and spaghetti, penne and smoked mackerel. And that enormous bright house cat you'll see prowling around is a pet ocelot.

Restaurante El Dorado, near the church in the centre of town, **t** 656 0145. Just as the Al Manglar specializes in pasta/ seafood combos, so this pulls off the same trick with pizzas and seafood, serving up thin crust bases topped with mussels, lobster and other briney selections. There's also a good dessert menu, featuring a killer tiramisu.

Restaurante Las Brasas, t 656 0546. Perhaps the town centre's most upscale offering, this authentic Spanish place serves up a whole galaxy of Iberian favourites, including the expected (paella, gazpacho, potato tortillas, plenty of good Spanish wines) and the slightly less expected (whole suckling pig, which understandably must be ordered in advance). There are two levels, with the upstairs offering good views of the beach.

Restaurante Wana Wana Acuario. Great beachfront pit stop – sit down to quick plate of fresh seafood at the outdoor counter.

Where to Stay and Eat in Carrillo

Club Carrillo, t 656 0316, *pkdufner@ racsa.co.cr.* ($$; $30). In town at the top of a steep hill, which offers a choice of well-equipped rooms (with private showers and fans) and separate self-catering villa with kitchens that sleep up to four ($50).

Cabinas El Colibrí, on the main road, **t** 656 0656 ($; $25). An Argentine-owned complex with a few small, clean cabins with private bathrooms (some have kitchenettes) and an Argentine restaurant, specializing, as you might have guessed, in steaks.

South of Sámara: Playa Carrillo and Beyond

About 6km (or a 10min drive, or a 1½-hour walk along a paved road) southeast of Sámara is **Playa Carrillo**, which offers a charming collection of archetypal tropical beach pleasures – white sands overlooked by gently swaying palm trees, good swimming, and spectacular sunset views. Though it has been getting more built up of late, this is still a relatively quiet and unspoilt place with just a handful of beachfront hotels and restaurants. You'll find more in the small town of **Carrillo** itself, set on a hill above the beach, which is also home to a few surf shops and sports fishing operators.

As far as most tourists are concerned, Carrillo marks the furthest extent of this stretch of coast. You can continue further south if you wish, but you'd have to be pretty adventurous to do so. Roads, if you can call them such – rough pathways through the vegetation might be a more accurate description – do extend along the southern shore, albeit in the most uneven, higgledy-piggledy fashion imaginable. If asked to devise a course designed to provide the most testing driving conditions imaginable, you might well come up with something like this. And, if all that sounds like a challenge, then you'll need to come prepared. Get yourself the sturdiest 4WD you can find (with as high a clearance as possible) and get ready to be banged and buffeted about (and quite probably lost). The 70km between Carrillo and the town of **Cóbano** (which will mark your re-emergence into civilization) offers some pretty hairy driving, the rewards of which will be access to some of the peninsula's most gorgeously untamed beaches, including **Punta Islita**, **Playa San Miguel** and **Playa Coyote**.

The Southern Tip: Puntarenean Nicoya

While the opening of the Puente La Amistad (*see* p.191) has made gaining access from the mainland to the centre of the Nicoya Peninsula significantly easier, Nicoya's southern tip is still more readily accessed via the ferry service from Puntarenas to Paquera (for details of ferry times, *see* p.213).

It's a lazy one-hour journey, during which time the landscape of the peninsula will gradually emerge into focus. From near the mainland, Nicoya appears as just a rough outline punctuated by blocks of colour – mainly great expanses of brown (much of this section of the peninsula is now pastureland) surrounding intermittent bursts of green that represent the peninsula's few remaining pockets of jungle. Indeed, the distribution of land in this region would seem to neatly demonstrate the conflicts inherent in the 'Costa Rican problem' – how to find a way to balance the needs of mass tourism, environmental conservation and agriculture. All three concerns are strongly represented here: the coastal towns of Montezuma and Tambor are two of the country's leading resorts (the latter has become a byword for ruthless environmental exploitation); the Reserva Natural Absoluta Cabo Blanco, on the peninsula's southernmost tip, was the country's first ever protected area and has become an emblem and touchstone for the conservation movement; while the peninsula's inner expanses are home to some of Costa Rica's largest cattle ranches.

Refugio Nacional de Vida Silvestre Curú

Refugio Nacional de Vida Silvestre Curú
t 641 0590, refugiocuru@yahoo.com; open 7–3.30, adm

There was a time when you had to phone up at least a week in advance if you wanted to visit this 80ha reserve near the eastern tip of the peninsula, 7km southeast of the small town and ferry terminal of **Paquera**. It's a little more accessible now, although it might still be an idea to call/drop them an e-mail in advance, just in case they have a party of naturalists or students staying and have decided to shut their gates to the general public for a few days.

Owned by the Schutts, a local Tico family who are prominent figures in the peninsula's conservation movement, Curú represents something of a last stand of nature in this most agricultural of regions. For the many species of bird who have been recorded here (including hummingbirds, kingfishers, woodpeckers and trogons), it provides a rare island of habitable forest amid a sea of barren pastureland. Though not particularly large, the refuge contains a number of different habitats, with marked trails leading through areas of deciduous forests (home to monkeys, agoutis and pacas) over hills and down to a series of beaches, where iguanas, phantom crabs and sea turtles have been spotted and which

Where to Stay near the Refugio Nacional Curú

In the Refuge

Provided it's not being occupied by a group, you can stay at the rather basic **lodge** for $30 a day (which includes three meals); book well in advance.

Paquera

Otherwise, the closest accommodation is in the village of **Paquera**. **Cabinas Ginana, t** 641 0119 ($; $20). Has simple, clean rooms (with private bathrooms and a choice of either fans or air-conditioning) and a decent restaurant.

Getting to the Refugio Nacional Curú

The most convenient option is to go on an **organized trip** with one of Montezuma's various tour operators for around $25, including transport and meals (*see* p.204), which will at least guarantee that the refuge will be open when you turn up.

Buses travelling between Paquera and Tambor pass by the entrance. Ask the driver to let you off.

If **driving**, look for the signs around 7km southeast of Paquera, 20km northeast of Tambor.

offer good snorkelling. The owners organize their own snorkelling excursions to the **Isla Tortuga**, a pair of uninhabited islands just out to shore, for $20.

Tambor

Considering all the hoo-ha (*see* box, below), and its reputation as a flagship for mass tourism, Tambor town is much quieter and less

Tourism Unleashed

Though greater environmental outrages have been committed elsewhere in the years since, the story surrounding the building of the Hotel Barceló Playa Tambor in the early 1990s is still the one most often cited as the ultimate example of cold-hearted business interests ransacking a pristine environment in search of the almighty tourist dollar.

To be honest, told slightly differently, the story could equally well be used to illustrate a rather more heart-warming moral, showing how formidable and determined local communities can become when they band together to fight a common enemy. Essentially, what happened was this.

In 1991, the Spanish Barceló hotel group began constructing a new beachfront property just outside Tambor, which up to that point had been a rather quiet, secluded fishing village. Perhaps this seclusion gave the group a false sense of confidence, but the plans it came up with were almost ridiculously grandiose, involving the construction of a 2,000-room resort boasting every facility and creature comfort known to man. Nothing was to be allowed to stand in the way of the Barceló group's vision. Unfortunately, that nothing included sections of preserved mangrove swamp (which were destroyed), pristine beaches (which were encroached upon, violating laws which state that there can be no development within 50m of the shore) and local rivers (from which the group removed large amounts of sand, leading to the erosion of their banks).

So insensitive, and more to the point, so obvious were the group's transgressions that they inspired the local community to form a protest group dedicated to halting the resort's construction. Barceló was ordered to stop building while an official investigation was held, which eventually found the group guilty of flouting environmental laws, for which it was fined a grand total of $14,000, a paltry sum rightly held up as indicative of how the legal system fails to adequately punish environmental violaters (it probably cost more than that to rip out the mangroves).

However, what is not often mentioned is that, while the protestors may not have succeeded in halting the juggernaut of mass tourism in its tracks, they did at least get it to cut its speed a little. The Barceló Playa Tambor that finally opened in 1992 was a considerably scaled-down version of what had originally been planned, with just 400 rooms and fewer facilities. Though the protestors' victory was not total, it was far from being the abject defeat it is often portrayed as. Indeed, there were many positives to be drawn from the campaign. It certainly brought the abuses of over-eager developers to national attention, and served notice to any other hotel groups tempted to flout environmental laws that they were being watched, and would be zealously opposed.

Today, as if ashamed of its own existence, the Barceló Playa Tambor sits brooding on its own at the end of a private access road to the north of Tambor, a sort of separate satellite community rather than an intrinsic part of the town itself.

Getting to Tambor

Both Sansa and NatureAir operate daily **flights** (*see* p.104) to Tambor's airstrip, located 5km north of town, near the Hotel Barceló Playa Tambor, from where you can catch the Paquera–Montezuma **bus** to Tambor (6 per day 6am–6pm; make sure you get one going the right way).

developed than you might expect. That is not to say that it's entirely pristine, but with most of the major hotel complexes lying outside the town proper, this is still a rather relaxed and laid-back place. Indeed the centre can feel almost villagey at times.

It also enjoys a rather beautiful setting flanked by verdant tree-lined hills and overlooking the calm waters of the **Bahía Ballena**, a large bay where whales are often spotted. The beach is long, sandy – a strange but not unappealing browny-grey colour – and often practically empty. The town certainly makes a good, leisurely base from which to explore the Refugio Nacional Curú to the north and the more bustling resort of Montezuma and the Cabo Blanco wildlife reserve to the south.

Services in Tambor

Tambor isn't exactly awash with facilities, but you will find a super-market, a police station, plus cheap cafés and sodas on its street.

However, for Internet cafés (if your hotel doesn't provide access), banks, post offices and pharmacies, you'll have to head inland to **Cóbano**, 20km southwest, the area's major service town.

Where to Stay in Tambor

Hotel Tambor Tropical, t 683 0013, *www.tambortropical.com* ($$$$$; $175). This adult-orientated getaway (no children under 16) is set in lush, landscaped grounds. Its ten suites are split between five hexagonal wooden cabins and come with fans, kitchen-ettes, private bathrooms and balconies. The complex also boasts a swimming pool, a Jacuzzi, a bar and a restaurant. Tours and activities, including horse-riding and snorkelling at Isla Tortuga, are offered. Includes breakfast.

Hotel Tango Mar Beach Resort, Southwest of town towards Cóbano,

t 683 0001, *www.tangomar.com* ($$$$$; $165). Occupying an idyllic stretch of beachfront, this is one of the area's more developed mega-resorts, offering large rooms, even larger suites ($245) and positively enormous villas ($465). Additional facilities include a seafront restaurant, tennis courts and a nine-hole golf course – $25 for a day of unlimited rounds. Tours offered.

Hotel Costa Coral, t 683 0105, *www.costacoral.com* ($$$; $65). This mid-range choice on the main street is particularly good value if you're travelling as part of a group, as its brightly coloured villas sleep up to four and come equipped with satellite TV, telephones, kitchenettes, private showers and terraces (with a choice of fan or air-conditioning). There's also a swimming pool, a Jacuzzi, a laundry service and a restaurant/bar. The room rates include breakfast.

Hotel Dos Lagartos, t 683 0236, *aulwes@costarica.net* ($; $20). Friendly budget hotel by the beach offering smallish, simply furnished rooms with fans (choice of shared and private bathrooms) and a lovely jungly garden with hammocks. Tours are offered by the hotel.

Getting to Montezuma

Sansa and NatureAir both operate daily **flights** from San José to Tambor (*see* p.104), from where you can take a **taxi** the 18km south to Montezuma ($25) or catch one of six **buses** a day, passing through from Paquera (where the Puntarenas **ferry** arrives, *see* p.213) from 6am–6pm. Buses drop passengers at Chico's Bar at the southern end of the main street.

Montezuma

⭐ Montezuma

Montezuma, near the southern tip of the Nicoya Peninsula, welcomed its first tourists in the early 1980s when a community of North American travellers – intent on hanging by the beach and generally chilling the summer away – arrived and decided that this remote, sleepy fishing village was just about perfect for their needs. It has been the unofficial headquarters for Costa Rica's free and easy, dropping out, slacker culture ever since, its streets full of New Age remedy stores and health food shops, its beaches thick with dreadlocked backpackers, and its evening air redolent of marijuana smoke. Though largely shunned by the more upmarket resort brigade (they're all at Manuel Antonio), it attracts a steady stream of itinerant 'alternative' types, who presumably like to practise being alternative by hanging around in large groups of like-minded people.

Though it can get very crowded in the season, the town's relaxed vibe means that it never feels overwhelmingly so. And, with most of its businesses aimed at the lower and middle end of the market, the town has managed to pull off the cunning trick of seeming much less developed than it actually is. Despite the predominantly American sensibility of its culture, Montezuma still feels part of its surroundings and not cut off like so many of the region's resorts. If you are not expecting too high a level of comfort, and don't mind a bit of noise, this can be a very enjoyable place and is certainly much less brashly commercial. It is also very handy, lying within easy reach of a number of day trip s, including a set of waterfalls (*see* overleaf), the Reserva Natural Absoluta Cabo Blanco, 10km south (*see* p.208), the Isla Tortuga (*see* p.204) and the Curú Wildlife Reserve (*see* p.200)

Despite having been around for a long time (at least in tourist terms), Montezuma's infrastructure remains at a very basic level, wholly in keeping with its 'taking life easy' image, with the whole town consisting of just a few dirt roads. The main drag stretches in a curve along the seafront for around 300m from the **Bakery Café** in the north to **Chico's Bar** in the south, where buses pull in and which marks the unofficial town centre. From here, a road heads inland to a T-junction. The right fork heads towards Cóbano, the left towards Cabo Blanco, passing the town's football field.

Just south of Chico's is the town's main **beach**, a beautiful palm-fringed stretch of sand. Unfortunately, though the waters here may look inviting, the area is plagued by riptides, making swimming a rather risky proposition. At low tide you can walk further south around the rocky headlands to where there are a series of **tide pools**.

North of town is another collection of fine-looking beaches, including **Playa Grande**, which is usually less crowded than Montezuma's main strip, and reachable via a road that connects with the northern end of the main drag.

The Waterfalls

The most popular day trip from town is to a set of waterfalls that lies about a 30–45min hike away. Take the road heading south out of town towards Cabo Blanco for a couple of kilometres till you reach the Hotel Amor de Mar, near where there's a signed turn-off for the waterfall (the sign says '*Catarata*'). From here, it's a 20-minute, rather slippery ascent to the 25m fall. There's another small fall further downstream. Despite this area's undoubted beauty, the popularity of the trip – you're unlikely to have the falls to yourself – seems to have bred a certain overfamiliarity in the minds of many visitors, and when you come you may well see people attempting to climb the falls. Avoid following suit; this is an extremely dangerous pursuit, up slippery moss-covered rocks, and many would-be climbers have been seriously injured over the years (some even killed) and there are no lifeguards on hand to help should you get into difficulties. Content yourself with the views, a swim in the plunge pool (keeping a safe distance from the falls itself) and an exploration of the surrounding forest where monkeys can often be spotted.

There are also a couple of more inaccessible waterfalls in the area which can only be reached on horseback in the company of a guide provided by one of the town's numerous tour operators.

Services in Montezuma

The town has **Internet cafés**, **laundries**, **pharmacies**, **supermarkets**, a **post office** and a very good **ookstore**, Librería Topsy, which sells English-language (mostly American) books, magazines and newspapers, and operates a small lending library.

There's no **bank** (although most businesses will accept small denomination dollar bills), the nearest being at Cóbano, around 6km inland.

Activities in Montezuma

There are a number of operators in town offering guided tours to the local **waterfalls** (from $25 on horseback), the

Cabo Blanco Wildlife Reserve (from $25, *see* p.200), the **Curú National Wildlife Refuge** (from $25, *see* p.208), as well as kayaking (from $25) and **snorkelling**, both in the local vicinity and out at **Isla Tortuga**, a pair of uninhabited islands lying just offshore where there's a particular abundance of marine wildlife (from $35).

Aventuras en Montezuma, t 642 0050, *www.aventurasenmontezuma.com*.

Montezuma Eco Tours, t 642 0467, *www.playamontezuma.net*.

Montezuma Expeditions, t 642 0919, *www.montezumaexpeditions.com*.

Waterfalls Canopy Tour, t 642 0911. Offers a new twist on the canopy tour – zip-lines directly over the river.

Where to Stay in Montezuma

Catering mainly to its core 'slack-packer' clientele, Montezuma's accommodation tends to fall mainly in the budget and mid-range categories, with just a handful of high-end places. Those establishments in the centre of town, particularly around the perennially popular Chico's Bar, can be rather noisy in high season when the bars blast out their music till the early hours, although quieter places can be found on the outskirts, e.g. on the road heading south towards Cabo Blanco. Montezuma can be crowded in peak months, but with so much accommodation available, you'd be unlucky not to find a room somewhere.

Camping is officially prohibited on the beach, though lots of people do it.

Nature Lodge Finca Los Caballos, 3km northwest of town uphill on the road to Cóbano, **t** 642 0124, *www.nature lodge.net* ($$$$; $80). In a luxuriant tropical garden, with great elevated views over surrounding area, Finca Los Caballos offers ranch-style rooms (with private hot-water bathrooms and patios), a two-bedroom self-catering bungalow sleeping up to four ($440, minimum three nights), a pool, a good restaurant/bar (open to the public by reservation only) and a range of tours, including horse-riding and bird-watching. Bikes can be hired.

El Sano Banano Beach Hotel, **t** 642 0638, *www.elbanano.com* ($$$$; $100). The town's most secluded accommodation. You can't drive here, but must instead pop into its sister property, **El Sano Banano Village B&B**, in the centre of town (where there's a very good restaurant, *see* 'Eating Out') and report to reception. Staff will transfer your bags while you take a 10-minute stroll up the beach to the property. It's an extremely pretty place with eight luxurious circular bungalows (all decorated with pictures of local fauna) set in tropical gardens, the highlight of which is the waterfall-fed swimming pool. There's also a two-storey self-catering property with three bedrooms and a kitchenette.

Hotel Amor de Mar, right on the shorefront, near the turn-off to the waterfall, a 5–10min walk south of town, **t** 642 0262, *www.amordemar.com* ($$$; $40). This German-owned complex is peaceful and rather swish, with a large garden leading down to the beach where you'll find a natural seawater plunge pool. The wood-panelled superior rooms have private baths ($75), balconies and sea views, while the standard ones have shared. There's also a self-catering house for rent with four bedrooms, and a great snack bar overlooking the ocean.

Hotel El Jardin, just above the T-junction leading to the centre of town, **t** 642 0548, *www.hoteleljardin. com* ($$$; $60). In a lush hillside garden, this Italian-owned choice has 15 cabins ranging in size and price: from medium-sized/medium-priced with fans and tile bathrooms; to large/expensive with air-conditioning and terraces, rocking chairs and hammocks overlooking the ocean ($80), all bedecked with attractive hardwood furniture and pretty picture windows. There's also a self-catering house ($100, minimum stay 3 nights).

Hotel Luz de Mono, **t** 642 0090, *www. luzdemono.com* ($$$; $75). Much more luxurious than anything you'll find in the centre for the same price, this grand establishment on the outskirts of town is surrounded by dense woodland (home to monkeys and various wildlife – there are trails), and has large, comfortable and extremely well-equipped rooms – all with ceiling fans, fridges, coffee- makers, minibars, safes, CD players (with a selection of Costa Rican music CDs) – as well some self-catering houses with kitchenettes ($170). There's also a Jacuzzi and an excellent restaurant/ bar, the **Blue Congo**, where works by local artists are displayed and live music is staged. The food (despite the restaurant's name) is Italian-influenced and among the best in Montezuma.

Hotel Aurora, on a hill by the northern entrance to town, **t** 642 0051 ($$; $30). The Aurora offers a variety of budget options: small rooms with fans and shared baths (cold water), slightly larger ones with private baths, air-conditioning and hot water ($50), and a large apartment with a separate living area, kitchen and terrace that

⊛ Hotel Luz de Mono >>

⊛ El Sano Banano >

sleeps up to six ($250 per week). There's also a communal kitchen and hammocks, which are available to all guests. Some of the rooms are a bit old and tired-looking, but the hotel was one of the area's very first.

Hotel Los Mangos, on the road heading south, t 642 0384, *www.hotellos mangos.com* ($$; $30). This grand (for Montezuma) complex occupies large, neat gardens and offers a choice of basic, brightly coloured rooms with shared baths, more expensive ones with private baths, and some separate octagonal thatch-roofed cabins ($60), with fans, fridges, private baths, balconies and rocking chairs. There's also a pool, a Jacuzzi and a very good Mediterranean restaurant. Yoga classes and massages are offered.

Hotel Montezuma Pacífica, on a quiet street just inland from the town's church, t 642 0204 ($$; $30). Away from the worst of the centre noise, this has basic, clean rooms. Those at the front have balconies and views, and there's a choice of fan or air-conditioning. Breakfast included.

Hotel Lucy, 10 minutes south of town, t 642 0273 ($; $14). Right on the beachfront (in fact, technically illegally so, as it lies within 50m of the shore, but it has managed to get away with it so far), this is one of the town's cheapest choices. Most of the rooms are small, but scrubbed and dusted, with shared cold-water showers, although a couple reserved for more fancy guests have private bathrooms. Extra facilities include a sea-facing terrace. The good, cheap restaurant next door is run by the same owners.

Luna Loca Hostel, on the road heading north out of town, t 642 0390 ($; $25–10). Strangely, despite the town's reputation as a backpacking haven, hostels (that ultimate form of backpacker accommodation) are actually rather thin on the ground. This is the town's only example, offering more or less exactly what you'd expect: simple, functional dorms with metal bunk-beds, shared bathrooms ($10 per bed), and (more importantly) a lively communal area with beanbags and hammocks where you can meet up with fellow travellers. There are also a couple of private rooms available ($25).

Hotel Montezuma, on the front, t 642 0058 ($; $20). This hotel's main attraction is its location, by the beach, right at the heart of the action, as the actual standard of accommodation is nothing special. You're offered a pretty ordinary choice of very stark rooms in an old building, and slightly less stark ones in newer annexe across the street, all with fans, fridges and balconies. Don't expect to get much sleep when things start heaving at the nearby bars. There's a good attached restaurant serving Spanish cuisine.

Cabinas El Tucán, north of the soccer field, back from the beach, t 642 0284 ($; $13). This is one of most budget-conscious places in what is, after all, a very budget-conscious town. The rooms are small, basic and rather austere, but tidy and (crucially) very cheap. Shared cold water bathrooms.

Eating Out in Montezuma

If Montezuma were a restaurant, it would be a vegetarian sandwich shop with funky décor, a relaxed (albeit slightly earnest) attitude and a menu of ethically concerned, organically friendly snacks. The establishing of a sizeable expat American community over the past couple of decades has added a Western-orientated veneer to the existing seafood, fish and *comida tipica* base. As well as all the health food options, you'll also find a number of decent gourmet choices, most of which are located in the hotels outside the centre of town. The Hotel Amor de Mar (light snacks), Hotel Luz de Mono ('international gourmet') and Hotel Los Mangos ('Mediterranean') all operate very good restaurants.

Bakery Café. Enjoying rather stylish surrounds at the northern end of the beach, this vegetarian snack bar serves up large, filling sandwiches packed full of vegetables, vegetarian *casados*, and some very good breakfasts – pancakes muffins, etc.

El Sano Banano Natural Foods Restaurant and Coffee Shop. Another typically Montezuman restaurant set beneath the El Sano Banano Village B&B in the centre of town, this places a strong emphasis on organic produce, serving pesticide-free vegetarian dishes, hormone-free meat dishes and locally caught seafood dishes, plus fruit-crammed smoothies. Its showing of a US film every night attracts lively crowds, and is officially 'free', although you do have to buy $5 worth of food in order to be allowed to sit down. There's an Internet café next door.

Iguana Café. Another very good sandwich shop in the centre of town, the Iguana's offerings are very large, generously filled and made with home-baked bread ($4). It also serves a range of juices and coffees, as well as muffins and cakes flavoured with tropical fruit.

Playa de los Artistas. A couple of mins' walk south of the village, this is one of the town's more refined choices, enjoying an elegant, lantern-lit, alfresco dining space overlooking the beach. The food is Italian-influenced (plenty of home-made pasta, plus a range of meat, fish and vegetarian choices), very good and rather expensive – mains $10–15. No phone.

Restaurant Lucy. It's a bit of a walk, 10 mins south of town, but well worth it if you're looking to save a bit of money. This serves tasty seafood and Costa Rican staples on a breezy terrace overlooking the ocean at very reasonable prices. It's located next to the hotel of the same name.

Nightlife in Montezuma

The focus of Montezuma's social life, now as always, is **Chico's Bar** in the centre of town where the music is loud and the beer plentiful until 2am most nights. **Bar Montezuma, Shangrilá** and the **El Sano Banano** restaurant (which shows English-language movies each night) are also lively, although not overwhelmingly so. The scene here is more laid-back than full on.

Around Montezuma

Cóbano, Malpais and Santa Teresa

The town of **Cóbano** lies around 5km northwest inland from Montezuma. Though by no means a tourist town, the number of services it offers, including a post office and the only bank in the area, a branch of the Banco Nacional, means that it still welcomes its fair share of visitors.

From here a road heads west to the coast, from where you can access a couple of decent surfing towns, **Malpais** to the south and **Santa Teresa** to the north, which have recently been colonized by communities of tourists looking to get away from it all and obviously having deemed that Montezuma was no longer the place to do it. Unfortunately, the popularity of this stretch of coast, with new hotels seemingly springing up by the month, means that this may not be the place to do it for much longer either. Expect the next 'getting away from it all' place to have been discovered a few kilometres further up the coast in the next few years.

Activities and Where to Stay in Malpais and Santa Teresa

As with Montezuma, both towns have a laid-back, almost hippyish atmosphere and offer very good surfing. There are several hotels and operators offering lessons and hiring out boards, including **Pura Vida Surf School, t** 640 0118, and the **Malpais Surf Camp, t** 640 0061, *www.malpais surfcamp.com*, which also hires out decent *cabinas* for $25–35 – with a mixture of shared and private baths.

Getting to the Reserva Cabo Blanco

The 10km road from Montezuma to Cabo Blanco is very rough and uneven. If **driving**, you'll need a 4WD. Even suitably equipped, the road sometimes becomes impassable in the wet season.

Buses leave for the park three times daily at 8am, 10am and 2pm, returning at 9am, 1pm and 4pm. You can also take a **taxi** (of the 4WD kind) from Montezuma to the reserve for around $10.

Reserva Natural Absoluta Cabo Blanco

🌟 Reserva Natural Absoluta Cabo Blanco
t 650 0607;
open Wed–Sun 8–4; adm

1963 represents year zero in the history of conservation in Costa Rica, for it was in that year that the expat Scandinavian couple, Olaf and Karen Morgenson, succeeded in turning this section of forest right on the southern tip of the Nicoya Peninsula into the country's first officially recognized protected area of land. In fact, back then there wasn't as much forest here as there is now, just a small, dwindling patch surrounded by ever-encroaching farmland, the plight of which spurred the Morgensons into action. Over the past four decades the trees have gradually reclaimed their lost territory and forest now blankets the whole area once again.

The Morgensons were extremely prominent members of the conservation movement throughout the '60s and early '70s, loudly ringing the ecological bell, and their lobbying was instrumental in the setting up of the national parks system in 1969. Tragically, Olaf was murdered in 1975 while scouting on the Osa Peninsula to determine the borders of what would be Corcovado National Park. The work he started has continued, however, and today the reserve provides a fitting memorial to his efforts. In addition to a large swath of forest – home to howler monkeys, white-faced capuchins, squirrels, armadillos, coatis, peccaries, anteaters, sloths and many other types of animal – the reserve also contains a large stretch of coast, which provides an important nesting sites for numerous birds, including brown boobies, pelicans and frigate birds. Once the most zealously protected – until 1989, it really was an 'absolute' wildlife reserve, with no members of the public allowed in at all – it is now rather more visitor-friendly, with regular opening times and marked trails, although it is closed on Mondays and Tuesdays and there is talk of limiting visitor numbers to protect the wildlife. There's no accommodation in the park, and camping is not permitted.

For the best overview of what the reserve has to offer, follow the main 5km **trail** leading from the **ranger station** all the way down to the **beach** – a 4hr round trip. You'll pass through dense forest and travel up and down a hill before emerging onto the white sands of the coast. As tempting as the waters look, it's best not to swim here, as strong currents flow around the tip of the peninsula. Bring raingear and, if possible, rubber boots, as the forest receives a lot of rainfall and this trail can get very muddy. Conversely, you'll also need sunblock, a hat and plenty of water for when you emerge onto the beach, as summer temperatures can exceed 30°C.

The Central Pacific Coast

and Monteverde

The Central Pacific coast represents both the best and the worst of the Costa Rican holiday experience. For tourists looking for a luxurious tropical getaway, it could hardly be improved upon, with its miles of pristine, palm-lined white-sand beaches, fabulously well-equipped hotels, lively resort towns and wealth of activities on offer – sports fishing, surfing, zip-lining, etc. From an ecological perspective, however, the region demonstrates how, in the delicate balancing act between trying to improve and expand the tourist infrastructure while protecting the natural environment, it's usually the environment that ends up getting dropped. Development has been so intense here, with resorts hungrily competing for beach space, that the most visited 'ecological' tourist attraction, the Parque Nacional Manuel Antonio, now represents the region's only sizeable area of coastal rainforest.

11

Don't miss

⭐ **Ethereal beauty**
Monteverde Cloudforest Reserve **p.241**

⭐ **Nightlife and surfing**
Jacó **p.217**

⭐ **Crocodiles and scarlet macaws**
Parque Nacional Carara **p.215**

⭐ **Glorious tropical beaches – and monkeys too**
Parque Nacional Manuel Antonio **p.234**

⭐ **Treetop thrills**
Selvatura Canopy Tour **p.248**

See map overleaf

The Central Pacific

Volcán Arenal
La Fortuna
Muelle San Carlos
Rio Sardinal

Parque Nacional Arenal
Reserva Santa Elena
Cordillera de Tilarán
Bosque Eterno de los Niños
Ciudad Quesada (San Carlos)
La Virgen
San Miguel

Santa Elena
Monteverde
Juntas

Reserva Biológica Bosque Nuboso Monteverde
Bajo del Toro
Volcán Poás
Parque Nacional Volcán Poás
Parque Nacional Braulio Carrillo

Yomale
San Rafael
Zarcero
Volcán Barva

Rancho Grande
Miramar
Angeles
San Ramón
Naranjo
Sarchí
Grecia
Alajuela
Barva

Esparza
Atenas
Garita

Puntarenas
San Mateo
Rio Virilla
SAN JOSÉ

Naranjo
PUNTARENAS
Orotina
Santiago de Turiscal

Paquera
Refugio Nacional de Vida Silvestre Curú
Isla Tortuga
San Ignacio de Acosta
SAN JOSÉ

Tárcoles
Parque Nacional Carara

Playa Herradura
Isla Herradura
Jacó
PUNTARENAS

Playa Hermosa

N

20 km
10 miles

Pacific Ocean

Quepos
Manuel Antonio
Playa Espadilla
Punta Catedral
Playa Manuel Antonio
Parque Nacional Manuel Antonio

p.160

NICARAGUA
Caribbean Sea
COSTA RICA
Pacific Ocean
PANAMA

Don't miss

1 Monteverde Cloudforest Reserve **p.241**

2 Jacó **p.217**

3 Parque Nacional Carara **p.215**

4 Parque Nacional Manuel Antonio **p.234**

5 Selvatura Canopy Tour **p.248**

Getting around the Central Pacific Region

For once, the advice here is relatively encouraging. With the Central Pacific coast possessing a good, regularly repaired road network, there is no need to issue the dire warnings that have featured in other regions.

Two main roads lead from San José to the coast, both of which are pretty well maintained: the main Interamericana (HWY-1), which wends its way over the Cordillera Central and down to the Pacific lowlands before heading north just east of Puntarenas; and HWY-3, which leads via Alajuela down to the southern end of the region to Jacó and Manuel Antonio, a very scenic drive. Neither route should require a 4WD, even in the wet season. Road coverage gets poorer the further north you go. In order to preserve the reserve, the roads surrounding Monteverde have been kept unpaved and are very bumpy (for these you will need a 4WD).

The Nicoya Peninsula (see pp.175–208), which sits opposite the Pacific coast to the west, can be reached via a ferry service from Puntarenas or via the Puente la Amistad ('Friendship Bridge'; see p.191) across the Río Tempisque, further north. Be warned that some of the roads in the southern half of the peninsula are very poor; some become practically impassable in the wet season (4WD or no).

Thankfully, the Monteverde area to the north away from the coast has managed to redress the environmental balance slightly, its 30,000 hectares (and growing) of preserved cloudforest representing the country's largest privately funded conservation project. There's still plenty of fun to be had here – canopy tours, horse-riding, not to mention treks through the magical cloudforest itself – but local communities have taken pains to make sure that this doesn't come at too high an environmental cost, fending off attempts to have the smaller local roads paved, a move they feel would lead to the area's being opened up to greater development.

The cost of having luxury on tap – of knowing that you're never too far from your next cold beer, or dip in a Jacuzzi or lively night out – is that it places the natural wonders of Costa Rica further out of reach. Even those few surviving 'wild' areas seem to have been sanitized and commercialized for public consumption. This particularly applies to Manuel Antonio. Undeniably beautiful with its shimmering sweeps of sand, it nonetheless represents the wilderness in its safest and most easily palatable form, with its well-worn paths and beach resorts crowding in on all sides. Of course, there's no point in being too curmudgeonly about things. Development has brought an economic vibrancy to the area and has provided many locals with a good standard of living.

Easy as it is to blame all environmental problems on the search for the US tourist dollar, it is worth pointing out that the Central Pacific coast's touristification has been driven as much by Ticos, with whom this is an extremely popular tourist destination (certainly much more so than the Caribbean coast), as foreigners. This popularity is partly due to the ease of access – there is a network of well maintained roads leading from the capital plus frequent bus services – and partly due to the reliability and stability of the coastal climate. Whereas the Caribbean coast has no true dry season, with downpours likely at any time, this stretch of the Pacific coast is guaranteed several months of very dry, extremely hot weather between December and March, when daytime temperatures will rarely drop below 30°C and sunscreen becomes a necessity. Away from the coast, heading north towards the Monteverde Cloudforest Reserve, the climate gets increasingly wetter; the reserve's higher elevations are pretty much sodden all year round.

The Central Pacific Coast

Puntarenas

Ah, what might have been. For a while it seemed as if Puntarenas was set to dominate the region's tourist industry and become a major resort. After all, what other town was better qualified? Set on the coast and enjoying a particularly balmy climate, Puntarenas was the regional capital, home to the largest population, a port with good transport links (ferry, road, rail) and the proud possessor of a long sandy beach (Puntarenas translates literally as 'sandy point'). Unfortunately, nobody else seemed to agree that these features made it prime resort material. Though Puntarenas has always attracted a smattering of loyal Tico holidaymakers, foreign visitors just couldn't be persuaded of its charms. They found it crowded, its beaches dirty and its transport links supremely efficient – for getting to almost anywhere else. While the region's southern resorts, particularly Jacó, thrived, Puntarenas declined. Its beaches became polluted, its businesses went under and crime levels soared.

Come the turn of the century, however, and the city authorities decided that it was time to try again. A millennial makeover was instigated which saw the beach cleaned, the main boulevard (the Paseo de los Turistas) spruced up and a new dock opened, aimed at the cruise liner market. It's had some effect. True, much of the town is still a bit grim, filled with dilapidated buildings, rusty machinery and peeling paint (and its dock and market area are not the sort of place you want to do much walking around after dark), but things are improving. The town's new marine park, a decent collection of restaurants and a lively, bustling and (for the first time in years) hopeful atmosphere make it well worthy of a day trip.

Puntarenas lies 110km west of San José on a narrow sandy peninsula jutting out from the Central Pacific shore into the Gulf of Nicoya. Its streets are laid out according to the same grid pattern as most other Costa Rican towns with *avenidas* running east–west and *calles* north–south. However, being much longer than it is wide, there are just five main *avenidas* but over 20 *calles*.

Though just a few blocks apart, the northern and southern sides of town have quite distinct characters. The northern side is very much the working area, home to the banana docks, the ferry dock, the fishing fleet and the central market. The whole area is a veritable

Getting to and around Puntarenas

Buses for Puntarenas leave San José hourly from 6am–7pm from C 16, Av 10/12. The journey costs c995 and takes around 2hrs 20mins, arriving at Puntarenas' main bus terminal on the Paseo de los Turistas (Av 4, C 2).

Most of the town's attractions are grouped within a few blocks of each other, making walking the easiest way of getting around. Buses and taxis are available for journeys to the western tip of the peninsula along the Avenida Central.

Getting away from Puntarenas

Puntarenas may not be very good at getting visitors to stay in town, but it continues to be adept at processing their departure to other destinations, acting as the region's major transport hub.

Ferries leave from the main terminal on the town's northwestern tip every day to the Nicoya Peninsula towns of Paquera (every 2hrs 4.30–8.30; 1hr; passengers $1.75, cars $12), from where you can catch **buses** to the other major southern peninsula towns of Montezuma and Tambor. If travelling by **car**, you should arrive at the docks at least an hour before departure to be sure of getting a ticket. The town's main **bus terminal** is located on the corner of Av 4, C 2. Services depart from here to all the major regional destinations including San José, Alajuela Airport, Nicoya, Monteverde, Santa Elena, Quepos, Jacó and Liberia.

cacophony of sounds and smells from dawn till dusk. The southern side is more touristy, with a sandy beach, the **Playa Puntarenas**, running along its length. The most pleasant stretch is at its western end where the water has been deemed safe enough for swimming. Bordering the beach is Avenida 4, rechristened long ago (rather optimistically) as the **Paseo de los Turistas** – although it is currently making a better attempt at living up to its name than at any time in its past following the opening of a new cruise ship terminal, which has in turn inspired the creation of a number of new hotels and restaurants.

In between these two areas is the town centre, marked by two of the town's main cultural attractions, which occupy a former port building: the **Casa de la Cultura**, which stages plays, concerts and art exhibitions (and also has a collection of historic photographs of the town) and the **Museo Histórico Marino** (Marine History Museum), which tells the story of the town and its relationship with the sea, focusing in particular on the glory years of the 19th century when Puntarenas was Costa Rica's main coffee port (a status it would eventually lose to Limón).

Casa de la Cultura
t 661 1394

Museo Histórico Marino
t 661 5036; www.museosdecostarica.com; open 9.45–5.15

Parque Marino del Pacífico
t 661 5272, www.parquemarino.org; open Tues–Sun 9–4.30; adm

The town's latest attraction is the **Parque Marino del Pacífico**, which lies 500m east of the cruise ship terminal. Funded largely with government money, its creation has been a quite deliberate attempt to drive the town's image in a more upmarket direction. The 2.5ha site is home to 22 indoor aquaria, inhabited by a variety of Pacific marine life (including sharks), as well as several outdoor pools designed to replicate coastal wetlands, where you'll find crocodiles and turtles. The park still has a slightly unfinished look to it and there aren't quite as many animals here as you might hope, but it's still early days and it seems to have given the city a much-needed injection of pride.

Tourist Information and Services in Puntarenas

There's a small **tourist office** opposite the main ferry terminal, which can provide basic maps and information as well as Internet access.

Banks: Banco Nacional Av 3, C 1; Banco de Costa Rica Av 3, C 0. Both have 24hr ATMs.

Hospital: Hospital Monseñor Sanabria, 8km east of town, **t** 663 0033.

Internet access: Internet Café Puntarenas, Av 1, C3; Millennium Cyber Café Av 4, C 13/15.

Police: Av 3, C 0/2, **t** 661 0640.

Post office: Av 3, C 1/0, **t** 661 2156.

Tour Operators

Puntarenas may not have that many attractions of its own, but it is home to a number of tour operators offering trips to some of the surrounding area's prime draws including the Parque Nacional Manuel Antonio, the Monteverde Cloudforest Reserve, the Parque Nacional Carara and the pristine Isla Tortuga (*see* p.204).

Bay Island Cruises, **t** 258 3536.

Tortuga Island Tours, **t** 661 2508.

Calypso Tours, **t** 256 2727, *www.calypsotours.com*.

Coonatramar, **t** 661 9011, *www.coonatramar.com*.

Where to Stay in Puntarenas

There's plenty of choice, particularly at the budget end of the spectrum, although you should exercise some caution. The very cheapest places, located around the Mercado Central, tend to be seedy dives and the whole area is rife with prostitutes after dark. The more upmarket (and safer) places are located on and around the Paseo de los Turistas.

Hotel Tioga, Av 4, C 17/19, **t** 661 0271, *tiogacr@racsa.co.cr* ($$$$–$$$; $98–59). On the main tourist boulevard, this offers rooms in a variety of shapes and sizes (hence the difference in price): some have air-conditioning, some have sea-facing balconies, but all are *en suite* with TVs and telephones. Extra facilities include a garden, games room, casino, pool and bar. The price includes breakfast.

Hotel Las Brisas, Av 4, C 31/33, **t** 661 4040, *hbrisas@racsa.co.cr* ($$$; $69). A nice, two-storey waterfront option right at the western (i.e. the more pleasant) end of the peninsula near the ferry docks. All rooms have TV, air-conditioning and private bathrooms and some have balconies offering great sunset views of the Gulf of Nicoya. There's also a small pool and a restaurant serving a slightly peculiar hybrid Greek-Mexican menu. Secure parking and Internet access available.

Costa Rica Yacht Club, 3km east of town, **t** 661 0784, *www.costarica yachtclub.com* ($$$; $75–45). Overlooking a 200-berth marina, this caters principally to its own members, but, as there never seem to be enough in attendance to fill the place, they usually have room (although you should check in advance). The facilities are not quite as grand as you might expect, with rather bare, under-furnished (though clean) rooms, all with private bathrooms and ceiling fans (those with air-conditioning are around $20 more than those without), but you have access to a reasonable restaurant and swimming pool.

Hotel Portobello, 3km east of town centre, **t** 661 1322 ($$$; $50). Near the yacht club, set in nice landscaped gardens, this is a charming mid-range choice with good-sized rooms, all with private bathrooms (the more expensive have air-conditioning) and an Italian restaurant overlooking the estuary. Sports fishing tours and trips to Isla Tortuga (*see* p.204) are offered.

Eating Out in Puntarenas

The eating out advice depends very much on how much money you have at your disposal. If price is not a major concern, then head straight to the Paseo de los Turistas where there are several excellent (albeit rather pricey) fish restaurants. The more thrifty among you will have to make do with the sodas and snack bars that surround the Mercado Central and ferry terminal.

Restaurante Aloha, Av 4, C 19, t 661 0773. Next door to the more upmarket La Yunta (*see* below), this is a more relaxed affair, serving large plates of seafood and rice at a terrace overlooking the beach.

La Caravelle, Av 4, C 19/21, t 661 2262. A mixture of top-notch French cuisine, an elegant antique-adorned interior and lovely beach views make the 'carousel' one of the town's top dining experiences. Good wine list.

Restaurante Kahite Blanco, Av 1, C 15/17, t 661 2093. Offering simpler fare than the restaurants on the front, this back-to-basics eaterie by the docks is particularly popular with the locals, who pack its restricted confines each evening to tuck into *bocas*, *ceviche*, shrimps and rice, and lobster. You can get a filling meal for less than $4.

Restaurante La Yunta, Av 4, C 21/23, t 661 3216. This Puntarenas stalwart has a nice old-fashioned feel, with its starched white tablecloths and ever attentive waiters. It specializes in seafood, which you can eat either in the indoor dining room overlooked by a mounted ox head (Yunta means 'oxen') or on the shady verandah – a great people-watching sport.

Nightlife in Puntarenas

Nightlife tends to consists mainly of drinking at one of the various bars lining the Paseo de los Turistas, some of which turn into discos as the evening wears on. The Casa de la Cultura hosts regular concerts and several of the town's hotels also operate casinos.

Parque Nacional Carara

Parque Nacional Carara
t 383 9953; open daily 7–4; adm

The 4,700ha Parque Nacional Carara lies 50km southeast of Puntarenas, 90km west of San José at the mouth of the Río Tárcoles. Almost entirely surrounded by farmland, the park provides a welcome refuge for the region's wildlife, of which, considering the park's somewhat diminutive size, there is a surprisingly large amount. This abundance is principally due to the fact that the park lies in the centre of what is officially known as a 'transition zone'. The vegetation here is a sort of cross between the tropical dry forests of Guanacaste to the north, and the humid, sultry tropical wet forests of the Pacific south, producing conditions suitable for the animals and plants of both. As a result, the park is home to a great many of the country's species of mammal, including monkeys, racoons, coatis, tapirs and armadillos; four species of cat (jaguars, pumas, ocelots and margays); no fewer than 19 of Costa Rica's 22 species of poisonous snakes, as well as a veritable cornucopia of birds, including toucans, trogons and hummingbirds, as well as one of the country's most significant communities of scarlet macaws – it's renowned as one of the country's leading birdwatching destinations. The park's mangrove swamps and mudbanks also support a large population of crocodiles, for whom the best viewing spot actually lies just beyond the park's borders on the road to Puntarenas where the Río Tárcoles Bridge (more commonly known as **Crocodile Bridge**) provides elevated views of the scaly beasts as they bask on the banks.

Despite this abundance of wildlife, animal sightings are by no means guaranteed. The park's relative proximity to (and easy accessibility from) San José means that it can sometimes seem as

Getting to the Parque Nacional Carara

The park can easily be reached by **car** along the coastal highway. You should have no trouble spotting the turning by the Río Tárcoles Bridge, as it's usually lined with parked cars and sightseers trying to get a look at the crocodiles. The entrance to the park and the ranger station lies 3km south of here. Be warned that, a while back, there was a spate of car break-ins both near the bridge and at the ranger station. Although the situation seems to have been rectified by employing scouts to watch the cars, you should be careful and make sure you don't leave any valuables lying in your car.

All **buses** trundling the coastal highway, north from Jacó or south from San José, pass by the park, although you may have to ask the driver to let you off as there's no official bus stop. Similarly, you'll have to flag down a bus on the highway once you leave.

if it's as full of people as it is of animals. At peak times, it can be difficult to see anything as the park's inhabitants slink back into the forest depths away from the crowds. For the best chance of encountering the wildlife, try to visit as early in the morning as possible, when you'll have fewer human companions and the animals (particularly the birds) will be more inclined to put in an appearance.

Unless you get caught in a downpour, the early morning will also be the most pleasant time to visit. The park's status as a transition zone may be good for its wildlife quota, but it poses its fair share of problems for visitors as the climate here can at times be as hot as the north (over 30°C at midday) and as wet as the south (it receives over 3m of rain annually). The dry season is from December to April.

Two **trails** lead from the **ranger station** into the forest, the first of which, a short 1.7km trek through primary rainforest, is the only wheelchair-accessible trail in the entire national parks system. The other, longer trail connects with a further looping trail that follows part of the route of the Río Tárcoles, and which is reckoned to be the best for wildlife-watching (probably because it's less visited).

In addition to all its natural wonders, the park also contains several pre-Columbian archaeological sites dating from the first millennium AD, although these are currently out of bounds to the public.

Where to Stay and Eat in the Parque Nacional Carara

It's not a great area for anyone on a tight budget. Camping is not permitted in the park and budget accommodation is pretty thin on the ground until you reach Jacó itself, some 15km south. However, if you have a bit of cash to play with, you'll find the nearby town of **Tárcoles** home to a couple of superior eco-lodges, both of which specialize in birdwatching tours.

Tarcol Lodge, 5km north of Tárcoles, t 297 4134 ($$$$$; from $198 all-inclusive). One of the most famous birdwatching lodges in the country, the Tarcol overlooks the Río Tárcoles tidal mudflats, which provide a home for (and a larder to) hundreds of species of bird throughout the year. As a free birding tour to Carara National Park is also offered to anyone staying three nights or more, you can see why this is generally regarded as a spotters' delight. The lodge itself is simple and rustic, but very comfortable (all rooms have private bathrooms and fans) and the owners (who also operate a sister property in Turrialba) are welcoming, enthusiastic and very knowledgeable.

(★) Tarcol Lodge >

Villa Lapas Lodge, just south of Tárcoles, t 637 0232, *www.villalapas. com* ($$$$$; from $146 inclusive). The Villa Lapas owns its own swath of 'transitional' forest where you can, depending on how active (or brave) you feel – sit spotting birds, hunt for wildlife along ground-level trails or (not for the faint-hearted) go on an elevated treetop tour along a series of suspension bridges, some of which are set over 55m off the ground. Should you be able to open your eyes, there is apparently plenty of wildlife to be spotted up here. The lodge's rooms are large and well-equipped (if a bit boxy), all with air-conditioning and private bathrooms, and there is also a pool and a restaurant where displays of traditional Costa Rican dance are staged at weekends.

Jacó

🟡 Jacó

Jacó is no johnny-come-lately resort created on the back of the country's 1990s tourism boom. As the possessor of the closest and most easily accessible beach to San José (a mere 120km jaunt down the motorway), this has been a popular holiday destination with Ticos (and Josefinos in particular) for decades. American surfers have also been coming here since the late 1970s when the then surfing bible, *Surfing* magazine, first brought the region's now famous waves to its countrymen's attention. It could therefore be said that the recent huge growth in tourism, which has had such a transformative effect on the surrounding area, has, in Jacó, merely accelerated a process that was already well under way. Today Jacó is firmly established as one of the most popular resorts on the entire Pacific coast, welcoming a swarming mass of humanity – surfers, backpackers, package tourists and Tico holidaymakers – throughout its peak months, although it can be strangely, almost eerily quiet out of season.

Its attractions are simple: the beach, which despite its rather unappealing grey-brown colour is these days relatively clean (there are regular litter patrols); the waves, which are challenging rather than nerve-jangling (though rip-tides can make swimming some-what hazardous); and the nightlife, which keeps getting bigger and louder year on year. Aside from the surfing, which, according to those who know, is supposedly better at nearby Playa Hermosa, there are plenty of other activities to be enjoyed in and around town, including canoeing, horse-riding, sports fishing, zip-lining or just sitting on the beach at the end of the day with a beer watching one of the region's remarkable sunsets.

Orientation

Finding your way around Jacó is a pretty straightforward process. The town consists of a main road (Avenida Pastor Díaz) which runs north–south for around a kilometre parallel to the sea, a smattering of side streets leading down to the sea that connect at seemingly random intervals, and not much else. Some of the streets do have names, although almost nobody uses them when giving directions, preferring, as is customary throughout the country, to rely on landmarks, such as the Mas X Menos supermarket and the Best Western Jacó Beach Hotel.

Getting to and around Jacó

Buses leave San José's La Coca-Cola bus terminal, C 16, Av 1/3, five times daily at 7.30am, 10.30am, 1pm, 3.30pm and 6.30pm, arriving three hours later at the bus stop opposite the Best Western Jacó Beach Hotel, 1km north of the town centre. The journey costs c990. A **taxi** from the bus stop to the town centre should cost little more than $1. Buses from Puntarenas to the north and Quepos to the south arrive at a different bus stop on Jacó's main drag in the centre of town.

To get to **Playa Herradura**, take a taxi from Jaco's main street ($5). No bus runs nearer than a 4km walk (along an unpaved road) away.

To get to **Playa Hermosa**, take any bus heading south from town towards Quepos and ask the driver to let you off. The journey should take less than 10 minutes.

Getting away from Jacó

Five **buses** a day travel between Jacó and San José at 5am, 7.30am, 11am, 3pm and 5pm. The bus stop is 1km north of the town centre opposite the Best Western Jacó Beach. Bus services to Quepos and Manuel Antonio in the south and Puntarenas in the north can be picked up in the centre of town.

Car Hire

National Costa Rica, Av Pastor Díaz, just north of Mas X Menos supermarket, **t** 290 0431, *www.natcar.com*. **Payless Car Rental**, Av Pastor Díaz, 400m north of Mas X Menos supermarket, **t** 643 3224, *www. paylesscarrental.com*.

The town itself could hardly be described as one of Costa Rica's prettiest – a ragtag collection of often hastily erected shops, hotels, restaurants and tour operators straggling for a kilometre or so alongside the beach – but it's well equipped and one of the liveliest, with hordes of bars, discos and clubs. Indeed, its nightlife is so revered that each weekend busloads of Josefinos arrive to sample it.

Of course, the town's brash hedonism – with the unfortunately inevitable rise in petty crime, drug-taking and prostitution that accompanies it – is not to everyone's taste. Thankfully, there are quieter stretches of coast within easy reach. Seven km north, the horseshoe-shaped black sand **Playa Herradura** offers good swimming and a more relaxed environment – at least for now. Completely unspoilt and undiscovered until a decade ago, the beach's north side is now taken over by the Los Sueños Resort, a vast hotel complex

Surfing in Jacó

Experts may prefer the more rip-roaring waves of the outlying beaches (particularly Playa Hermosa), but Jacó's main beach offers reasonably good surfing conditions – the waves here aren't exactly gentle but neither are they too fearsome – where the less able can build up their confidence and technique before moving on to more challenging areas. While many tourists pitch up in Jacó sporting all the gear, it is quite possible to hire (or buy) all the necessary equipment – including boards – as well as a course of lessons at one of the plethora of surf shops and schools lining the main drag. Try the **Academia de Surfing C.R., t** 643 1948, which offers lessons for all ages, **Chosita del Surf, t** 643 1308, *chucks@racsa.co.cr* (ask for Chuck) or the **Mother of Fear Surf Shop, t** 643 2002, which stocks the town's best-value second-hand boards. Lessons start at around $40 for 3hrs, including board rental.

The downside of Jacó's status as a surfing mecca is that its beaches can get very crowded (despite all the talk of Playa Hermosa having 'purer' waves, most surfers still seem to end up in Jacó itself) and you may have to wait in line for quite some time before being able to catch a wave of your own.

aimed at wealthy Americans, with a yacht marina, a golf course (offering the rather unconvincingly named 'eco-golf') and a growing network of privately owned condominiums. While the south side of the beach is less developed, with a few nice budget hotels and restaurants, there's a bit of an 'end of an era' feel to the whole place.

Five km south of Jacó is **Playa Hermosa** (not to be confused with the Nicoya Peninsula beach of the same name, *see* p.180), a serious surfers' beach where the waves are bigger, the breaks fiercer and the surfing a good deal more intense than at Jacó. The southern end of the beach is a protected reserve for green turtles, who come here each year to nest.

Tourist Information and Services in Jacó

Jacó does not have an official tourist information office, although there's no shortage of tour operators willing to offer (hardly impartial) advice, *see* 'Sports and Activities' below.

Banks: Banco Nacional, Av Pastor Díaz, adjacent to the Mas X Menos supermarket; Banco Popular, Av Pastor Diaz, 100m south of Banco Nacional. Both have 24hr ATMs.

Internet access: Mexican Joe's Internet Café, Av Pastor Díaz, just south of Mas X Menos supermarket, **t** 643 2141, *open 9am–10pm daily*.

Supermarket: Mas X Menos, Av Pastor Díaz. With its large sign, this is one of the town's most prominent landmarks, often used when giving directions.

Police: At the southern end of town, **t** 643 3011.

Post office: Beyond the centre, at the southern end of town.

See box, left, for details about surfing in the area.

Green Tours, **t** 643 2773, *juniorbenito@ racsa.co.cr*. Sports fishing, horse-riding, rafting, kayaking and snorkelling are all offered, as well as trips to Carara National Park, Manuel Antonio National Park and the Monteverde Cloudforest Reserve.

Intense Sunset Tours, **t** 643 1222. Offers horse-riding, jungle trekking, rafting and more.

Jacó Equestrian Center, **t** 643 1569, *www.horsetours.com*. Horse-riding tours for all abilities along the coast and up into the nearby hills.

Kayak Jacó, **t** 643 1233, *www. kayakjaco.com*. Experts in all sorts of water-based activities – sea kayaking, outrigger canoeing, white-water rafting and snorkelling, etc.

King Tours, **t** 643 2441. Leads tours to the Monteverde Cloudforest Reserve, Manuel Antonio National Park and Isla Tortuga, as well as snorkelling and horse-riding trips.

Sports and Activities in Jacó

There are a huge number of activities available in Jacó and the surrounding area – cycling, horse-riding, sports fishing, rafting, kayaking, snorkelling, jet-skiing, surfing, canopy tours, jungle trekking and more – and an almost equally huge number of tour operators offering them. As a rough guide, horse-riding tours should start at around $35, canopy tours from $45, national park trips from $45 and surfing from $40, but shop around for the best deals.

Where to Stay in Jacó

As well stocked with accommodation options as Jacó is, with plenty of choice in all price categories, the sheer popularity of the place is such that it's still advisable to book in advance at peak times (Dec–April). This pressure on beds has also served to drive prices up, although out of season you should be able to negotiate some significant discounts, particularly at the more expensive places. The very cheapest accommodation is provided by the **campsites** to the north and south of town, where it costs around $4 to pitch a tent. Most are pretty well equipped with showers, toilets and so forth. The centre of town is dominated by budget and mid-range *cabinas* aimed at the surfing and partying community, while most of the town's high-end places are located on the outskirts of town. Because many people (again, particularly surfers) visit Jacó on extended stays, the town also has a number of self-catering places, some of which represent significant value for groups.

Noise can be a problem here, both from the traffic on the main road, and from the music pumping out of the bars and discos. Places near the seafront tend to be slightly less overbearing, although there's nowhere in town that could be described as quiet.

Luxury ($$$$$)
Hotel Canciones del Mar, Calle BriBrí, right on the beach, **t** 643 3273, *www.cancionesdelmar.com* ($195). Set as close to the waterfront as regulations will allow, the delightfully named 'Songs of the Sea' hotel offers a stylish apartment complex set amid lush tropical foliage. Each individual condo has a kitchenette (complete with fridge and cooker), air-conditioning, sofa, and a terrace with either garden, pool or sea views. Wireless Internet access, a laundry service and a variety of tours are also offered.

★ Hotel Club del Mar >

Hotel Club del Mar, south of town centre, on the road towards Playa Hermosa, **t** 643 3194, *www.clubdelmar costarica.com* (condos $203, rooms $139). At the recently revamped and expanded Club del Mar, you can choose between the lavishly appointed hotel rooms, which have private bathrooms and balconies with sea views, and the even more luxurious two-bedroom self-catering condos which come with tile floors, hardwood furniture, kitchens, fridges, air-conditioning, TVs and telephones. Set right on the beach, the English-owned complex is surrounded by lovely gardens and boasts one of the town's very best restaurants as well as a spa, a large pool, a library and games room.

Expensive
Best Western Jacó Beach, 1km north of town centre, opposite San José bus stop, **t** 643 1000, *www.bestwestern costarica.com/locations_jaco.html*

($115). One of the town's major landmarks, this offers a good level of generic, chain-hotel, first-world comfort, if not exactly the most 'real' of Costa Rican experiences. All rooms have air-conditioning, cable TV, telephones and large bathrooms. Extra facilities include a large pool, tennis courts, a casino, a disco (at weekends) Internet access and complimentary bike hire. The hotel is the sister property of the **Best Western Irazú** in San José, guests of which have use of the facilities here and are bussed in daily. Tours offered.

Jacó Fiesta Resort, south of the town centre, on the front, **t** 643 3147 ($103). Very comfortable all-inclusive hotel offering every facility you could wish for, but little in the way of genuine atmosphere. All rooms have air-conditioning and there are three pools, tennis courts and a beachside restaurant. A range of tours is offered.

Expensive–Moderate ($$$$–$$$)
Aparthotel Flamboyant, town centre, south of Mas X Menos, at end of road facing beach, **t** 643 3146 ($60–90). Smart rather than flamboyant, this is a good option for groups, with its large apartments comfortably sleeping up to six people. All come equipped with TV, kitchen, fridge, private bathrooms and ceiling fans (air-conditioning on request), as well as small terraces overlooking the garden and pool area (where there's a Jacuzzi). And, if you don't fancy self-catering, there's a pretty good on-site restaurant.

Moderate
Mar de Luz Garden Suites, town centre, just back from main street, behind Subway, **t** 643 3259, *www.mardeluz. com* ($70). Another good option for groups, the Dutch-owned 'Sea of Light' has well-equipped apartments (the new split-level ones sleep up to five) all with air-conditioning, kitchenettes (including microwaves), TV and terraces overlooking a landscaped garden where there are two pools and a Jacuzzi. There's also a games room. Tours and car hire can be organized.

Hotel Pochote Grande, north of the town centre, **t** 643 3236 ($64). Good, mid-budget choice set in neatly tended gardens. Overlooking the beach, the rooms come with private bathrooms, air-conditioning and fridges, and there's a pool, restaurant and bar.

Hotel Poseidon, Calle Bohio, town centre, half a block from beach, t 643 1642, *www.hotel-poseidon.com* ($75). This 'boutique-style' hotel recently changed management and has had a much-needed refit. The rooms are now spick and span and very well equipped with private bathrooms, minibars, TVs and fans. Elsewhere, there's a pool with a swim-up bar and a very good Asian-influenced seafood restaurant/bar that's become a popular late-night hangout. Further eating options are provided by the very good Italian restaurant next door. Breakfast is included. A range of tours is offered.

Inexpensive–Budget ($$–$)

Cabinas Antonio, 1km north of town centre, near bus stop, t 643 3043 ($25). There's nothing frilly or fancy about the Cabinas Antonio. It offers no-nonsense accommodation aimed at people who are going to spend the majority of their time here taming the waves and touring the bars, and want nothing more at the end of the day than somewhere simple and clean to sleep. The rooms here are pretty spartan, but the beds are comfy, the bathrooms have hot water and there's a restaurant and small pool.

Cabinas La Cometa, Av Pastor Díaz, town centre, t 643 3615 ($32–22). Your level of comfort here will depend largely on how much roughing it you're prepared to do. The hardcore will be happy with shared bathrooms and cold water, while the more faint-hearted may be tempted to shell out extra for a private bathroom with hot water and air-conditioning. Located right in the heart of the action on the main road, this can get rather noisy, though it also has a great atmosphere.

Cabinas Playa Hermosa, Playa Hermosa, 7km south of Jacó, t 643 2640 ($15 per person). Run by a couple of surfing-mad brothers (who hire out boards), this offers simple, basic, surfer-friendly accommodation with en suite rooms, a pool and restaurant.

Chuck's Cabinas and Board Repair, Calle Anita, on beach at northern end of town, t 643 3328 (dorms $9, shared bathroom $17). Another set of surfer-orientated *cabinas* offering dorm beds

⭐ Colonial
Steakhouse »

and basic rooms with shared bathrooms at decent rates. There are also a couple of superior doubles with private baths (with hot water), TV and air-conditioning for $50. Chuck is an inexhaustible supply of information on all things surfboard-related.

Eating Out in Jacó

Unsurprisingly given its status as one of the country's major resorts, Jacó has no shortage of restaurants. While it may not have quite the culinary diversity you'll find in San José, there are still plenty of different cuisines to choose from, including Mexican, Italian and American, although fish and seafood are by far the most common options (and, indeed, some of the best to be found in the entire region). In the main, prices are a little higher than you'd pay in some of the region's lesser resorts, with mains typically costing around $6–8.

BBQ Tangeri, Av Pastor Díaz, just south of Copey Bridge, t 643 3669. Be careful when walking past this restaurant, as the enticing scents emanating from its outdoor barbecue are almost impossible to resist. Meat is the speciality here – pork ribs, thick steaks – though they also do a good selection of fish, including grilled marlin. There's a nice, leafy outdoor eating area.

Chatty Cathy's, Av Pastor Díaz, opposite Mas X Menos, t 643 1039. Long-established pit-stop for surfers, who pile in here each morning to load up on generous portions of eggs, pancakes and muffins after a few hours spent riding the early waves.

Colonial Steakhouse, Av Pastor Díaz, just south of Copey Bridge, t 643 3326. It's a touch on the expensive side, but has a deserved reputation for serving up the best steaks and burgers in town. The excellent range of wines and cigars offered in the classy next door bar give it an added touch of class.

Gilligan's, Av Pastor Díaz, 200m north of and on opposite side to Mas X Menos, t 643 2874. There's not a great deal of choice here with the kitchen preparing just a handful of dishes each day, but what there is tends to be of the highest quality – fresh fish, delicately spiced chicken, etc.

Bar & Restaurante Marisquería El Barco, Av Pastor Díaz, just north of Mas X Menos, **t** 643 2831. As well as serving a wide array of excellent fish and seafood dishes, this Jacó stalwart also does a fine line in pizzas. Finish your meal with a cone from the renowned ice cream parlour, 'Pop's', next door.

Restaurante La Ostra, Av Pastor Díaz, just south of Copey Bridge, **t** 643 1318. One of the town's most celebrated fish and seafood eateries, serving up the catch of the day – sea bass, lobster or tuna – in a simple, unfussy style.

Pizzeria Rioasis, Av Pastor Díaz, off a side street just north of Mas X Menos. This serves over 20 different types of pizza, including several 'tropical' varieties (such as pineapple, coconut and ham), all cooked in a traditional brick oven. The slightly eclectic menu also includes a few Mexican dishes. The front patio is good for people-watching, and there's a popular bar with pool tables at the back that sells imported beer as well as the ubiquitous native Imperial. Look out for the restaurant's regular '2 for 1' deals.

Sunrise, Av Pastor Díaz, just north of Copey Bridge, **t** 643 3361. Another good breakfast choice beloved of US surfers (probably because they specialize in 'American' breakfasts).

Nightlife in Jacó

It's pretty full-on. No matter how many new bars, clubs and discos open each year, there always seem to be enough people here to fill them. During the season, the whole town positively crackles with energy as the streets become a seething mass of tourists and Ticos on the look out for a good time. Things are much quieter in the low season, when many bars close down.

A couple of notes of caution before you head out – prostitution is rife in Jacó and in several bars, particularly those favoured by gringos, you may find (as a man) much of your evening taken up with fending off the advances of scantily clad ladies. Their behaviour is rarely aggressive or persistent, but it can quickly become tiresome. A firm 'no' is usually sufficient to get them to take their hand off your leg and send

them on their way. The Beatles Bar, on the main road north of the town centre, is one of the more notorious 'pick-up joints', although despite its well-known reputation, it always seems strangely full of US expat men in the evening.

The second thing to be aware of is that night-time Jacó is a very loud place to be. Most of the downtown bars believe that the best way to attract custom is to blast out their music louder than the neighbouring bars, resulting in a cacophonous aural war that can only be ended by mutually assured eardrum destruction. If you want to talk, you'd be better off heading to a restaurant (one that doesn't have a bar attached).

As with all resort towns, the scene in Jacó changes quickly. The bars and clubs listed below have been around for a few years, but it's always a good idea to ask around in town about the newest 'hottest' place.

La Central, near beach, on a side street, south of Mas X Menos, **t** 643 3076. Big traditional, generic disco pumping out a mix of Latin and American hits. This large dance floor positively heaves at weekends, but really this could be anywhere. However, its air-conditioning is a unique luxury among the town's clubs. *Open till 5am Fri and Sat.*

Club Ole, Av Pastor Díaz, 200m north of Copey Bridge, **t** 643 1576. *The* place to watch Latin dancing at its hip-shaking best. Sit yourself down at the bar and watch the salsa couples burn up the floor until you feel ready (i.e. drunk enough) to join in. It's a bit kitschy (there's a mechanical bull), but a lot of fun. It's open till 4am Friday and Saturday. The small cover charge of just over ¢100 is offset by pricey beer at over a dollar a bottle.

Onyx Bar, above Subway sandwich shop, Av Pastor Díaz, north of Copey Bridge. Lively, popular bar catering to those with a penchant for pool (they have five tables) and slightly naff 'classic' rock hits, which pump unceasingly from the jukebox, although not quite so overwhelmingly loudly.

Pancho Villa's, southern end of town. Open 24 hours, Pancho's has long been the place where everyone ends up when everywhere else is shut. It's the main wind-down bar offering cold beer, rather expensive food (but then it's catering to a captive audience) and subdued (by Jacó standards) music, allowing people to talk (perhaps for the first time that evening).

El Zarpe Bar, north of town centre, near bus stop, t 643 3473. One of the town's more relaxed nightspots, this is a good place to start the night off with some *bocas* (mini-snacks, a sort of Latin American version of tapas), a few beers and a little conversation before heading out into the aural maelstrom that makes up the rest of the town.

Quepos

There's something charmingly wheeler-dealerish about Quepos, 60km south of Jacó. There's not much to it, and what there is ain't much to look at (the word 'ramshackle' could almost have been invented for the town), but it always seems determined to make the best of things. If it were a person, you'd imagine that it would spend its time trying to convince you of the benefits of a second-hand car, or have a stall down the market selling 'solid gold watches for £1'. It's certainly been good at reinventing itself over the years, always on the lookout for the next opportunity as potential disaster looms.

It was originally part of a territory ruled over by the indigenous Quepoa people (from whom the name derives). Lords of the area for over a thousand years, they were swiftly removed from power, and indeed ultimately from existence, by a triple whammy of disease, defeat and enslavement following the arrival of the Spanish in the 16th century.

The preserve of small-scale farmers for several centuries, in the early 20th century the area underwent something of a boom following the introduction of industrial-scale banana production. United Fruit, the country's (and indeed Central America's) then dominant fruit-producing company, not only planted vast acres of labour-intensive plantations, they also invested a good deal in the region's infrastructure, building company villages for the thousands of workers they employed (some of which still stand). For a while Quepos thrived, becoming a major banana-exporting port. However, a devastating banana blight in the 1950s prompted United Fruit to relocate its operation, at a stroke undermining the entire local economy. Thankfully, Quepos's 'can-do' attitude helped it to keep its head above water. The region's banana plantations were turned over

Orientation

Because of its status as one of the region's main towns and a major base for exploring Manuel Antonio National Park, you might imagine Quepos to be rather bigger than it is. In fact, its docks aside (which lie 1km south of the town proper), the whole of Quepos is probably no bigger than around 20 football pitches, with everything occupying a small grid of around a dozen interconnecting streets. As is customary, directions are given using landmarks rather than the (non-existent in any case) street signs. The football field represents the town's eastern extent, the seafront and rather scrubby beach its western, while the centre is marked by the bus station and adjacent market.

Getting to Quepos

It all depends how eager you are. If you're very keen or need to get there in a hurry, your best option is to take a **plane**. Eleven flights a day link San José with Quepos: eight operated by Sansa (C 24, Av 0/1, **t** 221 9414, *www.flysansa.com*), and three by NatureAir (**t** 220 3054, *www.natureair.com*). Prices start at around $50 one-way, $96 return. Quepos **airport** lies 5km north of the town, from where taxis ($3–5) and minibuses ($2–3) run to the town and on to Manuel Antonio. For more details on domestic flights, *see* p.104.

The next quickest option is by **car**. It's a pretty straightforward 2½–3 hour drive between San José and Quepos, although this can be extended if you miss the turning for the town (which is quite easily done). If arriving from the north, remember to bear left as the road forks; the right-hand turning takes you down to the docks.

If taking the **bus**, four direct services leave San José, C 16, Av 3/5, daily, bound for Quepos at 6am, 12noon, 6pm and 7pm. They take 3½ hours and cost c1,640.

The slowest (and cheapest) option of all is via the regular, stopping bus service, which takes 5 hours, costs just c1,280 and leaves at 7am, 10am, 2pm, 4pm and 5pm. Both the direct and stopping bus services carry on to Manuel Antonio.

Getting away from Quepos

For getting to the Parque Nacional Manuel Antonio, south of Quepos, *see* p.233. It is an easy journey, with **buses** every half-hour.

Heading north is slightly more complicated, but only slightly. Buses leave for Jacó at 4.30am, 7.30am, 10.30am and 3pm, and should arrive around 1½ hrs later, after which they head on to Puntarenas (another 1½hrs further on).

Buses do also head south to Dominical, 44km south, although, as this journey is along an unpaved road, you should be aware that it's slow, uncomfortable and liable to cancellation in bad weather.

---

to the production of palm oil (not as labour-intensive as bananas, but still a viable crop), while Quepos itself, no longer able to function as a major industrial port, reinvented itself as both a sports fishing destination (it's now one of the leading centres in Costa Rica) and, in recent decades, as one of the main bases for (budget) tourists visiting the Parque Nacional Manuel Antonio.

The town is small and somewhat dilapidated in parts, but lively, with a good collection of bars and restaurants. It's also a pretty friendly place, its residents having long ago worked out that the best way to do business with people is to charm them. There are plenty of tour options to choose from (not all of them fishing-based) and a pretty good range of accommodation choices. Places here are in the main less well equipped than those nearer Manuel Antonio, but are also considerably cheaper.

Services in Quepos

Banks: Banco Nacional, northern end of beachfront road; Banco de San José, on beachfront road, one block south of bus station; Banco de Costa Rica, just east of bus station.

Supermarket: Mas X Menos, one block west of the bus station.

Internet access: There are Internet cafés dotted throughout town, including **Quepos Diner and Internet Café**, **t** 777 2189, a block and a half south of the bus station; **Quepos Internet Café**, northwest of the bus station, **t** 777 2183; or **Arte Net**, **t** 777 3447, two and a half blocks west of the football field.

Police: Just north of the bus station.

Post office: On the beachfront road, one block north of the bus station.

Sports and Activities in Quepos

Activity tours are big business in Quepos. It is one of the country's major centres of sports fishing, with dozens of operators offering trips out to snare the big game fish of its coastal waters, which include sailfish, tuna, wahoo and marlin. Most companies operate a fleet of boats, for both charter and regular tours, and offer both fly and conventional fishing. Half-day charter rates start at around $350; the quoted fee does not usually include the necessary fishing licence ($15). It's not a cheap pastime, but the waters are so fertile, although the number of fishing operators and competition for fish is growing all the time. The fishing season runs from December to April.

As important as fishing is to the local economy, not everything here revolves around lines and hooks. Plenty of other activities are also offered by the town's plethora of tour operators, including tours of the Parque Nacional Manuel Antonio (from $45 with transport and lunch), tours of the Parque Nacional Carara (from $65), white-water rafting (from $65, more if the trip includes lunch), sea kayaking (from $65), horse-riding (from $35), canopy tours (from $60) and dolphin-watching (from $65).

Specialist Sports Fishing Operators

Bluefin Sportfishing, t 777 2222, *www.bluefinsportfishing.com.*

Flounder Sportsfishing, t 777 1060, *www.floundersportfishing.com.*

Blue water Sportsfishing, t 777 1596, *bluewat@racsa.co.cr, www.sportsfishingcostarica.com.*

General Tour Operators

Adrenaline Tours, t 777 0117, *www.adrenalinetours.com.* ATV/quad biking.

Costa Rica Flying Boat Tours, t 368 1426, *www.flyingboatcostarica.com.* Trips on a sort of microlight-dinghy.

Fourtrax Adventure, t 479 8444, *www.fourtraxadventure.com.* ATVs.

Gaytours Costa Rica, t 297 3556, *www.gaytourscostarica.com.* Unusually for Costa Rica, Quepos (and more particularly Manuel Antonio) has a (relatively) open gay scene. There are several gay-friendly hotels on the road between Quepos and Manuel Antonio, and even a gay-friendly beach at the northern end of Playa Espadilla, near Manuel Antonio. Helps organize gay-friendly excursions in the local area and throughout the country.

H₂o, t 777 4092,. Watersports specialist offering white-water rafting, sea kayaking and more.

Iguana Tours, t 777 1262, *www.iguanatours.com.* This company's experienced guides are some of the best people to tour Manuel Antonio National Park with. Iguana also offer trips to the Parque Nacional Carara, as well as rafting, sea kayaking, dolphin-watching, canopy tours, horse-riding and sports fishing.

Jungle Coast Jets, t 777 1706, *www.junglecoastjets.com.* Jet-skiing.

Lynch Travel, t 777 0161, *www.lynchtravel.com.* One of Quepos' major players, Lynch's remit covers everything from the local – horse-riding, sports fishing, white-water rafting, canopy tours plus a host of other activities – to the regional (tours to Bahía Drake and Corcovado in the Pacific south) – and even countrywide: they sell NatureAir and Sansa flights, can provide car hire and even deal with visa extensions. And, even if you're not in the market for a tour, the shop is a great place just to stop by and browse with a good selection of guides and maps.

Planet Dolphin, t 777 1647, *www.planetdolphin.com.* Dolphin-watching tours in Manuel Antonio's coastal waters. The trips cost $65, which includes lunch and stops for swimming and snorkelling (plus equipment hire). They also offer sunset cruises.

Platoon Paintball, t 777 2984, *www.platooncostarica.com.* Paintballing fun.

Rainmaker Tours, t 777 3565, *www.rainmakercostarica.com.* This offers only one tour, but it's a goodie. Guides pick you up from your hotel and transport you to a 600ha jungle reserve, known as Rainmaker, 20km south of Quepos in the Fila Chonta Mountains. Though not quite as spectacular as Manual Antonio, it's usually considerably less crowded. You can tour the forest both at ground level along a series of clearly marked trails, and at tree level, teetering your way across a collection of six canopy-strung suspension bridges (Rainmaker was the first reserve in the country to install these now ubiquitous aerial walkways). According to some estimates, the refuge may be home to as much as 70 per cent of country's known species of flora and fauna, so you should spot something of interest during your explorations. The tour costs $65 and includes lunch.

Where to Stay in Quepos

There's plenty of choice. This region has one of the highest concentrations of hotels in the entire country, with the road between Quepos and Manuel Antonio providing a veritable *smorgasbord* of accommodation, much of it aimed at the luxury end of the market (*see* pp.229–31). Quepos itself, however, though not short of options, caters mainly to a less high-falutin' clientele, with most of its hotels aimed pretty directly at either fishermen or budget travellers. Facilities tend to be of a more basic standard than you'll find on the road south but, on the positive side, prices are also a good deal lower. Those establishments in the centre of town near the bars can suffer at times from excessive noise.

Best Western Hotel Kamuk, on the seafront, t 777 0811, *www.kamuk.co.cr* ($$$$–$$$; superior $95/standard $70). Despite being one of the town's more upmarket hotels, the Kamuk could hardly be described as luxurious (but, then, none of Quepos' in-town choices is). Nonetheless, it provides a good standard of chain-hotel accommodation. The standard rooms have private bathrooms, air-conditioning, TVs and phones, while the superior rooms boast balconies and ocean views. Aimed very much at the fishing fraternity, its seafood restaurant operates under the slogan 'you catch it, we cook it', and there's a casino (the only one in town). It's very popular, although if you're not on a fishing holiday you may find yourself left out of the bar room conversation somewhat. Price includes breakfast.

Hotel Malinche, just northwest of the bus station, t 777 0093 ($$$–$; $45–20).

The cosy and convenient (if a touch noisy) Malinche offers two categories of accommodation: budget rooms in an older building which have a mixture of shared and private bathrooms (cold water only), ceiling fans and balconies (although the views aren't too spectacular); and mid-range rooms in a new extension, which can offer cleaner, fresher looking décor, air-conditioning and private bathrooms with hot water. All rooms have cable TV. Tours (particularly fishing tours) are offered and there's parking available

Hotel Ceciliano, 100m west of the football field, on south side of street, t 777 0192 ($$–$; shared bathroom $15, private $30). Decent budget choice offering a range of accommodation options from very basic (small, featureless, bathroom-less rooms) to the moderately comfortable (slightly larger rooms with air-conditioning, private bathrooms and hot water). There's also a small Spanish restaurant and laundry service.

Hotel Mar y Luna, northwest of the bus station, t 777 0394 ($; $8 per person with shared bathroom, doubles private $12). The 'sea and moon' is a touch tatty, but this backpacker favourite has a really friendly atmosphere, with a comfy communal area with a TV and plants (a good place to meet fellow travellers). The rooms are a bit cramped, but spotless, and there's a choice of shared or private bathrooms (hot water). The friendly owner is a good source of information on the town and area. Breakfast, which is extra ($3), is served in a small courtyard. A laundry service is also available.

Hotel Melissa, northwest of bus station, a few doors down from Hotel Malinche, t 777 0025 ($; $20). The very basic and very cheap Melissa is recommended only to budget travellers looking to save a few dollars (or if everywhere else is full). Rooms have private bathrooms and ceiling fans, but are a bit grim.

Hotel Quepos, just west of the football field, on the opposite side of the road, t 777 0274 ($; $15). Away from the centre, where noise from the bars can be a problem, this simple choice is nothing special, but the rooms are

Eating Out in Quepos

In the main, Quepos' restaurants don't offer the most refined or authentic of cuisines, with most places aimed squarely at the town's principal gringo, sports fishing clientele (who, to be fair, are the town's main source of tourist revenue). So, you'll find plenty of places serving up burgers, steaks and Tex-Mex platters.

Happily, Quepos' location means that it is also a great source of fish and seafood, although this can be a touch on the expensive side (unless you catch it yourself; several restaurants offer a 'cook what you catch' option).

As always, the cheapest meals are provided by the sodas; there are several around the bus station.

For more upmarket, gourmet options, *see* the 'Where to Stay' and 'Eating Out' entries for the 'Quepos to Manuel Antonio' section, pp.229–32.

Dos Locos, just south of the bus station, t 777 1526. Large, open-sided restaurant serving a rather generic international approximation of Mexican food – burritos, fajitas, etc. – in generous portions. In the daytime it's a good place to watch the comings and goings at the bus station just up the road, while at night it becomes one of the town's more happening bars. It's a fun place with kitschy touches (toilets marked '*locos*' and '*locas*') and live music is put on some nights during the high season.

Escalofrio, southwest of the bus station, t 777 0833. Quality Italian cusine – including great pizzas cooked up in a wood-fired oven – plus a nice terrace at the front and a lively bar at the back make up Escalofrio's charms. They're particularly renowned for their desserts, especially ice cream.

El Gran Escape, on the seafront, t 777 0395. This is aimed squarely at the eating and drinking habits of American fishermen, its kitchen serving up a hotchpotch of eager-to-please US cuisine: American breakfasts, burgers, chicken wings, Tex-Mex platters, etc., as well as fish, with a standing promise to cook up anything caught. At night the bar reverberates to tall tales of the ones that got away. The food isn't terrible, just uninspired.

El Patio, at the northern end of the seafront, t 777 4982, *www.cafemilagro.com*. The town's most refined culinary experience is provided by the new open-air café-cum-restaurant of Café Milagro, the American-owned coffee-roasters located next door (they also operate a café on the Manuel Antonio road, *see* p.232). Menu buzz phrases, such as 'latino fushion', warn you that this is a restaurant with pretensions. Thankfully, that doesn't make it pretentious. The owners' infectious enthusiasm has helped them to pull it off, and the food is genuinely innovative, a mixture of traditional and tropical influences – a salad of green mango, purple cabbage and greens with passion fruit vinagrette, or beef tenderloin with yucca purée and grilled *chayote*. They also have a lively bar serving *bocas* and cocktails and you can purchase bags of roasted coffee beans next door.

Pizza Gabriel, northwest of the bus station, t 777 1085. A local stalwart serving up simple, inexpensive pizzas ($4) in a simple, unpretentious dining room. Just west of the bus station, this makes a good inter-journey pit-stop.

Nightlife in Quepos

It's not exactly Jacó, but Quepos has a decent smattering of bars. These can get lively in peak months, though they tail off dramatically in low season.

Other than the bars mentioned in the 'Eating Out' section (particularly Dos Locos), the best places are: the **Hard Croc Café** on the seafront, a bustling bar/diner where live music is often staged; the long-standing **Wacky Wanda's Bar**, just north and inland, where the recently installed air-conditioning doesn't seem to have cooled the ever lively atmosphere; the rather more mundane **El Banco Bar**, the next street over, which is seemingly permanently filled with sports-lovers tucking into Tex-Mex food and watching soccer matches on its plethora of TVs (which usually seem to be showing about eight different games simultaneously); and the **Sargento Bar**, a couple of blocks south, which attracts a young, happy crowd.

Nature under Threat:
Quepos to Manuel Antonio

Despite the much-advertised eco-charms of the Parque Nacional Manuel Antonio – a pristine stretch of coastal rainforest providing a home to the country's largest remaining population of squirrel monkeys – there are many who consider it to be fast becoming something of an ecological nightmare. It's the country's smallest national park but, because of the ease of access here, also one of the most visited, a situation which has led to severe overcrowding and placed intense pressure on the park's limited resources. The park authorities often have great difficulty coping with the vast numbers of visitors tramping the trails here in what at times can resemble an almost unbroken chain of humanity.

Measures are at long last being taken to address these problems (*see* pp.234–6). Unfortunately, the situation is much less clear-cut beyond the park's borders, where the development of the surrounding area would seem to confirm every fear ever expressed about how the lack of management of the tourism boom might adversely affect the environment. The road that stretches the 7km south from Quepos to the town of Manuel Antonio and the entrance to the park is undeniably beautiful, rising over a series of hills, the tops of which afford wonderfully grand views of the beaches, forest and ocean below. It's also undeniably overdeveloped. The beauty has not gone unnoticed, and the road is now lined nose to tip by a large and growing number of hotels and lodges, the vast majority of which have been constructed in the past couple of decades. Unsurprisingly, this has caused some serious environmental problems, not just in terms of the amount of forest that has had to be cleared for construction, but in the provision of infrastructure, particularly sewage and waste disposal, which has at times struggled to keep up with the pace of change.

For all the hand-wringing about the current situation, everyone – even the most ardent environmentalist – realizes that there can be no turning the clock back. Things can't be reversed (i.e. all the hotels pulled down), only improved. This may not be beyond the realms of possibility, but it's going to require the co-operation of the region's hotel owners. Outside the national park, most of the area's remaining patches of forest are either in private refuges (where they are of course protected) or in the grounds of hotels. From a preservation perspective, this is not necessarily a bad thing: hotel owners are well aware that having a patch of genuine jungle on your doorstep is a great draw for tourists and so have a vested interest in its continued survival. The problem lies, not so much in the amount of forest that is left – which, if added together, would still be considerable – but more in the haphazard, unmanaged way in which it has been cleared. Lack of planning has led to the 'island-ization' of the forest, with areas separated from each other, often not by great distances, but large enough to prevent easy access between them by wildlife. To help combat this, conservationists have started campaigning for the creation of 'life corridors' between the areas of forest. One of their first initiatives has been to string ropes and wooden bridges between separated areas of forest canopy – particularly those either side of a road – to allow monkeys to cross.

For the situation to improve, there needs to be much tighter regulation of the region's development – hotel owners need to act more responsibly, while the government needs to be more willing to use its powers to punish those who flout the laws. A ban on the creation of new hotels wouldn't hurt either, but is unlikely.

The problems facing the area are not solely the result of tourism. Take the other road south from Quepos, towards Dominical, and you'll find yourself bumping along an unpaved road amid a seemingly endless sea of oil palms, where the only wildlife you'll encounter will be the vultures perched by the roadside carefully watching your car for signs of an imminent breakdown.

Caught in an ever-tightening pincer grip between the pressures of tourism and agriculture, this is an area where nature is struggling to hold its own. It's certainly an area where, if you are concerned about preserving the environment, you should make a determined effort to visit in as responsible, low-impact a way as possible.

Where to Stay between Quepos and Manuel Antonio

Over the past couple of decades, the road leading from Quepos to Manuel Antonio has been turned into a great unbroken procession of accommodation, with almost every scrap of land now home to some sort of lodge or hotel, all boasting of their proximity to nature (by no means untrue, since most hotels do border forest, but their adverts might be a touch more honest if they also boasted of their proximity to a bunch of other hotels) or, if perched on a hill, of 'ocean views'. Despite the environmental cost of this overcrowding, there's no doubt that many of the hotels here offer an unparalleled level of luxury – at a price. You certainly shouldn't go expecting to find any great bargains in high season; there may be an abundance of accommodation, but the sheer popularity of

the place means that hotel owners can charge pretty much what they like at peak times. Prices come down in the low season when you may be able to barter yourself a good rate even at one of the very high-end establishments – the sort of place perched on a hill with its own stretch of rainforest, 'horizon' pool, Jacuzzi, gourmet restaurant, helipad and stunning views overlooking the Punta Catedral and the Pacific. Otherwise, the cheapest accommodation is found in the towns at each end of the road: Quepos to the north (see pp.226–7) and Manuel Antonio to the south (see p.233).

The hotels below are not listed alphabetically or by price, but rather by location – i.e. in the order in which they appear on the road as you head south from Quepos.

Cabinas Pedro Miguel, t 777 0805, *www.cabinaspedromiguel.com* ($$$–$$; $75–$25). Just out of Quepos, but already well into jungle territory, this represents something of a bargain for this otherwise rather overpriced area. It offers nice, simply furnished rooms (complete with mosquito nets) in a large block facing out over a pool and onto a stretch of forest where monkeys are often spotted. The larger rooms sleep up to five and have kitchenettes, balconies and hammocks. Its popular restaurant takes the form of a do-it-yourself barbecue, where you pick out cuts of meat and fish and then cook them up on a communal grill. The complex also operates a well-respected language school.

⭐ Hotel Plinio >

Hotel Plinio, t 777 0055, *www. hotelplinio.com* ($$$; $65). Great for nature-spotters, the Hotel Plinio is set in its own private jungle reserve where there are 10km of marked trails and a 10m-high wildlife observation platform. Large rooms are decorated with quirky 'native' art and have private bathrooms, balconies and hammocks. Those with air-condition-ing are $10 more than the quoted price. For groups, they also have a 2-storey 'duplex' suite ($85), a 3-storey suite ($110) and a 3-bed house with ocean views ($100). There's also a pool, a poolside bar and one of the region's very best gourmet restaurants, which serves an eclectic international menu made up mainly of Thai and Indian cuisines, but with a few Costa Rican, Indian and even German dishes thrown in for good measure. It's a touch on the expensive side, with main courses typically $8–10, but well worth it for the standard of cooking.

Hotel El Mono Azul, t 777 1548, *www. monoazul.com* ($$$$–$$$; $60–$100). The 'Blue Monkey' is one of the region's most celebrated hotels, not just because of its well-equipped rooms with private bathrooms, TVs, jungle views and ceiling fans ($20 more will get you air-conditioning and there are also self-catering villas and a long-stay condo for hire), two swimming pools, Internet access, gym and award-winning restaurant (which serves an absolute hotchpotch of different cuisines – choose from chicken provençal, spaghetti bolognese, enchiladas and *casados*), but because of the active role it plays in local conservation efforts. This is the HQ of 'Kids Saving the Rainforest', *www.*

kidssavingtherainforest.org, a not-for-profit organization, set up in late 1990s by two (then) schoolchildren concerned with the plight of the region's squirrel monkeys. Its aim is threefold: to raise awareness, to educate local children and to help preserve the environment. To this end, they have purchased 10 hectares of rainforest, are building an education centre and have helped to erect over 40 'monkey bridges' across the Quepos road, thereby helping to reduce the number of squirrel monkeys lost each year to road accidents.

Hotel Las Tres Banderas, t 777 1478, *www.hotel-tres-banderas.com/ costa-rica* ($$$; $69). This is pretty much a perfect example of what more or less every hotel in this region is trying to offer – luxury in the middle of the jungle; the trappings of civilization amid the lush wilderness. You can choose between standard rooms, which are elegantly furnished and come with private showers, balconies and air-conditioning, and lavish suites ($110) with bathtubs, kitchenette (complete with fridge and microwave) and an extra sofabed. Extra facilities include a games room, swimming pool, a poolside bar, Jacuzzi and, of course, a surrounding swath of picture-perfect jungle.

La Colina, t 777 0231, *www.lacolina.com* ($$$; $55). Not quite as luxurious as some of its competitors but still well fitted out, La Colina's rooms are a touch on the small side, but come with fans and hot-water bathrooms, while its larger suites ($85) have air-conditioning, TVs and balconies (some have ocean views). There's also a spa, a pool with a swim-up bar and an excellent Italian(ish) restaurant, **Bruno's Sunset Grill**, where live music staged on Tuesdays and Saturdays. Mains (lasagne, grilled tuna, jumbo shrimp, roast chicken) are around $5–8. Breakfast is included in the price.

Tulemar, t 777 0580, *www.tulemar.com* ($$$$$; $270, plus $25 per extra guest). The Tulemar is only recommended for families, groups or couples who want a lot of space and are willing to pay through the nose for it. Its 20 octagonal luxury bungalows sleep up to six people. Each comes with a separate living room, sofabeds, minibar, kitchenette, TV (with VCR) and air-conditioning. Huge windows provide great jungle or ocean views. And if you consider that to be slumming it, then you can always hire the four-bedroom villa instead, although this is only rented out for minimum stays of five nights (from $4,400 for seven low-season nights). If you don't fancy self-catering, there's a gourmet, 'multi-ethnic' cuisine restaurant that provides great views of the hotels' 33 acres of private forested grounds. A path leads from the hotel down to the beach, where there's a bar and (so long as you don't spend too much time at the bar) you have the use of complimentary kayaks and snorkelling equipment.

Makanda by the Sea >

Makanda by the Sea, t 777 0442, *www. makanda.com* ($$$$$; $350). Set well back from the main road in extensive grounds, this offers a haven of 'getting-away-from-it-all' grown-up luxury (they don't allow children; in fact, they make quite a big thing about its being 'adults only'). Each of its super-expensive, super-comfortable villas comes with its own kitchenette, minibar, coffee-maker, TV, CD player, terrace and amazing views. There are also a couple of smaller, but just as well-equipped, studios. You and your fellow adults can also enjoy a 'horizon' pool, a poolside restaurant, Jacuzzi and, just half a kilometre away via a winding path, the beach. It's expensive, but prices do drop to a practically giveaway $265 (!) per night in low season. Breakfast is included in the price (you'd hope so).

Hotel Parador, t 777 1437, *www. hotelparador.com* ($$$$$). Perhaps nowhere exemplifies the unsettling paradox of the Manuel Antonio area better than the Parador. It's the absolute last word in glamorous luxury, its lavish facilities attracting millionaire patrons who touch down at its on-site helipad, before moving on to enjoy the stylishly decorated rooms filled with colonial-era antiques, wondrous views, twin Jacuzzis, 'horizon' pool with swim-up bar, tennis courts and two restaurants. The prices ensure that only the best kind of people (i.e. the richest) get to stay here. Suites start at $350, the presidential suite at $780. However, for all its

qualities, you can't help feeling a twinge of regret that all of this should have come at the expense of removing an entire hill's worth of forest.

La Mariposa, t 777 0355, *www. lamariposa.com* ($$$$$; $280–130). La Mariposa has a lot to answer for. This was Manuel Antonio's first luxury hotel and it's still going strong, with a large complex of nearly 60 rooms providing a mixture of standard rooms, deluxe rooms and suites. There's also a penthouse suite with a private Jacuzzi, three pools, a bar, a restaurant, a spa and a gift shop. Tours of Manuel Antonio National Park are offered.

Hotel Si Como No, t 777 0777, *www. sicomono.com* ($$$$$; rooms $160, suites $250). If you want to stay in the lap of luxury but feel guilty about the environmental impact that this might have, then perhaps this hotel might provide a suitable compromise. It's certainly luxurious; its architecturally innovative painted concrete suites (nicer than they sound) have a nice Mediterranean feel to them and enjoy a lush rainforest setting, perched high on a hill overlooking Manuel Antonio National Park. All rooms have fans (or air-conditioning), minibars, telephones, coffee-makers and balconies, and there are two pools (one for kids, one for adults) as well as a Jacuzzi, spa, poolside bar and seafood restaurant. However, for all its many and various facilities, the hotel does still make a concerted effort to be eco-friendly, relying on solar-heating and energy-efficient air-conditioning as much as is possible. Breakfast is included.

Hotel Costa Verde, t 777 0584, *www. costaverde.net* ($$$$$; $155). At the end of the Quepos road, near Manuel Antonio town, the Costa Verde is beautifully set in wildlife-filled jungle where monkeys are commonly spotted. Its studios range in size and have either ceiling fans or air-conditioning, and jungle or ocean views (those overlooking the Punta Catedral are particularly impressive), but all are prettily decorated. There are also a couple of suites with kitchenettes, as well as three restaurants, the pick being the **Anaconda**, just across the Quepos road, which serves good-quality international cuisine.

Eating Out between Quepos and Manuel Antonio

With almost every hotel along this uber-touristy road operating an open-to-the-public restaurant, you'll never be short of somewhere or something to eat. In the main, you can expect to find a good standard of cuisine with eclectic, international menus and the odd gourmet star turn. You can also expect to pay a fair bit, with most hotel restaurants charging $8–10 for mains. Thankfully, the Quepos–Manuel Antonio road also has a number of stand-alone places where prices are usually a good deal cheaper. Like the hotels, the restaurants below are listed in geographical order heading south from Quepos. For details of the best hotel restaurants, *see* above.

★ **El Avión >>**

Barba Roja, t 777 0331. The food at this long-established bar and restaurant is nothing special – the usual American-based menu of hamburgers, steaks, Tex-Mex platters, seafood and nachos – but you come for the atmosphere and views, both at their best around sunset. Coincidentally enough, this is also when the bar has its 'happy hour' to help get the party started.

Billy Beach's Karola's Bar and Restaurant, t 777 1557. Just back from Barba Roja's is this good-quality, Mexican restaurant serving up burritos, enchiladas and tacos, as well as killer margaritas and its renowned macadamia nut pie. There's also a good vegetarian selection and, at night, a lively bar.

Café Milagro, t 777 3535. It seems strange to say it, but coffee shops in Costa Rica often disappoint, as the really good stuff is often held back for export. Not here. Here it's the *grano de oro* freshly roasted at the café's own plant in Quepos (*see* p.227). They serve a huge range of brews, from the straightforward (espresso, capuccino, etc.) to the more unusual (chocolate-raspberry latte, almond mocha) as well as a range of iced coffees including their speciality, the Quepoccino, a mixture of espresso, milk and chocolate. And, as if that weren't enough, they also operate an in-store bakery turning out a delicious array of cakes and sandwiches – banana nut muffin, focaccia with tomato, onion and olives, etc. Highly recommended.

El Avión, t 777 3378. The region's most distinctive eaterie is set inside the body of a converted bomber plane. Of course, it's not a Costa Rican bomber, Costa Rica having no armed forces, but an American one, bought with the intention of being passed on to the CIA-backed Contra forces fighting Nicaragua's socialist Sandinista regime in the 1980s. Unfortunately, for the USA, the Iran–Contra 'Arms for Hostages' controversy erupted before the plane could be delivered. The plan was put on hold and the plane left in a San José hangar until 2000, when it was purchased by a couple of Costa Rican entrepreneurs and shipped to Manuel Antonio. Today, it sits proudly by the side of the road providing great views of the coast and turning the head of everyone who drives by. The food, though by no means bad, is pretty standard US-orientated surf 'n' turf fare, but considering the restaurant's story and setting, the menu was always going to be a secondary consideration. It's as good a place for a drink and a photo stop as you'll find in the country.

Manuel Antonio

The small village of Manuel Antonio lies at the end of the Quepos road, just before the park entrance. It consists of little more than a road loop where buses turn round, a collection of hotels and restaurants and a nice beach, **Playa Espadilla**, heading northeast from town. Though inevitably crowded near the town, this pleasant stretch of sand gets progressively less so the further north you walk.

Getting to Manuel Antonio

It couldn't be easier getting to Manuel Antonio. Over 25 **buses** a day (including the through services from San José), roughly every half-hour from 6am–8pm, leave Quepos central bus station south for the town of Manuel Antonio, at the entrance to the national park. They can also be hailed from the Quepos–Manuel Antonio road. The 7km journey takes just 7mins (providing it doesn't stop at any hotels to drop off/pick up passengers *en route*) and costs c100.

If that sounds too difficult, you can always take a **taxi** from opposite the bus station for around $3.

If **driving**, you can leave your car at the car park on Manuel Antonio's road loop for $3.

It's also sometimes patrolled by lifeguards, something of a necessity as it's plagued by dangerous rip-tides; if swimming, you should exercise extreme caution.

Tourist Information in Manuel Antonio

(i) **La Buena Nota >**
2km east of park entrance, t 777 1002, buennota@racsa.co.cr

The major local landmark of La Buena Nota is not an official tourist office, but is a great source of local information nonetheless. It's officially a souvenir shop, selling local hand-produced crafts, surfing gear and jewellery, but has transmogrified over the years into a 'jack of all trades' sort of a place, providing details of tours and stocking guidebooks, maps, US newspapers and magazines.

Where to Stay and Eat in Manuel Antonio

Though most places here are as overpriced as anywhere else, Manuel Antonio does also have a fair number of budget-orientated places. As a consequence, it attracts its fair share of backpackers and budget travellers, which in turn has led to its developing a lively nightlife scene.

Cabinas Espadilla, t 777 2113, *www.espadilla.com* ($$$$–$$$; $100–79). One of the town's pricier options, these reasonably large and well-equipped *cabinas* still represent pretty good value for groups. The more expensive ones have kitchenettes and air-conditioning, and there's a pool. There's an even more expensive hotel run by the same management just across the road.

Hotel Manuel Antonio, t 777 1237 ($$$; $70–50). Just a few steps from the park entrance, this is a very convenient choice. They offer two categories of accommodation: standard rooms ($50), which are smallish and rather dark, but perfectly well equipped; or deluxe rooms ($70) which are housed in a new building and have a bright, fresh feel to them with tile floors, private bathrooms, TVs, telephones, air-conditioning and small terraces. Internet access and a laundry service are available, and there's an all-day restaurant.

Hotel Vela Bar, t 777 0413, *http://velabar.com* ($$$; $45) Near the beach, the hotel itself is moderate at best – a few standard rooms with private baths and a choice of ceiling fan or air-conditioning – but it does have one of town's best and most celebrated (and, it has to be said, most expensive) restaurants, serving 'international cuisine', which translates as lots of seafood, although vegetarians are also well catered for.

Albergue Costa Linda, t 777 0304 ($$$–$; $45-plus–16). If the majority of hotels on the Quepos road seem dauntingly expensive, then this backpackers' favourite will come as something of a relief to your wallet, offering simple rooms with shared bathrooms for $16, or apartments (with TV and kitchenette) from $45. Its restaurant makes a point of catering to vegetarians. Laundry service available.

Cabinas Piscis, t 777 0046, *vivipisc@racsa.co.cr* ($; $20). Another decent budget choice, just 100m from beach. The Piscis' rooms are a bit small and cheerless, with cold stone floors and even colder shared showers (no hot water), but if you're looking to save money (and round here, who isn't?), it's definitely the place to come, especially as its restaurant is equally budget-conscious. And, if you fancy upping the comfort level, you can also get a separate cabin ($40) or house ($70), which come with private baths, TVs, kitchenettes and air-conditioning. It's popular, so book early in high season. Discounts offered for groups.

Nightlife in Manuel Antonio

Bar and Restaurant Mar y Sombra, the only bar on the beach. Forget the food (which is snack-based), this is one of the town's major nightlife options, particularly at weekends when it hosts pumping discos.

Parque Nacional Manuel Antonio

Parque Nacional Manuel Antonio
t 777 0644; open Tues–Sun 7–4; adm

Depending on whom you talk to, the Parque Nacional Manuel Antonio is either Costa Rica's greatest treasure, the finest showcase of her natural wonders, or her most shameful ruin and a blot on a once pristine landscape. The park's supporters can point to its wondrous beauty and natural diversity; its more than 275 hectares of land and 220 hectares of sea; its gorgeous sweeping beaches and forests teeming with life. They can point to the quality of the transport and accommodation infrastructure that gives so many people the opportunity to enjoy the area. They can point out the almost guaranteed wildlife-spotting opportunities the park provides, with the resident animals – particularly the monkeys – having got so used to people that they no longer skulk off into the forest upon their arrival but happily interact with them.

Nay-sayers, on the other hand, can point to the overdevelopment of the area, the stretches of forest outside the park that are no longer there because they have been cleared to create hotels and roads. They point to the increased levels of pollution and the shrinking numbers of squirrel monkeys, already Central America's rarest simian. They point out that animals 'interacting' with visitors is a negative trait, not a positive one. They could also argue, with some justification, that at its worst extremes Manuel Antonio represents the theme-parking of nature, the cosy packaging of what was once wilderness into acceptable, easily managed bundles, and how its success may well lead to the rest of the country being packaged in a similar way. There is merit in both arguments, although it has to be said that, for all the area's many and various charms, overdevelopment is a serious threat that needs to be addressed sooner rather than later. Still, there's no need to get too gloomy. Whatever troubles there may be, there's still much about this place to be enjoyed, and the park authorities are at last doing something to try and tackle the problem of overcrowding within the park. They have banned camping, restricted visitor numbers to just 600 on weekdays, 800 at weekends, and have even taken the bold step of completely shutting the park on Mondays so as to give the animals some respite from the constant inspection.

Those animals include an absolute mass of birdlife (including pelicans, hawk-eagles and trogons), plenty of mammals (racoons, sloths, agoutis and more) and a smattering of reptiles (including both black and green iguanas as well as the odd green turtle). However, as interesting as these are, there's no doubt that it's the **monkeys** that are the main wildlife enticement for visitors. Manuel Antonio's forests support both a community of white-faced capuchins and one of only two sizeable populations of squirrel monkey (or 'mono titi') left in the entire country. To give some idea of their rarity, there are estimated to be no more than 1,500 remaining here, and this is the larger of the two populations. Both types of monkey are very cute and highly inquisitive, often descending to the lower branches of trees to examine the human interlopers in their jungle, thereby providing great photo opportunities (although that's as far as your 'interaction' should go; see box, below).

Along with the monkeys, the park is also famed for its lovely **beaches**, of which there are three, not including Playa Espadilla, which actually lies north of the park's borders (see p.232). The park's longest beach, **Playa Espadilla Sur**, lies just south of the park's entrance and ranger station (just south of Manuel Antonio town). It's long, pretty and sandy, but not great for swimming as there are fierce currents here. A marked trail leads from the park entrance through the jungle backing the beach. At the end of the beach, you can either cut straight across a narrow neck of land to Playa Manuel Antonio, or follow a circular trail around the headland through the forest of the **Punta Catedral**, a former offshore island that has been reconnected to the mainland via the creation of a tómbolo – a sort of natural causeway formed from deposited sand and silt. **Playa**

Let the Wildlife Be

However cute and friendly they may look, and however much you might be tempted to 'interact' with them, you should resist feeding the monkeys, even (in fact, especially) if they beg for food, which they have been known to do. Not only will you be fined and ejected from the park if caught by a ranger, but your actions, though seemingly harmless, can actually cause very serious damage to the animals.

It's not just that monkeys are not designed to digest the most common offerings of crisps and sandwiches. Even if you were feeding them fresh fruit, the very act of providing them with nourishment can change their patterns of behaviour for the worse, causing them to start relying on humans for sustenance, which in time will make them less able to fend for themselves. On a more practical level, the feeding of monkeys in the past has led to them becoming overconfident, even aggressive to people (not so much begging for food as demanding it with menaces). Some have even been known to try and snatch purses and bags. Content yourself with a photo instead.

Manuel Antonio is probably the park's nicest beach, a lovely sweep of sand with relatively calm, sheltered waters, although you should still take care when swimming as it's usually unsupervised. Again, a marked trail skirts the jungle behind it. The park's third, rockier beach, **Playa Escondido**, is further east; you'll need to check with the ranger station before visiting as it often gets cut off by the tides.

It goes without saying that this is a park best visited in the less crowded off-season – both for your sake and the animals', although this may involve a few climatic problems. Conditions tend towards the wet here even in the dry months, and it pays to bring wet-weather gear with you. It's also worth stating that, despite the park's restricted dimensions, the ease of its trails and the presence of a refreshment stand (on Playa Manuel Antonio), you should still come prepared, as for any other park, with adequate supplies of food, water and warm clothing. Though it is easy to guide yourself along the park's trails – only the trek around the Punta Catedral could be regarded as even reasonably challenging – it's worth investing in the services of a **guide** at the ranger station ($20 for two hours), as this will greatly increase your wildlife-spotting options.

Monteverde and Santa Elena

If Manuel Antonio, in the southern Central Pacific region, repre-sents the way an area of once pristine natural beauty can rapidly become overdeveloped, then Monteverde, to the north, would seem to show how it is still possible for communities working together to protect an area's environmental integrity. That's not to say that the Monteverde area has survived entirely untouched by human hands. The three main protected areas here, the **Reserva Biológica Monteverde**, the **Reserva Santa Elena** and the **Reserva Bosque Eterno de los Niños**, together represent a sort of last stand of nature, comprising, as they do, the final remaining swaths of one of Costa Rica's rarest habitats – cloudforest – which once upon a time blanketed the entire Cordillera de Tilarán region. Development has taken place here, but thanks to the efforts of the local people – not least a community of Quakers ('Cuáquers') who have been living here since the early 1950s – the future and security of the reserves and their precious habitats look to have been assured. Remarkably, this has mostly been done via private, locally led initiatives, rather than with the help of the government or national parks system. In fact, these private schemes have often put the efforts of the (admittedly severely underfunded) national parks system to shame. Since the 1970s, thanks to a series of national and international fundraising campaigns, over 30,000 hectares of land have been purchased and preserved.

Getting to Monteverde and Santa Elena

Monteverde's road network has been kept at a very basic level for a reason – local communities don't want to make it too easy for people to get here. As long as access remains relatively difficult, then, so the theory goes, only those with a genuine interest in and concern for the area will bother making the trip. The only flaw in this logic is that, so long as you've got enough money, you don't really need to make that much effort. Pretty much every San José-based tour operator offers tours to the region, usually based on a 3-day, 2-night trip (see pp.68–70). Nonetheless, travelling independently is still something of a chore.

By Bus

Transportes Tilarán, t 222 3854, operates just two services a day from San José to Monteverde at 6.30am and 2.30pm, leaving from C12, Av 9/11. These fill up quickly and, to be sure of getting a seat, you should ideally book well in advance – at least a day (or even two) before during the dry season. Buses stop first in Santa Elena, at the top of the 'triangle', before heading off, at no great speed, down the unpaved Monteverde road, dropping passengers off at their hotels *en route* before finally coming to rest at the town's cheese factory. The entire journey takes around 3½ hours, longer in the rainy season. Be warned, as most of the route is unpaved once you leave the Interamericana, the going can be extremely bumpy and extremely slow. It costs around c1,475.

If you fancy travelling with a degree more comfort, **Beltours, t** 645 5978, offer a private minibus service for around $30 return. There are two direct bus services a day from Puntarenas at 1pm and 2pm, and one a day from Tilarán at 1pm.

By Road

If you like your driving off-road, winding, bumpy, full of obstacles and, above all, challenging, Monteverde is the drive for you. You'll need a 4WD, whatever time of year. In fact, once you've informed your rental company that you're going to be travelling to Monteverde, they'll probably insist on your taking one. The Santa Elena–Monteverde road, in particular, can become an absolute quagmire in the rainy season.

Daunting as it may seem, the first two hours of the drive from San José aren't actually that bad. Once out of the city, you simply head north up the Intermericana. It's once you're off the motorway that the fun begins. There are three turnings to the right for Santa Elena if travelling from the south: at **Rancho Grande**, **Yomale**, and just south of **Limonal** (look for signs to Las Juntas). If you miss all three, the town can also be reached from the north via Cañas. All routes offer extremely concentration-heavy driving along winding, pothole-riven roads.

Monteverde's battle to keep development at arm's length has been aided by the community's long-standing refusal to countenance the paving of the region's roads. By deliberately keeping the region's infrastructure low-tech, the Monteverde communities, as represented by the Monteverde Conservation League, have so far managed to see off the advances of the major international hotel chains who might otherwise have descended here *en masse*.

Make no mistake, despite the difficulty of access this is still a heavily visited area, attracting thousands of tourists each year. However, unlike the regions to the south – such as Jacó, where the emphasis is on beach life and hedonism, or Manuel Antonio National Park, where nature seems to be regarded less as a wonder in itself than as a beautiful backdrop for man-made luxury – in Monteverde the stress is very much on conducting your trip in harmony with the environment.

The region is home to two main towns, **Monteverde** and **Santa Elena**, which lie at either end of a narrow, extremely potholed and tyre-scarred unpaved road, carefully nursing their respective cloudforest reserves. They are very different in character – the Quaker-founded Monteverde is still relatively undeveloped, while

Getting away from Monteverde and Santa Elena

Return **bus** services to San José, which again during the peak months should be booked at least a day in advance, depart from the cheese factory in Monteverde at 6.30am and 2.30pm. One service a day leaves for Punterenas at 6am, and one for Tilarán at 7am.

One of northwest Costa Rica's other main tourist destinations, **La Fortuna** (*see* pp.265–71), lies just 25km northeast of Monteverde as the crow flies. Unfortunately, as that crow has to fly over several unbridged rivers, a huge lake and a towering volcano to get there, the journey is a touch more tricky for people. There's been talk of building a road link between Monteverde and La Fortuna for years, but up to now that's all it's been talk. For the time being the quickest and most popular way to get to La Fortuna is via the explanatorily named **Jeep/Boat/Jeep** route: a 4WD taxi takes you from Santa Elena/Monteverde to the Río Chiquito where a boat whisks you across the Laguna de Arenal (Lake Arenal) beneath the towering bulk of Volcán Arenal to where another taxi awaits ready to take you on the final leg to La Fortuna. Any hotel in town can arrange the trip, which takes three hours and costs $30, or you can call **t** 645 5051.

It is also possible to reach La Fortuna on **horseback**, although this will take around twice as long and cost around twice as much. There are several companies in town offering trips along the **El Castillo Trail**, as it is known; *see* p.248.

the more solidly Tico Santa Elena is more built-up – but together they seem to have come up with a working *modus operandi* for an effective form of genuine eco-tourism, i.e. tourism that aims to protect, educate and conserve, rather than just provide the tourist with an experience regardless of the environmental impact. Solar power and organic farming are more than just advertising slogans here; they're an intrinsic part of day-to-day life.

All three reserves offer great wildlife-spotting opportunities. Their sultry, dripping depths (humidity can reach 100 per cent) are thick with all manner of things that slide, slither, crawl and glide, though the denseness of the vegetation cover can make it difficult to pick out some of the better-camouflaged creatures (including, unfortunately, the resplendent quetzal). Being the least well known, the Reserva Santa Elena and the Reserva Bosque Eterno de los Niños tend to be less crowded and more rewarding in term of wildlife-spotting than the main Monteverde reserve.

Spiritual History

Monteverde's first significant community was founded by around two dozen Quakers who arrived here from the USA in the early 1950s. These were no eco-tourists, but rather conscientious objectors (Quaker teaching forbids any form of violence), several of whom had already spent time in prison for refusing to be conscripted into the US Army. They came looking for a tolerant, peaceful, fertile and safe land where they could practise their beliefs free from persecution. Costa Rica, which had recently abolished its army, certainly fitted the 'tolerant' and 'peaceful' criteria, while the Monteverde area was unmistakably fertile. It was also, crucially, 'safe', its high elevations putting it largely out of reach of malaria- and yellow fever-carrying mosquitoes. To make ends meet, the Quakers purchased a small dairy herd with the intention of making and selling a little cheese,

The factory they founded way back in 1953, La Lechería, is now one of Costa Rica's largest and most famous cheese producers, churning out over 1,400 kilos of the stuff each week. Despite this economic success, the Quakers maintain a simple rural existence, ensuring their activities have as little environmental impact as possible.

Natural History

Unlike so many other parts of the country, which have seen areas of protected land gradually encroached upon, their buffer zones whittled away, the Monteverde story is of a small area of protected land that has – almost against the odds – been vastly expanded in the decades since its creation. The first conservation efforts here were undertaken in the early 1970s by a combination of the Quaker community, local residents and concerned ecologists, who teamed up to purchase a small portion of the area's watershed in order to protect it against development by the then-increasing number of migrants.

The Monteverde Reserve's initial 328ha would soon grow when the World Wildlife Fund (now the World Wide Fund for Nature), recognizing the opportunity this scheme offered to protect the region's fauna, provided money to buy more land. Soon a movement had begun, dedicated to purchasing and protecting as much of the cloudforest as possible. Sometimes the amount of newly protected land grew by just a little; at other times, it grew by rather a lot, as was the case with the creation of the Bosque Eterno de los Niños ('Children's Eternal Rainforest') in the 1980s. This extraordinary piece of conservation came about, remarkably enough, as a result of a project by a group of Swedish schoolchildren, whose plans to raise money for the purchase of a tract of forest were picked up and emulated by children from all over the world (including the USA, Canada, the UK and Japan). A preliminary allocation of just 15ha would, as the money began pouring in, soon swell to an astonishing 20,000ha, making the children's rainforest the largest private reserve in the whole of Costa Rica. In the 1990s a further 310ha were added to the general pot when the Santa Elena Reserve was set up. Today, the Monteverde Conservation League (MCL), the body charged with overseeing the area's reserves, manages one of the most successful conservation projects in the country, responsible for over 30,000 hectares of land.

The Towns

Santa Elena may be the lesser known of the region's two towns, but it's the first you'll encounter and, if you've got any business to attend to – money to take out, e-mails to send – the one you'll probably spend more time in. It is the more built-up of the two,

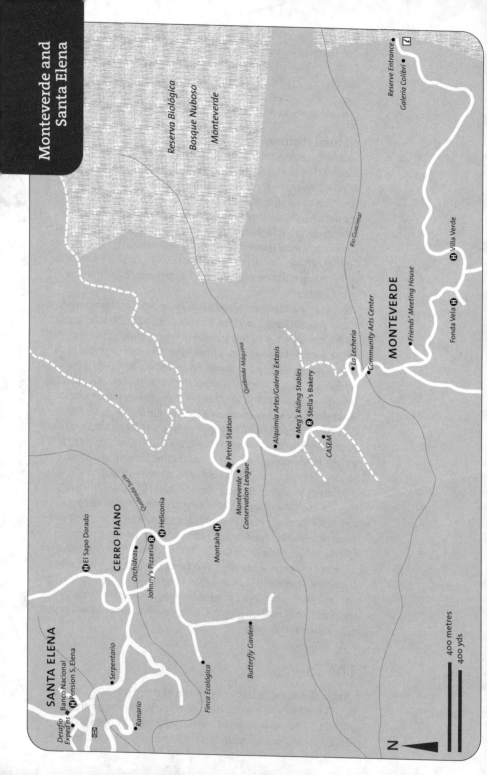

Monteverde and
Santa Elena

Reserva Biológica
Bosque Nuboso
Monteverde

SANTA ELENA

Desafío
Exped'ns
Banco Nacional
Pension S. Elena

Serpentario

Ranario

Finca Ecológica

CERRO PIANO

Orchideas

Johnny's Pizzeria

Heliconia

Butterfly Garden

Montaña

Monteverde
Conservation League

Petrol Station

Quebrada Máquina

Alquimia Artes/Galeria Extasis

Meg's Riding Stables

Stella's Bakery

CASEM

La Lechería

Community Arts Center

MONTEVERDE

Friends' Meeting House

Fonda Vela

Villa Verde

Río Guacimal

Reserve Entrance

Galeria Colibrí

El Sapo Dorado

Quebrada Sucia

400 metres
400 yds

N

having become increasingly touristified over the past decade, its streets now lined with banks, Internet cafés, budget hotels and restaurants. Despite this growth, however, development seems, for the time being, to be more or less under control. Indeed, in a way, Santa Elena could be regarded as a sort of regional safety valve, attracting development that might otherwise spread towards the reserves. The town's roads are laid out in a simple triangular pattern, with the apex to the north, where you'll find the **Banco Nacional**, one of the town's major landmarks.

To the east is the poorly maintained road to the Monteverde Reserve, alongside which the town of **Monteverde** is spread out in a rather haphazard manner. The town's centre, such as it is, is **La Lechería**, the cheese-making factory that was the town's economic lynchpin for much of the past five decades (until it was succeeded by tourism). Its shop sells fresh cheeses and you can take a 2hr tour of the factory to see the cheese-making process.

If you're intrigued by the Quaker way of life here, you can pay a visit to the **Friends' Meeting House** (Quakers are also known as the 'Society of Friends') to get an introduction to the Quakers' uniquely unfussy, unpushy form of religion. The meeting house isn't really a house of worship in the traditional sense, having no minister or order of service. Rather, pews are arranged in a circle and people are invited to speak on whatever topic they want (there's no official agenda) as, when and if the mood takes them. Interested visitors can attend the meeting on the first Sunday of each month.

La Lechería
t 645 5436; open Mon–Sat 7.30–4, Sun 7.30–noon; adm

The Reserves

Reserva Biológica Bosque Nuboso Monteverde

⭐ **Reserva Biológica Bosque Nuboso Monteverde**
t 645 5122, www.cct.or.cr; open daily 7–4; adm

Cloudforest (*bosque nuboso*), of which this reserve is the country's (and, indeed, Central America's) most famous example, is well named. A combination of geographical factors – winds, rainfall, elevation, topography, etc. – creates a near 100 per cent humidity, blanketing the region in thick mists. Permanently sodden (there's no true dry season, just a slightly less wet one, with the stress on the slightly), this great soggy forest provides the most astoundingly fertile environment, thick with a superabundance of life. It's not just that every square metre of ground seems to be home to myriad plants, but that those plants that can't find any ground to take root in have simply taken to living on top of other plants. From forest floor to leafy canopy, it's just layer upon layer of plant life – mosses, lichens, ferns, trees, strangler vines, lianas, bromeliads, orchids and more, over 2,500 species in total. At times the forest seems to be almost at war with itself, a mass of battling greenery, hungrily competing for each rare shaft of sunlight.

Getting to the Monteverde Cloudforest Reserve

The most scenic and pleasant way to get to the reserve (providing you're already in Santa Elena or Monteverde; if not, see p.237) is to **walk** along the paths running adjacent to the main road. Obviously, if coming all the way from Santa Elena, this will involve a relatively arduous 6km uphill hike, and certainly isn't recommended if you want to get there early, or are in a hurry. However, if you've got the time, it's a lovely way to pass the day, the jungle-fringed road providing lots of wildlife- (particularly bird-) watching opportunities.

Otherwise, **buses** connect Santa Elena with Monteverde at 6.15am and 1.15pm (returning at 11.15am and 4pm). A 4WD **taxi** from Santa Elena should cost around $5.

From a visitor's perspective, this low level of visibility caused by the combination of mists and extremely dense vegetation can make it rather difficult to spot the resident wildlife. According to the experts, the park is home to over 400 species of bird and over a hundred species of mammal but, with so much jungle for them to hide in, you could easily spend an entire afternoon here and not see much at all – the countless insects of the forest floor excepted.

For this reason, it is best to visit the reserve in the company of an experienced guide. You can either book an independent guide (see p.247 for details); or else the reserve offers its own 3hr **tours**, open to all, which leave from the visitor centre near the entrance. For spotting purposes, the night-time torchlight tours (you'll need to bring your own torch), which leave at 7.15pm, are the preferred option, as a good 70 per cent of the reserve's animal residents are nocturnal. Though it may sound early, the 7.30am morning tour is actually a little late (not to say a little too crowded) to provide favourable conditions for seeing the animals. Both tours should be booked at least a day in advance in the dry season.

Tours of the reserve
both tours cost $15, in addition to the reserve entrance fee

You'll certainly need to arrive early if you're hoping to track down the park's most famous resident – the resplendent **quetzal**. These dazzling green and red birds have long held a near-mythic status in the region (see p.43) and attract hordes of eager spotters throughout the year. They are most commonly viewed during the March–June breeding season, when the males are busy displaying their plumed finery and the females descend to lower elevations to lay their eggs. A good guide will be able to lead you to **aguacatillo** (a sort of avocado) trees that are the birds' primary source of food. Be under no illusions: spotting a quetzal is difficult, but with suitable amounts of patience and determination, by no means impossible. Spotting one of the forest's few remaining **jaguars**, however, no matter how patient or determined you are, probably is impossible. Other, more easily spotted forest critters include peccaries, coatis, white-faced capuchins, dozens of different types of amphibian (including poison arrow frogs) and over 30 types of hummingbird. These last are particularly easy to spot as there's a dedicated hummingbird gallery, **Galería Colibrí**, near the visitor centre at the park's entrance, where you can see the iridescent whirligigs sipping from special feeders filled with sugared water.

Galería Colibrí
open Mon–Sat 9.30–4.30, Sun 10–2

Tips for Visiting the Monteverde Reserve

• Get there early. Not only do the best wildlife-spotting opportunities arise just after dawn, but visitor numbers are limited to a maximum of 160. If you arrive after the limit has been reached, the authorities may take pity on you and let you in, or they may not, obliging you to sit and wait until somebody (or bodies, depending on how many of you there are) leaves. The park fills up quickly after 7.30am, especially in the dry season, when the official guided tour leaves and the tour groups arrive *en masse*. Though the ticket office to the reserve doesn't open until 7am, you can enter the park earlier and simply pay your fee when you leave.

• Bring wet-weather gear. Rubber boots, a waterproof jacket and an umbrella are essentials in the rainy season, and highly recommended in the 'dry' (it may not actually be raining, but it will still be very wet).

• Be prepared for changes in temperature. You may be in the tropics in the midst of a Hollywood-style jungle, but you're also very high up (as much as 1,680m up at the top of the highest trail) and temperatures tend to hover around the 15°C mark – think dank and clammy rather than hot and steamy. That said, in areas of open country when the sun comes out, temperatures can rise rapidly. Dress in layers.

• Bring plenty of DEET-based insect repellent, and use it. Bugs love the wet.

While Monteverde may be the epitome of dense, impenetrable, primeval jungle, it's also surprisingly user-friendly, with a well-run, well-stocked **visitor centre** (selling maps, wildlife-spotting guides and a range of souvenirs – T-shirts, postcards, etc.) and nine clearly marked **trails** (amounting to some 13km of hiking). The three most popular trails – the **Sendero Bosque Nuboso** (Cloudforest Trail, 2km), the **Sendero Pantanoso** (Swamp Trail, 1.6km) and the **Sendero Río** (River Trail, 1.9km) – together form a large triangular route known, inevitably, as **El Triángulo**. Owing to the extreme slipperiness of the ground, many of the walkways are fitted with wooden and concrete supports, which, though diminishing the romance of the thing rather, do at least make it a lot easier to keep your footing. Without these aids, El Triángulo would be severely challenging; as it is, it's a moderately taxing day's hike.

The more hiking you do, the more you'll realize that the term 'forest' actually covers a multitude of different environments and ecosystems. You'll certainly encounter thick, almost cartoonish jungle – particularly on the Sendero Bosque Nuboso – but there are also stretches of almost European-style oak and pine forest, sinister-looking swamp forests as well as winding rivers and waterfalls. Climb the **Chomogo Trail**, the reserve's highest, which ascends 150m to an elevation of 1,680m, and you'll find dense vegetation giving way to the scrappier fare of elfin forest, where stunted trees huddle on exposed ledges, struggling for existence against the biting winds. Up here you can see the so-called Continental Divide, with the great stretches of canopy on the Pacific and Caribbean slopes stretching out before you on either side. Of the reserve's other trails, **El Camino** ('The Road') is renowned for its bird- and butterfly-watching opportunities, while the **Sendero El Puente** offers stupendous views from a 100m suspension bridge.

Getting to the Reserva Santa Elena

The reserve lies 5km northeast of Santa Elena village. **Shuttle buses** leave for the reserve at 6.45am and 11am, making the return journey at 10.30am and 3.30pm. A **taxi** from town to the reserve should cost in the region of $6.

Reserva Santa Elena

Reserva S. Elena
t 645 5390, www.
monteverdeinfo.com/
reserve; open daily
7–4; adm

The Santa Elena reserve is almost never described in its own right, but only in terms of how it compares to its more famous sibling, the Monteverde Reserve. So, for the record, Santa Elena is two decades younger than Monteverde, having been founded in 1992 (as compared to 1972), much smaller (preserving 300 hectares of cloudforest as compared to over 10,500) and a bit higher (with an average elevation of 1,650m).

So far, so what? you might think – from this description, Santa Elena's lack of fame would seem to be wholly justified. Facts and figures aren't everything, however. The reserve's relative obscurity means that it's also much less visited than Monteverde, and that means that its wildlife-spotting potential is actually (whisper it quietly) rather better, its emptier, quieter trails proving just that bit more attractive to the resident animals. It certainly offers better chances of encountering a quetzal than Monteverde's more crowded confines. Its four marked **trails** comprise a total of 12km of relatively easy hiking through pristine jungle. Because of its high elevation, the park has several lookout points where on a rare clear day you can see all the way to Volcán Arenal.

The park was founded by and is still administered by Santa Elena High School, whose students regular perform litter patrols of its trails. It's entirely self-funding with all profits going towards the upkeep of the reserve (additional donations gratefully received).

Tours of the reserve
day tours cost $15;
night tours $13

The small **visitor centre** at the entrance can provide maps, has a cafeteria and offers **guided tours** at 7.30am and 11.30am (both 3hrs), as well as torchlight **night tours** at 7pm. These should be booked well in advance, as numbers are extremely limited.

Bosque Eterno de los Niños

Bosque Eterno de los Niños
via Monteverde
Conservation League,
t 645 5003;
open daily
7.30–5.30; adm

Ah, the younger generation. When they're not experimenting with illegal substances, playing their music too loud or generally breaking taboos, they're banding together to save the rainforest. These kids, they just don't know they're born.

The 'Children's Eternal Forest', a Swedish children's school project that became Costa Rica's largest private reserve (*see* p.239 for more information on the background), borders the Monteverde reserve and is made up of much the same vegetation, including large swaths of primary cloudforest, as well as areas of reclaimed agricultural land that are being left to return to a wild state. Much of the reserve, which is managed by the Monteverde Conservation

Where to Stay in the Reserves around Monteverde

Reserva Biológica Bosque Nuboso Monteverde

The reserve can offer a few simple accommodation options. You can hire a bunk in the 40-bed dorm near the entrance for $10 (shared bathroom), or book a space in one of three shelters within the reserve for $3.50. The latter have kitchen areas and gas supplies for cooking, as well as cold water showers, but you'll need to bring your own sleeping bag, food and toilet paper.

Bosque Eterno de los Niños

Dormitory accommodation is available in a couple of field stations within the reserve, although places tend to be reserved for scientific groups. However, if there's space, these can be rented out to independent travellers, but must be booked several weeks in advance.

League, is deliberately kept out of bounds to visitors – the children have been quite fundamentalist about this, insisting that the forest should primarily be a refuge for nature rather than a tourist attraction – but there is a short 3.5km **trail** by the Bajo de Tigre entrance. Here the forest is a bit more open and sparse than in Monteverde, making wildlife-spotting that bit easier.

Smaller Reserves

Valle Escondido
t 645 5156; adm

Reserva Sendero Tranquilo
t 645 5010; adm exp

Finca Ecológica
t 645 5554, www.finca ecologicamonteverde. com; open 7–5; adm

Aside from the 'Big Three', Monteverde also has a few smaller, privately operated reguges, reserves and eco-farms, including the **Valle Escondido** or 'Hidden Valley', which has a nature trail leading through an 11ha private forest; the 80ha **Reserva Sendero Tranquilo** bordering the Monteverde Reserve, whose 'tranquil paths' are deliberately kept narrow and overgrown and can only be explored in the company of a guide (included in the admission price) in groups of no more than six; and the **Finca Ecológica**, a former banana and coffee plantation that has been left to return to a state of secondary forest, with four looping trails taking you past waterfalls, lookout points and areas of premontaine forest, home to coatis, sloths, monkeys and porcupines. The last-named is best viewed on one of the twilight walks which leave every evening at sunset ($14). The spotting here tends to be quite good (principally because the farm cheats slightly by leaving food out for the animals).

Other Attractions

The reserves may be the big draws but they are by no means the region's only attractions. Monteverde has a fine collection of wildlife exhibits, as well as a surprisingly lively arts and crafts scene.

Wildlife and Nature Attractions

Jardín de Mariposas
t 645 5512; open 9.30–4; adm

Though they have managed to get their name above the title, butterflies are not the only stars of the **Jardín de Mariposas** (Butterfly Garden). In addition to the hundreds of fluttering beauties

Who's the King of the Swingers? Problems in the Treetops

It's not all sweetness and light in the world of zipping (see 'Canopy Tours', p.248). The ubiquitousness of the tours, which have spread at startling speed, has given rise to some serious safety concerns. As professionally run and safety-conscious as most operations are, there are still dangers inherent in the practice. After all, you're a long way up and often moving at quite a speed. Also, it's sometimes difficult, with some of the lesser-known operators, to establish just how rigorous their safety procedures are. It's relatively easy to set up a canopy tour, and official regulation of the industry is by no means as stringent as it might be.

There's also another oft-overlooked danger that particularly applies to canopy tours located in areas of lowland forest, where trees are very tall (perfect for zip-lining), but also very fast-growing. The consequence for any life form that is fast-growing is that it also tends to be short-lived. Few lowland rainforest trees make it past a hundred. Zip-lines have to be attached to the tallest trees, i.e. the ones nearing the end of their life...you can see where the logic is going. For this reason, canopy touring is a practice perhaps best avoided in the rainy season, when the majority of tree falls happen, as the root systems get undermined by water. Stick to the better-known companies and don't agree to anything unless you're one hundred per cent satisfied with the safety precautions.

There are also problems within the industry itself. Its burgeoning success has brought little pleasure to the man who 'claims' to have invented the pursuit, the Canadian, Darren Hreniuk, of the tellingly named Original Canopy Tour. In fact, so incensed has he become at what he sees as people 'ripping off' his idea that he has instigated legal proceedings to try to force other operators to pay him licensing rights – not, it has to be said, with a great deal of success. In fact his attempts to close down rival businesses have not gone down well in a country that these days derives a significant amount of income from this high-adrenaline eco-sport.

inhabiting four tropical gardens (not including the pupae being hatched in a separate greenhouse), the centre also has displays of leaf-cutter ants, beetles, stick insects and tarantulas. The admission price includes a free guided tour.

Orquídeas de Monteverde
t 645 5510;
open 8–5; adm

The **Orquídeas de Monteverde**, a haven of beautifully coloured, exquisitely fragranced tranquillity, is home to over 400 species of orchid, including examples of the smallest orchid in the world. Guided tours in English are available.

Ranario
t 645 6320; open
9–8.30; adm

The **Ranario** (Frog Pond) is home to over 20 brightly coloured native species of frog and toad, who live in a collection of terraria (as aquaria for land animals are officially known). Your admission price includes a free 45-minute guided tour – handy for pointing out some of the better-camouflaged inhabitants. Unfortunately, one former local resident you definitely won't be seeing is the golden toad. Once common in the region, the creature hasn't been spotted since 1989, and its disappearance has been a source of major concern to naturalists, who think it may be indicative of some small but profound shift in the environmental balance of the area. One theory suggests that, as toads absorb oxygen through their skin, they may be particular susceptible to airborne toxins and that their demise could therefore be attributable to an increase in air pollution. The 'pond' is definitely best visited in the early dusk when the previously motionless inhabitants start gearing up for the night ahead with a spring in their step and a croak in their throat.

Serpentario de Monteverde
t 645 5238; adm; open 8–5

Finally in the area, the **Serpentario de Monteverde** houses over 40 species of snake, including numerous native venomous varieties (think of it as a handy reference tool as to what to avoid when out in the jungle), as well as an assortment of other reptiles, including turtles, frogs and lizards. Guided tours in English are available.

Art Galleries

All that surrounding natural beauty must have an inspiring effect. Monteverde has had a thriving arts and crafts scene since the early 1980s when **CASEM** (the Cooperativa de Artesanía Santa Elena Monteverde) was founded to represent and market the creations of a handful of local female artists. Today, the co-operative has over a hundred artists on its books (still mostly women), selling everything from paintings and sculptures to handicrafts – embroidery, clothes, wooden homeware, jewellery, etc. – and souvenirs.

CASEM
t 645 5190

In the past two decades, it has been joined by well over a dozen other galleries and showrooms, including **Galería Extasis**, which specializes in figurative wooden sculptures (mostly animals), and **Alquimia Artes**, which sells a wide selection of brightly coloured jewellery and ceramics. And if you find the scenery inspiring you too, and fancy having a go at producing a work of art yourself, the **Monteverde Studio of the Arts** and the **Community Arts Center**, both offer art classes.

Galería Extasis
t 645 5548, galeria extasis@racsa.co.cr

Alquimia Artes
t 645 5847, alquimiaartes@ racsa.co.cr

Monteverde Studio of the Arts
t 645 5434, www.mvstudios.com

Community Arts
t 645 6121, mviarte@mvinstitute.org

Tourist Information in Monteverde and Santa Elena

There's no official tourist office, but any local hotel or tour operator should be able to provide you with all the relevant information. You can get information about the reserves from their visitor centres.

Services in Monteverde and Santa Elena

Banks: Banco Nacional, at the top of the Santa Elena 'Triangle', just north of the bus stop. There's an ATM. This is one of the town's major landmarks, and is often used as a reference point by locals giving directions.
Bookstore: Chunches, just southeast of the Banco Nacional, **t** 645 5147. It sells guidebooks, US newspapers and a variety of Spanish and English language second-hand paperbacks.
Internet: Internet Pura Vida, opposite the Banco Nacional.

Police: t 645 5127, south of the Banco Nacional.
Post office: Towards Monteverde.
Supermarket: At the southern end of the 'Triangle'.

Tours around Monteverde and Santa Elena

General Tours

For individual guides, contact your hotel (nearly all offer tours) or the **Asociación de Guías de Monteverde** (Monteverde Guides Association), **t** 645 5483, whose members offer tours to all the local reserves. Prices start at $30 per person for an individual tour, $15 per person for groups.

For tours to more far-flung destinations – Volcán Arenal, Manuel Antonio, etc. – again try your hotel or some of the area's specialist tour operators, including **Desafío Expeditions**, **t** 645 5874, *www.monteverdetours.com*; **Green Trails**, **t** 364 1710, *greentrailssgt@ yahoo.com*; and **Pensión Santa Elena**, t 645 5051, *www.monteverdeinfo.com*, the last of whom is generally regarded as running one of the best tour desks in town, particularly aimed at budget travellers.

Horse-riding Tours

With the local roads in such poor condition, horse-riding is actually one of the most sensible and pleasant ways of getting around locally. Several firms in the area offer horse treks (suitable for all abilities) through the local countryside for around $15 an hour. Desafio, listed on the previous page, also organizes horse tours.

The operators listed below also offer overnight camping trips plus longer trips to La Fortuna along the **El Castillo Trail**. As romantic as this sounds, you should exercise a degree of caution before committing. A few years back, this became rather controversial, with several operators accused of maltreat-ing their animals. As competition on the route grew, so, the protestors claimed, the welfare of the horses began to suffer. Some were old animals bought in cheaply that were simply no longer up to the task, while others, to save money, were being pushed too hard or being used on too many jobs. Thanks to a good deal of negative publicity, there's been a drastic over-haul of the industry, and standards are now a lot better. It goes without saying that you should only use recom-mended stables, such as those listed here, and be sure to check the health of your horse before saddling up. If you're at all unhappy, resist the sales pressure and use another operator.

Meg's Stables, t 645 5052, *www.stellasbakery.com*.

Sabine's Smiling Horses, t 645 5051, *horseback@monteverdeinfo.com*.

Coffee Tours

Cielo Verde Coffee Tour, t 645 5641, *tinas_casitas@hotmail.com*. Offers 2hr tours of the Finca Cielo Verde, a local coffee farm, 2km west of Santa Elena, for $15, or $50 including transport and meals.

Canopy Tours

Canopy, or 'zip-line', tours, of which there are dozens available throughout the country, were pioneered right here

⭐ Selvatura Canopy Tour >>

in Monteverde. The idea behind them is simple. You ascend to a platform set at the top of a very tall tree. Then, using the sort of harness traversing system common in caving, you are connected via a pulley to an overhead cable, along which (following a safety briefing and a quick summoning up of your courage), you will zip to the next tree-set platform – and so on.

The number of 'zips' depends on the operator.

Though this all takes place in the forest, and there's a distinct eco-veneer to the advertising, zip-lining has very little to do with nature-watching (you're moving much too fast and much too noisily for that). It's about a speed- and vertigo-induced adrenaline rush, nothing more – although that's not to say it's not a lot of fun.

The three major local canopy tour companies all have good reputations for safety (*see* box, p.246). Prices are around $35–45. Which one you choose depends on how much zipping you want to do.

The Original Canopy Tour, t 645 5243, *www.canopytour.com*. Seven zip-trips.

Sky Trek, t 645 5238, *www.skywalk.co.cr*. Offers 11 zip-trips.

Selvatura, t 645 5929, *www.selvatura. com*. Offers a mighty 18 zips (including one that's a heart-attack-inducing 770m long). For the slightly less brave, Selvatura also has a series of aerial walkways (as does Sky Trek's sister concern, **Sky Walk**).

Where to Stay in Monteverde and Santa Elena

Though there is some overlapping, Santa Elena and Monteverde tend to provide opposing types of accom-modation. Santa Elena is the site of all the best budget options – cheery, locally owned *pensiones* and B&Bs, whose amenities often don't stretch much beyond four walls, a bed and a limited supply of hot water. Monteverde, on the other hand, tends to specialize in much grander fare; the sort of places that have indi-vidually decorated rooms, Jacuzzis, gourmet restaurants and private stretches of forest.

You'll probably need to book ahead for the mid-range and top-end places during the peak months of December to April (particularly Christmas and Easter), when many will be full of tour groups. However, if you do arrive unannounced, and are willing to lower your standards a little, you should be able to find space somewhere. Indeed, in the quieter months you may find the accommodation coming to you, with touts noisily and persistently soliciting for your custom as you step off the bus.

For accommodation in the reserves, see p.245.

Expensive ($$$$)

Hotel Fonda Vela, on the Monteverde road, 1.5km from the reserve entrance, t 645 5125, www.fondavela.com ($99). The Fonda Vela is owned by one of Monteverde's original Quaker families, but don't go expecting something sober, stark and simple. Despite nods towards environmental friendliness – the water is solar-heated, the furniture from sustainable sources – this offers luxury on tap: bright and airy rooms with minibars and phones, suites with air-conditioning and balconies (some rooms have wheelchair access) and an outstanding French restaurant (with a very good wine list). There are also over 12ha of grounds with 2km of trails (they hire out horses if you don't fancy walking).

Hotel Heliconia, on the road to Monteverde, t 645 5109 ($87). The rooms at this fetching wood-heavy mountain lodge are pretty nice – large, well equipped with good views – while the suites ($115) situated further up the hill are simply sumptuous – two double beds, large bathtubs and even better views. There's also a Jacuzzi with views out over the forest, a spa offering a range of health treatments and an excellent Italian-esque restaurant, **Mediterráneo**, serving pizzas from a traditional wood-fired oven. A range of tours is offered.

Monteverde Cloud Forest Lodge, southwest of Santa Elena, off the Monteverde road, t 645 5058 ($85). Secluded, charming and elegant, the lodge is set amid a 30ha forest with 5km of trails. The lovely cabins (two of which have wheelchair access) all have TVs, large bathrooms, and terraces with sweeping views. A section of the hotel's grounds is occupied by the Original Canopy Tour (see p.248) with whom you get a 25 per cent discount. Horses can be hired.

Hotel El Sapo Dorado, east of Santa Elena, t 645 5010, www.sapodorado. com ($105). The Sapo Dorado is one of the area's most luxurious hotels, offering a choice of: 'mountain' suites, perched on a hill with fireplaces and views of the coast; 'sunset' suites, set a little lower and facing due west (hence the name); and bungalows in the leafy grounds (there are trails). The restaurant is one of the most renowned around, serving up a tasty array of fish and vegetarian dishes.

Moderate ($$$)

Arco Iris Eco Lodge, in Santa Elena, t 645 5067, www.arcoirislodge.com ($65–$35). The Arco sits perched on a hill in its own grounds, at the end of a side road just north of the Santa Elena 'triangle'. On clear days you can see all the way to the coast, but when the clouds descend, you'll have a job picking out Santa Elena. There are 12 good-sized cabins, all with private bathrooms and terraces, as well as a couple of smaller, less well-equipped (but cheaper) rooms. Breakfast is an extra $7.

Hotel de la Montaña, 0.5km south of Santa Elena, on the Monteverde road, t 645 5046, www.monteverdemountain hotel.com ($67). One of the region's older hotels, the Montaña oozes rustic charm. Set in over 35 acres of grounds (there are trails), the nicely decorated rooms have balconies overlooking well-tended gardens and out towards coast. The deluxe rooms have bathtubs and minibars, and there's a Jacuzzi, a sauna and a good seafood restaurant. Tours are offered.

Trapp Family Lodge, near the reserve entrance, t 645 5858, www.trappfam. com ($75). As snug and safe as a Sunday afternoon in front of the telly, these appropriately Alpine-looking (given the name) mountain chalets are very handy for the Monteverde Reserve, which is just a short walk away. A mass of wood-panelling

★ Hotel Heliconia >

★ Pensión
Santa Elena >>

adorns the high-ceilinged A-frame rooms, which have huge windows (providing good views of the surrounding forest) and very large bathrooms. The very good restaurant is unfortunately not open to non-residents. The friendly Chilean owners are a mine of local information. You really need your own car to stay here, as it lies beyond the last bus stop by several kilometres.

Hotel Villa Verde, about 1km from the reserve entrance, on the Monteverde road, **t** 645 5025, www.villaverdehotel. com ($65). Near the reserve, in lovely forested grounds with good bird-spotting potential, the Villa Verde is cosy but not exactly opulent (the furniture is a touch spartan), but there's a swimming pool and the suites have fridges and fireplaces. The restaurant is a bit tour-groupy but serves decent enough fare. The price includes breakfast.

Moderate–Inexpensive ($$$–$$)

La Colina Lodge, on the Monteverde road, a couple of km from the reserve entrance, **t** 645 5009 ($46–34). This lovely rustic lodge, decorated with an assortment of antiques, has a distinctly American feel to it, as if it would be more at home on the American prairies, rather than nestling against the rainforest. Formerly owned by Quakers, but now under new manage-ment, it offers 11 rooms – some in a lodge, some in a carriage house – with a mixture of shared and private bath-rooms, as well as a good restaurant serving plenty of fish and vegetarian dishes. You can also camp in the grounds for $7. The large US-style breakfast is included in the price.

Inexpensive–Budget ($$–$)

Hotel Camino Verde, Santa Elena, **t** 645 5916 ($20–10). Basic, unfussy, no-frills (but crucially clean) accommodation, with simple rooms (a choice of shared or private bathrooms) and a communal kitchen. Tours of the area can be arranged by the friendly front desk.

Pensión Colibri, Santa Elena, **t** 645 5682. Nestling among the trees on the road off the main Santa Elena 'triangle', this very cheap and very basic *pensión* offers small rooms with shared bathrooms for $5, and slightly

larger ones with balconies and private bathrooms for a very competitive $10. The friendly owners also rent out horses. Breakfast is an extra $1.50.

Pensión Santa Elena, Santa Elena, **t** 645 5051, www.monteverdeinfo.com ($15–10). The Santa Elena is not just a popular backpackers' hangout, it's also one of the town's best tour operators, offering a range of options for budget-conscious travellers. The accom-modation it supplies is simple and basic, designed with thriftiness not luxury in mind – small rooms with shared baths and a couple of dorms ($5). With Internet access, a communal kitchen, an events noticeboard and a great community atmosphere, this is *the* place in Monteverde to meet fellow travellers.

Hotel El Sueño, Santa Elena, **t** 645 5021 ($30–15). Right in centre of town, 'The Dream' hotel offers small, cheap rooms with shared bathrooms in an old building ($15) and much more fancy two-storey rooms with private bathrooms and forest views in a new annexe ($30). The tasty breakfasts are an extra $3.

Pensión El Tucán, Santa Elena, **t** 645 5017 ($20–10). There's not much to the Tucán, but then its customers, who are principally money-conscious back-packers, aren't looking for frills and fancies, but savings, which the *pensión* can certainly offer, especially if you decide to take one of its rather small rooms with shared bathrooms ($10). Rooms with private bathrooms are $10 more, but are only slightly less small. Continuing the money-saving theme, there's also a reasonably priced Tico restaurant.

Eating Out in Monteverde and Santa Elena

The advice for 'eating out' is pretty much the same as for accommodation – for budget places, stick to Santa Elena, for something more fancy, head to Monteverde.

In addition to the stand-alone places listed below, many of the region's upscale hotels operate gourmet restaurants (*see* 'Where to Stay' for details), most of which will require reservations in high season.

Restaurants typically tend to close early, around 9.30–10pm, so don't leave it too long before making your mind up. Most restaurants do serve alcohol in this Quaker town, although it's often rather overpriced.

Café Rainforest, Santa Elena, t 645 5841. Opposite the church, this tranquil café is one of Santa Elena's less bustling eateries and a nice place to sit and contemplate. The open-air balcony on the first floor is a particularly good people-watching spot (provided it's not too cold). And, if that wasn't enough, they also serve some of the region's best coffee, made with locally harvested beans, as well as fruit drinks, sandwiches and pastries.

 Johnny's Pizzeria >

Johnny's Pizzeria, on Monteverde Road, just east of Santa Elena, **t** 645 5066. Rather fancy, with candlelit tables, attentive waiters and top-notch cuisine, Johnny's renowned pizzas are cooked in a traditional wood-fired oven ($5–8). The restaurant also does a range of pasta (including delicious home-made ravioli), meat, fish and vegetarian dishes, and has a good wine list. The outdoor patio overlooking the forest is one of the most romantic spots in town and the popular bar serves (for temperate Monteverde) rather potent cocktails.

Moon Shiva, just off the Monteverde road, on the next turning past Stella's Bakery, **t** 645 6270. For something a bit different, this charming Middle Eastern-influenced restaurant is particularly good for vegetarians with plenty of falafel, hummus and tahini on the menu, as well as a few Tico dishes. They also do a good range of ice creams for dessert.

Morpho's, Santa Elena, **t** 645 5607. This two-floor establishment is more like a café during the day, serving breakfasts and snacks from 9am to a steady stream of customers, before, in the evening, whipping out the good linen and candles and offering a hearty menu of fish, steaks, burgers and Tico favourites. There are always plenty of imaginative specials on offer and a good selection of wines. Mains are around $5–8.

Restaurante El Campesino, Santa Elena. There's no mistaking El Campesino, with its ceiling adorned with stuffed toys. The friendly, chatty owner serves up good Tico cuisine – *casados*, etc. – as well as steaks and seafood for gringos. It's got a nice homey atmosphere.

Restaurante El Nido, Santa Elena, **t** 645 6111. There are two factors which make El Nido one of the most popular eateries with budget travellers: one, obviously, is its prices, with nothing on its simple soda menu (*casados*, sandwiches, *gallo pinto*) costing more than $3; the other is its location, just across from the Banco Nacional with a good vantage point looking out over the street, allowing you to see the town's comings and goings as you eat.

Sabores, just east of Santa Elena. This lovely little ice-cream parlour in Cerro Plano is a great place to cool down on a hot day, serving a wide variety of flavours.

Stella's Bakery, Monteverde road, **t** 645 5560. Stella's has long been a favourite pit stop for travellers *en route* to the Monteverde Reserve. It opens at 6am, allowing you to stock up before an early morning cloudforest hike on jumbo-packed sandwiches made with tasty home-made bread, as well as soups, salads, rolls, muffins, pastries (sweet and savoury), fruit juices and light pasta dishes. Many of the ingredients are grown in the organic garden out the back. They also serve a good range of coffees. Stella's daughter runs Meg's Stables (*see* p.248).

Entertainment and Nightlife in Monteverde and Santa Elena

Monteverde is one of the few communities outside San José with a lively and varied cultural scene, playing host to one of the county's top cultural events, the **Monteverde Music Festival** (*www.mvinstitute.org*), during February and March. Organized by the Monteverde Institute, the concerts, which are mainly classical, jazz and Latin, are held at venues nightly throughout the region.

The implicit Quaker disapproval of alcohol does seem to have had a distinct influence upon the local nightlife, however, of which there is very little.

Most restaurants serve alcohol, and there are a handful of bars and a couple of half-hearted clubs aimed squarely at the gringo market. The most popular places include the **Amigos Bar** in Santa Elena, and **La Taberna Valverde**, 300m west of Banco Nacional, which has a small dance floor and offers perhaps the area's closest approximation of Jacó-style nightlife (i.e. not very close).

The North

Costa Rica's least populous, least glamorous and least visited region sits between the more attention-grabbing Pacific and Caribbean coasts. Stretching from the Nicaraguan border to the Cordillera Central, it's a no-nonsense sort of a place, with most of its acreage given over to the intensive production of crops – bananas, pineapples, sugar cane, rice – and the rearing of cattle. While the rest of the country has been busy over the past couple of decades transforming itself for visitors, the people of the north, whose sparse numbers are mainly made up of rugged farmers, seem to have decided that they have better things to do than cater to the capricious whims of tourists.

That's not to say that a visit here isn't worthwhile. While you may have to work harder and search longer for your thrills, you will, if you are willing to put the effort in, find much that's rewarding.

12

Don't miss

⭐ **Top-class windsurfing**
Lake Arenal p.273

⭐ **A birdwatchers' paradise**
Refugio Nacional de Vida Silvestre Caño Negro p.277

⭐ **Foaming rapids**
White-water rafting on the Río Sarapiquí p.262

⭐ **Cocktails, baths and volcano views**
Tabacón hot springs p.267

⭐ **Nature's fireworks**
Volcán Arenal p.271

See map overleaf

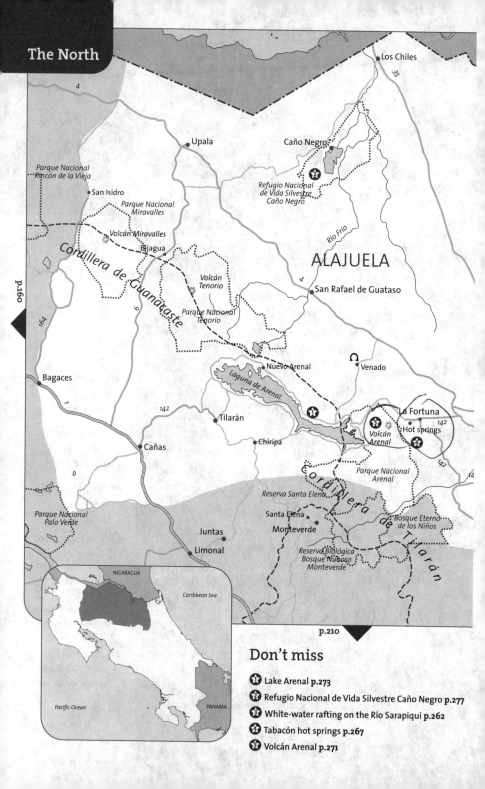

Los Chiles

4

Upala

Caño Negro

Parque Nacional Rincón de la Vieja

San Isidro

Parque Nacional Miravalles

Volcán Miravalles

Bijagua

Refugio Nacional de Vida Silvestre Caño Negro

Río Frío

Volcán Tenorio

ALAJUELA

4

San Rafael de Guataso

Parque Nacional Tenorio

Cordillera de Guanacaste

164

Bagaces

142

Nuevo Arenal

Venado

La Fortuna

142

Tilarán

Laguna de Arenal

Hot springs

Volcán Arenal

142

Cañas

Chiripa

14

Parque Nacional Arenal

Parque Nacional Palo Verde

Reserva Santa Elena

Cordillera de Tilarán

Juntas

Santa Elena

Monteverde

Bosque Eterno de los Niños

Limonal

Reserva Biológica Bosque Nuboso Monteverde

p.210

NICARAGUA

Caribbean Sea

Pacific Ocean

PANAMA

Don't miss

1 Lake Arenal **p.273**
2 Refugio Nacional de Vida Silvestre Caño Negro **p.277**
3 White-water rafting on the Río Sarapiquí **p.262**
4 Tabacón hot springs **p.267**
5 Volcán Arenal **p.271**

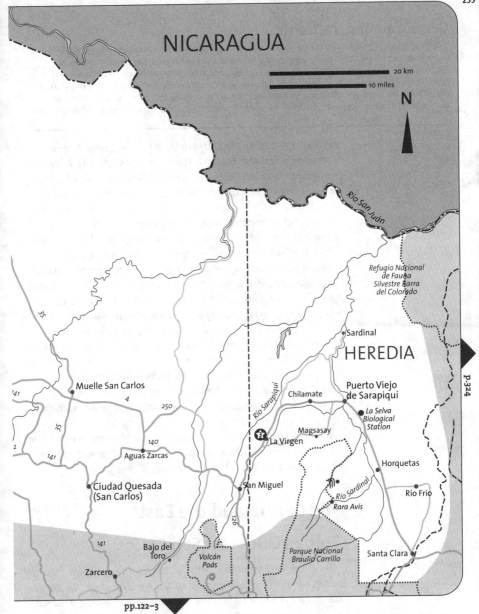

If travelling north from San José via Alajuela, the first sizeable settlement you'll come to will be the 'beef and milk' town of **Ciudad Quesada** (also known rather confusingly as **San Carlos**), which neatly divides the region in two: to the east is the major transport hub of **Puerto Viejo de Sarapiquí**, which can be used as a base to explore both the Río Sarapiquí, one of the country's prime white-water rafting destinations, and some of the area's few remaining swaths of

Getting around the North

Getting to and from the main tourist centres – Puerto Viejo de Sarapiquí and La Fortuna – is relatively easy. To these at least, there are relatively well-maintained **roads** and good, regular **bus** connections. Travelling further afield, however, particularly to the more sparsely populated north, can be a little bit more tricky. What bus services there are tend to be few and far between, and the roads are often in a quite shocking state of repair. Travelling by car will afford you greater peace of mind than trying to use the public transport system, but you'll need to keep your wits about you to safely negotiate the pothole-ravaged roads – relaxing it is not.

rainforest, including the northern tip of Braulio Carrillo National Park and the **La Selva Research Station**, one of Costa Rica's most respected eco-research centres; while to the west is one of the country's most spectacular natural sights (presuming the weather is clear enough for you to see it, which is by no means guaranteed), the ever-active **Volcán Arenal**, spewing out its seemingly endless torrent of lava, and its attendant tourist village of La Fortuna. Most of the north of the region is made up of a flat landscape of agricultural plains, the major exception being the **Refugio Nacional de Vida Silvestre Caño Negro** in the northwest, a vast area of wetlands that provides a home to one of the country's highest concentrations of indigenous and migratory birds. Once a destination visited only by super-determined birders, the refuge is becoming an increasingly common stop on the tourist trail, with most visitors now coming on tours from La Fortuna. North of here, the only real point of interest is the small border crossing point at **Los Chiles**, which processes the arrival and departure of a limited but steady drip of humanity, as compared to the torrent of migratory traffic that passes each day through Peñas Blancas further west (*see* pp.173–4).

As the region's climate encompasses both the wetter east and the drier west, the best advice is to say that the weather is changeable, the only constant being the searing heat.

The Centre and the East

Ciudad Quesada (San Carlos)

The locals here seem have little fondness for the city's official name, preferring to call it by the jauntier moniker of San Carlos, which can make asking for directions a little bewildering. And, just to add to the confusion, regional buses have adopted an either/or approach to displaying their destination. Still, should you manage to make it here, you'll find a pleasant rural community of around 30,000 people at the heart of one of the country's most important centres of milk and beef production. Ciudad Quesada essentially acts as a service town and meeting point for this vast farming region, providing all those little essentials – banks, Internet access, casinos, bars, other people – not available out on the open plains. It's

Getting to Ciudad Quesada

Ciudad Quesada lies about 95km northwest of San José. If travelling by **car**, follow the Interamericana (HWY-1) north to the Naranjo exit, then head north along HWY-141. **Buses** from San José leave hourly between 5am–7.30pm, from C 12, Av 7/9. The journey takes 3 hours and costs c820.

Getting away from Ciudad Quesada

By bus: Return services to San José leave hourly from 5am–6.15pm from the town's main **bus terminal** 1km north of the Parque Central. Five buses a day link Ciudad Quesada with Puerto Viejo de Sarapiquí (4.50am, 6am, 10am, 3pm and 5.30pm); the journey takes 2½ hours and costs c550. There are seven services a day between Ciudud Quesada and La Fortuna (6am, 10.30am, 1pm, 3.30pm, 5.15pm, 6pm and 8pm). There are also two services a day from San José to Los Chiles, leaving from C12, Av 7/9 (5.30am and 3.30pm), which stop in Ciudad Quesada.

By car: HWY-142 leads west to La Fortuna; HWY-140 heads northeast to Aguas Zarcas where you can connect with HWY-4 east to Puerto Viejo de Sarapiquí; while HWY-141 heads north to Muelle de San Carlos (usually abbreviated to Muelle) from where HWY-35 meanders its way all the way up to Los Chiles at the border.

also a major transport hub (which is the principal reason why most tourists come here – to pass through to somewhere else), with good connections to La Fortuna, Los Chiles and Puerto Viejo de Sarapiquí.

Not being a great tourist draw in itself, nor sitting on the doorstep of any major attractions – the nearest, Volcán Arenal, is over 40km away – the city's charm lies instead in its simplicity, in the chance it gives you to see a traditional agricultural community going about its business – browsing the stalls of the Saturday **market** piled high with locally grown produce (particularly fruit); popping into one of town's famous **saddle shops** (*talabarterías*) to order an intricately crafted leather creation, or enjoying a hearty supper at one of the town's renowned **steakhouses**. Indeed, it's this very lack of excitement that attracts a modest but steady stream of visitors throughout the year. The most touristy pursuits are provided by the hotels located on the lower volcanic slopes to the northeast of town, a couple of which have their own thermal pools. One also has a small branch of the Original Canopy Tour in its grounds.

The town's few streets huddle around its rather pretty **Parque Central**, in the northwest corner of which you'll find the town's arts and crafts market, the **Mercado de Artesanía**. The town's covered food market is one block south. There are banks with ATMs just north of the park and an Internet café just northeast.

Where to Stay in Ciudad Quesada

Considering that Ciudad Quesada isn't a major tourist town, there's a surprisingly decent number of options. In the town centre, most of the hotels tend to come under the category of either 'budget' or 'business' (sometimes both), with the grander places located on the outskirts, particularly on HWY-140 heading northeast out of town (which is where you'll find the hotels with thermal pools). Pre-booking is not really essential apart from in April, when the town plays host to Costa Rica's largest **cattle fair**, attracting bovine enthusiasts from all over the country.

Termales del Bosque, 7km northeast of town, **t** 460 1356, *termales@racsa.co.cr* ($$$; $53). At first glance, this would appear to be no different from dozens of other rural lodges in the region, with 19 snug cabins, all with fans and private bathrooms, nestling in a forested setting. What sets it apart, however, is its collection of seven hot volcanic springs around a 1km walk from the hotel. Set in tropical vegetation, with birds singing in the trees and butterflies fluttering, this offers as idyllic an experience as you could wish for as you hop from pool to pool (lower in temperature the further from the source you get). There's also a branch of the **Original Canopy Tour** (*www.canopytour.com*) on-site (*see* p.246), with five platforms set in the treetops and a very good restaurant, **La Casona**, serving traditional Tico fare.

El Tucano Resort, 8km northeast of town, **t** 460 6000, *www.occidental tucano.com* ($$$; $50). Owned by the Spanish Occidental group, this well-equipped resort has a rather generic European feel to it. It has all the facilities – leafy grounds, over 80 rooms equipped with TVs, fans and telephones and a good international restaurant, **El Torréon**, but there's no doubt that it's the thermal pools that are the big draw here. The hotel's two swimming pools, Jacuzzis and sauna are all fed by a natural volcanic hot spring, and there's an on-site spa providing pampering procedures: mud baths, facials, hydrotherapy, etc. Non-guests can use the pools for $12.

Hotel Conquistador, 600m south of Parque Central, **t** 460 0546 ($$; $32). Perched on a slight hill to the south of the town centre, the Conquistador is one of the town's grander choices, although that still doesn't make it that grand. The rooms behind the orange and blue façade are large and reasonably comfortable, with fans, TVs and private bathrooms. Some have decent views of the town and surrounding countryside.

Hotel La Central, west side of Parque Central, **t** 460 0301, *www.hotella central.net* ($$; $26). This big red modern building caters mainly to business travellers, hence the on-site casino. Its comfy rooms come equipped with fans, TVs, telephones and private bathrooms. There's also a good steakhouse, **Coca Loca**, next door.

Eating Out in Ciudad Quesada

There's little in the way of gourmet fare available, but you'll find plenty of decent, cheap places. With fresh produce in abundance, the meals served here are actually a cut above what you might normally expect in a town of this size and type. The local speciality is steak, '*lomito*', hardly surprising for somewhere plum at the centre of a major beef-rearing region. It comes served in a variety of different ways; the restaurants typically list over 20 different steak recipes on their menus, from the basic (grilled in oil) to the very fancy – *filet mignon* in spicy marinades, or tenderloin stuffed with ham and cheese. Prices are pretty reasonable: even a mighty half-kilo T-bone won't set you back more than about $7 (you'll pay in other ways, once the meal is over; this would test the constitution of even the hardiest cowboy). A more typical portion of 300g will cost around half that. Some of the best steakhouses include **Coca Loca**, **t** 460 3208, by the Hotel Central on the west side of the Parque Central, and **La Terraza**, **t** 460 5287, a couple of blocks northeast of the park by the petrol station, which attracts hordes of locals.

Cheap, filling eats are also provided by the sodas at the covered market and bakeries by the Parque Central.

Puerto Viejo de Sarapiquí

Eighty-five kilometres northeast of San José, Puerto Viejo de Sarapiquí, to give it its full name (and to distinguish it from the Puerto Viejo de Talamanca on the Caribbean coast), is still a major transport hub, with good connections to San José and the coast.

Getting to Puerto Viejo de Sarapiquí

By car: The quickest route from San José is along the Guápiles Highway through Braulio Carrillo National Park (HWY-32) which should take around 90mins in relatively light traffic. Alternatively, you can take the 'scenic' route via Heredia and Varablanca north along HWY-9, and then northeast along HWY-4 from San Miguel, which, though slightly shorter at 83km, will take around twice as long, particularly as you'll probably keep slowing down to admire the views as you pass through the valley bisecting volcanoes Poás and Barva.

By bus: Bus services offer the same two options: the main highway route, which takes 2hrs, and the scenic route, which takes 4hrs. As both services are marked simply 'Puerto Viejo', you'll need to check with the driver which route is being taken, although it's more likely to be the quicker one, which departs roughly every hour between 7am–6pm. There are just three scenic services via Heredia each day leaving at 6.30am, 1pm and 5.30pm. All services depart from San José's Caribbean bus terminal at C 0, Av 11.

Getting away from Puerto Viejo de Sarapiquí

As the hub around which much of the northeast's transport system revolves, Puerto Viejo has links to pretty much everywhere in the vicinity. All **buses** leave from the station just north of the soccer field. Services to San José, via the Guápiles Highway, depart at 5.30am, 7am, 8am, 11am, 1.30pm, 3pm, 5.30pm and 6.30pm, and via Varablanca at 5am, 7.30am, 11.30am and 4.30pm; to Guápiles at 5.30am, 7am, 9am, 12noon, 2.30pm, 4pm and 6.30pm, and to Ciudad Quesada at 5.30am, 9am, 12noon, 2pm and 3.30pm (2½ hrs).

Back in the mid-19th century, however, it was one of the most important ports in the entire country, the central cog in a vast export industry where boats loaded with coffee were sailed north up the Río Sarapiquí and then east along the Río San Juan to the coast. The opening of the Jungle Train in 1891, and the subsequent development of Puerto Limón as the country's main Caribbean port (*see* pp.326–8), put paid to much of this activity. Though Puerto Viejo managed to avoid going into an outright decline, and continues to serve as a major dormitory town for the region's plantation workers (with a small resident population of around 6,000), it has never since been able to find for itself a similar focus of purpose.

True, it welcomes its fair share of tourists, but almost none of these comes to town for what Puerto Viejo has to offer. Most of the area's attractions lie beyond the town's borders: **La Virgen**, the main centre of white-water rafting, to the southwest; the best eco-lodges, including Selva Verde, to the west; and the most impressive swaths of rainforest to the southeast. The town itself has been reduced to a cipher, offering little beyond the handiness of its location and its still excellent transport links. Like a railway turntable, its only purpose seems to be to redirect traffic. This basic functionality is reflected in the town's appearance, which has a make-do, unloved aesthetic to it – dusty, unkempt and slightly down-at-heel. It's basically a one-street town, which leads from the highway past a football field (the main landmark) to the dock.

Boat Trips
trips can be booked in town at Souvenirs Río Sarapiquí, t 766 6727, opposite the Banco Nacional, for around $15

The main activity offered in town even involves leaving it. It's a motorized **boat trip** up the Sarapiquí and San Juan rivers, following the old commercial coffee route. Bear in mind that, as the Río San Juan lies wholly within Nicaragua (Costa Rica only extends as far as the south bank of the river), you'll need to show your passport at

Migraciónes before departing, although, as Costa Ricans have the right to travel freely on the river, you probably won't be challenged once under way. It's a lovely journey, giving you the chance to appreciate the subtly changing landscape, something that is not always possible in a car (you have to pay too much attention to upcoming potholes) or on a crowded bus. North of Puerto Viejo, it's mainly pastureland, which gradually gives way to more forested areas as you get closer to Nicaragua. There's plenty of wildlife to be spotted *en route*, from crocodiles and turtles sunning themselves on logs to sloths and monkeys in the treetops.

Services in Puerto Viejo de Sarapiquí

Along the main road you will find ATM machines (at the Banco Popular), a post office (*correo*), an Internet café (Internet Sarapiquí) and a couple of supermarkets.

Where to Stay in Puerto Viejo de Sarapiquí

★ Centro Neotrópico Sarapiquí >>

★ Hotel Selva Verde Lodge >

In town there are plenty of budget options, many of which are aimed squarely at the region's plantation workers and are, in truth, rather dire, although there are a couple with decent facilities. At the other end of the scale, the countryside beyond the town's borders, particularly heading west towards the white-water rafting centre of La Virgen, is home to some of the best eco-lodges in the country, set in grand sweeping swaths of jungle with great wildlife-spotting potential. **Hotel Selva Verde Lodge**, 7km west of town, near Chilamate, **t** 766 6800, *www.holbrooktravel.com* (\$\$\$\$\$; \$135). One of the country's most celebrated eco-lodges, the Selva Verde enjoys an idyllic location on the banks of the river set amid 200ha of land (much of it made up of premontane rainforest). The lodge provides a supremely relaxing, supremely sedate environ-ment in which to get acquainted with nature (this low-key atmosphere is partly due to the fact that much of its clientele is made up of senior citizen tour groups). It's also supremely luxurious – there's no question of roughing it here. Its 40 standard rooms are all very large, with fans, verandahs

and jungle views, and there are also five superior bungalows. Marked trails lead through the grounds (an absolute mecca for birdwatchers), which can be explored either on your own or in the company of one of the lodge's guides (\$15). Additional facilities include a herb garden, a butterfly garden and an education centre. Horse-riding and trips along the Río Sarapiquí (either animal-spotting or white-water rafting depending on your inclination) are offered.

Centro Neotrópico Sarapiquí, 2km north of La Virgen, **t** 761 1004, *www. sarapiqui.com* (\$\$\$\$; \$85). This is much more than just another eco-lodge (although it's certainly very 'eco', using solar-heated water and its own biological sewage-treatment plant), it is also an important historical site, home to the **Alma Ata Archaeological Park and Museum of Indigenous Cultures** where the remains of a pre-Columbian village and burial ground are displayed. The public can visit the park daily from 9am–5pm for the not inconsiderable sum of \$19, although this does also entitle you to entry to the adjoining **Tirimbina Rainforest Centre**, a 750-acre reserve that is reached via a suspension bridge across the Río Sarapiquí. The lodge's 36 bungalows have been designed (appropriately enough) to resemble indigenous circular huts, while its **Palenque** restaurant aims to replicate dishes from pre-Columbian times.

Posada Andrea Cristina B&B, 1km west of Puerto Viejo, **t** 766 6265, *www. andreacristina.com* (\$\$\$; \$40). This small complex of just six simply-furnished, garden-set cabins (all with private bathrooms and fans) has a nice family-friendly atmosphere. It sits next to the ABAS conservation group (Asociación Para el Bienestar Ambiental de Sarapiquí), which was founded by the hotel's owner, Alex Martínez, who is as good a guide and source of information on environmental matters as you're likely to find in the area. A range of tours is offered.

El Bambú, in town, on the main road, t 766 6359, *www.elbambu.com* ($$$; $52). Long established as the town's most fancy accommodation, this can fill up quickly at peak times. Its 16 nicely furnished rooms all have air-conditioning and TVs and there's a small pool, a gym and, overlooked by the eponymous bamboos, a good restaurant/bar serving a slightly strange Costa Rican/Chinese menu.

El Gavilán Lodge, 1km south of Puerto Viejo, t 234 9507, *www.gavilanlodge.com* ($$$; $50). Set in a 100ha riverside nature reserve made up mainly of secondary forest (it was formerly a cattle farm), this offers 12 rooms in a two-storey building, all with private (albeit small) bathrooms, fans and terraces. The nice al fresco restaurant serving *comida típica* is popular with locals. Birding tours, horse-riding and river trips are offered. Breakfast is included in the price.

La Quinta de Sarapiquí Country Inn, 5km north of La Virgen, t 761 1300, *www.laquintasarapiqui.com* ($$$; $58). Occupying a swath of jungle next to the Río Sardinal that's become a renowned bird-watching destination, La Quinta offers a good restaurant (open to the public), a butterfly garden, a pool and a small museum (also open to the public) containing native artefacts and specimens of strange and alarming-looking insects. Paths lead through the jungle to various lookout points and a variety of tours are offered – jungle treks, horse-riding, fishing trips, even a tour to a nearby pineapple farm. Its 23 rooms all have fans, private bathrooms and terraces.

Hotel Ara Ambigua, 2km west of Puerto Viejo, t 766 6401, *www.sarapiquirainforest.com* ($$; $26). Good low-price choice with 13 rustic-style rooms, a very good restaurant and a swimming pool. Rafting and kayaking trips on the river available.

Mi Lindo Sarapiquí, in town, next to the football field, t 766 6281 ($; $21). The town's best, cleanest and most welcoming budget choice. The rooms are large, simple and spotless with fans and private bathrooms – all you could want, really. There's also a pretty decent restaurant. Parking is available.

Rancho Leona, La Virgen, 19km west of Puerto Viejo, t 761 1019, *www.rancholeona.com* ($; $9 per person). This is hugely popular with backpackers, for whom it offers the perfect combination of cheap, simple accommodation – five dorm-style rooms with shared bathrooms and camping space in the grounds – and lots of activities. The hotel has a communal area with computer games, a plunge pool and a hot tub, and adjoins an 30ha forest (with trails). It also hires out kayaks and, slightly bizarrely, has an on-site glass workshop where the owner produces Tiffany-style creations.

Restaurante y Cabinas Tia Rosita, La Virgen, 19km west of Puerto Viejo, t 761 1032 ($; $13). This popular budget choice next to the Rancho Leona is usually filled with truck drivers and plantation workers, so you can expect some pretty earthy company. You'll also need to book in advance whatever the time of year. If offers four dinky little *cabinas* at very competitive rates, all with private showers (with hot water), TVs and fans. There's a good attached soda.

Eating Out in Puerto Viejo de Sarapiquí

The advice for eating out is much the same as for finding somewhere to stay. If you want something basic, head into town where most things are geared towards the budget tastes of plantation workers and truck drivers. You'll find a number of cheap, though hardly inspiring, sodas around the football field and along the main road. There's not much variety to the cuisine – *casados* are the mainstay – but it is cheap and filling. A much better standard of cuisine is provided by the all-inclusive eco-lodges of the surrounding area, some of which are open to the public (*see* above).

Nightlife in Puerto Viejo de Sarapiquí

Entertainment consists of a small collection of slightly grim, slightly seedy bars which can get very boisterous on Friday nights (pay day for plantation workers). Monday is probably your best bet for a quiet drink, if that's what you prefer.

Around Puerto Viejo de Sarapiquí

La Virgen

White-water Rafting

The area's main **white-water rafting** centre is the small banana town of La Virgen, 19km west of Puerto Viejo. The waters here aren't quite as fearsome and foamy as those of the Río Pacuare (see p.155), but are quite challenging enough if this is your first rafting trip.

. The stretch between the town and the village of **Chilamate** downriver has been designated a Class III section of rapids – perfect for beginners. The more intense IV–V class rapids further upriver are perhaps best left to experienced rafters and adrenaline junkies.

If that all sounds a bit frenetic, it's also possible to take gentler wildlife-spotting kayak tours along the river's lower course. The peak rafting months are August–November, when increased levels of rainfall make the rapids even more rapid, although trips are available all year round.

Tour Operators
Rancho Leona,
t 761 1019, www.
ranchaleona.com
Aventuras del
Sarapiquí, t 766 6768,
www.sarapiqui.com
Sarapiquí Outdoor
Centre, t 761 1123

There are several **tour operators** in town offering trips (see left), with prices ranging from $40–75 depending on the difficulty and length of the trip. It's also possible to book through several San José-based operators (see p.69), which should include pick-up from your San José hotel and lunch, although it will cost a good $30 more.

Jardín de Serpientes
t 761 1059; open
9–6.30; adm

The town's other major attraction is its **Jardín de Serpientes** or 'snake garden', which has over 40 species of snake, as well as reptiles and frogs.

Estación Biológica La Selva

Estación Biológica La Selva
t 766 6565,
laselva@sloth.ots.ac.cr

Run by the Organization for Tropical Studies and funded by universities from all over North and South America, the not-for-profit La Selva Research Station, 3km southwest of Puerto Viejo, oversees a 1,500ha territory on the border of the Parque Nacional Braulio Carrillo, including areas of both primary premontaine rainforest and secondary forest on reclaimed agricultural land. This forest acts as a sort of natural laboratory for the station, whose main purpose is to study the flora and fauna of the local environment in order to devise new and sustainable methods of managing the country's tropical resources. The centre's work is hugely respected, its experimental gardens attracting visiting scientists and biologists from all over the world.

As admirable as all this is, however, it's not really the reason why you're here; that's to visit and explore the outdoor laboratory itself,

Getting to La Selva

From San José, you'll need to catch either the 7am **bus** (for the 8.30am tour) or the 11am bus (for the 1.30pm tour) from the Caribbean bus terminal at C 0, Av 11. The destination on the front of the bus will say 'Río Frío'. Ask to be let off at the station. The driver will drop you on the main road, from where it's a 1.5km walk to the station entrance (signposted). Alternatively, you can take a **taxi** direct to the station from Puerto Viejo.

whose variety of habitats – including forest, swamps and rivers – provide a home to over 400 species of bird (it welcomes birders from all over the world), 500 species of butterfly and 200 species of mammal (including over 70 species of bat alone). It's a doggedly wet environment, receiving over 4m of rain year. Even with the sun out, there are parts of the forest that never truly dry out, so bring raingear with you (and, ideally, rubber boots). Thankfully, around a fifth of the station's 50km of trails are concrete, making walking that bit easier. The station's grounds can only be explored as part of a pre-booked **guided tour** (unless staying at the on-site lodge, *see* below), which leave at 8am and 1.30pm every day and cost $25 for a four-hour hike. The station also offers less regular dawn and twilight walks ($40), which offer the best opportunities for getting a look at all those bats.

Rara Avis

Rara Avis
t 764 3131,
www.raraavis.com

Rara Avis seems to pride itself on its hardcore approach to nature-watching. This private 160ha reserve high on the northeastern slopes of the Central Mountains, 17km south of Puerto Viejo, does not welcome casual visitors. Only the most dedicated tourists, willing to stay at least one night and brave an incredibly bumpy ascent in a tractor-drawn cart, make it here. The reserve sits on the border of Braulio Carrillo National Park (*see* pp.143–6) and has much

Where to Stay in La Selva

You'll need to reserve ahead if you're hoping to stay in the station's own accommodation, which tends to be booked up right through the high season. This is surprising, given that's it's hardly cheap, and hardly luxurious. Your $65 per person will get you a room in a university-like communal dormitory, three meals a day (served in a refectory), a guided walk and, best of all, access to the station's trails.

Where to Stay at Rara Avis

⭐ **Rara Avis ≫**

Your level of comfort here will depend on how much roughing it you're prepared to do, and the size of your bank balance.

If you decide to continue the puritan approach, as exemplified by the tractor ride, you can take a basic, forest-set **cabin** (albeit for the not very basic price of $90 for two) with kerosene lamps (there's no electricity) and cold-water showers.

An extra $40 will get you access to hot water in the **Waterfall Lodge** ($130), while the top-of-the-range **River Edge Cabin** ($180) has access to solar-powered electricity and hot water and has become a popular honeymoon option. Prices include transport (i.e. the tractor ride), guided tours and all meals, which, thankfully dispensing with the puritan theme, are great *comida típica* feasts served in a communal restaurant.

Getting to Rara Avis

There's only one option. Be sure to inform the reserve in advance of your arrival time, then take the 'Río Frío' **bus** at 7am from San José, C 0, Av 11, to the small village of **Horquetas** (ask the driver to let you off at Rara Avis) where you'll be met by the tractor driver. If there's a problem, the Rara Avis office is located just down the road opposite the village school. You'll enjoy some wonderful views as you ascend; that's if you can focus on anything while you attempt to stay upright in the bumping, banging cart as it makes its slow climb up the sodden track. If it's too wet, the driver may ask you to get out and walk for a while (bring some rubber boots with you).

the same climate (albeit even wetter) and vegetation (only even denser). Over 350 species of bird, as well as plenty of mammals – including monkeys, sloths, coatis and tapirs – make their home here among the forest depths. There are over a dozen marked **trails** – one of the best, the **Sendero Platanill**, provides a good three hours' worth of challenging hiking and leads to a **waterfall** with adjacent swimming hole – as well as a **butterfly house** and **orchid garden**.

Volcán Arenal and Around

After several centuries spent lying dormant, Volcán Arenal came back to life with a bang on 29 July 1968, literally blowing its top to send a superheated torrent of gas, ash and lava (technically but not quite so emotively known as a 'pyroclastic flow') spewing over the surrounding area destroying two villages, numerous farms and killing over 80 people (none of whom had the least expectation of what was about to befall them). It's been awake and active ever since, although not always in an entirely uniform way. Sometimes the volcano is fully alert, bright-eyed and bushy-tailed, flinging rocks high into the air and oozing molten lava. At other times, it seems happy to slumber dozily, contenting itself with the odd threatening rumble and belch of sulphurous gases. Thankfully, from a visitor's perspective, the next spectacular show is never too far away.

For the most part, this activity poses little danger to the local communities. Still, it pays to show a healthy respect. Volcanoes are notoriously unpredictable. The last major eruption in 1998 damaged roads and hotels thought at the time to lie way beyond the volcano's reach, providing a timely reminder of the potential power and fury waiting to be unleashed by this most brutal and unforgiving of natural phenomena. More tragically, in 2000, a local guide and his charges were killed when lava erupted out of the volcano's previously 'safe' east side (note: there is no safe side). Don't be fooled by the locals' affectedly casual disregard for the constant seismic growls; this is potentially a very dangerous area and you should exercise the utmost caution during your visit here. Stay clear of the volcano's slopes and, whatever you do, make no attempt to climb to the summit. It's bad enough that you'd be risking your own life, but unforgivable that you should be putting in danger the lives of those who would be obliged to attempt a rescue.

To give yourself the best chance of seeing the volcano in all its fiery glory, you should ideally aim to stay in the region for a couple of days or more. The dampness of the climate means that it can be pretty much guaranteed that the summit of the volcano will be obscured by cloud and mist on at least one of these days (in the rainy season, probably more than one). The best views tend to be at night, when you may be able to see the bright red lava flow glowing against a jet-black sky (it can be harder to pick out in the day), a natural firework display more impressive than anything you'll see on 5 November or 4 July.

The former farming community of La Fortuna, just 6km east of the summit, is the main tourist base for viewing Arenal, its small rural confines now filled with hotels, restaurants and tour operators.

La Fortuna

It's not easy to go from being a small, relatively isolated farming community to one of the country's most visited and high-profile tourist towns in just a couple of decades and still maintain a sense of identity. But La Fortuna seems to be managing it (just about). Despite its huge success, as shown by the wealth of businesses lining its streets, the town has retained a distinct rural Tico feel to it. Many of its hotels, bars and restaurants are lovely, quiet family-run places where you can sit and chat with the locals. The flip side to this relaxed, friendly vibe is the slightly unpleasant in-your-face commercialism you'll encounter out on the streets. Here, you'll often find yourself besieged and beseeched by an army of touts all trying to get you to sign up with their particular tour operator (whatever bargains they may be offering, these are best avoided; see p.269).

The reason for all this activity lies just 6km west. On a clear day (and even more so on a clear night), the town offers spectacular views of one of the most active volcanoes in the entire western hemisphere, a mighty vent leading straight down into the bowels of the earth (or, as it's technically known, a magma chamber) out of which floods of flaming hot lava regularly pour. Sadly, the crucial clause of that last sentence is 'on a clear day'. This is a very wet, cloudy region where clear days are by no means guaranteed. In the rainy season, the summit can remain submerged in mist for days at a time. Indeed, many visitors, perhaps as many as half, never catch sight of the volcano's peak during the entire duration of their stay.

This situation would be more frustrating than it sounds were it not for the fact that the town and the region offer such a wealth of alternative attractions and activities. The volcano may be the biggest and brightest spectacle around, but it's by no means the only show

Getting to La Fortuna

There are three direct **bus** services a day between San José and La Fortuna, leaving at 6.15am, 8.40am and 11.30am from C 12, Av 7/9. The journey takes 4½hrs and costs c1,130. Alternatively, for around c100 extra, plus an extra hour and a half or so's travelling time, you can catch the bus to Ciudad Quesada from the same stop (hourly from 5am–7.30pm, 3 hrs, c820), and then connect with one of the seven daily La Fortuna services at 6am, 10.30am, 1pm, 3.30pm, 5.15pm, 6pm and 8pm (2hrs, c405). All buses pull up on La Fortuna's main road on the south side of the Parque Central.

If **driving** from San José, follow the Interamericana (HWY-1) north to the Naranjo exit, then head north along HWY-141 to Ciudad Quesada, from where you can follow the tourist signs (they're marked with a volcano icon) west to the town. If coming from the northwest, be aware that the motorway around the northern shore of Lake Arenal is in a particularly poor state of repair.

Getting away from La Fortuna

Depending on your inclination (and financial reserves), travelling from La Fortuna to Monteverde can either be quite an adventure, or just another bus journey (albeit just another bus journey offering magnificent views of a volcano and the largest lake in the country).

Cash-strapped **bus** travellers will need to catch the 8am or 5pm service, which will take them all the way along the northern and western shores of Lake Arenal to the town of Tilarán (3hrs), from where you can pick up a connecting service to Santa Elena (a further 3hrs away) – quite a round-trip to get to somewhere that actually lies around 25km directly southwest. If you've got $30 to spare, you can reach Monteverde in around 3hrs using the **Jeep/Boat/Jeep** service. A 4WD taxi takes you from La Fortuna to Lake Arenal, where a boat will whisk you across the water to another 4WD taxi waiting on the other side, in which you will complete the final leg of your journey to Santa Elena. Any hotel or tour operator in town can arrange it, or call t 645 5051.

It's also possible to reach Monteverde on **horseback**, although this will take around twice as long and cost around twice as much. For details, see p.248.

You can also catch **bus** services from Tilarán to Liberia and the Nicoya Peninsula beaches. Six buses a day run from La Fortuna to Ciudad Quesada, at 5am, 6.30am, 7.30am, 12.30pm, 3.30pm and 5.30pm, from where you can connect with services to Puerto Viejo de Sarapiquí and San José. There are also two direct services from La Fortuna to San José a day at 12.45pm and 2.45pm. The journey takes 4½hrs and costs c1,130.

in town. To the south is a set of spectacular waterfalls, **La Catarata de Fortuna**; to the west a collection of volcanic hot springs and beyond that the **Laguna de Arenal** (Lake Arenal), where you can enjoy windsurfing and fishing, while slightly further afield are the wildlife refuge of **Caño Negro** (to the north) and the cloudforests of **Monteverde** (to the southwest; see pp.236–52). With La Fortuna filled with tour operators, you can also really pack in the activities here – rainforest hikes, birdwatching, mountain-biking, horse-riding, sailing, canyoning, canopy tours, white-water rafting, canoeing, windsurfing, fishing, quad-biking... the list goes on. Indeed, you may find that, in amongst the hurly- burly of doing other things, you've forgotten to do any volcano-viewing at all.

Despite its emergence over the past couple of decades as one of the country's leading tourist towns, La Fortuna remains a relatively small, compact place of just a dozen or so interconnecting streets, although that's not to say that it has remained completely unchanged or undeveloped. Its few streets are now all packed nose-to-tail with hotels, restaurants and, above all, tour operators. Some of the roads do have (recently added) names: there's an **Avenida Central** (the main road), an **Avenida Fortuna** and an **Avenida Arenal**,

Getting to the Catarata

If you want to get to the waterfalls a bit quicker than walking, you could hire a bike from **Bike Arenal** (t 479 9454), book a horse-riding tour with **Pura Vida Tours** (*see* p.269) or, the quickest (but also the least romantic) option, take a **taxi** from town (around $4).

but almost nobody uses them (hardly surprising, given that the town's official name, 'La Fortuna de San Carlos', is hardly used either). As with almost everywhere else in the country, directions here are given using landmarks, the most prominent being the **Parque Central**, which more or less marks the centre of the town, and the pretty **Iglesia de San Juan Bosco** on its western side. And if you do get at all disorientated, just remember, the volcano is directly west. The view of the little church with the volcano looming menacingly behind it has become the souvenir snapshot of the town, and indeed has become a sort of icon of the country (albeit a slightly ironic one given that the picture appears to show something man-made being overwhelmed by nature; the exact opposite of what's actually happening throughout much of the country).

12 The North | La Fortuna

La Catarata de Fortuna (Fortuna Waterfall)

La Catarata
de Fortuna
open 8–5; adm

6km south of La Fortuna are two spectacular waterfalls, where the Río Fortuna tumbles over a couple of heavily forested escarpments. Reaching them involves a challenging, but ultimately rewarding, hike. Head south along the road one block west of the Parque Central for about a kilometre, then follow the signs along a fairly steep path that wends its way past local farms to the entrance (around a 2hr walk in total). From here, it's a further 20–30min trek down a narrow path (often rather slippery, so watch your step), after which you'll be rewarded with great views of a tumbling river of water seemingly erupting out of the forest canopy. The tallest waterfall drops over 70m and looks like someone's idea of a fairytale tropical cascade – a sheer white torrent crashing down into a frothing plunge pool (be sure to wear waterproof clothing). As inviting as the pool looks, and despite the fact that people will inevitably be doing it when you visit, you should really obey the signs and refrain from swimming here – the water is travelling at quite some velocity when it hits the bottom, stirring up all manner of currents. There are some safer swimming holes downstream.

Hot Springs

 Tabacón Resort
*t 256 1500, www.
tabacon.com; open
daily 10–10; adm
10–7 $29, 7–10 $19*

Several bathing complexes have been built around La Fortuna in the past couple of decades to take advantage of the natural volcanic hot springs that dot the area.

The most popular (and most expensive), the **Tabacón Resort**, is located 12km west of town and is often visited as part of a combined tour with the Parque Nacional Volcán Arenal. It offers a sort of kitschy luxuriousness with 10 pools, ranging in temperature from the steamy (40°C) to the merely lukewarm (25°C), occupying a lush landscaped setting adorned with artificial waterfalls, cascades and caves. There's also a gourmet restaurant and a swim-up bar, where you can order a drink, settle back in your pool and hope the mists clear long enough (and you stay sober enough) for you to enjoy the views of the pyrotechnics atop the volcano. To be honest, it can feel a bit cheesily decadent, sitting at the poolside in your swimming costume drinking cocktails waiting for a volcano to explode, like a 1970s Martini advert, but it's undeniably enjoyable. The resort also has a spa offering a range of beauty treatments – mud packs, hydrotherapy, etc. – as well as a rather fancy hotel, the junior suites of which have Jacuzzis for guests who just can't get enough superheated water.

Las Fuentes Termales, just across the road and operated by the same management, offer slightly cheaper volcanic bathing, principally because you can't see the volcano from here. The closest springs to town are the **Baldi Termae**, just 4km west, next to the Volcán Look disco, which boasts the region's hottest pools (the very hottest is a bright-pink-skin-inducing 67°C), and the new, rather swish **Eco Termales**, just across the road.

Las Fuentes Termales
t 256 1500, www. tabacon.com; adm $10

Baldi Termae
t 479 9051; adm $10

Eco Termales
t 479 8484; adm $14

Choosing a Tour Operator

There's plenty to do in and around La Fortuna. Unfortunately, most of it costs money and, as you pile in the activities, the bills can quickly start to mount up. For this reason, the tour touts who approach you on the street (and they will approach you, probably within a few minutes of your arrival in town) can seem like a godsend, offering a range of tours and activities for a fraction of what you might normally expect to pay – and with a free lunch thrown in.

The trouble is, whatever the touts may say, there's no such thing as a free lunch. While some of these hustlers do represent genuine, professionally run tour operators, there are an awful lot who represent ones who are neither. Finding yourself on a poorly managed, slipshod tour is a pretty vexing experience, but it's nothing compared to discovering (once you've handed over your money, of course) that there isn't even a tour to go on. Unfortunately, over the past few years La Fortuna seems to have become the unofficial headquarters of the Costa Rican scamsters' union, with groups of conmen signing up tourists for non-existent tours, getting the cash in advance and then taking off as soon as their 'clients' are out of sight.

As a basic rule of thumb, don't buy anything from anyone until you've first visited their offices (to check, apart from anything else, that they do indeed have an office where you can return to take up any grievance). For your own peace of mind, deal only with established, reputable organizations. They may cost a bit more, but at least you know you'll get what you pay for. The larger your group, the better the discount you'll be able to negotiate.

The most popular tour, offered by every operator in town, involves a hike around Volcán Arenal, a visit to (and a dip into) the hot springs at Balneario Tabacón, followed by dinner. This should cost between $45–55 per person, depending on how many of you there are, including all entrance fees (which will otherwise add another $30 or so). Most tour operators will also be able to offer all, or at least some, of the following: windsurfing and fishing on Lake Arenal; day trips to the Monteverde Cloudforest Reserve (*see* pp.241–3), Venado Caves (*see* p.275) and Caño Negro (*see* p.277); white-water rafting on the Río Sarapiquí; canopy tours, quad-biking and horse-riding. Most of the town's hotels can offer tours. Otherwise, some of the town's most respected and longest-established operators are listed in the box, right.

Tourist Information in La Fortuna

There's no official tourist office, but La Fortuna's streets are lined with tour operators (and indeed filled with their representatives hustling for custom) who can provide you with details of the area's attractions, plus the inevitable sales pitch for their own services. For the best (and safest) advice, stick to well-known established operators (see box, 'Choosing a Tour Operator', left, and 'Tours', below).

Services in La Fortuna

All the services you need, including banks with ATMs (including branches of the Banco Popular and Banco Nacional), Internet cafés, supermarkets and car rental offices can be found on the main road (Avenida Central) on or around the Parque Central.

Tours around La Fortuna

You need to be very careful when choosing a tour operator; see box, left. Most of the hotels can offer tours. Some of the town's most respected and longest-established operators are:

Desafio Adventure Center, t 479 9464, *www.desafiocostarica.com*. As well as all the mainstays, Desafio offers white-water rafting, horse-riding (as far as Monteverde, if you have the stamina for it) and trips to the Guatuso Indigenous Reserve. It also has an Internet café and a book exchange.

Jacamar Naturalist Tours, t 479 9767, *www.arenaltours.com*. Offers a wide variety of tours: rainforest hikes, canoeing, tree-planting, night-time torchlit nature walks, birdwatching...

Pura Vida Tours, t 479 9045, *puravidatours@racsa.co.cr, www.pura vidatrips.com*. 'Pure Life' tours offers horse-riding trips to local waterfalls, among numerous other options.

Sunset Tours, t 479 9800, *www. sunsettourscr.com*. Highly experienced, long-established tour operator providing all the major tours as well as canoeing trips and tours to Guatuso Indigenous Reserve (see p.275).

Where to Stay in La Fortuna

In La Fortuna, as is customary in many of Costa Rica's major tourist centres, there is a strict demarcation between budget accommodation, which tends to be situated in town, and the more expensive places, which are mainly found on the outskirts. The area's very best lodges are located west of town towards the Parque Nacional Volcán Arenal and on the road running north around Lake Arenal (see pp.274–5), several of which offer stupendous volcano views.

In La Fortuna itself, the ever-increasing competition for custom has led to many hotel owners trying to pre-empt their rivals by meeting the public buses as they arrive in town in order to solicit for custom (or employing touts to do so on their behalf). While this was once a relatively innocent way of drumming up extra business, there have been increased instances of touts using a variety of scams in order to secure their commissions – telling you the hotel at which you're booked if full/closed down, etc. As such, you're probably best off ignoring them all, which is a bit of a shame for honest hoteliers.

Though most in-town choices are just simple *cabinas* with few of the facilities you'll find in the out of town places (some of which are very luxurious), La Fortuna has some lovely family-run establishments with friendly owners who'll go out of their way to get you the best prices on local tours. Every hotel, whether big, small, budget, luxury or otherwise, can arrange tours.

Hotel Arenal Country Inn, 1km south of La Fortuna on San Ramón Road, t 479 9670, *www.arenalcountryinn.com* ($$$$; $96). Nice, bright modern cabins occupying the extensive grounds of a former ranch, all with two queen-sized beds, air-conditioning, minibar, telephone and, last but not least, patios with volcano views. There are two pools (one for adults, one for children) and an open-air restaurant occupying the ranch's former stables, where breakfast (included in the price) is served.

Luigi's Lodge, La Fortuna, main road, three blocks west of Parque Central, **t** 479 9909, *www.luigislodge.com* ($$$; $70). One of the town's more upmarket offerings, Luigi's offers perhaps the best volcano views in town. Its 23 rooms all have carpets, private bathrooms (with marble bathtubs), air-conditioning, minibars, coffee-makers and balconies with volcano views. Some also have TVs. There's also a pool, a Jacuzzi, a gym (open to non-guests) and a pizza restaurant (also open to the public). Internet access and laundry service available. The price includes breakfast.

(★) Cabinas Cerro Chato >

Cabinas Cerro Chato, west of La Fortuna, **t** 479 9494, *www.geocities. com/cerrochato.cr* ($$; $35). Located at the end of a dirt track around 1km from the main Arenal road (phone for a free transfer from La Fortuna), this rural jewel represents something of a bargain. The rooms are simple but comfortable, all with private bathrooms, and you can also camp in the grounds for $3. A variety of tours (including horse-riding, $25) are offered. Breakfast is $2 extra.

Cabinas Adriana, La Fortuna, one block south and three blocks west of Parque Central, **t** 479 9454 ($; $6–4). Simple accommodation, aimed squarely at the backbacker market with clean well-maintained dorms ($4 per person) and, for those wanting to splash out a little, a couple of decent doubles with private bathrooms (cold water only) for $6 per person. Bikes can be hired. Breakfast is an extra $2.

Cabinas El Bosque, La Fortuna, one block west of Parque Central, **t** 479 9365 ($; $20). This looks a touch tatty from the outside, but it's clean and tidy within. The rooms are spick and span with TVs and private bathrooms (hot water). A range of tours is offered.

Cabinas Carmela, La Fortuna, main road, across from southwest corner of Parque Central, **t** 479 9010, *cabinascarmela@racsa.co.cr* ($; $25). Near the bus stop, this family-run hotel is a good budget self-catering choice; its well-equipped apartments come with fridges, cable TV, fans and hot showers. Some also have balconies (the views are only of the Parque Central rather than the volcano, but still) and

there's a communal kitchen. Parking is available.

Cabinas Sissy, La Fortuna, one block south, one and a half blocks west of Parque Central, **t** 479 9256 ($; $18). The Sissy's 12 rooms come in two categories: basic, which means a bed, access to a shared bathroom and the communal kitchen, and little else; and slightly less basic, which have private bathrooms, fans, TVs and coffee-makers, although these still aren't exactly the height of luxury. You can also camp in the grounds for $3. The friendly owners offer a range of tours. Laundry service available

Hotel La Posada Inn, La Fortuna, main road, three blocks east of Parque Central, **t** 479 9793 ($; $5 per person). The town's absolutely rock-bottom cheapest accommodation, the Posada is where backpackers looking to save their few remaining dollars tend to end up. The rooms are pretty small and can be quite noisy, but are perfectly acceptable for the price (with fans, albeit not much else), and you have access to a shared bathroom (with hot water) and a communal kitchen – a great place to meet fellow cash-strapped travellers and swap tales of budgetary woe. And, if you can't stretch to the $5 (and providing you've brought your tent with you), you can camp in the grounds for just $1.50. Internet access available.

Eating Out in La Fortuna

Starting with the cheapest options: there are two **supermarkets** in La Fortuna, one on the southeast corner of the Parque Central, the other one block south and one block east. There are also several decent **bakeries** and **cafés**, as well as quite a few reasonably priced Tico restaurants offering the usual (if hardly inspiring) *gallo pinto/ casado* standards, and catering mainly to locals, hence the relative cheapness of the prices. More elaborate gourmet fare is provided by the area's upmarket lodges, some open to the public.

Restaurante La Brasitas, main road, two blocks west of Parque Central, **t** 479 9819. On the road heading out of town towards the national park, this serves up spicy Mexican/Costa Rican fare – fajitas, *casados*, etc. – as well as some good roast chicken. The garden seating offers volcano views.

Rancho La Cascada, in the northeast corner of the Parque Central, **t** 479 9145. Under a large thatched roof in the corner of the town's main square, this is probably the most visible restaurant in town. It's a bit touristy – its interior is adorned with the 'flags of all nations' and the menu employs a equally scattergun approach to cuisine encompassing everything from *casados* and *empanadas* to pasta, pizzas, steaks and American breakfasts, which you eat at long refectory style tables (mains $6–8). There's a large upstairs bar that becomes a popular club at weekends.

La Choza de Laurel, one block west of Parque Central, **t** 479 9231. Opening early for people *en route* to the volcano, La Choza has a sort kitschy, ersatz authenticity with its thatched roof, rustic décor and traditional wood-fired oven. It serves a standard, not to say slightly overpriced, Tico/ international menu (main courses from $7–10), although it does do excellent steaks. It's on the main road, so it can get crowded.

Lava Rocks, main road, just west of Parque Central, **t** 479 8039. Trendy café serving an imaginative selection of fish and seafood (for around $3–5) at its open-air counter.

Soda La Parada, on main road on south side of Parque Central, **t** 479 9547. This 24-hour soda (the only such soda in town) is the place to fortify yourself with coffee if you're trying to catch the 5am Tilarán bus. It does a good line in cheap pizzas ($2–4) and sandwiches ($1.50), which you can eat at the counter alongside similarly bleary-eyed locals.

Nightlife in La Fortuna

There's not much nightlife, but there are a few places to go – in terms of liveliness, you'd probably pitch La Fortuna somewhere between Jacó and Monteverde. Some of the best places include the **Rancho La Cascada** restaurant, **t** 479 9145, on the northeast corner of the Parque Central, which has an attached club that gets full at weekends; the disco pool bar (it's also a pretty decent pizza restaurant) **Vagabondo**, **t** 479 9565, 5km west of the town centre, which is open till 2am daily and stages live music on some weekends; and **Volcán Look**, **t** 479 9690, slightly further out, which claims to be rural Costa Rica's biggest disco (the biggest disco outside of San José) and has a dance floor 'booming with volcanic music', apparently.

Parque Nacional Volcán Arenal

⊕ **Parque Nacional Volcán Arenal**
t 461 8499; open daily 8–4; adm

Arenal is a classically volcanic-looking volcano: a giant sawn-off mountain housing a huge crater out of which red-hot lava regularly flows. It sits on what is known as, in geological terms, a subduction zone. This is where two tectonic plates push against each other until one plate is gradually (over millions of years) forced down beneath the other. As the rock making up the plate is pushed deep under-gound, it melts, becoming magma (liquid rock), which may in time be forced back up to the surface through a weak point in the crust, as has happened at Arenal. The 12,000ha park surrounding **Volcán Arenal** was created in 1995, not so much to protect the volcano, or even to protect local communities *from* the volcano (although this has been an important side effect), but in order to protect the watershed area feeding Lake Arenal to the west, and specifically to maintain the water supply to the **Arenal Dam**, the country's largest producer of hydroelectricity.

Getting to the Parque Nacional Volcán Arenal

Most people visit the park as part of a **guided tour**, although it is possible to visit independently. The park's main **ranger station** is located southwest of the volcano. To reach it, follow the road west out of La Fortuna for around 15km, then take the signed turn-off towards the park. The entrance is a further 2km on. You can also catch the Tilarán **bus** to the turn-off, and then walk to the entrance. A **taxi** from town will cost around $7.

Visiting the park after dark (which is when you'll get the best views) is only possible as part of an official tour group.

Reasons for visiting the park are twofold: to see the volcano close up (albeit still at a safe distance) and to trek the areas of dense forest that surround the great cone, which are home to a good deal of wildlife. Once upon a time this forest stretched right up to the volcano's summit, but its higher sections were, as you might imagine, completely vaporized following the 1968 eruption.

From the **ranger station**, three **trails** lead out into the forest and across lava fields to a number of **lookout points**. While the quality of the views will depend largely on the amount of cloud cover, you'll certainly hear a good deal. From inside the park, the explosions, as the volcano coughs up its daily expectoration of gases and boulders, can seem very loud (and not a touch unnerving). Just in case you don't see anything, the park's **visitor centre** (located west of the volcano near Lake Arenal) shows videos of some of the most spectacular past eruptions.

Where to Stay and Eat near the Parque Nacional Volcán Arenal

Hotel Jungla y Senderos Los Lagos, 6km west of La Fortuna, **t** 479 8000, *www.hotelloslagos.com* ($$$$; $85). There are probably safer places to stay, but then the same could be said of the entire area. In 2000, about 3km towards the volcano from here, a guide and his charges were caught and tragically killed by an unexpected eruption. A slightly larger one in the same direction might make it to the hotel next time or, of course, might miss it completely. In any case, the air of expectation gives the place a frisson of danger and excitement, exacerbated by its on-site **crocodile farm**. Otherwise, this is pretty standard lodge fare, with decent cabins set in attractive grounds (all with air-conditioning, fridges, cable TV), 2 pools (with connecting water slide), one heated via a natural hot spring, a swim-up bar and a good restaurant, **Las Palmas**.

Hotel Volcano Lodge, 7km west of La Fortuna, **t** 460 6080, *www.volcanolodgecostarica.com* ($$$$; $95). In lush grounds, this offers large, pleasantly furnished rooms, all with volcano views (they'd hardly be able to call themselves a 'Volcano Lodge' if things were otherwise), air-conditioning, cable TV, telephone, hairdryer and terraces with rocking chairs (so you can enjoy the vistas in comfort). Extra facilities include a swimming pool, a Jacuzzi, laundry service and a decent restaurant. Pice includes breakfast.

Montana de Fuego Resort and Spa, 9km west of La Fortuna, **t** 460 1220, *www.montanadefuego.com* ($$$$; $95). This large resort has 50 stylish hardwood cottages. You have a choice of standard (private bathroom, cable TV, ceiling fan) or, for $30 more, deluxe rooms (with air-conditioning, private porches, rocking chairs). All have volcano views. There's also a pool with a swim-up bar, a Jacuzzi, a fully equipped spa and a very good restaurant, **Acuarelas**, serving a hybrid Tico/international menu.

★ Arenal Observatory Lodge >

Arenal Observatory Lodge, 4km past entrance to park, signposted, **t** 290 7011, *www.arenal-observatory.co.cr* ($$$; $70). This lodge, founded in the 1980s by the US Smithsonian Institute, lies just 1.7km from the crater, which is about as close as you can legally get, making it the place to stay if you're really serious about volcano-watching. The rooms are nicely furnished, although, as they also have giant windows looking directly out onto Arenal (which looks almost close enough to touch), you probably won't notice. Extra facilities include a swimming pool, Jacuzzi and restaurant (all, of course, with stunning views). Even if you don't stay at the lodge, you can still tour its grounds, which are open to the public for $4 (or free if you eat in the restaurant, which would be considerably overpriced were it not for the fact that it looks directly onto an active volcano). Savings can be made if you can rustle up nine friends to stay at the **Villa**, which costs $350 a night.

Laguna de Arenal (Lake Arenal)

⓫ Lake Arenal

Costa Rica's biggest lake, measuring some 88 sq km, lies around 18km west of La Fortuna. It's largely man-made, most of it having been created in 1974 following the construction of a hydroelectric dam that now supplies much of the energy for the northwest of the country (the lake grew to such a size that it actually engulfed and submerged two entire villages). Today, the lake offers a number of activities for tourists, including fishing, sailing and, above all, windsurfing. Owing to the metronomic consistency of the winds here (in terms of both direction and strength), the lake has become one of the leading windsurfing destinations, not just in Costa Rica but in the whole of the Americas, with international teams decamping here to practise during the December–April season.

The lake's major town, **Nuevo Arenal** (New Arenal), lies on its northern shore, 29km west of La Fortuna. It was built in the 1970s to replace the original Arenal, which now lies at the bottom of the lake, and is home to a sizeable and growing number of hotels, many with volcano/lake views, as well as several windsurfing companies.

Arenal Botanical Garden

t 694 4305; open Mon–Sat 9–5; adm; fee includes guided 1hr tour

Hanging Bridges of Arenal

t 479 9686, www. hangingbridges.com; adm $20, or with guided tour $30, or with transport and tour $40

Other local attractions include: the **Arenal Botanical Garden**, 4km east of town, which has a pretty collection of tropical blooms, including numerous orchids, a butterfly garden and serpentarium; and the **Hanging Bridges of Arenal** (Puentes Colgantes de Arenal), near the Arenal Dam, a collection of canopy-set platforms giving you elevated views of a 250ha swath of forest. The complex can be visited independently, though for the best wildlife-spotting opportunities it's advisable to join one of the daily tours at 6am and 6pm.

The journey around the north shore of the lake to (and past) Nuevo Arenal is particularly scenic, offering great views of the volcano. You'll certainly have plenty of time to take it all in, as the road here is one of the worst maintained in the region, making driving necessarily slow and cautious. As you go, look out for the wind farms, set up on the northern shore to exploit the area's famous breezes.

Getting to Lake Arenal

One of the best ways to appreciate the lake's beauty is via the **Jeep/Boat/Jeep** crossing to Monteverde (*see* p.266). With somebody else obliged to concentrate on navigating and steering for a while, you're free to enjoy the majestic spectacle of the volcano rising up above the lake.

Two **buses** a day leave from La Fortuna to Tilarán, at 8am and 5.30pm, stopping at Nuevo Arenal *en route*.

From Nuevo Arenal, on the north shore of Lake Arenal, the main road continues west before looping around the far edge of the lake and then heading south to **Tilarán**, a small whitewashed village that has, like Nuevo Arenal, become a major centre of white-water rafting in recent years. It's also something of a regional transport hub, offering connections south to Monteverde and west to Cañas and on to Guanacaste. White-water rafting lessons and board rental are available from the Hotel Tilawa (*see* box, below).

Southwest of Tilarán, the dusty cowboy town of **Cañas** marks your return to the Interamericana and the start of Guanacaste, Costa Rica's driest province. Though of little interest in itself, it can serve as a base for trips to the Parque Nacional Palo Verde, 30km west (*see* p.174), and the Tenorio and Miravalles to the north (*see* p.276).

Sports and Activities around Lake Arenal

There are several companies in and around Nuevo Arenal and Tilarán offering windsurfing lessons, as well as board and wetsuit (the waters can be quite chilly) rental. Prices start at $40 for a half-day, $70 for a full day.

Tico Wind, Nuevo Arenal, t 692 2002, *www.ticowind.com*.

Rock River Lodge, Nuevo Arenal, t 692 1180.

Hotel Tilawa, Tilarán, t 695 5050, *www.hotel-tilawa.com*.

Where to Stay around Lake Arenal

Some of the area's very best lodges are located on the road running north around Lake Arenal. Most cater principally to all-inclusive tour packages, so you'll need to book well in advance to secure a booking in high season, particularly for those establishments near Nuevo Arenal.

La Ceiba Tree Lodge, 6km east of Nuevo Arenal, t 692 8050, *ceibaldg@ racsa.co.cr* ($$$; $64). Named in honour of a giant 500-year-old ceiba tree in its lovely gardens, which also provide a home to a multitude of birds and flowers, the lodge has five nicely decorated cabins, all with private baths and lake views, as well as a self-catering apartment. There are trails through the grounds, and fishing and sailing trips can be organized. Mountain bikes can also be hired.

Chalet Nicholas B&B, 2km east of Nuevo Arenal, t 694 4041, *nicholas@ racsa.co.cr, www.chaletnicholas.com* ($$$; $68). Canophobes beware: the owners of this charming B&B have five simply enormous Great Danes who like nothing better than jumping up at guests as they arrive (in a friendly fashion, of course; the hotel's ban on children under 10 is presumably nothing to do with an aversion to kids, rather a precaution to prevent them being squashed). There are just three large rooms perched on a hilltop in extensive gardens, all with private bathrooms, hot water and views of the lake and volcano. There isn't a restaurant, but the nearby **Restaurante Caballo Negro**, which serves up a slightly odd German/vegetarian combination menu, is recommended. The owners hire out horses and organize birdwatching trips, and also have a small orchid house. No smoking throughout.

Los Héroes Hotel, 14km west of La Fortuna, t 692 8012, *www.hotel losheroes.com* ($$$; $55). Swiss-style chalet hotel with spacious Alpine-esque rooms, all with private bathrooms and TVs. The large complex also incorporates a restaurant, a farm, a pool and a Jacuzzi as well as apartments that sleep up to six ($115). The price includes breakfast.

Lake Coter Eco-Lodge, 4km northeast of Nuevo Arenal, t 440 6768, *www. ecolodgecostarica.com* ($$$; $62). This smart lodge overlooking the region's 'other' lake is only accessible via a 3km unpaved track leading off from the main Arenal road. It caters mainly to all-inclusive packages, rather than casual trade, specializing in outdoor activity and nature-watching holidays. There's certainly plenty to do: guided tours through the lodge's own small private cloudforest reserve, horse-riding, kayaking, canopy tours, etc. Hopefully, you'll be so exhausted after all that, you won't notice that the rooms are a bit small and shabby-looking. Still, they all come with private bathrooms, coffee-makers and decent views of the lake.

Hotel Tilawa, Tilarán, t 695 5050, *www.hotel-tilawa.com* ($$$; from $60). Located 8km north of Tilarán, this is pretty easy to spot, having been designed to resemble an ancient Greek palace – all kitschy neoclassical columns and arches. It also offers a range of other activities including sailing, kite-surfing, tennis and even skateboarding (it's home to Central America's largest skate park).

Eating Out around Lake Arenal

Tom's Pan, Nuevo Arenal, t 694 4282. More than just a restaurant, Tom's Pan German bakery/delicatessen is a local meeting point and landmark, serving up a range of German dishes including sausages, breads (including pumpernickel), pastries (including strudel) and a range of tasty sandwiches. It also offers Internet access and there's even a room to rent at the back (which the owners claim has the only waterbed in the area).

North of Volcán Arenal

Venado Caves
t 478 8071; open daily
7–4; closed in wet
season; adm

Not far north of La Fortuna lie the **Venado Caves**, which have become an increasingly popular day (or more accurately half-day) excursion in recent years. This small network of intestinal limestone caverns would seem to conform to the dictionary definition of labyrinthine, its narrow, twisty passages adorned with floor-to-ceiling stalactites and stalagmites. It's a very wet environment, with dripping water everywhere, and can be a touch unnerving, especially if a giant spider or a disturbed bat decides to put in an appearance. Trips to the caves are offered by every tour operator in town for around $45, including lunch and transport. It's considerably cheaper to visit the caves on your own, although as the only bus serving the caves doesn't leave La Fortuna until 2pm, you won't actually get that much time to look around (but then the caves are quite small, so this shouldn't be too much of a problem).

Some tour operators also offer trips to the recently established **Guatuso Indigenous Reserve**, which lies just north of the caves. You can buy Guatuso crafts – carvings, instruments, etc. – in the small town of **San Rafael de Guatuso** which borders the reserve. The volcanoes Tenorio and Miravalles lie northwest of here.

Getting to Volcán Tenorio and Volcán Miravalles

Though the Tenorio park lies due north of the western end of Lake Arenal, getting to the entrance from here is much more complicated than you might imagine. As you can't actually travel due north, the park can only be accessed either by skirting around its western edge via a very poorly maintained dirt track connecting the lake road with HWY-6, or by backtracking, via Tilarán and Cañas, to the Interamericana, and then taking HWY-6 up towards **Bijagua**, the nearest town – a round trip of over 60km. Driving from San José is much more straightforward. You just head up the Interamericana past Cañas to HWY-6 and then follow the signs.

There's a regular **bus** service between Cañas and Upala that stops *en route* in Bijagua, as well as one service a day from San José, leaving at 3pm from C 12, Av 3/5. Unless you have your own transport, you'll have to take a taxi from Bijagua – a $24 round trip.

A **taxi** from **Bagaces** to the hot spring complexes of Volcán Miravalles will cost around $8.

The Northern Volcanoes

Parque Nacional Tenorio

**Parque Nacional
Tenorio**
*t 200 0135;
open daily 7–4*

Created in 1996, this is one of Costa Rica's newest national parks, and so has fewer facilities than many of its more established siblings. Encompassing an area of over 3,000 hectares, it surrounds the 1,916m **Volcán Tenorio**, which like Arenal is currently active, albeit in a much less spectacular way than its southern neighbour. Whereas Arenal spends its time regurgitating lava and flinging boulders into the air, Tenorio's activity takes the more sedate form of hot springs, bubbling mud pools and gaseous belches.

From the **ranger station**, two relatively short trails explore the volcano's lower reaches, which include sections of cloudforest, punctuated by numerous steam vents. One leads to the **Río Celeste**, whose startling blue colour is a result of dissolved volcanic minerals (there's a waterfall and swimming hole). Be sure not to stray from the officially designated areas, as much of the ground around here is superheated. The two-day hike required for the round-trip to the summit (which, unlike Arenal, is safe to visit) can only be undertaken with the explicit permission of the ranger station, and is best undertaken in the company of an official guide.

Volcán Miravalles

Volcán Tenorio is not the only volcano bordering HWY-6. To the west is its twin, the 2,028m Volcán Miravalles, Guanacaste's highest peak. As with Tenorio, Miravalles is active in a low-key sort of a way, its southern slopes, in particular, home to a number of steam vents and bubbling mud pools. The giant silver pipes you'll see sticking out of the ground here are part of the **Proyecto Geotérmico Miravalles**, the government's attempt to harness this subterranean energy to produce electricity, which was set up in the early 1990s. As most of the volcano lies out of bounds to the public, the only way you'll get to appreciate this thermal activity is by visiting some of the hot

(★) Albergue
Ecoturistico
Heliconia >>

Where to Stay near Volcán Tenorio

There are a few basic *cabinas* in Bijagua. However, to get the most out of the area, you'd be best off staying at one of the lodges nearer to the park, both of which offer rustic but comfortable rooms and a range of tours.

La Carolina Lodge, 6km from Bijagua, t 380 1656, *www.lacarolinalodge.com* ($$$; $90 including meals and tours). Its 100ha contain a dairy farm, forest, waterfalls and thermal springs (which

provide all the hot water), and are renowned for their birding.

Albergue Ecoturístico Heliconia, 3km from Bijagua, t 286 4204, *www. agroecoturismo.net* ($$$; $45 including breakfast). A six-room lodge, whose forested grounds have canopy-set hanging bridges, a butterfly garden and a snake collection and which offer sweeping panoramic views (on a clear day you can see Lake Nicaragua).

Cabinas Bijagua, Bijagua, t 466 8050 ($). Simple, clean rooms with private baths for around $10.

Thermo Mania
t 673 0233; adm

Yökö Hot Springs
t 673 0410; adm

spring complexes that have been erected around the volcano's base, including **Thermo Mania**, a sort of hot spring aquapark with pools, chutes, slides and even a go-cart track; and **Yökö Hot Springs**, which offers slightly more refined, sedate bathing.

The Northern Border Regions

Refugio Nacional de Vida Silvestre Caño Negro

(12) Refugio
Nacional de
Vida Silvestre
Caño Negro
*t 471 1309; open
6–4; adm*

The 26,000ha Caño Negro Refuge is renowned as one of the best birdwatching and fishing destinations in the entire country and, following the improvement of the local road system in recent years, has begun to welcome an increasing number of visitors. However, its relative isolation – less than 20km from the Nicaraguan border – and the difficulty of access here for much of the year means that it still lies some way off the main tourist trail.

Much of the park is made up of an enormous flood plain around the **Río Frío**. Every year during the wet season, the river bursts its banks to form a 8,000ha **lake** that attracts a vast agglomeration of resident and migratory wildfowl including storks, herons, anhingas, cormorants, ducks and egrets, as well as several rare species particularly sought after by dedicated birders, the roseate spoonbill and Nicaraguan grackle among them. Birds may be the most visible inhabitants, but they're by no means the refuge's only residents. Its watery depths also provide a home to an abundance of reptiles – iguanas, snakes, fresh water turtles, Jesus Christ lizards, caiman, crocodiles – plus plenty of fish (including the giant snook and tarpon so beloved of sports-fishermen) and (apparently) even a relatively healthy population of jaguars (not that you stand any chance of seeing them, of course, but it's nice to know they're there).

Getting to the Refugio Caño Negro

The advice changes according to the season. In the wet season, you can reach the refuge only via **boat** from Los Chiles or Puerto Viejo de Sarapiquí. In the dry months it is possible to **drive** to Caño Negro, which lies on the Los Chiles–Upala Road. Although local roads have been improved in recent years, the region's yearly deluge does take its toll on the road surfaces, and you should exercise caution. There are two **bus** services from San José, both leaving from C 12, Av 7/9. The first, to Upala, leaves twice a day at 3pm (via Cañas, 4hrs) and 3.45pm (via Ciudad Quesada/San Carlos, 5½hrs). You'll probably have to stay the night in Upala, where you can either book a tour or a taxi to the refuge. There's also a bus to Caño Negro from Upala at 11am. Buses from San José to Los Chiles take 5hrs and leave at 5.30am (which still gives you enough time to visit the park) and 3.30pm (which doesn't). Two buses connect Los Chiles with Caño Negro a day at 5am and 2pm.

From a viewing perspective, the refuge is actually best visited during the dry season, December to February, when the pounding heat effects a profound change upon the landscape. As parched and baked as the wet season is sodden and soggy, the dry season sees the park's vast sheet of water virtually disappear, contracting down to just a few pools, while the river itself is reduced to a virtual trickle. In all, the water level drops by an astonishing three metres in just a few months. This aids wildlife viewing in a number of ways: firstly, it makes it easier to get to the refuge, which during wetter periods can only be accessed via a boat journey of several hours; it allows you to explore parts of the refuge on foot, rather than having to remain entirely boat-bound as you must during the wet season; the dry season also happens to coincide with the arrival of the highest concentrations of migratory birds; and, last but not least, the drying up of the refuge's lakes serves to push the bird colonies into ever-closer proximity, making it much easier for visitors to spot them.

Entrance to the park is via the **ranger station**, which sits next to the dock in the tiny town of **Caño Negro**. Owing to the inconvenience of getting here, and because of the need to arrive as early in the morning as possible – birds are at their most active shortly after dawn – you should ideally come as part of an organized tour or, failing that, in the company of a guide who will be able to identify some of the more similar-looking species. Major tour operators and lodges in La Fortuna offer trips, as do many San José-based operators. You can also book tours locally in Caño Negro village – try **Cabinas Martin Pescador, t** 471 1369 – or in the border town of Los Chiles. A 2hr trip should cost around $40 (for five people or more).

Where to Stay in the Refugio Caño Negro

You can stay at the Caño Negro **ranger station** for $6 (book well in advance). The accommodation is basic (cold showers), but at least you'll be on hand for the optimum dawn viewings. You can also camp in the grounds for $2. You'll need to bring your own tent.

There are also a few lodges in the area. A couple of the best include the **Caño Nego Natural Lodge, t** 265 6370, www.canonegrolodge.com ($$$$; $86); and the **Caño Negro Fishing Club, t** 656 0071, www.canonegro.com ($$$; $55).

If staying in **Upala**, the **Hotel Upala, t** 470 0169 ($; $12) and the **Cabinas Maleku, t** 470 0142 ($; $16) both have clean, simple rooms.

Getting to Los Chiles

It's a pretty straightforward **drive** to Los Chiles from Ciudad Quesada. Head north along HWY-141 to Muelle, from where it's a straight 70km journey, passing a few minor villages and a great many sugar cane planta-tions, to the town.

Two **buses** a day make the journey from San José, at 5.30am and 3.30pm (returning at 5am and 3pm). It takes 5hrs and costs c1,515, leaving from C 12, Av 7/9. Buses depart hourly to the town from Ciudad Quesada.

Los Chiles and the Nicaraguan Border

The northern zone's most northerly town lies just 3km from Nicaragua. Though an important crossing point, it's still considerably less busy than Peñas Blancas (*see* pp.173–4) to the west on the Interamericana. This is partly because the crossing from here into Nicaragua has to be made by boat along the Río Frío, the road crossing being reserved for government officials (although there are apparently plans to open up the land route at some indeterminate point in the future).

The small town, which is home to just 8,000 inhabitants, conforms to the simple template repeated throughout the country of a few dusty streets surrounding a football field. As provincial, rural and innocent as the town now looks, it did enjoy a somewhat politically charged status in the 1980s when it was used to shuttle supplies (including guns) to Contra rebels fighting the Sandanista govern-ment in Nicaragua (around 40 per cent of the town's population is of Nicaraguan descent).

Today, the town still has a slightly edgy atmosphere to it, perhaps best described as sleepy but watchful, like a lightly dozing guard dog whose tail continues to twitch.

They've only been allowing foreign nationals to cross the border here since the 1990s, and you get the feeling they're still not entirely used to it, although the town's recent transformation into a minor tourist centre servicing travellers en route to the Caño Negro refuge has helped it to relax a little.

There is a branch of the Banco Nacional in town, although you shouldn't necessarily count on its ATM working.

Crossing into Nicaragua

So long as you remain courteous and polite to the officials and have all the relevant documentation with you, your crossing should be smooth and untroubled. You'll need some US dollars in order to pay the entry tax into Nicaragua (the land exit tax from Costa Rica was abolished a few years ago).

To cross, you must first present your passport to *Migración*, which is situated near the dock, open 8am–5pm. The Nicaraguan entry tax currently stands at $9 till noon, $12 after that and at weekends.

The crossing boat timetable is not fixed, and is liable to change according to demand, but in high season, when the border sees a lot of day-trippers travelling to Lake Nicaragua and back, there are around five sailings a day, at 9am, 11am, 1pm, 2.30pm and 4pm, although this can drop to just two sailings (1pm and 4pm) during less busy times of year.

Where to Stay in Los Chiles

There are several hotels in town, including **Cabinas Jabiru**, **t** 471 1055 ($; $10), which has clean rooms with TVs; and the **Rancho Tulipan**, **t** 471 1414 ($$; $30), the town's most upmarket hotel, which is located right next to the docks. Both offer tours to the nearby Caño Negro refuge.

The South and the Osa Peninsula

Traditionally one of the country's least visited regions, Costa Rica's southern zone is becoming an increasingly popular destination, particularly with nature-watchers en route to the Parque Nacional Corcovado in the Osa Peninsula, which contains some of the largest and best-preserved swaths of primary rainforest to be found anywhere outside of the Amazon Basin. As a whole, the region still welcomes just a fraction of the holidaymakers who pour into the North Pacific resorts each year, but visitor numbers, and levels of development, are growing steadily.

13

Don't miss

1 Sunsets and luxury
Bahía Drake **p.315**

2 Coral reefs and ancient mysteries
Isla del Caño **p.317**

3 Costa Rica's highest peak
Chirripó **p.287**

4 Wildlife-spotting supreme
Parque Nacional Corcovado **p.319**

5 Whale-watching
Parque Nacional Marino Ballena **p.294**

See map overleaf

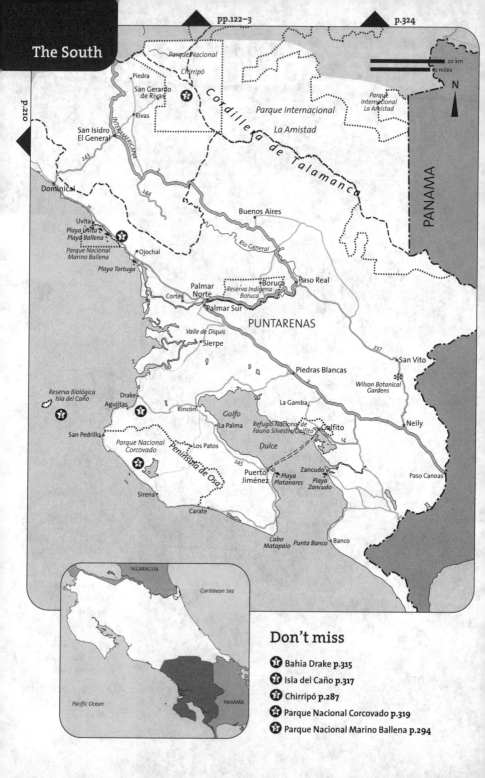

The South

pp.122–3
p.324
p.210

20 km
10 miles

N

Parque Nacional
Chirripó

Piedra

San Gerardo
de Rivas

Rivas

Cordillera de Talamanca

Parque Internacional
La Amistad

Parque
Internacional
La Amistad

PANAMA

San Isidro
El General

INTERAMERICANA

Dominical

244

Buenos Aires

Uvita
Playa Uvita
Playa Ballena

Parque Nacional
Marino Ballena

Ojochal

Río General

Playa Tortuga

Palmar
Norte

Boruca
Reserva Indígena
Boruca

Paso Real

Cortes

Palmar Sur

PUNTARENAS

Valle de Diquís

Sierpe

237

San Vito

Piedras Blancas

Wilson Botanical
Gardens

Reserva Biológica
Isla del Caño

Drake
Agujitas

Rincón

Golfo

La Gamba

Neily

San Pedrillo

Parque Nacional
Corcovado

Península de Osa

La Palma

Los Patos

Refugio Nacional de
Fauna Silvestre Golfito

Dulce

Golfito

245

14

Sirena

Puerto
Jiménez

Playa
Platanares

Zancudo

Playa
Zancudo

Paso Canoas

Carate

Cabo
Matapalo

Punta Banco

Banco

NICARAGUA

Caribbean Sea

Pacific Ocean

PANAMA

Don't miss

⭐ Bahía Drake **p.315**

⭐ Isla del Caño **p.317**

⭐ Chirripó **p.287**

⭐ Parque Nacional Corcovado **p.319**

⭐ Parque Nacional Marino Ballena **p.294**

It certainly looks as if mass tourism – and all its attendant environmental problems – has begun to make its inexorable progress south. Every year the creeping fog of resort culture spreads a few more kilometres further down the coast. First comes the improvement of the roads, then the introduction of power and phone lines, then the buying up of coastal land ready for the construction of hotels, lodges, restaurants, supermarkets, surf schools and every other business and facility that together make the tropics palatable for Western, first-world tastes. Turn your head for a moment, and when you look back you'll probably find that yet another 'peaceful, traditional fishing village' has been transformed into the latest 'tropical beachfront resort'. For now, the southern zone stands on the threshold of change. It still boasts some of the most remote and unspoilt stretches of coast in the entire country, but, with eager developers poised to pounce, it's debatable how much longer this will remain the situation. The surfing centre of Dominical is currently mass tourism's frontier town, marking the outer reaches of a sustained campaign of development that, without better official regulation, could in a few decades engulf the entire Pacific seaboard.

Of course, there's much more to the southern zone than coastline, as you might expect from a region that stretches from just south of Cartago in the Valle Central all the way down to the Panamanian border, and from the Pacific coast right across the country almost to the Caribbean lowlands – and which can comfortably fit within its boundaries the country's largest national park, the **Parque Internacional La Amistad**, a giant life corridor linking Costa Rica with Panama. The southern zone encompasses a huge variety of landscapes, from the mountains of the Cordillera de Talamanca – which include the 3,819m Cerro Chirripó, Costa Rica's highest peak – to the lowland forests of the Osa Peninsula; and an almost equally varied number of climates. Generally speaking, the northern half of the region, particularly its coastal areas, enjoys a standard two-season year: wet from May to November; dry from December to April. The region's southern half, however, has a much less uniform climate, perhaps best characterized as a sort of permanent wet season – the Osa Peninsula can receive over 5m of rain a year – punctuated by unpredictable but sustained periods of dry weather.

Major attractions, aside from the aforementioned national parks of Corcovado and La Amistad and their copious wildlife, include: the beautiful remote settlements of **Bahía Drake**, which can offer some of the most stunning sunset views to be enjoyed anywhere along the Pacific coast; the tax-free haven of **Golfito**; and, offshore, the **Reserva Biológica Isla del Caño**, with its famous lithic spheres – giant stone balls carved by the Diquis indigenous tribe that represent some of the only significant physical evidence remaining of the country's pre-Columbian past.

Getting around the South

The Osa Peninsula aside, where road coverage is minimal and road maintenance almost non-existent, getting around the southern zone is pretty straightforward. The **Interamericana** runs south from San José straight through the centre of the region down to the Panamanian border at Paso Canoas. For most of its length, this represents relatively hassle-free driving, although it should be noted that the northern section between Cartago and San Isidro El General, which ascends 2,000m over the **Cerro de la Muerte** ('The Mountain of Death'), offers one of the hairiest stretches of motoring to be found anywhere in the country (*see* box, opposite page).

San Isidro El General is the region's main transport hub, where you can catch buses to all the principal mainland towns. Reaching the southern zone's beaches has become a lot easier in the past few years, following the paving of the coastal road.

In the **Osa Peninsula**, different transport rules apply. The roads here have understandably been kept in a poor condition so as to prevent the delicate environment of Corcovado National Park from being overwhelmed. Getting around will require a little more dedication than on the mainland. The bus network only runs as far as Puerto Jiménez, after which you'll either have to make your own way in the sturdiest of 4WDs – although be aware that, in the wet season, the road to Carate may become completely impassable – or by taking the region's open-back truck-taxis which trundle the roads collecting passengers as they go, and are known, appropriately enough, as *colectivos*.

If your budget can stretch to it, it's worth paying the extra to fly into Osa. Costa Rica's main domestic airlines operate services to Bahía Drake (which is otherwise reachable only by boat from Sierpe), Puerto Jiménez and Carate.

History

The Bahía Drake region of the Osa Peninsula was home to perhaps the country's best-known – albeit by no means best understood – pre-Columbian tribe, the **Diquis**. Of all their contemporaries, the Diquis certainly left the most visually arresting evidence of their existence. They were skilled goldsmiths, panning for the metal in local rivers and fashioning delicate, intricate pieces of jewellery and animal-shaped charms (jaguars, hawks, snakes, etc.), which it is believed were used to ward off evil spirits. You can see examples of their work at the Museo de Oro Precolombino in San José (*see* pp.104–5). The Diquis also carved an abundance of **lithic spheres**, perfectly round blocks of stone ranging in size from a tennis ball to a car, which they left in carefully arranged patterns all over southeast Costa Rica (particularly in Palmar and on the Isla del Caño, the precise meaning and purpose of which nobody has ever been able to decipher (*see* p.298).

The Diquis disappeared soon after the arrival of the Spanish in the 16th century, their demise probably resulting more from exposure to new European diseases such as smallpox and influenza than from conquest. Indeed, little active settling was done of this region until well into the 20th century. When the Interamericana was carved through here in the 1950s, the southern zone's entire population probably numbered no more than a few thousand people, with most journeys undertaken either by boat or horse. It was these centuries of isolation that enabled the Osa Peninsula's Corcovado rainforest to survive more or less unmolested, its once ignored biological diversity now regarded as one of the country's greatest treasures.

The Centre

San Isidro El General

San Isidro El General, which lies just shy of 140km south of San José, is the southern zone's main transport hub, meeting point and administrative centre. Set amid rolling agricultural country, the town is the public face of the region, its interface with the outside world. Everyone and everything in the province with business to conduct – farms, ranches, plantations, tour operators, hotels, the national parks service – has an office and representatives here. It's a mid-sized town of around 45,000 inhabitants and, architecturally, much of a muchness, designed with business, not beauty in mind. It's the sort of place to stop while you have a coffee, check your e-mails and plan the next stage of your journey. The only occasions when you might consider sticking around for a few days are in February, when there's a large agricultural fair, or for the week around May 15 when the town's patron saint, San Isidro, is commemorated with parades.

The town's layout can most accurately be described as a lopsided grid, with the Interamericana cutting off the northeast corner of what would otherwise be a sort of rough square. Streets are numbered in the standard fashion, with *calles* running north–south and *avenidas* east–west. The **Parque Central** sits at the town's centre. As precious few of these streets have signs, directions tend to be given using landmarks, the principal ones being the Parque Central and the Interamericana itself.

Museo Regional del Sur
t 771 5273; opening hours are erratic, although officially posted as Tues–Sat 8–5

If you're stuck in town for a while awaiting a connection, there are a few things you can do, including visiting the town's bustling **Mercado Municipal** at Av 4, C 0/2, or its one small cultural offering, the **Museo Regional del Sur** (Regional Museum of the South), which has a small display on the history of farming in the area as well as a

---

Over the Mountain of Death

Unless coming via the unpaved coastal road linking Quepos and Dominical, or flying into one of the southern towns bordering the Parque Nacional Corcovado, you will enter the southern zone via the Interamericana – and it's quite some entry. South of Cartago, the highway climbs to elevations of over 3,000m as it rises over the top of the chillingly named Cerro de la Muerte (which translates as the 'Mountain of Death' and not in an ironic way). This has to be the most dangerous and unpleasant stretch of highway in the entire country: frighteningly narrow, sick-makingly winding and prone to both landslides and pea-souper fogs that descend in seconds. If driving, you'll probably spend most of your journey either backed up behind a convoy of crawling lorries, furiously braking to avoid colliding with the car embarking on the seriously midjudged overtaking manoeuvre up ahead, or frantically weaving out of the way of the next landmine-blast-like pothole. And, after an hour and a half's worth of furious, wet-browed concentration, you'll begin the gentle descent to San Isidro El General, the region's largest town. By any objective criteria, San Isidro is not much to look at, but after that drive it will probably look like the most beautiful place on earth. Whatever you do, don't attempt the drive in the dark.

The bus journey is a good deal less scary – especially if you close your eyes.

Getting to San Isidro

Driving from San José involves tackling the ascent over the Cerro de la Muerte (*see* box, p.285). Otherwise, buses leave from Co, Av 22/24 every hour between 5.30am and 6.30pm. The journey nominally takes 3½hrs, but this can be significantly extended if you get stuck in a particularly fearsome tailback. It costs c1,140.

Buses drop their passengers off at the main bus terminal at Av 6, C 0/2, next to the Mercado Municipal.

Getting away from San Isidro

At the centre of a major regional crossroads, San Isidro offers four main travelling options: **north** to San José, which will involve ascending over the Cerro de la Muerte either by **car** or **bus** (which leave every half-hour 5am–7.30am and then every hour till 5.30pm from the Interamericana, C 0/2); **west** to Dominical and the Pacific coast (buses leave the main terminal daily at 7am, 9am, 1.30pm and 4pm; the 9pm and 4pm services continue on to Uvita; if driving, you want the Calle Central, which lies on western edge of the Parque Central); **east** to San Gerardo de Rivas and Chirripó National Park (buses leave at 5am from the Parque Central, 2pm from the main bus terminal, or you can take a taxi to the park entrance for around $15); or **south** down the Interamericana, for southern destinations such as Golfito (services leave at 10am and 6pm from the corner of the Interamericana, C 3), Puerto Jiménez (at 6.30am, 12 noon and 3pm from the main terminal) and Paso Canoas and the Panamanian border (8.30am, 10.30am, 2pm, 4pm, 7.30pm and 9pm from the corner of the Interamericana, C 3).

collection of local art. There's a small handicrafts showroom, the **Tienda de Artesanía**, next door.

Incidentally, locals tend to refer to their town either by its diminutive name, San Isidro, or, more confusingly, by the name of the local district, Pérez Zeledón, which is usually abbreviated to just Zeledón.

Tourist Information in San Isidro

(i) **MINAE, San Isidro El General** ›
*Av 2, C 2, t 771 3155;
open Mon–Fri 8–4*

There is no information office, but you can book tickets and accommodation for the Chirripó and La Amistad national parks at the **MINAE** office.

Tour Operators

See also the lodges mentioned under 'Where to Stay', below.

Selva Mar, C 0, Av 2/4, t 771 4582, *www.exploringcostarica.com*. Offers tours to the nearby national parks as well as trips further afield to Bahía Drake, Isla del Caño and Corcovado, in addition to providing a booking service for many of the region's coastal hotels, many of which still don't have phones.

Ciprotur, C 4, Av 1/3, t 771 6096, *www.ecotourism.co.cr*. Tours to local attractions as well as cheap Internet access.

Services in San Isidro

Banks: Banco Nacional, Parque Central, Av 0, C 1; Banco de Costa Rica, Av 4, C 0. Both have ATMs.

Internet access: Brunc@NetCafé, Parque Central, Av 0, C 0/1; *see also* Ciprotur above.

Post office: C 1, Av 4/6.

Where to Stay in San Isidro

San Isidro's accommodation options are principally made up of budget and business hotels, although there are also some nice lodges on the outskirts out towards San Gerardo de Rivas, the main base for exploring the Parque Nacional Chirripó.

The Cerro de la Muerte does have slightly more to offer than fabulously dangerous driving. Its higher elevations also support a wide range of bird life (including those most sought-after of all Costa Rican birds – quetzals) and there are now a few rural lodges lying off the Interamericana specializing in birdwatching tours. Some of the best include the **Albergue de Montaña Tapanti**, 62km from San José, t 232 0436 ($$$; $55) and the tellingly named **Mirador de Quetzales**, 70km from San José, **t** 771 4582, *www.exploringcostarica.com/mirador/quetzales* ($$$; $40).

Rancho la Botija del Sur Mountain Lodge, 6km northeast of San Isidro, **t** 351 3329 ($$$; $54). There are 8 rustic but comfortable cabins (two of which are wheelchair-accessible) on this working ranch/organic farm. The grounds also contain forest (nature hikes offered) where pre-Columbian petroglyphs have been found (non-guests can visit them for $5). There's also a good restaurant. Kayaks can be hired. Non-smoking throughout.

Hotel Diamante Real, Av 3, C 4, **t** 770 6230 ($$$; $50). Offering a better class of accommodation than what you normally find in San Isidro, the recently opened Diamante is a decent business hotel. All rooms have shiny new furniture and private bathrooms (with a regular supply of hot water). And for the businessman looking to splash out a little (literally), there's a superior suite with a Jacuzzi.

Talari Mountain Lodge, 7km northeast of San Isidro, **t** 771 0341, *talaripz@racsa.co.cr* ($$$; $55). On the road to San Gerardo de Rivas, this lodge boasts extensive grounds with fruit orchards and hiking trails that are particularly renowned for their birdlife (over 200 species have been spotted). The owners offer birding tours as well as horse-riding and hiking treks to Chirripó. The rooms aren't exactly luxurious, but they are clean, tidy and welcoming – each comes with a free booklet explaining what there is to do in the area – and there's a restaurant with an adjoining piano bar, and a swimming pool.

Hotel Chirripó, Parque Central, Av 2, C 0/1, **t** 771 0529 ($; $10 shared bathroom, $15 private). The Chirripó is the town's best budget choice. The rooms are a bit spartan, but clean and tidy, and some have private bathrooms with hot water showers (in theory anyway, although you may find that the little death-trap heater thing isn't working). There's also a good, cheap soda on site. Internet access available.

Eating Out in San Isidro

There's a fair bit of choice. San Isidro's status as a major agricultural town means that its restaurants are never going to run short of fresh produce. There are also a number of good cheap sodas at the Mercado Municipal, Av 4, C 0/2. And, if you just can't shake that hankering for US fast food, there's a branch of McDonald's at C 0, Av 0/1, north of the Parque Central.

Some of the best places include:

Soda Chirripó, Av 2, C 0/1 (next to the Hotel Chirripó). Opens early and serves tasty staples – *gallo pinto*, *casados*, *empanadas*, etc.

Marisquería Marea Baja, C 2, Av 4/6. A very good seafood restaurant.

Pizzería el Tenedor, C 0, Av 0/1. Serves generous and reasonably priced pizzas.

Parque Nacional Chirripó

Parque Nacional Chirripó
t 771 3155; open 5am–5pm; adm

Chirripó National Park, 20km northeast of San Isidro El General, provides access to Costa Rica's most accessible (and highest) mountain range. Not only does the 2,500ha park contain Costa Rica's tallest mountain, **Cerro Chirripó** (standing at either 3,819m or 3,820m high, depending which source you believe), which marks the topmost part of the Cordillera de Talamanca; there are also another three peaks over 3,500m. Indeed, there's not much of the park that isn't mountain (or at least very tall hill), with most of its area lying at elevations way above 2,000m.

The park entrance, just outside the small town of **San Gerardo de Rivas** (where many visitors to the park base themselves), is by comparison set at an almost laughably low 1,350m. From here, it's

Getting to Chirripó

From San Isidro, if travelling by **car**, head south out of town on the Interamericana, albeit at not too swift a pace as you'll have to make a turn-off to the left after about 1km. Look for the sign marked 'San Gerardo'. The road (more like a gravel track) ascends steeply from here towards the town, which is around a 20min drive away. The park is a further 3km beyond this.

Two **buses** a day leave San Isidro for San Gerardo at 5am from the Parque Central, and 2pm from the main bus terminal, Av 6, C 0/2. The journey takes 1½hrs. Return services leave at 7am and 4pm.

A 4WD **taxi** from San Isidro will cost around $16.

---

a 16km hike to the summit, by the end of which you will have ascended over 2.5km vertically. Though challenging and only recommended for people with a good level of fitness, the mountain hike is still just that – a hike: there's no actual climbing involved, although there will be an awful lot of pretty gruelling walking. In its entirety, the hike can take anything from 6–12hrs, depending on the weather and your pace, and perhaps half that on the way down. And just to make you feel suitably inferior, there's an annual race to the summit in February, which is usually won in a little over three hours.

Tips for Visiting Chirripó

• **Be sure to book early**. Chirripó is not a turn-up-and-pay sort of a park. If planning to hike to the summit, you must first reserve a bunk at its mountaintop lodge through either the San Isidro MINAE office (*see* p.286) or the San José MINAE office (*see* p.112). Somewhat confusingly, you are not allowed to book through the Chirripó ranger station, although you must check in here before entering the park in order to confirm your reservation, pay your park fees (*$15 for two days, $10 per day after that if overnighting*) and pick up a map. In the high season, you should ideally book several weeks in advance. If there's no space, you can bed down in San Gerardo on the park's doorstep in the hope of taking the place of a cancellation or a no-show, but this is a risky strategy. Even if you don't want to stay the night, you must still reserve your place in the park, as only 40 hikers are allowed in at any one time.

• **Aim to travel light**. You can store your luggage at the ranger station free, or hire a porter (either human or equine) to carry it for you, but this can be expensive. Horses cost $18 (maximum weight 35kg), people just $17 (but they can only carry a maximum of 14kg). It's a good idea to place waterproof covers over all your luggage and equipment.

• **Bring appropriate clothing and footwear**. This is not quite as straightforward as it sounds, as you may, during your time in the park, have to deal with everything from torrential rains (particularly between Sept and Nov) to blasting heat of over 30°C at midday during the dry season and, at night in the wet season, sub-zero temperatures. Bring light raingear that can quickly be removed and carried once the downpour stops, waterproof hiking boots, and plenty of layers to put on when temperatures start to drop (or take off when they start to rise), plus gloves and a woolly hat. Keep an umbrella and sunblock handy.

• **Don't go hungry**. Remember, if you're climbing to the summit you will have to stay overnight, so be sure to bring suitable supplies of energy-rich food and water.

• **Bring a torch with you**. The electricity at the mountaintop lodge goes off early in the evening (at 8pm).

• **Try to quit smoking before you arrive**. Because of the risk of forest fires, the trail is a no-smoking area. If you are a smoker, you'll have to wait till you get to the lodge before lighting up (there's a designated smoking area), by which time you'll be absolutely gasping (for various reasons).

• **Come at the right time**. The best time to visit is June–August. Though officially part of the 'rainy season', the rains don't come into full effect here until September. The dry season, December–April, offers the best weather, but midday temperatures will be roasting, and at weekends you'll probably struggle to get accommodation in the lodge. The park is closed in May, and during prolonged rainy periods.

Owing to its length, the climb will necessitate an overnight stay at the park's **mountaintop lodge** (*see* below and below left). However, if you don't feel up to the full mountain hike, the park is still well worth visiting. Though it will garner you plenty of disapproving or pitying looks from other hikers as they set off in determined fashion towards the summit, walking the mountain's lower slopes can be just as rewarding. Without the deadline and pressure of reaching the summit to distract you, you've got more time to appreciate the magnificent views and to go looking for the numerous species of bird (including hawks, trogons and quetzals), butterfly and mammal (including monkeys, coatis and tapirs) who make the park their home. As long as you start early enough, it's quite possible to climb about halfway up the mountain and return before nightfall; an **emergency shelter** marks the halfway point. As you ascend you'll find yourself passing through a variety of habitats, including cloud-forest, oak forest and, at higher elevations, a stunted, sparse form of Alpine-esque vegetation known as *páramo*. The mountaintop lodge doesn't actually mark the official summit; that's another 5km further on (or a 2hr round hike), although the ascent is considerably more gentle than what you will have experienced up to here. The morning after your ascent, just before you begin your descent, will probably be your most pleasant time on the mountain. Now that you no longer have to concentrate on the build-up of lactic acid in your legs, you can fully take in the views. From here, you should be able to pick out the mountain's small glaciers, the remnants of Ice Age giants that scoured the landscape around 30,000 years ago.

Where to Stay and Eat around Chirripó

Other than at the lodge atop the mountain, where you'll be obliged to spend at least a night if you're planning to climb to the summit of Chirripó, the majority of people bed down at one of the various budget hotels in San Gerardo de Rivas, 3km west of the park entrance, most of which have decent, if basic facilities. Many also operate cheap on-site restaurants and sodas.

In the Park

The park's mountaintop lodge, **Los Cretones**, which is the only accommodation available inside the park (camping is not allowed), offers basic dormitory-style lodging for around 60 people. Solar-powered electric lights are switched on between 6pm and 8pm only, after which you'll have

to rely on torches (which you must bring yourself). Though it's recommended that you bring your own sleeping bags, cooking equipment and gas, all of these items can be hired from the lodge. A word of warning – the lodge's showers are freezing cold. In fact, it's probably an idea to forgo ablutions for a night and reward yourself with a hot shower at your hotel upon your return. Book your stay at the MINAE office in San Isidro or San José well in advance.

San Gerardo de Rivas

Río Chirripó Retreat, t 771 7065, *www. riochirripo.com* ($$$; $40). San Gerardo's most upmarket accommodation lies just outside the town proper. It's certainly a relaxing place, with part of the complex given over to a Tibetan meditation area. It specializes in yoga retreats, but the less spiritual will still find much to enjoy with its cosy two-storey wooden cabins, restaurant/bar, heated pool and terrace overlooking the river.

Albergue y Restaurante Urán, t 388 2333, www.hoteluran.com ($$–$; $35–$7). The Urán is the closest hotel to the park entrance and, after a couple of days spent walking all the way up and down the mountain, you'll probably want your bed as close by as possible. It provides a choice of simple rooms with shared bathrooms ($7 per person), and much more fancy ones with private facilities ($35), as well as a large cabin, with a private bathroom, that sleeps up to five people. There's a simple but very good Tico restaurant and they offer free transfer and pick-up to the park.

Cabinas y Restaurante El Bosque, t 771 4129 ($; $15–8). Near the river, this is a relaxing spot with hammocks on balconies, decent budget rooms, most with shared bathrooms ($8), a couple with private ($15) and a friendly restaurant/bar that stays open till midnight.

Cabinas El Descanso, t 375 3752, eldescanso@ecotourism.co.cr ($; $10 per person). A reasonable budget choice, the Descanso's 12 rooms are quite small, and only have shared bathrooms, but they do have hot water (an absolute necessity after a night on the mountain). The friendly owners offer guided tours (including birding tours) to the park and hire out horses, and there's a small garden at the back where you can camp for $3.50. There's also a good on-site vegetarian restaurant. Free transport to the park.

Hotel Bar y Restaurante Roca Dura, t 771 1866, luisrocadura@hotmail.com ($; $20). In the centre of town, built into the side of a giant boulder, the Roca Dura offers nine rooms with shared baths, a couple of superior cabins with private baths (hot water in both) and a garden around the back near the river where you can camp for $4. They also operate a self-catering house in the village ($200 a month) and an inexpensive restaurant. Parking.

South along the Interamericana

From San Isidro, the Interamericana trundles south for around 80km, more or less following the course of the Río de El General, to the small town of **Paso Real**, whereupon it changes direction, heading west for 20km until it reaches **Palmar**. Here, having connected with the Pacific coastal highway, it once again resumes its journey southwards down towards the Panamanian border. If driving from San Isidro to Palmar, you'll find precious little cause to break your journey; this stretch of the highway boasts few attractions. You might choose to pull over at the pineapple town of **Buenos Aires**, which lies 3km off the highway, around 60km south of San Isidro (and just south of a Del Monte processing plant), but this would only be to have a coffee and recharge your batteries, rather than because the town has anything of specific interest to offer.

Other than this, the area's main draw is the **Reserva Indígena Boruca**, which can be accessed via the small village of Boruca, northwest of Paso Real, just north of the Interamericana. It's home to the Boruca indigenous tribe who are famed for their crafts, particularly clothes and scarves which they weave on small looms, and balsa wood 'little devil' masks, used during the New Year's *Fiesta de los Diablitos*. During this three-day festival, the men of the village don the masks in order to engage in a stylized battle with a man dressed as a bull, supposed to represent the Spanish *conquistadores*. The whole thing is a symbolic retelling of the Spanish invasion – a slightly revisionist one, as the bull always loses. The festival is the only time when the reserve welcomes significant numbers of visitors. For the rest of the year, you're free to visit the town and browse its craft stalls and, should you desire it, will probably be able to arrange some form of accommodation – there are a few rooms available to rent, or you may get permission to camp.

The Pacific Coast

Dominical

In terms of its character, its level of development and the type of visitors it attracts, the surfing and general-all-round-partying town of Dominical, just over 50km southwest of San Isidro, would seem to have more in common with Jacó and the Central Pacific resorts to the north than it does with the quiet fishing villages of Uvita and Ojochal to the south, who are its more immediate neighbours. Indeed, there are a number of people in the region who probably wish that Dominical could somehow be relocated further north to join its spiritual cohorts. For, since its discovery by the surfing community just over a decade or so ago, its transformation from sleepy coastal village to major resort, filled with budget hotels, bars and restaurants, would seem to provide an unpleasant foretaste of things to come along this stretch of the Pacific coast.

The problem is not just that this development has been rapid (which has caused its share of environmental problems) or largely uncontrolled, but that it seems to have been done in spite of, rather than in partnership with, the local community. Dominical now offers an overwhelmingly US-orientated experience: most of its businesses are US-owned, most of its hotels and restaurants cater to US tastes, and you could easily spend an entire afternoon walking the streets here and not hear any Spanish spoken at all. Sad to say, but many of the people buying land or investing in businesses here are not so much participating in another culture as importing their own, rewriting their cultural needs over those of the existing population (think Brits on Spain's Costa del Sol by way of comparison). These days, the symbol of the town is not so much its surfing beaches, but its plethora of real estate agents all hungrily buying up land from (often impoverished) local Ticos to be sold on to rich US investors. If only there were some sort of guarantee that this development could be controlled and contained, then the situation wouldn't look so bad. There's a place for a Dominical-like town on this coast. The fear, of course, is that one day Dominical will be the name not just of the town, but of the entire stretch of seaboard.

Getting to Dominical

The **drive** from San Isidro to Dominical is very twisty and turny, but not too taxing, certainly not when compared with the drive over the Cerro de la Muerte. It should take around an hour and a half. The only problem may be finding the right road out of San Isidro, where the signposting is poor. You want the Calle Central, which lies on the western edge of the Parque Central.

By way of contrast, the 44km drive south from Quepos, though more or less straight, is extremely taxing: a bumpy, banging, rumbling ride along an unpaved, rock-ridden road through a seemingly endless palm oil plantation (your back won't thank you for it).

Buses from San Isidro leave the main terminal daily at 7am, 9am, 1.30pm and 4pm; the 9pm and 4pm services continue on to Uvita. The bus service from Quepos follows the same route and is equally uncomfortable. It nominally departs four times a day, but is liable to cancellation in bad weather.

That said, and its influence on the future development of the area notwithstanding, there is still much about the town to be enjoyed. The surfing is among the best on the entire Pacific coast (although the swimming can be a bit hairy); it offers a range of services – supermarkets, Internet cafés, etc. – not repeated until you reach Palmar, and if you're looking for somewhere to party – in its most simplistic form of getting drunk and dancing – this is definitely the place to be, spending your days frolicking in the waves and sunbathing on the sandy beach and then, as evening approaches, retiring to watch the sunset with a beer from a beachfront bar. Its heady high season programme of film screenings (Cheech and Chong movies are popular), rowdy discos and beach parties may not be exactly what you came to Costa Rica for, but they can be fun.

While its number of businesses is growing all the time, the town's fundamental infrastructure remains at a rather basic level. There are no paved roads, just a handful of somewhat ill-defined muddy tracks – which must make getting planning permission for all those new businesses that much easier. There are essentially two major arteries: a main street, lined with an assortment of hotels and restaurants (there's a football field about halfway down); and a parallel beachfront road, with a higgledy-piggledy collection of paths, alleyways and tracks connecting the two. The **beach** is long and sandy, although more brown than golden in colour.

Tourist Information and Services in Dominical

ⓘ **Dominical** >
t 787 4027,
www.dominical.biz

The town's **tourist office** is in a new office by the San Clemente Bar and Grill, by the football field, with an Internet café above, all staffed, as you might expect, by US expats, which can provide information on the entire southern region.

At the junction between the turn-off leading from the coastal highway and the main street sits a large, purpose-built construction housing an **Internet** café and a **supermarket** as well as several estate agents. There are no **banks**, although you can change money at the **San Clemente Bar and Grill**, also as the town's **post office**.

Tour Operators

As inward-looking a community as you'll find throughout the whole of Costa Rica, Dominical does nonetheless have a number of tour operators catering to those visitors who do want to leave its confines. Try **Southern Expeditions**, by the entrance to town, t 787 0100, *www.costarica-southern-expeditions.com*, who offer trips to the Parque Nacional Corcovado and the Isla del Caño as well as kayaking trips; or the long-established **Don Lulo's**, t 787 0198, *www.ecotourism.co.cr/docs/nauyacawaterfalls*, who run popular trips to a set of local waterfalls (some of the highest in the entire country).

Sports and Activities around Dominical

It seems slightly strange, given that this is the activity that put Dominical on the tourist map, but the **surfing** can actually be rather dangerous here. The waves are certainly pretty fearsome, offering lots of late breaks, but the profusion of rip-tides means that you must keep a wary eye out for red flags, which are regularly displayed to indicate that the currents have become too strong. **Swimming** is recommended only in the calmest of conditions. The beach is patrolled by lifeguards.

There are a number of **surf schools** in town offering lessons and board rental. The best is probably the **Green Iguana Surf School**, t 787 0033, which offers lessons from $50 per person for two hours, or $40 for two or more people.

Where to Stay in Dominical

There's a superabundance of places to stay in Dominical. Most are cheap and cheerful *cabinas* aimed at the surfing community, with little in the way of stylish décor or ambience (although you can usually guarantee that they'll have hammocks and boogie-boards). As you might expect, these can be pretty noisy in the high season. There are some nicer, quieter places beyond the town's borders, including a few with their own private forest reserves and beach access.

Hotel Villas Río Mar, just outside town, 500m east of the Barú river bridge, t 787 0052, *www.villasriomar.com* ($$$$; $82). This pleasant little complex is set on 6ha of land just outside town, with 40 wooden bungalows, all with private bathrooms, mini-bars, ceiling fans and balconies with hammocks. There is also a restaurant, a bar, a swimming pool

and tennis courts. Surfboards can be hired.

Finca Brian y Milena, 3km south of town, t 396 6206 ($$$$–$$$; from $40 per person). This 10ha property contains a working farm, a rainforest wildlife reserve and a botanical garden. Accommodation options run the comfort gamut from the very luxurious Ocelot House, which sleeps up to four and has its own private bathroom, the more basic Bird House which only has a shared bathroom, and camping space in the grounds. Rates include all meals and a free guided tour of the grounds. Two-week volunteer programmes working on the farm and reserve are also available.

Hacienda Barú, 1km north of town, t 787 0003, *www.haciendabaru.com* ($$$; $68). Providing quite a contrast to the first-world hedonistic pleasures of Dominical just to the south, this offers natural wonders in abundance. One of the area's top eco-lodges, the Hacienda Barú occupies a 300ha nature reserve comprising a variety of landscapes – beach, mangroves, rainforest – that provides a home to over 350 species of bird and over 50 species of mammal (around half of them bats). The large, comfortable rooms have fans, kitchenettes, living cabins and hammocks. There's a great open-air restaurant and a variety of tours are offered, including zip-line canopy tours, horse-riding and night tours. The price includes all meals.

Diuwak Hotel and Beach Resort, between the main street and the beach at the southern end of town, t 787 0087, *www.diuwak.com* ($$$; $65). Aimed primarily at self-caterers (they offer good long-term rates), this offers a wealth of facilities, if not exactly the most authentic of ambiences. The rooms have kitchens, private bathrooms and living rooms; and there's a supermarket, an Internet café, a bar, a restaurant and a car rental office on site, as well as a swimming pool and Jacuzzi. You can hire kayaks and snorkelling gear. Private parking.

Cabinas San Clemente, on the beachfront, t 787 0026 ($; $25–10). Run by the same management as the bar/grill of the same name on the main street, this consists of two adjacent buildings: one containing dorms with shared bath ($10) and communal kitchen; the other providing slightly fancier hotel accommodation. The rooms have private bathrooms and, in certain instances, ocean views ($25).

Cabinas Sun Dancer, on the main street, t 787 0189 ($; $21). One of town's quieter budget options, set back from the main street. The rooms are small, but clean with shared bathrooms, and there's a communal kitchen, a pool and nice secluded gardens.

Tortilla Flats, on the seafront, t 787 0033, *tortflat@racsa.co.cr* ($; $25). The hammocks and boogie-boards adorning the balconies tell you all you need to know – this is a surfing hangout with all the benefits (great atmosphere) and problems (sometimes there's a bit too much atmosphere) that this entails. The rooms are brightly painted and come with private bathrooms. A couple even have air-conditioning. As comfortable as the rooms are, don't count on getting much sleep if the regulars are making a night of it at the beachfront bar.

Eating Out and Nightlife in Dominical

The restaurants and cafés of Dominical tend to have menus aimed at US tastes, with the odd Costa Rican dish added almost as an afterthought. Some of the more upmarket hotels do offer a better standard of cuisine, but in the main Dominical provides simple fare for people who regard food more as a fuel to aid their activities, than a pleasure in itself.

The town has lots of decent bars – 'decent' in this instance meaning loud, lively and patronized almost exclusively by Americans – and there are numerous parties and events (beach parties, Hallowe'en parties, film screenings, etc.) throughout the year. The tourist office can provide details.

Bar y Restaurante El Rincón, on the right as you enter town, t 787 0048. This hybrid Italian/Argentinian restaurant is one of the town's more upmarket offerings, providing a good standard of cuisine and a decent wine list. If nothing else it offers a welcome respite from the ubiquitous burgers and Tex Mex platters.

San Clemente Bar and Grill, on the main street, past the football pitch, t 787 0055. This popular meeting spot – it also provides a money-changing facility and acts as the town's post office – serves up decent Tex-Mex fare, as well as beer for the patrons of its pool table, and on Friday nights transforms into a pumping disco.

Thrusters, on a road linking the main street with beach, next to the police station, t 787 0127. This is the sort of bar where the management seem scared that people might get bored if obliged to talk to each other, and so provide TVs showing an endless stream of football matches, pool tables and dartboards so as to prevent them from having to. The menu is none too challenging – pizzas, *burritos*, etc. – but perfectly acceptable.

Tortilla Flats, on the seafront. Noisy, popular bar with tables on the beach. It's *the* place to watch the sunset with a few beers after a hard day's surfing.

Parque Nacional Marino Ballena

Parque Nacional
Marino Ballena
t 743 8236; adm

There's a problem with the Parque Nacional Marino Ballena, 20km south of Dominical. This problem has nothing to do with what the park is trying to achieve. It was set up in 1990 with the noble intention of trying to protect, in order of size: humpback whales (*ballena* in Spanish), who have long used the waters here as a breeding and calving ground (incidentally, the longest-ever recorded animal migration was undertaken by a humpback whale travelling from the Antarctic to here); dolphins, who are also common in these waters; shrimps, the population of whom has come under threat from commercial trawling; and the tiny polyps that make up one of the few sizeable remaining areas of coral reef off Costa Rica's Pacific coast. Nor is the problem to do with the park's aquatic extent, which covers over 800 hectares of ocean. In fact the problem has nothing to do with what's going on offshore at all; it's onshore where there's cause for concern. Put simply, the park doesn't extend far enough inland. Although it stretches for a good 15km along the coast, this amounts to a combined area of just 95ha, or just over one square kilometre. This includes some important territory, including the nesting sites of olive ridley and hawksbill turtles (from May to October), as well as habitats for tropical seabirds, such as pelicans, brown boobies and frigate birds, but this is still just the tip of the ecological iceberg. For the sake of the local environment, it would help if a few more square kilometres could be included within the park's boundaries; after all, this is one of the most pressurized stretches of coast in the entire country. Since the paving of the coastal highway half a decade ago, and even more so since the laying down of power and electricity lines in the past few years, this has become a veritable real estate smorgasbord. Pristine stretches of sandy beach backed by great swaths of coastal rainforest that had previously sat way off the beaten track have suddenly become easily accessible and developable. Much of this land belongs to small-scale landowners – farmers, fishermen, etc. – who can be persuaded to sell up for what must seem at the time like a sizeable amount of money – not realizing that some developers have been able to increase their investment by over 1,000 per cent in just a few years, such is the demand for land. From an economic perspective, you can see why the government and local communities might welcome a certain managed level of development, in order to bring jobs, money and opportunities into an area that was formerly somewhat impover-ished. But without proper official regulation, this can quickly take on the appearance of a 19th-century US land-grab. There are plenty of locals with tales to tell of hard-nosed real estate agents putting undue pressure on fishermen to relinquish their holdings, or of hotel chains offering financial inducements to council officials to get them to pass a building project without first subjecting it to a proper environmental impact study. Of course, the reason why this area is attracting so much interest is precisely because it remains so pristine and unspoiled. But there's only so much development it can take before it becomes well and truly spoiled, after which the golden goose will have been pretty much cooked for everyone.

Thankfully, the park still has a way to go before it reaches Manuel Antonio levels of development (see pp.234–6). And, until that moment arrives, this is still a lovely area with some great beaches, particularly those lying within the confines of the national park. At the park's northern extent is **Playa Uvita**, which stretches along the

Punta Uvita, an offshore island that's been reconnected to the mainland via the creation of a *tómbolo* – a sort of natural causeway formed by deposited sand. The thin bar of sand widening out to the rocky island actually (and rather appropriately) resembles a whale's tail. Six kilometres south of here is **Playa Ballena** (Whale Beach), an idyllic sweep of sand inhabited by thousands of scuttling tiny crabs that scatter aside in great clacking synchronized formations as you pass, while 8km further south is **Playa Tortuga** (Turtle Beach) and the small, but increasingly developed town of **Ojochal**, which offers wonderful views of this stretch of coast.

The park's **ranger station** at **Playa Bahía**, just south of Uvita, is only intermittently staffed (in fact 'station' is a rather grand description for what is essentially a trestle table). As over 90 per cent of the park is out at sea, there are no marked land trails and you are free to wander the beaches and fringing rainforest, although it is requested that you clear up your litter, particularly if you camp. The rangers may hand you a plastic bag when you arrive, to dispose of garbage.

There are a number of **activities** you can enjoy out in the main body of the park. You can hire a boat at Playa Bahía for around $30 to go snorkelling or dolphin-/whale-watching (trips are also offered by many of the area's lodges), although, during the main whale-breeding season of December to April (which handily corresponds to the main tourist season), it's also possible to spot whales from the shore as they breach the surface.

(★) La Cusinga >>

Where to Stay around the Parque Nacional Marino Ballena

As wonderful as many of the hotels bordering the park are, often offering their own beach access, swaths of rainforest to explore and luxurious rooms, you can't help but feel a twinge of regret as each new lodge opens and another piece of coast is turned from eco-wilderness to eco-resort. The best that can be hoped for is that these establishments are ecologically friendly, work in harmony with (and help to preserve) the environment and are supportive of local communities. Many are and do, and it goes without saying that you should not patronize any that aren't and don't.

There is no purpose-built accommodation available within the park itself (there's not really room), although you can camp at a specially designated area a few hundred metres from the ranger station.

La Cusinga, 22km south of Dominical, 35km north of Palmar, on Finca Tres Hermanas, t 770 2549, *www.lacusinga lodge.com* ($$$$; $94). Perhaps the benchmark by which all the area's lodges should be judged, La Cusinga (a type of toucan) is owned and operated by a local Costa Rican family (itself something of a novelty for these parts) and offers eco-tourism at its most eco, eco-tourism squared. It's probably best to start the description by listing all the things you won't find here – no heated pool, no Jacuzzi, no bar, no games room, no alcohol (unless specifically requested) – and yet this is still one of the best places to stay in the whole of Costa Rica. Occupying a great swath of secondary coastal rainforest bordering the national park, which is home to both howler and white-faced monkeys, the lodge sits on the brow of a small hill overlooking a stunning sweep of ocean where you can clearly see the '*tres hermanas*' that gave the farm that formerly occupied this site its name (they're actually three adjacent rocks jutting out of the sea). The grounds contain a stream with a natural swimming hole as well as access to a tiny pristine beach. Everything about the lodge has been done in as scrupulously an environmentally friendly way as possible: its simple, rustic but very comfortable wooden cabins, plus all their interior furniture, have been built on-site at the lodge's own workshop using lumber from its own sustainable plantation; low-level lighting is provided by hydro and solar power; while the lovely meals served in the communal dining area are made largely from produce from the lodge's own organic farm (the price includes all meals). The lodge also takes pains to work closely with the local community, helping to administer the national park and running an education centre where local children are invited to learn about preserving the environment. This is the sort of place where you have to re-tune your body clock to be up at dawn (the howler monkeys will help with this), so as to get the most out of the day – exploring the rainforest, whale-watching out in the park (the lodge offers boat trips) and strolling the jungle-fringed beach, before settling in the rocking chair of your cabin balcony to enjoy the nightlife – the constant pulsing shimmer of a million insects.

(★) **Balcón de Uvita** >

Balcón de Uvita, Uvita, 17km south of Dominical, **t** 743 8034, *www.balconde uvita.com* ($$$; $55). The very antithesis of a large, modern, pack-'em-in hotel complex, the Balcón de Uvita is sparing with its facilities. It doesn't do much, but what it does, it does very well. Its partly forested grounds are home to three nicely decorated *casitas* (two

sleep up to four, one sleeps up to three) with large bathrooms and views out over Uvita Bay, while its renowned Indonesian restaurant has just six tables. Be sure to book yours early, as it serves up great spicy cuisine and offers fantastic views from its eponymous balcony. It's a 3km walk to the beach.

Hotel Villas Gaia, 14km south of Uvita, at Playa Tortuga, **t** 256 9996, *www. villasgaia.com* ($$$; $75). A much more conventionally luxurious choice than La Cusinga, the hotel is set in a swath of forest just back from the beach, which provides a home to white-faced capuchins, toucans, sloths and various other wildlife, and in which you'll find 12 cheery, brightly decorated *casitas*, all with tile floors, hardwood furniture, private bathrooms and terraces overlooking the jungle. There's also a slightly grander two-bedroom house with air-conditioning and TV, as well as a very good restaurant and a swimming pool with marvellous coastal views from its poolside bar. The beach is a 20min walk away along a forested trail. Tours of the area and beyond to Bahía Drake, Caño Island and Corcovado are offered.

Eating Out around the Parque Nacional Marino Ballena

Most of the area's lodges operate restaurants, some of which are open to the public. Otherwise, you can choose between Dominical's US-flavoured eateries (see p.294), or the more authentic (but hardly more inspiring) roadside sodas you'll find lining the coastal highway.

The South

Palmar

A trip to Palmar is at best a necessary evil. There are really only two reasons why you might end up here. The first is to get somewhere else – it's the site of one of the region's main airports; it marks the junction of the Pacific coastal highway, the Interamericana and the Sierpe road; and it has numerous bus connections. The second is to see one of the southern zone's best collections of lithic spheres (*see*

Getting to Palmar

Both the major domestic carriers, Sansa and NatureAir, operate daily **flights** to Palmar from San José (*see* p.104). You'll have to take a taxi from the airfield in Palmar Sur to Palmar Norte, which should cost around $3.

Seven **buses** a day also link the capital with Palmar, leaving from C 14, Av 5, at 5am, 7am, 8.30am, 10am, 1pm, 2.30pm and 6pm, and dropping passengers at the Tracopa bus stop on the Interamericana (this is also where you can catch services to Golfito, Pasa Canoas and Puerto Jiménez). The journey takes 6hrs and costs c2,000.

Getting away from Palmar

Buses for Sierpe leave from Supermercado Térraba, one block east and one block south from the Tracopa stop at 8am, 9am, 9.30am, 12noon, 2.30pm and 5.30pm. The journey takes around 45mins and costs c300.

box). The town itself basically provides a service centre for the surrounding banana plantations, with banks, Internet cafés, supermarkets, etc. It's as functional and ugly as you might expect with just a few very basic accommodation and eating options. The town is divided into northern and southern halves by the Río Grande de Térraba: the southern half (**Palmar Sur**) is where you'll find the airport; the northern half (**Palmar Norte**) most of the services. If forced to stay the night, try **Cabinas Tico Alemán**, **t** 786 6232 ($; $13) on the Interamericana, or, for somewhere a little quieter, the **Casa Amarilla** near the football field, **t** 786 6251 ($; $16).

Golfito and the Golfo Dulce

There's something a bit Norma Desmond, a bit *Sunset Boulevard*-like about Golfito. Once the grandest of *grandes dames*, the country's biggest and most important banana-exporting port, it became for a while the most has-been of has-beens, before staging something of

---

A-round in the Past

Lithic spheres (or *esferas de piedra* as they are known locally) are strange, almost perfectly spherical carved stones, ranging in size from an orange to a space hopper and beyond, that were fashioned by the Diquís, the dominant indigenous tribe here in pre-Columbian times, and deposited all over the region. A particularly high concentration can be seen in the area bordering the road between Palmar and Sierpe, and on the Isla de Caño, 20km off the shore of the Osa Peninsula (*see* p.317). The sheer effort it must have taken to erect these great granite monoliths – the stone was quarried from the central Talamancan mountains and then transported significant distances – shows that they must have played an important role in Diquí culture, although exactly what remains a mystery. Various theories have been put forward. It has been suggested that they may have been symbols of wealth and prestige – the higher your social status, the bigger your stone. Or that they may have been used in funerary rites, perhaps acting as indicators of the deceased's life, like giant spherical tombstones (small ones for children, big ones for adults). Or that perhaps their arrangement was supposed to mirror the constellations and served some sort of astrological or religious purpose. Or perhaps their function was purely navigational – some stones have been found arranged in patterns pointing due north. These are all educated guesses at best. A slightly less educated notion held that they might have been repositories for prehistoric treasure, like giant stone safes, but the smashing open of a couple of stones quickly put paid to that hypothesis. All other conjectures, however, are still open to debate.

Getting to Golfito

One of the country's two main domestic carriers, Sansa, operates daily **flights** from San José to Golfito's tiny airstrip, which lies just north of the Zona Americana (*see* p.104 for more details).

There are regular **bus** services from San Isidro El General and Palmar, as well as a daily **ferry** service from Puerto Jiménez at 6am (see 'Getting away' below). It's also possible to catch a bus all the way from San José, some 340km to the north, although this is undoubtedly the most hardcore (although also ultimately the cheapest) option. Two buses a day leave the Tracopa Terminal, C 14, Av 5, at 7am and 3pm. The journey costs c2,420 and takes the best part of 8 hours. Any service in the run-up to Christmas will need to be booked in advance, to prevent your seat being taken by an eager shopper on route to the Depósito Libre.

Otherwise, Golfito lies a short **drive** from the Interamericana. Look out for the turning at Río Clara.

Getting away from Golfito

One passenger **ferry** a day, known as *La Lancha*, connects Golfito with Puerto Jiménez across the Golfo Dulce. It departs at 11am from the Muellecito ('little dock') by the Pueblo Civil and takes 1½hrs (c1,000). You can also catch a **water taxi** from just north of here to a variety of local destinations, including Playa Cacao, Playa Zancudo and Playa Pavones.

Buses leave for San José every day from the main bus stop near the Muelle Bananero at 5am and 1.30pm.

a comeback in recent years. Its story is a familiar one in Costa Rica. When United Fruit, the country's biggest firm and the largest banana-exporter in the whole of the Americas, set up for business here in the late 1930s, it dramatically transformed the fortunes of the area. 'Yunai', as it is known locally, repeated the trick it had first performed in Puerto Limón on the Caribbean coast, providing employment for thousands and building houses, schools and hospitals for the local community. Unfortunately, it also repeated the endgame, which saw the firm and its unions enter into a series of increasingly bitter disputes over workers' rights which finally resulted in United pulling the plug on the whole operation, abandoning the town virtually overnight in 1985. Shorn of its main economic provider, Golfito fell into a sudden and serious decline, with high unemployment and its accompanying side effects of increased drug use and prostitution. Tossed aside, ignored and forgotten, for a while the town could get nobody to take its calls.

Golfito's revival began in the 1990s when the government established a tax-free zone here, known as the Depósito Libre, where anyone in the country could come and buy imported consumer durables from Panama without having to pay the normally pro-hibitive (up to 100 per cent) import tax. And, because it has been cunningly arranged so that tickets for the zone can only be bought a day in advance, potential shoppers are obliged to spend a least a night (and with any luck some money) in town. Golfito has also managed to establish itself in recent years as a major sports fishing destination and, to a lesser extent, as a low-cost base from which to visit the Parque Nacional Corcovado across the Golfo Dulce.

These measures might not make the town as glamorous as when it was the biggest player in one of country's biggest industries, but they bring in much-needed visitors and much-needed currency. As with so many other places in Costa Rica, Golfito's ultimate salvation may lie in its ability to sell itself to the outside world, to convince tourists that it's a place worth visiting. The process is already well under way. It's not quite ready for its close-up yet, but Mr De Mille should definitely be on standby.

Golfito, which translates as 'small gulf', is the name both of the town and the small body of water on which it sits, which in turn feeds into the **Golfo Dulce**, the much larger body of water separating the mainland from the Osa Peninsula. On a fine day, the town offers great views out across the gulf to the peninsula, which from here seems be entirely swaddled in forest. Unfortunately, it rains a lot around here, and fine days are by no means guaranteed.

Golfito is basically a one-street town that straggles for around 3km along the waterfront with various tributaries intersecting here and there. In the good old days the town's focus was obviously its **Muelle Bananero** (Banana Dock), which lies slap bang in the middle of town, where crates of 'yellow gold' were once packed up and shipped out by the million. Today, this area is the town's least prosperous, supporting the fewest number of businesses – perhaps people are fearful of trying anything here in case the bad luck still lingers. A few banana boats are still loaded up at the dock, but this is just a fraction compared to the activity that went on before. Any big boat you see here now is more likely to be part of the US coastguard or Navy fleet, who regularly dock here – and whose sailors boisterously (to put it mildly) patronize the local bars.

These days the town's focus is split between the **Pueblo Civil** to the south, its downtown area where you'll find most of the budget hotels, restaurants and shops as well as some particularly unsavoury bars; and the more residential **Zona Americana** to the north, site of the Depósito Libre, and generally regarded as the more upmarket side of town, albeit still considerably faded from its banana-exporting heyday when this was the playground of big-shot US executives. The tax-free shopping haven of the **Depósito Libre** is the main reason the majority of Ticos come to town, particularly in the period leading up to Christmas . Would-be shoppers must buy their tickets (*boletos*) a day in advance from the **booking office**, a deliberate device to encourage them to spend a little extra cash in town overnight. Ticos are permitted just one trip here every six months, during which they can spend up to a maximum of $500, although there are restrictions on certain items (they can only buy one TV a year, and a fridge only every three years).

With the opening of its tax-free zone and the setting up of a number of sports fishing operators, Golfito has been doing it's best to raise its image in the past few years, but there's still a distinct whiff of seediness about the place. Certain streets in the Pueblo Civil become an almost unofficial red light district at night. Avoid any bar

Depósito Libre
open Tues–Sat 8–4.30, Sun 7–2;
booking office *open 8–8*

where a sign has been positioned outside to stop you from seeing what's inside – you don't want to know.

The town isn't exactly the most lively you can visit in the region, but it does provide a useful and relatively inexpensive place to base yourself *en route* to the Panamanian border, 58km south. It's certainly much more pleasant than the border town itself, Paso Canoas (*see* pp.303–304). It's also within easy reach of several decent beaches, including **Playa Cacao** just across the little gulf (take a water taxi from the **Muellecito**, or 'little dock', by the Pueblo Civil); **Playa Zancudo** (as exotic as this sounds, its English translation, Mosquito Beach, is not quite so appealing) 15km southeast, which is another major sports fishing destination whose gentle waves are perfect for swimming; and, 10km beyond that, **Playa Pavones**, one of Costa Rica's plethora of renowned surfing locales, which has one of the longest left-hand wave breaks in the world, apparently (and where swimming definitely isn't recommended).

Services in Golfito

Most of the services you require are located in the **Pueblo Civil**. There's a **petrol station**, an **Internet café** (next to the petrol station), a **supermarket** and a **post office** (*correo*) just back from main road.

The main **bank**, Banco Nacional, which has an ATM, is situated opposite the main bus stop, near the Muelle Bananero.

Sports and Activities in Golfito

Since the demise of the banana-exporting business, sports fishing has become one of the region's biggest earners, with several firms in and around town offering trips out onto the high seas on the hunt for marlin and sailfish. Three-day fishing packages, including all transport, accommodation and meals, cost from between $2,500 and $4,500, depending on the desired level of comfort.

Arena Alta Sportsfishing, Playa Zancudo, t 766 0115, *www.costarica sailfish.com*.

Golfito Sportsfishing, Playa Zancudo, t 776 0007.

Land-Sea Tours, in Golfito itself, just south of the Pueblo Civil, on the main road, t 775 1614, *landsea@racsa.co.cr*. A long-established tour operator which also arranges jungle hikes to the Refugio Nacional de Fauna Silvestre Golfito, just northeast of Golfito (otherwise quite difficult to access), and generally acts as a sort of unofficial tourist office for the town.

Where to Stay in Golfito

Golfito's best accommodation options tend to be located outside the town centre. Those places in the Pueblo Civil lean towards the very basic, aimed primarily at people looking to stay just a single night before visiting the Depósito Libre and wanting to save as much money as possible. There are some very good eco-lodges to the north of Golfito out towards the Refugio Nacional de Fauna Silvestre Golfito.

Luxury ($$$$$)
Esquinas Rainforest Lodge, 8km north of Golfito along an unpaved road, near the small community of La Gamba, t 775 0901, *www.esquinaslodge.com* ($190). Owned by the Austrian government, this lodge conducts a good deal of important scientific research into conservation techniques, welcoming naturalists and scientists from all over the world to its 100-plus hectare swath of primary rainforest bordering the little-developed **Parque Nacional Piedras Blancas**. It's ostensibly run as a not-for-profit

★ **Esquinas Rainforest Lodge >>**

operation, with any money that it does make redirected towards educating and aiding the local community of La Gamba, which provides most of the lodge's employees. As 'eco' as the lodge is, it doesn't stint on the comfort – its 10 large cabins all have private bathrooms, fans and porches. There are marked trails through the grounds and you can hire horses. Trips to Corcovado are also offered. The price includes all meals.

Playa Nicuesa Rainforest Lodge, north of town, t 735 5237, *www. nicuesalodge. com* ($130). Though you can pamper yourself silly at this luxurious 60ha private coastal rainforest reserve on waterfront, you can still feel good about yourself, as it's also supremely environmentally friendly, using electricity supplied by solar power. You can choose between large rooms decorated with indigenous handicrafts in a two-storey wooden lodge, or even larger hexagonal cabins in its grounds, and enjoy a delicious *comida típica* feast served up in its open-air restaurant. A range of guided tours are offered to the nearby **Casa de Orquídeas**, a private botanical garden that is home to over a hundred varieties of orchid, and you can also go kayaking, fishing and sailing.

Rainbow Adventures Lodge, north of the town centre, t 380 2650, *www. rainbowcostarica.com* ($168). It's not cheap, but you do get a lot for your money. The price includes transfer from Golfito, all meals (including drinks) plus a tour of the 400ha private rainforest reserve on which the lodge sits, which is home to over 250 species of bird. The rooms in the main lodge are supremely luxurious – all handmade furniture, hardwoods and antiques – and there are a couple of even grander cabins nestling amongst the foliage overlooking the beach. A variety of activities is offered, including kayaking, snorkelling, dolphin-watching and fishing. All the electricity is provided by solar power.

Moderate ($$$)

Las Gaviotas, t 775 0062, *www. costaricasur.com/lasgaviotas* ($42). Like Golfito, Las Gaviotas has seen better

(★) **Cabinas Playa Cacao >>**

days. Stuck out on the southern edge of town, this 'resort', as it likes to style itself (it's more of a glorified chalet complex), feels a bit out of the way, although at least that means it's quiet. It's quite a walk into town from here. The pool and bar area are the highlights of the complex, with views out over the gulf. The rooms, which occupy long blocks, are OK but in need of a re-fit – all come with ceiling fans, cable TV and private bathrooms. There are also three slightly swisher bungalows with kitchenettes ($84). The hotel caters to a large list of regular patrons – mainly older Americans and Europeans – who return year after year (and presumably don't want anything changed). The popular restaurant is open to the public and offers weekend buffets.

Cabinas Playa Cacao, Playa Cacao, t 221 1169, *www.kapsplace.com* ($40). On the quiet Playa Cacao, just across the water from the town, this is run by Isabel Arias, the mother of Karla Arias who runs Kap's Place, San José's best budget choice, and she is equally welcoming. It offers a grand combination of simple, thatch-roofed, indigenous-style huts, all with bathrooms and plug-in fans, and the chance to listen to Isabel tell fascinating stories of her life in Costa Rica and beyond. You can hire canoes and Isabel will go out of her way to recommend and organize activities for you.

Budget ($)

Cabinas Mar y Luna, t 775 0192 ($15). A decent budget choice. All rooms have private bathrooms (although the supply of hot water can be somewhat intermittent) and cable TV, and there is a choice of ceiling fan or, for a mere $6 more, air-conditioning. The restaurant is one of best in town, serving a good selection of fish and seafood, with outdoor seating overlooking the gulf.

Cabinas El Tucán, t 775 0553 ($10). There are now two El Tucáns: an older, slightly more threadbare version in the Pueblo Civil, and a brighter, newer version 200m north. The accommodation in both is pretty basic, but perfectly adequate for a night or two.

La Purruja Lodge, t 775 1054, *www. purruja.com* ($25). Just south of the centre, La Purruja is owned and run by a Swiss/Tico couple. It offers just five cabins, all with ceiling fans and private bathrooms set in nice gardens (where you can camp for $2), as well as a wealth of tours, from jaunts to the local wildlife refuge to trips all the way across to Corcovado.

Eating Out in Golfito

For the best cuisine, you'll need to head to the hotels and lodges away from the town centre.

Try the excellent fish and seafood restaurant at **Cabinas Mar y Luna** or the nearby **Las Gaviotas**, which serves all-you-can-eat barbecues on Friday and Saturday evenings.

Things are a bit more basic in town. You'll find plenty of sodas and cheap eats in the Pueblo Civil, including **Soda Muellecito**, **La Cubana** and the Chinese **Restaurant Hong Kong**.

Nightlife in Golfito

There are plenty of bars in town, but for safety's sake you should probably stick to those on the seafront; the drinking holes of the Pueblo Civil tend to fill with prostitutes come sundown.

Samoa del Sur is one of the most popular and can get pretty raucous, particularly because it's the favoured haunt of US marines. The **Coconut Café** and **8°Latitude** offer a more relaxed drinking experience.

Paso Canoas and the Panamanian Border

In keeping with all border crossings, life at Paso Canoas moves at a slow, shuffling, inching-forward kind of a pace. As you might expect for somewhere directly on the Interamericana, it's a very popular crossing, particularly with Ticos on the hunt for cheap consumer

Crossing the Border

The crossing point may look slightly chaotic, but the procedure for getting over the border is relatively straightforward, if not quite as clear as it might be. Be prepared to ask questions if in any doubt as to what to do.

First, make sure you have a **return ticket** out of Panama, as you'll have to present this at the crossing point. Unless exiting Panama via a different border point, this will probably entail a visit to the Tracopa office in Paso Canoas, where you can purchase a return bus ticket to David, the first major town in Panama, which lies around 50km past the border, for c1,000.

Next, you must show your **passport** as well as any other relevant **documentation** – which for Canadian, Australian and New Zealand citizens may include a visa – at *Migración* (open 7am–10pm), before moving on to the **Instituo Panameño de Turismo** (*open 6–11 and 1–5*) where you must purchase a $5 **Tourist Card**, after which you can proceed to the crossing point itself. Before being allowed to enter Panama, you may be asked to prove you have independent means and are not seeking work in the country, although these sorts of questions are usually reserved for Ticos. A couple of hundred dollars in your wallet or a few credit cards should convince the authorities of your honourable intentions. There are banks with ATMs on either side of the border.

On the Panamanian side you will no doubt be besieged by the **money-changers** (*bolsijeros*) with their bum-bags full of *balboas*, the Panamanian currency, ready to change up your spare *colones*. Be sure to haggle down the exchange rate before agreeing to any transactions.

There are several **customs** posts on either side of the border, so keep your passport with you, as you may be asked to present it several times. However, as these are mainly concerned with picking up illegal immigrants and preventing the smuggling of goods from Panama, they'll probably quickly let you on your way once they realize you're a tourist – so as long as you're polite and co-operative, of course. **Buses** run from the border to David every 10 minutes.

Getting to Paso Canoas

You can't take rental cars out of Costa Rica, so you'll probably arrive here by **bus**. Services leave San José's Tracopa terminal at Av 5, C 14 every day at 5am, 7.30am, 11am, 4.30am and 6pm. However, as the journey takes over 9hrs, you should ideally begin your trip slightly further south.

Over 20 buses a day link Neily, 17km north, with the border between 6am–7.30pm.

---

durables in the run-up to Christmas, and Americans looking to renew their three-month tourist visas – a process which, if repeated often enough, effectively allows them to live permanently in the country. Ideally, you should aim to get here as early as possible, so as to give yourself enough time to deal with any potential bureaucratic hiccups (*see* box, p.303).

It won't exactly be your most luxurious or memorable night in the country, but there are sleeping options in Paso Canoas if you find yourself having to spend the night. The **Hotel Azteca, t** 732 2217 ($; $5 per person), and **Cabinas Interamericano, t** 732 2041 ($; $10),have decent, clean rooms. Slightly more upmarket accommodation is provided in the town of Neily (try the **Hotel Andrea**, **t** 783 3784; $20) and Golfito (*see* pp.301–303).

San Vito and Around

A little piece of Italy transplanted to the tropics, San Vito was founded in the early 1950s by Italian settlers who turned the surrounding forested hills into coffee plantations and farms. It retains a distinctly Mediterranean flavour, with many families still using Italian as their first language and Italian restaurants lining its streets. Indeed, the townspeople have made a concerted effort to maintain close links with the 'motherland', establishing a cultural centre where Italian lessons are offered, and erecting a **Fuente de Fraternidad** (Fountain of Fraternity) in the town's **Parque Central** in order to celebrate the strong spirit of friendship that exists (apparently) between Costa Rica and Italy.

Occupying an elevated location nearly 1,000m above sea level, the town enjoys a slightly cooler, breezier climate than many of its more low-lying southern neighbours, making it a pleasant base from which to explore the nearby attractions of the Wilson Botanical Gardens (6km south) and the Parque Internacional La Amistad (25km north). It's a neat, compact little place, its few basic roads intersecting with a main street, Calle Dante Alighieri, alongside the southern end of which you'll find the town's cultural centre, the

Centro Cultural Dante Alighieri
t 773 3570; call for opening times; free

Centro Cultural Dante Alighieri, which was built on the site of a giant ceibo tree felled by the first settlers. In fact you can see pictures of the settlers caught in the very act of felling at an exhibition of historic photographs within the centre.

Getting to San Vito

Getting to San Vito has become a lot easier in recent years since the paving of the road to Paso Real. Four **buses** a day leave San José's Tracopa terminal, Av 5, C 14, for the town at 5.45am, 8.15am, 11.30am and 2.45pm. The journey takes around 7hrs and costs c2,300.

Getting to the Wilson Botanical Gardens

From San Vito, you'll need to catch the Neily **bus** via Agua Buena which leaves the main bus terminal at 7am and 9am. The journey takes just over 10mins. There's no official bus stop for the gardens, so you'll have to ask the driver to let you off.

Wilson Botanical Gardens

Wilson Botanical Gardens
t 773 4004, www.ots. ac.cr; open daily 8–4; to sleep here, see below

These internationally renowned botanical gardens 6km south of San Vito were founded in 1963 by a couple of US biologists, but have been administered since the early 1970s by the Organization for Tropical Studies in San José. They provide a home to a dazzling variety of plant life, with what seems like a country's (if not a continent's) worth of diversity crammed into a 10ha site. Here you'll find not just Central America's largest collection of bromeliads, but the world's second largest collection of palms, numbering over 700

★ **La Amistad Ecolodge >>**

ⓘ **MINAE, San Vito >**
open 9–4, t 773 4090

Tourist Information and Services in San Vito

There's a **MINAE** office at the northern end of town, which can provide information on, book hostel space within, and arrange the services of a guide for the Parque Internacional La Amistad.

The town has all the facilities and services necessary for a stay of a few days: two **banks**, both with ATMs, a **supermarket**, a couple of **Internet cafés** and a **post office**.

Where to Stay and Eat in San Vito

As well as sleeping in San Vito, it is possible to stay at **Las Cruces Biological Station** adjoining the Wilson Botanical Gardens, which like the gardens is overseen by the Organization for Tropical Studies, but you'll need to book your place well in advance, **t** 773 4004. The rooms are simple but perfectly adequate with private bathrooms, and cost $75 including all meals and a tour of the gardens.

La Amistad Ecolodge, just east of San Vito, towards Sabalito, **t** 228 8671, *www.laamistad.com* ($$$$; $88). If you want to experience the region's forests, but don't yet quite feel up to tackling La Amistad's mighty Valle del Silencio trail (*see* p.307), then this eco-lodge set on an organic coffee farm and vast area of rainforest adjoining the park is probably your best bet. It offers luxurious hardwood rooms, all with private bathrooms, and there are guided tours available through its grounds – home to an abundance of wildlife – which feature well-equipped tent camps allowing you to overnight in the forest. All room rates include meals.

Hotel El Ceibo, just east of the town centre, **t** 773 3025 ($$; $30). Named after the (now felled) tree around which the town was built, the Ceibo is by far and away the town's best choice. There are 40 good-quality, nicely decorated rooms – all with private bathrooms, ceiling fans and TVs, some with balconies offering views over the surrounding country-side – and a good restaurant offering an Italian-influenced menu.

Hotel Rino, just north of the Parque Central, **t** 773 3071 ($; $21). On the second floor of a small shoppng plaza, this offers reasonably sized, reasonably priced rooms, all with cable TV and private bathrooms (hot water). Breakfast in the adjacent soda is included in the price.

Pizzeria Liliana, west of Parque Central, **t** 773 3080. The town's most celebrated Italian restaurant was also its first, and is still serving a delicious array of (very large) pizzas, plus a few pasta dishes, served on a leafy terrace. A little taste of Italy.

species. Marked grassy **trails** take you on a 2hr trek through the gardens, past all manner of tropical blooms: giant bamboo plants, great floppy bananas, delicate orchids and heliconias, plus an attendant fluttering orchestra of butterflies and hummingbirds. There's also a trail through an adjoining swath of secondary forest on the banks of the Río Java. To find out more, you can book a **tour** with the centre's resident botanist.

Tours
$10; best done in advance

Parque Internacional La Amistad

Parque Internacional La Amistad
t 773 4090; adm

The proud claim, endlessly repeated by the tourist board, that 25 per cent of Costa Rica's territory is protected against future development, does not tell the whole conservational story. While this 25 per cent may be the total amount of preserved land, it does not represent a single area, but rather a disparate collection of national parks and private refuges, some big, some small, that for the most part lie separated from each other. And for the country's larger animals, particularly its big cats who need sizeable territories in which to hunt effectively, it is this parcelling up of the environment into sections – with islands of forest surrounded on all sides by farmland – that poses one of the biggest threats to their existence. Which is why the Parque Internacional La Amistad is so important, as it is one of the few Costa Rican parks to provide proper big-cat-sized spaces.

In fact, it's so big, it's gone international, encompassing not just well over 2,000 sq km (or well over 200,000 hectares or half a million acres) of Costa Rican territory, but another 2,000-plus sq km of Panamanian territory. It's by far the biggest protected area in Costa Rica, but also one of the least visited, and it's deliberately being kept that way. With few official access points, amenities or

Where to Stay in La Amistad

The **refuge** at Cerro Kamuk has 20 bunks and cold-water showers, but not much else. You'll have to bring everything else you might need with you – a sleeping bag, food, cooking equipment, cooking gas, a source of heat, a torch, a shoulder to cry on. You'll need to reserve your bunk and your guide in advance at the San Vito MINAE office (*see* p.305), although it's not necessary to book if you're just visiting for the day. It is also possible to **camp** in the park for $2, although there are almost no amenities.

Getting to La Amistad

Altamira lies 25km north of San Vito at the end of a very rough and rocky unpaved **road**. A 4WD is recommended in dry weather and is obligatory in the wet.

If hoping to travel by **bus**, you'll need to catch one of the regular services from San Vito to Las Tablas, then change for one of the two daily services to Altamira at 12.30pm and 5pm.

---

trails, most of the park lies well out of reach of all but the hardiest adventurers, thereby affording the greatest level of protection for its vast collection of wildlife.

At the park's heart is the mighty Cordillera de Talamanca, stretching all the way down to the border and beyond, around which is arranged a myriad different landscapes and life zones, from lowland rainforest to mountaintop *páramo*, and everything in between. Almost all of Costa Rica's superstar animals are here, including the country's largest population of tapirs, over 500 species of bird (that's over half the total number for the country), over 200 species of reptile and all five of the big cats – margay, ocelots, jaguarundis, pumas and, of course, jaguars. Indeed, so much flora and fauna is protected in this giant international life corridor that in the 1980s it was designated a World Heritage Site by UNESCO.

For tourists, the only accessible entrance to the park is via the small hamlet of **Altamira**, 25km north of San Vito, where there is a permanently staffed **ranger station**. From here, two marked trails head into the depths. The first, the **Sendero Gigantes del Bosque**, provides 3km worth of relatively challenging but not too difficult hiking through lowland primary and secondary forest. No part of the trail ascends above 1,500m. The second trail, the **Sendero Valle del Silencio**, is a different proposition altogether. If tackled in its entirety, it will take you on an extremely gruelling 20km yomp through forests, past rivers and up and over a number of peaks (some over 3,000m high) to the park's refuge at **Cerro Kamuk**, where you'll have to spend the night (*see* box, left). The trail can take well over 10 hours to hike in its entirety and should only be attempted in the company of an experienced guide.

The Osa Peninsula

Viewed on a map, Costa Rica's two peninsulas, the Nicoya in the northwest and the Osa in the southwest, have largely similar, dangling-trunk-like shapes, although Osa is a good deal smaller. There, however, the similarities would seem to end. For while the Nicoya Peninsula has long been a byword for overdevelopment and mass tourism, with beaches that are among the most built-up in the country, Osa has so far managed to escape the worst ravages of the tourism boom. That said, it has, as with everywhere else in Costa

Rica, seen more development and welcomed more visitors in the past 20 years than in the previous 200 combined.

The major attraction here, accounting for around a third of the peninsula's area, is the Parque Nacional Corcovado, which contains the country's largest remaining section of virgin tropical wet forest, a vast swath of concentrated natural diversity that provides a home to a countless array of flora and fauna. If you've come to Costa Rica in the hope of seeing some of the country's showpiece animals, i.e. the ones that always seem to feature prominently if not a touch misleadingly on the covers of guidebooks – scarlet macaws, tapirs, pumas, jaguars, etc. – then this park represents your best chance.

The peninsula has historically been one of the country's most isolated and least visited, something that made its later conservation that bit easier. Until the second half of the 20th century, precious few Costa Ricans, let alone tourists, had set foot here. Blanketed in forest and with almost no roads, Osa had come to be regarded as an untameable wilderness, best left to the hardy handful of gold-prospectors who made up its principal population. By the time people began to wake up to its potential, the conservation movement was already well established, allowing Corcovado to be swiftly incorporated into the national parks system before developers could begin staking their claims. There's been some pressure on the land since. The closure of United Brands' Golfito operation in 1985 and consequent mass unemployment in the area led to many families arriving in the region in the hope of setting up smallholdings on the edge of the forest – they're particularly evident on the road between Rincón and Puerto Jiménez. Other former workers tried to alleviate their plight by panning for gold within the park, until forcibly ejected in the late 1980s. However, for the most part this is one of the most scrupulously maintained natural environments in the country, with most of the hotels, lodges and locals taking great pains to help preserve the forest.

There are three main bases for exploring the park: Puerto Jiménez, the peninsula's largest town, located on its eastern side, which offers a rather basic, backpacker-orientated experience; and the more upscale areas of Carate and Bahía Drake on the western side of the peninsula, which specialize in very luxurious, jungle-set eco-lodges. Indeed, the peninsula would seem to cater best to the extremes of the market: either budget travellers willing to sit on endless bumpy bus/open-back truck journeys and rough it in cold-water *cabinas*; or wealthy jet-set vacationers who can fly into one of the three main base airports, whereupon they will be chauffeured to their luxury accommodation to enjoy the finest facilities – giant beds, fabulous restaurants, ocean views, wildlife on tap – that the jungle can provide. Mid-range travellers will have to decide whether

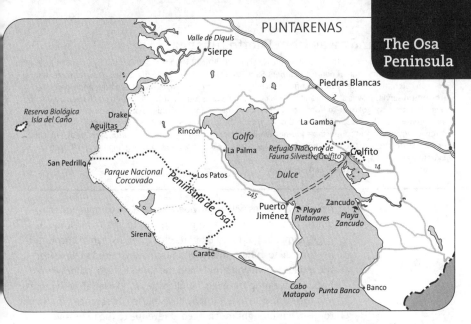

they want to live below or above their means, as visiting the peninsula would seem to entail spending either next to nothing or your entire life savings.

Puerto Jiménez

For a long time, Puerto Jiménez marked the very outpost of civilization, the furthest frontier of Costa Rican Man. The only people who regularly passed through here were gold-prospectors, a few farmers, and the odd fugitive escaping justice.

What a difference a couple of decades make. Today 'Jim' (as it's known locally) is the peninsula's largest town and its main link with the outside world (partly because this marks the furthest extent of the phone lines).

Of course, these things are relative and you certainly shouldn't go expecting some sort of major metropolis. It may be Osa's big city, but it still comprises little more than a few ramshackle streets. Still, on these streets you'll find all the services necessary to keep you going if making your own way around the peninsula to Corcovado National Park – a bank, a petrol station (the only one on the entire peninsula), a post office, Internet cafés, tourist information, laundries and supermarkets, as well as plenty of restaurants and hotels aimed directly at the lower end of the market. This is back-packer country – dusty, potholed and slightly ramshackle, but with a great laid-back, friendly atmosphere. If staying in one of the area's fancy lodges, you'll probably never set foot in the place as you're whisked from the airport to your tropical hideaway where all the

Getting to and away from Puerto Jiménez

There are a number of options, each progressively more difficult than the last. You can **fly** from San José (both of the country's major domestic carriers, Sansa and NatureAir, operate flights, *see* p.104 for more details); you can catch the daily **ferry** from Golfito, which leaves at 11am and arrives around an hour and a half later (the return service leaves at 6am, and it costs c1,000 one-way); you can **drive**, although you'll need a 4WD to negotiate the final 30km or so from Rincón, which is unpaved and very rough going; or you can catch the **bus**. One service a day leaves San José from C 12, Av 7/9 for the gruelling 8hr haul to Puerto Jiménez (it costs c2,225). A more convenient and comfortable journey would see you breaking your trip *en route*, perhaps at San Isidro or Palmar, from where there are more frequent services. Again, be aware that the going beyond Rincón will be extremely bumpy.

To get to Corcovado National Park, *see* p.320.

necessary services will be provided. Some have complained that, during its transformation from frontier outpost to tourist town, Puerto Jiménez has lost a bit of its character. Instead of encountering grizzled fortune-hunters with fascinating tales to tell, visitors to the modern town will simply find the same T-shirt-, trainer- and backpack-wearing travellers familiar the world over, all with more or less the same tale to tell. It may have diluted its essence slightly, but tourism has brought much-needed revenue to the town and area, and certainly a much more regular supply of income than gold-prospecting ever could (even if it is less romantic).

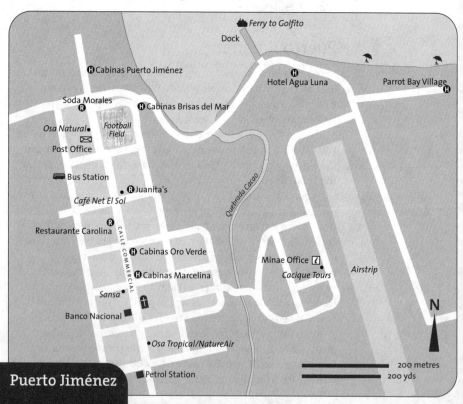

Puerto Jiménez

The town is made up of a small network of streets. Its northern extent is marked by a **football field**, next to which you'll find the post office and the tour operator Osa Natural (*see* below). From here, the main street, **Calle Comercial**, runs south down to the petrol station and the turn-off for the Carate road. The **dock**, where the ferry for Golfito arrives/departs, the town's small **airstrip** and its slightly scrubby **beach** all lie to the east of the town centre.

South of Puerto Jiménez, an extremely bumpy road (*see* 'Getting to Corcovado') winds its way around the bottom of the peninsula and up the other side to the village of **Carate**. It's along here that you'll find some of the region's most upmarket accommodation.

Tourist Information in Puerto Jiménez

Next to the football field is the **post office** (*correo*) and the tour operator **Osa Natural, t** 735 5440, *www. osanatural.com*, which acts as a sort of unofficial tourist office, providing a wealth of information about the area, and a booking service for the *colectivo* (*see* 'Getting away') and the Parque Nacional Corcovado.

The Parque Nacional Corcovado's **MINAE office** is located by the airstrip to the east of town. Here you can engage the services of a guide and book space at any of the park's four ranger stations, although in high season you're best off doing this well before you reach town, at the San José office (*see* p.112).

(i) MINAE, Puerto Jiménez >>
t 735 5036; open Mon–Fri 8–4

Tour Operators

As the peninsula's major base for travellers hoping to explore Corcovado, Puerto Jiménez is home to several tour operators (to make your way independently to the park, *see* p.320). All of the following offer hikes of varying lengths through the national park.

Aventuras Tropicales, t 735 5195, *www. aventurastropicales.com*. Offers a wide range of tours, including kayaking, mangrove tours, birding, dolphin-watching, snorkelling and multi-day hikes into the park.

Cacique Tours, near the airstrip, **t** 735 5440. Personalized tours to Corcovado, particularly popular with birdwatchers.

Escondido Trex, in Restaurante Carolina, main street, **t** 735 5210, *www.escondidotrex.com*. One of the town's longest-established operators,

offering a whole range of trips: multi-day hikes through Corcovado, dolphin-watching, waterfall rapelling, snorkelling, fishing, horse-riding and more.

Everyday Adventures, several km south of the town on the Carate road (best to call in advance), **t** 735 5138, *www.everydaycostarica.com*. Run by 'action' naturalist Andy Pruter, this offers 'psycho' tours, catering to travellers who want a little high-adrenaline activity with their nature-watching: waterfall-rapelling; tree-climbing (to the top of 40m fig trees); hard-core hiking, etc. You'll need to be extremely fit to keep up.

Osa Aventura (no physical office), **t** 735 5670, *www.osaaventura.com*. A specialist in longer, more intense tours under the leadership of its main guide, Mike Boston, including trips out to the Isla del Caño.

Services in Puerto Jiménez

Banks: The town's sole bank, a new, rather large branch of the Banco Nacional, lies just north of the petrol station. It can change money and travellers' cheques and has an ATM.

Internet access: Café Net El Sol on the main street, as well as at the post office and Osa Natural, although connections can be tortuously slow.

Laundry: You can get your laundry done at **Soda Marisquería** at the north end of the main street. Turnaround time is around 2hrs, depending on the level of business, allowing you to stick around and have a meal while you wait.

Where to Stay in Puerto Jiménez

As popular as Puerto Jiménez has become in recent years, its hotels still cater mainly to the budget end of the spectrum, with many places still only able to offer cold-water showers. A couple of more upmarket choices have opened lately near the beach, but for true upscale lodging you'll need to head out of town to the lodges lining the road to Carate.

Puerto Jiménez Town/Beach

Iguana Lodge, 5km east of town at Playa Platanares, t 735 5205, *www. iguanalodge.com* ($$$$$; $210). Well outside the town proper, this beach-side property provides a foretaste of the accommodation you can expect on the road leading to Carate. These four luxury cabins overlooking the gulf have every facility you could want – hardwood furniture, Egyptian cotton sheets, large tiled bathrooms and terraces overlooking pretty gardens. A range of activities is offered, including sea kayaking, swimming, yoga and even salsa lessons. Rates include all meals, which are lavish buffet affairs.

Parrot Bay Village, by the airstrip, close to the beach, t 735 5180 ($$$$; $98). The town's highest-quality accommodation is, coincidentally enough, furthest from the village centre. Nestling in gardens near mangroves where crocodiles are often spotted, the Parrot Bay has eight octagonal cabins, all with huge ornate mahogany doors, elegantly crafted wooden furniture, outdoor (screened) hot showers and air-conditioning or fans. With each cabin sleeping up to eight, considerable savings can be made if you come as a group. The open-air restaurant/bar in the centre of the complex is open to the public and attracts a lively crowd throughout evening. A range of tours, including sports fishing packages, is offered. Guests can use the lodge's kayaks free.

Hotel Agua Luna, on the seafront near the ferry dock, t 735 5393, *agualu@ racsa.co.cr* ($$$–$; $45–25). One of town's more refined choices, albeit still catering to the lower–middle end of the market. Its best rooms ($45) are pretty large, with telephones, cable TV, air-conditioning, fridges and private bathrooms, while its more basic ones are smaller, but still have private bathrooms ($25).

Cabinas Puerto Jiménez, on the front, just north of the football field, t 735 5090, *cabinasjimenez@yahoo.com* ($$$–$; $55–20). Another formerly rock-bottom budget choice that's decided to reupholster itself in the hope of attracting a (slightly) more upmarket clientele. Hot water has been added, even to cheaper rooms, while the more expensive ones have new décor, furniture, bathrooms and air-conditioning (and now cost in excess of $50).

Cabinas Brisas del Mar, overlooking the Golfo Dulce, t 735 5028 ($$–$; $40–10). This offers the basics for its traditional backpacker customers – dorm-style rooms sleeping up to six with fans and shared cold water bathrooms for $10 per person – as well as a couple of better-equipped 'deluxe' rooms for $40, aimed at a more upmarket clientele, which have good- quality furniture, mosquito nets, air-conditioning and private bathrooms (with hot water). Student discounts.

Cabinas Marcelina, on the main street, around halfway between the football field and the petrol station, t 735 5007, *cabmarce@hotmail.com* ($; $24). This was a rather down-at-heel place just a few years ago, but has been completely overhauled, and now offers eight large, spick-and-span rooms (a fresh coat of paint can perform wonders), tiled private bathrooms (hot water) and even air-conditioning in a couple of rooms. Tours can be arranged and discounts are available for 'Hostelling International' members.

Cabinas Oro Verde, main street, t 735 5241 ($; $7 per person). Centrally located, slap bang in the middle of the main road, the Oro Verde is as good a choice as you can expect for the price, offering basic, simple rooms, all with fans and private bathrooms (cold water only) and there's a laundry service and a decent (and cheap) Tico restaurant.

Puerto Jiménez to Carate

The hotels and lodges adjoining the 43km unpaved and rather uneven (to put it mildly) road running around the tip of the peninsula to Carate are considerably more well-to-do than anything you'll find in Puerto Jiménez. Indeed, some are among the best-equipped and most luxurious places in the whole country, and have become popular honeymoon destinations. Cabo Matapalo on the very tip of the peninsula has acquired a reputation as a sort of upscale surfing destination, catering to élite break-riders who want to catch the waves but not necessarily slum it. Do be aware, when booking, that the phone network doesn't extend this far out, and mobile phone coverage is poor. Most hotels receive all their communications (including e-mail and faxes) via Puerto Jiménez, so there may be a delay of a few days before they return your messages. And, just to complicate matters further, RACSA, the state phone company, occasionally goes down, during which time its servers will often 'swallow' e-mails. Try to book as far in advance as possible, so as to avoid any crossed wires.

The following options are listed in the order you encounter them on the road from Puerto Jiménez to Carate. Prices include all meals, and usually a range of tours.

⭐ **Lapa Rios >**

Lapa Ríos, 20km south of Puerto Jiménez, t 735 5130, www.laparios.com ($$$$$; $420). In a region dominated by luxurious eco-lodges, the Lapa Ríos takes the concept to a whole new level. Set on a hill with gorgeous ocean views, it boasts absolutely huge thatched bungalows – all with hardwood furniture, four-poster beds (with mosquito nets), sumptuous bathrooms, private gardens and terraces – a fantastic restaurant serving up all manner of opulent creations fashioned from local produce. It has also thoughtfully provided a 160ha private nature reserve, home to a similar array of wildlife as can be found in Corcovado (over 320 species of bird have been recorded here), that can be toured either on foot or on horseback in the company of a guide. Or, if that sounds too energetic, you can simply admire it from the panoramic viewing platform above the restaurant. A range of other pursuits, including fishing, snorkelling, swimming, yoga and massage therapy, is also offered. And, before you start complaining about the effect all this must be having on

the environment, it's worth noting that the owners are committed conservationists, actively involved in the local community (they helped to finance the building of a nearby school) and are the only hotel in the country to have been awarded five 'leaves', the tourist board's top award for ecological sustainability. In fact, it's hard to find fault with the whole operation, apart from that's it's exceptionally expensive, but it is exceptionally well equipped.

Bosque del Cabo, Cabo Matapalo, t 735 5206, www.bosquedelcabo.com ($$$$$; $135). Bosque del Cabo is not quite as luxurious as the Lapa Ríos, but it's not far off, and can at least content itself with having the slightly larger nature reserve – 220 hectares. Owned and run by a friendly American couple, the accommodation is spread out over nicely landscaped gardens, with 10 stylish cabins and two rental houses, all designed and built to very high specifications out of a combination of cement, stucco and hardwoods. Located on a hill right on the southern tip of the peninsula, some of the cabins offer superb ocean views (the best are from the terrace of the 'Congo' cabin perched high above the waves). You can actually see the point where the currents of the Golfo Dulce and Pacific meet, forming a long white foamy line stretching to the horizon. Top-quality meals made from local produce are served in the open-air restaurant beneath a thatched indigenous-style roof, and there's a swimming pool and bar. The grounds are home to an array of wildlife including several species of monkey – who often venture boldly into the inhabited parts of the compound – and there's a trail leading down to a private beach. The lodge even boasts its own short (one zip-line long) canopy tour, which you can use as a practice run before tackling some of the more challenging tours elsewhere around the country. All electricity is provided by hydro and solar power.

Terrapin Lodge, 40km from Puerto Jiménez, just south of Carate, t 735 5207, www.terrapinlodge.com ($$$$; $110). One of the few places in this area to be owned by Costa Ricans, rather than Americans, the Terrapin is, as you'd expect, a bit smaller and more basic than many of its competitors, but nonetheless comfortable. On 8ha of forested land sit five simple cabins, all with terraces with hammocks, a small pool and an open-air restaurant. Trails lead down to the beach and up to a waterfall in the grounds. Kayaks and horses are available for hire.

Lookout Inn, Carate, t 735 5431, *www. lookout-inn.com* ($$$$$; $198). Another of the region's superbly luxurious choices, this offers a large lodge with four well-appointed rooms (and very plush bathrooms) plus a couple of stand-alone cabins in the grounds adorned with bespoke artwork ($240). As the name suggests, there are plenty of wonderful vistas of the ocean and forest, both from a special observation deck and from the terrace of the gourmet restaurant. There's a pool and a Jacuzzi and guests have free use of the lodge's kayaks. Fishing and horse-riding trips are available. A seriously steep trail through the grounds leads to two waterfalls.

Luna Lodge, less than 2km from Carate, t 380 5036, *www.lunalodge.com* ($$$$$; $85 per person). If possible, fly in to Carate and arrange for a pick-up, as the final ascent to this lodge is among the leading contenders for the most challenging section of road in the entire country. Its isolated position, right at the end of the coastal road, is perfectly in tune with its retreat-like, getting-away-from-it-all, spiritual vibe. The lodge's defining feature is its yoga platform, set looking out over the forest on which Tai Chi, meditation, and (just to liven things up a bit) salsa lessons are offered. Lovely hardwood bungalows are set into the hill of this elegantly landscaped complex, and there's a great open-air restaurant set under an enormous indigenous-style thatched roof, where lavish feasts, mostly made from produce taken from the lodge's own organic garden (a necessity in these secluded parts) are served. All the energy here is derived from solar power with lights switched off at 10pm in order to conserve it. In truth, you might find the spiritual earnestness of the place slightly overwhelming (not to say off-putting), but with a 25ha reserve to explore, there's no need to get any more yogic than you want to. And the lodge can arrange horse-riding on the beach, sea-kayaking, and tours of nearby Corcovado in the company of knowledgeable guides.

Corcovado Lodge Tent Camp, 2km west of Carate, t 257 0766, *www.costarica expeditions.com* ($$$$; $49 per person). The name makes it sound more rustic than it actually is, although it's still a step down from the region's super-resorts. It offers superior camping in a complex owned and run by Costa Rica Expeditions, the country's pre-eminent tour operator. Enjoying an idyllic setting right on the beach en route to the La Leona entrance to Corcovado, it has 20 platform-set tents with shared bathrooms, mosquito screens (a necessity in these bug-infested climes), a small restaurant where communal meals are served, and a 140ha private reserve adjoining the national park where a 33m-high wildlife-observation platform has been erected, around half an hour's hike away. You'll need to bring a torch as the tents have no lights – they're reserved for the communal areas only.

La Leona Ecolodge and Tent Camp, t 735 5705, *www.laleonalodge.com* ($$$$; $60 per person). The last rung of civilization, La Leona is located on the beach right by the entrance to the park. This offers much the same fare as the other beach camp described above: platform-set tents, mosquito nets, shared bathrooms, a private nature reserve (30ha) and a range of tours – night hikes, birding, horse-riding on the beach, etc. Electricity, a precious commodity around here, is used only to illuminate the public areas, so you'll need to bring a torch with you. The camp's restaurant is open to the public and is a great place to rest after hard morning's hiking in the park. Boogie-boards for hire.

Eating Out and Nightlife in Puerto Jiménez

There's not a huge array of dining options in Puerto Jiménez. The restaurant scene, such as it is, consists of a few traditional sodas aimed at locals, plus a number of 'international' places aimed at tourists. There are also a few late opening bars, some of which can get pretty boisterous at weekends, but this is no party town.

Restaurante Agua Luna, on the front, near the ferry dock, **t** 735 5393. This hotel restaurant offers a slightly peculiar Chinese-Tico hybrid menu, with the odd random Italian dish thrown in for good measure. Its bar overlooking the gulf is a popular nightspot, serving an array of powerful tropical cocktails, and can get pretty packed at weekends. Mains from $4–6.

Restaurante y Cabinas Carolina, in the middle of the main street in the middle of town, **t** 735 5185. Located where it is, Carolina's is more than just a restaurant, it's a sort of unofficial social crossroads, a central meeting point where everyone in Puerto Jiménez, both locals and tourist alike, seems to pop in over the course of a day to check out the latest happenings. If you want to find something, track someone down or book a trip somewhere (it's the headquarters of Escondido Trex, one of the town's main tour operators, *see* p.311), this is the place to do it. And, what's more, you can have a bite to eat while you pursue your enquiries. The food is perfectly decent *comida típica* fare, and there are also a couple of basic **cabins** to rent (cold water only, $15).

Juanita's Mexican Bar and Grill, just off the main street, **t** 735 5056. A relaxing place to wind down in the late afternoon (4–6pm is happy hour) with a beer or one of their special recipe (and potent) margaritas, watching the comings and goings from the outside terrace. As the evening progresses you can move inside (through the kitschy hacienda-style swing doors) to sample some of the Tico-style Mexican cuisine, which includes decent tacos, burritos and a very fiery chilli. Its cheap prices (most mains from $3–5) and regular 'fun' (i.e. studenty) events – hula-hoop competitions, eating races, etc. – make it very popular with the backpacking community. *Open from breakfast till late, closing at 1am (sometimes later) Fri and Sat.*

Soda Morales, opposite the northern end of the football field. Good solid, typical soda serving good solid, typical soda food, including a renowned *ceviche* (a combination of fish and seafood 'cooked' in lime juice, not for the faint-hearted), plus decent *casados*. *Open till 10pm daily.*

Bahía Drake

⭐ Bahía Drake

The idyllic Bahía Drake ('Drake Bay'), tucked away in the Osa Peninsula's northwestern corner, provides a classy, exclusive, isolated yin to to Puerto Jiménez's rough, ready and accessible yang. The bay itself is stunning – a gorgeous sweep of forested coast, overlooking a pristine, postcard-perfect beach, on to which lap the clear blue waters of the Pacific where yachts bob up and down and dolphins

The Pirate's Bay

Though pronounced in the Spanish manner ('Dra-Kay'), the bay is named after that most English of adventurers, Sir Francis Drake, who visited the area in 1579 either, according to official reports, to rest or, according to local legend, to bury some of the excess treasure he'd looted from the Spanish during his various raids along the Central American coast. Drake's piracy had achieved mythic proportions by this time, with the great buccaneer regularly sending ships weighed down with stolen gold and silver back across the ocean to England. In 1585 he stole so much from Spain's West Indian territories that the Bank of Spain went bankrupt, an event which largely influenced King Philip II of Spain's decision to build an armada with which to attack England a few years later – which was ultimately, not to say rather poetically, defeated by Drake himself, of course.

While Drake may well have had plenty of treasure to bury here, he certainly hid it well if he did, as nobody has been able to find it in over four centuries of searching.

Getting to Bahía Drake

You'll need to put your thinking cap on. Bahía Drake does not lend itself to ad hoc, spur-of-the-moment visits. It's too isolated and the transport options are much too limited for that.

As is often the case, there is an easy way to get here, plus a couple of much more difficult ones. The easy way consists of **flying** into Drake's small airfield, located at the northern edge of the bay, from where you'll be picked up by your lodge and either driven or sailed to your accommodation. NatureAir and Sansa both operate daily flights (*see* p.104 for details).

In the dry season, it is just about possible to **drive** from Rincón to Agujitas, although the road is pretty shocking and you'll have to negotiate carefully the crossing of a couple of rivers. Even with a 4WD, this route will probably still be impassable during the wet season.

The most common way in to Drake is by **boat**. For this, you'll need to get to the town of **Sierpe**, 15km south of Palmar, where you can board a motorized *lancha* for the 30km, 2hr journey down the Río Sierpe and along the Pacific coast to the bay. This is normally arranged by your lodge and included in the price (by far the most stress-free option), although it is possible to arrange your own trip. Boats depart according to no fixed timetable (as and when there are enough passengers to make it worthwhile) from in front of the Restaurante Las Vegas on the waterfront, which is also the best place to find and engage the services of a boat captain. If none is present, try asking Sonia Rojas at the El Fenix *pulpería* if she knows where you might be able to track one down. If you're lucky, and can turn on the charm, you may be able to inveigle your way onto another hotel's boat for around $15; otherwise, you'll have to negotiate a price. The more of you there are, the better; if travelling alone, you may have to pay in excess of $60. The journey itself along the jungle-fringed river is beautiful, but a touch nerve-racking, especially at the point where the river meets the ocean, which can be decidedly choppy. Make sure your captain has lifejackets and put yours on as soon as you get in the boat.

Try to get to Sierpe as early as possible, as the waters get progressively rougher over the course of the day. The last boats leave at around 3pm. This may mean staying the night in Palmar (*see* p.298) or Sierpe itself, which has a few accommodation options – the **Hotel Oleaje Sereno**, **t** 786 7580 ($$; $35) on the waterfront is most convenient, the **Estero Azul Lodge**, **t** 786 7422 ($$$; $60), around 2km north, the most comfortable.

The bus/boat combo is not the most difficult way to make it here. It is also possible, although by no means recommended, to **hike** all the way through the Parque Nacional Corcovado from La Leona to San Pedrillo, and then continue up the coast to the bay – a total hike of over 70km (or at least three days).

---

frolic and play. Any description inevitably ends up sounding like a tourist brochure, but that doesn't make it any less true. The accommodation in these parts, some of the grandest the country has to offer, tends to inspire equally purple prose. In addition to all their lavish facilities, most of the lodges here offer a wealth of activities and tours, from hiking in the Parque Nacional Corcovado around 20km south (they can also arrange drop-off and pick-up at the park entrance if you want to travel independently, otherwise it's a good 4–6hr hike away), to snorkelling at the Isla del Caño National Reserve, 20km offshore, as well as scuba-diving, sports fishing, horse-riding and birding. Bahía Drake doesn't welcome very many backpackers and budget travellers – it's too difficult to get here, and too expensive once you have – but if you've got the money it's well worth it, offering the perfect combination of luxurious living and nature-watching with which the country as a whole is attempting to market itself to the world.

The 'community' of **Drake** is spread out over several kilometres along the coast, with the tiny village of **Agujitas** at its centre. Actually, Agujitas isn't much of a village (to call it a hamlet would be a bit of an exaggeration), consisting of little more than a *pulpería*, a school, a phone box and a few budget cabins, but then few visitors spend any time here, being whisked off to their lodges almost as soon as they arrive.

② Reserva Biológica Isla del Caño
adm $6, usually covered in tour price

Reserva Biológica Isla del Caño

Most of the lodges in Bahía Drake offer trips to the tiny, uninhabited **Caño Island**, 20km due west of (and clearly visible from) the bay. Actually, 'tiny' is not quite the right adjective; only a small area of land, some 3km by 2km, lies above the surface of the Pacific Ocean, but this represents the tip of a huge underwater mountain. The island, which has been classified as a biological reserve, offers three main attractions: evergreen forest, which blankets the interior and offers good hiking; lithic spheres, those strange circular carved stones shipped here in pre-Columbian times by the Diquis, the local indigenous tribe, and placed on top of the island's central ridge for some important purpose (nobody is sure exactly what; *see* p.298); and, the main draw, offshore coral reefs, which provide some of the country's very best snorkelling and scuba-diving, with warm, clear waters that are home to a myriad fish. Other than the small **ranger station**, where the entrance fees are paid if not covered by of a tour, there are no facilities on the island. Camping is not permitted.

Where to Stay in Bahía Drake

Most of the lodges in Bahía Drake specialize in all-inclusive packages, offering transport (from San José or Sierpe), meals and a range of tours (to Corcovado, the Isla del Caño, etc.) as part of the price. As with the entire west coast of the peninsula, telephone links here are somewhat erratic, with many places only having access to radio phones, and picking up their e-mails in Sierpe. Book as far in advance as possible and keep trying till you get a response. The area's isolation also means that many places have a limited supply of electricity (some of the more basic places don't have any at all), provided by a combination of generators, solar and hydro power.

The following are listed north to south as you encounter them, arriving either by air or *lancha*.

Mirador Lodge, t 387 9138, *www.mirador.co.cr* ($$$; $35 per person). Perched on a forested hill (the entrance is up a steep path) with good views of the bay, this is one of Drake's cheaper options, although it's still hardly a bargain, especially as there's no electricity, obliging you to make do with cold water and candlelight. You'll soon get used to it, however, and will probably find the friendly, helpful staff's infectious, can-do spirit rubbing off on you. The seven basic but comfortable cabins sleep up to four and you can camp in the grounds for $5. A wide range of tours is offered and the great home-cooked meals are included in the price.

Rancho Corcovado Lodge, t 350 4866 ($$$; $45 per person). Clean and simple accommodation near the beach, the Rancho's rooms are large enough to sleep four, but are a touch basic, although all have bathrooms (cold water only) and balconies with hammocks where you can relax, taking in the views of the bay. Camping space is available in the grounds for $6 (which entitles you to use the bathrooms) and a range of tours, including horse-riding, is offered. Rates include all meals.

Aguila de Osa Inn, t 296 2190, *www.aguiladeosainn.com* ($$$$$; $240). Superbly well-equipped, the Aguila offers 13 huge rooms – all with hardwood furnishings and lavish tiled bathrooms – plus a very good open-air restaurant overlooking the bay, and (a real luxury for these parts) 24hr electricity. The lodge specializes in sports fishing packages and has its own fleet of boats, also used for dolphin-watching and scuba-diving trips.

Drake Bay Wilderness Resort, t 770 8012, *www.drakebay.com* ($$$$$; $180). One of the bay's oldest established lodges, this also enjoys one of the area's best locations, perched on a point sticking out into the bay, providing great 180-degree ocean views. There are 19 cabins – all with terraces, mosquito screens, large beds and showers (solar-heated water) – as well as a restaurant/bar overlooking the bay. Night time electricity is provided, as are a couple of cheaper tents during the high season. Tours include fishing, dolphin-watching, mountain biking and kayaking.

★ La Paloma Lodge >

La Paloma Lodge, t 293 7502, *www. lapalomalodge.com* ($$$$$; $160). Nestling among the trees at the top of a hill, La Paloma offers several large bungalows, all with two beds, ceiling fans, mosquito nets and balconies (with hammocks) and outdoor (but screened) bathrooms, allowing you to ablute while gazing out over the rainforest. The thatch-roofed restaurant has a special sunset terrace, as well as a bar serving potent tropical cocktails. A variety of tours and activities are offered, including sea-kayaking, horse-riding, boogie-boarding, night hikes and the lodge's particular speciality, scuba-diving – La Paloma has its own dive shop, as well as a dive boat that undertakes trips to the Isla del Caño.

Corcovado Adventures Tent Camp, 2km south of Agujitas, **t** 396 2451, *www.*

corcovado.com ($$$$; $110). A way south of town, 1–1½hrs' walk. Though the name,'Tent Camp', makes it sound rather basic, this complex, a long walk south of town, is still a pretty fancy option, with nine platform-set tents overlooking the sea, a nice restaurant and a range of tours offered – fishing, snorkelling, hiking, etc. You can also use the camp's boogie-boards free.

Poor Man's Paradise, 8km southwest of Bahía Drake, **t** 771 4852, *www. mypoormansparadise.com* ($$$$–$; $100–7). Right on the beach, just a few kilometres from the park entrance, this offers three levels of accommodation: nice rustic tent cabins for $100 with private baths (with cold water only); a couple with shared baths for $45; and, the only option liable to tempt a poor man, camping space for $7. There's also a thatch-roofed restaurant and a range of tours, including sports fishing and snorkelling. Lights out at 9pm.

Casa Corcovado, t 256 3181, *www.casa corcovado.com* ($$$$$; $430 plus). The closest accommodation to the national park, which may go some way towards explaining its extraordinarily high prices, this only offers multi-day packages (with a minimum stay of two nights) with three-night deals starting at around $1,300. It's fabulously well equipped, with its own 70ha reserve of land bordering the national park; 12 luxuriously appointed circular bungalows – all with ceiling fans, tasteful Oriental-style furniture, bathrooms with hot water and private terraces with hammocks – plus two swimming pools, a sunset bar and a beach bar. A wide range of tours is offered, including Corcovado hikes undertaken in the very early morning – the best time to see the animals.

Parque Nacional Isla del Coco

It seems strange that the Isla del Coco isn't more well known than it is. After all, it's got some pretty impressive statistics. Measuring around 12km long and 5km wide, it's the largest uninhabited island on earth. It's also the only tropical Pacific island with a climate wet enough to support genuine rainforest, in which live several species found nowhere else on earth.

And its clear coastal waters are thick with a superabundance of marine life – hammerhead sharks, bottlenose dolphins, manta rays

Getting to the Isla del Coco

If you want to visit – and it's supposed to be absolutely magical – a few diving operators and cruise ships do make the journey each year, but it's going to cost you. The ***Okeanos Aggressor***, **t** (257) 8686 800, *www.okeanoscocoisland.com*, which runs 10-day diving trips to the island throughout the year for the not inconsiderable sum of $3,500 per person, is probably the cheapest option going.

and a sweetshop assortment of brightly coloured tropical fish – making it a highly respected diving destination. It was even briefly a film star, assuming the role of 'Dinosaur Island' at the beginning of the film *Jurassic Park*.

But for all these manifold charms, the island's isolation – it lies nigh on 500km southwest of Costa Rica – puts it out of reach to all but the most dedicated (and richest) of adventurers. It was seemingly ever thus. Though there is some evidence to suggest that people visited the island in prehistoric times, it seems pretty clear that it has never managed to sustain a permanent community. Costa Rica claimed the island in the mid-19th century (not that there was much competition for it) presumably with the intention of colonizing it, but never got round to it, eventually turning the whole thing into a national park in 1978.

Parque Nacional Corcovado

Parque Nacional Corcovado
open daily 8–4; adm

This is it. This is the motherlode. If you've come to Costa Rica in the hope of watching wildlife, then the Parque Nacional Corcovado is the main show on the biggest screen, the most biologically diverse part of the world's most biologically diverse country. Comprising over 55,000 hectares, or around a third of the Osa Peninsula's total area, including most of its western coast, the park is home to a huge variety of different habitats – from soft sandy beaches and mangroves at its margins, passing through secondary forest and swamps at its outer flanks to the country's largest swath of virgin rainforest, which blankets its central hump-like hill (Corcovado literally translates as 'hunchback').

At least 50 per cent of the country's entire biodiversity can be found here, although, with many species of insect and plant yet to be identified, the final figure could end up being much higher. No matter how long you spend here – and many travellers spend up to three days trekking the forest depths – you're going to see something remarkable. Here's a list of the animals I saw during my first hike into Corcovado which lasted just half a day – scarlet macaws (dozens of them), Hallowe'en crabs, howler monkeys, white-faced capuchins, coatis, a red-leg honey-creeper, Jesus Christ lizards, iguanas, a pair of curassows, lots of butterflies and (wait for it, drum roll, please...) a tapir.

Getting to Corcovado from Puerto Jiménez

If not part of an official **tour** (*see* 'Puerto Jiménez', p.311), you've got your work cut out. Puerto Jiménez may be the main base for travellers visiting the park, but it doesn't exactly lie on the doorstep. You can reach two of the park's three entrances from there, although it's not particularly straightforward getting to either.

To Los Patos

The nearest, Los Patos, in the park's northeast corner, is actually the most difficult to access, and as a consequence the least used. You must catch one of six **buses** a day to **La Palma**, 24km north of Puerto Jiménez, from where it's a 12km, 3–4hr hike to the park. You'll need to set off early if you're hoping to return the same day. An overnight stay is the more likely option, in which case you'll need to book space at the ranger station well in advance. You may also be able to get a 4WD **taxi** to drive you from Puerto Jiménez to Los Patos for around $60.

To La Leona via Carate

Most independent travellers use the La Leona entrance on the western side of the peninsula, a couple of kilometres north of the village of **Carate**, southwest of Puerto Jiménez. Carate is a village in name only, consisting of little more than an airstrip and a *pulperia* – local store – where you can stock up on water and supplies before the one and a half-hour trek along the jungle-fringed beach to La Leona ranger station. To get here, you'll either have to fly, drive or use the *colectivo*, the principal means of public transport in these parts – it's a sort of open-back truck taxi that trundles along collecting passengers as it goes (hence the name).

Both Sansa and NatureAir operate daily **flights** to Carate in the high season (*see* p.104). If you're feeling particularly flush, it's also possible to charter a small 5-seater plane with Alfa Romeo Aero Taxis (t 735 5353) for around $250 for the short hop from Puerto Jiménez to either Carate or Sirena, which lies within the park itself.

If **driving**, you'll need the sturdiest 4WD you can lay your hands on. The 43km road from Puerto Jiménez around the tip of the peninsula to Carate may well be the worst in the entire country, although apparently it's been 'much improved' of late, which makes you wonder just how bad it was before. Once you've got used to the constant bumping over rocks and debris, you'll then be obliged to wheel-spin up several steep hills and splash your way through several small rivers (which become large impassable rivers in the wet season). The final section of the road, past Carate out towards the Luna Lodge, is the *pièce de résistance*, ascending almost vertically. Even the locals consider this a bit tricky, strapping chains to their tyres during the wet season.

The drive is therefore probably best left to professionals. Two *colectivos* leave Puerto Jiménez every day for Carate at 6am and 1.30pm from the street running parallel to the west of the Calle Comercial (the main street), just back from the football field. Tickets can be booked at Osa Natural, next to the football field. Return services from Carate leave at 8.30am and 4pm. It costs $10 one-way. There's also a less regular *colectivo* service to Bahía Drake at 12 noon on Mondays and Fridays. All services are liable to cancellation in the wet season. The driver will drop you anywhere you want along the route, provided you can get his attention.

You can also hire a 4WD taxi from the main street in Puerto Jiménez to take you to Carate, although this can be expensive if travelling alone – up to $70; try joining up with some fellow travellers to spread the cost a little. Unfortunately, it looks as if taxi prices may well be set to rise in the future. Most of the current fleet of taxis are great pick-up trucks, in which up to eight people can travel sitting in the back. However, a recent law requiring that all passengers wear seatbelts has rendered these officially illegal. Taxi drivers are gradually switching over to all-seater vehicles, but somewhat grudgingly, as this means they can carry fewer passengers at a time, thereby obliging them to increase their fares.

Getting to Corcovado National Park from Bahía Drake

Most lodges in Bahía Drake will arrange tours and transport to the park. Otherwise, depending on which lodge you're staying in, the entrance can lie as far as 25km, or a 6–8hr hike, south. There's no public transport. If planning on walking to the entrance, you'd be best off arranging to stay overnight at the ranger station and beginning your hike into the park the next day.

According to the latest estimates, the park provides leafy accommodation for over 400 species of bird; 140 species of mammals (including sloths, white-lipped peccaries, anteaters, pumas, jaguars and margays); over 120 species of reptile and amphibian; and literally countless species of insect.

Though the animals are understandably the park's main draw, once here you'll probably find yourself becoming just as fascinated by the abundance of plant life – giant tree-shaped strangler vines (with the 'murdered' tree now long since rotted away), bromeliads,

Tips for Visiting Corcovado

• **Be careful**. Though many (if not most) visitors come on organized tours, it is perfectly possible to explore Corcovado independently, although you'll need to keep your wits about you. It may be a 'tourist attraction' but this is still a dangerous, wild place full of all manner of deadly beasties – sharks, poisonous snakes, crocodiles, jaguars. Not that you're likely to have a close encounter with any of them, but the potential is there. Of more immediate concern is the extreme nature of the tides in this region, particularly because hiking the park's trails will involve a good deal of beach walking, not to mention the crossing of a couple of rivers. Indeed, certain waterways and sections of beach become completely impassable at high tide. Pick up a tidal chart from the ranger station and study it carefully. Ideally, you should hire the services of an experienced, knowledgeable guide (*see* below), but failing that, do at least travel with a companion who can raise the alarm should something untoward happen. The rangers make a careful note of how many people are on each trail and, if you haven't reached your destination by the expected time, will go looking for you, but by then, of course, it may already be too late.

• **Be sure to bring plenty of water** (at least five litres per hike; you can re-fill at the ranger stations) and sunscreen. Try to rest out of the sun during the midday heat when temperatures may exceed 30°C and humidity can reach nearly 100 per cent.

• **Bring lots of DEET-based repellent** and regularly reapply in order to keep the park's vast numbers of biting, burrowing, irritating insects at bay (at least for a few more seconds).

• **Be physically prepared**. Though short day hikes are possible from all three entrance stations, the park lends itself best to a visit of several days. And, considering the difficulty of getting here in the first place, it does seem a shame to restrict the amount of exploring you can do once you've finally arrived. Many people choose to spend up to three days here – hiking to Sirena on the first day, exploring the forest depths on the second, and then hiking out again on the third. It may seem obvious, but if this is what you're planning to do, it's going to involve an awful lot of hiking, and you need to make sure that you're physically up to the task. There have been too many examples of couch potatoes arriving in Corcovado to undertake their first serious piece of exercise in years, only to succumb to exhaustion after just a few kilometres. If you know you're coming, get in training early.

• **Try to travel as light as possible**. Even if you are fit, the going can still be hard. Indeed, on a particularly gruelling hike, you may find the appeal of the rainforest beginning to wear off slightly. As you walk the trails, you might occasionally spot some overloaded, red-faced, sodden-shirted hikers plodding along, clearly no longer interested in the natural vistas around them, but instead simply concentrating on putting one foot in front of the other and getting to the next ranger station by sundown. Try to avoid becoming one of them.

• **Hire a guide**. If travelling independently, it's certainly worth investing in the services of an experienced guide. The MINAE office in Puerto Jiménez (*see* p.311) will be able to put you in touch with one. Guides justify their cost ($20–45 a day depending on what's required) on a number of levels. Firstly, from a safety perspective, they can help prevent you getting lost, eaten, drowned or succumbing to any other potential disaster in the jungle. A guide I was hiking with helped me to make it safely through the day by preventing me from resting against a 'mountain lily', a delicate name for an absolute brute of a tree, whose seed pods can weigh up to 5kg and dangle from the canopy about 100ft above your head. If one of those drops while you're sitting under it, it's going to do a lot of damage. A good guide is also invaluable in spotting animals camouflaged in the undergrowth, recognizing that log-shaped silhouette for what it truly is, as well as identifying tracks and calls. They often also have a good knowledge of the local plants, many of which are used in traditional herbal remedies – leaves that you can boil up for kidney infections, barks that can be used to treat anaemia, etc. In fact, it seems as if every ailment has its own curative plant to be found somewhere in the rainforest.

Where to Stay in the Parque Nacional Corcovado

All four stations are well equipped, offering accommodation (bunks and camping areas at La Leona and Sirena, small campgrounds at the other two), dining facilities, water and bathrooms. Space is limited at each, so if you're hoping to stay the night you'll need to book as far in advance as possible, through the MINAE office in Puerto Jimenez, see p.311.

epiphytes, orchids and hundreds and hundreds of species of tree. Corcovado has a density of trees unmatched anywhere outside the Amazon basin, some of which have truly outlandish shapes. Because the soil here (as is often the case with rainforests) is thin, many trees in Corcovado support themselves by bolstering their root systems with giant overground, undulating, Gaudí-esque buttresses.

Trails through Corcovado

Corcovado has four **ranger stations**, linked by a network of trails: **La Leona** on its southwest border; **San Pedrillo** on its northwest border; **Los Patos** on its northeast border; and **Sirena**, which is located within the park itself, on the coast roughly a third of the way between La Leona and San Pedrillo.

Most of the trails traverse the outskirts of the park, hugging the coast, with just the Sirena–Los Patos route running through the heart of the forest.

Much of the route from **La Leona to San Pedrillo** is made up of large sections of unshaded beach.

The **La Leona–Sirena** trek (18km), which starts off on the beach before heading inland through the secondary forest of a former banana plantation, is one of the best areas to see scarlet macaws, which regularly roost in the coastal trees, as well as howler and white-faced monkeys. It's a pretty challenging hike, but, being mostly flat, can still be considered the park's easiest trail.

The 20km **Sirena–Los Patos** trail, a part of which ascends a hill in the centre of the park, is much harder going, even in the dry season, and can be particularly gruelling in the wet, although it does afford perhaps the best chance of seeing some of the park's larger mammals, who tend to confine themselves to the forest depths.

The 25km **Sirena–San Pedrillo** trail is only open in the dry season (December to April) and, even at this time, will involve the careful fording of a couple of pretty treacherous rivers, including the Río Sirena, where (just to make things interesting) bull sharks come upstream to scavenge at high tide. As with the La Leona–Sirena section, most of this trail hugs the coast. Indeed, sizeable chunks simply follow the beach.

The Caribbean Coast

Less built-up and certainly much less aggressively touristy than many other areas of the country, Costa Rica's Caribbean coast offers a wealth of relaxed, sedate pursuits – sunbathing on palm-lined beaches, snorkelling in among coral reefs, drifting along jungle-fringed rivers on the lookout for wildlife.

The area's historic isolation – many of its communities have only acquired reliable transport and communications links in the past couple of decades – and its diverse racial mix have helped it to develop a unique character.

14

Don't miss

⭐ **Snorkelling at the best coral reef**
Cahuita **p.351**

⭐ **Jungle cruises by day, turtle-spotting by night**
Parque Nacional Tortuguero **p.335**

⭐ **Surfing and bar-hopping**
Puerto Viejo de Talamance **p.353**

⭐ **Carnival time**
Puerto Limón **p.331**

⭐ **Hiking off the beaten track**
Reserva Biológica Hitoy Cerere **p.352**

See map overleaf

20 km
10 miles

N

NICARAGUA

Barra del Colorado

*Refugio Nacional
de Fauna Silvestre
Barra del Colorado*

Tortuguero

Parque Nacional Tortuguero

Caribbean Sea

Cariari

LIMON

Parismina

Guápiles
128 Río Jiménez
Guácimo
• *Rainforest Aerial Tram*

Río Reventazón

Río Pacuare

*Parque Nacional
Braulio Carrillo*

Siquirres

*Parque Nacional
Volcán Turrialba*

*Reserva Forestal
Río Pacuare*

Cordillera Central

Portete
Moín
PUERTO LIMÓN

Turrialba
Pacayas

*Parque Nacional
Barbilla*

*Parque Nacional
Cahuita*

Cachi
Orosi

CARTAGO

Valle la Estrella

Fortuna
Pandora
Cahuita
Punta Cahuita

*Parque Nacional
Tapantí*

*Reserva Biológica
Hitoy Cerere*

Puerto Viejo
de Talamanca
Playa Chiquita
Manzanillo

INTERAMERICANA

*Parque
Internacional
La Amistad*

LIMON

Bribri

*Refugio Nacional
Gandoca-Manzanillo*
Gandoca

*Parque Nacional
Chirripó*

*Parque
Internacional
La Amistad*

PANAMA

San Gerardo
de Rivas

Sixaola

p.282

NICARAGUA

Caribbean Sea

Pacific Ocean

PANAMA

Don't miss

PP.254-5

PP.122-3

Getting around the Caribbean Coast

With the possible exception of the Osa Peninsula, this is perhaps the most difficult region in the whole of Costa Rica to get around. **Road** coverage is by no means total. Indeed, some areas, most notably Barra del Colorado and Tortuguero in the northeast, do not have roads at all and can only be reached either via **boat** (usually via Moín) or **plane** from San José. That said, if you can afford it, plane travel is quick, efficient and largely hassle-free. In the south, the transport infrastructure is more developed, but only comparatively so. The main **Braulio Carrillo Highway** (HWY-32) runs from San José through the Caribbean lowlands to Puerto Limón, from where a coastal road heads south to the Caribbean villages of Cahuita and Puerto Viejo de Talamanca. The road south of here is unpaved.

The Braulio Carrillo Highway itself, though greeted with mass fanfare upon its completion in the 1970s when it was held up as a sign of Costa Rica's growing modernity, poses its fair share of problems. Its surface may be well maintained, certainly in comparison with many of the country's other 'major' roads, but its course, particularly in the section northeast of San José cut into the slopes of the region's volcanoes, has made it susceptible to landslides. At higher elevations, fog is also a major hazard. The thick mists that descend in a matter of minutes can make it difficult to see even a few metres in front of your windscreen. Combine this with the fact that this is one of the country's most congested arteries, permanently choked with cars, buses and lorries, and you'll understand why the authorities urge you to use the utmost caution when driving here. Accidents are worryingly common and have led to its being given the nickname 'The Highway to Heaven'.

The road it superseded, HWY-10, which runs through Turrialba, is if anything even worse – narrow, poorly maintained and exceptionally winding. The only advantage it has over its modern rival is that it conveys far less traffic. Neither road should be driven in the dark.

In racial and cultural terms, most of Costa Rica displays an overwhelming homogeneity. Because there were so few indigenous people remaining by the time Spain got round to colonizing Costa Rica – most having either fled or died of diseases of European origin – the Costa Rican population that emerged over the succeeding centuries was drawn from a very narrow racial stock, with the vast majority of people able to trace their origins directly back to Spain. Limón province, however, which comprises the entire Atlantic coast, is different. Until the late 19th century, this was a largely underpopulated area, home to just a few small indigenous tribes, the perceived harshness of the environment having deterred many Ticos from settling here. Thus, the first sizeable community to emerge here was actually made up of Afro-Caribbean workers who had been brought over from Jamaica in their thousands to help construct the 'Jungle Train' linking San José with the coast. Many stayed on to work in the region's banana and pineapple plantations, and today around a third of the province's population is of Afro-Caribbean descent. Their influence can be felt in all aspects of the local culture: in the language – Caribbean English is spoken almost as widely as Spanish; the food – your tastebuds will welcome the change from *típico* cooking provided by the creole cuisine of the restaurants; and, of course, in the music, as Latin rhythms give way to reggae beats.

The cultural diversity of the region is further enhanced by the continued presence of the Bribrí and Cabécar tribes to the south, representative of the country's small remaining indigenous peoples who now make up less than two per cent of the entire population. Unfortunately, this cultural diversity has not always been welcomed by the rest of the country. Despite the help they provided in constructing the country's infrastructure, black people were officially discriminated against until 1949, with laws preventing them from travelling into the central highlands or becoming Costa Rican citizens, while indigenous tribes were denied their own separate reserves of land until the 1970s. Sad to say, you may still encounter prejudice directed towards the region and its inhabitants as you travel around the rest of the country. **Puerto Limón**, the provincial capital, is sometimes portrayed by highland Ticos as a crime-ridden slum inhabited almost exclusively by thieves and conmen. In truth, Limón does have a problem with petty crime (as do most Costa Rican cities) and parts of it are seriously run-down, but this is principally because of the economic hardships the region has suffered since the United Fruit Company relocated to the Pacific coast in the 1930s. Certainly, the area and its people could use the investment currently being thrown at the country's Pacific resorts by the tourist industry.

The consequence of this lack of funding is that the Caribbean coast is much less developed than the Pacific and welcomes far fewer tourists. Ticos overwhelmingly favour the more bloated Pacific resorts for their vacations. The upside to this coastal bias is that it has enabled the authorities to preserve around half the Caribbean coastline in a network of parks and refuges. It has also helped the region's towns to retain their low-key charm. **Cahuita** and **Puerto Viejo de Talamanca**, in particular, do pretty good approximations of laid-back Caribbean island beach towns – the former is renowned for its snorkelling, the latter for its surfing. Other attractions include, in the far north, **Barra del Colorado**, a sports fishing paradise, and the **Parque Nacional Tortuguero**, which offers wonderful wildlife-spotting opportunities along jungle-fringed canals, not to mention, from July to October, the sight of nesting sea turtles.

There are a couple of things to bear in mind before you come. It is a very wet region. Unlike the rest of the country, the Caribbean coast's 'dry season', December to March, tends to be dry in name only, so be sure to bring suitable waterproof clothing with you. Thankfully, the rain tends to take the form of sharp, sudden downpours that drench everything thoroughly for their duration but quickly pass, although lingering pockets of still water can provide the perfect breeding conditions for mosquitoes. For this reason, if you're planning on spending a long time in the area, it's worth investing in an appropriate course of antimalarial drugs.

History: The Jungle Train

While Limón province may have witnessed the first European footfall on Costa Rican soil, when Columbus landed at Isla Uvita near the site of present-day Puerto Limón in 1502, it took over four centuries for the first sizeable settlement to be established here.

The twin threats of malaria – the coast's swampy depths proving fertile breeding grounds for mosquitoes – and piracy, which was rife all along the Central American isthmus in the 16th and 17th centuries, led the Spanish to establish their colony in the relative safety of the Central Valley highlands. For the next few hundred years, the Spanish colonists found life even in these relatively protected climes such hard going that little effort was expended on trying to settle more challenging areas.

Following the introduction of **coffee** in the early 19th century, and the subsequent growth of the economy as Costa Rica became a major international exporter, the government began to become less entrenched in its outlook. Nothing is liable to broaden your horizons more than the promise of profit, and for the first time it looked as if there might be a way of making money out of the Caribbean lowlands. From the 1860s onwards, the country's coffee-growers, who had come to dominate the political scene, began to speculate whether it might be possible to replace the slow, inefficient method of transporting coffee to the coast by river with a speedy railway, thus raising revenues. In 1871, convinced of its practicality, the government employed the American **Minor Keith** to build a railway between San José and Puerto Limón. Though the railway only had to stretch for 165 kilometres, its construction through the swamp-ridden lowlands was to prove a hellishly difficult task that would take nigh on two decades to complete. Much of the immigrant labour (including several thousand Chinese and Indian workers) brought over to work on the project died of yellow fever (as did two of Keith's brothers), leading to the hiring of over 10,000 Jamaicans who, it was believed, were immune to the disease.

When the **Jungle Train**, as it came to be called, was finally completed in 1890, many of these workers stayed on, employed in the **banana** plantations that Minor Keith had foresightedly planted alongside the tracks as he went. These workers provided the founding communities from which many of the region's coastal towns developed, including Cahuita and Puerto Viejo de Talamanca. Interestingly, it was these 'afterthought' bananas, rather than the railway itself, which would prove the real success story, at least as far as Minor Keith was concerned (especially as he had been awarded the land for free by the government, in lieu of payment for the railway). They proved so profitable that the company Keith formed to export the bananas, **United Fruit Company** (also known from 1970 onwards as United Brands, or locally as 'Yunai'), would go on to dominate the industry, not just of Costa Rica, but of the whole of the Americas. At one point, the company was responsible for 75 per cent of banana sales in the USA. The Afro-Caribbean community also benefited from the company's success, at least early on. They gained jobs throughout the fledgling export industry, helped in no small part by being English-speakers, a skill which could be utilized by United Fruit as they tried to make inroads into the US market. The company, for its part, built schools, hospitals and housing in the community. It seemed like a perfect relationship, but it had a sinister side. United were perfect employers so long as there was no disagreement over their methods. They were fiercely opposed to any form of unionization and often paid their workers in redeemable vouchers rather than money, thereby stopping them from saving what they earned. Unfortunately, when the emergence of a devastating banana blight in the 1930s coincided with an increased militancy among the company's workforce as they sought to have their concerns addressed (they went on strike, demanding that Yunai provide them with antimalarial drugs and make all wage payments in cash), United Fruit took the opportunity to pull out of Limón entirely and relocate to the Pacific coast. With laws in place restricting black people from moving out of Limón province, the company workers were unable to relocate to search for new jobs.

A period of mass unemployment followed during which the Afro-Caribbean population endured severe hardship. The Jungle Train itself, that almost forgotten catalyst for the creation of United Fruit, was still a source of employment, albeit on a much smaller scale and with the inevitable accompanying discrimination: until 1949, black train drivers were only allowed to take their trains as far as Siquirres on the border of the Valle Central, where a white counterpart would have to take over for the final journey into the 'pure' heartland.

What economic benefits the train was able to bring to the area came to a dramatic end in 1991, 101 years after the railway's completion, when a devastating earthquake destroyed many of the tracks. As most of the country's exports were by this time trans-ported by road, it was decided that it simply wasn't economically viable to repair it, and so it was abandoned. Recently, a section of the track has been reopened for passenger trips.

Today, as with much of the country, the Caribbean coast derives a significant portion of its revenue from tourism. At present, it specializes in a more eco-friendly, sustainable form of tourism than that practised by many of the northern Pacific resorts. Its showpiece in this regard is Tortuguero in the far northeast, which has been transformed from a village dependent on logging to one dependent on preserving and showcasing the environment, particularly its beaches, where nesting sea turtles return each year.

Along the Braulio Carrillo Highway

Several of the towns that lie along the Braulio Carrillo Highway, including **Guápiles** (50km northeast of San José), **Guácimo** (62km northeast) and **Siquirres** (100km northeast), were once important

Getting along HWY-32

Buses depart for Puerto Limón every half-hour from 5am to 7pm from San José's Caribbean bus terminal at C 0, Av 11, stopping at Guápiles, Guácimo and Siquirres *en route*.

---

stops on the now defunct Jungle Train that used to transport bananas (and passengers) from San José to the coast. Siquirres, in particular, holds the notorious claim to fame of having been the line's white/black exchange point where Afro-Caribbean drivers from Limón would give way to their Tico counterparts for the final journey into the Valle Central, where black people were legally forbidden from travelling until 1949.

A decade and a half after the train was put out of commission by the earthquake, the towns still play a significant role in the transit cycle of the region's bananas, now serving as service stations and watering holes for the truck drivers hauling the seemingly endless convoys of fruit along the highway. None of the towns is particularly geared up for the tourist trade, though all can offer a range of fairly basic accommodation and simple restaurants – not to mention plenty of petrol stations – aimed at their principal clients. The situation may change one day soon, however, following the recent decision to reopen a stretch of the train track for tourist rides. There are also a number of more upmarket lodges to be found in the surrounding countryside.

Siquirres is the most visited of the towns, as it is still a major transport hub, particularly for tour groups heading to Tortuguero, who board boats here for their trip along the Río Reventazón.

Sights around Guácimo

EARTH

EARTH
*t 713 0000,
www.earth.ac.cr;
open for official tours
only, advance booking
necessary; adm*

You can't help but think that they thought of the acronym first and then tried to work out what it could stand for. In the end, they came up with the Escuela de Agricultura de la Región Tropical Húmeda, or the School of Agriculture for the Tropical Humid Region. It's essentially a not-for-profit college dedicated to researching and promoting the sustainable management of tropical resources, with particular emphasis on developing ecologically friendly pesticides and fertilizers – a vitally important project in a country that has suffered severe environmental damage from the intensive use of pesticides, particularly on banana plantations.

Of course, this is all very admirable, but not really the reason why you're here; that's to visit the institute's 160ha tract of forest, birding trails and experimental banana plantation where much of the college's work is carried out. The 4hr **tour** also takes in the classrooms and laboratories where the students go about their

Getting to EARTH

EARTH is located a few kilometres east of Guácimo, just off the main Braulio Carrillo Highway. Over a dozen **buses** a day leave from San José's Caribbean bus terminal, C o, Av 11, passing through Guácimo. Ask the driver to let you off at the entrance to the EARTH complex. If you are **driving**, it's signposted from Guácimo.

work. The institute also operates a small on-site **lodge** with rooms available for around $45 a night.

Costa Flores

Costa Flores
t 716 6457; open daily 5.30am–3pm; adm exp

A garden centre with a difference, Costa Flores, 3.5km north of Guácimo, has a lot to answer for. Many of the tropical blooms that have come to dominate modern flower displays started their life here. The centre's vast nursery is home to a huge array of riotously coloured flowers, including over 120 varieties of heliconia (their speciality) as well as bromeliads and palms.

Tours (1½hrs, in English) through the gardens are given, on which you can see how the blooms are intensively reared and then packed ready for export. Your admission price includes a gift of a tropical flower bouquet. There's also a pretty decent restaurant.

Where to Stay along Highway-32

Guápiles

Casa Río Blanco, 6km west of town, just past the Restaurant La Ponderosa, **t** 710 4124, *www.casarioblanco.com* ($$$; $65). Well-to-do, Dutch-owned eco-lodge set on its own 20ha stretch of forest, containing hiking trails and waterfalls and home to over 300 species of bird. Its well (if simply) equipped *cabinas* nestle attractively in amongst the greenery. Some are perched on a cliff overlooking the eponymous Río Blanco and all have balconies with hammocks. Tours to local attractions, including the Rainforest Aerial Tram and the Braulio Carrillo National Park (*see* pp.143–6) are offered.

Hotel Country Club Suerre, 2km east of town centre, **t** 710 7551, *www. suerre.com* ($$$$; $90). It's a bit of a tour mill, but a very comfortable one, especially as it's located out of the town centre away from the worst of the choking diesel fumes. Set in neatly tended gardens, its 55 rooms have air-conditioning, private bathrooms and cable TV, and there's an Olympic-size swimming pool, a Jacuzzi, a sauna, tennis courts, two restaurants offering typical Costa Rican cuisine, buffet-style for its tour groups, two bars, a disco and a casino.

Hotel Wilson, next to the Soda El Banco, 1 block east of the church, **t** 710 2217 ($; with bathroom $18, without $10). Basic it may be, but this is also a comfortable, well-maintained and very cheap town centre choice. Some of its large doubles have air-conditioning and cable TV.

Guácimo

Hotel Río Palmas, a couple of km east of town, 400m past the entrance to EARTH, **t** 760 0330, *riopalmas@ hotmail.com* ($$$; $40). Enjoying a lush tropical garden setting, this *hacienda*-style hotel offers 30 charming whitewashed *cabinas* – each with TV and private bathroom – and a pretty tiled restaurant laid out around a central courtyard where there's a waterfall and swimming pool. Fishing tours and Tortuguero trips, as well as rafting and kayaking trips on the Pacuare, Reventazón and Sarapiquí rivers, are offered.

Getting to Puerto Limón

Buses leave for Limón from San José's Caribbean bus terminal, C 0, Av 11, every half-hour from 5am to 7pm, arriving some 3hrs later at C 7, Av 1/2. The journey should cost around $3 (payable in *colones* only).

If you fancy arriving in style, NatureAir operates **flights** from San José to Limón's small airport, 4km south of the centre (*see* p.104 for details), from where you'll have to take a **taxi** to the centre.

Getting away from Puerto Limón

Buses leave Limón's main bus terminal, Av 2, C7, for Moín, 8km north, every hour from 6am to 7pm, from where you can board a *lancha* (shallow-bottomed boat) for the journey north to Tortuguero. There's no official timetable of *lancha* departures; it's more a question of negotiating with the respective boatmen, who will usually wait until they have a full passenger load before leaving. It should cost around $10 per person for a group of six, more if there are not enough people to fill the boat or if you want to pay extra for an early departure. Bear in mind that because of the length of the journey (3–4hrs) the last boats leave at around 2pm.

Bus services south, to the towns of Cahuita and Puerto Viejo de Talamanca, leave from Av 4, C 3/4 every hour from 7am to 6pm; as do services for Bribrí and the border town of Sixaola, roughly every 40mins, 5am–6pm.

Puerto Limón

⭐ Puerto Limón

The coastal port of Puerto Limón has long served an almost metaphorical purpose in Costa Rican society. Whenever a highland Tico wants to highlight just how bad the social situation is getting somewhere, or just how high the crime rate is, or just how deprived a place is becoming, he or she will compare it with Limón (it's usually referred to by the diminutive form), which for many seems to represent the ultimate sordid underbelly of Costa Rican life. Unfortunately, you can't help but think that sometimes – not always but sometimes – these remarks are born of a prejudice somewhat more sinister than an aversion to derelict buildings. After all, there are several other Costa Rican towns with similar levels of deprivation, but these, unlike Limón, do not have a population that is predominantly black. Limón certainly has its problems, but the antipathy directed against the town by much of the rest of the country can sometimes make these seem like self-fulfilling prophecies, as if the city has been told for so long that it's awful that it somehow feels an obligation to continue being so.

Slums, drug-taking, urban deprivation and crime are part of the Puerto Limón story, but they are not the whole story. This was once a prosperous, almost bourgeois place. Founded in 1871 on the site of Cariari, an indigenous tribal settlement, it grew significantly during

Orientation

As with most of the country's major towns, Limón is laid out according to a grid system, with numbered *calles* running north–south and *avenidas* east–west. The only difference is that the numbers of the roads ascend sequentially (1, 2, 3, etc.) rather than alternately (2,4,6, etc.) as is the case with most other towns. In practice, this makes very little difference, as Limón also shares the characteristic with most other Costa Rican towns of having few road signs. Locals use landmarks to give directions, the main ones being the Mercado Central and Parque Vargas, which lie a couple of blocks apart from each other on Av 2.

Staying Safe in Puerto Limón

Considering its reputation, it's worth saying a word or two about personal safety in Limón. While it is understandable to approach your time in the city with a degree of trepidation – especially if you've spoken to some Ticos before you arrive and have heard terrible tales of what might befall – the truth is, Limón's bark (or at least the warning bark of its neighbours) is considerably worse than its bite. Puerto Limón may have a reputation as a crime-ridden hellhole, but its problems and crime levels are no worse than any other major Costa Rican town. Petty thievery, street muggings and car theft do happen, but so long as you take the normal safety precautions you would anywhere – not walking around unfamiliar areas alone after dark, not wearing or carrying items of conspicuous wealth, not leaving valuables on display in your car – you should avoid them happening to you.

the next 60 years as several thousand Afro-Caribbean workers, brought over from Jamaica to work on the construction of the Jungle Train and, later, United Fruit's banana plantations, settled here. During the early decades of the 20th century, when it was the country's main fruit-exporting port and United Fruit was pouring money into the local infrastructure, it could even have been described as thriving. However, United Fruit's relocation to the Pacific coast in the 1930s and the discriminatory laws of the time, which prevented black workers from moving inland to find work, precipitated a long and slow decline, culminating in a devastating earthquake in 1991 that destroyed many of the city's buildings.

Though the town's fortunes have improved over the past decade or so, this is still a place where few tourists choose to linger. That's not to say it doesn't welcome its fair share of visitors; its continuing importance as a transport hub sees hordes of tourists arriving daily. The trouble is, most leave again pretty quickly, either for the city's twin port of Moín, 8km north, to catch a boat to Tortuguero, or by bus to the southern beach resorts of Cahuita and Puerto Viejo de Talamanca. The only time the town gets a significant influx of visitors willing to stay for a few days is during its annual week-long carnival leading up to Columbus Day on October 12. But things may be about to change ('*Limón cambia*', as the locals say). For one thing, for the first time in decades the city is receiving a significant and sustained amount of government investment, the first fruits of which have seen the creation of a new dock, the Termal de Cruceros, which it is hoped will welcome the arrival of a dozen or so cruise ships (and more importantly their passengers) each winter. The heart of the town centre, around Parque Vargas and Avenida Dos, has been spruced up and now forms a pleasant, bustling open space. Further-more, the town is home to several great Caribbean restaurants and has a pleasant beach, a little way north of the centre. It's not exactly Puerto Vallarta yet, but, if it keeps improving at the current rate, it's not beyond the realms of fancy to suggest that it might be a rival one day. It's certainly a lot better than a lot of Ticos give it credit for.

While Limón itself is a reasonably sized town of around 80,000 inhabitants with outskirts that sprawl for several kilometres, tourist

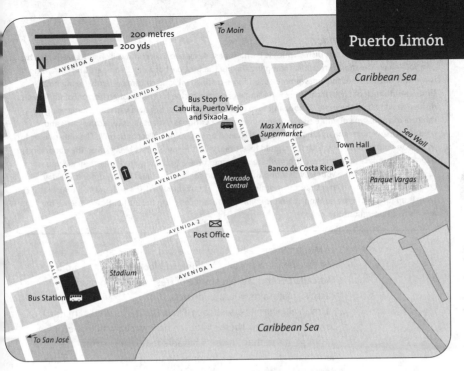

Puerto Limón

Caribbean Sea

Sea Wall

To Moín

200 metres
200 yds

N

AVENIDA 6

AVENIDA 5

Bus Stop for
Cahuita, Puerto Viejo
and Sixaola

Mas X Menos
Supermarket

Town Hall

AVENIDA 4

Banco de Costa Rica

Parque Vargas

CALLE 5

CALLE 4

CALLE 3

CALLE 2

CALLE 1

AVENIDA 3

Mercado
Central

CALLE 6

CALLE 7

AVENIDA 2

Post Office

AVENIDA 1

Stadium

CALLE 8

Bus Station

To San José

Caribbean Sea

Limón isn't very big at all. Pretty much everything you might want to visit lies within a few blocks of the seafront, either side of Avenida 2.

Starting our tour at the **seafront**, you'll notice on the eastern side a colourful (though in places rather flaky) semicircular **mural** by local artist Guadalupe Alvarea, depicting some of the major events in the region's history – Columbus' arrival, the conversion of the native population by Catholic missionaries, the building of the Jungle Train, etc. The mural borders **Parque Vargas**, the city's most pleasant open space, a neatly laid-out park lined with tall palm trees and benches. Sit yourself down and see if you can spot any of the resident sloths in the treetops. From here, take a walk along Avenida 2, also known

---

Limón Carnival

It seems entirely appropriate that the country's most culturally diverse city should play host to its most culturally diverse event, the Limón Carnival, which takes place during the week leading up to 12 October (Columbus Day). At this time, Ticos from throughout the rest of the country put aside whatever pre-conceptions they may have regarding Limón to join in the revelry, which comprises a heady concoction of music, dancing, parades, fireworks and, of course, plenty of drinking.

Consciously modelled on the Río Carnival, Limón's version began in earnest in the 1950s and is officially held in honour of the anniversary of Columbus' arrival in the New World, although its name, *El Día de la Raza* (the Day of the People) betrays its true purpose – it's an excuse for the people to have fun, which is exactly what they do. These days the celebrations don't take place on the city streets but, for safety and sanitation's sake, on a specially set aside section of the docks where food stalls and sound systems are set up. It's a hugely popular occasion and if you want to attend you'll have to arrange your trip early, as accommodation can get snapped up weeks in advance.

Don't Rush Your *Rondón*

The region's most famous dish – which is perhaps best described as coconut milk fish stew – is also the one you'll have the most difficulty in sampling. Taking the best part of a day to prepare and cook, *rondón* is the very antithesis of the mass-produced, uniform-tasting fast food culture currently taking hold throughout much of Costa Rica. There is no single or official recipe for this most archetypal of Caribbean dishes (making it all the more Caribbean). Each cook will have his or her own variation, comprising a mixture of some type of white fish – often red snapper – Caribbean vegetables (typically yams and breadfruit), green bananas, garlic and onion all cooked up in lashings of coconut milk. The only rule, as far as *rondón* preparation goes, is that it should take time, with the ingredients being given the opportunity to gradually reduce or 'run down' (from where the name comes) to the required consistency. If you want to sample *rondón* during your travels along the Caribbean coast, you should ideally order it the day before, and certainly no later than the morning of the night of your meal. If a restaurant claims that it can whip it up for you there and then, it ain't *rondón*. Restaurants offering the authentic experience are mentioned throughout this chapter.

as **Market Street**, a bustling boulevard of shops and cafés that marks the true heart of the city. A couple of blocks west is the vibrant **Mercado Central**, a great source of fresh Caribbean produce – cassava, plaintains, yucca, *chayotes*...

Limón also has its own beach, **Playa Bonita**, located 4km north of town. You can walk there along the narrow **sea wall** (*malecón*), although it's perhaps more advisable to take a bus from the Gran Terminal del Caribe. Look for ones heading to Moín and ask the driver to let you off at the beach. It's a pleasant stretch of sand where the waves are fierce enough to attract the attention of a small surfing community.

Services in Puerto Limón

Banks: Banco de Costa Rica, Av 2, C 1; Banco Nacional Av 2, C 3.
Internet access: Net Café Av 4, C 5/6.
Post office: Av 2, C 4.
Supermarket: Mas X Menos, Av 3, C 3.

Where to Stay in Puerto Limón

Puerto Limón's hotels are, in the main, pretty reasonably priced, though you should avoid the absolute bargain-basement places. Their low cost tends to come with an accompanying lack of security. Noise can be a problem, particularly for those near the Mercado Central. Quieter hotels are available near the seafront and at Playa Bonita. It can be very difficult to find rooms during Christmas and Easter, and nigh on impossible in Carnival week.

Cocori, Playa Bonita, t 795 1670 ($$$; $45). Overlooking the ocean, this is a good choice to set up camp for a few days, as its rooms have kitchenettes (and air-conditioning), although there's also a pretty decent beachfront restaurant, with live music at weekends.

Maribu Caribe, Playa Bonita, t 795 4010 ($$$; $45). One of the few 'get-away-from-it-all' places that Limón offers, the luxurious Caribe offers thatched, indigenous-style bungalows set on a hill overlooking the sea, as well as two pools, a restaurant and bar.

Park, Av 3, C 1, t 798 0555 ($$$; $45). Rather good (for Limón) business hotel right on the front. Several rooms offer sea views and there's a good restaurant. Private parking available.

Acón, Av 3, C 2/3, t 758 1010 ($$; $32). A lively choice – it operates a disco at weekends – but a welcoming one. All rooms have TV, air-conditioning, phones and private bathrooms.

Miami, Av 2, C 4/5, t 758 0490 ($$; $38). Just across the road from the market, this inevitably suffers from a good deal of noise, but the rooms are reasonable. The pricier ones have cable TV, fans and private bathrooms.

Teté, Av 3, C 4/5, t 758 1122 ($$; $35). Another somewhat noisy choice just west of the market. It's well-equipped with private bathrooms and a large communal lounge. The rooms facing the street have balconies.

Eating Out in Puerto Limón

There are, as you might expect, a number of Caribbean-influenced restaurants, including one of the region's most celebrated, Springfield. The Mercado Central is also, as is usually the case, a great source of cheap eats, with numerous sodas selling such regional delicacies as *pan bon* and *patí*.

BioNatura, Av 4, C 6. If there's another macrobiotic Caribbean restaurant in Costa Rica, we have yet to find it, making this a unique experience for that reason alone. The food is good, made from local organic ingredients and served up with tasty fruit shakes.

Brisas del Caribe, Hotel Caribe, C 1, Av 2. It's not the most authentic Caribbean experience you can enjoy – the menu is a 'calling all cuisines' hotchpotch of *casados*, burgers, sandwiches and seafood, with even a few Chinese dishes thrown in for good measure –

but it has a nice setting on the north side of the Parque Vargas (there's an outside terrace) and enjoys a laid-back, relaxed vibe.

Kimbambu, Playa Bonita, t 795 4850. Good-quality fish and seafood eaterie overlooking the beach.

Soda la Estrella, C 5, Av 3/4. A local institution in the northwest corner of the market, this serves up tasty *gallo pinto*, *casados* and sandwiches, all for a couple of dollars, as well as pretty decent coffee.

Springfield, on the road north of Limón towards Portete. The best Caribbean cuisine in town – try the rice and beans cooked in coconut milk, or, if you've got time to hang around, *rondón* – dished up in a charming wood-panelled interior. A pumping reggae and salsa disco is held here on weekends.

Entertainment in Puerto Limón

The city's bars, however, apart from those places on the main drag, notably Brisas del Caribe, are perhaps best avoided (particularly at night) as many serve a dual purpose as pick-up joints for the city's prostitutes. If in doubt, look to see whether the bar has a board outside blocking your view of the interior (it's being blocked for a reason). Otherwise, there are a few relaxed bars overlooking the water at Playa Bonita, and Springfield transforms into a hot and sweaty disco on weekend evenings.

The Northern Coast

Parque Nacional Tortuguero

⭐ **Parque Nacional Tortuguero**
open daily 6–6; adm

Tortuguero means 'turtle region', the name deriving from the park's beaches, which together are one of the most important nesting sites for sea turtles (including hawksbill, loggerhead, leatherback and, above all, green turtles) in the world. Though the park, which lies on the northern Caribbean coast, comprises nearly 200,000 hectares (split roughly 60/40 per cent between marine and inland areas), traversed by dozens of waterways and featuring areas of thick jungle and mangroves, it's these narrow, sandy beaches and, in particular, the sight they afford nightly from July to October of thousands of

Getting to Tortuguero

Getting to Tortuguero is either quick and easy or rather lengthy and really quite difficult, depending on how you travel and whom you travel with.

By Organized Tour

If you are coming as part of a tour, it should be a doddle, especially if you arrive by **plane**. Small, 12-seater aircraft take just 35mins to travel from San José to Tortuguero. The flight itself can be a little hairy, as the plane has to land on a tiny strip of land set between the sea and the canal that only become visible beneath the trees a few seconds before touchdown. Still, it's an experience, providing wonderful views on the way of Braulio Carrillo National Park and the region's volcanoes.

The **boat** journey is a lot calmer, if no less scenic as you make your way up jungle-fringed canals past stilt-set, pastel-coloured villages, but will take a good deal longer. Most packages travel via the Río Reventazón, boarding at Siquirres, 100km northeast of San José, taking (door-to-door, San José–Tortuguero) around 4hrs.

Independently

Travelling independently will involve a degree of planning. The easiest, and most expensive, option is by **plane**, travelling with Sansa (C 24, Av 0/1, **t** 221 9414, *www.flysansa.com*) out of Juan Santamaría International Airport, or NatureAir (**t** 220 3054, *www.natureair.com*) out of Tobías Bolaños airport in Pavas, 7km west of San José. *See* p.104. From Tortuguero airfield, unless you're staying at a lodge (which will send a *lancha* to pick you up), you'll have to walk the 4km along the beach to the village.

The most time-consuming and complicated route involves catching a **bus** to Limón (from San José, C 0, Av 11; every half-hour 5am–7pm), another to the port of Moín 8km north (Av 2, C 7; every hour 6am–7pm) and then negotiating transport on a *lancha* with the boat captains stationed there. It should cost around $10 per person for a group of six, more if there are not enough people to fill the boat or if you want to pay extra for an early departure. If travelling from San José, the entire journey should take around 6 or 7hrs.

mother turtles clambering clumsily ashore, digging their nests and laying their eggs, that are the main attraction.

Tortuguero may today be synonymous with the preservation and celebration of turtles, but this was by no means always the case. At one time, a more likely scenario would have seen the area witnessing the creatures' extinction. Indeed, the story of the creation of Tortuguero National Park is the story of a region pulled back from the brink of environmental disaster. So successful has this process been that the park, and the small village of the same name that sits on its border, would now seem to provide an object lesson in sustainable conservation, and in particular how to get a local community to both participate in and benefit from the protection of the environment.

Indigenous peoples had hunted turtles in this region for centuries before the arrival of Europeans from the 16th century onwards, but never in a way that threatened the continued survival of the population. Things began to change, however, in the late 19th century when the growing popularity of turtle soup in the USA and

When to Go

Costa Rica's traditional high-low season is reversed in Tortuguero, with the park receiving the greatest number of visitors during the traditional low (or 'green' season) of July–October, which also corresponds to the period of highest rainfall, so be sure to bring plenty of wet-weather clothing. However, it should be noted that, as with most of the Caribbean coast, there is no true dry season in Tortuguero, and you should expect rainfall whatever time of year you visit.

Getting around Tortuguero

Outside of your hotel or lodge, most of your journeys will be undertaken in shallow-bottomed boats, or *lanchas*. With no roads, the area's rivers, streams and canals make up the area's main transport network. Within the park's confines, boats must be navigated by certified guides. However, some lodges and hotels hire out **canoes** and **hydro-bikes** allowing you to explore the waterways beyond the park's borders independently. Such **walking** as you do do will be restricted to the village – where there are no cars or scooters – and the beach.

Swimming is not permitted in either the canal (currents and crocodiles) or the sea (sharks).

Europe led to the reptiles (both adults and eggs) being harvested on an industrial scale, causing a dramatic fall in their numbers. To make matters worse, the mass logging of the region's coastal forests began in the 1940s – the village of Tortuguero was actually established to provide homes for workers in the logging industry – severely damaging the reptiles' habitat. Threatened by such a devastating onslaught, the region's turtles would probably have vanished entirely had it not been for the efforts of one man, the US biologist Archie Carr, who in the 1950s established the Caribbean Conservation Corporation (CCC) in Tortuguero with the intention of bringing the turtles' plight to national attention. Sustained lobbying by Carr and his colleagues over the next decade lead to the creation of Tortuguero National Park in the 1970s, finally bringing some much-needed respite to the area and its marine visitors.

One of the most significant aspects of this process, and a major contributor towards its success, has been the way in which the village of Tortuguero has managed to adapt to the changes – the logging community, once bent on exploiting the coastal forest, transformed into its most ardent protector. Today, most of the town's 600 or so inhabitants are involved in some way or another in preserving and showcasing the environment, working as guides, hotel operators and restaurateurs (sometimes all three).

The area's environmental recovery has also been aided by its historic isolation and the continuing lack of a modern transport infrastructure. Despite recent attempts by vested interests to open up a land route through the park to the coast (thankfully resisted by the local people), the park remains accessible only by air or water. That's not to say that it doesn't attract its fair share of tourists. This is actually one of Costa Rica's most visited parks (after all, if the aim is to get the area to sustain itself via eco-tourism, then there have to be enough eco-tourists to make it worthwhile). However, the majority of visitors come as part of highly organized tours that follow strictly observed itineraries. Independent travellers often have to undertake a long and arduous boat journey to get here, which serves to keep their numbers down. This has enabled the authorities to keep the development of the area relatively low-key. With no road linking it to the outside world, Tortuguero village remains small and largely self-sustaining; the most touristified area is the stretch of

canal just north of the village where half a dozen or so upmarket jungle lodges are located, although there are regulations in place preventing the building of any more. Entrance to the park via its waterways is only permitted in the company of a guide and, while you're free to explore the beaches during the day, access is heavily restricted at night during the laying season.

As successful as the project has been, all is still not entirely well in eco-paradise. The park just about copes with the number of visitors it currently receives, but there is constant pressure from within the tourist industry (as well as from a few locals) to bring in even more. Logging firms and multinational fruit companies have taken advantage of lax laws to exploit the land on the park's boundaries, much of which has now been deforested and turned into banana and oil palm plantations, the pesticides from which run off into the park's water system. But despite these problems, it's fair to say that things are a lot better now (especially for the turtles) than they were 50 years ago.

Turtle-watching

The '*desove*', or turtle-laying season, is at its height from roughly mid-July to the end of October, though some individual turtles may start laying as early as April. It's a fascinating, not to say rather wondrous event, watching these great aquatic beasts using their flippers to haul themselves up the shore, finding a suitable patch of sand – which must be of an optimum temperature to make sure their young incubate correctly – carefully excavating a hole and then depositing their shining white brood of up to a hundred eggs, before shuffling back to the ocean for another year.

Four species of turtle lay their eggs here, including hawksbill, loggerhead and giant leatherback turtles, although it's the green turtles (the plight of whom prompted the creation of the park) who are the most numerous, and thus the most likely to be seen.

Turtles almost invariably lay their eggs at night – which is also when the hatchlings emerge – so as to afford the greatest protection from predators, who, in addition to people, include coatis and racoons. During the season, **tours** leave for the beaches from the village information kiosk in two waves, at 8pm and 10pm. All visitors must be in the company of an officially certified guide. While package tourists will have their guides provided by their respective lodge, independent travellers will need to engage the services of one of the guides working out of the village, who can usually be found touting for custom near the kiosk from around 5pm onwards. A tour should cost around $10, in addition to the $7 park admission fee.

Everything about the tours is carefully regulated, so as to ensure the safety and wellbeing of the turtles. The number of visitors allowed on the beach each night is limited to just 400 (no more than 200 at one time), so arrive early to be sure of getting a place.

As magical as the experience may be, don't count on immortalizing it for posterity. Cameras are banned on the beach, as are torches (only the guides are allowed to carry weak, red-tinted flashlights), brightly coloured clothing or anything else (such as cigarettes) liable to disturb the turtles and send them scurrying back to the sea. All tours end, regardless of whatever fascinating activity the turtles may currently be engaged in, at midnight.

In truth, despite these regulations, problems do still arise. On nights when there are large numbers of turtles laying, things tends to run smoothly with everyone able to get a view of the proceedings. However, on those nights when just a few turtles put in an appearance, arguments can break out as guides try to muscle in on each other's territory to get their charges the best views (and themselves the tips on which their livelihoods depend).

If visitor numbers have been reached for a particular evening before you've had a chance to secure your place on a tour, you may find an independent guide offering to 'sneak' you on to the beach unofficially. As tempting as this may seem – you'll get to see the turtles and help out a guide stuck without work for a night – you should resist. Such deceptions are looked on extremely unfavourably by the authorities. If caught, the guide will probably be punished by having his licence revoked for anything up to two weeks, which will cause significantly greater damage to his livelihood than just a single workless night.

Jungle Cruises

Turtles may be the headline act, but they're by no means the only show in town. The park's great swath of humid, sultry forest and network of natural and man-made waterways supports a great abundance of wildlife, much of it aquatic. Around half of all Costa Rica's known species of reptile can be found here, including freshwater turtles, snakes, basilisks (more commonly referred to as Jesus Christ lizards because of their ability to use their large, webbed feet to 'run' across bodies of water to escape from predators), caimans and, usually spotted on the mudbanks near the sea, crocodiles. The jungle floor is home to all manner of amphibians, including marine toads and poison arrow frogs.

The most common variety in this region have red bodies and blue legs and are referred to locally as 'blue jeans frogs'. As cute as they are, avoid touching them, as their poison can be transmitted through the skin. The canopy supports around 400 species of bird – again, around half the number that have been recorded in the entire country. Kingfishers, green macaws, cormorants and herons are all common – in fact, you'll be lucky to go two minutes without spotting some representative of the heron family (egrets, ibis, spoonbills, storks). Resident mammals include manatees (an extremely rare aquatic mammal that looks a bit like a giant seal), otters, coatis, peccaries, sloths and three types of monkey (howler, spider and white-faced capuchin) who can often be spotted in the trees fringing the waterways, as well as (in theory) jaguars, although there have been few sightings in recent years.

Most of the lodges offer boat cruises as part of their tour packages. Alternatively, you can engage the services of an independent guide in the village for around $10 (plus $7 park admission). Several lodges also have canoes and hydro-bikes for hire, enabling you to tour the waterways to the north of the park on your own, where there is still a lot of wildlife to be spotted (entrance to the park is only allowed in the company of a guide). Do be careful, if paddling your own canoe, to maintain a safe distance from the wildlife; don't end up misjudging the currents and careering into a caiman that, until that moment, had been happily basking on a log.

Tortuguero Village

Of all Tortuguero's charms, the village itself could be regarded as the least of them – a small, slightly ramshackle affair of rather tatty-looking wood-panelled houses with little in the way of infrastructure. Spend some time here, however, and you'll probably find it growing on you. It may not be able to offer the slick, ever-attentive service of the lodges (see 'Where to Stay', pp.341–2), but you might find that counting in its favour. Life here is more relaxed and, as a consequence, more atmospheric than that experienced among the lodges' stricter, more orderly, more antiseptic confines.

Occupying a narrow stretch of land in between the sea and the canal, the layout of the town is best described as a sort of blurry line, with an unpaved 'main street' (really just a track) running north–south from the museum to the park entrance, either side of which sits a hotchpotch agglomeration of buildings and gardens.

Natural History Museum
t 710 0547, www. ccturtle.org; open daily 10–5.30; adm

The small **Natural History Museum**, a mainstay of most lodge tours, is run by the Caribbean Conservation Corporation, the organization whose campaigning led to the park's creation. It provides a good introduction to the world of turtles, with a range of displays – photos, maps, turtle shells, etc.– and an audiovisual presentation on the organization's work. Recently, the CCC has been conducting a study of the turtles' migratory patterns using satellite tagging. It has produced some pretty startling results – turtles that have nested in Tortuguero have turned up a few months later off the shores of Africa. The study has also provided the inspiration for the organization's latest fund-raising wheeze, the 'adopt a turtle' scheme, whereby for $25 you receive a certificate plus regular updates on the global whereabouts of your chosen creature.

Services in Tortuguero

Banks: There are no banks or money-changing offices in Tortuguero, so be sure to bring adequate funds with you.
Supermarket: Super Morpho, by the football field.

Tourist Information in Tortuguero

Tourist information and tickets for the nightly turtle tours (which go on sale from 5pm onwards) are available from the **information kiosk** in the centre of the village. It's easy to find, standing opposite the main souvenir shop, outside of which stand lifesize fibreglass replicas of a green and a leatherback turtle.

The nearby **Tortuguero Safaris Information Office**, run by the committed Canadian environmentalist Daryl Loth, can provide information on jungle tours, turtling, activity hikes and more. It's also the location of the town's Sansa ticket office (and can provide Internet access for around $4 an hour). Loth also operates (and can often be found) at the next-door B&B, **Cabinas Marbella**, *see* p.342.

Where to Stay in Tortuguero

There are two types of accommodation offered in Tortuguero: at the **canalside lodges**, which cater mainly to tour packages (though they do sell rooms on an individual basis if space is available); and **in the village**, aimed primarily at independent travellers. Both have advantages and drawbacks.

The lodges guarantee a certain level of comfort, all having decent en suite rooms and restaurants, and providing knowledgeable guides for tours into the park. Some also have swimming pools, games rooms and gardens. However, in order to maintain the turnover of guests necessary to ensure profitability, their service can at times have something of a production-line quality to it. Guests are shuttled in, fed and taken on tours in great orderly crocodiles (to see the crocodiles) according to strict itineraries, before being efficiently despatched ready for the next set of arrivals.

The accommodation available in the village tends to be a good deal more basic, with some places unable to provide bathrooms or even hot water. And there's not a swimming pool in sight. On the plus side, life is more relaxed here, giving you more opportunities to get to know the area and its people. Furthermore, staying in the village allows you to sample what nightlife there is, as most of the lodges do not provide transport to the village after 8pm outside the turtle-laying season. That said, village accommodation does tend to be a degree more expensive than you'd pay for something similar in a less isolated community.

The Canalside Lodges

Prices, unless otherwise indicated, are for 3-day, 2-night packages including transport (from San José), meals and tours.

Mawamba Lodge, 1km north of the village on the same side of the canal, **t** 223 2421, *www.grupomawamba.com* ($$$$$; $262). All the package comforts you could want on this 6ha site: well-equipped *cabinas* with fans and private bathrooms; hiking trails through the grounds; a butterfly garden; a large pool with Jacuzzi, a restaurant, a canalside bar and a range of tours. And if you're still not satisfied, it's just a short walk to the beach and ocean.

Laguna Lodge, 1km north of the village on the same side of the canal, **t** 223 3740, *www.lagunatortuguero.com* ($$$$$; $250). The Laguna Lodge oversees a very slick operation processing the arrival of several large tour groups every day, who are all housed in long dormitory-like blocks (divided into 71 large, but rather featureless en suite rooms, all with ceiling fans), fed over several sittings in a vast refectory-like dining room, shown presentations in a new turtle-shaped conference centre (the creation of which is a sign of the lodge's success) and taken on an assortment of tours. When not assembling at various muster points, guests can enjoy the pool, a nice canalside bar, neatly laid out gardens and walks along the adjacent beach.

Pachira Lodge, opposite the village on the other side of the canal, **t** 256 7080, *www.pachiralodge.com* ($$$$$; £269). The latest and, so the authorities would have us believe, the last lodge to be built on the canal rivals the Tortuga for the title of most luxurious, with lush grounds (where there are 2km of marked trails) in which are set several large, beautifully designed almond-wood *cabinas* – all with bespoke furniture, king-size beds and huge bathrooms. The turtle-shaped pool (complete with Jacuzzi) is a nice kitschy touch.

⭐ **Tortuga Lodge** >

Tortuga Lodge, 2km north of the village, on the opposite side of the canal, directly across from the airfield, **t** 710 8016, *www.costaricaexpeditions. com* ($$$$$–$$$$; from $110 per night inclusive). Owned and operated by Costa Rica Expeditions (the country's largest tour operator), the 'Turtle' lodge offers supremely efficient, supremely slick service. Your every whim is catered for as you are picked up at your San José hotel, driven to the airport and then flown to Tortuguero, where a *lancha* awaits your arrival ready to ferry you across the canal to the lodge. Upon setting foot on dry land, you're immediately handed a fruit cocktail (the lodge's customer feedback form features a tick-box asking you to confirm that this has taken place), before being shown to your elegantly decorated, *hacienda*-style room (with ceiling fan and en suite bathroom, of

course). The lodge is set in large grounds with its own hiking trail and serves up lavish buffet dinners full of Costa Rican treats at its restaurant. A variety of tour options, plus kayak and hydro-bike hire, are offered. The whole thing is a bit like being hermetically sealed in a tropical garden with your own butler service.

Jungle Lodge, 1km north of the village on the same side of the canal, **t** 233 0133 ($$$$; $230). Archetypal all-inclusive lodge, ferrying you door-to-door from San José via a minibus ride and then a boat trip from Siquirres. Guests – most of whom are here courtesy of the lodge's owner, the tour operator Cotur – have the use of a swimming pool and a games room, and can hire canoes for trips on the canal. The *en suite* rooms are furnished in a vague rustic style, and there's a good restaurant where discos are held in high season.

El Manati, 1.5km north of the village, on the opposite side of the canal, **t** 383 0330 ($$$; $50 per night including meals). This is unlike the other lodges in that it caters as much to independent travellers as tour groups and is pretty reasonably priced. It therefore seems entirely appropriate that it's named after one of the region's most endangered inhabitants, the manatee, dwindling numbers of which still live in the region's waterways. There are just eight simple *cabinas*, all with private bathrooms, ceiling fans and mosquito nets. Canoes are for hire.

In the Village
Prices are per night.

Cabinas Marbella, on the main street, next to the Tortuguero Safaris Office, **t** 709 8011, *safari@ racsa.co.cr* ($$; $30). Perhaps the best place to stay if you're keen to find out more about the natural history of the region. The Marbella, and the next-door information office, are operated by Daryl Loth, a committed Canadian-born environmentalist and guide. It offers four large, simply decorated and furnished en suite rooms and a nice canalside terrace where breakfast is served.

Cabinas Tortuguero, southern end of the village, *tinamon@racsa.co.cr* ($$; $30). Set in a pretty garden, the Tortuguero offers five reasonably spacious *cabinas*, all with hot-water showers, fans and hammocks. The rates include breakfast and tasty dinners at the adjacent Italian-inspired restaurant.

Miss Junie's, at the northern end of the village, just in front of the Natural History Museum, **t** 710 0523 ($$; $35). Things are obviously going well for the town's most celebrated cook, who has recently expanded and refurbished her premises. The rooms are spick and span as always, but now have hot-water showers and fans. You can sample Miss Junie's famous cooking at the restaurant next door . Breakfast is included in the price.

Cabinas Aracari, south of the information kiosk, turn left at La Culebra bar, **t** 798 3059 ($; $20). Simple, basic but spotlessly clean *cabinas*, all with private baths (cold water only) and ceiling fans.

Eating Out in Tortuguero

Despite its reduced dimensions, Tortuguero can offer plenty of eating options, with several good Caribbean restaurants.

La Casona, by the football field. As relaxed a meal as you could want – dine on a variety of spicy fish dishes (the shrimp with rice is recommended) and sink some cold beers at the restaurant's long, refectory-style tables. There's also a bakery for snacks on the go.

Miss Junie's, north end of the village, just before the Natural History Museum. The ever-resourceful Miss Junie operates a constantly changing menu based on whatever the day's catch has brought in. If you want to request a specific dish, you'll have to order it well in advance (this particularly applies to *rondón, see* p.334). In fact, it's a good idea to book a table early in any case, as this is a very popular place during the season. Miss Junie's open-air dining room may be new (it was constructed in the past couple of years) but it's part of a tradition going back half a century (Fidel Castro was reportedly one of the restaurant's early patrons).

Miss Miriam's, by the football field. Tasty Caribbean concoctions – such as rice and beans in coconut milk – cooked up by the Nicaraguan-born Miss Miriam, another of the town's celebrated cooks.

Nightlife in Tortuguero

Entertainment is provided by a number of riverside bars, including the **Tropical Lodge Bar**, the slightly down-at-heel **La Culebra Bar** and the **Bar Brisas del Mar**. The last two hold regular reggae discos with pumping sound systems.

Parismina

Tortuguero village is not the only entry point for the Parque Nacional Tortuguero. The smaller, less well-known and certainly much less visited village of Parismina lies at the park's southern end, on a thin strip of land set between the Caribbean coast and the Río Parismina. It seems strange that Parismina should continue to be so overlooked. Though, like Tortuguero, it is inaccessible by road (and, unlike Tortuguero, by plane), the boat journey to Parismina is considerably quicker than that to its more northerly counterpart. Furthermore, the town offers just as many wildlife-spotting opportunities as Tortuguero, with similarly large numbers of nesting green, leatherback and hawksbill turtles arriving here each year. Perhaps it's the town's reputation as a major sports fishing destination, with most of the lodges here offering tarpon- and snook- hunting trips, that puts off those visitors who would rather

Getting to Parismina

There are no road or air options. The only way to reach Parismina is by **bus and boat**, although the journey is considerably less arduous than the one to Tortuguero. From San José, catch a bus from the Caribbean bus terminal, C 0, Av 11, to **Siquirres** (1½hrs), where you can connect either with the rather intermittent bus service (at 1pm Mon–Fri, 6am and 2pm Sat and Sun; 2hrs) or, more likely, take a taxi ($25; 1–1½hrs) to the town of Caño Blanco. Here, a regular boat service will ferry you the short journey to Parismina ($1.50; 10mins). The last boat leaves at 6pm.

You can also travel to Parismina via Moín, using the same method as you would to get to Tortuguero (just making sure your captain knows to drop you off early).

observe than catch their wildlife. That said, nature trips along Tortuguero National Park's waterways and turtle-watching trips are also available.

The town itself consists of little more than a dock, a church and a dirt track, around which is grouped a small collection of budget hotels and sodas. Most of the all-inclusive lodges, which welcome the majority of the town's visitors, lie to the north of the village.

Tourist Information and Services in Parismina

Tourist information is provided by the **Asociación Salvemos Las Tortugas de Parismina kiosk** in the centre of the village.

There are no **banks**.

Where to Stay in Parismina

Although there are a few budget options in town (with more being added all the time), most accommodation options lie outside the village and cater to all-inclusive packages. If you've booked independently, you'll need to call ahead to arrange boat pick-up from the town.

Jungle Tarpon Lodge, 2km north of town, t 800 544 2261, *www. jungletarpon.com* ($$$$$). As the name suggests, this lavish lodge set in 40 hectares of land caters both to those looking to explore the forest depths, and to those looking to bag themselves a scaly beauty out at sea. It's a pretty high-falutin' place, with air-conditioned rooms all with large bathrooms and wooden furniture, a pool, and a restaurant where, even if you don't get lucky out on the ocean waves, you can be sure of finding a regular supply of fresh fish. The lodge

offers plenty of tours, including jungle trips and turtle-watching, but tends to specialize in longer, all-inclusive packages (with transport, meals and tours included), typically 9 days/8 nights, from $1,095 for eco-tours, and from $1,195 (rising to over $3,000) for fishing packages.

Río Parismina Lodge, t 229 7597, *www. riop.com* ($$$$$). An ever-popular choice with fishermen hoping to spend a day out on the high seas wrestling with an industrial-sized tarpon, this offers luxurious rooms with huge comfy beds (old men of the sea need their rest), private bathrooms, TV and fans, and there's also a pool and Jacuzzi. Sports fishing isn't the only draw here. The lodge is set in over 20ha of forested land and offers a variety of tours including boat trips into Tortuguero National Park and horse-riding. It's not cheap (packages from $425 a day to $2,950 for 7 days), but you do get a lot for your money, with all transport, meals, tours, fishing trips and even an open bar thrown in.

La Rosa Espinosa, 200m north of the dock, t 711 0974 ($; $20). A good in-town budget option if your resources won't stretch to one of the more luxurious out-of-town lodges, this has good-sized rooms, all with private baths (hot water) and a pleasant restaurant.

Barra del Colorado and the Nicaraguan Border

The small town of Barra del Colorado, tucked away in Costa Rica's northeastern corner near the border with Nicaragua, is famous above all for one thing – sports fishing. As this is one of the most isolated locations in the whole of the country, your inclination to visit will probably depend largely on how big a fan you are of hauling in jumbo-sized (so the publicity blurb would have you believe) snook and tarpon. This is a shame, because in theory Barra should be able to offer much the same wildlife-spotting opportunities as Tortuguero. It lies within the 900 sq km (90,000ha) **Refugio Nacional de Fauna Silvestre Barra del Colorado** that stretches right up to the Río San Juan and the border with Nicaragua, making it the largest refuge in Costa Rica, home to much the same abundance of wildlife as the Parque Nacional Tortuguero (minus the turtles, who tend not to nest this far north). The trouble is, the people here have done the maths and realized that sports fishing is a much more profitable enterprise than nature-watching, with lodges able to charge, on average, at least 10 times as much for a fishing trip as a nature tour. As a result, almost everything about the town is tailored towards the tastes of hardcore American fishing enthusiasts, with nature-watching very much relegated to the status of a secondary activity. Most of the lodges here offer nature tours, but almost as an afterthought or *apéritif* to the main event; everything here is geared towards getting you out on the ocean with a rod in your hand.

The town itself, which is dusty and dilapidated, is made up of two parts: **Barra Sur**, where you'll find the dock and airstrip, and **Barra del Norte**, the main residential area, which sit opposite each other either side of the Río Colorado. As most visitors are shuttled in and out by their lodges, there are few tourist facilities in town: no banks, no Internet cafés and just a handful of eating and sleeping options, principally aimed at the town's sizeable Nicaraguan population.

The Nicaraguan Border

The northern border of the Refugio Nacional de Fauna Silvestre Barra del Colorado is marked by the **Río San Juan**, which also forms the official border between Costa Rica and Nicaragua. Technically, Costa Rica only extends as far as the river's southern bank, with the river itself lying wholly within Nicaraguan territory. However, Costa Rican citizens are entitled to travel on the river free from interference by the Nicaraguan authorities, which in effect means that tourists travelling with Costa Rican guides should be able to do so as well, although you should bring your passport with you just in case. While it's hardly a major tourist route, boat trips along the river can be arranged from Puerto Viejo de Sarapiquí (the Río Sarapiquí

Getting to Barra del Colorado

As with Tortuguero, there's an easy way to get to Barra del Colorado, and a hard way. The easy way, naturally enough, is also the most expensive – by **plane** from San José, travelling either with Sansa (C 24, Av 0/1, t 221 9414, *www.flysansa.com*), out of Juan Santamaría International Airport, or NatureAir (t 220 3054, *www.natureair.com*) out of Tobias Bolaños airport in Pavas, 7km west of San José. The journey takes just over an hour and should cost around $130–140 return.

The hard way involves a combined **bus/boat** trip, either via Tortuguero (bear in mind, when planning your trip, that the bus/boat journey from San José to Tortuguero takes a good 7hrs, from where it's another 1–1½hrs to Barra; for details of how to get to Tortuguero, *see* p.336), or Puerto Lindo. To get to Puerto Lindo, you'll need to take a bus from San José's Caribbean bus terminal, C 0, Av 11, to Cariari, where you can pick up a connecting service. It may also be possible to arrange boat transport from Puerto Viejo de Sarapiquí (*see* p.346).

connects with the Río San Juan), but you should be aware that you cannot cross into Nicaragua from the river as there's no official border post; the closest is at Los Chiles (*see* p.279).

As isolated as it is, the river and its surrounding area have occasionally come to the forefront of Costa Rican affairs. Running all the way to the Lago de Nicaragua (Lake Nicaragua), prior to the construction of the Panama Canal the river formed part of an important Atlantic–Pacific trade link with ships sailing up to the lake, where their cargo would be unloaded on to railroad trucks to complete the journey to the western seaboard. In the 1980s, the Costa Rican side of the river became a notorious hideout for the CIA-backed Contra rebels fighting Nicaragua's Sandinista regime. Indeed, Barra del Colorado was for several years the base in exile for the Contra leader Edén Pastora, more commonly known as Comandante Cero (Commander Zero). Today, this sparsely populated region has become a concern because of the activities of illegal loggers who have succeeded in deforesting large areas of the riverbank, particularly on the Costa Rican side near the confluence of the Río Sarapiquí and Río San Juan.

If you do decide to take a trip up the river, resist the temptation to go for a swim, as the waters are home to a sizeable population of bull sharks who patrol the river all the way up to Lake Nicaragua – though how they cope with the transition from salt water to freshwater and back again continues to baffle naturalists.

Where to Stay in Barra del Colorado

Barra lacks the independent budget hotels you'll find in Tortuguero. Almost all the accommodation is provided by all-inclusive sports-fishing lodges and, as a result, tends to be quite expensive. However, most lodges are willing to accept independent travellers (at reduced rates) outside the main fishing seasons of Jan–May and Sept–Oct.

Río Colorado Lodge, Barra Sur, riverfront, t 232 4063, *www.sportsmanweb. com/riocolorado* ($$$$$). Despite its impeccable sports fishing credentials (it operates a veritable fleet of modern, highly equipped boats), this is also a pretty decent option for independent travellers and nature tour enthusiasts, offering non-fishing accommodation for $120 per night (although, considering the difficulty and expense of getting to Barra, you'll really have to pack the activities in to make this worth your while) and boat tours into Tortuguero National Park. All rooms come with air-conditioning, TV, private bathrooms and twin beds (this is buddy, not couple, country). There are lovely views from the riverfront restaurant. All-inclusive fishing tours from $1,430 for 6 days/5 nights.

Silver King Lodge, Barra Sur, t 381 1403, *hal@silverkinglodge.com* ($$$$$). Fish in luxury at this rather grand place aimed directly and unashamedly at the US market with large rooms equipped with ceiling fans, large bathrooms and

TVs showing American channels. There's a pool, Jacuzzi and restaurant. Three-day packages from $1,850.

Tarponland, Barra Sur, near the airstrip, t 710 2141 ($). This is another reasonable choice for independent travellers, allowing you to book its rooms ($20), fishing trips ($140) and nature tours ($15) separately. The rooms are by no means the most luxurious in town, but are perfectly adequate, all with screens, fans and private bathrooms (with hot water).

The Southern Coast

Cahuita and the Parque Nacional Cahuita

Cahuita, 44km south of Puerto Limón, is perhaps the most archetypally Caribbean village on this stretch of coast, offering a wealth of simple, laid-back pleasures – snorkelling on a coral reef, sunbathing on sandy beaches, tucking into rice and beans and a cold beer at a beachfront bar. It also has the added attraction of the Parque Nacional Cahuita (site of the aforementioned coral reef) and its expanses of coastal rainforest right on its doorstep.

Cahuita

Perhaps unsurprisingly, given the town's relaxed nature and hedonistic charms, Cahuita has become extremely popular with backpackers, and many of the hotels cater primarily to this trade. Despite the inevitable commercialization that this entails, the town still manages (more or less) to retain the authenticity of its Creole culture. After all, for the first hundred years or so of its existence, this was a place little visited by the rest of the country, with whom it had precious few transport or communications links. On the streets you may still hear its inhabitants exclaiming the traditional greetings: 'Allright' (which means 'hello') and 'Okay' (which means 'goodbye').

For a while Cahuita had a reputation for drug-taking and petty thievery. In truth, drugs were no more prevalent here than they were

Orientation

Cahuita is not laid out according to the grid pattern that characterizes so many other Costa Rican towns, but then it's so small, it hardly needs to. The whole town is composed of just a few unpaved, sandy streets next to the shore that interconnect in a somewhat haphazard pattern. There are no street signs (no point, there are no street names), so directions are usually given in relation to major landmarks – police station, beach, bus stop, etc. (although, if you do manage to get lost in Cahuita's minimal confines, you deserve some sort of special disorientation medal). The entrance to the national park lies just south of the village at Kelly Creek, while the village's northernmost extent is marked by a football field.

Getting to Cahuita

Though travelling along this stretch of coast has its problems – road coverage is minimal – it's still a big improvement on what went before. Prior to the opening of the Río Estrella Bridge and the coastal highway in the 1980s, Cahuita was accessible only to those willing to undertake a train ride, a canoe ferry and a bus journey along an unpaved, extremely bumpy road. Today, four direct **buses** for the town leave daily from San José's Caribbean bus terminal, C 0, Av 11, at 6am, 10am, 1.30pm and 3.30pm. They arrive 4hrs later and disgorge passengers onto the main street opposite Turistica Cahuita, before heading on to Puerto Viejo de Talamanca and Sixaola on the Panamanian border. Alternatively, you can take a bus to Limón, every 30mins 5am–7pm, and then catch a connecting service from Av 4, C 3/4 to Cahuita (they leave roughly once every hour, 7am–6pm).

If travelling by **car**, be aware that the village lies off the main road and in the wet season you'll need a 4WD (it's probably quite a good idea in the dry season, too, as rarely a week goes by without at least some rain). Furthermore, Cahuita's streets are not paved, but made of sand. Drive carefully and cut your speed accordingly so as not to send up clouds of dust.

in any of the country's other resorts that attract large numbers of young, itinerant travellers. An increased police presence on the village's streets seems to have brought these problems under control. Regarding drugs, it goes without saying that the official advice is to steer clear. Drug-taking is illegal. Not only do you not know what you might be purchasing, you can't be sure who you're purchasing from, and it has been known for the police to set up sting operations to catch would-be buyers.

There may not be much to Cahuita beyond a few dusty streets, but it has managed to cram a lot into a small space, with dozens of hotels, cafés and tour operators – not to mention the odd residential wood-panelled house. It's a pleasant place to wander – in among bouts of sunbathing, hiking and snorkelling – popping in and out of shops, checking out the tour options and settling down to a plate of something freshly caught and prepared. And at night, when the town's bars and discos get into gear, it's definitely the place to be.

There are beaches either side of the town: **Playa Blanca**, just to the south, actually lies within the confines of the national park (entrance is free via the Kelly Creek ranger station, although you may be asked to make a donation) and is patrolled by lifeguards; while **Playa Negra** (Black Sand Beach) lies to the north of the village. Bikes (the best way to get around), surfboards (the waves are better further south at Puerto Viejo de Talamanca) and snorkelling gear can all be rented at the town's plethora of tour operators.

Tourist Information in Cahuita

The town does not have an official tourist information office. However, there are tour operators in town who can provide information about local attractions and tours – snorkelling, surfing, touring Cahuita National Park, visiting the Keköldi Reserve, etc.

Tour Operators

Cahuita Tours, 100m north of the bus stop, t 755 0000, *cahuita@racsa.co.cr*. Rents out surfboards, snorkelling gear, binoculars, etc., and offers tours to Cahuita National Park and the Hitoy Cerere Biological Reserve, as well as white water rafting trips.

Mr Big J, just south of the bus stop and central crossroads, t 755 0328. The

★ Aviarios del
Caribe >>

town's pre-eminent tour operator, with most trips run by Big Joseph himself, offers tours – horse-riding on the beach, snorkelling, jungle hikes, fishing trips and more, as well as excursions to Cahuita National Park, the Hitoy Cerere Biological Reserve and Tortuguero. Also sells guidebooks and maps.

Roberto Tours, just south and across from the bus stop, **t** 755 0117. Sports fishing specialist Roberto offers you the chance to catch your own meal, which he will serve up for you that evening at his adjacent seafood restaurant. Snorkelling and dolphin-watching tours also offered.

Turística Cahuita, opposite the bus stop, **t** 755 0017, *dltacb@racsa.co.cr*. Offers river-rafting, snorkelling and sports fishing as well as tours to the Keköldi Reserve.

Services in Cahuita

Banks: There are no banks in Cahuita; the nearest are in Puerto Limón and Bribrí. There are exchange offices at Cabinas Safari and Cahuita Tours (which also has a Western Union office), while the Safari supermarket can change (small amounts) of cash.

Internet access: Ciber Café, opposite the bus stop, next to Turística Cahuita.

Police: On the main road at the north end of the village, by the beach.

Post office: Opposite the police station.

Where to Stay in Cahuita

To make the most of your money, it's best to travel as a group. The town's *cabinas* (you'll soon discover that there's precious little else but *cabinas*) are usually charged per room, regardless of the number of occupants. For groups of four and over this can represent a significant bargain; for couples and independent travellers less so (though it does provide an incentive to start making friends). Before accepting a room, make sure it has an undamaged mosquito net – a necessity in this humid, bug-infested part of the country. While none of the in-town choices is particularly luxurious, there are a few grander choices on the road north.

Expensive ($$$$)

Aviarios del Caribe, 11km north of town, follow the signs, **t** 750 0775, *www.ogphoto.com/aviarios* ($75). The well-equipped jungle lodge located here is just part of this organization's operation. As the name suggests, this is also a birding reserve with a number of trails traversing its tracts of forest, linked by a network of observation platforms, where you can try try and spot some of the 300-plus species that have been recorded here. It also rehabilitates injured or abandoned sloths, who can be viewed at the on-site sanctuary. Three-hour canoe tours of the Río Estrella are offered for around $30. The rooms themselves are lovely and bright with tiled floors, ceiling fans, private bathrooms and balconies, but are a touch pricey and they don't allow children. They also don't have an on-site restaurant (though they do offer breakfast), so you'll have to head into town each night to eat.

Magellan Inn, 3km north of town by Playa Negra, **t** 755 0035, *http://magellaninn.toposrealestate.org* ($79). A peaceful, secluded (not to say rather upmarket) choice away from the bustle of the town. Pretty gardens adorned with pre-Columbian statues surround a small sunken pool. The bungalows are elegantly furnished with tile floors, bespoke wooden furniture, original artwork and balconies (some have air-conditioning, some ceiling fans), and there's a highly respected French Creole restaurant, **La Casa Creole**. The price includes breakfast. A variety of local tours is offered.

Moderate ($$$)

Atlántida Lodge, 1km north of the village, next to the football field, **t** 755 0115, *www.atlantida.co.cr* ($64). Rather fancy with jungly (but carefully tended) gardens, a pool (with Jacuzzi and that ultimate decadant touch, a poolside bar) and 30 large, tastefully decorated rooms, all with ceiling fans and private bathrooms, as well as a separate self-catering house sleeping up to six ($116). It likes to emphasize its Costa Rican credentials by offering free coffee and bananas. Playa Negra is just a short walk away. Breakfast is included in the price. Tours offered.

⭐ **Miss Edith's** ››

El Encanto B&B, on the main road north out of the village, between the police station and the football field, t 755 0113, *www.elencantobedand breakfast.com* ($59). It's got a bit of a hippyish vibe, offering yoga classes, oriental massages and a 'Zendo-style' meditation room, but this Canadian-owned place is supremely comfortable, with three large, well-equipped bungalows in landscaped gardens (complete with Buddhas peering out of the foliage) and a separate self-catering house with its own kitchen that sleeps up to six. Snorkelling, dolphin-watching, horse-riding and birdwatching tours are offered.

Hotel-Restaurante Kelly Creek, next to the park entrance to the south of the village, t 755 0007, *www.hotelkelly creek.com* ($45). This Spanish-owned wooden house hotel has four very large rooms (sleeping up to four), all with two double beds, ceiling fans, mosquito nets, private baths and terraces. There's also a pretty good Spanish restaurant on site (if you want the paella, order it by 2pm).

Inexpensive–Budget ($$–$)

Cabinas Iguana, north of the village, t 755 0005, *www.cabinas-iguana.com* ($35). The three-bedroom house ($65) of this popular beachfront low-priced choice always seems to have an extended family of backpackers ensconced within. There are also stilt-set bunga-lows with private bathrooms and fridges, as well as a couple of smallish rooms with shared bathrooms. Additional facilities include a small swimming pool and a laundry service.

Cabinas Jenny, by the beach, t 755 0256, *cabinasjenny@rasca.co.cr* (shared bathroom $15, private $25). Unlike many of the town's other establish-ments, this beachfront hotel offers a range of accommodation choices from basic rooms with shared bathrooms to large, high-ceilinged rooms with decent-sized beds, ceiling fans and patios with hammocks and sea views.

Linda's Secret Garden, off the main road, at the southern end of the village, t 755 0327 ($35–20). Backpacker favourite set in a cheery garden with a range of colourfully decorated rooms – the largest sleeps up to four – and a communal kitchen. Secure parking.

Eating Out in Cahuita

Plenty of freshly caught fish, Creole spices, plus the odd international gourmet flourish are the hallmarks of Cahuita's rather fine restaurant scene.

Cha Cha Cha! Gourmet fare with flair served up under the auspices of a trained French chef. Despite the hotch-potch nature of the global cuisine menu – *burritos*, Jamaican jerk chicken, Thai curry, etc. – all the dishes are lovingly prepared. The dining room, bedecked with fresh flowers and paintings by local artists, isn't bad, either. There's an outdoor terrace.

Miss Edith's, east of the police station. The town's most celebrated restaurant is still presided over by the redoubtable Edith (the 'Miss' is not a sign of youth, but rather age, only being given to elder, respected members of the Creole community), even if these days she no longer prepares all the dishes herself – the restaurant's popularity would make this impossible. In a charming dining room, this serves up Caribbean cuisine at its finest – lobster, fish with coconut, curry and yucca, and of course the famous *rondón* (*see* p.334), which must be ordered in advance. It's rela-tively expensive (mains from around $8), but definitely worth it. No alcohol.

Restaurante Roberto, next to the tour operator of the same name. This gives you the chance to go on a fishing trip with Roberto himself, who will then cook up your catch Caribbean-style at his restaurant. A great experience.

Sobre Las Olas, on the beachfront. 'Over the Waves' is an excellent Italian eaterie serving a wide range of pasta, pizza and seafood dishes. Try the fresh lobster or octopus.

Nightlife in Cahuita

The town's bars are all much of a muchness, all serving cold beer and, as the evening wears on, cranking up the music. Pick an inviting-looking one overlooking the front and settle back. If you fancy something a bit more lively, head to the twin discos of **Coco's** and **Serafina's** on the main road (more or less opposite the bus stop), where heaving reggae and salsa parties take hold on weekends.

Parque Nacional Cahuita

❶ Parque Nacional Cahuita
t 755 0302; open Mon–Fri 8–4.30, Sat and Sun 7–5; adm or free, depending on which entrance you use

The coastal stretch south of Cahuita village was designated a national park in the early 1970s in order to protect the country's largest coral reef, which lies just offshore from here. Indeed, of the park's 23,500 hectares, over 21,000 lie out to sea, encompassing the reef plus much of the ocean beyond. The rest of the park is made up of a thin strip of coastal rainforest that, despite its relatively small size, is home to a surprising abundance of wildlife.

Access to the park is via two **ranger stations**, the first of which is at **Kelly Creek**, just 50m or so south of Cahuita. Though you must sign in at Kelly Creek, you aren't required to pay an entrance fee (though donations are actively encouraged). Entrance via the ranger station at **Puerto Vargas**, several kilometres south, however, will cost $8. It's possible to camp at the Puerto Vargas ranger station, which is pretty well equipped with showers and toilets. It can get crowded, however, so it's best to check in advance that they have space.

From Kelly Creek, a coastal **trail** heads past the beach and into the rainforest, taking you on a trip to the end of a small promontory jutting out to sea, **Punta Cahuita** (which forms the bedrock for the reef), past **Playa Vargas**, a lovely secluded white-sand beach, and on to Puerto Vargas, a total hike of around 9km. It's a pretty easy walk, the trail having been cleared and widened to almost road-like dimensions. Your only difficulty may come at high tide when you'll have to cross a couple of semi-deep rivers, and when parts of the beach may become impassable. You'll also have to deal with

The Coral Reef of Cahuita

As with all coral reefs, Cahuita's has been formed slowly over many hundreds of years by communities of polyps – single-cell animals – who filter their food, principally algae, from the water and excrete calcium carbonate, which they use to form the hard, supportive base on which they grow. Because of the time it takes coral to grow, and because coral needs to be near the surface in order to catch the algae (which relies on photosynthesis to survive), reefs are extremely fragile ecosystems, susceptible to even the slightest environmental damage and rapidly withering following even the most minor changes to their habitat and conditions. Sadly, contamination of the water here by pesticides used on the area's banana plantations, and an increased build-up of sediment caused by inland deforestation, combined with the natural disaster of the 1991 earthquake which pushed parts of the coral up above sea level, have killed off a significant portion of the reef. Still, there's enough remaining to make a snorkelling trip here well worth your while, although you should avoid doing so after heavy rains, when churned-up sediment will severely reduce visibility.

All the corals here have wonderfully descriptive, evocative names, not least **brain coral**, one of the most common forms, whose spongy ridged surface does indeed look like the outside of a brain. Other relatively common species include **moosehorn coral**, **deerhorn coral** and **fan coral**. Among the various other types of creature who make their home on the reef – including octopuses, angelfish, crabs, lobster, sponges, anemones and sea urchins (do avoid coming into contact with the relatively common black sea urchin, whose sharp spines can get lodged beneath the skin) – look out for **blue parrot fish**, who have been indirectly responsible for creating many of the region's beaches. The fish actually eat the coral skeleton, crunching it up with their specially adapted, super-strong beaks and excreting what they can't digest in the form of sand, which eventually ends up on the shore.

mosquitoes and bugs. As wet weather is a near-constant here, it's also advisable to bring waterproof clothing, whatever the state of the skies. Howler monkeys and white-faced capuchins are often spotted in the coastal trees here, particularly later in the day (when howler monkeys will certainly be heard) and coatis and lizards (notably Jesus Christ lizards) are fairly common sightings on the trail itself. Do also look out for the cawi trees, after whom the park and town are named (the 'ta' suffix means 'point'), which have a gnarly, folded appearance. They're also known as sangrilla trees locally because of their thick red, blood-like sap.

The park's main attraction, Costa Rica's largest **coral reef**, spreads for around 580 hectares around Punta Cahuita in a vaguely anvil-shaped pattern, its 35 species of coral providing a home to over 120 species of fish. Though snorkelling independently is allowed, it is best to go in the company of a knowledgeable guide (all the tour operators in town offer a service, as do many of the hotels), who can show you the best places, where the coral coverage is still strong.

Reserva Biológica Hitoy Cerere

Reserva Biológica Hitoy Cerere t 758 5855; adm

The name of this 22,000ha reserve, 67km south of Puerto Limón, about 22km west of Cahuita, which translates as 'fuzzy water', is not quite as nonsensical as it might first appear. The 'water' refers to the plethora of rivers and streams that unsurprisingly fill an area that receives between 4–6m of rain a year, while the 'fuzzy' is a fairly accurate description of the thick carpet of mosses that cover much of this sodden environment. The relative difficulty of access to the park, plus its lack of facilities – there's only one, very challenging official trail – means that this is off the more beaten tourist track. However, anyone who makes the trip here is usually glad that they did. This is a real wilderness, thick with lush tropical vegetation and all manner of wildlife, although you should be aware that its lack of development makes it a challenging place to negotiate. Waterproof clothing, proper hiking shoes and a good degree of fitness (plus, for preference, at least some previous hiking experience) are vital requirements for a visit here.

The reserve lies between three indigenous reserves, the Talamanca to the south, the Telire to the west and the Tayni to the north. The Río Estrella valley also lies to the north, its slopes thick with banana plantations, and it's here, in the park's northeast corner, that you'll find the only (and only intermittently staffed) **ranger station**. From the station, the park's lone **Espavel** ('Cashew Tree') **Trail** heads south for around 4.5km to the Río Moín. Despite the trail's relative brevity, the denseness of the vegetation and the steepness of the gradient mean that a return trip can take the best part of a day, and you should be sure to leave yourself enough time to get back before nightfall. The hike can be arduous, particularly after heavy rain, when

Getting to the Reserva Biológica Hitoy Cerere

Getting to the reserve by public transport is going to take a bit of perseverance. You'll need to take a **bus** from Limón to the small banana plantation village of **Fortuna**, a 2½hr trip, from where you should be able to hire a 4WD taxi from the plantation office to take you the 15km to the park entrance. You'll also need to arrange a pick-up time with the driver, as the ranger station may well not be staffed. The total journey should set you back around $20. **Driving** yourself offers slightly greater peace of mind as you don't have to worry about getting stranded, although finding your way through the mass of banana plantations to the entrance – with roads heading off in all directions – can be a challenge.

The costliest but also the safest option is to take an **organized tour** out of Cahuita, as offered by most of the town's tour operators (*see pp.348–9*), which should set you back around $50.

the ground becomes muddy and the moss covering the various boulders, stones and fallen tree trunks that line the trail especially slippery. As for what flora and fauna you may see as you make your slow progress along, it's difficult to say. As no thorough study of the park has ever been done, nobody knows exactly what animals live here, although plenty of birds (including hummingbirds and kingfishers) have been recorded, as have monkeys, sloths and lots of frogs, who thrive in the humid conditions. You should also see plenty of orchids, bromeliads and, of course, the eponymous cashew trees.

The ranger station does have a few bunks available for people, but these must be booked in advance. Camping may also be permitted but, again, advance reservation is necessary.

Puerto Viejo de Talamanca

⭐ **Puerto Viejo de Talamanca**

Similar in nature to Cahuita, but prettier and, if anything, even more laid-back, Puerto Viejo de Talamanca is famed for its beaches and its surfing. Great 7m-high waves known as 'La Salsa Brava' batter the coast here between December and March, producing, according to those in the know, surfing conditions unequalled along the entire Caribbean coast, but only safe for experienced surfers.

The town itself more or less corresponds to the template set out by Cahuita with a main road running parallel to the shore, a few unpaved tracks intersecting here and there, and not much else. However, there's a lot more to it (and a lot more going on) than first impressions might suggest. Locals and, it has to be said, a good many more newly arrived Europeans and Americans have taken advantage of the town's increasing popularity to open businesses, and these days almost every building seems to house a concern of some kind: a shop, tour operator, restaurant or hotel.

Following the town's discovery by the surfing community a few years ago, Puerto Viejo has developed a rather hippyish, bohemian vibe to it, hence the large number of New Age remedy stores and health food shops you'll see. However, while meditation (and of course sunbathing and surfing) may be the order of the day, at night Puerto Viejo turns into a veritable party town as numerous bars and

Getting to Puerto Viejo

All **buses** serving Puerto Viejo have first passed through Cahuita. Four direct buses a day (at 6am, 10am, 1.30pm and 3.30pm) link San José's Caribbean bus terminal, C 0, Av 11, with Puerto Viejo. They take around 4½hrs, dropping passengers on the seafront in the town. You can also catch a bus to Limón, every 30mins 5am–7pm, and then a connecting service from Av 4, C 3/4 to Puerto Viejo (they leave hourly, 7am–6pm).

If travelling by **car**, be aware that the road leading east out of the village towards Manzanillo is unpaved, unlit and very bumpy, and you'll need a 4WD.

Getting around Puerto Viejo

While it's perfectly easy to explore the town's limited confines on foot, if you're staying at one of the hotels on the unpaved road to the east (some of which lie several kilometres from town), hiring a **bike** does make a sensible (not to say enjoyable) way of getting around. Many of the town's hotels and most of the its tour operators offer a bike-hire service for around $3–4 a day.

discos crank into gear. Things are calmer along the unpaved road heading east out of town, where you'll find the area's most upmarket accommodation as well as a series of pristine white-sand beaches. These begin 2km southeast at **Playa Cocles**, which turns into **Playa Chiquita** at around the 4km mark before ending up, 15km southeast, at the small town of **Manzanillo**, gateway to the Refugio Nacional de Vida Silvestre Gandoca-Manzanillo. There's also a good black sand beach to the north of the town.

Finca La Isla Botanical Gardens
t 750 0046, www.greencoast.com/ garden; open 10–4; adm $5 self-guided, $10 with guide; price includes a fresh fruit drink

Half a kilometre west of town at **Playa Negra**, **Finca La Isla Botanical Gardens** is a working 4ha tropical fruit, spice and herb farm on an old cacao plantation. You can take tours through the grounds to see the crops (which include black pepper, cinnamon, chocolate, vanilla and ginger) being grown. The farm is also home to a bromeliad garden as well as a good deal of wildlife, including sloths and poison arrow frogs.

Just inland towards the Talamancan mountains lies one of the country's largest and most important indigenous reserves, the **Keköldi Indigenous Reserve**, which can be visited as part of a tour run under the auspices of ATEC, a local eco-tourism and conservation initiative which has an office in the centre of town on the main road (*see* 'Tour Operators', right). The reserve is home to around two hundred Bribrí and Cabécar people, and ATEC is its public face, its aim being to educate the population – both national and international – about the lives of the people who live here and to help the tribes sell their handicrafts (they're particularly renowned for their carvings) and benefit from the increase in tourism to the area in a way that causes as little disturbance to the environment and the tribes' way of life as possible. To this end, ATEC employs guides drawn from the tribes' ranks and conducts most of its tours of the heavily forested reserve either on foot or on horseback, so as to lessen the environmental impact. Most of the organization's profits go towards supporting the environment and local tribes.

Tourist Information in Puerto Viejo

Puerto Viejo does not have an official tourist office. Tour operators can provide you with information.

Tour Operators

ATEC, main street, t 750 0398, *www.greencoast.com/atec*. The Talamanca Ecotourism and Conservation Association provides information on and organizes tours to the Keköldi Reserve (*see* left). In the village centre, the office also gives information on the rest of the region and offers general tours – rainforest hikes, snorkelling, nature walks, etc. Most of the organization's profits go towards supporting the environment and local tribes.

Puerto Viejo Tours, on the seafront, west of the bus stop, t 750 0398, *puertoviejotours@yahoo.com*. Offers snorkelling trips to Cahuita National Park and Gandoca-Manzanillo Refuge, hiking tours of the Hitoy Cerere Biological Reserve, as well as rafting and kayaking excursions. It also hires out surfboards, bikes and scooters.

★ Cariblue >>

Reef Runner Tours, on the seafront, east of the bus stop, t 750 0480, *reefrunnerdivers@hotmail.com*. Diving specialist offering excursions to the Gandoca-Manzanillo Refuge.

Terraventuras, main street, two blocks west of the ATEC office, t 750 0750, *www.terraventuras.com*. A wealth of tours, including snorkelling in Cahuita National Park, rafting on the Pacuare river, quad-biking in the Talamancan forests, hiking in the Gandoca-Manzanillo Refuge and Keköldi Reserve and cruising the Tortuguero canals.

Xtreme Caribe, Playa Cocles, t 750 0507. Specialist in adrenaline-fuelled tours – horse-riding, zip-lining, kayaking, jungle hikes, etc. It also offers surfing lessons and rents out boards and bikes.

Services in Puerto Viejo

Banks: There are no banks. The nearest are in Puerto Limón and Bribrí.

Internet access: There's an Internet café, Video Mundo, on the main street next to the ATEC office. The ATEC office can also provide Internet access.

Laundry: There's a laundromat located next to the post office.

Post office: Just inland of the main street, on the road just west of the main street.

Where to Stay in Puerto Viejo

Accommodation in the town tends to be all of a type – i.e. simple *cabinas* aimed at the backpacker market and surfing community – though there are some exceptions. The better-quality places lie on the unpaved road that heads east (then south) out of town towards Manzanillo, where you'll find some extremely lush accommodation enjoying forest settings, fancy restaurants, swimming pools and more. Do bear in mind, however, that this road is largely unlit; if you're heading into town for the evening, be sure to bring a torch with you or you might fall into a stream you mistook for the path to your lodge.

Cariblue, Playa Cocles, 1.5km from Puerto Viejo, t 750 0035, *www.cariblue.com* ($$$$; $90). One of the area's most luxurious choices. Around a central indigenous-style thatch-roofed building are a collection of exquisitely rendered wooden bungalows, all with large beds, indigenous artwork on the walls, sumptuous bathrooms and wide verandahs (with hammocks). There's a pool (with poolside bar), games room and an excellent Italian restaurant. The white sand of Playa Cocles is just across the road.

Cabinas Casa Verde, just back from the main road, t 750 0015, *www.cabinascasaverde.com* ($$$; shared bathroom $40, private $60). A funky little place with a small tropical garden in which sit six comfortable *cabinas* (private bathrooms) and a block of seven rooms (shared bathrooms), all decorated with curios and bric-a-brac – shells, wind chimes, colourful mosaics, tapestries. Bike hire and parking.

La Costa de Papito, Playa Cocles, 2km from Puerto Viejo, t 750 0080, *www.greencoast.com/papito.htm* ($$$; $50). Overseen by American Elvis lookalike, Eddie Ryan, this has a nice kitschy vibe to it. Its 10 large wooden bungalows set in wooded tropical gardens, all have tiger- and leopard- print bedspreads and groovy multicoloured bathrooms. Breakfast, which is included in the price, is served either in the new snack bar area or on your bungalow's verandah. You can hire bikes for the journey back into town.

Cabinas Grant, on the main road, **t** 750 0292 ($; $25). Right at the heart of the action. The rooms are basic but clean; those on the ground floor are a touch cramped, while those on the first floor have balconies providing you with a ringside seat for all the comings and goings on the main road.

Cabinas Jacaranda, 1½ blocks back from the main road, **t** 750 0069, *www.cabinasjacaranda.com* ($; $25). Perfectly attuned to the town's New Age sensibilities, this offers reiki and shiatsu massages at its 'pagoda'. The large, two-bed *cabinas* (private and shared bathrooms) have a quirky charm, adorned with brightly coloured fabrics, and there's a good restaurant overlooking the hotel's tropical garden.

Hotel Pura Vida, two blocks back from the main road, just across from the football field, **t** 750 0002 ($; $25). The 'pure life' is one of the town's better budget choices, offering a quiet atmosphere away from the centre, clean basic rooms, all with fans and mosquito nets (the more expensive have private bathrooms) laid out around a central garden.

Eating Out in Puerto Viejo

There's plenty of choice. While it may be difficult to track down authentic, traditional Caribbean cuisine, the number of 'international' eateries is growing all the time.

Animoda, east of the town centre, past nightspot Bambú. Italian recipes with Caribbean ingredients – swordfish pasta, shrimp ravioli, etc.– make this something of a gastronomic adventure. It has a lovely beachside terrace.

Café Coral, just back from the main road. It was the first restaurant to serve pizza to the people of Puerto Viejo way back in the late 1980s (when it apparently caused something of a stir) and it still cooks up the best slices

in town, with generous toppings and spicy sauces.

Soda Lidia, two blocks inland from the ATEC office. Excellent cheap soda selling Tico staples – *casados*, etc.– with a Caribbean twist.

El Loco Natural, on the main road, west of the ATEC office. Above a souvenir shop, this offers a Caribbean restaurant, a healthfood store and New Age boutique. So in among herbal remedies and abstract sculptures you can enjoy some delicately spiced, locally sourced organic dishes (their coconut-infused curries are particularly recommended). There are vegetarian and even vegan choices available.

Miss Sam's, two blocks inland from the ATEC office. The town's longest-established Caribbean restaurant is your best source of *rondón* (*see* p.334), which must be ordered in advance, as well as Creole-style rice and beans with beef, chicken or fish.

Salsa Brava, east of the town centre, just past Bambú. Named after the town's infamous wave, so beloved of surfers, this is a great beachside restaurant-bar offering a wealth of fish and seafood – tuna, lobster, etc.– plus a range of very potent cocktails. A good place to fill up before dancing the night away at nearby Bambú.

Nightlife in Puerto Viejo

After a hard day spent taming the waves, the town's surfers need to unwind. Thankfully, as Puerto Viejo has one of the best nightlife scenes on the Caribbean coast, there are more than enough places to help them do it. The streets are thick with bars – **Tamara** on the main road is a good spot to begin the festivities watching the revellers emerge – and as the evening wears on the town's reggae discos come to life pumping their sounds out.

The town's two most popular nightspots are **Stanford's** and **Bambú**, which lie close to one another at the eastern edge of town. The décor may be nothing special – basically a glitter ball – but the crowds who flock here (particularly on Monday and Friday nights) don't care, dancing to the beats till dawn.

Getting to the Refugio Nacional Gandoca-Manzanillo

All the **tour companies** in Puerto Viejo provide tours of the refuge. You can also contact **Aquamoor, t** 759 9012, who specialize in diving trips, and **MANT, t** 759 9064, a co-operative of local guides working under the aegis of MINAE, in Manzanillo itself.

If you're not travelling as part of an organized tour, you can easily reach the refuge by **bus** to Manzanillo; four leave daily from Puerto Viejo at 7.30am, 12noon, 4.30pm and 7.30pm. Follow the main trail which sets out from the village and along the beach for several kilometres before heading into the forest depths. Though the coastal stretch is a relatively easy hike, the trail becomes increasingly difficult – and increasingly poorly maintained – once you head inland. It will involve a good three hours of walking just to reach the entrance, and is perhaps inadvisable if you're planning a sustained trek into the forest depths. It can also get pretty humid, so be sure to bring plenty of water.

You can also **cycle**.

Refugio Nacional Gandoca-Manzanillo

Refugio Nacional Gandoca-Manzanillo
t 750 0398;
open daily 7–4

Around 15km southeast of Puerto Viejo, almost at the farthest extent of the coastal road, is the tiny village of **Manzanillo**. Despite its small size, the town has become increasingly touristy in recent years owing to the growing popularity of the Refugio Nacional Gandoca-Manzanillo, which lies right on its border. The 20-year-old, 9,000ha refuge's appeal lies in the large number of different habitats – both marine and terrestrial – it encompasses and, more particularly, the amount of wildlife-spotting opportunities it affords.

Starting offshore, and accounting for around half the park's area, is a well-preserved **coral reef**, which, though smaller than the one in Cahuita, offers perhaps better snorkelling. Bottle-nosed and Atlantic dolphins are common in these waters. The park's **beaches** are important nesting sites for marine turtles, while the **mangrove swamps** near the Gandoca estuary (some of the best-preserved in the entire country) are home to crocodiles and caimans as well as rare and endangered manatees.

Inland, thick **forest** stretches all the way to the Panama border, providing a home to pumas, monkeys, sloths, poison dart frogs and over 300 species of bird.

Where to Stay in Manzanillo

There are several places to stay in Manzanillo town. Camping is also permitted on the refuge's beach, although you should check in advance with the ranger station.

⭐ **Almonds and Corals Lodge >**

Almonds and Corals Lodge, t 222 2024, *www.almondsandcorals.com* ($$$; $66). The area's best accommodation, actually located within the refuge itself, comprises a network of supremely comfortable, stilt-set tents right in the forest, all with locally produced furniture and large bathrooms. The complex also boasts a Jacuzzi and a very good restaurant (who said jungle trips were all about roughing it?).

Cabinas Pangea, t 759 9004, *pangea@racsa.co.cr* ($$; from $650 a month, otherwise $35 a day). Set in a lovely tropical garden and specializing in long-term stays.

Cabinas Something Different, t 759 9014 ($$; $30). Next door to Pangea, and more basic.

Crossing the Border

To make your crossing as hassle-free as possible, aim to arrive early in the morning, which will probably mean staying the night at one of the nearby towns of Cahuita, Puerto Viejo or, at a pinch, Bribri, some 34km north. The earliest bus from San José leaves at 6am (see p.103), but won't arrive at Sixaola till around noon (you cannot drive; Costa Rican rental cars cannot be taken out of the country). The border is open 7am–5pm Costa Rican time, 8am–6pm Panama time.

Bring a plentiful supply of **US dollars** with you. Panama's currency is so closely tied to the US dollar that it basically *is* the dollar, although the country clings to some nominal notion of fiscal independence by minting its own coins. Furthermore, Panamanian officials may ask you to prove you have adequate means to support yourself during your stay in the country and are not seeking work (although these questions are usually reserved for Ticos). A wallet containing around $200 should persuade them of your honourable intentions. Sixaola doesn't have a bank, so if you haven't brought enough cash with you, you'll need to stop off in Bribri and hope that the ATM of the town's only bank is working.

Unless you've already picked one up at the Panamanian consulate in San José (C 38, Av 5/7, **t** 281 2442), you'll need to purchase a **tourist card** for $5 from the pharmacy in Sixaola, after which officials will stamp your passport, leaving you free to walk across the border to the small village of **Guabito** on the other side – basically a Panamanian facsimile of Sixaola, with almost no facilities for tourists. You'll need to take the bus (every 30mins while the border post is open) or a taxi (around $15) to **Changuinola**, the nearest sizeable village with any sort of sleeping options. From here you can catch a *lancha* to the Bocas del Toro.

Sixaola and the Panamanian Border

The end of the line, as far as Costa Rica is concerned, comes in the shape of the tiny town of Sixaola, which, were it not for the fact that it marks the border with Panama, would be almost entirely unremarkable. With services aimed principally at the workers of the banana plantations in which it lies, Sixaola seems to treat its status as a border town almost as an afterthought, possessing little in the way of decent accommodation or eating options.

Crossing the border can be a bit of a rigmarole – particularly at weekends when the pharmacy selling the necessary tourist card may be closed – but it's not as bad as it could be (*see* above). And at least you can usually count on having a fair bit of company. Many foreigners, especially Americans, manage to unofficially 'live' in Costa Rica via the expedient of staying up to the limit of their three-month visa and then popping over to Panama for 72 hours, after which they are issued with a new visa entitling them to another three-month stay.

It's principally American visitors to Panama who have helped to popularize the **Bocas del Toro**, an archipelago of beach-fringed islands just across the border in the northeast of the country that offer a Caribbean-tinged holiday experience similar to the resorts of Cahuita and Puerto Viejo de Talamanca.

Language

Spanish is the country's official language and the mother tongue for the majority of Costa Ricans. As it is taught in all schools, even those people who do not use it as their first language – including a few thousand Afro-Caribbeans on the Atlantic coast who speak Creole English, and similar numbers of Bribrí and Cabécar Indians who speak in their own native tongues – will be able to understand it and converse in it.

The next most commonly spoken language is English, the use of which is growing all the time as tourism, particularly from the USA, increases. You'll find it spoken in almost all upscale tourist-related businesses – hotels, restaurants, tour operators, etc. However, you shouldn't assume that everyone speaks English. As a basic rule of thumb, the more rural the area, and the less tourist-orientated the business, the less likely it is that you'll be able to find someone who speaks English. You should certainly bring a Spanish phrase book with you, and try to memorize a few basic phrases. And for politeness' sake, even in high-end places where you can be fairly confident of finding an English speaker, you should always begin conversations in Spanish, even if you can't get much further than the greeting. Costa Ricans will appreciate the effort made and will happily oblige you by switching to English once you start to flounder.

If want to learn Spanish, there are schools throughout the country offering lessons.

Pronunciation

Costa Rican Spanish is first and foremost a version of Latin American Spanish, rather than European Spanish, which means that 'c' and 'z' sounds are pronounced with a crisp 'seh' sound, rather than a lispy 'theh' one, and the letter 'r' is rarely rolled. Other than that,

Costa Rican Spanish follows more or less the same pronunciation rules as Spanish spoken everywhere. It's essentially a 'say what you see' approach, with pretty much every letter of each word pronounced phonetically and consistently, with none of the 'ough' pronunciation variety you get in English. In general the **stress** is put on the penultimate syllable.

Vowels

A is pronounced with short 'ah' sound, as in 'rather'.

E is pronounced with short 'eh' sound, as in 'set'.

I is pronounced with a long 'ee' sound, as in 'police'.

O is pronounced with a short 'o' sound, as in 'got'.

U is pronounced with a long 'oo' sound, as in 'fuel'.

Consonants

C is pronounced with a 'seh' sound, as in 'cement', when preceding an 'e' or an 'i', otherwise with a hard 'k' sound.

G is pronounced with a soft 'ch' sound when preceding 'e' and 'i', otherwise with a hard 'g' sound.

H is always silent, as in 'hour'.

J is always pronounced with a soft 'ch' sound

LL is pronounced with a 'yur' sound, as in 'yacht'.

Ñ is pronounced with a 'ny' sound, as in 'canyon'.

QU is pronounced with a hard 'k' sound.

R is usually pronounced in the English fashion and not rolled.

V is often pronounced with a soft 'b' sound.

Z is pronounced with a short 'seh' sound.

Costa Rican Spanish Words

Ticos use a whole range of slang words and colloquialisms, many of which are used throughout Latin America, although some are unique to the country. In fact **Tico**, the very word Costa Ricans use to describe themselves, is itself a colloquialism. Its precise origin is unclear. One theory has it deriving from the Costa Rican habit of referring to things by their diminutive form, via use of the (colloquial) *'itico'* suffix, by which, for instance, *hermano* (brother) becomes *hermanitico* (little brother). Others contend that it's a corruption of a specific diminution, *'momentico'* (meaning 'in a little while') and is a (not unkindly meant) comment on Costa Ricans' procrastinatory habits.

Other *'tiquismos'*, as Costa Rican colloquialisms are known, to listen out for include: *'pura vida'*, which means literally 'pure life' and has both been adopted as a sort of unofficial motto of the country, and is used in general conversation to mean 'good' or 'okay'; *'maje'*, which is used primarily by young males and means 'mate' or 'buddy'; and *'chunche'*, which perhaps translates most accurately as 'whatya-callit' or 'thingamajig', being used mainly when the speaker can't remember (or doesn't know) the correct word. Costa Ricans also use *'vos'*, an archaic version of the informal 'you', in preference to the more common *'tu'*.

Useful Words and Phrases

Greetings and Farewells

Hello *Holá*
Pleased to meet you *Mucho gusto*
Good morning *Buenos días*
Good afternoon *Buenas tardes*
Good evening/night *Buenas noches*
Goodbye *Adiós*
See you later *Hasta luego*
What is your name? *¿Cómo se llama usted?/¿Cómo se llama?*
My name is... *Me llamo...*
Where are you from? *¿De dónde es?*
I'm from... *Soy de...*
How are you? *¿Cómo está?*
Well, thank you, and you? *¿Muy bien, gracias, y usted?*

Queries and Responses

What?/Who?/Where? *¿Qué?/¿Quién?/ ¿Dónde?*
How? *¿Cómo?*
When?/Why? *¿Cuándo?/¿Por qué?*
Excuse me *Con permiso*
Do you speak English? *¿Habla inglés?*
Please *Por favor*
yes/no *sí/no*
OK *De acuerdo*
I don't know *No sé*
I don't understand *No entiendo*
I don't speak Spanish *No hablo español*
Speak slowly *Hable despacio*
Thank you *Gracias*
Many thanks *Muchas gracias*
You're welcome *De nada*
I am sorry (apology) *Disculpe/Perdón*

Days

Monday *lunes*
Tuesday *martes*
Wednesday *miércoles*
Thursday *jueves*
Friday *viernes*
Saturday *sábado*
Sunday *domingo*

Months

January *enero*
February *febrero*
March *marzo*
April *abril*
May *mayo*
June *junio*
July *julio*
August *agosto*
September *septiembre*
October *octubre*
November *noviembre*
December *diciembre*

Numbers

one *un/uno/una*
two/three/four *dos/tres/cuatro*
five/six/seven *cinco/seis/siete*
eight/nine/ten *ocho/nueve/diez*
eleven/twelve *once/doce*
thirteen/fourteen *trece/catorce*
fifteen/sixteen *quince/diez y seis*
seventeen/eighteen *diez y siete/diez y ocho*
nineteen *diez y nueve*
twenty *veinte*
twenty-one *veinteuno*
thirty *treinta*
thirty-one *treinta y uno*

forty *cuarenta*
fifty *cincuenta*
sixty *sesenta*
seventy *setenta*
eighty *ochenta*
ninety *noventa*
one hundred *cien*
one hundred and one *ciento uno*
two hundred *doscientos*
one thousand *mil*

Time

What time is it? *¿Qué hora es?*
It's one o' clock/two o'clock/three o'clock
  Es la una/Son las dos/Son las tres
When? *¿Cuándo?*
now/later *ahora/más tarde*
yesterday *ayer*
today/tomorrow *hoy/mañana*
this week *esta semana*
next week *la semana que entra*

Transport Vocabulary

airport *aeropuerto*
plane *avión*
bus stop *parada de autobuses*
bus station *estación de autobuses*
bus *autobús*
taxi *taxi*
ticket *boleto/tiquete*

Buying Tickets

A ticket to San José, please *Un boleto a San José, por favor*
one way *de ida*
return (round-trip) *de ida y vuelta*
How do I get to...? *¿Por dónde se va a...?/¿Cómo llego a...?*
How much is it? *¿Cuánto cuesta?*
Where does the bus to San José leave from? *¿De dónde sale el autobús para San José?*
When does it leave? *¿A qué hora sale?*
When does it arrive? *¿A qué hora llega?*

Driving and Directions

Is it far? *¿Está lejos?*
left/right *izquierda/derecha*
straight on *derecho*
Is this the way to...? *¿Por aqui se va a...?*
petrol station *gasolinera/bomba*
Fill the tank, please *Lleno, por favor*
diesel *diesel*

The car has broken down *El auto se ha averiado*
leaded petrol *gasolina con plomo*
unleaded *gasolina sin plomo*
puncture *agujero*
map *mapa*
bicycle *bicicleta*
car *auto/carra*
motorcycle *motocicleta*
four-wheel drive *doble tracción/todo terreno*
garage *garaje*

Road Signs

Acceso Entrance
Ceda el paso Give way
Despacio Slow
Escuela School
No adelantar No overtaking
No hay paso No entry
Pare/Stop Stop
Peligro Danger
Puente Bridge
Salida Exit
Una vía One way

Shopping Services and Sightseeing

What is that? *¿Qué es eso?*
How much is it? *¿Cuánto cuesta?*
I want... *Quiero...*
I would like... *Quisiera...*
Give me... *Deme...*
Is there...? *¿Hay...?*
Do you have... *¿Tiene...?*
What do you call this in Spanish? *¿Com se llama éste en español?*
good *buen/bueno/buena*
bad *mal/malo/mala*
big *grand/grande*
small *pequeño/pequeña*
here/there *aquí/allí*
this/that *este/eso*
more/less *más/menos*
Where is...? *¿Dondé está...?*
open/closed *abierto/cerrado*
ATM *cajero automático*
bank *banco*
beach *playa*
church *iglesia*
city hall *palacio municipal*
laundry *lavandería*
market *mercado*

museum *museo*
park *parque*
pharmacy *farmacia/botica*
post office *correo*
supermarket *supermercado*

Accommodation

I'd like a double room, please *Quisiera una habitación doble, por favor*
I'd like a single room, please *Quisiera una habitación individual, por favor*
with bath *con baño privado*
May I see the room? *¿Podría ver la habitación?*
It's OK, I'll take it *Está bien, la tomo*
Is breakfast included? *¿Incluye el desayuno?*
camping area *area de acampar*
key *llave*

Menu Reader

Basics

carta/menú menu
cuenta bill/check
helado ice cream
hielo ice
huevos eggs
pan bread
queque cake
queso cheese
salsa sauce
Soy vegetariano/a I am a vegetarian

Carne (Meat)

bistec/lomito beef steak
cerdo pork
jamón ham
pollo chicken

Verduras y Legumbres (Vegetables and Herbs)

aceituna olive
ajo garlic
cebolla onion
cilantro coriander
elote corn on the cob
enslada salad
frijoles beans
palmito palm hearts
pimiento pepper
plátano plantain

Pescado y Mariscos (Fish and Seafood)

atún tuna
camarone shrimp
cangrejo crab
corvina sea bass
langosta lobster
ostiones clams
pargo snapper
pulpo octopus

Frutas (Fruit)

ackee small pink Jamaican fruit
aguacate avocado
anona custard apple
carambola starfruit
cas small sharp-tasting fruit, often used to liven up *refrescos*
cereza cherries
coco coconut
frambuesa raspberry
fresa strawberry
grandilla/maracuya passion fruit
guanábana soursop – large green fruit with sweet, creamy, rather fibrous flesh. It's often served in *refrescos* and ice creams.
guayaba guava, a sweet fruit that grows as long banana-shaped pods filled with seeds. Only the flesh surrounding the seeds is eaten. Often added to salads.
higo fig
lima lime
limón lemon
mamone small spiny fruit with a delicate grape-like flavour
maní peanut
manzana apple
marañón cashew fruit, a very juicy but rather tart pear-like fruit
mora blackberry
naranja orange
pasa raisin
pejibaye an orangey-coloured nutty-flavoured fruit, occasionally served in salads
pera pear
piña pineapple
plátano banana
sandía watermelon
tamarindo tamarind, a rather sharp-tasting fruit, occasionally added to *refrescos*
uva grape

Drinks

agua water

café coffee

Café Rica a Kahlúa-like coffee flavoured liqueur produced by the country's state-owned distillery

cerveza beer

chocolate chocolate

leche milk

guaro extremely potent sugar cane-based drink produced by the country's state-owned distillery. Its effects are as severe as its taste is rough. Best mixed with considerable portions of cola or fruit juice.

pipa coconut water

refrescos fruit shakes made by blending up crushed ice, milk (or water) and several varieties of fruit.

vin wine, not widely sold, although most upmarket restaurants will stock Chilean or Argentine imports

zumo juice

Dishes

arroz con carne/frijoles/mariscos/pescado/ pollo rice with meat/beans/seafood/fish/ chicken

bocas snacks traditionally served as free accompaniments to drinks in bars, much in the manner of tapas, although, as with tapas, a small charge tends to be levied these days

casado a 'marriage' of rice and beans, a selection of vegetables and a piece of chicken, meat or fish

ceviche a mixture of fish, seafood, onions, peppers and spices 'cooked' in lime juice

chorreado cornflour pancake, often served with sour cream

empanada deep-fried turnover with either a savoury or sweet filling

enchilada pastry filled with savoury filling, typically vegetables, potatoes, cheese and meat

ensalada salad

gallo a small tortilla sandwich, usually filled with beans, vegetables, cheese or meat

gallo pinto the country's traditional breakfast dish – a mixture of rice, beans, sweet peppers and coriander, often served with a portion of scrambled eggs

olla de carne a stew of beef and various vegetables, such as potatoes, squash and yucca

pan bon traditional Caribbean bread, often served stuffed with fruit

patacones thinly sliced deep-fried plantain

plato del día dish of the day

pozol corn and pork soup

rondón this slow-cooked coconut fish stew is a Caribbean coast speciality (*see* p.334 for more information)

rosquillos corn doughnuts

sopa negra thick soup made with black beans and chicken stock

tamales a mixture of ground cornmeal, vegetables, meat and raisins wrapped in a banana leaf, traditionally served at Christmas

tortillas Mexican-style cornflour pancakes, usually stuffed with various concoctions of vegetables, meat and cheese, then fried

15 | Language | Menu Reader

Glossary

agua potable drinking water

ave bird

ballena whale

barrio neighbourhood or suburb

bomba petrol station

bosque forest

bosque nuboso cloudforest

botica pharmacy

campesino agricultural worker/rural smallholder

carretas colourfully painted, decorative ox-carts

catarata waterfall

cerro mountain

chepe nickname for San José and, indeed, anyone called José

cocina kitchen

colectivo open-back truck taxi service used in rural areas, such as the Osa Peninsula, where the roads are too bad to support proper buses

cordillera mountain range

correo electrónico e-mail

costarricense Costa Rican

cueva cave

Dios God

fauna silvestre wildlife

finca farm

gringo someone from North America, the term can be used in a friendly or a hostile fashion, but is most commonly used purely descriptively

ICE the commonly used acronym for Costa Rica's electricity company, the Instituto Costarricense de Electricidad.

ICT the commonly used abbreviation for the Costa Rican tourist board, the Instituto Costarricense de Turismo.

Interamericana the Pan-American Highway

Josefino someone who lives in San José

lancha a small flat-bottomed boat used for negotiating the country's rivers and canals

lapa parrot

malecón sea wall

mercado central central market

mestizo someone of mixed indigenous/ Spanish ancestry

MINAE the commonly used acronym for the Ministerio del Ambiente y Energía, the Ministry of Energy and the Environment, which oversees the national parks system

mirador lookout point or viewing area

mono monkey

mono carablanca/colorado/congo/titi white-faced capuchin/spider monkey/ howler monkey/squirrel monkey

muelle dock

murciélago bat

Nica someone from Nicaragua

OTS the abbreviation for the Organization for Tropical Studies

parque central central park or plaza

puerto port

puesto a ranger station at a national park.

pulpería a small general store.

RACSA the commonly used acronym for Costa Rica's main phone company and Internet provider, Radiográfica Costarricense SA

refugio nacional de vida silvestre national wildlife refuge

río river

sabanero Costa Rican cowboy

sendero a trail

serpiente snake

soda a small, often family-run restaurant or café, aimed at the local population

Tico a native inhabitant of Costa Rica

tortuga turtle

zancudo mosquito

Further Reading

Beletsky, Les, *Travellers' Wildlife Guides – Costa Rica* (Interlink Books, 2004). In-depth guide to wildlife-spotting, ecotourism and conservation; endorsed by the Wildlife Conservation Society.

Biesanz, Mavis, Richard Biesanz and Karen Zubris Biesanz, *The Ticos: Culture and Social Change in Costa Rica* (Lynne Rienner Publishers, 1998). Detailed examination of Costa Rican society, focusing in particular on the family, politics, education and religion.

Booth, John A., *Costa Rica: Quest for Democracy* (Westview Press, 1999). A history of the development of the country's democratic institutions.

Calderon, Gloria, *The Life of Costa Rica* (Editores Villegas, 2001). Hardback photographic study of the country with over 300 pictures of its peoples, towns, animals and environments.

Carr, Archie, *The Windward Road* (University Press of Florida, 1979). Evocative description of the search for green turtles by the naturalist who was the prime impetus behind the foundation of Tortuguero National Park and its protected turtle nesting sites.

Fogden, Susan C. L., *Photographic Guide to the Birds of Costa Rica* (Ralph Curtis, 2005). Slightly less exhaustive than the Stiles book, but lighter and more easily manageable, this has over 250 colour photographs.

Henderson, Carrol L., *Field Guide to the Wildlife of Costa Rica* (University of Texas Press, 2002). Good practical guide to the country's fauna.

Howard, Christopher, *New Golden Door to Retirement and Living in Costa Rica*, 14th edn (Costa Rica Books, 2005). In-depth guide on how to retire to the '*pura vida*' from an expat who has done exactly that.

Kavanagh, James, *Costa Rican Wildlife: An Introduction to Familiar Species* (Waterford Press, 2001). Fold-out chart providing pictures and identifying descriptions for the country's most commonly encountered animals.

Palmer, Steven (ed), *A Costa Rica Reader: History, Culture, Politics* (Duke University Press, 2004). A collection of scholarly essays on various aspects of Costa Rican society.

Ras, Barbara (ed), *Costa Rica: A Traveler's Literary Companion* (Whereabouts Press, 1993). 26 stories set in locales around the country, translated into English from the original Spanish.

Solorzano, Alejandro, *Serpientes de Costa Rica – Snakes of Costa Rica* (INBio, 2005). Glossy hardback publication featuring colour pictures of all the country's many snake species, with text by its leading snake expert and backing by INBio, the country's leading institute of biodiversity.

Stiles, F. Gary and Alexander F. Skutch, *A Guide to the Birds of Costa Rica* (Cornell University Press, 1990). Comprehensive, exhaustive guide to the country's birdlife.

Theroux, Paul, *The Old Patagonian Express* (Mariner Books, 1989). The intensely told tale of the author's 1979 railway journey from Massachusetts to Patagonia, by way of Costa Rica along its now defunct railroad.

Van Rheenen, Erin, *Living Abroad in Costa Rica* (Avalon Travel Publishing, 2004). Practical advice for people looking to move to the country.

Zuchowski, Willow, *A Guide to Tropical Plants of Costa Rica* (Zona Tropical, 2005). Large, comprehensive tome illustrated with 540 photos by the suitably arboreally named author.

Useful Websites

www.bruncas.com offers a variety of web links to Costa Rican services

www.costaricabureau.com the official website of the Costa Rica Tourism and Travel Bureau

www.dominical.biz Dominical-based site containing information and links for much of the southern zone

www.ecotourism.co.cr the site of Ciprotur, a branch of the Costa Rican Chamber of Commerce, providing information on conservation, tours and volunteer projects in southern Costa Rica

www.fores.com information on Spanish language courses in Costa Rica

www.infocostarica.com travel information portal

www.1costaricalink.com large tourist website with over 5,000 available pages of online information

www.nacion.co.cr the website of *La Nacion*, the country's pre-eminent Spanish language newspaper

www.ticotimes.net the website of the *Tico Times*, the country's leading English language newspaper, and an excellent resource for anyone hoping to learn more about the daily narrative of Costa Rican life

www.visitcostarica.com the official Costa Rican Tourism Board site

Index

Main page references are in **bold**. Page references to maps are in *italics*.